STRATEGIC MARKETING
MANAGEMENT

The Practice of Management Series

HARVARD BUSINESS SCHOOL PUBLICATIONS

The Craft of General Management
Readings selected by Joseph L. Bower

The Entrepreneurial Venture
Readings selected by William A. Sahlman and Howard H. Stevenson

Managing People and Organizations
Readings selected by John J. Gabarro

Strategic Marketing Management
Readings selected by Robert J. Dolan

STRATEGIC MARKETING MANAGEMENT

READINGS SELECTED BY

Robert J. Dolan

Harvard Business School

HARVARD BUSINESS SCHOOL PUBLICATIONS
Boston, Massachusetts

Library of Congress Cataloging-in-Publication Data

Strategic marketing management / edited by Robert J. Dolan.
  p. cm.—(Practice of management series)
  Includes index.
  ISBN 0-87584-310-7 (pbk.)
  1. Marketing—Management. I. Dolan, Robert J. II. Series.
HF5415.13.S878 1991
658.8'02--dc20   91-31903
                                                      CIP

The Harvard Business School Publications Practice of Management Series is distributed in the college market by McGraw-Hill Book Company. The readings in each book are available individually through PRIMIS, the McGraw-Hill custom publishing service. Instructors and bookstores should contact their local McGraw-Hill representative for information and ordering.

"An Issue of Trust: Ethics in Marketing Management" by Marilyn Nadelhaft, *HBS Bulletin*, December 1990. Copyright © by Marilyn Nadelhaft. Reprinted by permission of author.

Printed in the United States of America.

95   5 4 3 2

ROBERT J. DOLAN

Robert J. Dolan is the Edward W. Carter Professor of Business Administration and Chair of the Marketing area at the Graduate School of Business Administration, Harvard University. He was appointed the Carter Professor in 1990 at the retirement of the first holder of the chair, Theodore Levitt. Formerly, Dolan taught at the Graduate School of Business of the University of Chicago, where he held a joint appointment in the Marketing and Management Science areas.

His major research interests are in the areas of product policy and pricing. He has published widely on these topics in such journals as the *Bell Journal of Economics, Industrial Marketing Management, Journal of Business, Journal of Marketing, Marketing Science,* and *Sales and Marketing Management.* His article in *Marketing Science,* "Quantity Discounts: Managerial Issues and Research Opportunities," was honored in the Best Marketing Paper of the Year competition. He is the editor of the Field Studies section of *Marketing Science.* He also serves on the Editorial Board of the *Journal of Marketing* and has served on the Publications Review Board of the Harvard Business School Press.

At Harvard, Dolan initiated and developed the second-year MBA elective course "New Product Development: An Analytical Approach" and recently completed a book, *Managing the New Product Development Process,* based on the course. He previously published a three-volume series on marketing management with John A. Quelch and Benson P. Shapiro. Since 1987, he has been faculty chairman of the Strategic Marketing Management Program, a summer course for senior marketing executives at Harvard Business School.

He is a member of the Board of Directors of Warnaco, Inc., and a corporator of Mt. Auburn Hospital in Cambridge, Massachusetts. He consults on product policy and pricing to a wide variety of clients ranging from Domino's Pizza to NASA's Office of Space Flight to the New York Stock Exchange.

CONTENTS

PART SEVEN
ISSUES FOR THE 1990s

SECTION A
SERVICES

SECTION B
MULTINATIONAL MARKETING

SERIES PREFACE

The Harvard Business School has a long and distinguished publishing history. For decades, the School has furnished original educational materials to academic classrooms and executive education programs worldwide. Many of these publications have been used by individual managers to update their knowledge and skills. The Practice of Management Series, developed by Harvard Business School Publications, continues this tradition.

The series addresses major areas of the business curriculum and major topics within those areas. Each of the books strikes a balance between broad coverage of the area and depth of treatment; each has been designed for flexibility of use to accommodate the varying needs of instructors and programs in different academic settings.

These books also will serve as authoritative references for practicing managers. They can provide a refresher on business basics and enduring concepts, and also offer cutting-edge ideas and techniques.

The main objective of the Practice of Management Series is to make Harvard Business School's continuing explorations into management's best practices more widely and easily available. The books draw on two primary sources of material produced at the School.

Harvard Business School is probably best known for its field research and cases. Faculty members prepare other material for their classrooms, however, including essays that define and explain key business concepts and practices. Like other classroom materials produced at Harvard Business School, these "notes," as they are called at the School, have a consistent point of view—that of the general manager. They have a common purpose—to inform the actual practice of management as opposed to providing a theoretical foundation. The notes are an important source of selections for the books in this series.

The *Harvard Business Review* has long been recognized by professors and managers as the premier management magazine. Its mix of authors—academics, practicing executives and managers, and consultants—brings to bear a blend of research knowledge and practical intelligence on a wide variety of business topics. *Harvard Business Review* articles challenge conventional wisdom with fresh approaches and often become a part of enlightened conventional wisdom. The magazine speaks primarily to the practice of management at the level of the general manager. *Harvard Business Review* articles are another essential source of selections for this series.

Finally, this series includes selections published by other distinguished institutions and organizations. In instances where there were gaps in coverage or viewpoint, we have taken the opportunity to tap books and other journals besides the *Harvard Business Review*.

——— ACKNOWLEDGMENTS

The books in this series are the products of a collaborative effort. Robert J. Dolan, the Harvard Business School faculty member who wrote the introduction to *Strategic Marketing Management*, worked closely with a Harvard Business School Publications editor, Polly Glasser, to select and arrange the best available materials. Professor Dolan's content expertise, teaching experience, and diligence, together with Ms. Glasser's editorial skill and commitment, have been crucial to the development of the book.

The Harvard Business School faculty whose work is represented in the books have generously taken the time to review their selections. Their cooperation is much appreciated.

Each of the books has been evaluated by practitioners or by professors at other institutions. We would like to thank the following individuals for their careful readings of the manuscript for the collection on marketing: James A. Narus, Babcock Graduate School of Management, Wake Forest University; Youjae Yi, School of Business Administration, The University of Michigan; and Paul Root, president of the Marketing Science Institute in Cambridge, Massachusetts. Their evaluations and many useful suggestions have helped us develop and shape this book into a more-effective teaching instrument.

We would like to thank Maria Arteta, former Director of Product Management for Harvard Business School Publications; Bill Ellet, Editorial Director of Harvard Business School Publications; and Benson P. Shapiro, Malcolm P. McNair Professor of Marketing and former faculty adviser to Harvard Business School Publications. The Practice of Management Series would not have materialized without their support, guidance, and insight.

INTRODUCTION

This is, in many respects, the Age of Marketing. Indeed, the title of a recent *Harvard Business Review* article proclaimed that "Marketing Is Everything."[1] Other leading business magazines apparently share this view. Every issue, it seems, features yet another article on some company's efforts to become "market oriented," or the financial success of companies that were able to make the customer the focal point of their operations, or the financial problems of those that could not make the desired transition. Marketing has become so important to companies that we are told it can no longer be left to just those in the marketing department. Rather, marketing is everybody's job, and marketing's job is "to integrate the customer into the design of the product and to design a systematic process for interaction that will create substance in the relationship."[2]

This view of marketing corresponds to our philosophy at Harvard Business School. We generally do not seek to develop functional specialists in our MBA or executive program classrooms. Instead, our goal is to educate general managers. Although we rely heavily on the case method of instruction, we also know that other methods of learning can greatly benefit from a vintage collection of teaching materials such as those included here.

---

1. Regis McKenna, "Marketing Is Everything," *Harvard Business Review* (January–February 1991), pp. 65–79.
2. Ibid., p. 69.

We devote a great deal of our research and development resources to actual business situations and problems and to crafting teaching materials that address those situations in a manner suitable for classroom use. This collection of carefully selected readings does just that: it brings into our classrooms what is most important to managers from a variety of marketing contexts. We consider these readings to be a powerful knowledge-dissemination mechanism that will enhance the student's ability to capture vital information and viewpoints necessary to a keener understanding of the field of marketing. They can stand alone as an important teaching vehicle, or they can provide a solid background for entering case discussions in classrooms where cases are used. The knowledge in these readings is enduring however they are used. The student can only benefit as his or her base of knowledge is broadened.

We have drawn our materials from two major sources: the *Harvard Business Review* and the collection of writings produced by the Harvard Business School. The *Harvard Business Review* publishes the works of a variety of authors, executives, consultants, and academics both at Harvard Business School and other institutions. This work is designed to inform, stimulate, and induce executives to act. The Harvard Business School readings are a product of the School's faculty and are primarily designed to provide background information on an industry, topic, or concept. They can be used to enrich the students' base of knowledge in a particular subject or area or to complement the case studies where those are used. These readings range from a two-page description of some basic marketing calculations to much longer, more-complex prescriptions on the development of marketing strategy.

This volume contains work contributed by 20 Harvard Business School faculty and 16 other writers. Our objective in bringing together these *Harvard Business Review* articles and Harvard Business School faculty-authored readings is to provide the reader with a broad-based overview on marketing management. Our attempt to cover the full range of marketing issues in one volume naturally leads to a sacrifice of some depth within each topic. Taken together, however, the readings in each section not only provide a good overview of the topic, but in some cases they also provide reference to additional readings for those wishing to pursue a topic in more depth. The readings share a common characteristic: they are written with the idea of impacting practice. Thus, while our Part and Section headings resemble those of popular marketing management textbooks, their impact on the reader will be quite different. While some of the authors in this volume are fine theorists—and this influences all they write —little in the way of marketing's theoretical underpinnings shows up in these readings. Consequently, this book will benefit three audiences:

1. Students will be able to use it as a companion volume in a case-based marketing course at either the undergraduate or graduate level.
2. Students taking a marketing management course with a theoretical orientation will find that it complements that training by stressing

managerial concerns and positioning marketing as a general management activity.
3. Executives can use it as a resource book of both classic and current thinking on marketing management issues.

To reinforce the learning process, we have included a set of discussion questions after each reading. These questions are designed to stimulate discussion by encouraging a variety of viewpoints, whether they oppose or agree with the ideas presented. Therein lies the challenge of learning.

——— ORGANIZATION OF THE BOOK

The book has seven parts and an appendix. Parts One through Four deal with the issue of how a manager thinks about marketing. They develop the rationale for a market-driven organization and the processes for achieving a market orientation. One key component analyzes consumer behavior, another focuses on the "New Wave" in marketing—the growing diversity among what consumers want in a product and allied services, how much they are willing to pay for that product, and where they would like to acquire it. Part Five considers the tools at the disposal of the marketer—referred to as the "marketing mix." All the readings are concerned with managerial action, but Part Six focuses on the execution of a marketing strategy. Salient issues for the 1990s are highlighted in Part Seven.

The following is a brief introduction to each part and section, suggesting how the reader could best utilize the book.

PART ONE: MARKETING: AN OVERVIEW

This is a short section of just one selection written by Harvard Business School Professor Benson P. Shapiro to explain the proper domain of marketing. Certainly, marketing is not "everything"; nor is it a Madison Avenue phenomenon designed to get some unfortunate consumer to accept that he or she ought to buy what some powerful manufacturer has decided to produce and support with an advertising budget. Shapiro sets the stage for what follows by articulating the proper marketing-related concerns of the general manager.

PART TWO: THE MARKET-DRIVEN ORGANIZATION

"We're in deep trouble. . . . The only way to get out of this mess is for us to become customer driven or market oriented. I'm not even sure what that means, but I'm damn sure that we want to be there." This executive, featured in one of the selections in this section, is not alone. It seems that "market driven" is the panacea of the 1990s. The pathway to this "paradise" is strewn with slogans: "the customer is king," "just worry about customer satisfaction, profits will come later," "the customer is always right," and so on. Yet we know that life is a series of trade-offs. What does it mean to be market driven? What are the benefits? What are the costs? What are the primary barriers to such an orientation and how are they overcome?

The three selections in Part Two deal with these key issues. Written over a span of almost 30 years, from 1960 to 1988, these readings indicate what's enduring and what's new about the nature of marketing. Much of what is being said today was said in Ted Levitt's 1960 classic, "Marketing Myopia," namely, "The DuPonts and the Cornings have succeeded not primarily because of their product-research orientation but because they have been thoroughly customer oriented also." The other two selections in Part Two cut through the barrier of cliches dominating management literature to provide substantive ideas on how to attain a market orientation. Shapiro helps to define what it means to be market oriented. Kenichi Ohmae, the head of McKinsey's Tokyo office, explains the factors that have led many firms to drive their strategy off competitive analysis and suggests ways to get back to "strategy [that] takes shape in the determination to create value for customers."

PART THREE: DEVELOPING THE MARKETING PLAN

The two selections in Part Three deal with the nuts and bolts of properly balancing customer, competitor, and company considerations when formulating an overall set of objectives and plans. The conceptual framework of Part Three is more fully fleshed out in a discussion of the customer in Part Four and a look at the marketing mix in Part Five. The "Marketing Strategy" selection presents the analytical areas that should be investigated when developing a strategy. "Marketing Planning and Organization" then deals with the reality of how this does or does not happen within an organization.

PART FOUR: UNDERSTANDING THE NEW CONSUMER

One of the most apparent and important changes in marketing strategy over the past decade has been an increased attention to the differing wants of customers. The age-old notion of developing a product and offering it to some idealized "average" consumer is dead. In the 1970s, a total of six toothpaste formulations suited us all quite well; there were no major outcries and demonstrations at shopping centers about the lack of suitability of toothpaste offerings. Yet today, the number of brands and points of differentiation among brands of toothpastes are staggering. "Marketing in an Age of Diversity" tells why this is happening and sets out the challenges it presents to marketers. The other four selections in Part Four similarly deal with analyzing a potential set of customers to develop the most useful segmentation scheme and look at how to manage a marketing program in the face of such deeply segmented markets.

"Marketing and Its Discontents" shows the difficulty in properly aligning a marketing program and its target market. The reading on "Local Marketing" discusses the problems and opportunities in the trend toward more regional variation in programs. Finally, the two articles by Tom Bonoma and Bonoma with Ben Shapiro—"Who *Really* Does the Buying?" and "How to Segment Industrial Markets"—present a useful framework for analyzing buyers and segmenting industrial markets.

These selections can help managers understand the issues that are necessary to develop a winning marketing plan: the driving forces behind customer segmentation; how to analyze the customer population to distinguish the difference between a consumer-selling and industrial-selling situation; the costs and benefits of a segmentation strategy; and the importance of selecting the target market and understanding its buying behavior.

PART FIVE: THE MARKETING MIX

Part Five introduces the concept of the marketing mix and the inter-relationship of its elements. Four sections follow, each devoted to one of the four major mix elements: product, pricing, channels of distribution, and communications. The authors' expertise provides a keen insight into the variables that accompany these issues.

In describing the marketing mix concept some years ago, Neil Borden observed that there was wide variation among different firms in what they spent on advertising, how large their received gross margins were, how widely they distributed their products, and so on. He concluded that the "elements of marketing programs can be combined in many ways" and that a marketer's success came from "skill in devising a 'mix' of marketing methods...." Borden's mix notion has become pervasive in marketing. The selection that follows it by Shapiro extends some of Borden's ideas and suggests methods for devising an optimal mix.

Section A. Product Decisions
Product policy encompasses determining which products or services a firm will offer, the characteristics of those offerings, and the relationships among the different offerings. The opening selection, "Product Policy" by Professor John Quelch, provides an overview and discussion of these issues. Levitt's "Marketing Success Through Differentiation—of Anything" provides an important description of the four aspects of a product: the generic product, the expected product, the augmented product, and the potential product.

By expanding differentiation possibilities beyond the core or generic product, the selection notes the proper scope for a firm's efforts to attract and retain customers.

Shapiro's "Product Line Planning" deals with the interrelationship among the individual products offered by a firm. He describes the issues in both vertical and horizontal relationships. The section closes with two articles specifically related to new product development. "The New Product Development Map" provides a descriptive tool to chronicle the development of a product line over time in a way that leads to insight about key development factors. "The New New Product Development Game" focuses on the process by which new product ideas can be developed quickly and effectively.

Section B. Pricing Decisions

This section covers pricing—the function by which a firm takes back from its customers part of the value that its marketing efforts have created. Ray Corey's "Pricing: The Strategy and Process" provides a conceptual framework for pricing options. Joel Dean's "Pricing Policies for New Products" is a classic and describes the key choice between "skimming" and "penetration" strategies. Although it does not deal explicitly with customer diversity, this selection does address how price is changed over time to reflect the changing composition of buyers in the market.

In keeping with the theme of increasing customer diversity, the last two pricing selections consider more-effective price management based on this diversity. Elliot B. Ross's "Making Money with Proactive Pricing" describes a pricing system that will yield superior profits to a reactive or passive cost-based strategy. Several years later, Ross collaborated with three Harvard Business School professors to develop a pricing management system based on the recognition of customer diversity on both product value and cost-to-serve. This is described in "Manage Customers for Profits (Not Just Sales)."

Section C. Distribution Decisions

This section discusses a number of ways for the manufacturer to connect with the end consumer. The opener, "Strategic Issues in Distribution," presents the issues in (1) designing the system to interact with customers and (2) managing that system. While this reading cites one factor that affects channel design as "buyer behavior," the next selection, "Customer-driven Distribution Systems," presents an eight-step approach for deriving a system to match customer segments rather than convenient logistical arrangements.

The last two readings in this section address the two major trends in channel management. First, historically, there has been a love/hate relationship between manufacturers and distributors, as both recognize the need to cooperate but each wants a greater proportion of the profits. The method for achieving a better cooperative arrangement is presented in "Turn Your Industrial Distributors into Partners." Second, the diversity of customer segments is leading firms to use a variety of approaches to the market. This multiplicity of approaches presents management challenges, which are addressed in "Managing Hybrid Marketing Systems."

Section D. Communications Decisions

Marketers communicate with consumers in a number of ways and for a variety of purposes. This section focuses on what is needed to communicate in a systematic, integrated way. "Communications Policy" examines the six tasks in developing a communications program. "New Ways to Reach Your Customers" describes the wide variety of devices for communicating.

One way to communicate is through personal selling. "Aspects of Sales Management: Key Themes" looks at the issues involved in sales situations that affect sales-management requirements. Both "After the Sale Is Over . . ." and "Close Encounters of the Four Kinds" concern the expanded job of marketing— that of establishing and maintaining a relationship with the account. "Close Encounters" presents four different kinds of relationships and the requirements for effective account management.

PART SIX: MARKETING IMPLEMENTATION AND CONTROL

While the readings in Parts One through Five all address management action, Part Six looks at key issues in getting the job done. Tom Bonoma's "Making Your Marketing Strategy Work" differentiates those effective at marketing implementation from those who are not. Philip Kotler's "From Sales Obsession to Marketing Effectiveness" provides a checklist for assessing the marketing effectiveness of an organization.

PART SEVEN: ISSUES FOR THE 1990s

The issues that might warrant special considerations for the 1990s are open to debate. The readings in Parts One through Six were selected with an eye to the future; that is, to focus on issues of increasing importance to marketing managers. However, we believe three areas of marketing will play an even more prominent role in the next decade:

1. marketing of services
2. multinational marketing
3. ethical and legal issues

In the first area, economies are becoming more service-based than product-based. In the second, competition will continue to move to a global basis. In the third, marketing managers will confront more legal and ethical issues in the conduct of business. Part Seven highlights these three areas.

Section A. Marketing of Services

The role that services will play in the 1990s is vital to satisfying evermore demanding customers. This section recognizes the "customization" concept: delivering the services that customers want and managing the process so both the customer and the company benefit.

The two readings in this section complement one another. Jim Heskett's "Lessons in the Service Sector" adopts the point of view that "whatever your business, services have something to teach." Heskett provides examples from the service sector, noting some common themes and practices shared by leading service companies that yield important lessons for managers. In "Service Companies: Focus or Falter," William Davidow and Bro Uttal apply familiar product-market thinking on market segmentation: focus on a particular market segment and meet the needs of that segment. This reading presents the special challenges posed by the nature of the service sector.

Section B. Multinational Marketing

With the face of Eastern Europe and the Far East changing, it becomes increasingly clear that the world is the marketer's playing field for the 1990s. The prospect of entering new markets will bring a new awareness of the basic approaches to multinational marketing. The three selections in this section look at what a global strategy means and debate the extent to which that strategy can be standardized across geographic markets. First, Ted Levitt exhorts marketers to exploit the underlying similarity of markets in "The Globalization of Markets." John Quelch and Ted Hoff argue for a more situational approach in assessing the trade-offs involved in standardization versus customization in "Customizing Global Marketing." Finally, Gary Hamel and C. K. Prahalad differentiate between global tactics and a global strategy and provide a new competitive framework in "Do You Really Have a Global Strategy?"

Section C. Ethical and Legal Issues

The 1980s were plagued by the downfalls of prominent managers who did not have the proper internal compass on ethical and legal issues. We're all familiar with many of those memorable episodes. The environment of the 1990s will present even more strain on the individual's basic values and moral compass. This section presents no new ethical principles but, rather, renews our awareness of the legal and ethical pitfalls "out there." The moral expectations of the 1990s could leave marketing management more vulnerable than ever to the blurrings that are rampant in the ethics arena.

Pat Kaufmann's "Legal Restrictions on Marketing Management" is an overview of the legal issues and concerns that affect the decision-making process. "An Issue of Trust" documents the discussions of a leading group of scholars gathered at Harvard Business School in May 1990 for the seminar "The Impacts of Marketing Decision Making: A Workshop on Ethics in Marketing." This wide-ranging discussion focused on key ethical issues facing today's managers, and also on the principles that can be used in their resolution.

APPENDIX

The appendix contains two selections: one on basic calculations for marketing analysis and one that provides a glossary, or dictionary, of commonly used marketing terms.

Taken together, the readings in this volume provide an overview on the best thinking about marketing management. All the readings have been individually tested with executive and student audiences; bringing them together in this collection should serve to make each more useful. All have been drawn from the wealth of teaching materials at the Harvard Business School and compiled with the intention of disseminating that knowledge among a broader-based community. It is our hope that by sharing these materials, the benefits for students and practitioners of marketing management will be far-reaching.

ROBERT J. DOLAN

PART ONE

MARKETING: AN OVERVIEW

Marketing à la Agatha Christie? Considering the mysteries that surround the creation of the perfect marketing program, it might as well be. The elements of the marketing mix are the players. You can call them the four Ps: Product, Pricing, Place, and Promotion. Which ones to choose and how much of each? What combination will accomplish your goals? Striking just the right mix to create the most beneficial marketing strategy is indeed the work of a true marketing sleuth, and it is possible only through compiling and analyzing the correct market data to arrive at the best possible decision.

An introduction to marketing can by no means cover all the core elements of marketing thought—the mix, the participants, and the process itself, from analysis and strategy to planning and implementation. The first reading is intended only as an overview of the dynamic world of marketing and the application of its skills and concepts. The rest is up to the reader.

An Introduction to Marketing   1

BENSON P. SHAPIRO

This basic introductory reading gives a brief introduction of the marketing function and discusses some of the reasons for a perspective beyond marketing's traditional "four Ps." It stresses the importance of learning to integrate the various marketing concepts into an effective marketing plan that solves a specific problem.

Many people who come to the subject of marketing with little or no business experience picture it as the study of selling and advertising. While marketing certainly includes selling and advertising, it encompasses much more. Broadly speaking, the marketing function of a company—or nonprofit organization—is responsible for serving customers and for dealing with intermediaries and such external support organizations as distributors and advertising agencies. Perhaps the best way to explain the scope and nature of marketing is to consider a specific example and review some of the decisions marketers have to make.

━━━ THE SUBSTANCE OF MARKETING

Assume for a moment that you have decided to enter the watch business. You will need to make a set of important marketing-related decisions, which might include the following:

1. To which consumers should I sell my watches? How should I define the consumer I hope to serve? Should I think in terms of geography—perhaps the country or region of the country in which my consumer lives? Or maybe the consumer's income or sex or fashion orientation is more important?
2. What product or products should I offer? For example, should I offer digital or analog, ornate or simple, multifunction or single-function watches?
3. How much should I charge for each watch? Should I offer discounts to people who pay cash or who buy in large volumes?
4. Should I sell direct to consumers or through stores? If through stores, what type of stores? Drugstores, gift shops, department stores, jewelry stores, other outlets? Should I offer my product in several types of outlets or only in one type? And how do I select

and service the outlets I choose? Finally, how do I convince the stores to carry my brand?

5. How should I communicate with the people to whom I wish to sell? Do I use advertising, and if so, in what media? Television, radio, magazines, newspapers, other media? How do I reach the stores? Do I use salespeople? Should the salespeople visit the stores, or should they just telephone them?

These decisions help to explain two important marketing concepts. The first is perhaps the most important decision in marketing—*market selection*. Market selection is the choice of which customer needs to attempt to fill and which customer needs *not* to attempt to fill. Any organization has a finite set of abilities and resources and, thus, can serve only a certain group of customers and fill only a limited set of needs. It is impossible for any organization to succeed in being all things to all people. The market selection theme pervades good marketing practice.[1]

The other four decisions (items 2 through 5 above) relate to the second key concept—the *marketing mix*. The marketing mix is the tool kit of the marketer and consists of four elements:

1. *Product policy*—designing the characteristics of the product to be offered to the customer, which includes the physical product and all its service enhancements. Sometimes the "product" is purely a service.
2. *Pricing policy*—determining the total financial cost of the product to the customer, including discounts, rebates, and so forth, and the price to the wholesalers or retailers who carry the product.
3. *Distribution policy*—choosing intermediaries through which a product flows to reach consumers. These include retail stores, wholesalers, and industrial distributors, as well as a wide range of other organizations.
4. *Communications policy*—selecting the means by which the organization "talks to" its customers, prospective customers, and other people important to the organization, such as distributors. Although this is the most visible part of marketing because it includes advertising and personal selling, it is only one element in the marketing mix.

The four elements of the marketing mix are important. One easy way to remember the elements was popularized by E. J. McCarthy[2] as the four Ps.

1. Product
2. Price

---

1. For more on this topic, *see* E. Raymond Corey, "Key Options in Market Selection and Product Planning," *Harvard Business Review* (September–October 1975).
2. E. Jerome McCarthy with Andrew A. Brogowicz, *Basic Marketing: A Managerial Approach*, 8th ed. (Homewood, Ill.: Richard D. Irwin, 1984), pp. 46–49.

3. Place (distribution channels)
4. Promotion (communication)

We prefer the term *distribution* because the channel provides much more than a place to buy. Also, we use *communication* instead of *promotion* because promotion means a short-term cut in price usually accompanied by increased communication.

─── THE PARTICIPANTS

In addition to the four Ps, there are also four Cs. This useful mnemonic device points to the participants in the marketing arena:

1. *Company.* The protagonist organization, which can be a nonprofit organization or a governmental entity as well as a business.
2. *Consumers.* The people who use, buy, or influence the purchase of a product or service.
3. *Channels.* The distribution channels through which the product reaches consumers. The channels are also components of the marketing mix.
4. *Competitors.* Other organizations that attempt to satisfy the same consumer needs.

Some nonbusiness programs have produced highly visible advertising programs, such as the antismoking, antidrug, and Armed Forces recruitment campaigns. Nonprofit organizations and government agencies, like businesses, have to consider all four elements of the marketing mix as well as the market-selection decision.[3]

The consumer is the raison d'être of all marketing. In fact, the idea that the key to marketing is to satisfy the consumer has been called the *marketing concept.*[4] Consumer is actually a catchphrase for a total purchasing unit that sometimes includes several or more individuals and is often referred to as a *decision making unit* (DMU). To understand the DMU concept, consider the different types of marketing. In consumer and consumer-goods marketing, products travel through a distribution channel, then are bought by ultimate consumers. Industrial marketing, on the other hand, is the marketing of products to companies, institutions, and governments. Sometimes the same product is sold as both a consumer good and an industrial good. Mattresses, for example, are sold to ultimate consumers as well as to hotels, hospitals, and prisons (governments).

---

3. On the study of nonbusiness marketing, *see* Benson P. Shapiro, "Marketing for Nonprofit Organizations," *Harvard Business Review* (September–October 1973), and Christopher H. Lovelock and Charles B. Weinberg, *Marketing for Public and Nonprofit Managers* (New York: John Wiley & Sons, 1984).

4. J. B. McKitterick, "What is the Marketing Management Concept?" in *The Frontiers of Marketing Thought and Science,* ed. Frank M. Bass (Chicago: American Marketing Association, 1957), pp. 71–82.

The industrial DMU is often large and complex, sometimes involving over 10 people. It is not unusual for a large purchase to be made by a formal committee or task force or for many individuals to play important roles in a very complex decision-making process (DMP). Even consumer goods can involve multiperson DMUs. In the purchase of plumbing fixtures for a home, the actual purchaser may be influenced by users (perhaps children in the family), experts (an architect, for example), and installation personnel (the plumber). A more common case might be a vacation or automobile purchase in a family of four, where each member has different needs and criteria.

Consumer analysis is a difficult, endless, and critically important task, for the consumer is the focus of almost all marketing action.

The channel, the third participant, is an active player in the marketing process. Products often succeed or fail based on whether or not they attract trade (or channel) support. The channel is typically presented with far too many products to carry, so only a subset is carried, a smaller number receive active support, and many are not even carried. If the company's marketing plan assumes that stores will carry a product, and they do not, the result is either failure or a change in the distribution plan. The channel, therefore, justifies the same type of careful analysis as the consumer.

The fourth participant is the competition. Few products face no competitors. Sometimes the competition is very direct, as between Pepsi-Cola and Coca-Cola. At other times it is more subtle, as when trade associations for different fruits compete with one another. It is unlikely that consumers will simultaneously and for long periods increase their consumption of all fruits. Consequently the trade associations for peaches and apples compete with one another for "share of stomach," as it is called in the food industry. At a broader level, all uses of the consumer's funds compete with one another because both money and time are limited, even for the affluent. If a wealthy consumer has purchased a yacht, a villa on the Italian Riviera is probably out of the question, at least for the moment.

Generally, competition is viewed in terms of substitution for a given product need. Thus, gas ranges are viewed as competitive with electric ranges. But the competition among electric ranges is generally more intense than competition between the two types of ranges. Defining the competition is an art in itself.

Marketing is a blend of science and art, and the conceptual structures are far from perfect. They are good if they are useful; they do not have to be perfect. Marketing, furthermore, is not studied according to one overarching, unified theory. There are many concepts, but each is useful in only some situations. The art of marketing is to apply each concept (the science) to the right situation and only to the right situation, which is one reason case study is so appropriate in marketing. It emphasizes the situation-specific nature of marketing without detracting from theory building and concept generation.

——— THE MARKETING PROCESS

The marketing process enables us to study what marketers do. The first stage of marketing is *analysis*. Along with a healthy balance of quantitative and qualitative approaches, analysis usually focuses on the company, consumer, channels, and competitors. It helps the marketer select the right markets to approach and the right elements of the mix to use.

Two forms of analysis deserve special attention here. The first, *market segmentation*, is the process of dividing a market into groups of consumers who in some important way are more like one another than they are like members of another segment. An apparel maker might, for example, group people by age, income, height, height/weight combination, fashion interest, and so forth. Or it might combine several descriptors. A manufacturer of expensive suits might focus on wealthy urban consumers with strong fashion interest. Market segmentation is a part of consumer analysis and a demanding art form. The segmentation approach must fit the marketing decision being made.

A second form of analysis is relatively straightforward quantitative analysis and includes *break-even analysis* and *profitability projections*.[5] Effective decisions cannot be made without careful quantitative analysis based on well-developed assumptions.

Market analysis leads to the development of *strategies, plans,* and *programs*. These differ from one another in terms of their scope and time impact. Strategies are broad and are intended to have long-term influence. Programs are detailed and have short-term impact. In the middle of both dimensions are plans, which tie programs and strategies together.

Developing strategies, plans, and programs is not enough. What follows is *implementation*—the execution of the marketing activities.

Finally, marketers must *monitor* and *audit* what has taken place. Because the world changes, and consumers, channels, competitors, and even companies themselves change, a firm must audit its plans and monitor the external environment to more effectively repeat the cycle of analysis, formulation of strategy, plan and program, and implementation.

Since marketing is a combination of art and science, no amount of creativity or cleverness can replace careful, disciplined analysis, formulation, and implementation. Marketing, like invention, is 90% perspiration and 10% inspiration.

---

5. *See* Robert J. Dolan, "Basic Quantitative Analysis for Marketing," Harvard Business School No. 9-584-149.

——— DISCUSSION QUESTIONS

1. Would you say that marketing is mainly executed through advertising and selling? Why or why not?

2. The marketing function gets the product or service to the customer, usually through intermediaries. Of the four major elements involved in this function, do you consider some to be more important than others? Explain which ones and why.

3. Who are the participants in the marketing arena? Describe the function of each one. Are there any instances when one of these participants can be eliminated and still effect a successful marketing campaign?

4. The marketing process enables marketers to study what they do through analysis. Describe the various stages of the process and the integration that is necessary to develop a marketing program. Once this process has proved to be successful, can it be effectively repeated? Why or why not?

5. What are the marketing-related concerns that face the typical marketing manager in consumer goods? How do these differ from those in industrial goods?

THE MARKET-DRIVEN ORGANIZATION

E*very organization should have a market philosophy that guides the planning and implementation of its marketing functions. For example, if a company's goal is growth, its marketing strategy should guide it toward taking advantage of all growth opportunities. In addition, the entire organization should be involved in the marketing strategy so that all units can participate in a shared commitment to company goals by becoming market focused and customer sensitive. These viewpoints are presented in the first two readings. The last reading in Part Two puts the spotlight on today's competitive environment and on how different strategies capture different markets by catering to customers' real needs.*

Marketing Myopia   2

THEODORE LEVITT

This time-tested reading was first published in 1960, and a retrospective commentary was added by the author in 1975. Its success testifies to the validity of its message: To ensure continuing growth, organizations need to define their industries as broadly as possible to take advantage of growth opportunities. Using the archetype of the railroads, the author shows how they declined inevitably as technology advanced because they defined the business they were in too narrowly (i.e., the railroad business instead of the transportation business). To continue growing, companies must ascertain and act on their customers' needs and desires, not bank on the presumed longevity of their products.

Every major industry was once a growth industry. But some that are now riding a wave of growth enthusiasm are very much in the shadow of decline. Others which are thought of as seasoned growth industries have actually stopped growing. In every case the reason growth is threatened, slowed, or stopped is *not* because the market is saturated. It is because there has been a failure of management.

Fateful purposes. The failure is at the top. The executives responsible for it, in the last analysis, are those who deal with broad aims and policies. Thus:

- The railroads did not stop growing because the need for passenger and freight transportation declined. That grew. The railroads are in trouble today not because the need was filled by others (cars, trucks, airplanes, even telephones) but because it was *not* filled by the railroads themselves. They let others take customers away from them because they assumed themselves to be in the railroad business rather than in the transportation business. The reason they defined their industry incorrectly was that they were railroad-oriented instead of transportation-oriented; they were product-oriented instead of customer-oriented.

- Hollywood barely escaped being totally ravished by television. Actually, all the established film companies went through drastic reorganizations. Some simply disappeared. All of them got into trouble not because of TV's inroads but because of their own myopia. As with the railroads, Hollywood defined its business incorrectly. It thought it was in the movie business when it was actually in the entertainment business. "Movies" implied a specific, limited product. This produced a fatuous contentment which from the beginning led producers to view TV as a threat. Hollywood scorned and rejected TV when it should have welcomed it as an opportunity—an opportunity to expand the entertainment business.

Today TV is a bigger business than the old narrowly defined movie business ever was. Had Hollywood been customer-oriented (providing entertainment) rather than product-oriented (making movies), would it have gone through the fiscal purgatory that it did? I doubt it. What ultimately saved Hollywood and accounted for its resurgence was the wave of new young writers, producers, and directors whose previous successes in television had decimated the old movie companies and toppled the big movie moguls.

There are other less obvious examples of industries that have been and are now endangering their futures by improperly defining their purposes. I shall discuss some in detail later and analyze the kind of policies that lead to trouble. Right now it may help to show what a thoroughly customer-oriented management *can* do to keep a growth industry growing, even after the obvious opportunities have been exhausted; and here there are two examples that have been around for a long time. They are nylon and glass—specifically, E. I. DuPont de Nemours & Company and Corning Glass Works.

Both companies have great technical competence. Their product orientation is unquestioned. But this alone does not explain their success. After all, who was more pridefully product-oriented and product-conscious than the erstwhile New England textile companies that have been so thoroughly massacred? The DuPonts and the Cornings have succeeded not primarily because of their product or research orientation but because they have been thoroughly customer-oriented also. It is constant watchfulness for opportunities to apply their technical know-how to the creation of customer-satisfying uses which accounts for their prodigious output of successful new products. Without a very sophisticated eye on the customer, most of their new products might have been wrong, their sales methods useless.

Aluminum has also continued to be a growth industry, thanks to the efforts of two wartime-created companies which deliberately set about creating new customer-satisfying uses. Without Kaiser Aluminum & Chemical Corporation and Reynolds Metals Company, the total demand for aluminum today would be vastly less.

Error of analysis. Some may argue that it is foolish to set the railroads off against aluminum or the movies off against glass. Are not aluminum and glass naturally so versatile that the industries are bound to have more growth opportunities than the railroads and movies? This view commits precisely the error I have been talking about. It defines an industry, or a product, or a cluster of know-how so narrowly as to guarantee its premature senescence. When we mention "railroads," we should make sure we mean "transportation." As transporters, the railroads still have a good chance for very considerable growth. They are not limited to the railroad business as such (though in my opinion rail transportation is potentially a much stronger transportation medium than is generally believed).

What the railroads lack is not opportunity but some of the managerial imaginativeness and audacity that made them great. Even an amateur like Jacques Barzun can see what is lacking when he says:

> I grieve to see the most advanced physical and social organization of the last century go down in shabby disgrace for lack of the same comprehensive imagination that built it up. [What is lacking is] the will of the companies to survive and to satisfy the public by inventiveness and skill.[1]

———— SHADOW OF OBSOLESCENCE

It is impossible to mention a single major industry that did not at one time qualify for the magic appellation of "growth industry." In each case its assumed strength lay in the apparently unchallenged superiority of its product. There appeared to be no effective substitute for it. It was itself a runaway substitute for the product it so triumphantly replaced. Yet one after another of these celebrated industries has come under a shadow. Let us look briefly at a few more of them, this time taking examples that have so far received a little less attention:

Dry cleaning. This was once a growth industry with lavish prospects. In an age of wool garments, imagine being finally able to get them safely and easily clean. The boom was on.

Yet here we are 30 years after the boom started, and the industry is in trouble. Where has the competition come from? From a better way of cleaning? No. It has come from synthetic fibers and chemical additives that have cut the need for dry cleaning. But this is only the beginning. Lurking in the wings and ready to make chemical dry cleaning totally obsolescent is that powerful magician, ultrasonics.

Electric utilities. This is another one of those supposedly "no-substitute" products that has been enthroned on a pedestal of invincible growth. When the incandescent lamp came along, kerosene lights were finished. Later the water wheel and the steam engine were cut to ribbons by the flexibility, reliability, simplicity, and just plain easy availability of electric motors. The prosperity of electric utilities continues to wax extravagant as the home is converted into a museum of electric gadgetry. How can anybody miss by investing in utilities, with no competition, nothing but growth ahead?

---

1. Jacques Barzun, "Trains and the Mind of Man," *Holiday*, February 1960, p. 21.

But a second look is not quite so comforting. A score of nonutility companies are well advanced toward developing a powerful chemical fuel cell which could sit in some hidden closet of every home silently ticking off electric power. The electric lines that vulgarize so many neighborhoods will be eliminated. So will the endless demolition of streets and service interruptions during storms. Also on the horizon is solar energy, again pioneered by non-utility companies.

Who says that the utilities have no competition? They may be natural monopolies now, but tomorrow they may be natural deaths. To avoid this prospect, they too will have to develop fuel cells, solar energy, and other power sources. To survive, they themselves will have to plot the obsolescence of what now produces their livelihood.

Grocery stores. Many people find it hard to realize that there ever was a thriving establishment known as the "corner grocery store." The supermarket took over with a powerful effectiveness. Yet the big food chains of the 1930s narrowly escaped being completely wiped out by the aggressive expansion of independent supermarkets. The first genuine supermarket was opened in 1930, in Jamaica, Long Island. By 1933 supermarkets were thriving in California, Ohio, Pennsylvania, and elsewhere. Yet the established chains pompously ignored them. When they chose to notice them, it was with such derisive descriptions as "cheapy," "horse-and-buggy," "cracker-barrel storekeeping," and "unethical opportunists."

The executive of one big chain announced at the time that he found it "hard to believe that people will drive for miles to shop for foods and sacrifice the personal service chains have perfected and to which [the consumer] is accustomed."[2] As late as 1936, the National Wholesale Grocers convention and the New Jersey Retail Grocers Association said there was nothing to fear. They said that the supers' narrow appeal to the price buyer limited the size of their market. They had to draw from miles around. When imitators came, there would be wholesale liquidations as volume fell. The high sales of the supers were said to be partly due to their novelty. Basically people wanted convenient neighborhood grocers. If the neighborhood stores would "cooperate with their suppliers, pay attention to their costs, and improve their service," they would be able to weather the competition until it blew over.[3]

It never blew over. The chains discovered that survival required going into the supermarket business. This meant the wholesale destruction of their huge investments in corner store sites and in established distribution and merchandising methods. The companies with "the courage of their convictions"

---

2. For more details *see* M. M. Zimmerman, *The Super Market: A Revolution in Distribution* (New York: McGraw-Hill Book Company, Inc., 1955), p. 48.

3. Ibid., pp. 45–47.

resolutely stuck to the corner store philosophy. They kept their pride but lost their shirts.

Self-deceiving cycle. But memories are short. For example, it is hard for people who today confidently hail the twin messiahs of electronics and chemicals to see how things could possibly go wrong with these galloping industries. They probably also cannot see how a reasonably sensible businessperson could have been as myopic as the famous Boston millionaire who early in the twentieth century unintentionally sentenced his heirs to poverty by stipulating that his entire estate be forever invested exclusively in electric streetcar securities. His posthumous declaration, "There will always be a big demand for efficient urban transportation," is no consolation to his heirs who sustain life by pumping gasoline at automobile filling stations.

Yet, in a casual survey I took among a group of intelligent business executives, nearly half agreed that it would be hard to hurt their heirs by tying their estates forever to the electronics industry. When I then confronted them with the Boston streetcar example, they chorused unanimously, "That's different!" But is it? Is not the basic situation identical?

In truth, *there is no such thing as a growth industry*, I believe. There are only companies organized and operated to create and capitalize on growth opportunities. Industries that assume themselves to be riding some automatic growth escalator invariably descend into stagnation. The history of every dead and dying "growth" industry shows a self-deceiving cycle of bountiful expansion and undetected decay. There are four conditions which usually guarantee this cycle:

1. The belief that growth is assured by an expanding and more affluent population.
2. The belief that there is no competitive substitute for the industry's major product.
3. Too much faith in mass production and in the advantages of rapidly declining unit costs as output rises.
4. Preoccupation with a product that lends itself to carefully controlled scientific experimentation, improvement, and manufacturing cost reduction.

I should like now to examine each of these conditions in some detail. To build my case as boldly as possible, I shall illustrate the points with reference to three industries—petroleum, automobiles, and electronics—particularly petroleum, because it spans more years and more vicissitudes. Not only do these three have excellent reputations with the general public and also enjoy the confidence of sophisticated investors, but their managements have become known for progressive thinking in areas like financial control, product research, and management training. If obsolescence can cripple even these industries, it can happen anywhere.

—— POPULATION MYTH

The belief that profits are assured by an expanding and more affluent population is dear to the heart of every industry. It takes the edge off the apprehensions everybody understandably feels about the future. If consumers are multiplying and also buying more of your product or service, you can face the future with considerably more comfort than if the market is shrinking. An expanding market keeps the manufacturer from having to think very hard or imaginatively. If thinking is an intellectual response to a problem, then the absence of a problem leads to the absence of thinking. If your product has an automatically expanding market, then you will not give much thought to how to expand it.

One of the most interesting examples of this is provided by the petroleum industry. Probably our oldest growth industry, it has an enviable record. While there are some current apprehensions about its growth rate, the industry itself tends to be optimistic.

But I believe it can be demonstrated that it is undergoing a fundamental yet typical change. It is not only ceasing to be a growth industry, but may actually be a declining one, relative to other business. Although there is widespread unawareness of it, it is conceivable that in time the oil industry may find itself in much the same position of retrospective glory that the railroads are now in. Despite its pioneering work in developing and applying the present-value method of investment evaluation, in employee relations, and in working with backward countries, the petroleum business is a distressing example of how complacency and wrongheadedness can stubbornly convert opportunity into near disaster.

One of the characteristics of this and other industries that have believed very strongly in the beneficial consequences of an expanding population, while at the same time being industries with a generic product for which there has appeared to be no competitive substitute, is that the individual companies have sought to outdo their competitors by improving on what they are already doing. This makes sense, of course, if one assumes that sales are tied to the country's population strings, because the customer can compare products only on a feature-by-feature basis. I believe it is significant, for example, that not since John D. Rockefeller sent free kerosene lamps to China has the oil industry done anything really outstanding to create a demand for its product. Not even in product improvement has it showered itself with eminence. The greatest single improvement—namely, the development of tetraethyl lead—came from outside the industry, specifically from General Motors and DuPont. The big contributions made by the industry itself are confined to the technology of oil exploration, production, and refining.

Asking for trouble. In other words, the industry's efforts have focused on improving the *efficiency* of getting and making its product, not really on improving the generic product or its marketing. Moreover, its chief product has continuously been defined in the narrowest possible terms, namely, gasoline, not energy, fuel, or transportation. This attitude has helped assure that

- Major improvements in gasoline quality tend not to originate in the oil industry. Also, the development of superior alternative fuels comes from outside the oil industry, as will be shown later.
- Major innovations in automobile fuel marketing are originated by small new oil companies that are not primarily preoccupied with production or refining. These are the companies that have been responsible for the rapidly expanding multipump gasoline stations, with their successful emphasis on large and clean layouts, rapid and efficient driveway service, and quality gasoline at low prices.

Thus, the oil industry is asking for trouble from outsiders. Sooner or later, in this land of hungry investors and entrepreneurs, a threat is sure to come. The possibilities of this will become more apparent when we turn to the next dangerous belief of many managements. For the sake of continuity, because this second belief is tied closely to the first, I shall continue with the same example.

IDEA OF INDISPENSABILITY

The petroleum industry is pretty much persuaded that there is no competitive substitute for its major product, gasoline—or if there is, that it will continue to be a derivative of crude oil, such as diesel fuel or kerosene jet fuel.

There is a lot of automatic wishful thinking in this assumption. The trouble is that most refining companies own huge amounts of crude oil reserves. These have value only if there is a market for products into which oil can be converted—hence the tenacious belief in the continuing competitive superiority of automobile fuels made from crude oil.

This idea persists despite all historic evidence against it. The evidence not only shows that oil has never been a superior product for any purpose for very long, but it also shows that the oil industry has never really been a growth industry. It has been a succession of different businesses that have gone through the usual historic cycles of growth, maturity, and decay. Its overall survival is owed to a series of miraculous escapes from total obsolescence, of last-minute and unexpected reprieves from total disaster reminiscent of the Perils of Pauline.

Perils of petroleum. I shall sketch in only the main episodes.

First, crude oil was largely a patent medicine. But even before that fad ran out, demand was greatly expanded by the use of oil in kerosene lamps. The prospect of lighting the world's lamps gave rise to an extravagant promise of growth. The prospects were similar to those the industry now holds for gasoline in other parts of the world. It can hardly wait for the underdeveloped nations to get a car in every garage.

In the days of the kerosene lamp, the oil companies competed with each other and against gaslight by trying to improve the illuminating characteristics of kerosene. Then suddenly the impossible happened. Edison invented a light which was totally nondependent on crude oil. Had it not been for the growing use of kerosene in space heaters, the incandescent lamp would have completely finished oil as a growth industry at that time. Oil would have been good for little else than axle grease.

Then disaster and reprieve struck again. Two great innovations occurred, neither originating in the oil industry. The successful development of coal-burning domestic central-heating systems made the space heater obsolete. While the industry reeled, along came its most magnificent boost yet—the internal combustion engine, also invented by outsiders. Then when the prodigious expansion for gasoline finally began to level off in the 1920s, along came the miraculous escape of a central oil heater. Once again, the escape was provided by an outsider's invention and development. And when that market weakened, wartime demand for aviation fuel came to the rescue. After the war the expansion of civilian aviation, the dieselization of railroads, and the explosive demand for cars and trucks kept the industry's growth in high gear.

Meanwhile, centralized oil heating—whose boom potential had only recently been proclaimed—ran into severe competition from natural gas. While the oil companies themselves owned the gas that now competed with their oil, the industry did not originate the natural gas revolution, nor has it to this day greatly profited from its gas ownership. The gas revolution was made by newly formed transmission companies that marketed the product with an aggressive ardor. They started a magnificent new industry, first against the advice and then against the resistance of the oil companies.

By all the logic of the situation, the oil companies themselves should have made the gas revolution. They not only owned the gas; they also were the only people experienced in handling, scrubbing, and using it, the only people experienced in pipeline technology and transmission, and they understood heating problems. But, partly because they knew that natural gas would compete with their own sale of heating oil, the oil companies pooh-poohed the potentials of gas.

The revolution was finally started by oil pipeline executives who, unable to persuade their own companies to go into gas, quit and organized the spectacularly successful gas transmission companies. Even after their success became painfully evident to the oil companies, the latter did not go into gas transmission. The multibillion-dollar business which should have been theirs went to others. As in the past, the industry was blinded by its narrow preoccupation with a specific product and the value of its reserves. It paid little or no attention to its customers' basic needs and preferences.

The postwar years have not witnessed any change. Immediately after World War II, the oil industry was greatly encouraged about its future by the rapid expansion of demand for its traditional line of products. In 1950 most companies projected annual rates of domestic expansion of around 6% through at least 1975. Though the ratio of crude oil reserves to demand in the Free World was about 20 to 1, with 10 to 1 being usually considered a reasonable working ratio in the United States, booming demand sent oil explorers searching for more without sufficient regard to what the future really promised. In 1952 they "hit" in the Middle East; the ratio skyrocketed to 42 to 1. If gross additions to reserves continue at the average rate of the past five years (37 billion barrels annually), then by 1970 the reserve ratio will be up to 45 to 1. This abundance of oil has weakened crude and product prices all over the world.

Uncertain future. Management cannot find much consolation today in the rapidly expanding petrochemical industry, another oil-using idea that did not originate in the leading firms. The total United States production of petrochemicals is equivalent to about 2% (by volume) of the demand for all petroleum products. Although the petrochemical industry is now expected to grow by about 10% per year, this will not offset other drains on the growth of crude oil consumption. Furthermore, while petrochemical products are many and growing, it is well to remember that there are nonpetroleum sources of the basic raw material, such as coal. Besides, a lot of plastics can be produced with relatively little oil. A 50,000-barrel-per-day oil refinery is now considered the absolute minimum size for efficiency. But a 5,000-barrel-per-day chemical plant is a giant operation.

Oil has never been a continuously strong growth industry. It has grown by fits and starts, always miraculously saved by innovations and developments not of its own making. The reason it has not grown in a smooth progression is that each time it thought it had a superior product safe from the possibility of competitive substitutes, the product turned out to be inferior and notoriously subject to obsolescence. Until now, gasoline (for motor fuel, anyhow) has escaped this fate. But, as we shall see later, it too may be on its last legs.

The point of all this is that there is no guarantee against product obsolescence. If a company's own research does not make it obsolete, another's will. Unless an industry is especially lucky, as oil has been until now, it can easily go down in a sea of red figures—just as the railroads have, as the buggy whip manufacturers have, as the corner grocery chains have, as most of the big movie companies have, and indeed as many other industries have.

The best way for a firm to be lucky is to make its own luck. That requires knowing what makes a business successful. One of the greatest enemies of this knowledge is mass production.

───── PRODUCTION PRESSURES

Mass-production industries are impelled by a great drive to produce all they can. The prospect of steeply declining unit costs as output rises is more than most companies can usually resist. The profit possibilities look spectacular. All effort focuses on production. The result is that marketing gets neglected.

John Kenneth Galbraith contends that just the opposite occurs.[4] Output is so prodigious that all effort concentrates on trying to get rid of it. He says this accounts for singing commercials, desecration of the countryside with advertising signs, and other wasteful and vulgar practices. Galbraith has a finger on something real, but he misses the strategic point. Mass production does indeed generate great pressure to "move" the product. But what usually gets emphasized is selling, not marketing. Marketing, being a more sophisticated and complex process, gets ignored.

The difference between marketing and selling is more than semantic. Selling focuses on the needs of the seller, marketing on the needs of the buyer. Selling is preoccupied with the seller's need to convert the product into cash, marketing with the idea of satisfying the needs of the customer by means of the product and the whole cluster of things associated with creating, delivering, and finally consuming it.

In some industries the enticements of full mass production have been so powerful that for many years top management in effect has told the sales departments, "You get rid of it; we'll worry about profits." By contrast, a truly marketing-minded firm tries to create value-satisfying goods and services that consumers will want to buy. What it offers for sale includes not only the generic product or service but also how it is made available to the customer, in what form, when, under what conditions, and at what terms of trade. Most important, what it offers for sale is determined not by the seller but by the buyer. The seller takes cues from the buyer in such a way that the product becomes a consequence of the marketing effort, not vice versa.

Lag in Detroit. This may sound like an elementary rule of business, but that does not keep it from being violated wholesale. It is certainly more violated than honored. Take the automobile industry.

Here mass production is most famous, most honored, and has the greatest impact on the entire society. The industry has hitched its fortune to the relentless requirements of the annual model change, a policy that makes customer orientation an especially urgent necessity. Consequently, the auto companies annually spend millions of dollars on consumer research. But the fact that the new compact cars are selling so well in their first year indicates that Detroit's vast researches have for a long time failed to reveal what customers really wanted. Detroit was not persuaded that people wanted anything different from what they had been getting until it lost millions of customers to other small-car manufacturers.

How could this unbelievable lag behind consumer wants have been perpetuated so long? Why did not research reveal consumer preferences before

---

4. *The Affluent Society* (Boston: Houghton Mifflin Company, 1958), pp. 152–160.

consumers' buying decisions themselves revealed the facts? Is that not what consumer research is for—to find out before the fact what is going to happen? The answer is that Detroit never really researched customers' wants. It only researched their preferences between the kinds of things which it had already decided to offer them. For Detroit is mainly product-oriented, not customer-oriented. To the extent that the customer is recognized as having needs that the manufacturer should try to satisfy, Detroit usually acts as if the job can be done entirely by product changes. Occasionally attention gets paid to financing, too, but that is done more in order to sell than to enable the customer to buy.

As for taking care of other customer needs, there is not enough being done to write about. The areas of the greatest unsatisfied needs are ignored or, at best, get stepchild attention. These are at the point of sale and on the matter of automotive repair and maintenance. Detroit views these problem areas as being of secondary importance. That is underscored by the fact that the retailing and servicing ends of this industry are neither owned and operated nor controlled by the manufacturers. Once the car is produced, things are pretty much in the dealer's inadequate hands. Illustrative of Detroit's arms-length attitude is the fact that, while servicing holds enormous sales-stimulating, profit-building opportunities, only 57 of Chevrolet's 7,000 dealers provide night maintenance service.

Motorists repeatedly express their dissatisfaction with servicing and their apprehensions about buying cars under the present selling setup. The anxieties and problems they encounter during the auto buying and maintenance processes are probably more intense and widespread today than many years ago. Yet the automobile companies do not seem to listen to or to take their cues from the anguished consumer. If they do listen, it must be through the filter of their own preoccupation with production. The marketing effort is still viewed as a necessary consequence of the product—not vice versa, as it should be. That is the legacy of mass production, with its parochial view that profit resides essentially in low-cost full production.

What Ford put first. The profit lure of mass production obviously has a place in the plans and strategy of business management, but it must always *follow* hard thinking about the customer. This is one of the most important lessons that we can learn from the contradictory behavior of Henry Ford. In a sense Ford was both the most brilliant and the most senseless marketer in American history. He was senseless because he refused to give the customer anything but a black car. He was brilliant because he fashioned a production system designed to fit market needs. We habitually celebrate him for the wrong reason, his production genius. His real genius was marketing. We think he was able to cut his selling price and therefore sell millions of $500 cars because his invention of the assembly line had reduced the costs. Actually he invented the assembly line because he had concluded that at $500 he could sell millions of cars. Mass production was the *result*, not the cause, of his low prices.

Ford repeatedly emphasized this point, but a nation of production-oriented business managers refuses to hear the great lesson he taught. Here is his operating philosophy as he expressed it succinctly:

> Our policy is to reduce the price, extend the operations, and improve the article. You will notice that the reduction of price comes first. We have never considered any costs as fixed. Therefore we first reduce the price to the point where we believe more sales will result. Then we go ahead and try to make the prices. We do not bother about the costs. The new price forces the costs down. The more usual way is to take the costs and then determine the price; and although that method may be scientific in the narrow sense, it is not scientific in the broad sense, because what earthly use is it to know the cost if it tells you that you cannot manufacture at a price at which the article can be sold? But more to the point is the fact that, although one may calculate what a cost is, and of course all of our costs are carefully calculated, no one knows what a cost ought to be. One of the ways of discovering . . . is to name a price so low as to force everybody in the place to the highest point of efficiency. The low price makes everybody dig for profits. We make more discoveries concerning manufacturing and selling under this forced method than by any method of leisurely investigation.[5]

Product provincialism. The tantalizing profit possibilities of low unit production costs may be the most seriously self-deceiving attitude that can afflict a company, particularly a "growth" company where an apparently assured expansion of demand already tends to undermine a proper concern for the importance of marketing and the customer.

The usual result of this narrow preoccupation with so-called concrete matters is that instead of growing, the industry declines. It usually means that the product fails to adapt to the constantly changing patterns of consumer needs and tastes, to new and modified marketing institutions and practices, or to product developments in competing or complementary industries. The industry has its eyes so firmly on its own specific product that it does not see how it is being made obsolete.

The classic example of this is the buggy whip industry. No amount of product improvement could stave off its death sentence. But had the industry defined itself as being in the transportation business rather than the buggy whip business, it might have survived. It would have done what survival always entails, that is, change. Even if it had only defined its business as providing a stimulant or catalyst to an energy source, it might have survived by becoming a manufacturer of, say, fanbelts or air cleaners.

What may someday be a still more classic example is, again, the oil industry. Having let others steal marvelous opportunities from it (e.g., natural

---

5. Henry Ford, *My Life and Work* (New York: Doubleday, Page & Company, 1923), pp. 146–147.

gas, as already mentioned, missile fuels, and jet engine lubricants), one would expect it to have taken steps never to let that happen again. But this is not the case. We are now seeing extraordinary new developments in fuel systems specifically designed to power automobiles. Not only are these developments concentrated in firms outside the petroleum industry, but petroleum is almost systematically ignoring them, securely content in its wedded bliss to oil. It is the story of the kerosene lamp versus the incandescent lamp all over again. Oil is trying to improve hydrocarbon fuels rather than develop *any* fuels best suited to the needs of their users, whether or not made in different ways and with different raw materials from oil.

Here are some things which nonpetroleum companies are working on:

- Over a dozen such firms now have advanced working models of energy systems which, when perfected, will replace the internal combustion engine and eliminate the demand for gasoline. The superior merit of each of these systems is their elimination of frequent, time-consuming, and irritating refueling stops. Most of these systems are fuel cells designed to create electrical energy directly from chemicals without combustion. Most of them use chemicals that are not derived from oil, generally hydrogen and oxygen.

- Several other companies have advanced models of electric storage batteries designed to power automobiles. One of these is an aircraft producer that is working jointly with several electric utility companies. The latter hope to use off-peak generating capacity to supply overnight plug-in battery regeneration. Another company, also using the battery approach, is a medium-size electronics firm with extensive small-battery experience that it developed in connection with its work on hearing aids. It is collaborating with an automobile manufacturer. Recent improvements arising from the need for high-powered miniature power storage plants in rockets have put us within reach of a relatively small battery capable of withstanding great overloads or surges of power. Germanium diode applications and batteries using sintered-plate and nickel-cadmium techniques promise to make a revolution in our energy sources.

- Solar energy conversion systems are also getting increasing attention. One usually cautious Detroit auto executive recently ventured that solar-powered cars might be common by 1980.

As for the oil companies, they are more or less "watching developments," as one research director put it to me. A few are doing a bit of research on fuel cells, but this research is almost always confined to developing cells powered by hydrocarbon chemicals. None of them are enthusiastically researching fuel cells, batteries, or solar power plants. None of them are spending a fraction as much on research in these profoundly important areas as they are on the usual run-of-the-mill things like reducing combustion chamber deposit in gasoline engines. One major integrated petroleum company recently took a tentative look at the fuel cell and concluded that although "the companies actively working on it indicate a belief in ultimate success . . . the timing and magnitude of its impact are too remote to warrant recognition in our forecasts."

One might, of course, ask: Why should the oil companies do anything different? Would not chemical fuel cells, batteries, or solar energy kill the present product lines? The answer is that they would indeed, and that is precisely the reason for the oil firms' having to develop these power units before their competitors do, so they will not be companies without an industry.

Management might be more likely to do what is needed for its own preservation if it thought of itself as being in the energy business. But even that would not be enough if it persists in imprisoning itself in the narrow grip of its tight product orientation. It has to think of itself as taking care of customer needs, not finding, refining, or even selling oil. Once it genuinely thinks of its business as taking care of people's transportation needs, nothing can stop it from creating its own extravagantly profitable growth.

Creative destruction. Since words are cheap and deeds are dear, it may be appropriate to indicate what this kind of thinking involves and leads to. Let us start at the beginning—the customer. It can be shown that motorists strongly dislike the bother, delay, and experience of buying gasoline. People actually do not buy gasoline. They cannot see it, taste it, feel it, appreciate it, or really test it. What they buy is the right to continue driving their cars. The gas station is like a tax collector to whom people are compelled to pay a periodic toll as the price of using their cars. This makes the gas station a basically unpopular institution. It can never be made popular or pleasant, only less unpopular, less unpleasant.

To reduce its unpopularity completely means eliminating it. Nobody likes a tax collector, not even a pleasantly cheerful one. Nobody likes to interrupt a trip to buy a phantom product, not even from a handsome Adonis or a seductive Venus. Hence, companies that are working on exotic fuel substitutes which will eliminate the need for frequent refueling are heading directly into the outstretched arms of the irritated motorist. They are riding a wave of inevitability, not because they are creating something that is technologically superior or more sophisticated, but because they are satisfying a powerful customer need. They are also eliminating noxious odors and air pollution.

Once the petroleum companies recognize the customer-satisfying logic of what another power system can do, they will see that they have no more choice about working on an efficient, long-lasting fuel (or some way of delivering present fuels without bothering the motorist) than the big food chains had a choice about going into the supermarket business, or the vacuum tube companies had a choice about making semiconductors. For their own good the oil firms will have to destroy their own highly profitable assets. No amount of wishful thinking can save them from the necessity of engaging in this form of "creative destruction."

I phrase the need as strongly as this because I think management must make quite an effort to break itself loose from conventional ways. It is all too easy in this day and age for a company or industry to let its sense of purpose become dominated by the economies of full production and to develop a dangerously lopsided product orientation. In short, if management lets itself drift, it invariably drifts in the direction of thinking of itself as producing goods and services, not customer satisfactions. While it probably will not descend to the depths of telling its salespeople, "You get rid of it; we'll worry about profits," it can, without knowing it, be practicing precisely that formula for withering decay. The historic fate of one growth industry after another has been its suicidal product provincialism.

——— DANGERS OF R&D

Another big danger to a firm's continued growth arises when top management is wholly transfixed by the profit possibilities of technical research and development. To illustrate I shall turn first to a new industry—electronics—and then return once more to the oil companies. By comparing a fresh example with a familiar one, I hope to emphasize the prevalence and insidiousness of a hazardous way of thinking.

Marketing shortchanged. In the case of electronics, the greatest danger which faces the glamorous new companies in this field is not that they do not pay enough attention to research and development, but that they pay *too much* attention to it. And the fact that the fastest growing electronics firms owe their eminence to their heavy emphasis on technical research is completely beside the point. They have vaulted to affluence on a sudden crest of unusually strong general receptiveness to new technical ideas. Also, their success has been shaped in the virtually guaranteed market of military subsidies and by military orders that in many cases actually preceded the existence of facilities to make the products. Their expansion has, in other words, been almost totally devoid of marketing effort.

Thus, they are growing up under conditions that come dangerously close to creating the illusion that a superior product will sell itself. Having created a successful company by making a superior product, it is not surprising that management continues to be oriented toward the product rather than the people who consume it. It develops the philosophy that continued growth is a matter of continued product innovation and improvement.

A number of other factors tend to strengthen and sustain this belief:

1. Because electronic products are highly complex and sophisticated, managements become top-heavy with engineers and scientists. This creates a selective bias in favor of research and production at the expense of marketing. The organization tends to view itself as making things rather than satisfying customer needs. Marketing

gets treated as a residual activity, "something else" that must be done once the vital job of product creation and production is completed.

2. To this bias in favor of product research, development, and production is added the bias in favor of dealing with controllable variables. Engineers and scientists are at home in the world of concrete things like machines, test tubes, production lines, and even balance sheets. The abstractions to which they feel kindly are those which are testable or manipulatable in the laboratory or, if not testable, then functional, such as Euclid's axioms. In short, the managements of the new glamor-growth companies tend to favor those business activities which lend themselves to careful study, experimentation, and control—the hard, practical realities of the lab, the shop, the books.

What gets shortchanged are the realities of the *market*. Consumers are unpredictable, varied, fickle, stupid, shortsighted, stubborn, and generally bothersome. This is not what the engineer-managers say, but deep down in their consciousness, it is what they believe. And this accounts for their concentrating on what they know and what they can control, namely, product research, engineering, and production. The emphasis on production becomes particularly attractive when the product can be made at declining unit costs. There is no more inviting way of making money than by running the plant full blast.

Today the top-heavy science–engineering–production orientation of so many electronics companies works reasonably well because they are pushing into new frontiers in which the armed services have pioneered virtually assured markets. The companies are in the felicitous position of having to fill, not find, markets; of not having to discover what the customer needs and wants but of having the customer voluntarily come forward with specific new product demands. If a team of consultants had been assigned specifically to design a business situation calculated to prevent the emergence and development of a customer-oriented marketing viewpoint, it could not have produced anything better than the conditions just described.

Stepchild treatment. The oil industry is a stunning example of how science, technology, and mass production can divert an entire group of companies from their main task. To the extent the consumer is studied at all (which is not much), the focus is forever on getting information which is designed to help the oil companies improve what they are now doing. They try to discover more convincing advertising themes, more effective sales promotional drives, what the market shares of the various companies are, what people like or dislike about service station dealers and oil companies, and so forth. Nobody seems as interested in probing deeply into the basic human needs that the industry might be trying to satisfy as in probing into the basic properties of the raw material that the companies work with in trying to deliver customer satisfactions.

Basic questions about customers and markets seldom get asked. The latter occupy a stepchild status. They are recognized as existing, as having to be taken care of, but not worth very much real thought or dedicated attention. No oil company gets as excited about the customers in its own backyard as about the oil in the Sahara Desert. Nothing illustrates better the neglect of marketing than its treatment in the industry press.

The centennial issue of the *American Petroleum Institute Quarterly*, published in 1959 to celebrate the discovery of oil in Titusville, Pennsylvania, contained 21 feature articles proclaiming the industry's greatness. Only one of these talked about its achievements in marketing, and that was only a pictorial record of how service station architecture has changed. The issue also contained a special section on "New Horizons," which was devoted to showing the magnificent role oil would play in America's future. Every reference was ebulliently optimistic, never implying once that oil might have some hard competition. Even the reference to atomic energy was a cheerful catalogue of how oil would help make atomic energy a success. There was not a single apprehension that the oil industry's affluence might be threatened or a suggestion that one "new horizon" might include new and better ways of serving oil's present customers.

But the most revealing example of the stepchild treatment that marketing gets is still another special series of short articles on "The Revolutionary Potential of Electronics." Under that heading, this list of articles appeared in the table of contents:

- "In the Search for Oil"
- "In Production Operations"
- "In Refinery Processes"
- "In Pipeline Operations"

Significantly, every one of the industry's major functional areas is listed, *except* marketing. Why? Either it is believed that electronics holds no revolutionary potential for petroleum marketing (which is palpably wrong), or the editors forgot to discuss marketing (which is more likely and illustrates its stepchild status).

The order in which the four functional areas are listed also betrays the alienation of the oil industry from the consumer. The industry is implicitly defined as beginning with the search for oil and ending with its distribution from the refinery. But the truth is, it seems to me, that the industry begins with the needs of the customer for its products. From that primal position its definition moves steadily backstream to areas of progressively lesser importance, until it finally comes to rest at the "search for oil."

Beginning and end. The view that an industry is a customer-satisfying process, not a goods-producing process, is vital for all businesspeople to understand. An industry begins with the customer and his or her needs, not with a patent, a raw material, or a selling skill. Given the customer's needs, the industry develops backwards, first concerning itself with the physical *delivery* of customer satisfactions. Then it moves back further to *creating* the things by which these satisfactions are in part achieved. How these materials are created is a matter of indifference to the customer, hence the particular form of manufacturing, processing, or what-have-you cannot be considered as a vital aspect of the industry. Finally, the industry moves back still further to *finding* the raw materials necessary for making its products.

The irony of some industries oriented toward technical research and development is that the scientists who occupy the high executive positions are totally unscientific when it comes to defining their companies' overall needs and purposes. They violate the first two rules of the scientific method—being aware of and defining their companies' problems, and then developing testable hypotheses about solving them. They are scientific only about the convenient things, such as laboratory and product experiments.

The customer (and the satisfaction of his or her deepest needs) is not considered as being "the problem"—not because there is any certain belief that no such problem exists, but because an organizational lifetime has conditioned management to look in the opposite direction. Marketing is a stepchild.

I do not mean that selling is ignored. Far from it. But selling, again, is not marketing. As already pointed out, selling concerns itself with the tricks and techniques of getting people to exchange their cash for your product. It is not concerned with the values that the exchange is all about. And it does not, as marketing invariably does, view the entire business process as consisting of a tightly integrated effort to discover, create, arouse, and satisfy customer needs. The customer is somebody "out there" who, with proper cunning, can be separated from his or her loose change.

Actually, not even selling gets much attention in some technologically minded firms. Because there is a virtually guaranteed market for the abundant flow of their new products, they do not actually know what a real market is. It is as if they lived in a planned economy, moving their products routinely from factory to retail outlet. Their successful concentration on products tends to convince them of the soundness of what they have been doing, and they fail to see the gathering clouds over the market.

── CONCLUSION

At the turn of the century American railroads enjoyed a fierce loyalty among astute Wall Streeters. European monarchs invested in them heavily. Eternal wealth was thought to be the benediction for anybody who could scrape a few thousand dollars together to put into rail stocks. No other form of transportation could compete with the railroads in speed, flexibility, durability, economy, and growth potentials.

As Jacques Barzun put it, "By the turn of the century it was an institution, an image of man, a tradition, a code of honor, a source of poetry, a nursery of boyhood desires, a sublimest of toys, and the most solemn machine—next to the funeral hearse—that marks the epochs in man's life."[6]

Even after the advent of automobiles, trucks, and airplanes, the railroad tycoons remained imperturbably self-confident. If you had told them 60 years before that in 30 years they would be flat on their backs, broke, and pleading for government subsidies, they would have thought you totally demented. Such a future was simply not considered possible. It was not even a discussable subject, or an askable question, or a matter which any sane person would consider worth speculating about. The very thought was insane. Yet a lot of insane notions now have matter-of-fact acceptance—for example, the idea of 100-ton tubes of metal moving smoothly through the air 20,000 feet above the earth, loaded with 100 sane and solid citizens casually drinking martinis—and they have dealt cruel blows to the railroads.

What specifically must other companies do to avoid this fate? What does customer orientation involve? These questions have in part been answered by the preceding examples and analysis. It would take another article to show in detail what is required for specific industries. In any case, it should be obvious that building an effective customer-oriented company involves far more than good intentions or promotional tricks; it involves profound matters of human organization and leadership. For the present, let me merely suggest what appear to be some general requirements.

Visceral feel of greatness. Obviously the company has to do what survival demands. It has to adapt to the requirements of the market, and it has to do it sooner rather than later. But mere survival is a so-so aspiration. Anybody can survive in some way or other, even the skid-row bum. The trick is to survive gallantly, to feel the surging impulse of commercial mastery; not just to experience the sweet smell of success, but to have the visceral feel of entrepreneurial greatness.

No organization can achieve greatness without a vigorous leader who is driven onward by a pulsating *will to succeed.* A leader has to have a vision of grandeur, a vision that can produce eager followers in vast numbers. In business, the followers are the customers.

In order to produce these customers, the entire corporation must be viewed as a customer-creating and customer-satisfying organism. Management must think of itself not as producing products but as providing customer-creating value satisfactions. It must push this idea (and everything it means and requires) into every nook and cranny of the organization. It has to do this continuously and with the kind of flair that excites and stimulates the people in it. Otherwise, the company will be merely a series of pigeonholed parts, with no consolidating sense of purpose or direction.

---

6. Jacques Barzun, "Trains and the Mind of Man," *Holiday*, February 1960, p. 20.

In short, the organization must learn to think of itself not as producing goods or services but as *buying customers,* as doing the things that will make people *want* to do business with it. And the chief executive has the inescapable responsibility for creating this environment, this viewpoint, this attitude, this aspiration. The chief executive must set the company's style, its direction, and its goals. This means knowing precisely where he or she wants to go and making sure the whole organization is enthusiastically aware of where that is. This is a first requisite of leadership, for *unless a leader knows where he is going, any road will take him there.*

If any road is okay, the chief executive might as well pack his attaché case and go fishing. If an organization does not know or care where it is going, it does not need to advertise that fact with a ceremonial figurehead. Everybody will notice it soon enough.

* * * * *

Fifteen years after the publication of this classic article, which has been widely quoted and anthologized—and subject to many interpretations—the author added the following commentary.

———— RETROSPECTIVE COMMENTARY

Amazed, finally, by his literary success, Isaac Bashevis Singer reconciled an attendant problem: "I think the moment you have published a book, it's not any more your private property. . . . If it has value, everybody can find in it what he finds, and I cannot tell the man I did not intend it to be so." Over the past 15 years, "Marketing Myopia" has become a case in point. Remarkably, the article spawned a legion of loyal partisans—not to mention a host of unlikely bed-fellows.

Its most common and, I believe, most influential consequence is the way certain companies for the first time gave serious thought to the question of what businesses they are really in.

The strategic consequences of this have in many cases been dramatic. The best-known case, of course, is the shift in thinking of oneself as being in the "oil business" to being in the "energy business." In some instances the payoff has been spectacular (getting into coal, for example) and in others dreadful (in terms of the time and money spent so far on fuel cell research). Another successful example is a company with a large chain of retail shoe stores that redefined itself as a retailer of moderately priced, frequently purchased, widely assorted consumer specialty products. The result was a dramatic growth in volume, earnings, and return on assets.

Some companies, again for the first time, asked themselves whether they wished to be masters of certain technologies for which they would seek markets, or masters of markets for which they would seek customer-satisfying products and services.

Choosing the former, one company has declared, in effect, "We are experts in glass technology. We intend to improve and expand that expertise with the object of creating products that will attract customers." This decision has forced the company into a much more systematic and customer-sensitive look at possible markets and users, even though its stated strategic object has been to capitalize on glass technology.

Deciding to concentrate on markets, another company has determined that "we want to help people (primarily women) enhance their beauty and sense of youthfulness." This company has expanded its line of cosmetic products, but it has also entered the fields of proprietary drugs and vitamin supplements.

All these examples illustrate the "policy" results of "Marketing Myopia." On the operating level, there has been, I think, an extraordinary heightening of sensitivity to customers and consumers. R&D departments have cultivated a greater "external" orientation toward uses, users, and markets—balancing thereby the previously one-sided "internal" focus on materials and methods; upper management has realized that marketing and sales departments should be somewhat more willingly accommodated than before; finance departments have become more receptive to the legitimacy of budgets for market research and experimentation in marketing; and salespeople have been better trained to listen to and understand customer needs and problems rather than merely to "push" the product.

A MIRROR, NOT A WINDOW

My impression is that the article has had more impact in industrial-products companies than in consumer-products companies—perhaps because the former had lagged most in customer orientation. There are at least two reasons for this lag: (1) industrial-products companies tend to be more capital intensive, and (2) in the past, at least, they have had to rely heavily on communicating face-to-face the technical character of what they made and sold. These points are worth explaining.

Capital-intensive businesses are understandably preoccupied with magnitudes, especially where the capital, once invested, cannot be easily moved, manipulated, or modified for the production of a variety of products—e.g., chemical plants, steel mills, airlines, and railroads. Understandably, they seek big volumes and operating efficiencies to pay off the equipment and meet the carrying costs.

At least one problem results: corporate power becomes disproportionately lodged with operating or financial executives. If you read the
charter of one of the nation's largest companies, you will see that the chairman
of the finance committee, not the chief executive officer, is the "chief." Executives with such backgrounds have an almost trained incapacity to see that
getting "volume" may require understanding and serving many discrete and
sometimes small market segments rather than going after a perhaps mythical
batch of big or homogeneous customers.

These executives also often fail to appreciate the competitive changes
going on around them. They observe the changes, all right, but devalue their
significance or underestimate their ability to nibble away at the company's
markets.

Once dramatically alerted to the concept of segments, sectors, and
customers, though, managers of capital-intensive businesses have become more
responsive to the necessity of balancing their inescapable preoccupation with
"paying the bills" or breaking even with the fact that the best way to accomplish
this may be to pay more attention to segments, sectors, and customers.

The second reason industrial-products companies have probably been
more influenced by the article is that, in the case of the more technical industrial
products or services, the necessity of clearly communicating product and
service characteristics to prospects results in a lot of face-to-face "selling" effort.
But precisely because the product is so complex, the situation produces
salespeople who know the product more than they know the customer, who are
more adept at explaining what they have and what it can do than learning what
the customer's needs and problems are. The result has been a narrow product
orientation rather than a liberating customer orientation, and "service" has
often suffered. To be sure, sellers said, "We have to provide service," but they
tended to define service by looking into the mirror rather than out the window.
They *thought* they were looking out the window at the customer, but it was
actually a mirror—a reflection of their own product-oriented biases rather than
a reflection of their customers' situations.

A MANIFESTO, NOT A PRESCRIPTION

Not everything has been rosy. A lot of bizarre things have happened as
a result of this article:

- Some companies have developed what I call "marketing mania"—
  they've become obsessively responsive to every fleeting whim of
  the customer. Mass-production operations have been converted to
  approximations of job shops, with cost and price consequences far
  exceeding the willingness of customers to buy the product.
- Management has expanded product lines and added new lines of
  business without first establishing adequate control systems to run
  more complex operations.

- Marketing staffs have suddenly and rapidly expanded themselves and their research budgets without either getting sufficient prior organizational support or, thereafter, producing sufficient results.

- Companies that are functionally organized have converted to product-, brand-, or market-based organizations with the expectation of instant and miraculous results. The outcome has been ambiguity, frustration, confusion, corporate infighting, losses, and finally a reversion to functional arrangements that has only worsened the situation.

- Companies have attempted to "serve" customers by creating complex and beautifully efficient products or services that buyers are either too risk-averse to adopt or incapable of learning how to employ—in effect, there are now steam shovels for people who haven't yet learned to use spades. This problem has happened repeatedly in the so-called service industries (financial services, insurance, computer-based services) and with American companies selling in less-developed economies.

"Marketing Myopia" was not intended as analysis or even prescription; it was intended as manifesto. It did not pretend to take a balanced position. Nor was it a new idea: Peter F. Drucker, J. B. McKitterick, Wroe Alderson, John Howard, and Neil Borden had each done more original and balanced work on "the marketing concept." My scheme, however, tied marketing more closely to the inner orbit of business policy. Drucker—especially in *The Concept of the Corporation* and *The Practice of Management*—originally provided me with a great deal of insight.

My contribution, therefore, appears merely to have been a simple, brief, and useful way of communicating an existing way of thinking. I tried to do it in a very direct, but responsible, fashion, knowing that few readers (customers), especially managers and leaders, could stand much equivocation or hesitation. I also knew that the colorful and lightly documented affirmation works better than the tortuously reasoned explanation.

But why the enormous popularity of what was actually such a simple preexisting idea? Why its appeal throughout the world to resolutely restrained scholars, implacably temperate managers, and high government officials, all accustomed to balanced and thoughtful calculation? Is it that concrete examples, joined to illustrate a simple idea and presented with some attention to literacy, communicate better than massive analytical reasoning that reads as though it were translated from the German? Is it that provocative assertions are more memorable and persuasive than restrained and balanced explanations, no matter who the audience? Is it that the character of the message is as much the message as its content? Or was mine not simply a different tune but a new symphony? I don't know.

Of course, I'd do it again and in the same way, given my purposes, even with what more I now know—the good and the bad, the power of facts, and the limits of rhetoric. If your mission is the moon, you don't use a car. Don Marquis's cockroach, Archy, provides some final consolation: "An idea is not responsible for who believes in it."

——— DISCUSSION QUESTIONS

1. One enduring requirement of marketing over the years has been to "give the customer what the customer wants." This philosophy is alive and strong today, but the ways it is being executed are different, varied, and complex. What are the benefits to be gained? What are the costs entailed? What are the obstacles to implementing this strategy? How can management overcome them?

2. To take advantage of growth opportunities as markets and technologies change, a company must define the business it is in as broadly as possible. The reading gives examples of industries that did not do this and suffered the consequences. What industries exist today that could face the same problem? If you were a decision maker in this industry, what would you do to prepare your company for the future?

3. According to the author, there is no such thing as a growth industry. He cites four pitfalls that blur the vision of marketing executives causing them to miss signs of decay. Do you agree with the author's analysis? The author gives the example of the movie industry nearly being "totally ravished by television." Why did this happen? What did Hollywood do to turn it around? Looking into the future, how should the encroachment of the VCR into both of these industries be viewed?

4. The solutions to many growth problems, suggests the author, can have their own caveats. What might those be, and how can they be resolved?

5. Do you agree that a superior product will sell itself and create a successful company? In your view, should a company devote its major resources to its product or to the people who consume it? Why?

6. The reading states that the chief executive of an organization must set the company's style, direction, and goals. What does the author mean when he says, "This is a first requisite of leadership, for unless [the chief executive] knows where he is going, any road will take him there. [And] if any road is okay, the chief executive might as well pack his attaché case and go fishing."?

What the Hell Is "Market Oriented"?   3

BENSON P. SHAPIRO

Becoming market oriented means more than encouraging the marketing group to get close to the customer, as Wolverine Controller Company learned. This reading describes how Wolverine, a company "in deep trouble with both domestic and foreign competition," developed a market orientation. The effort involved dispersing information about customers, potential customers, and competitors throughout the organization; spreading strategic and tactical decision making so that all key divisions participated; and instilling a shared sense of commitment toward flawless service of the company's markets. Finally, the company recognized that success could lead to smugness. The fear of complacency, when market share and earnings are headed upward, is also part of being market oriented.

The air hung heavy in French Lick, Indiana. A tornado watch was in effect that morning, and the sky was black. In a meeting room in one of the local resort hotels, where top management of the Wolverine Controller Company had gathered, the atmosphere matched the weather. Recent results had been poor for the Indianapolis-based producer of flow controllers for process industries like chemicals, paper, and food. Sales were off, but earnings were off even more. Market share was down in all product lines.

As the president called the meeting to order, he had fire in his eyes. "The situation can't get much more serious," he proclaimed. "As you all know, over the past couple of years everything has gone to hell in a handbasket. We're in deep trouble, with both domestic and foreign competition preempting us at every turn. The only way to get out of this mess is for us to become customer driven or market oriented. I'm not even sure what that means, but I'm damn sure that we want to be there. I don't even know whether there's a difference between being market driven and customer oriented or customer driven and market oriented or whatever. We've just got to do a hell of a lot better."

"I couldn't agree with you more, Frank," the marketing vice president put in. "I've been saying all along that we've got to be more marketing oriented. The marketing department has to be more involved in everything that goes on because we represent the customer and we've got an integrated view of the company."

The CEO scowled at him. "I said *market* oriented, not marketing oriented! It's unclear to me what we get for all the overhead we have in marketing. Those sexy brochures of yours sure haven't been doing the job."

There followed a lively, often acrimonious discussion of what was wrong and what was needed. Each vice president defended his or her function or unit and set out solutions from that particular standpoint. I will draw a curtain over their heedless and profane bickering, but here are paraphrases of their positions:

Sales VP: "We need more salespeople. *We're* the ones who are close to the customers. We have to have more call capacity in the sales force so we can provide better service and get new product ideas into the company faster."

Manufacturing VP: "We all know that our customers want quality. We need more automated machinery so we can work to closer tolerances and give them better quality. Also, we ought to send our whole manufacturing team to Crosby's Quality College."

Research and development VP: "Clearly we could do much better at both making and selling our products. But the fundamental problem is a lack of *new* products. They're the heart of our business. Our technology is getting old because we aren't investing enough in R&D."

Finance VP: "The problem isn't not enough resources, it's too many resources misspent. We've got too much overhead. Our variable costs are out of control. Our marketing and sales expenses are unreasonable. And we spend too much on R&D. We don't need more, we need less."

The general manager of the Electronic Flow Controls Division: "We aren't organized in the right way—that's the fundamental problem. If each division had its own sales force, we would have better coordination between sales and the other functions."

Her counterpart in the Pneumatic Controls Division: "We don't need our own sales forces anywhere near as much as we need our own engineering group so we can develop designs tailored to our customers. As long as we have a central R&D group that owns all the engineers, the divisions can't do their jobs."

As the group adjourned for lunch, the president interjected a last word. "You all put in a lot of time talking past each other and defending your own turf. Some of that's all right. You're supposed to represent your own departments and sell your own perspectives. If you didn't work hard for your own organizations, you wouldn't have lasted long at Wolverine, and you couldn't have made the contributions that you have.

"But enough is enough! You aren't just representatives of your own shops. You're the corporate executives at Wolverine and you have to take a more integrated, global view. It's my job to get all of you coordinated, but it's also the job of each of you. I don't have the knowledge, and nothing can replace direct, lateral communication across departments. Let's figure out how to do that after we get some lunch."

──── ALL RIGHT, WHAT IS IT?

Leaving the Wolverine bunch to its meal, I want to make a start in dispelling the president's uncertainty. After years of research, I'm convinced that the term "market oriented" represents a set of processes touching on all aspects of the company. It's a great deal more than the cliché "getting close to the customer." Since most companies sell to a variety of customers with varying and even conflicting desires and needs, the goal of getting close to the customer is meaningless. I've also found no meaningful difference between "market driven" and "customer oriented," so I use the phrases interchangeably. In my view, three characteristics make a company market driven.

1. *Information on all important buying influences permeates every corporate function.* A company can be market oriented only if it completely understands its markets and the people who decide whether to buy its products or services.

In some industries, wholesalers, retailers, and other parts of the distribution channels have a profound influence on the choices customers make. So it's important to understand "the trade." In other markets, nonbuying influences specify the product, although they neither purchase it nor use it. These include architects, consulting engineers, and doctors. In still other markets, one person may buy the product and another may use it; family situations are an obvious illustration. In commercial and industrial marketplaces, a professional procurement organization may actually purchase the product, while a manufacturing or operational function uses it.

To be of greatest use, customer information must move beyond the market research, sales, and marketing functions and "permeate every corporate function"—the R&D scientists and engineers, the manufacturing people, and the field-service specialists. When the technologists, for example, get unvarnished feedback on the way customers use the product, they can better develop improvements on the product and the production processes. If, on the other hand, market research or marketing people predigest the information, technologists may miss opportunities.

Of course, regular cross-functional meetings to discuss customer needs and to analyze feedback from buying influences are very important. At least once a year, the top functional officers should spend a full day or more to consider what is happening with key buying influences.

Corporate officers and functions should have access to all useful market research reports. If company staff appends summaries to regular customer surveys, like the Greenwich commercial and investment banking reports or the numerous consumer package-goods industry sales analyses, top officers are more likely to study them. That approach lets top management get the sales and marketing departments' opinions as well as those of less biased observers.

Some companies that have customer response phones—toll-free 800 numbers that consumers or distributors call to ask questions or make comments—distribute selected cassette recordings of calls to a wide range of executives, line and staff. The cassettes stimulate new ideas for products, product improvements, packaging, and service.

Reports to read and cassettes to hear are useful—but insufficient. High-level executives need to make visits to important customers to see them using their industrial and commercial products, consuming their services, or retailing their consumer goods. When, say, top manufacturing executives understand how a customer factory uses their products, they will have a more solid appreciation of customer needs for quality and close tolerances. Trade show visits provide valuable opportunities for operations and technical people to talk with customers and visit competitors' booths (if allowed by industry custom and show rules).

In my statement on the first characteristic, I referred to "important" buying influences. Because different customers have different needs, a marketer cannot effectively satisfy a wide range of them equally. The most important strategic decision is to choose the important customers. All customers are important, but invariably some are more important to the company than others. Collaboration among the various functions is important when pinpointing the key target accounts and market segments. Then the salespeople know whom to call on first and most often, the people who schedule production runs know who gets favored treatment, and those who make service calls know who rates special attention. If the priorities are not clear in the calm of planning meetings, they certainly won't be when the sales, production scheduling, and service dispatching processes get hectic.

The choice of customers influences the way decisions are made. During a marketing meeting at Wolverine Controller, one senior marketing person said, "Sales and marketing will pick out the customers they want to do business with, and then we'll sit down with the manufacturing and technical people and manage the product mix." Too late! Once you have a certain group of customers, the product mix is pretty much set; you must make the types of products they want. If sales and marketing choose the customers, they have undue power over decisions. Customer selection must involve all operating functions.

2. *Strategic and tactical decisions are made interfunctionally and inter-divisionally.* Functions and divisions will inevitably have conflicting objectives that mirror distinctions in cultures and in modes of operation. The glimpse into the meeting at French Lick demonstrates that. The customer-oriented company possesses mechanisms to get these differences out on the table for candid discussion and to make trade-offs that reconcile the various points of view. Each function and division must have the ear of the others and must be encouraged to lay out its ideas and requirements honestly and vigorously.

To make wise decisions, functions and units must recognize their differences. A big part of being market driven is the way different jurisdictions deal with one another. The marketing department may ask the R&D department to develop a product with a certain specification by a certain date. If R&D thinks the request is unreasonable but doesn't say so, it may develop a phony plan that the company will never achieve. Or R&D may make changes in the specifications and the delivery date without talking to marketing. The result: a missed deadline and an overrun budget. If, on the other hand, the two functions get together, they are in a position to make intelligent technological and marketing trade-offs. They can change a specification or extend a delivery date with the benefit of both points of view.

An alternative to integrated decision making, of course, is to kick the decision upstairs to the CEO or at least the division general manager. But though the higher executives have unbiased views, they lack the close knowledge of the specialists. An open decision-making process gets the best of both worlds, exploiting the evenhandedness of the general manager and the functional skills of the specialists.

3. *Divisions and functions make well-coordinated decisions and execute them with a sense of commitment.* An open dialogue on strategic and tactical trade-offs is the best way to engender commitment to meet goals. When the implementers also do the planning, the commitment will be strong and clear.

The depth of the biases revealed at the French Lick gathering demonstrates the difficulty of implementing cross-functional programs. But there's nothing wrong with that. In fact, the strength of those biases had a lot to do with Wolverine's past success. If the R&D vice president thought like the financial vice president, she wouldn't be effective in her job. On the other hand, if each function is marching to its own drum, implementation will be weak regardless of the competence and devotion of each function.

Serial communication, when one function passes an idea or request to another routinely without interaction—like tossing a brick with a message tied to it over the wall—can't build the commitment needed in the customer-driven company. Successful new products don't, for example, emerge out of a process in which marketing sends a set of specifications to R&D, which sends finished blueprints and designs to manufacturing. But joint opportunity analysis, in which functional and divisional people share ideas and discuss alternative solutions and approaches, leverages the different strengths of each party. Powerful internal connections make communication clear, coordination strong, and commitment high.

Poor coordination leads to misapplication of resources and failure to make the most of market opportunities. At one point in the meeting at French Lick, the vice president for human resources spoke up in this fashion: "Remember how impressed everyone was in '86 with the new pulp-bleaching control we developed? Not just us, but the whole industry—especially with our fast response rate. Even though the technology was the best, the product flopped. Why? Because the industry changed its process so that the response rate was less important than the ability to handle tough operating conditions and higher temperatures and pressures. Plus we couldn't manufacture to the tight tolerances the industry needed. We wasted a lot of talent on the wrong problem."

Probably the salespeople, and perhaps the technical service people, knew about the evolving customer needs. By working together, manufacturing and R&D could have designed a manufacturable product. But the company lacked the coordination that a focused market orientation stimulates.

——— ACTION AT WOLVERINE

Just about every company thinks of itself as market oriented. It's confident it has the strength to compete with the wolf pack, but in reality it's often weak and tends to follow the shepherd. In marketing efforts, businesses are particularly vulnerable to this delusion. Let's return to French Lick to hear of such a sheep in wolf's clothing.

"Look at Mutton Machinery," the vice president of manufacturing was saying. "They've done worse than we have. And their ads and brochures brag about them being customer oriented! At the trade show last year, they had a huge booth with the theme 'The Customer Is King.' They had a sales contest that sent a salesperson and customer to tour the major castles of Europe."

The sales vice president piped up. "They should send their salespeople for technical training, not to look at castles. We interviewed two of their better people, and they didn't measure up technically. The glitzy trade show stuff and the sexy contest don't make them customer oriented."

No, slogans and glossy programs don't give a company a market orientation. It takes a philosophy and a culture that go deep in the organization. Let's take a look at Wolverine's approach.

It's unlikely that any company ever became market oriented with a bottom-up approach; to make it happen, you need the commitment and power of those at the top. In gathering everybody who mattered at French Lick, Wolverine was taking the right step at the start. And from what we have heard, clearly they were not sugarcoating their concerns.

By the end of the first day, the executives had decided that they knew too little about their own industry, particularly customers and competitors. After a mostly social dinner meeting and a good night's sleep, they began at breakfast on day two to develop a plan to learn more. They listed 20 major customers they wanted to understand better. They designated each of the ten executives at the meeting (CEO, six functional heads, and three division general managers) to visit the customers in pairs in the next two months; the sales force would coordinate the visits. All ten agreed to attend the next big trade show.

They assigned the marketing vice president to prepare dossiers on the 20 customers plus another 10, as well as prospects selected by the group. Besides these data, each dossier was to include an examination of Wolverine's relationship with the customer or prospect.

Finally, the group singled out seven competitors for close scrutiny. The marketing vice president agreed to gather market data on them. The R&D vice president committed herself to drawing up technical reviews of them, and the financial vice president was to prepare analyses of financial performance. The seven remaining executives each agreed to analyze the relative strengths and weaknesses of one competitor.

Spurred by the president, the group concluded on day two that barriers had arisen among Wolverine's functional departments. Each was on its own little island. The human resources vice president took on the responsibility of scrutinizing cross-functional communication and identifying ways to improve it.

Back at headquarters in Indianapolis, the top brass did another smart thing: it involved all functional leadership so that line as well as staff chieftains would contribute to the effort. Top management quickly pinpointed the management information system as a major point of leverage for shaping a more integrated company view. Therefore, the president invited the MIS director to join the team.

Top management also decided that the bonus plan encouraged each function to pursue its own objectives instead of corporate-wide goals. So the controller teamed up with the human resources vice president to devise a better plan, which won the approval of top management.

As a new interest in communication and cooperation developed, the president perceived the need to make changes in structure and process. Chief among these were the establishment of a process engineering department to help production and R&D move new products from design into manufacturing and the redesign of managerial reports to emphasize the total company perspective.

The management group, more sensitive now to the ways people deal with each other, awoke to the power of informal social systems. To make the salespeople more accessible to headquarters staff, the sales office at a nearby location moved to headquarters (over the objections of the vice president of sales). The effort to promote interfunctional teamwork even extended to the restructuring of the bowling league. Wolverine had divided its teams by function or division. Now, however, each team had members from various functions. Some old-timers snorted that that was taking the new market orientation too far. But in a conversation during a bowling league party, the head of technical field service and a customer-service manager came up with an idea for a program to improve customer responsiveness. Then even the skeptics began to understand.

The analyses of customers and competitors identified an important market opportunity for Wolverine. The management group diverted resources to it, and under the direction of the Pneumatic Controls Division general manager, a multifunctional task force launched an effort to exploit it. Top management viewed this undertaking as a laboratory for the development of new approaches and as a showcase to demonstrate the company's new philosophy and culture. Headquarters maintained an intense interest in the project.

As the project gained momentum, support for the underlying philosophy grew. Gradually, the tone of interfunctional relationships changed. People evinced more trust in each other and were much more willing to admit responsibility for mistakes and to expose shortcomings.

Unfortunately, some people found it difficult to change. The sales vice president resisted the idea that a big part of his job was bringing customers and data about them into the company as well as encouraging all functions to deal with customers. He became irate when the vice president of manufacturing worked directly with several major customers, and he told the president that he wouldn't stand for other people dealing with *his* customers. His colleagues couldn't alter his attitude, so the president replaced him.

Wolverine's sales and earnings slowly began to improve. The market price of its stock edged upward. Internally, decision making became more integrative. Some early victories helped build momentum. Implementation improved through cooperation very low in the ranks, where most of the real work was done.

────── IMITATE LARRY BIRD

A year after Wolverine's first meeting in the French Lick hotel, the management group gathered there again. A new sales vice president was present, and the newly promoted MIS vice president/controller was also there.

This time the executives focused on two concerns. The first was how to handle the inordinate demands on the company resulting from the new push to satisfy important customers. The second was how to maintain Wolverine's momentum toward achieving a market orientation.

Attacking the first item, the group agreed to set major customer priorities. At hand was the information gathered during the year via industry analysis and executives' visits to top accounts. Available to the executives also were several frameworks for analysis.[1] Some accounts fit together in unexpected ways. In some situations, a series of accounts used similar products similarly. In others, the accounts competed for Wolverine's resources.

It took several meetings to set priorities on customers. The hardest part was resolving a dispute over whether to raise prices drastically on the custom products made for the third largest account. Wolverine was losing money on these. "Maybe not all business is good business," the R&D vice president suggested. That notion was pretty hard for the team to accept. But the CEO pushed hard for a decision. Ultimately, the group agreed to drop the account if it did not accede to price increases within the next six to eight months.

On the second matter, the management group decided it needed a way to measure the company's progress. The approach, everybody understood, had to be grounded in unrelieved emphasis on information gathering, on inter-

---

1. They used the account profitability matrix described by Benson P. Shapiro, V. Kasturi Rangan, Rowland T. Moriarty, and Elliot B. Ross in "Manage Customers for Profits (Not Just Sales)," *Harvard Business Review* (September–October 1987): 101.

functional decision making, and on a vigorous sense of commitment throughout the organization. They recognized how easy it is to become complacent and lose detachment when examining one's own performance. Nevertheless, the executives drew up a checklist of customer-focused questions for the organization to ask itself (see the *Exhibit*).

Two years after the company changed its direction, a major customer asked the president about Wolverine's efforts to become market oriented. Here is the response:

"It's proved to be harder than I had imagined. I had to really drive people to think about customers and the corporation as a whole, not just what's good for their own departments. It's also proved to be more worthwhile. We have a different tone in our outlook and a different way of dealing with each other.

"We use all kinds of customer data and bring it into all functions. We do much more interfunctional decision making. The hardest part of all was account selection, and that really paid off for us. It also had the most impact. Our implementation has improved through what we call the three Cs—communication, coordination, and commitment. We're getting smooth, but we sure aren't flawless yet.

"Last night I watched the Pacers play the Boston Celtics on TV. The Celtics won. Sure they've got more talent, but the real edge the Celtics have is their teamwork. At one point in the game, the Indiana team got impatient with each other. They seemed to forget that the Celtics were the competition.

"That's the way we used to be too—each department competing with each other. A few years ago we had a meeting down at French Lick where everything came to a head, and I was feeling pretty desperate. There's a real irony here because French Lick is the hometown of Larry Bird.

EXHIBIT
Self-examination Checklist

1. **Are we easy to do business with?**
   Easy to contact?
   Fast to provide information?
   Easy to order from?
   Make reasonable promises?
2. **Do we keep our promises?**
   On product performance?
   Delivery?
   Installation?
   Training?
   Service?
3. **Do we meet the standards we set?**
   Specifics?
   General tone?
   Do we even know the standards?

4. **Are we responsive?**
   Do we listen?
   Do we follow up?
   Do we ask "Why not," not "Why"?
   Do we treat customers as individual companies and individual people?
5. **Do we work together?**
   Share blame?
   Share information?
   Make joint decisions?
   Provide satisfaction?

"When I think about the Celtics and Bird, what working together means becomes clear. If each Wolverine manager only helps his or her department do its job well, we're going to lose. Back when the company was small, products were simple, competition was unsophisticated, and customers were less demanding, we could afford to work separately. But now, our individual best isn't good enough; we've got to work as a unit. Bird is the epitome. He subverts his own interest and ego for the sake of the team. That's what I want to see at Wolverine."

——— DISCUSSION QUESTIONS

1. Do you believe that to increase earnings and market share more emphasis should be placed on marketing? Why or why not?
2. What distinctions would you make between "market oriented" and "marketing oriented"? Discuss the benefits of each. How does management achieve market orientation?
3. According to the author, aggressive teamwork throughout an organization becomes necessary when a commitment is made to serve the customer and satisfy customer needs: decisions affecting the customer should be made by all units at all levels. Do you agree with this philosophy? Do you see any drawbacks to this approach?
4. Different units within an organization will approach marketing problems in different ways. Sales will manipulate prices or step up pressure to sell more product. Marketing will develop elaborate marketing plans to reach more customers in more ways. Top management will want more information about potential customers in order to serve them better and give them the products they want. Which approach do you favor for meeting the demands of the marketplace? Explain.
5. A company gathers information on customer needs, turns the information over to research and development, which then designs a product according to the data. Is this a desirable scenario for effective product development? Why or why not?

Getting Back to Strategy 4

KENICHI OHMAE

This reading challenges the idea that the goal of strategy is to beat the competition. Responses to competitors' moves may be appropriate, argues the author, but they are reactive. They come second, after real strategy—which means avoiding competition whenever possible and focusing instead on creating value for customers. Using a series of case examples, ranging from automobile to piano manufacturing, the author demonstrates what that commitment entails: asking fundamental questions about how customers use your product and, if necessary, rethinking what your product is, what it does, and how you can design, build, and market it. Getting back to strategy, in other words, means rediscovering the primary importance of paying painstaking attention to customers' needs.

Competitiveness" is the word most commonly uttered these days in economic policy circles in Washington and most European capitals. The restoration of competitive vitality is a widely shared political slogan. Across the Atlantic, the unification of the Common Market focuses attention on European industries' ability to compete against global rivals. On both continents, senior managers, who started to wrestle with these issues long before politicians got hold of them, search actively for successful models to follow, for examples of how best to play the new competitive game. With few exceptions, the models they have found and the examples they are studying are Japanese.

To many Western managers, the Japanese competitive achievement provides hard evidence that a successful strategy's hallmark is the creation of sustainable competitive advantage by beating the competition. If it takes world-class manufacturing to win, runs the lesson, you have to beat competitors with your factories. If it takes rapid product development, you have to beat them with your labs. If it takes mastery of distribution channels, you have to beat them with your logistics systems. No matter what it takes, the goal of strategy is to beat the competition.

After a painful decade of losing ground to the Japanese, managers in the United States and Europe have learned this lesson very well indeed. As a guide to action, it is clear and compelling. As a metric of performance, it is unambiguous. It is also wrong.

Of course, winning the manufacturing or product development or logistics battle is no bad thing. But it is not really what strategy is—or should be—about. Because when the focus of attention is on ways to beat the competition, it is inevitable that strategy will be defined primarily in terms of the competition. For instance, if the competition has recently brought out an electronic kitchen gadget that slices, dices, and brews coffee, you had better get one just like it into your product line—and get it there soon. If the competition has cut production costs, you had better get out your scalpel. If they have just started to run national ads, you had better call your agency at once. When you go toe-to-toe with competitors, you cannot let them build up any kind of advantage. You must match their every move. Or so the argument goes.

Of course, it is important to take the competition into account, but in making strategy that should not come first. It cannot come first. First comes painstaking attention to the needs of customers. First comes close analysis of a company's real degrees of freedom in responding to those needs. First comes the willingness to rethink, fundamentally, what products are and what they do, as well as how best to organize the business system that designs, builds, and markets them. Competitive realities are what you test possible strategies against; you define them in terms of customers. Tit-for-tat responses to what competitors do may be appropriate, but they are largely reactive. They come second, after your real strategy. Before you test yourself against the competition, your strategy takes shape in the determination to create value for customers.

It also takes shape in the determination to *avoid* competition whenever and wherever possible. As the great Sun Tzu observed 500 years before Christ, the smartest strategy in war is the one that allows you to achieve your objectives without having to fight. In just three years, for example, Nintendo's "family computer" sold 12 million units in Japan alone, during which time it had virtually no competition at all. In fact, it created a vast network of companies working to help it succeed. Ricoh supplied the critical Zylog chips; software houses produced special games to play on it, like Dragon Quest I, II, and III. Everyone was making too much money to think of creating competition.

The visible clashing between companies in the marketplace—what managers frequently think of as strategy—is but a small fragment of the strategic whole. Like an iceberg, most of strategy is submerged, hidden out of sight. The visible part can foam and froth with head-to-head competition. But most of it is intentionally invisible—beneath the surface where value is created, where competition is avoided. Sometimes, of course, the foam and froth of direct competition cannot be avoided. The product is right, the company's direction is right, the perception of value is right, and managers have to buckle down and fight it out with competitors. But in my experience, managers too often and too willingly launch themselves into old-fashioned competitive battles. It's familiar ground. They know what to do, how to fight. They have a much harder time seeing when an effective customer-oriented strategy could avoid the battle altogether.

——— THE BIG SQUEEZE

During the late 1960s and early 1970s, most Japanese companies focused their attention on reducing costs through programs like quality circles, value engineering, and zero defects. As these companies went global, however, they began to concentrate instead on differentiating themselves from their competitors. This heavy investment in competitive differentiation has now gone too far; it has already passed the point of diminishing returns—too many models, too many gadgets, too many bells and whistles.

Today, as a result, devising effective customer-oriented strategies has a special urgency for these companies. A number of the largest and most successful face a common problem—the danger of being trapped between low-cost producers in the newly industrialized economies (NIEs) and high-end producers in Europe. While this threat concerns managers in all the major industrial economies, in Japan, where the danger is most immediate and pressing, it has quickly led companies to rethink their familiar strategic goals. As a consequence, they are rediscovering the primary importance of focusing on customers—in other words, the importance of getting back to what strategy is really about.

In Japan today, the handwriting is on the wall for many industries: the strategic positioning that has served them so well in the past is no longer tenable. On one side, there are German companies making top-of-the-line products like Mercedes or BMW in automobiles, commanding such high prices that even elevated cost levels do not greatly hurt profitability. On the other side are low-price, high-volume producers like Korea's Hyundai, Samsung, and Lucky Goldstar. These companies can make products for less than half what it costs the Japanese. The Japanese are being caught in the middle: they are able neither to command the immense margins of the Germans nor to undercut the rock-bottom wages of the Koreans. The result is a painful squeeze.

If you are the leader of a Japanese company, what can you do? I see three possibilities. First, because Korean productivity is still quite low, you can challenge them directly on costs. Yes, their wages are often as little as one-seventh to one-tenth of yours. But if you aggressively take labor content out of your products, you can close or even reverse the cost gap. In practice, this means pushing hard—and at considerable expense—toward full automation, unmanned operations, and totally flexible manufacturing systems.

Examples prove that it can be done. NSK (Nikon Seiko), which makes bearings, has virtually removed its work force through an extensive use of computer-integrated manufacturing linked directly with the marketplace. Mazak Machinery has taken almost all the labor content out of key components in its products. Fujitsu Fanuc has so streamlined itself that it has publicly announced that it can break even with as little as 20% capacity utilization and can compete successfully with a currency as strong as 70 yen to the dollar. This productivity-through-automation route is one way to go. In fact, for commodity products such as bearings it may be the only way. Once you start down this path, however, you have to follow it right to the end. No turning back. No stopping. Because Korean wages are so low that nothing less than a total commitment to eliminating labor content will suffice. And China, with wage rates just one-fifth of those in the newly industrialized economies, is not far behind Korea and Taiwan in such light industries as textiles, footwear, and watchbands. Although the currencies of the newly industrialized economies are now moving up relative to the dollar, the difference in wage rates is still great enough to require the fiercest kind of across-the-board determination to get rid of labor content.

A second way out of the squeeze is to move upmarket where the Germans are. In theory this might be appealing; in practice it has proven very hard for the Japanese to do. Their corporate cultures simply do not permit it. Just look, for example, at what happened with precision electronic products like compact disc players. As soon as the CD reached the market, customers went crazy with demand. Everybody wanted one. It was a perfect opportunity to move upscale with a "Mercedes" CD player. What did the Japanese do? Corporate culture and instinct took over, and they cut prices down to about one-fifth of what U.S. and European companies were going to ask for their CD players. Philips, of course, was trying to keep prices and margins up, but the Japanese were trying to drive them down. The Western companies wanted to make money; the Japanese instinct was to build share at any cost.

This is foolishness—or worse. Of course, it is perfectly clear why the Japanese respond this way. They are continuing to practice the approach that served them well in the past when they were playing the low-cost market entry game that the Koreans are playing now. It's the game they know how to play. But now there's a new game, and the Japanese companies have new positions. The actions that made sense for a low-cost player are way off course for a company trying to play at the high end of the market.

There is another reason for this kind of self-defeating behavior. Sony is really more worried about Matsushita than about Philips, and Matsushita is more worried about Sanyo. This furious internal competition fuels the Japanese impulse to slash prices whenever possible. That's also why it's so difficult for Japanese companies to follow the German route. To do so, they have to buck their own history. It means going their own way, and guarding against the instinct to backpedal, to do what their domestic competitors are doing.

Hard as it is, a number of companies *are* going their own way quite successfully. Some, like Seiko in its dogfight with Casio and Hong Kong–based watchmakers, had been badly burned in the low-price game and are now moving to restore profits at the high end of the market. Others, like Honda, Toyota, and Nissan in the automobile industry, are launching more expensive car lines and creating second dealer channels in the United States through which to compete directly for the upscale "German" segment. Still others, like Nakamichi in tape recorders, have always tried to operate at the high end and have never given in on price. Such companies are, however, very rare. Instinct runs deep. Japanese producers tend to compete on price even when they do not have to.

For most companies, following the Korean or German approach is neither an appealing nor a sustainable option. This is true not only in Japan but also in all the advanced industrial economies, if for different reasons. What sets Japanese companies apart is the consideration that they may have less room to maneuver than others, given their historical experience and present situation. For all these companies, there is a pressing need for a middle strategic course, a way to flourish without being forced to go head-to-head with competitors in either a low-cost or an upmarket game. Such a course exists—indeed, it leads managers back to the heart of what strategy is about: creating value for customers.

——— FIVE-FINGER EXERCISE

Imagine for a moment that you are head of Yamaha, a company that makes pianos. What are your strategic choices? After strenuous and persistent efforts to become the leading producer of high-quality pianos, you have succeeded in capturing 40% of the global piano market. Unfortunately, just when you finally become the market leader, overall demand for pianos starts to decline by 10% every year. As head of Yamaha, what do you do?

A piano is a piano. In most respects, the instrument has not changed much since Mozart. Around the world, in living rooms and dens and concert halls and rehearsal halls, there are some 40 million pianos, and for the most part they simply sit. Market growth is stagnant, in polite terms. In business terms, the industry is already in decline, and Korean producers are now coming on-line with their usual low-cost offerings. Competing just to hold share is not an attractive prospect. Making better pianos will not help much; the market has only a limited ability to absorb additional volume. What do you do? What can you do?

According to some analysts, the right move would be to divest the business, labeling it a dog that no longer belongs in the corporate portfolio. But Yamaha reacted differently. Rather than selling the business, Yamaha thought long and hard about how to create value for customers. It took that kind of effort—the answers were far from obvious.

What Yamaha's managers did was look—they took a hard look at the customer and the product. What they saw was that most of these 40 million pianos sit around idle and neglected—and out of tune—most of the time. Not many people play them anymore—and one thing learning to play the piano takes is lots of time. What sits in the homes of these busy people is a large piece of furniture that collects dust. Instead of music, it may even produce guilt. Certainly it is not a functioning musical instrument. No matter how good you are at strategy, you won't be able to sell that many new pianos—no matter how good they are—in such an environment. If you want to create value for customers, you're going to have to find ways to add value to the millions of pianos already out there.

So what do you do? What Yamaha did was to remember the old player piano—a pleasant idea with a not very pleasant sound. Yamaha worked hard to develop a sophisticated, advanced combination of digital and optical technology that can distinguish among 92 different degrees of strength and speed of key touch from pianissimo to fortissimo. Because the technology is digital, it can record and reproduce each keystroke with great accuracy, using the same kind of 3 ½-inch disks that work on a personal computer. That means you can now record live performances by the pianists of your choice—or buy such recordings on a computerlike diskette—and then, in effect, invite the artists into your home to play the same compositions on your piano. Yamaha's strategy used technology to create new value for piano customers.

Think about it. For about $2,500 you can retrofit your idle, untuned, dust-collecting piece of oversized furniture so that great artists can play it for you in the privacy of your own home. You can invite your friends over and entertain them as well—and showcase the latest in home entertainment technology. If you are a flutist, you can invite someone over to accompany you on the piano and record her performance. Then, even when she is not there, you can practice the piece with full piano accompaniment.

Furthermore, if you have a personal computer at home in Cambridge and you know a good pianist living in California, you can have her record your favorite sonata and send it over the phone; you simply download it onto your computer, plug the diskette into your retrofitted piano, and enjoy her performance. Or you can join a club that will send you the concert that a Horowitz played last night at Carnegie Hall to listen to at home on your own piano. There are all kinds of possibilities.

In terms of the piano market, this new technology creates the prospect of a $2,500 sale to retrofit each of 40 million pianos—not bad for a declining industry. In fact, the potential is even greater because there are also the software recordings to market.

Yamaha started marketing this technology in the late 1980s, and sales in Japan have been explosive. This was a stagnant industry, remember, an industry which had suffered an annual 10% sales decline in each of the previous five years. Now it's alive again—but in a different way. Yamaha did not pursue all the usual routes: it didn't buckle down to prune costs, proliferate models, slice overhead, or use all the other usual approaches. It looked with fresh eyes for chances to create value for customers. And it found them.

It also found something else: it learned that the process of discovering value-creating opportunities is itself contagious. It spreads. For instance, now that customers have pianos that play the way Horowitz may have played at Carnegie Hall, they want their instrument tuned to professional standards. That means a tuner visits every six months and generates substantial additional revenue. (And it is substantial. Globally, the market for tuning is roughly $1.6 billion annually, a huge economic opportunity long ignored by piano manufacturers and distributors.) Yamaha can also give factory workers who might otherwise lose their jobs a chance to be tuners.

As the piano regains popularity, a growing number of people will again want to learn how to play the instrument themselves. And that means tutorials, piano schools, videocassettes, and a variety of other revenue-producing opportunities. Overall, the potential growth in the piano industry, hardware and software, is much bigger than anyone previously recognized. Creating value for the customer was the key that unlocked it.

But what about people's reluctance today to spend the time to learn piano the old-fashioned way? We are a society that prizes convenience, and as the many years of declining piano sales illustrate, learning to play a musical instrument is anything but convenient. Listening to music, as opposed to making music, is more popular than ever. Look at all the people going to school or to the office with earphones on; music is everywhere. It's not interest in music that's going down; it's the interest in spending years of disciplined effort to master an instrument. If you asked people if they would like to be able to play an instrument like the piano, they'd say yes. But most feel as if they've already missed the opportunity to learn. They're too old now; they don't have the time to take years of lessons.

With the new digital and sound-chip technologies, they don't have to. Nor do they have to be child prodigies. For $1,500 they can buy a Klavinova, a digital electronic piano, that allows them to do all kinds of wonderful things. They can program it to play and then croon along. They can program it to play the left-hand part and join in with a single finger. They can listen to a tutorial cassette that directs which keys to push. They can store instructions in the computer's memory so that they don't have to play all the notes and chords simultaneously. Because the digital technology makes participation easy and accessible, "playing" the instrument becomes fun. Technology removes the learning barrier. No wonder this digital segment is now much bigger than the traditional analog segment of the market.

Most piano manufacturers, however, are sticking with traditional acoustic technologies and leaving their futures to fate. Faced with declining demand, they fight even harder against an ever more aggressive set of competitors for their share of a shrinking pie. Or they rely on government to block imports. Yamaha has not abandoned acoustic instruments; it is now the world leader in nearly all categories of acoustic and "techno" musical instruments. What it did, however, was to study its music-loving customers and build a strategy based on delivering value linked to those customers' inherent interest in music. It left nothing to fate. It got back to strategy.

—— CLEANING UP

This is how you chart a middle course between the Koreans and the Germans; this is how you revitalize an industry. More to the point, this is how you create a value-adding strategy: not by setting out to beat the competition but by setting out to understand how best to provide value for customers.

Kao is a Japanese toiletry company that spends 4% of its revenues on fundamental R&D, studying skin, hair, blood, circulation—things like that. (This 4% may, at first, sound low, but it excludes personnel cost. This matters because as many as 2,800 of the company's 6,700 or so employees are engaged in R&D.) Recently it developed a new product that duplicates the effect of a Japanese hot spring. A hot spring has a high mineral content under extreme pressure. Even the right chemical thrown into a hot bath will not automatically produce the same effect. Babu, Kao's new bath additive, actually produces the same kind of improvement in circulation that a hot spring provides. It looks like a jumbo-sized Alka-Seltzer tablet. When you throw one Babu into a bath, it starts to fizz with carbon dioxide bubbles as minerals dissolve in the hot water.

Kao's strategy was to offer consumers something completely different from traditional bath gel. Because of its effects on overall health and good circulation, Babu competes on a different ground. In fact, it wiped out the old Japanese bath gel and additives industry in a single year. It's the only product of its kind that now sells in Japan. There is no competition because potential competitors cannot make anything like it. Kao is playing a different game.

For the new breed of Japanese companies, like Yamaha and Kao, strategy does not mean beating the competition. It means working hard to understand a customer's inherent needs and then rethinking what a category of product is all about. The goal is to develop the right product to serve those needs—not just a better version of competitors' products. In fact, Kao pays far less attention to other toiletry companies than it does to improving skin condition, circulation, or caring for hair. It now understands hair so well that its newest hair tonic product, called Success, falls somewhere between cosmetics and medicine. In that arena, there is no competition.

——— BREWING WISDOM

Getting back to strategy means getting back to a deep understanding of what a product is about. Some time back, for example, a Japanese home appliance company was trying to develop a coffee percolator. Should it be a General Electric–type percolator, executives wondered? Should it be the same drip-type that Philips makes? Larger? Smaller? I urged them to ask a different kind of question: Why do people drink coffee? What are they looking for when they do? If your objective is to serve the customer better, then shouldn't you understand why that customer drinks coffee in the first place? Then you know what kind of percolator to make.

The answer came back: good taste. I then asked the company's engineers what they were doing to help the consumer enjoy good taste in a cup of coffee. They said they were trying to design a good percolator. I asked them what influences the taste of a cup of coffee. No one knew. That became the next question we had to answer. It turns out that lots of things can affect taste—the beans, the temperature, the water. We did our homework and discovered all the things that affect taste. For the engineers, each factor represented a strategic degree of freedom in designing a percolator—that is, a factor about which something can be done. With beans, for instance, you can have different degrees of quality or freshness. You can grind them in various ways. You can produce different grain sizes. You can distribute the grains differently when pouring hot water over them.

Of all the factors, water quality, we learned, made the greatest difference. The percolator in design at the time, however, didn't take water quality into account at all. Everyone had simply assumed that customers would use tap water. We discovered next that the grain distribution and the time between grinding the beans and pouring in the water were crucial. As a result, we began to think about the product and its necessary features in a new way. It *had* to have a built-in dechlorinating function. It *had* to have a built-in grinder. All the customer should have to do is put in water and beans; the machine should handle the rest. That's the way to assure great taste in a cup of coffee.

To start you have to ask the right questions and set the right kinds of strategic goals. If your only concern is that General Electric has just brought out a percolator that brews coffee in ten minutes, you will have your engineers design one that brews it in seven minutes. And if you stick with that logic, market research will tell you that instant coffee is the way to go. If the General Electric machine consumes only a little electricity, you will focus on using even less.

Conventional marketing approaches won't solve the problem. You can get any results you want from the consumer averages. If you ask people whether they want their coffee in ten minutes or seven, they will say seven, of course. But it's still the wrong question. And you end up back where you started, trying to beat the competition at its own game. If your primary focus is on the competition, you will never step back and ask what the customer's inherent needs are or what the product really is about. Personally, I would much rather talk with three homemakers for two hours each on their feelings about, say, washing machines than conduct a 1,000-person survey on the same topic. I get much better insight and perspective on what customers are really looking for.

——— TAKING PICTURES

Back in the mid-1970s, single-lens reflex (SLR) cameras started to become popular, and the popularity of lens-shutter cameras rapidly declined. To most people, the lens-shutter model looked cheap and nonprofessional, and it took inferior quality pictures. These opinions were so strong that one camera company with which I was working had almost decided to pull out of the lens-shutter business entirely. Everyone knew that the trend was toward SLR and that only a better version of SLR could beat the competition.

I didn't know. So I asked a few simple questions: Why do people take pictures in the first place? What are they really looking for when they take pictures? The answer was simple. They were not looking for a good camera. They were looking for good pictures. Cameras—SLR or lens-shutter—and film were not the end products that consumers wanted. What they wanted were good pictures.

Why was it so hard to take good pictures with a lens-shutter camera? This time, no one knew. So we went to a film lab and collected a sample of some 18,000 pictures. Next we identified the 7% or so that were not very good; then we tried to analyze why each of these picture-taking failures had occurred. We found some obvious causes—even some categories of causes. Some failures were the result of poor distance adjustment. The company's design engineers addressed that problem in two different ways: they added a plastic lens designed to keep everything in focus beyond three feet (a kind of permanent focus), and they automated the focus process.

Another common problem with the bad pictures was not enough light. The company built a flash right into the camera. That way, the poor fellow who left his flash attachment on a closet shelf could still be equipped to take a good picture. Still another problem was the marriage of film and camera. Here the engineers added some grooves on the side of the film cartridges so that the camera could tell how sensitive the film is to light and could adjust. Double exposure was another common problem. The camera got a self-winder.

In all, we came up with some 200 ideas for improving the lens-shutter camera. The result—virtually a whole new approach to the product—helped revitalize the business. Today, in fact, the lens-shutter market is bigger than that for SLRs. And we got there because we did a very simple thing: we asked what the customer's inherent ends were and then rethought what a camera had to be in order to meet them. There was no point slugging it out with competitors. There was no reason to leave the business. We just got back to strategy—based on customers.

——— MAKING DINNER

There is no mystery to this process, no black box to which only a few gurus have access. The questions that have to be asked are straightforward, and the place to start is clear. A while ago, some people came to me with a set of excellent ideas for designing kitchen appliances for Japanese homes. They knew cooking, and their appliances were quite good. After some study, however, I told them not to go ahead.

What I did was to visit several hundred houses and apartments and take pictures of the kitchens. The answer became clear: there was no room. Things were already stacked on top of the refrigerators; the counters were already full. There was no room for new appliances, no matter how appealing their attributes.

Thinking about these products, and understanding the customer's needs, however, did produce a different idea: build this new equipment into something that is already in the kitchen. That way there is no new demand for space. What that led to, for example, was the notion of building a microwave oven into a regular oven. Everyone looked at the pictures of 200 kitchens and said, no space. The alternative was, rethink the product.

—— ACHING HEADS, BAD LOGIC

Looking closely at a customer's needs, thinking deeply about a product—these are not exotic pieces of strategic apparatus. They are, as they have always been, the basics of sound management. They have just been neglected or ignored. But why? Why have so many managers allowed themselves to drift so far away from what strategy is really about?

Think for a moment about aching heads. Is my headache the same as yours? My cold? My shoulder pain? My stomach discomfort? Of course not. Yet when a pharmaceutical company asked for help to improve its process for coming up with new products, what it wanted was help in getting into its development pipeline new remedies for standard problems like headache or stomach pain. It had assembled a list of therapeutic categories and was eager to match them up with appropriate R&D efforts.

No one had taken the time, however, to think about how people with various discomforts actually feel. So we asked 50 employees in the company to fill out a questionnaire—throughout a full year—about how they felt physically at all times of the day every day of the year. Then we pulled together a list of the symptoms described, sat down with the company's scientists, and asked them, item by item: Do you know why people feel this way? Do you have a drug for this kind of symptom? It turned out that there were no drugs for about 80% of the symptoms, these physical awarenesses of discomfort. For many of them, some combination of existing drugs worked just fine. For others, no one had ever thought to seek a particular remedy. The scientists were ignoring tons of profit.

Without understanding customers' needs—the specific types of discomfort they were feeling—the company found it all too easy to say, "Headache? Fine, here's a medicine, an aspirin, for headache. Case closed. Nothing more to do there. Now we just have to beat the competition in aspirin." It was easy not to take the next step and ask, "What does the headache feel like? Where does it come from? What is the underlying cause? How can we treat the cause, not just the symptom?" Many of these symptoms, for example, are psychological and culture-specific. Just look at television commercials. In the United States, the most common complaint is headache; in the United Kingdom, backache; in Japan, stomachache. In the United States, people say that they have a splitting headache; in Japan it is an ulcer. How can we truly understand what these people are feeling and why?

The reflex, of course, is to provide a headache pill for a headache—that is, to assume that the solution is simply the reverse of the diagnosis. That is bad medicine and worse logic. It is the kind of logic that reinforces the impulse to direct strategy toward beating the competition, toward cutting costs when making traditional musical instruments or adding a different ingredient to the line of traditional soaps. It is the kind of logic that denies the need for a detailed understanding of intrinsic customer needs. It leads to forklift trucks that pile up boxes just fine but do not allow the operators to see directly in front of them. It leads to dishwashers that remove everything but the scorched eggs and rice that customers most want to get rid of. It leads to pianos standing idle and gathering dust.

Getting back to strategy means fighting that reflex, not giving in to it. It means resisting the easy answers in the search for better ways to deliver value to customers. It means asking the simple-sounding questions about what products are about. It means, in short, taking seriously the strategic part of management.

Copyright © 1988; revised 1991.

——— DISCUSSION QUESTIONS

1. A company does well to try to beat its competition by offering something better—quality, distribution, price, for example. Does this strategy always work? Are there instances where it has not proved effective? Are there costs to this strategy?
2. Assume a company's strategy is not predicated on beating the competition but on fulfilling customer requirements. Think of a product or service and describe how the strategy of meeting customer needs would differ from beating the competition.
3. The Japanese marketing philosophy tries to drive prices down to capture and build market share at any cost. Western companies' philosophy is to make money by keeping prices and margins up. Which philosophy do you favor, and why ?
4. Assume your company has launched a good product and it is not catching on in the market. What might be some of the reasons for this situation?
5. Using the ideas presented in this reading, describe your options for making a decision about the scenario given in question 4.

PART THREE

DEVELOPING THE MARKETING PLAN

Planning, organizing, and executing an effective marketing strategy covers a broad range of tasks, from market selection and product planning to pricing, distribution, and communicating the vision. A marketing plan must consider the issues of when to enter the market and when to exit; how to differentiate the product from the competition's; and how much flexibility is necessary to respond to a changing technological and demographic environment. These are but a few of the matters that need to be addressed before a marketing program is implemented. Once it is under way, on-going measures of marketing performance serve as an audit to "keep the ship on course."

Marketing Strategy— An Overview

5

E. RAYMOND COREY

This reading provides an elementary treatment of all aspects of marketing strategy and is as applicable today as when it was first written in 1978. It also provides a good opportunity to gain an historical perspective from which to understand changes in current thinking.

The reading first presents the basic elements of any marketing strategy— market selection, product planning, pricing, and distribution. It then focuses on various aspects of marketing communication, the purchase-decision process, and the push vs. pull strategies in selling. It concludes with a discussion of the stages of market growth and the analytical approaches used in formulating marketing strategies.

S*trategy* 1) The science or art of military command as applied to the overall planning and conduct of large-scale combat operations. Compare *tactics.* 2) A plan of action resulting from the practice of this science. 3) The art or skill of using stratagems in politics, business, courtship, or the like.[1]

As this dictionary definition suggests, the meaning of the word *strategy* developed originally in a military context. Strategy meant a plan for the deployment and use of military forces and materiel over certain terrain (which might or might not be of the military commander's choosing) to achieve a certain objective. The strategy had to be based on what was known of the enemy's strength and positioning, the physical characteristics of the battleground, the friendly or hostile sentiments of those who occupied the territory, and, of course, the strength and character of the resources available to the commander. Time was a factor too, and it was also necessary to anticipate changes that might significantly alter the balance of forces.

Strategy, then, is a plan of action carried out tactically. According to the same dictionary, a tactic is an expedient, or maneuver, for achieving a goal. Therefore, a plan of action (strategy) is carried out through a series of interrelated

---

1. *The American Heritage Dictionary of the English Language* (Boston: Houghton Mifflin Co., 1973), p. 1273.

maneuvers that are not always planned in advance and may represent responses to the unanticipated actions of either opposing or even friendly forces.

The analogy to business strategies is direct and useful. In business, and in marketing, the terrain is the marketplace in particular and the economic, political, social, legal, and technological environments in general. The resources are personnel with wide-ranging skills and expertise as well as factories, laboratories, transportation systems, financial resources, and the corporation's reputation.

It is important to distinguish between objectives (or goals) and strategies. A business objective is a desired end result; a strategy is a plan for getting there. Objectives may be set at various levels. For the enterprise as a whole, the objective may be to achieve a certain rate of growth in sales and earnings, or to sustain a target return on shareholders' equity. Goals may also be imposed on managers of individual divisions so that the enterprise as a whole meets its objectives; and division managers may see market share as an important measure of their own performance. Thus a key objective might be to increase a particular product line's share of its market by X percent. Conversely, the objective might be to increase profitability while yielding a limited amount of market share.

At the level of individual products and markets, objectives may be expressed in terms of market share, profits on sales, and return on investment. But the goals may also be of a different order. A company's primary objective for a certain product or service, for example, might be to help support sales of other products in the line. A newspaper might publish a Sunday edition primarily to help build its circulation for weekday editions.

The importance of explicitly defining objectives to give purpose and direction to strategies cannot be overestimated. How can we develop useful strategies unless we know what we are trying to accomplish?

Overall corporate strategies are often thought of as having several components, including:

- *A financial strategy.* What should be the debt-to-equity balance? What sources of capital should be utilized?
- *A manufacturing strategy.* What should we make and what should we buy from outside suppliers? Should we have a few large plants or several smaller ones? How should they be designed? Where should they be located?
- *A research and development strategy (R&D).* Will we attempt to be a technical leader in our field or should we depend on others for new technical developments? Will we undertake basic or applied research? In what fields of technology will we work? What level of spending should we sustain?

Depending on the nature of the business, strategy may have other dimensions as well. At the heart of any business strategy is a marketing strategy. Businesses exist to deliver products to markets. To the extent that they serve this purpose well and efficiently, they grow and profit. Other components of the overall strategy (financial, manufacturing, R&D) must support the business's marketing mission. By the same token, the firm's marketing strategy must be appropriate to its resources and its strategies in other major areas of the business and take account of their limitations. Financial resources and manufacturing facilities, for example, typically impose certain constraints on the range of objectives set. Marketing goals and strategies have to be developed within these limitations.

───── ELEMENTS OF A MARKETING STRATEGY

A marketing strategy is composed of several interrelated elements. The first and most important is *market selection:* choosing the markets to be served. *Product planning* includes the specific products the company sells, the makeup of the product line, and the design of individual offerings in the line. Another element is the *distribution system*: the wholesale and retail channels through which the product moves to the people who ultimately buy it and use it. The overall *communications* strategy employs *advertising* to tell potential customers about the product through radio, television, direct mail, and public print and *personal selling* to deploy a sales force to call on potential customers, urge them to buy, and take orders. Finally, *pricing* is an important element of any marketing program. The company must set the product prices that different classes of customers will pay and determine the margins or commissions to compensate agents, wholesalers, and retailers for moving the product to ultimate users.

Depending on the nature of the product and its markets, the marketing strategy may also include other components. A company whose products need repair and maintenance must have programs for *product service.* Such programs are often businesses in themselves and require extensive repair shops, technical service personnel, and inventories of spare parts. For some companies, the nature and amount of *technical assistance* provided to customers is critical to marketing success and therefore an important part of strategy.

In many businesses, *customer credit* is an important element of the marketing program. Companies that operate gasoline stations, retail stores, or travel agencies, for example, must extend credit simply to compete for business. So must companies selling industrial equipment, raw materials, and supplies.

In businesses where products can be shipped only a certain distance from the plant, *plant location* determines the company's available market. A container plant, for example, can serve only a limited geographic area because shipping costs are high in relation to the product's unit value. When transport over long distances becomes uneconomical, plant location becomes a strategic marketing decision.

Brand name can also be an important element of marketing strategy. A company may have to choose between using a family brand name (such as Kraft for cheeses, jams, jellies) or a distinct name (such as Lite for a beer made by Miller Brewing Company).

Other elements of strategy, especially for consumer goods companies, are *display* of the merchandise at the point of sale, and *promotions* to consumers (e.g., cents-off coupons, two-for-one sales, and in-package premiums), retailers, and wholesalers. The list of elements that might shape marketing strategy is long and will vary among products, markets, and companies. Moreover, emphasis on particular aspects of marketing strategy will vary considerably, even among competitors selling comparable products to the same markets. Emphasis will shift, too, over time as products mature and market conditions change. At one stage a company may gain a competitive edge through extensive new-product development; at another, it may rely on low prices.

Strategy formulation can be seen as the choice of a marketing mix:

> The "marketing mixes" for different types of products vary widely, and even for the same class of product, competing companies may employ different mixes. Over time a company may change its marketing mix for a product, for in a dynamic world the marketer must adjust to changing forces of the market...to find a mix that will prove profitable....The marketing mix refers to the apportionment of effort— the combination, the designing, and the integration of the various elements of marketing—into a program that, on the basis of an appraisal of the market forces, will best achieve the objectives of an enterprise at a given time.[2]

While the precise mix varies from one marketing plan to another, most strategies include five basic elements: market selection, product planning, pricing, distribution systems, and communications. It is useful to examine each of these elements, identifying some of the strategic options that may be open in each area, and exploring considerations that bear on managers' choices.

MARKET SELECTION

The most important choice made by any organization, whether a business, school, hospital, or government agency, is deciding what markets it will serve with what products. Market selection implies major commitments to particular customer groups, specific skills and fields of technology, and a certain competitive milieu. Many organizations, however, seem to make decisions in this important area almost by default and in hasty reaction to the market opportunities at hand.

---

2. Neil H. Borden, "Concept of the Marketing Mix," Harvard Business School No. 9-502-004.

Market Segmentation   A first step in market selection is the division of the market into segments according to some rational scheme. A market segment may be defined as a set of potential customers that are alike in the way they perceive and value the product, in their patterns of buying, and in the way they use the product.

Market segmentation has developed as production capabilities have expanded to permit product variations rather than a single, standardized product, and as heterogeneity in income and lifestyles has fostered subsegments of demand where only a single market was thought to exist. A good example is the progression from the early standardized black automobile to the plethora of colors and options in cars today. Experience has also shown that marketing success is more likely when communications—and products—are aimed at a more narrowly defined group. A good example is the decline of mass-circulation magazines and the rise of more specialized (targeted) publications.

Markets may be segmented along several dimensions:

- *Demography.* People in different income and age groups, occupations, and ethnic and educational backgrounds may exhibit characteristically different tastes, buying behavior, and consumption patterns.
- *Geography.* Some products are culturally sensitive. That is, their usage, the ways in which they are promoted, and government restrictions with regard to product form, advertising, and pricing may vary considerably from one geographic area to another. An example of a culturally sensitive product class is pharmaceuticals.
- *Lifestyle factors.* Going beyond demographic differentiation, so-called psychographic typologies attempt to segment markets according to individual lifestyles and attitudes toward self, work, homes, families, and peer groups. Career-oriented women, for example, may differ in these respects from those who see themselves primarily as homemakers. Marketers might usefully distinguish between the two groups in planning their product lines and advertising programs.
- *Product-use patterns.* Particularly for industrial customers, a useful segmentation scheme can often be developed on the basis of how purchasers use the product and how it fits into their processes and systems. For example, a firm that buys nylon fiber to make hosiery uses it in the manufacturing process very differently from one that buys it for use in rubber tires. Similarly, the customer who buys a small plane for crop dusting is in a different market segment from one who buys an executive jet.

There are, of course, other useful ways of segmenting markets. Industrial marketers may find it useful to distinguish between large and small accounts, or to differentiate government agencies, commercial companies, schools, and hospitals. In each category, the purchase-decision process is characteristically different and may be shaped by different rules, regulations, and measurement systems as well as by different levels of purchasing professionalism.

Consumer-goods marketers may find it valid to differentiate between those who buy something as a gift and those who purchase it for themselves, or between light and heavy users of a product.

Market segmentation is an art, not a science. The important criteria in selecting one or another dimension or combination are customers' needs and the distinctive and significant differences in their buying behavior.

It is also important to recognize that the segmentation scheme appropriate at one stage in the development of a market may be less relevant later and may need to be recast as a market grows and matures. Customers become educated in buying and using the product. Demand increases and new competitors enter. Retail and wholesale distribution channels develop in response to market growth and change in character. New product forms emerge to serve the needs of different kinds of customers. Such events change the way people buy and reshape the industry environment; as a result the original segmentation scheme becomes obsolete.

Market Selection Criteria   The development of a market segmentation scheme is just the beginning point. The next step is to select among market segments the particular targets of opportunity that are best suited to the company. A number of issues need to be considered.

- The organization's broad goals and their fit with the specific market opportunity under consideration;
- The firm's particular strengths and weaknesses vis-à-vis particular market segments (e.g., its financial strength, marketing skills and resources, technical expertise, and product advantages);
- Resource commitments required for product development, advertising, sales force development, and manufacturing and distribution systems;
- The strengths and weaknesses of competitors and their positions in the market;
- Whether demand is growing or leveling off;
- The possibility of taking a significant share of the market.

PRODUCT PLANNING

A product offering is the total package of benefits the customer obtains when making a purchase: the product itself; its brand name; its availability; the warranty, repair service, and technical assistance the seller may provide; the sales financing arrangements; and the personal relationships that may develop between representatives of the buyer and the seller. A watch, for example, is an instrument for telling time as well as a piece of jewelry. The purchaser may derive psychic satisfaction from its style, its content of precious metals, its brand name, the fact that it performs several time functions and has digital readout, and the prestige of the store in which it was purchased. Indeed, part of a product's meaning may be the pleasure the buyer derives from shopping for it and making a purchase selection.

Thus product meaning must be defined in terms of the benefits the buyer obtains with purchase and use. Regardless of what the seller thinks of the product, what counts for strategic planning purposes is the purchaser's opinion and the value he or she places on alternative competitive offerings. Thus the product package will have different meanings to different potential buyers. The technical assistance, for example, that a seller of industrial chemicals offers to customers may be especially valued by small firms with no R&D resources of their own. Large companies with extensive technical staffs may give it little weight in making a buying decision.

Product-Planning Options   Planning the product line is a key element in marketing strategy. The product is not a given, but a variable. Marketing programs are designed to develop markets and the product is a vehicle intended to serve that purpose. Some specific choices to consider are these:

- How broad or narrow should the product line be?
- Will it span a range of price points or be concentrated at the low end or at the premium-price level?
- What are the physical and performance specifications?
- Will it consist of standard off-the-shelf components or will products be designed to individual customer preferences?
- Will the company market endproducts ready for use or will it sell materials and components to other firms that manufacture the endproducts?
- Will customers be given warranties? Will field service be available for repair and product maintenance?

Other more general considerations are also relevant in planning the product line:

- First, and most important, does the proposed product line allow the seller to serve a customer need profitably?
- Does the product differ from competitive offerings in its design, quality, or performance characteristics? (Profit opportunities are typically greatest for differentiated products.)
- Can the product be manufactured in existing facilities? Can it be marketed through distribution systems now in place?
- Will the proposed offering enhance the company's reputation, its position with existing customers, and its strength in dealing with retailers and distributors? Or will the new product only cannibalize sales of existing products without increasing total profitability?

Market selection and product-planning choices must often be made together. The starting point may be the identification of a customer need not being filled as well as it might, or a new technical development that will make it possible to perform some function in a better way. Or the company may simply see an opportunity to add to the supply of available products to help satisfy a rapidly growing market.

It is useful to think of the market as a chessboard, with the squares representing market segments. Competitors are arrayed over the playing area, each seeking to occupy certain spaces with certain product offerings. The heart of marketing strategy is determining what squares to go after with what products. It may be that some spaces, previously unrecognized as market opportunities, now lie vacant and would be relatively easy to occupy. Some may be filled by weak competitors with inadequate product offerings; they can be attacked. But other squares are solidly dominated by strong competition and superior product lines; it would be risky to try to enter those spaces.

PRICING

At the simplest level, pricing is establishing the price at which a product will be sold to a customer. The true art of pricing is to make the price a quantitative expression of the value of the product to the customer. If the price is lower than the customer is willing to pay, the seller sacrifices potential profits. In addition to retail price, the price structure may need to provide for quantity discount schedules; functional discount schedules for different classes of buyers; retail and wholesale margins; and payment terms (e.g., a certain percentage off the billed price for payment within a specified period).

Price Discrimination   Because the product may be worth more to some customers than to others, the seller might sell the same product at different prices to different groups of buyers. Many firms, for example, establish different prices in different countries or make minor modifications to differentiate product offerings to different classes of buyers. Food products sold to hotels and restaurants are usually packaged in bulk and sold at lower unit prices than the same items sold through retail stores to consumers. In such ways, a seller discriminates among market segments, attempting to maximize the revenue derived from each.

In other cases it may not be possible to price discriminately either geographically or through packaging, use of different brand names, or minor (nonfunctional) design modifications. Then the price set for all customers must equal the lowest valuation placed on the product by any target customer group.

The seller may also fail to realize a price that equals the value of the product to the customer if competitors charge lower prices. Competitive prices then establish value, since the customer has the option of buying a competitive product. Hence, competition tends to set a ceiling on the price any one seller may charge.

To the extent, however, that a supplier can differentiate its product from others, it enjoys a degree of freedom in setting prices. If buyers can be persuaded that the product is superior, the seller can obtain a premium theoretically equal to the increment of value the buyer perceives.

Cost as a Factor in Pricing   If competitive price levels set the ceiling, cost sets the floor. A supplier cannot long sell below the costs of manufacture and still stay in business. But a company may elect to sell at a loss temporarily in the hope of gaining a foothold in the market and realizing profits as volume increases and unit costs decline. It may even temporarily sell the product at a price that covers the direct costs of labor and material but not fixed overheads such as plant depreciation, simply to keep the work force employed.

A manager also has some choice with regard to the period of time over which certain investments are amortized. Prices for a new product line, for example, may be set so as to recover the product-development costs in one, three, five, or even more years. The choice of amortization period significantly affects the product cost base and hence the basis for setting price.

The relative levels of fixed and variable costs also affect pricing strategy. If such fixed costs as depreciation on plant and equipment, research and development, and advertising are high relative to variable costs (labor and material), maximizing sales volume becomes an important strategic objective in order to spread fixed charges over as many units as possible. For example, in the airline and hotel businesses, where fixed costs are very high, managers set prices to achieve maximum utilization of capacity. Bargain rates may substantially increase profits if they result in significantly higher sales volume.

In contrast, if variable costs are a relatively high proportion of the total, maximizing unit margins is critical to profitability. In the packaged foods business, for instance, materials and packaging represent such a large part of total costs that profitability depends on increasing as much as possible the spread between these variable costs and unit selling price.

Skimming vs. Penetration Pricing   The question of skimming versus penetration pricing often arises in developing strategy for a new product. In a skimming mode, the seller initially prices high and focuses its marketing efforts on customers who are likely to value the product highly. Then, as this pocket of opportunity is exhausted, prices are reduced to reach a larger group of potential buyers who were unwilling to pay the higher price. This process is repeated until the seller reaches all potential customers at the lowest price it is willing to charge.

A penetration price strategy is just the opposite. The seller first enters the market at a low price, usually with the expectation of preempting competitors and establishing a dominant market position. It may also hope to achieve significant manufacturing-cost reductions with substantial production volumes. The cost of penetration pricing is the profits sacrificed by initially charging some groups of customers considerably less than they would be willing to pay. The potential gain is large market share.

Penetration pricing is generally regarded as a risky strategy. If it is to succeed, several conditions must be met:

- The product must be free of any defects that might create customer dissatisfaction and incur large costs for recall, repair, or retrofitting.
- Production capacity must be in place to satisfy anticipated demand.
- Distribution channels must be available for reaching potential buyers.
- The product should not be such that potential customers would require long periods of testing before adopting it; such lags would give competitors an opportunity to react.

Price Leadership   As the foregoing discussion implies, a key factor in setting prices is competitive response. Very often sellers are forced to adjust prices because of a competitor's moves in the market. By the same token, sellers often initiate price moves in the expectation that competitors will follow. This is called price leadership. The price leader is often the industry's largest firm, respected for its economical manufacturing costs, strong distribution, and, frequently, technical leadership. Its decision to raise price levels, perhaps in the face of rising material and labor costs, may be perceived as beneficial to the entire industry and is likely to be followed. On the other hand, if competitors do not follow its lead, the initiator usually must retract its announced price rise or risk significant sales losses.

Price reductions are often initiated by smaller competitors, usually in the hope of increasing market share. If prices then decline generally as competitors move to protect sales volumes, the market leader may formally recognize the new lower levels by publishing revised price schedules.

Given the exercise of price leadership and the fundamental motivations of competitors, there is a good deal of parallel pricing in any industry. As long as competitors do not communicate with each other directly, and pricing moves cannot be construed as predatory (intended to drive smaller competitors out of business), conscious price parallelism is not only legally acceptable but may be essential to survival.

DISTRIBUTION SYSTEMS

A distribution system is a complex of agents, wholesalers, and retailers through which a seller's product moves physically to its markets. For the most part, this system consists of independent middlemen, although some companies operate their own captive sales branches. Distribution may also be handled through a combination of owned and franchised outlets.[3]

Direct vs. Indirect Selling Systems   In designing a distribution system, a manufacturer must choose between selling directly to user-customers through its own sales force or going through independent agents, wholesalers, and retailers. Initially, the decision depends on whether the manufacturer has the sales-volume base needed to support a direct sales effort. These costs are largely a function of the number of potential customers in the market, how concentrated or dispersed they are, how much each buys in a given period, and the logistical costs, such as those associated with transporting the product and maintaining field stocks.

If the balance of distribution costs and sales volume is favorable, industrial-goods manufacturers often sell directly. Consumer-goods manufacturers seldom go direct, however, because potential customers are so numerous and so widely dispersed. Most sell to retailers or through wholesalers to retailers and rely on these middlemen to take the product to the ultimate consumer. This form of distribution works because wholesalers and retailers are able to spread their operating costs over a sales base that includes the products of a great many manufacturers—often thousands.

Another consideration in planning distribution systems is how the ultimate customer wants to buy. The customer may prefer the large selection and rapid delivery offered by an industrial distributor or a retail store. Alternatively, if technical assistance and product service are important, the buyer may prefer a direct relationship with the manufacturer.

A third area affecting the choice of distribution is the degree of control the manufacturer wishes to exert over sales strategy and execution as the product moves to the ultimate customer. Motivating independent retailers and wholesalers to stock the product, promote it effectively, and, perhaps, to provide product service is often difficult. In addition, legal limitations make it difficult, if not impossible, to control the prices wholesalers and retailers charge customers or to limit where and to whom these intermediaries sell.

Selective vs. Intensive Distribution   A key issue in distribution strategy is the intensity of retail coverage in any given market area. The primary argument for selective or even exclusive distribution (i.e., one retailer or wholesaler in each market area) is that the manufacturer's one representative will enjoy a large market potential and need not compete with other dealers. Presumably, he or she will

---

3. Franchised outlets (e.g., McDonald's, Kopy Kat, Midas Muffler) typically operate under the franchisor's brand name and performance standards, selling the products or services with which the franchising company is identified. The franchisee usually owns or leases the property, manages it, pays the franchisor a royalty based on sales, and takes the profit.

benefit from higher sales volume and unit margins and be motivated to work hard at market development. In general, exclusive or selective distribution is a good choice if (a) the unit costs of stocking and selling the product are high (as in furniture); and (b) buyers are inclined to shop for the product and will travel to outlets where they may see the product and talk to salespeople.

By contrast, intensive distribution is typically used when (a) convenience of purchase and minimal shopping effort are key considerations for potential buyers; and (b) the unit costs of stocking and display are relatively low. Bally Shoes, for example, which seeks a relatively small segment of affluent, highly fashion-conscious buyers, uses very selective distribution. Thom McAn, on the other hand, attempts to cover the market with its own retail outlets to attract the mass of middle-income, convenience-oriented shoe purchasers.

It is not unusual for products to move from exclusive or selective distribution to intensive distribution over the product life cycle. In the early stages, when potential customers need to learn about the product—what to consider in making a purchase and how to use it—it may be essential that sales personnel provide extensive help at the point of sale. Such assistance adds considerably to retail sales costs and indicates the desirability of selective distribution. As the product matures and total sales volume increases, buyers need less point-of-sale education. At the same time, shopping convenience and retail price become more important to the buyer, and resellers' unit sales costs decrease markedly. In response, competitors move to establish strong market exposure by expanding their representation at the retail level. These factors typically prompt the industry leader to shift from selective to intensive distribution. Handheld calculators made this transition relatively rapidly as one large manufacturer, Texas Instruments, led the way in shifting from college bookstores and office equipment stores to mass merchandisers (discount houses) and drug chains.

Like other elements of a marketing strategy, distribution strategies should evolve in response to changing market conditions. Nonetheless, of all the elements of marketing strategy, except perhaps market selection, distribution systems, which take a long time to build and involve complex relationships with a great many independent businesspeople, are the most difficult to change. They represent the link to important groups of customers, and disturbing these relationships is at best risky. But failing to restructure the channel system as markets change may be courting disaster.

MARKETING COMMUNICATIONS

A core marketing function is communications: informing people about your product, showing them how it can be useful, persuading them to buy. Marketers can reach potential customers through such public media as radio, television, newspapers, magazines, and billboards, or by direct mail. Or, they may rely on personal messages through field salespeople calling on customers, or on personnel at the point of sale. These options are like a kit of tools that may be used in combination, each of which is especially useful for certain purposes under certain conditions. The optimal communications mix depends on several factors.

The Process of Decision Making   The purchase-decision process typically moves through several stages: (1) initial awareness of need, (2) identification of options, (3) a search for information, (4) selection, and (5) post-purchase reaffirmation. These stages are likely to depend on the nature of the product, the purchaser's previous buying and use experience, and the involvement of others in the buying decision. The key point for marketers is that the communications vehicles needed to reach prospective purchasers and to influence the decision-making process may be different at different stages. Television and magazine advertising may stimulate the initial desire to buy, but talking to friends, visiting stores, and reading relevant publications may be more effective when identifying options and searching for information. During the final selection, the most powerful communicator might be the clerk behind the counter or a company's sales representative.

Often several people are involved in a purchasing decision; this complex of players is called the *decision-making unit* (DMU). For a major household purchase, such as a car or a vacation, the DMU may consist of a parent and child, or a wife and husband, or indeed the whole family. In industrial companies the DMU can include engineers; production personnel; controllers; financial, marketing, and general managers; as well as members of the procurement department. Which players are involved depends on the product being purchased, the importance of the commitment, and individuals' previous experience in buying and using similar products.

Of course, the various participants in the decision-making process have different concerns, and the marketer may need to address them separately, offering each one information that he or she believes is important and recognizing the biases that person brings to interactions among DMU members.

Media Advertising   As marketing vehicles, media advertising may be especially effective in performing particular tasks:

- Providing information on product specifications and prices;
- Informing potential purchasers where to buy;
- Introducing new products;
- Suggesting ideas on how to use the product;
- Assuring prospective buyers of product quality, reliability of the source, and rightness of a decision to buy;
- Creating a prestige image;
- Establishing brand and packaging familiarity to facilitate product identification at point of sale;
- Developing interest among dealers; and
- Positioning the product in reference to competitive offerings; that is, indicating the particular market segment for which it is best suited.

The use of media advertising, therefore, may be especially helpful in particular situations, as when (a) a specific medium (television, radio, newspaper, or magazine) is especially well suited for getting across the intended message; (b) the target audience can be most efficiently reached through the medium selected; (c) the volume of sales justifies advertising costs; and (d) prospective buyers are open to receiving and acting on promotional messages; that is, they can be persuaded to buy and are not so loyal to competitive brands that they are unwilling to try something new.

Personal Selling   Besides performing some of the same functions as media advertising, personal selling is especially useful in identifying prospective customers; providing personalized reassurance on the rightness of a purchase decision; and developing solutions tailored to buyer needs (e.g., in clothing, furniture, computers, and machine tools). Only through personal selling can a manufacturer deal with customer problems such as late deliveries, product failure, or the need for technical assistance.

At the same time, personal selling offers a unique means of gathering vital information on product performance, competitive activity, level of market demand, and new sales opportunities. Unlike media advertising, personal selling is a two-way channel of communication between buyer and seller.

Personal selling is usually preferable to media advertising when relevant information is difficult to communicate through mass media (either the message is too complex or the target audience is difficult to reach). It is also preferable when the sales base may be too small to support the cost of media advertising, especially when arrangements must be tailored to the individual customer. Finally, in some purchasing decisions it is important for prospective purchasers to "feel the goods."

For all those reasons marketing strategies vary considerably in the resources allocated to media advertising and personal selling. The appropriate balance hinges on the nature of the sales message and the suitability of different media to communicate that message efficiently to a target audience. It also depends on the relative costs of using alternative communications options. The cost per customer is typically much higher for personal selling than for mass media. On the other hand, the total cost of communicating a particular message to a target audience is usually much higher when advertising campaigns are used, particularly on a national scale.

Push vs. Pull Strategies   In the push strategy, effort is concentrated on selling to the intermediate customers—say, retailers—and providing these channels of distribution with strong incentives to promote the product vigorously to the ultimate purchaser. Incentives at this level may include high retail margins, sales aids, sales contests, and sales training programs. In a pull strategy, on the other hand, the seller focuses marketing expenditures on influencing the ultimate user, typically through advertising, to go into the store to buy. In effect it pulls the product through its distribution channels by creating demand at the consumer level. Push and pull are also relevant concepts for industrial marketers. Pursuing a pull strategy, a manufacturer of aircraft engines may concentrate its selling efforts on the airlines, who buy planes from the airframe manufacturers. It tries to persuade the airlines to specify its engines in the equipment they purchase.

In balancing marketing resources, the choice between push and pull strategies rests on many of the same considerations as the choice between emphasizing personal selling or media advertising—that is, on cost efficiency, the nature of the sales message, and volume of sales. Pull strategies, especially in consumer markets, can be tremendously costly, and only the largest companies may be able to afford them. Fundamentally, the choice depends on what kinds of messages influence people to buy, where and how they can be delivered in the buying-decision process, and at what cost.

Advertising and personal selling are, however, but two elements in the marketing mix. Effective communications cannot bring marketing success in the face of adverse economic, social, and technological trends. Nor can heavy outlays for advertising and selling assure the sale of products that do not represent good value for the customer.

—— MARKETING STRATEGY AND STAGES OF MARKET GROWTH

As product markets grow, mature, and decline over time, the marketing strategy must evolve in response to changing customer and competitive demands. For purposes of this discussion we identify four stages of growth: the introductory period, the rapid-growth phase, the leveling-off stage, and market maturity. The customer's comprehension of the product and its uses, and the degree of competitive intensity, are different at each stage. The marketing infrastructure (the channels of distribution and the media reaching relevant customer groups) may also differ.

INTRODUCTORY PHASE

A new market opportunity is often based on some new technology—for example, synthetic fibers, plastics, or computers—that creates possibilities for a range of new products. In the early stages marketing strategies typically stress market education—assisting industrial purchasers of new materials and components in end-product design and in the development of manufacturing processes. Market education also includes communicating with potential end-users regarding the use of the product and its advantages over the conventional product it is intended to replace. In pricing and market selection, the strategy is typically to skim, which serves to generate high margins with which to fund the costs of research and development and technical market development. At this stage the market tends to be relatively insensitive to price as long as the new product offers significant advantages over what it replaces.

The basic objective is to create primary demand, that is, to maximize total demand for the new product category by replacing, as fully and rapidly as possible, the market volume held by competing traditional products. At this stage patent protection may give the manufacturer a legal monopoly, so that it alone profits from the market it creates.

RAPID-GROWTH PHASE

As the new-product concept takes hold, market conditions change markedly. Buyers become more discriminating and sophisticated in their purchasing behavior and product-use patterns. They may demand products tailored to their individual requirements. As competitors enter the market, potential customers realize they have options with regard to price, quality, product form, and brand. The need for buyer education grows, particularly at the point of purchase, where choices must ultimately be made.

The innovating firm and its new competitors may at this stage focus on expansion of primary demand, which all may enjoy. Their strategies for building demand typically take the form of product proliferation—the development of a variety of product forms to meet the specific needs of identified market segments. Market skimming continues to be profitable in this phase. As product prices are gradually reduced, the new product comes into direct competition with the lower-priced traditional products, market potential broadens, and unit manufacturing costs may decline enough to outweigh the profit impact of price reductions.

LEVELING-OFF STAGE

At some point the strategic emphasis shifts from developing primary demand to maximizing selective demand. Having worked to make the pie as large as possible, each competitor now tries to claim as large a piece as possible for itself.

Strategies for holding or expanding a company's market shares at this stage often stress expanding distribution systems to get as wide a market exposure as possible. A supplier may try to preempt shelf space in retail stores and distributor warehouses, not only to build sales volume but also to reduce competitors' market exposure. Paralleling the grab for shelf space is the drive for consumer "share-of-mind" through increased outlays for advertising, personal selling, and promotions.

Product strategy at this stage focuses on achieving maximum differentiation to permit latitude in pricing and to provide substance for the advertising messages needed to establish brand loyalty. Product lines also tend to broaden, to fill shelf space and to get the maximum return from investments in advertising and distribution systems. At the same time, a wide range of product variations emerges to satisfy customers' diverse needs in increasingly segmented markets.

The marketing strategy evolves and elaborates as buyers become more concerned with tailored-to-use products, ease of purchase, and product availability, and more sensitive to market communications in all forms.

MARKET MATURITY

In the mature phase, the structure of the supply industry has taken shape. A few firms have staked out major shares of the market; other marginal firms have lost out in the race for market dominance and must adjust to follower roles. At this point, if not before, the strategies of leaders and followers typically diverge.

The goal of market leaders is primarily to preserve and, if possible, to expand their market share. Their strategies reflect an effort to increase sales volume, sometimes but not always by means of low prices. In addition, to develop a preferential position with their customer bases and gain a product edge, they stress service to their channels of distribution and user-customers, as well as technical leadership. A related objective is to optimize manufacturing and marketing costs by attaining a level of critical mass[4] in both areas.

Market leaders at this stage display a strong sense of territorial imperative. They often stake out particular accounts, channels of distribution, and customer groups and defend them aggressively, by service and pricing actions, from competitive attack. At the same time, dominant firms demonstrate a high degree of strategic interdependency. That is, each develops its own strategy in such areas as price, product, technical service, and promotion in clear recognition of its competitors' strategies. Decisions to add new plant capacity are now significantly influenced by competitors' additions, as preserving the firm's share of productive capacity is often thought necessary to retaining its market share.

At this point, leading firms are especially vulnerable to competitive developments that may make obsolete the technologies on which their product

---

4. The concept of critical mass is based on the idea that unit costs are, to a significant extent, a function of the total size of the operation. Up to a point, unit costs decline as plant size increases or as the marketing effort scales up. Further increases in scale beyond that theoretical point reduce costs more slowly, if at all, and may even create diseconomies as limits are reached in plant capacity and in the ability of management to implement strategies. The level of critical mass will vary considerably from one product to another, depending on process technology and the extent to which pull strategies and outlays for mass media are effective in building sales volume.

lines are based. Often new technologies are introduced from outside the industry, bringing in new competitors and new norms of industry behavior. An effective response to such threats is painful, since it often means discarding the old technology, manufacturing facilities, and distribution systems and cannibalizing profitable sales of existing products. Moreover, the rapid adoption of a new technology means abandoning psychological commitments to once-successful patterns of business in the manufacture, distribution, and marketing of the product.

By contrast, smaller companies in the industry focus primarily on survival. Since they typically lack the resources to fund extensive product-development and promotional programs, they survive by picking a specific market segment and concentrating on serving it well. The target market should be one to which the company can bring some particular strengths and that does not require a large critical mass of resources in manufacturing, research, and marketing. A follower's profitability is likely to depend on its ability to operate with low overheads and no frills.

For the follower, new technical developments may create new opportunities, perhaps the chance to win market share from large entrenched competitors intent on preserving their position. To the smaller firm, the risk of sacrificing investments in the old technology may not seem so great as the possible gain from moving quickly to embrace the new technology. What differentiates leaders from followers in this situation, then, is their perceptions of relative risk and gain and their ability to relinquish psychological commitments to past successes and systems.

———— ANALYTICAL APPROACHES IN FORMULATING MARKETING STRATEGY

The responsiveness of a firm's strategy to changing market conditions and cost factors will almost always be based on careful analysis of the following areas.

Environmental Factors   At the broadest level it is useful to assess the significance of such environmental elements as growth in population and disposable income, as well as government regulations that may influence how the company conducts its business. Also relevant are the directions of new technical developments, the availability of critical materials and other key resources, inflation rates, and evolving lifestyles. This listing is simply illustrative; the relevant environmental factors will depend on the products and markets under consideration.

Market Factors   Focusing on a particular market, strategists will need to determine its size, rate of growth, stage of development, trends in the distribution systems serving it, buyer behavior patterns, seasonality of demand, segments that currently exist or could be developed, and unsatisfied opportunities that might provide a market entry. Next they will ask what levels of investment and marketing spending will be required.

Competition   Strategists will also need to know who the competitors are, what product/market positions they occupy, what their strategies are, their strengths and weaknesses, their cost structures (to the extent that this can be determined), and their production capacity.

Self-analysis   The company's own strengths and weaknesses relative to competitors must be appraised in such areas as technology, financial resources, manufacturing skills, marketing strengths, and the existing base of customers. For purposes of market selection and strategy formulation, corporate strengths must correspond to the needs of the market. It is essential to ask, "What can *we* bring to the party? How are we uniquely qualified to add something that others do not currently offer?"

Buyer Behavior   The analysis of patterns of purchasing behavior is central to product design, pricing, choice of distribution channels, and communications strategy. To a large extent we can hypothesize about buyer behavior from our own purchasing patterns and those we observe in others. Beyond that, buyer behavior can be analyzed in considerable depth with the aid of sophisticated market research tools, including survey techniques (e.g., customer interviews, questionnaires) and statistical analysis of sales patterns. Market tests can assess potential demand for a new product, the appeal of a proposed brand name, or the relative pull of different advertising messages. Market research, one of the most technical areas in marketing, is generally expensive; its cost must always be weighed against the anticipated value of the information—which is often less definitive and revealing than expected and is, at best, subject to interpretation.

Trade Analysis   To the extent that a company relies on resellers to take the product to market, its strategy must consider the availability of distribution channels as well as their requirements. What are the operating-cost structures of wholesalers and retailers? What costs are they likely to incur in stocking, selling, and servicing the products? What kinds of margins will they require? To what extent must they be relieved of competition from other resellers of the product? What sales training and promotional support will they require? What commitments might they already have to competing suppliers? What alternative opportunities do they have for utilizing limited resources, in particular shelf space?

Economic Analysis   The summation of all marketing analysis is the profit-impact calculation. If the company goes ahead, how much profit can it

EXHIBIT
Strategic Marketing Planning Model

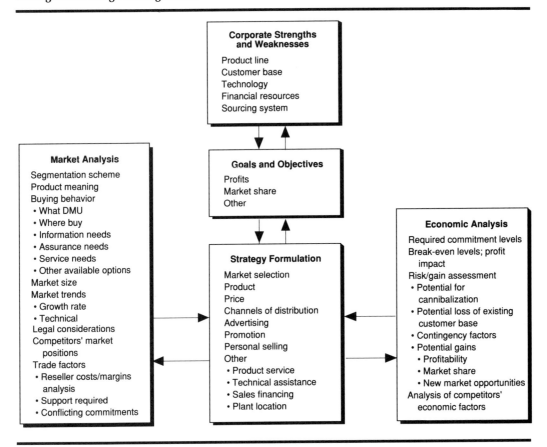

earn as compared with the profitability of other opportunities for utilizing limited resources? The profit-impact calculation assesses the fixed commitments needed to make and sell a new product, and then asks what contributions each unit sold will make toward amortizing these investments and generating an acceptable level of profit. Finally, it calculates the volume of sales that must be attained and compares that figure with the market potential for the product. Needless to say, such calculations are at best based on rough estimates. They are useful, however, in identifying and isolating the relevant variables and giving the marketing manager a framework within which to apply all the available information and his or her best judgment.

The *Exhibit* depicts graphically the analytical areas relevant to planning a marketing strategy.

Copyright © 1978; revised 1991.

——— DISCUSSION QUESTIONS

1. In your view, is there a difference between objectives (or goals) and strategies? Explain. In formulating an overall strategic marketing plan, what considerations go into the conceptual framework? What areas need to be analyzed?

2. Is it possible for two companies in the same business or industry to pursue two different marketing strategies and reach an equal level of success? What considerations would enter into developing each company's marketing strategy, and why might they differ?

3. Assume you have a new product you want to put on the market and you have already targeted the market for it. What other considerations need to be analyzed before developing a marketing plan? How would they affect market entry for your product?

4. What changes, if any, would you make to the segmentation scheme you used in the early stage of market entry as demand increases, the market grows, and the product matures? As competitors enter? As demand levels off? Would a changing environment have an effect on how people buy your product? Explain.

5. What options for response do you have when, after identifying your customers and providing the product that fills their need, the competition enters the market with a similar product, priced even lower?

6 Marketing Planning and Organization

ROBERT J. DOLAN AND ALVIN J. SILK

Marketing planning and organization in today's rapidly changing environment can benefit from the guidelines presented in this reading. The first section provides a general outline of the contents of a typical marketing plan and the process by which it is developed. In addition, it considers both the benefits that successful firms reap from their planning efforts and the problems that mark the efforts of not-so-successful planners.

The second section addresses marketing organization, setting forth a model for examining the relations between a firm's strategy and the design and structure of an organization to carry it out. The final paragraphs offer two principles to guide organization design.

A firm's marketing success depends on many factors. For instance, the size of various consumer segments, the preferences of those consumers, and the actions of competitors and distributors all interact to produce the results of a given marketing program. These factors are subject to change and uncertainty. For example, in developing its videodisc technology, RCA was uncertain about the advances that would be made by manufacturers of a competitive technology, videocassette recorders. According to reports in the press at the time of RCA's withdrawal from the market—at a loss of $580 million—RCA had not correctly anticipated the price decline of videocassette recorders, or measured accurately consumers' preference for dual-function machines—those that could record as well as play back material produced elsewhere.

Because of the number and uncertainty of factors influencing market success, a firm must have a systematic way of analyzing these factors, determining the impact of trends on its business, and designing a marketing program to meet present and future market conditions. The marketing planning process is the mechanism by which many firms accomplish these tasks.

EXHIBIT 1
Situation Analysis

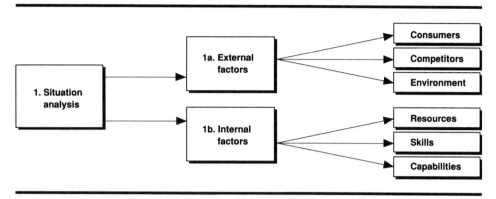

THE MARKETING PLAN—CONTENTS

There are many possible formats for a marketing plan; a 1981 Conference Board Report cites 38 examples of planning formats from consumer, industrial, and service companies.[1] While differences based on company type and competitive situations are appropriate, there is a common thread running through marketing planning documents. At their most general level, all plans require that the firm ask itself three questions: (1) Where are we now? (2) Where do we want to go? (3) How do we get there?

Essentially, the planning process forces the planner to imagine the desired future for the product (or service), recognizing the realities of the marketplace, and then to propose an action plan to reach the desired future. In structuring this effort, the following five-step format is useful.

1. Situation analysis
2. Problem and opportunity statement
3. Statement of objectives
4. Action plan recommendation
5. Statement of expected results, key risks

Step 1, the situation analysis, is the "Where are we now?" question. It is factual or descriptive, rather than normative—that is, it says how things are, not how they ought to be. It identifies key company strengths to be exploited, deficiencies to be remedied, or both. *Exhibit 1* illustrates graphically the components of the situation analysis.

---

1. David S. Hopkins, *The Marketing Plan* (New York: Conference Board Inc., 1981).

In the external-factors analysis (step 1a), the firm examines potential consumers to determine trends in primary demand, key market segments, and buyer behavior within various segments.

The second part of the external analysis is competitor analysis and asks such questions as the following:

- What segments do they serve?
- What products do they offer?
- What channels are used?
- What management resources do they have?
- What financial resources do they have?
- What are their objectives?
- How successful are they?

Finally, external analysis considers the other major environmental variables that may affect consumption behavior. These variables include economic factors such as interest rates, political factors such as trade barriers, and technological factors that may bring in new competitors. All external analysis is directed at understanding both the current situation and trends that may predict future positions.

Simultaneously, the firm completes the situation analysis by examining its own resources, skills, and capabilities in much the same way it analyzes competitors (step 1b). Although the internal assessment is easier because key data are more accessible, it is often difficult to be objective when looking inward. It may be hard, for example, to recognize that earlier new-product development efforts have failed to produce a viable product. Some firms find outside consultants particularly useful at this stage.

Step 2, the problem and opportunity statement, is largely a summary of step 1 analysis, except that management judgment is used to prioritize issues. There is real virtue in brevity at this point; a listing of 50 opportunities is foolish and wasteful if the firm has the money and staff to pursue only two or three. This stage might produce the following list for the hypothetical HAL Company.

Opportunity

1. The market for personal computers in the home is growing at 35% per year.
2. Consumers are confused by the proliferation of available brands and the types of retail outlets.
3. HAL Company has a microcomputer that is compatible with the IBM PC but, because it has a 32-bit processor, it is much faster than the IBM.

Problems

1. HAL has no marketing expertise, either in the sales force or at staff level.
2. HAL's financial resources are very limited.

Step 3, the statement of objectives, the "Where do we want to go?" phase, is the basis of the action plan in step 4. Objectives should be quantitative, in that they can be compared to actual performance and may be stated at both an overall marketing level and a function level. For example:

Primary Objectives

1. Increase to 70% by December the target consumers' awareness of HAL as a producer of personal computers for the home.
2. Ship first units to retail outlets by September. Ship 2,000 units between September and December.
3. Improve the market orientation of the entire HAL organization.

Function Objectives

1. Hire a marketing and sales manager by June.
2. Select an advertising agency by August.
3. Recruit 15 sales-representative organizations by December; set up program to monitor sales representatives' performance.

The first two primary objectives are quantitative; eventually, the actual performance results will be compared against these goals. The firm must also be willing to track data that are not generated through sales activities. Consumer awareness, for example, cannot be ascertained from shipping data; market research is needed to assess it. The next round of the planning cycle should include an audit of the firm's performance compared to its goals. The third primary objective (improve market orientation of entire HAL organization) is not easily quantified since market orientation measurements are ambiguous. Incorporating this objective into the plan is worthwhile, nonetheless, for the message it sends to all employees.

Step 4, action plan recommendation, is the "How do we get there?" phase based on the groundwork laid by steps 1–3. It states how the firm plans to remedy problems and achieve objectives by taking advantage of identified opportunities. Depending on industry characteristics, this plan may take from one year up to five years (or in rare cases even longer) to fulfill. For example, if a high-tech organization is undertaking a research and development effort, it may be five years before a product emerges.

This step details the actions, priorities, and time schedule needed to attain objectives. For example, if one objective is to ship 2,000 units to distributors by the end of the year, the action plan section assigns responsibilities to people, sets intermediate deadlines, specifies distributors to call on, and details such necessary marketing-support objectives as

- Print and mail HAL brochure to all computer retail chains of more than 50 stores by July 15.
- Offer exclusive distribution of HAL personal computers to these chains, emphasizing that the product will be available only in full-service outlets.

- Produce factory inventory of 2,500 units on September 1, with production capacity of 500 units per month by September 1.

Stating the action steps prompts an estimate of the resources required to achieve the goals. In step 5, statement of expected results and key risks, the firm assesses the plan's financial impact. Step 5 anticipates the impact of step 4 actions on the firm. It calculates key resource uses and costs, expected revenues, and, often, a pro forma or estimated income statement for the upcoming time period. Typical performance measures cited at this stage are

- Unit sales
- Sales revenue
- Cost of goods sold by product
- Gross margins by product
- Key account penetration
- Market share by segment

Since the plan of action is predicated on certain assumptions about uncertain events—competitive moves, for example—key risks and contingencies should be noted.

Although this five-step outline is typical, there is no one best way for all firms to put together a market plan. If a firm adopts a given format without thinking, it is unlikely that going through the motions of mechanically filling in prespecified forms will accomplish anything of value. The firm must also tailor the specific contents of the plan to its own needs.

——— THE MARKETING PLAN—PROCESS

Many newcomers to marketing planning think the major job in getting started is to specify the contents of the plan. Much has been written on this issue. Little has been written, however, on the equally important issue of how the planning is to get done.[2] There are four major questions to consider in structuring the planning job.

1. *Participation.* Who has overall responsibility for seeing that the planning gets done? Who does each segment of the job? Who acts as an advisor or information source for planners?
2. *Scheduling.* How often is planning done? Should planning be done on a fixed time schedule or as market developments warrant?
3. *Review.* Who reviews and approves proposed plans?

---

2. One exception is Stanley Stasch and Patricia Lanktree, "Can Your Marketing Planning Procedures Be Improved?" *Journal of Marketing* (Summer 1980): 79–90. This article considers in depth the contents and process issues in six large consumer goods organizations and traces the full process for one organization believed to be obtaining good results from its planning.

4. *Monitoring.* What is the best mechanism for ensuring that the plan is executed and desired results are achieved?

An important principle of issue 1 ("Who does what?") is that the people involved in the planning process are more committed to the plan once it is adopted than those who were not involved. Thus, if possible, people who will implement the plan should be involved in its development. This sounds clear enough, but in many organizations implementers feel that the plan is something imposed on them by top management and people in staff positions. If they consider the plan's goals or resource allocation to be unrealistic they will not be motivated to carry it out. To be effective, planning must be an integral part of managing the business; it should not be something to be got through as quickly as possible in order to get back to "real" work.

Issue 2, scheduling, is often not considered explicitly by planners. To fit in with the cycles for other reports, such as taxes and reports to stockholders, marketing planning is usually done annually. Although an annual marketing plan may indeed be the correct choice for the majority of firms, the planner should evaluate that choice in terms of the rhythms of a particular marketplace. Should the planning cycle for a producer of laundry detergents, for example, be the same as for the HAL Company, the hypothetical manufacturer of personal computers?

Most people argue that having a fixed, inflexible time schedule ensures that planning gets done. The major problem here is that requiring too much information in too little time may have unexpected consequences. Asking people to adhere to a strict schedule can encourage "filling in the form," regardless of the quality of the input.

Review and approval, issue 3, concerns the role of top management. Practice suggests that senior management be involved at a number of points in the process, rather than just to say "yea or nay" at the end. This ensures harmoniousness with management's overall conception of the business.

Finally, issue 4, monitoring, concerns how the plan is made a living document rather than an entry on an out-of-the-way bookshelf. To be effective the plan documentation should provide guidelines for actions and checkpoints on performance. Moreover, channels will need to be in place to allow for midcourse corrections in case an unexpected event occurs or inputs just do not yield desired outputs in spite of correct assessments of conditions.

DESIRED BENEFITS

According to David Hopkins,[3] the broad objective of planning is to encourage thinking about the future, improve performance, and keep the firm alive. But what specific benefits do companies derive from structuring their analysis of the market and writing everything down in a formal way?

---

3. David Hopkins, "Plan or Perish," *Sales and Marketing Management* (May 18, 1981): 45–46.

EXHIBIT 2
Intraorganization Communications

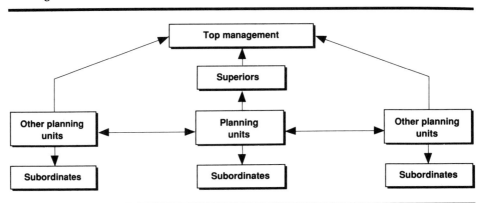

First of all, a plan can be a very effective communication device (see *Exhibit 2*). The planning unit's document facilitates three kinds of communication flow: (1) up to superiors for their concurrence with the plan; (2) down to subordinates so that they understand more clearly the mission of the unit; and (3) laterally to other planning units.

Second, the collection of plans from all planning units allows top management to check the consistency of the actions and synergies across units. A plan can also aid in evaluating managers. Since managers have asked for resources to perform activities in anticipation of certain results, they have produced a formal record of their "promises made, promises kept."

Third, the plan focuses people on the right questions. This is especially helpful when there are a number of new managers in the organization. Participation in the planning process can be an effective training device. Drawing up the plan provides an opportunity for many people to contribute facts. It also encourages constructive debate about alternative action plans in much the same way a good case study does.

Finally, the existence of a written plan with quantified objectives is a prerequisite to accurate assessment of the firm's performance. It serves as an audit and can (1) yield diagnostic information when objectives are not achieved, and (2) provide better understanding of how the market performs.

THREATS TO BENEFITS

Marketing planning is not a universally acclaimed activity. In some firms, the line people who implement the plan view it as a burdensome overload imposed by staffers trying to justify their existence. Some top managers view it in similar terms. In the words of the chief executive officer of a multibillion-dollar company, "Get rid of those planners and put in somebody who will *do* something." To a large extent, the criticism is unfair, for what is generally at fault is not the concept of marketing planning but the firm's execution of the planning function.

Charles Ames[4] found three major pitfalls in effective marketing planning:

1. Failure to fit the concept to the company
2. Overemphasis on the system and formats at the expense of content
3. Failure to recognize and consider alternative, creative plans of action (i.e., the tendency to base future plans on continuation of current policies with minor changes)

Although Ames's study was of industrial products, many failures in consumer goods and service industries also can be traced to the company's attempt to borrow intact the marketing planning procedures of another organization. Procedures must be based on specific market characteristics; required interfaces between the marketing, manufacturing, and finance functions; size of the organization; breadth of the product line; and so forth.

Ames's second point concerns separating planners of the process from implementers. Some organizations have planning-input requirements that appear to be based on the principle of "the more, the merrier." The forms are overly structured and detailed. They ask implementers to provide information that is totally useless for effective management. Some managers find that planning documents direct them to provide information about unimportant factors but allocate no space to write about critical areas.

——— MARKETING ORGANIZATION

Marketing plans establish objectives and recommend actions for achieving them. The plans' execution falls to the marketing organization where planning and organizing are inexorably intertwined. Thomas V. Bonoma describes the interrelation between strategy and implementation as a "cascade phenomenon," whereby goals and decisions flow down an organization hierarchy "much like water does from pool to pool in a Japanese garden."[5] Strategic plans formulated at one level in an organization are communicated to the level below, where they are interpreted and translated into actions undertaken to achieve the broader strategy. Thus, an organization's design and management become critical factors in the successful implementation of any strategy.

---

4. Charles Ames, "Marketing Planning for Industrial Products," *Harvard Business Review* (September–October 1968): 100–111.

5. Thomas V. Bonoma, *The Marketing Edge* (New York: Free Press, 1985), p. 9.

STRATEGY, STRUCTURE, AND PERFORMANCE

The premise that organization matters to economic performance and is realized through efforts to implement a chosen strategy is depicted in *Exhibit 3*, which also identifies the major classes of organization-design variables.

A key issue in appraising a marketing plan is the fit between the strategy embodied in the plan and the organization's design. In his landmark study of the evolution of large industrial corporations in the United States, Alfred Chandler shows how the pursuit of alternative product/market growth strategies posed special administrative challenges and therefore gave rise to distinct organization forms or structures. He summarizes his findings and thesis as follows:

> Strategic growth resulted from an awareness of the opportunities and needs—created by changing population, income, and technology—to employ existing or expanding resources more profitably. A new strategy required a new or at least a refashioned structure if the enlarged enterprise was to be operated efficiently. The failure to develop a new internal structure, like the failure to respond to new external opportunities and needs, was a consequence of over-concentration on operational activities by the executives responsible for the destiny of their enterprises, or from their inability, because of past training and education and present position, to develop an entrepreneurial outlook.[6]

Note that Chandler sees environmental change as the source of "new opportunities and needs." New strategies are adopted in response to shifts in external conditions, which leads to Chandler's famous proposition that "structure follows strategy" and to its corollary—that without structural adjustments, changes in growth strategy can lead to economic inefficiency.

A large body of empirical evidence supports these concepts. For example, after investigating the organizational practices of 10 large firms in different industries, Corey and Star concluded that "in successful companies, organization structure responds to market environment." At the same time, Corey and Star remind us, strategies do not grow out of an organizational vacuum: "Today's organization is an important influence molding tomorrow's strategy, which in turn shapes tomorrow's organization."[7]

Chandler's work provides the rationale for the strategy–organization–performance linkage shown in Galbraith and Nathanson's model (*Exhibit 3*). A firm's internal organization is represented by the large circle encompassing the five principal design variables that define an organization's structure and processes.

---

6. Alfred D. Chandler, Jr., *Strategy and Structure: Chapters in the History of American Industrial Enterprise* (Cambridge, Mass.: MIT Press, 1962), pp. 15–16.

7. E. Raymond Corey and Steven H. Star, *Organization Strategy: A Marketing Approach* (Boston: Division of Research, Graduate School of Business Administration, Harvard University, 1971), pp. 4, 5.

EXHIBIT 3
Strategy, Organization Design, and Performance

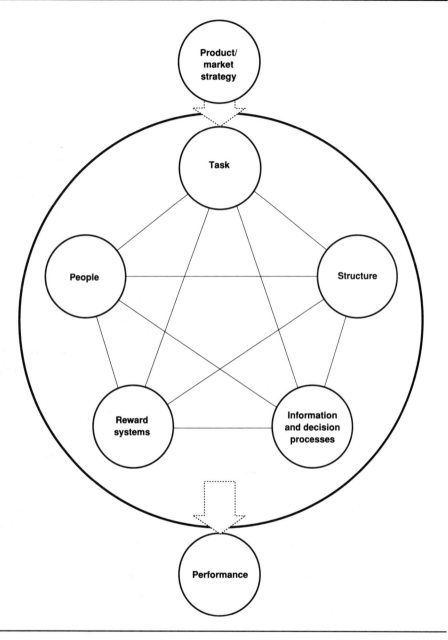

Source: From Jay R. Galbraith and Daniel A. Nathanson, *Strategy Implementation: The Role of Structure and Process* (St. Paul, Minn.: West Publishing Co., 1978), p. 2.

Task refers to the basic activities performed by employees and reflects the technology available for doing the organization's work. *Structure* denotes the arrangements among people for getting work done and can be conceptualized along two basic dimensions: differentiation and integration. Differentiation involves the division of labor or combining of tasks into roles and the assignment of roles to organizational units such as departments and divisions. Differentiation, however, gives rise to the need for integration, or means for achieving control and coordination of specialized roles and units so as to accomplish both specific and general organizational goals.

Two other mechanisms for effecting control and coordination in marketing organizations are *reward systems* and *information/decision processes*. These mechanisms may be thought of as relating to both the fundamental rationale for organizing and the basic limitation of organizations. As Herbert Simon observes: "It is only because individual human beings are limited in knowledge, foresight, skill, and time that organizations are useful instruments for the achievement of human purpose; and it is only because organized groups of human beings are limited in ability to agree on goals, to communicate, and to cooperate that organizing becomes for them a 'problem.'"[8]

Information and decision processes affect communication flows, decision making, and the distribution of influence within an organization. Decision processes may be designed to be more or less formalized in terms of who participates, how the search for and analysis of alternatives is conducted, and what criteria are invoked in selecting among them. Choices about the collection, maintenance, processing, and distribution of data determine the nature, quality, and timeliness of information available to support decision making. These choices thus have an important bearing on how an organization responds to environmental feedback and manages internal interdependencies.

Reward systems serve to motivate individuals to perform routine and nonroutine tasks essential for the functioning of the organization. Rewards include policies relating to compensation, performance appraisal, promotion, job design, and leadership style.

People, the final organization-design variable, are invariably a company's scarcest resource when developing an organization well matched to its strategic needs and opportunities. The time-honored maxim of "find good people and turn them loose" leads to a focus on policies relating to recruitment, selection, training and development, promotion, and transfer.

The challenge for management in setting these design variables is a dual one: the choices made with respect to tasks, structure, people, rewards, and decision/information systems should not only fit the strategy being pursued but must also be internally consistent. The latter point is reflected in *Exhibit 3* by the interconnecting lines of the five design variables.

Two implications of this condition deserve emphasis. First, while performance, in principle, may be affected by a change in any of these design

---

8. Herbert A. Simon, *Models of Man* (New York: Wiley, 1957), p. 199.

variables, their flexibility and leverage are likely to be dissimilar and situational. A design modification that works in one circumstance may be ineffective or even dysfunctional in another. Within a short planning horizon, certain design alterations may not be feasible and will constrain implementation of a new strategy. Second, the design variables are interdependent and a change in one may require changes in others, thereby making a piecemeal approach to organization design suspect if not hazardous. Thus the problem of organization design is highly complex, requiring continuing attention and frequent adjustment.

GENERIC MARKETING ORGANIZATION STRUCTURES

The structure of marketing organizations, like the units of a multi-product/service firm, can be differentiated either vertically or horizontally. Vertical differentiation is reflected in the number of different levels within an organizational hierarchy, while horizontal differentiation refers to differences in task and orientation among units at the same organizational level.

An important property of vertical organization is the extent to which decision-making authority is centralized or decentralized. The more discretion and participation in decision making granted to members at lower organization levels, the more decentralized is the organization structure.

Marketing organizations tend to be differentiated (or centralized) by product, market, geography, and function. With respect to function, there is a distinction between the internal activities of marketing management and related support services (advertising, sales promotion, new-product development, and market research) and external activities (sales force and customer services). These internal and external functions are typically further differentiated on the basis of product or market.

The three types of structures for marketing organizations are based on these dimensions of differentiation. The first, a product-based organization, differentiates both internal and external functions by product lines, while differentiation by markets characterizes a market-based structure. The hybrid form combines a product-based structure for internal functions with a market-based organization of the sales force and other external activities. Although these generic structures represent ideal types, they can help us understand the more complex organizational forms observed in practice. They can also serve as tools for analyzing organization-design problems.

In general, the more complex or diverse an organization's environment, the more differentiated will be its marketing structure. Hence, businesses producing diverse products for relatively homogeneous markets, such as consumer packaged goods and pharmaceutical firms, tend to adopt a product-based form of organization. Conversely, businesses producing a relatively homogeneous product line for diverse end-use markets, such as materials suppliers or equipment manufacturers, are more likely to operate through market-based structures. Finally, firms selling diverse products to a diverse set of markets, such as computer manufacturers, will often develop hybrid structures to cope with environmental complexity.

Consider, for example, the three-pronged hybrid structure IBM introduced in the mid-1960s for its Data Products Division, which was responsible for the firm's intermediate-to-large computer business.[9] Product marketing managers were assigned for each system in the division's product line; they had responsibility for identifying marketplace applications, working with engineering personnel on product design, and coordinating production scheduling with manufacturing people. They also participated in pricing decisions and in training the field sales force.

In addition, market managers, known as industry directors, were appointed for each of several end-user market segments. They planned strategy—including communications programs and sales force deployment—and were involved in hardware and software development.

Geographically, the division also created market regions and operated a number of branches within each, headed, respectively, by region managers and branch managers. The latter were specialized by end-user/industry market segments and were responsible for managing both sales and customer service personnel in their branches and for providing market intelligence to division management.

ORGANIZATION DESIGN AND CHANGE

The approach to organization design represented in *Exhibit 3* is known as "contingency theory." As summarized by Galbraith and Nathanson, "the theory states that there is no one best way of organizing, but all ways of organizing are not equally effective. That is, the choice of organization form makes a difference in terms of economic performance. The choice depends, however, on the situation."[10]

As the above discussion stresses, the key contingency that must be addressed to design an effective organization is environmental complexity and diversity. Hence, a basic requirement of organization design is that one begin analysis of such problems with an explicit segmentation of the firm's relevant markets. Marshall states it concisely when he advises: "Design your business from the outside to the inside."[11] A second key principle is "fit." Businesses are organized to execute strategies; therefore the problem of organization design

9. This example is taken from E. Raymond Corey, Christopher H. Lovelock, and Scott Ward, *Problems in Marketing*, 6th ed. (New York: McGraw-Hill, 1981), pp. 716–17.

10. Jay R. Galbraith and Daniel A. Nathanson, *Strategy Implementation: The Role of Structure and Process* (St. Paul, Minn.: West Publishing Co., 1978), p. 54; *See also* Jay R. Galbraith, *Organization Design* (Reading, Mass.: Addison-Wesley, 1977).

11. Martin V. Marshall, "Short Notes on Marketing," Harvard Business School, May 1988, p. 23 (unpublished).

is to match strategy with the key dimensions of organization structure and process.

Clearly, the search for an organization design that balances the interdependencies depicted in *Exhibit 3* is an on-going pursuit. Organizational changes initiated at Procter & Gamble serve to underscore this point. In 1988, P&G, a pioneer of the brand-management system, modified the structure of its decades-old marketing organization. John G. Smale, P&G's chair, announced to employees in a company newsletter that "our historical way of managing Procter and Gamble's business no longer fits the company we are today nor the business environment in which we must compete."[12]

Faced with slow growth, fragmentation of markets, and powerful retailers, P&G sought to shift its strategic focus toward management of product categories, rather than individual brands. Traditionally, brand managers had been encouraged to compete with one another in the same category. (For example, P&G markets numerous brands of bar soaps.) Under the restructured marketing management organization, brands are grouped into 39 categories, each with its own manager. The latter serves as a general manager to whom brand managers report, along with advertising, sales, manufacturing, research, and engineering.

In addition to this structural realignment, new performance measurement and compensation policies were introduced. Whereas volume and market share criteria had been emphasized under the previous brand-management system, category managers now have direct profit responsibility, and part of their compensation depends on the financial performance of their categories. P&G is apparently seeking better interfunctional coordination and reduction in the conflicts and inefficiencies resulting from brand managers' competition for the same resources.

P&G's restructuring illustrates the process of mutual adjustment of a firm's strategy and organizational design in response to a changing environment. Thus, market forces test the adaptability of even the most dominant and successful organizational forms, such as the brand-management system.

—— **CONCLUSIONS**

Marketing planning has made a fundamental contribution to the success of many firms. However, there are significant challenges in designing a plan's contents and development process so as to avoid the pitfalls noted here. There is no cookbook solution to planning; successful firms go beyond an understanding of the concept of planning to custom tailoring a plan to their own situation.

---

12. This discussion draws on Zachary Schiller, "The Marketing Revolution at Procter & Gamble," *Business Week* 3062 (July 25, 1988): 72–76; quote, p. 73.

Once a strategy and a marketing plan to pursue it have been formulated, attention must turn to the design of the organization responsible for executing the plan. Like marketing planning, organization design defies cookbook solutions. There are no simple answers to the question: What is the right organization structure? However, two principles to guide design choices are implicit in the above discussion. First, a marketing organization should be designed from the outside to the inside; hence the foundation for any effective organizational design is segmentation of the markets served by the firm. Second, businesses are organized to execute strategies and, therefore, must seek a fit between strategy and the entire set of key design variables that define an organization's form and processes: tasks, structure, information/decision systems, reward systems, and people.

Copyright © 1984; revised 1991.

——— DISCUSSION QUESTIONS

1. In formulating a marketing plan, a company first decides where it is now, where it wants to go, and how it can get there. Once the objectives are laid out, the considerations become complex. Should management be involved in developing the plan? Or should the planners do it and have management either approve or disapprove it at the end? Who is going to implement it? How does the plan get monitored to see that the desired results take place?

2. In spite of the benefits of planning, the authors acknowledge that "marketing planning is not a universally acclaimed activity." In fact many firms view it as "burdensome." While some companies strongly support formal marketing planning, others dispense with the planning process and instead just "do it." Which view do you take? Why?

3. What in your opinion are the pitfalls that could reduce the effectiveness of a marketing plan? Does involving a large number of people in the planning process assure a wide commitment in the organization? Or can a large group impede, delay, or at least dilute the process?

4. How does the design and management of an organization influence the execution of a marketing plan? What can management do to avoid or minimize the pitfalls when designing its marketing plan?

PART FOUR

UNDERSTANDING THE NEW CONSUMER

Effective marketing today is based first and foremost on understanding the needs and wants of particular groups of customers, whose tastes dictate product development and all other aspects of the marketing mix. The variations in tastes are almost as numerous as the customers themselves. Technology too has contributed largely to the proliferation of product offerings, thereby creating a greater need for customization of all parts of the marketing mix. Mass production and mass marketing have given way to custom products and carefully targeted marketing. Advertising may never be the same. As the readings in the following section demonstrate, today's marketer focuses increasingly on segmenting the market and customizing the product offering to meet the needs of particular segments.

Marketing in an Age of Diversity 7

REGIS MCKENNA

The days of mass production and mass marketing are over, according to this reading. Technology has combined with a diverse marketplace to create an array of products, services, and markets. From his experience in helping some of the country's most innovative high-tech ventures develop and market products, the author offers observations on today's fractured marketplace and stresses the need for managers and organizations to adapt to the new rules of marketing in the age of diversity. To succeed in this new world of variety and options, he argues, businesspeople must change the ways they act and think, abandoning old-style marketshare goals and instead tying the uniqueness of any product to the unique needs of the customer.

Spreading east from California, a new individualism has taken root across the United States. Gone is the convenient fiction of a single, homogeneous market. The days of a uniformly accepted view of the world are over. Today diversity exerts tremendous influence, both economically and politically.

Technology and social change are interdependent. Companies are using new flexible technology, like computer-aided design and manufacturing and software customization, to create astonishing diversity in the marketplace and society. And individuals temporarily coalescing into "micromajorities" are making use of platforms—media, education, and the law—to express their desires.

In the marketing world, for example, the protests of thousands of consumers, broadcast by the media as an event of cultural significance, were enough to force Coca-Cola to reverse its decision to do away with "classic" Coke. On the political scene, vociferous minorities, sophisticated in using communication technology, exert influence greatly disproportionate to their numbers: the Moral Majority is really just another minority—but focused and amplified. When we see wealthy people driving Volkswagens and pickup trucks, it is clear that this is a society where individual tastes are no longer predictable; marketers cannot easily and neatly categorize their customer base.

Since the early 1970s, new technology has spawned products aimed at diverse, new sectors and market niches. Computer-aided technologies now allow companies to customize virtually any product, from designer jeans to designer genes, serving ever narrower customer needs. With this newfound technology, manufacturers are making more and more high-quality products in smaller and smaller batches; today 75% of all machined parts are produced in batches of 50 or fewer.

Consumers demand—and get—more variety and options in all kinds of products, from cars to clothes. Auto buyers, for example, can choose from 300 different types of cars and light trucks, domestic and imported, and get variations within each of those lines. Beer drinkers now have 400 brands to sample. The number of products in supermarkets soared from 13,000 in 1981 to 21,000 in 1987. There are so many new items that stores can demand hefty fees from packaged-foods manufacturers just for displaying new items on grocery shelves.

Deregulation has also increased the number of choices—from a flurry of competing airfares to automated banking to single-premium life insurance you can buy at Sears. The government has even adapted antitrust laws to permit companies to serve emerging micromarkets: the Orphan Drug Act of 1983, for instance, gave pharmaceutical companies tax breaks and a seven-year monopoly on any drugs that serve fewer than 200,000 people.

Diversity and niches create tough problems for old-line companies more accustomed to mass markets. Sears, the country's largest retailer, is trying to reposition its products, which traditionally have appealed to older middle-class and blue-collar customers. To lure younger, style-minded buyers, Sears has come up with celebrity-signature lines, fashion boutiques, and a new line of children's clothing, McKids, playing off the McDonald's draw. New, smaller stores, specialty catalogs, and merchandise tailored to regional tastes are all part of Sears's effort to reach a new clientele—without alienating its old one.

Faced with slimmer profits from staples like detergents, diapers, and toothpaste, and lackluster results from new food and beverage products, Procter & Gamble, the world's largest marketer, is rethinking what it should sell and how to sell it. The company is now concentrating on health products; it has high hopes for a fat substitute called "olestra," which may take some of the junk out of junk food. At the same time that P&G is shifting its product thinking, it also is changing its organization, opening up and streamlining its highly insular pyramidal management structure as part of a larger effort to listen and respond to customers. Small groups that include both factory workers and executives work on cutting costs, while other teams look for new ways to speed products to market.

In trying to respond to the new demands of a diverse market, the problem that giants like Sears and P&G face is not fundamental change, not a total turnabout in what an entire nation of consumers wants. Rather, it is the fracturing of mass markets. To contend with diversity, managers must drastically alter how they design, manufacture, market, and sell their products.

Marketing in the age of diversity means:

- More options for goods producers and more choices for consumers.
- Less perceived differentiation among similar products.
- Intensified competition, with promotional efforts sounding more and more alike, approaching "white noise" in the marketplace.

- Newly minted meanings for words and phrases as marketers try to "invent" differentiation.
- Disposable information as consumers try to cope with information deluge from print, television, computer terminal, telephone, fax, satellite dish.
- Customization by users as flexible manufacturing makes niche production every bit as economic as mass production.
- Changing leverage criteria as economies of scale give way to economies of knowledge—knowledge of the customer's business, of current and likely future technology trends, and of the competitive environment that allows the rapid development of new products and services.
- Changing company structure as large corporations continue to downsize to compete with smaller niche players that nibble at their markets.
- Smaller wins—fewer chances for gigantic wins in mass markets, but more opportunities for healthy profits in smaller markets.

——— THE DECLINE OF BRANDING, THE RISE OF "OTHER"

In today's fractured marketplace, tried-and-true marketing techniques from the past no longer work for most products—particularly for complex ones based on new technology. Branding products and seizing market share, for instance, no longer guarantee loyal customers. In one case after another, the old, established brands have been supplanted by the rise of "other."

Television viewers in 1983 and 1984, for instance, tuned out the big three broadcasters to watch cable and independent "narrowcast" stations. The trend continued in 1987 as the big three networks lost 9% of their viewers—more than six million people. Small companies appealing to niche-oriented viewers attacked the majority market share. NBC responded by buying a cable television company for $20 million.

No single brand can claim the largest share of the gate array, integrated circuit, or computer market. Even IBM has lost its reign over the personal computer field—not to one fast-charging competitor but to an assortment of smaller producers. Tropicana, Minute Maid, and Citrus Hill actually account for less than half the frozen orange juice market. A full 56% belongs to hundreds of mostly small private labels. In one area after another, "other" has become the major market holder.

IBM's story of lost market share bears elaboration, in large part because of the company's almost legendary position in the U.S. business pantheon. After its rise in the personal computer market through 1984, IBM found its stronghold eroding—but not to just one huge competitor that could be identified and stalked methodically. IBM could no longer rely on tracking the dozen or so companies that had been its steady competition for almost two decades. Instead, more than 300 clone producers worldwide intruded on Big Blue's territory.

Moreover, IBM has faced the same competitive challenge in one product area after another, from supercomputers to networks. In response, IBM has changed how it does business. In the past, IBM wouldn't even bother to enter a market lacking a value of at least $100 million. But today, as customer groups diversify and markets splinter, that criterion is obsolete. The shift in competition has also prompted IBM to reorganize, decentralizing the company into five autonomous groups so decisions can be made closer to customers.

Similar stories abound in other industries. Kodak dominated film processing in the United States until little kiosks sprang up in shopping centers and ate up that market. In the late 1960s, the U.S. semiconductor industry consisted of 100 companies; today there are more than 300. In fact, practically every industry has more of every kind of company catering to the consumer's love of diversity—more ice cream companies, more cookie companies, more weight loss and exercise companies. In 1987, enterprising managers started 233,000 new businesses of all types to offer customers their choice of "other."

—— THE FALSE SECURITY OF MARKET SHARE

The proliferation of successful small companies dramatizes how the security of majority market share—seized by a large corporation and held unchallenged for decades—is now a dangerous anachronism. In the past, the dominant marketing models drew on the measurement and control notions embedded in engineering and manufacturing. The underlying mechanistic logic was that companies could measure everything, and anything they could measure, they could control—including customers. Market-share measurements became a way to understand the marketplace and thus to control it. For example, marketers used to be able to pin down a target customer with relative ease: if it were a man, he was between 25 and 35 years old, married, with two-and-a-half children, and half a dog. Since he was one of so many measurable men in a mass society, marketers assumed that they could manipulate the market just by knowing the demographic characteristics.

But we don't live in that world anymore, and those kinds of measurements are meaningless. Marketers trying to measure that same "ideal" customer today would discover that the pattern no longer holds; that married fellow with two-and-a-half kids could now be divorced, situated in New York instead of Minnesota, and living in a condo instead of a brick colonial. These days, the idea of market share is a trap that can lull businesspeople into a false sense of security.

Managers should wake up every morning uncertain about the marketplace, because it is invariably changing. That's why five-year plans are dangerous: Who can pinpoint what the market will be five years from now? The president of one large industrial corporation recently told me, "The only thing we know about our business plan is that it's wrong. It's either too high or too low—but we never know which."

In the old days, mass marketing offered an easy solution: "just run some ads." Not today. IBM tried that approach with the PC Jr., laying out an estimated $100 million on advertising—before the product failed. AT&T spent tens of millions of dollars running ads for its computer products.

In sharp contrast, Digital Equipment Corporation spent very little on expensive national television advertising and managed to wrest a healthy market position. Skipping the expensive mass-advertising campaigns, DEC concentrated on developing its reputation in the computer business by solving problems for niche markets. Word of mouth sold DEC products. The company focused its marketing and sales staffs where they already had business and aimed its message at people who actually make the decision on what machines to buy. DEC clearly understood that no one buys a complex product like a computer without a reliable outside reference—however elaborate the company's promotion.

━━━━ NICHE MARKETING: SELLING BIG BY SELLING SMALL

Intel was in the personal computer business two years before Apple started in Steve Jobs's garage. The company produced the first microprocessor chip and subsequently developed an early version of what became known as the hobby computer, sold in electronics hobby stores. An early Intel advertisement in *Scientific American* showed a junior high school student using the product. Intel's market research, however, revealed that the market for hobbyists was quite small and it abandoned the project. Two years later, Apple built itself on the hobbyist market. As it turned out, many of the early users of personal computers in education, small business, and the professional markets were hobbyists or enthusiasts.

I recently looked at several market forecasts made by research organizations in 1978 projecting the size of the personal computer market in 1985. The most optimistic forecast looked for a $2 billion market. It exceeded $25 billion.

Most large markets evolve from niche markets. That's because niche marketing teaches many important lessons about customers—in particular, to think of customers as individuals and to respond to their special needs. Niche marketing depends on word-of-mouth references and infrastructure development, a broadening of people in related industries whose opinions are crucial to the product's success.

Infrastructure marketing can be applied to almost all markets. In the medical area, for example, recognized research gurus in a given field—diabetes, cancer, heart disease—will first experiment with new devices or drugs at research institutions. Universities and research institutions become identified by their specialties. Experts in a particular area talk to each other, read the same journals, and attend the same conferences. Many companies form their own scientific advisory boards designed to tap into the members' expertise and to build credibility for new technology and products. The word of mouth created by infrastructure marketing can make or break a new drug or a new supplier. Conductus, a superconductor company in Palo Alto, built its business around an advisory board of seven top scientists from Stanford University and Berkeley.

Represented graphically, infrastructure development would look like an inverted pyramid. So Apple's pyramid, for instance, would include the references of influential users, software designers who create programs, dealers, industry consultants, analysts, the press, and, most important, customers.

Customer focus derived from niche marketing helps companies respond faster to demand changes. That is the meaning of today's most critical requirement—that companies become market driven. From the board of directors down through the ranks, company leaders must educate everyone to the singular importance of the customer, who is no longer a faceless, abstract entity or a mass statistic.

Because niche markets are not easily identified in their infancy, managers must keep one foot in the technology to know its potential and one foot in the market to see opportunity. Tandem Computers built its solid customer base by adapting its products to the emerging on-line transaction market. Jimmy Treybig, president and CEO, told me that the company had to learn the market's language. Bankers don't talk about MIPS (millions of instructions per second) the way computer people do, he said; they talk about transactions. So Tandem built its products and marketing position to become the leading computer in the transaction market. Not long before, Treybig said, he had been on a nationwide tour visiting key customers. "Guess who was calling on my customers just a few days ahead of me? John Akers"—chairman of IBM.

Many electronics companies have developed teams consisting of software and hardware development engineers, quality control and manufacturing people, as well as marketing and salespeople—who all visit customers or play key roles in dealing with customers. Convex Computer and Tandem use this approach. Whatever method a company may use, the purpose is the same: to get the entire company to focus on the fragmented, ever-evolving customer base as if it were an integral part of the organization.

THE INTEGRATED PRODUCT

Competition from small companies in fractured markets has even produced dramatic changes in how companies define their products. The product is no longer just the thing itself; it includes service, word-of-mouth references, company financial reports, the technology, and even the personal image of the CEO.

As a result, product marketing and service marketing, formerly two distinct fields, have become a single hybrid. For example, Genentech, which manufactures a growth hormone, arms its sales force with laptop computers.

When a Genentech salesperson visits an endocrinologist, the physician can tie into a data base of all the tests run on people with characteristics similar to his or her patients. The computer represents an extended set of services married to the original product.

Or take the example of Apple Computer and Quantum Corporation. These firms entered a joint venture offering on-line interactive computer services for Apple computer users. In addition to a long list of transaction services that reads like a television programming guide, Apple product service, support, and even simple maintenance have been integrated into the product itself. Prodigy, a joint venture between IBM and Sears, offers IBM and Apple users access to banking, shopping, the stock market, regional weather forecasts, sports statistics, and encyclopedias of all kinds.

In consumer products, service has become the predominant distinguishing feature. Lands' End promotes its catalog-marketed outdoorsy clothes by guaranteeing products unconditionally and promising to ship orders within 24 to 48 hours. Carport, near Atlanta, offers air travelers an ultradeluxe parking service: it drives customers to their gates, checks their bags, and, while they are airborne, services, washes, and waxes their cars. "Macy's by Appointment" is a free shopping service for customers who are too busy or too baffled to make their own selections.

With so much choice backed by service, customers can afford to be fickle. As a result, references have become vital to product marketing. And the more complex the product, the more complex the supporting references. After all, customers who switch toothpaste risk losing only a dollar or so if the new choice is a dud. But consumers buying a complete phone system or a computer system—or any other costly, long-term, and pervasive product—cannot afford to take their investments lightly. References become a part of the product, and they come in all kinds of forms. Company financial reports are a kind of reference. A person shopping for an expensive computer wants to see how profitable the company is; how can the company promise maintenance service if it's about to fold? Even the CEO's personality can make a sale. Customers who see the leader of Ford or Apple or Hewlett-Packard on a magazine cover feel assured that a real person stands behind the complex and expensive product.

In this complicated world, customers weigh all these factors to winnow out the products they want from those they don't. Now more than ever, marketers must sell every aspect of their businesses as important elements of the products themselves.

——— THE CUSTOMER AS CUSTOMIZER

Customer involvement in product design has become an accepted part of the development and marketing processes in many industries. In technologically driven products, which often evolve slowly as discoveries percolate to the surface, the customer can practically invent the market for a company.

Apple's experience with desktop publishing shows how companies and customers work together to create new applications—and new markets. Apple entered the field with the Macintosh personal computer, which offered good graphics and easy-to-use features. But desktop publishing didn't even exist then; it wasn't on anyone's pie chart as a defined market niche, and no one had predicted its emergence.

Apple's customers made it happen; newspapers and research organizations simply started using Macintosh's unique graphics capability to create charts and graphs. Early users made do with primitive software and printers, but that was enough to spark the imagination of other developers. Other hardware and software companies began developing products that could be combined with the Macintosh to enhance the user's publishing power. By visiting and talking to customers and other players in the marketplace, Apple began to realize desktop publishing's potential.

As customers explored the possibilities presented by the technology, the technology, in turn, developed to fit the customers' needs. The improved software evolved from a dynamic working relationship between company and customers, not from a rigid, bureaucratic headquarters determination of where Apple could find an extra slice of the marketing pie.

Technological innovation makes it easier to involve customers in design. For example, Milliken, the textile manufacturer, provides customers with computer terminals where they can select their own carpet designs from thousands of colors and patterns. Electronics customers, too, have assumed the role of product designer. New design tools allow companies like Tandem and Convex to design their own specialty chips, which the integrated-circuit suppliers then manufacture according to their specifications. Similarly, American Airlines designs its own computer systems. In cases like these, the design and manufacturing processes have been completely separated. So semiconductor companies—and many computer companies—have become raw-materials producers, with integration occurring all the way up the supply line.

The fact that customers have taken charge of design opens the door for value-added resellers, who integrate different materials and processes. These people are the essence of new-age marketers: they add value by understanding what happens in a doctor's office or a travel agency or a machine-tool plant and customize that service or product to the customer's needs. To capitalize on market changes, companies should follow these examples and work directly with customers—even before products hit the drawing boards.

———— THE EVOLUTION OF DISTRIBUTION

It's nearly impossible to make a prediction on the basis of past patterns. Perhaps many big institutions founded on assumptions of mass marketing and market share will disappear like dinosaurs. Or they'll evolve into closely integrated service and distribution organizations.

In fact, tremendous innovation in distribution channels has already begun in nearly every industry. Distribution channels have to be flexible to survive. As more flows into them, they have to change. Grocery stores sell flowers and cameras. Convenience stores rent out videos. And television offers viewers direct purchasing access to everything from diamonds to snowblowers to a decent funeral.

To get products closer to customers, marketers are distributing more and more samples in more ways. Today laundry detergent arrives in the mail, magazines enfold perfume-doused tear-outs, and department stores offer chocolate samples. Software companies bind floppy disk samples into magazines or mail out diskettes that work only until a certain date, giving customers the chance to test a product before buying.

Every successful computer retailer has not only a showroom but also a classroom. The large computer retailers are not selling just to off-the-street traffic. Most of their volume now comes from a direct sales force calling on corporate America. In addition, all have application-development labs, extensive user-training programs and service centers—and some have recently experimented with private labeling their own computer product brands. The electronics community talks more and more about design centers—places where customers can get help customizing products and applications.

Today the product is an experience. As customers use it, they grow to trust it—and distribution represents the beginning of that evolving relationship. That's why computer companies donate their systems to elementary schools: schools are now a distribution channel for product experience.

—— GOLIATH PLUS DAVID

Besides making changes in distribution channels, big corporations will also have to forge new partnerships with smaller companies. IBM, for example, already has ties to 1,500 small computer-service companies nationwide, offering help for IBM midsized machine owners. Olivetti makes personal computers for AT&T. All over the world, manufacturers are producing generic computer platforms; larger companies buy these, then add their own service-oriented, value-adding applications.

This approach seems almost inevitable considering what we know about patterns of research and development. Technological developments typically originate with basic research, move to applied research, to development, then to manufacturing and marketing. Very few U.S. companies do basic research; universities and various public and private labs generally shoulder that burden. Many big companies do applied R&D, while small companies concentrate on development. Basic and applied research means time and money. Consider the cases of two seminal inventions—antibiotics and television—the first of which took 30 years and the second 63 years from idea to the market.

Perhaps because of their narrow focus, small companies realize more development breakthroughs than larger ones. For example, the origins of recombinant DNA technology go back to the mid-1950s; it took Genentech only about six years to bring the world's first recombinant DNA commercial product to market.

A 1986 study by the Small Business Administration showed that 55% of innovations have come from companies with fewer than 500 employees, and twice as many innovations per employee come from small companies than from large ones. This finding, however, does not indicate that large companies are completely ineffective developers. Rather, the data suggest that small, venture-capitalized companies will scramble to invent a product that the market does not yet want, need, or perhaps even recognize; big companies will wait patiently for the market to develop so they can enter later with their strong manufacturing and marketing organizations.

The Japanese have shown us that it's wise to let small companies handle development—but only if large companies can somehow share that wisdom before the product reaches the market. From 1950 to 1978, Japanese companies held 32,000 licensing agreements to acquire foreign technology—mostly from the United States—for about $9 billion. In essence, the Japanese simply sub-contracted out for R&D—and then used that investment in U.S. knowledge to dominate one market after another.

If orchestrated properly, agreements between large and small com-panies can prove mutually beneficial. When Genentech developed its first product, recombinant DNA insulin, the company chose not to compete against Eli Lilly, which held over 70% of the insulin market. Instead, Genentech entered into a licensing agreement with Lilly that put the larger company in charge of manufacturing and marketing the products developed by the smaller company. Over time, Genentech built its own manufacturing company while maintaining its proprietary product.

This model worked so well that it has shaped the fortunes of Silicon Valley. Of the 3,000 companies there, only a dozen hold places on the lists of America's largest corporations. Most of the companies are small developers of new products. Like the Japanese, large U.S. companies are now subcontract-ing development to these mostly high-tech startups. In the process, they are securing a critical resource—an ongoing relationship with a small, innovative enterprise.

Giant companies can compete in the newly diversifying markets if they recognize the importance of relationships—with small companies, within their own organizations, with their customers. Becoming market driven means aban-doning old-style marketshare thinking and instead tying the uniqueness of any product to the unique needs of the customer. This approach to marketing demands a revolution in how businesspeople act—and, even more important, in how they think. These changes are critical to success, but they can come only gradually, as managers and organizations adapt to the new rules of marketing in the age of diversity. As any good marketer knows, even instant success takes time.

——— DISCUSSION QUESTIONS

1. Not too long ago most marketing was directed to the "average" consumer. Today, the idea of an average consumer has given way to targeting selected audiences and market segments. What challenges does this present to the marketing manager?

2. The author tells us that the face of marketing has been changed—from mass production and mass marketing to customized production and niche marketing. Do you agree that the days of mass marketing are over? Why or why not?

3. The author argues that most large markets evolve from niche markets—that by selling small, you can sell big. How would you explain this seeming contradiction?

4. How can a changing, fragmented market affect competitors who are all vying for market share? What effect would this have on marketing strategies? Are established, well-known brands safe from the unpredictable challenges of a changing marketplace? Give some examples to support your answer.

5. Why is the analysis of consumer behavior so important? What kinds of information are helpful? What benefits can management gain from this knowledge?

6. According to the author, today's customer has so many choices that a buyer's market prevails. What the customer wants, the customer gets—if not from your company, then from another. How will this "age of diversity" affect the way large organizations approach the various marketing functions in the future? Will smaller companies use a different approach? Explain.

8   Marketing and Its Discontents

STEVEN H. STAR

Marketers are often accused of trying to get people to want products they don't need and can't afford. Yet the driving force of modern marketing is the marketing concept, whose central premise is that business succeeds by giving customers what they truly want. This reading explores this conflict, focusing on the practical difficulties in implementing the marketing concept. For example, members of a market segment rarely group themselves into neat program targets. Even the most efficient marketing program will not reach all members of a target but will certainly reach people with no interest in the product: either they do not need or want or cannot afford the advertised product. The result is frustrated consumers and, eventually, angry social critics. To manage this conflict, the author suggests, marketers must recognize that the mechanics of modern media and the geographic dispersion of the target audience do not perfectly match—and sometimes result in discontent.

Business sometimes has a bad name, and marketing is particularly singled out, especially advertising. Even businesspeople often hold marketing in deep suspicion. It is widely suspected of trying, with all the intelligence, technology, and cunning it can command, to get people to want what they don't need, of overpromising and exaggerating what can be delivered, and, worst, of exploiting people's vulnerabilities to get them to value, want, and expect the unattainable and undesirable. This criticism amounts to an attack on the ethics of marketing and, by extension, on business itself.

What makes this situation remarkable is the fact that since the late 1950s the driving theme in the practice of modern marketing has been the marketing concept, whose central principle is that business succeeds best when it tries to serve customers by giving them what they truly want. Something seems not right, and it is useful to try to understand what is going on and going wrong.

Actually, marketing and its practices, especially advertising and selling, have always been subjects of criticism and controversy. Some of these complaints go back as far as the Bible, Confucius, and classical Greek literature. More recently, the introduction of "personal deodorants" in the 1960s was highly controversial—both the idea of the product itself and the way it was advertised. In the 1970s, there was bitter criticism of "war toys," advertising aimed at children, and the promotion of baby formula in Africa. Today it's junk mail, the glorification to the young of hedonic lifestyles, and the sheer abundance and intrusiveness of commercial communications.

Criticism of marketing focuses largely on two areas: its "excesses" and its "expertness." Excesses are about purposefully shoddy and objectionable products, inadequate warranties, deceptive or objectionable advertising, misleading packaging, questionable selling practices, and emphasis on tawdry values. These are the basis of what's broadly referred to as the consumer movement, or consumerism.

Expertness refers to the special ways marketing thinks about and approaches consumers. Most people define consumer needs or wants in terms of products and their functional attributes—what a product does, how it performs, tastes, or looks. Marketers do the same, but much more. They think also of how products perform in terms of consumers' psychological and psychosocial needs and wishes. These tend to be complex, subtle, and manipulatable. Individuals often don't perceive any need for particular products until they have been persuasively exposed to the possibility of having them—and it is marketing experts who expertly do the persuading. When an expert takes on an amateur, especially when money is involved, the general feeling is that it's unfair.

Remarkably, the debate about marketing has been silent about some of the mechanics of modern life that give rise to it, specifically, about the structure of modern media and audiences. Indeed, it can be argued that many of the social discontents, and even ethical issues, associated with marketing arise not from "excesses," "inappropriate" definitions of consumer wants and needs, or from greed or cunning, but rather from functional limitations on the implementability of the marketing concept.

The true practitioner of the marketing concept is supposed to find out what consumers want or need and try to satisfy these needs—if that makes economic and strategic sense. Assuming for the moment that one wants to cater carefully to consumer wants and needs (and that's not always a justified assumption—there are charlatans and sharpshooters everywhere, in all professions), if you think for a moment about the process of trying to practice the marketing concept carefully, you quickly see how things will necessarily go wrong.

First, the marketer identifies a market opportunity—an apparent consumer need discovered by research, intuition, technological innovation, or some combination of these. Then the marketer determines its size, its intensity (how much the people who have the need would be willing to pay for its satisfaction), and whether the need could be satisfied at a profitable cost. In other words, would it be feasible and profitable for the marketer's company to seek to satisfy this particular consumer need?

Then there is target identification—the specific groups in the population that the necessary marketing effort (usually called "program") will go after—not just people with the indicated need but also people with the wish, will, and money to try to satisfy it. Marketers identify potential consumers along demographic and, especially in consumer goods, psychosocial terms. If, for example, there are 500,000 potential consumers of the product, the marketer wants to know specifically who they are—young or old, male or female, rich or poor, urban or rural, "with-it" or "square," active or passive, confident or concerned.

A basic thrust of behavioral research in marketing is to suggest that psychosocial factors are at least as important as demographic factors in defining a market segment. In other words, consumers who share a common set of attitudinal, perceptual, and sociological characteristics are more likely to share a particular set of needs than, say, consumers in the same age or income group.

These findings are useful for developing communications themes and other marketing efforts aimed at the target audience. Unfortunately, the efforts usually cannot be closely matched to the audiences. There are few media or channels of distribution that allow the marketer to direct a marketing program exclusively to an audience that has the highly specific behavioral or psychosocial characteristics of the targeted audience. No matter how specialized our media, how carefully computerized our audience data, how sophisticated the protocols of market analysis, there remain, as always, major misfits among products, audiences, messages, and media. As one marketing executive recently said, "This consumer and behavior research is interesting, but in the end we still tell our advertising agencies to cast a wide net, to go after middle-income homemakers between 21 and 40."

In the end, the marketer develops a program to coincide, to the greatest extent possible, with the attributes of the consumer target group. Unfortunately, the "greatest extent possible" is always full of disjunctions and static. Given the target group, marketers must make trade-offs regarding specific product features, packaging, personal selling, copy strategy, distribution channels, attendant services, price, advertising media, and much more. And while marketers typically view the "audience" for the selected program as a function of a media plan, audience also depends on the choice of channels of distribution. And depending on how much personal selling is used either directly or through the distribution channels, audience is a function of the "call instructions" given to the sales force.

This brief look at what's involved in the development of a marketing program allows us to identify three groups of consumers who are affected by that process, and how it works. First, there is the *market segment*—people with the need in question. Second, there is the *program target*—people in the segment with the "best fit" characteristics for the product and program. (Lots of people may need trousers, but only a few qualify as likely buyers of Giorgio Armani.) Finally, there is the *program audience*—all people who are actually exposed to the marketing program, without regard to whether they are in the segment of its best-fit component.

These three groups are rarely synonymous. The exception occurs occasionally in industrial products where customers for a particular product may be few and easily identifiable. Such customers, all sharing a particular need (a market segment), are likely to group themselves into a meaningful target (for example, all companies with a particular application of the product in question, such as high-speed filling of bottles at breweries). In such circumstances, direct selling is likely to be economically justified, and highly specialized trade media exist to help expose the members of the program target (and *only* the members of the program target) to the marketing program. Under these circumstances, the marketing segment, program target, and program audience often will be virtually identical.[1]

Most consumer goods markets are significantly different. Typically, there are many rather than few potential customers. Each represents a relatively small amount of potential sales. Rarely do members of a particular market segment group themselves neatly into a meaningful program target. There are substantial differences among households or individual consumers with similar demographic characteristics.[2] Even with all the advances in information technology throughout the 1980s, in microsegmentation of consumers, in communications, and in specialized media and distribution systems, the economic feasibility of direct selling of consumer goods is rare. Mass marketing remains the predominant mode.

In consumer goods, the continued existence of significant differences between market segments and program targets, and between program targets and program audiences, is obvious enough. Assume that a market segment of one million household buyers has been determined to have a particular need— say for a heavy-duty laundry detergent. Seventy percent of these buyers share a particular set of demographic characteristics—they have small children who frequently play outdoors in muddy fields. The remaining 30% have demographic characteristics that are randomly distributed throughout the rest of the population—the households include adults who work as auto mechanics. Under these conditions, if the program target is demographically defined in terms of families with small children, it will include only 70% of the market segment.

Moreover, the set of demographic characteristics that provides a best-fit description of the market segment almost certainly also describes a group of

---

1. The overwhelming success of IBM in the computer mainframe business, from roughly 1957 to 1980, was based largely on the congruence of its market segments, program targets, and audiences. It divided its data-processing business into 16 major segments, most of which were further divided into subsegments. In general, these segments were defined by applications commonality: the distribution segment, for example, included all companies for which inventory and physical distribution costs represented a major component of controllable expense. A separate program was developed for each segment (or subsegment), and individual salespeople and sales offices specialized in those segments. Every potential purchaser of data-processing equipment in the United States was assigned to an IBM salesperson, who was expected to tailor marketing programs to the potential customer's specific needs. As a result, IBM achieved a high degree of congruence among segments, targets, and audiences, despite the fact that its market was highly varied. *See* E. Raymond Corey and Steven H. Star, *Organization Strategy: A Marketing Approach* (Cambridge, Mass.: Harvard University Press, 1971), pp. 108–155.

2. In theoretical terms, a consumer market segment consists of individuals who share psychological, sociological, and demographic characteristics, which together are likely to lead to a particular purchase act. In implementing a marketing program, however, it is frequently necessary to treat demographics as the sole variable of interest (except in copy formulation). Thus, while behavioral research in marketing helps explain the reasons for program-target incongruence, it has made remarkably little headway in helping marketers reduce the incongruence.

consumers who are not members of the market segment (they do not have the need in question because, say, their children don't play in muddy fields). If, for example, the small-children households total 1,500,000, then members of the muddy-fields market segment represent less than 50% of the members of the program target. The misfit is enormous.

Similar misfits accompany the translation of a program target into a program audience. The usual objective is to maximize advertising exposure of the program target for a particular budgetary expenditure. The most efficient media schedule will rarely reach all members of the program target. But it will almost certainly reach people who are not in the program target. The same kinds of misfits will almost certainly occur in distribution channels. From the marketer's perspective, these inefficiencies are unfortunate but totally unavoidable.

Thus marketing programs generate three partially overlapping groups of consumers: the market segment, the program target, and the program audience. Largely, these divide into six meaningful clusters:

1. Segment, target, and audience
2. Segment and audience
3. Target and audience
4. Audience
5. Segment and target
6. Segment[3]

The relative size of each of these clusters for a particular marketing program is a function of the level of congruence between the market segment, the program target, and the program audience (as shown in *Exhibit 1*).

Cluster 1 (segment, target, and audience) represents the social value of the marketing concept. Consumers in this cluster have had their needs identified, have had a marketing program designed specifically around their characteristics, and have been exposed to the marketing program. The marketing program has satisfied the needs of these consumers.

Cluster 2 (segment and audience) consists of consumers whose needs have been identified, who have had a product made available to them in the market, and who have been exposed to the marketing program. But unfortunately, neither the product nor the program has been designed with their particular characteristics in mind. The product may be too expensive or sold through inconvenient channels (outlets that exist only in large urban centers), or the copy strategy may make them feel uncomfortable (a youth theme when they are of advanced years). Members of this cluster may be partially satisfied (if they purchase the product though it doesn't quite fill their needs) or frustrated (if, for example, they can't afford the product).

Consumers in cluster 3 (target *and* audience) are exposed to the marketing program even though they have no interest in it (they don't feel the need to which it is addressed). The marketing program is likely to be distracting or even

---

3. A separate "target" cluster is also possible but is not relevant for the present purpose.

EXHIBIT 1
Marketing Effort and Consumer Discontent

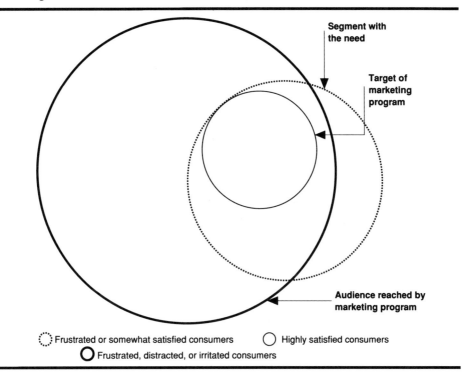

Segment with
the need

Target of
marketing
program

Audience reached by
marketing program

◌ Frustrated or somewhat satisfied consumers   ◯ Highly satisfied consumers

⬤ Frustrated, distracted, or irritated consumers

irritating, especially since it has been designed (copy, media, channels) to appeal to consumers with their particular characteristics.[4] Cluster 4 (audience only) is quite similar except that the marketing program is likely to be somewhat less distracting since it was not designed to appeal to members of this cluster (they are not members of the program target).

Clusters 5 (segment and target) and 6 (segment only) consist of consumers who have a need that a marketer has attempted to fill, but they are not aware of the product's availability because they are not members of the program audience. They've not heard or seen the message. They are the "dropped outs" of the marketing process. The marketing concept is not working for them. Behaviorally, these consumers are frustrated.[5]

---

4. Actually, a consumer who had the need but has satisfied it would also fall into this cluster. For example, a consumer who may have needed information prior to purchasing a watch may find such information distracting after having made the purchase, especially if it makes him or her question the purchase. Conversely, a product's advertising may reduce a customer's postpurchase cognitive dissonance, as would seem to be the case with automobiles.

5. Of course, segment-audience incongruence is not the only (or even major) source of consumer frustration. In many cases, consumer needs will not be satisfied because of (1) technological constraints—it can't be done; (2) economic constraints—it isn't profitable; (3) strategic constraints—companies choose not to do it; or (4) information constraints—companies have simply not yet identified the need. In this context, we may view segment-audience incongruence as a *process constraint* on consumer satisfaction.

EXHIBIT 2
Marketing Clusters and Consumer Reactions

CLUSTERS	REACTIONS
1. Segment, target, and audience	Highly satisfied
2. Segment and audience	Somewhat satisfied or frustrated
3. Target and audience	Highly distracted or irritated
4. Audience	Somewhat distracted
5. Segment and target	Frustrated
6. Segment	Frustrated

It is obvious that the number of possible mismatches is from three to six times greater than the number of possible close matches. (For a summary of the clusters, see *Exhibit 2*.) The possibilities of disaffection are abundant, not because of carelessness, indifference, irresponsibility, ineptitude, or cupidity, but because the world is imperfect.

While a well-conceived marketing program certainly provides satisfaction to some consumers (cluster 1 and some of cluster 2), it most likely will also distract some consumers (clusters 3 and 4) and frustrate others (clusters 5 and 6 and some members of cluster 2). And it is these consumers who almost surely give rise to much (though not all) of the criticism of marketing in our intensely commercial times.

It is quite possible that the effects of segment-target incongruence would be of little importance if they were randomly distributed through the population. A certain amount of dissatisfaction, distraction, and frustration seems inherent in the human condition, and—according to some psychologists—it may even be a necessary condition of psychological health. Unfortunately, certain segments of society probably encounter disproportionately large amounts of distraction and frustration. In particular, people whose needs differ significantly from the needs of others who have their particular demographic characteristics are likely to experience an unusually large amount of distraction. They are exposed to a great deal of marketing effort (mostly via mass communications) that is not intended for them. And so they get mad.

This possibility was documented in 1968 in the Harvard Business School study *Advertising in America*.[6] Users of products who encountered advertisements for those products had more favorable (or fewer unfavorable) attitudes toward those advertisements than did nonusers. And users of particular brands of those articles had even better attitudes toward ads featuring those brands than did users of other brands. Getting irritated or mad depends, as they say, on "where you're coming from."

---

6. Raymond A. Bauer and Stephen A. Greyser, *Advertising in America: The Consumer View* (Boston: Division of Research, Graduate School of Business Administration, Harvard University, 1968).

The likelihood of getting mad is almost surely greater in the better-educated sectors and among the professional commentators of our society. They fall disproportionately into cluster 3 (target and audience, but not segment), where they probably share many of the demographic characteristics of the dominant middle class (age, income, location) but differ significantly in values and perceived needs. This subgroup may be exposed to a great many marketing programs in which it has little interest, or which it perceives as alien to its values. It probably also has disproportionately greater access to the institutions and instruments of public commentary (via lectures, news reports, columns, and articles) and is likely therefore to make a disproportionately large amount of critical noise about modern marketing.

Another group of consumers who are exposed to marketing programs that bother them are those who have the needs that the programs address but not the demographic characteristics of the best-fit program targets. They may have, for example, a strong desire for a high-performance sports car or expensive toys for their children (as advertised on Saturday morning TV) but not the resources to pay for them. Such consumers are likely to experience an unusual amount of frustration. The same is also true of variously disadvantaged members of society—falling disproportionately into clusters 6 (segment only) and 2 (segment and audience).

Although their needs may be recognized and they may be exposed to relevant marketing communications, such consumers are rarely targets of the particular marketing programs. The marketing programs are rarely tailored specifically to their circumstances (low income, lack of "normal" credit, limited physical or psychological mobility), and so they are likely to be extremely frustrated. Presumably, this frustration would be higher for the segment-audience cluster (the urban disadvantaged) than for the segment-only cluster (the rural disadvantaged), but this is only conjecture. Nor is this to suggest that the frustrations of the disadvantaged are attributable to the marketing process. Clearly the causes are far more basic. But it does suggest some of the reasons why the practice of the marketing concept and the operations of the marketing process at least do not prevent, avoid, or minimize frustrations.

The marketing concept, like all good things that seem to make good sense, is burdened by process constraints that limit, in implementation, the achievement of its promises. In particular, the lack of congruence among segments, targets, and audiences seems a significant cause of consumer distraction and frustration. Marketing programs that produce social goods (consumer satisfaction) will almost surely also have dysfunctional social effects.

This line of reasoning takes us into the old, and not very reassuring, subject of welfare economics—a method of analysis that, like so much else in the rhetoric of the social sciences, suffers deeply from analysis paralysis. If a particular marketing program has both functional and dysfunctional effects, how does one make a trade-off between them? If a given program could be shown to have satisfied 1 million consumers, distracted 500,000, and increased the frustration of 300,000, would its net effect on society be negative or positive?

While the relative intensity of these several social effects would certainly have to be an important part of the equation, even this information would leave the question unanswered, since reasonable people would surely continue to dispute the social importance of a unit of satisfaction as compared with a unit of frustration.

The social effects of the marketing process must, like all social phenomena, be looked at in some sort of trade-off matrix. While there may never be agreement on the proper trade-offs among social effects, it would be useful to have a better picture of what these effects are. This would make it possible to determine the relative magnitudes of the effects occasioned by various marketing programs in each of the six clusters, to measure the intensity of the hypothesized behavioral effects of such clusterings, and to determine whether selected subgroups of society fall into particular clusters to a disproportionate degree. It should also be possible to identify specific points at which technical improvements in the marketing process would have significant social payoffs.

Of course, the analysis suggested here regarding marketing's sometimes bad reputation is independent of corrupt business practices, such as calculated duplicity, conscious misrepresentation, distortion, trickery, shoddiness, and the like—none of which is, in any case, unique to modern times. But there always will be misfits between products, segments, targets, and audiences. It is useful to understand their innocent origins and inevitability.

Still, any such understanding should not prevent asking what real problems are being missed because we argue about the wrong things. An explanation of a phenomenon is not its justification. Do we fail to exercise the self-restraint that civilized life requires? Do we become so intent on fighting our critics that we fail to honestly confront critical issues while avoiding the necessity to be honestly self-critical? Have we tried honestly to fix some of the misfits and alleviate some of the discontents?

▬▬ DISCUSSION QUESTIONS

1. There are some who say that marketers exploit people's vulnerabilities, manipulating them to buy what they don't really need or want. Do you agree or disagree with this view? Why? What are some reasons that contribute to this negative opinion?

2. Assume you have chosen to market your product to the widest possible audience. Does this audience target have inherent problems? Is it possible to design a strategy that will satisfy the entire audience? Why or why not?

3. The author states that "the true practitioner of the marketing concept is supposed to find out what consumers want or need and try to satisfy those needs. . . ." What difficulties does this pose for

marketers? How would you distinguish between market segment and market target?

4. Assume you have accurately selected the best audience for your particular product and have chosen excellent media and distribution channels to reach your target audience. What is the probability of achieving a proper fit between your marketing program and your target market—high, low, moderate? Why?

5. Describe some of the factors of the modern world that contribute to the dysfunction of the marketing process and result in consumer dissatisfaction.

9   Local Marketing

JOHN A. QUELCH

Marketers of national brands of consumer goods and services are increasingly being urged to adopt local marketing. This reading discusses the environmental trends that explain this emerging interest in local marketing and profiles the product categories that are most affected. It then identifies the principal costs and risks that manufacturers must consider before implementing local marketing programs. Finally, it offers guidelines for developing and implementing a local marketing strategy that goes well beyond an ad hoc collection of localized sales promotion events.

Local marketing means tailoring some aspects of a national marketing program (or supplementing it with local programs) to the needs of local consumers, wholesalers, or retailers. This "customizing" can be done at various levels of disaggregation on both a geographic basis—by region, city, or zip code—or on an account basis—a program for each retail chain, division of the chain, or individual store.

Local marketing is nothing new; the product formulas for national brands of coffee, for example, have long been tailored to regional tastes. Heavier investments in local advertising and promotion, as a percentage of sales, are often used to boost sales in less active market areas and encourage consumers to try a different brand. Sales forces frequently adjust their work plans to combat especially competitive regional brands of, for example, products with short shelf lives. In addition, most companies roll out new products region by region and adapt marketing programs to local conditions.

—— GROWING IMPORTANCE OF LOCAL MARKETING

In recent years local marketing has been especially evident in franchise service businesses. Fast food marketers like McDonald's encourage franchisees to establish close ties with local communities through promotions involving local media, sports teams, and charities. Convinced of the effectiveness of local promotions, other franchisees of everything from automobiles to fast foods are challenging the percentage of sales head offices devote to national marketing.

Such moves are symptomatic of the current surge of interest in local marketing and the tendency to allocate a higher percentage of marketing budgets to local programs. A 1987 Dechert-Hampe survey reported that 56% of consumer marketers planned to implement regional marketing programs in 1988, and that 43% of those already involved in regional marketing planned to spend more than 20% of their marketing budgets on local marketing efforts.[1] Here are some recent examples.

- Between 1985 and 1987, Frito Lay quadrupled the marketing budgets set aside for its zone sales managers.[2]
- In 1987 Lever Brothers offered Surf detergent only in liquid form in the northern United States, where liquid detergents are more popular, and only in powdered form in the southern states.
- Airlines regularly raise bonus mileage for frequent fliers on routes where their competitive position is weak.
- The Vons supermarket chain classifies stores into five groups on the basis of demographic analyses of patrons and adjusts product assortments accordingly.[3]
- Automobile manufacturers, often in association with regional dealer networks, develop special limited-edition models to cater to regional tastes; target direct mail to zip codes with demographics that fit the profiles of likely purchasers of particular models; and adapt media mixes to reflect regional lifestyles.[4]

CHANGES IN THE MARKETING ENVIRONMENT

Whereas in the past local marketing was largely seen as a necessary inconvenience, undertaken for defensive reasons, today it is viewed as a potential source of competitive advantage. Several changes in the marketing environment account for this shift.

First, consumer heterogeneity is more evident; the mass market has given way to a patchwork quilt of demographic, geographic, and lifestyle segments for which national programs do not work well. With national population growth running at less than 1% per annum, manufacturing marketers are customizing their marketing programs to specific segments in order to differentiate themselves from competitors and boost profit margins. Besides bringing the marketer closer to the end consumer, local marketing facilitates feedback, which permits further, more effective customization of the program.

The same environmental trends are also prompting retailers to pay more attention to market segmentation and local marketing. New retail

---

1. Michael Raffini, "Regional Marketing: Survey Shows Accelerating Interest," *DHC Viewpoint* (Winter 1987–88): 1.

2. Jennifer Lawrence, "Frito Play: New 'Basics' Strategy Takes On Regional Rivals," *Advertising Age* (March 30, 1987): 1.

3. Brad Edmondson, "America's Hot Spots," *American Demographics* (January 1988): 24–30.

4. Roger C. Olsen, "Regional Marketing's Comeback at Ford," *Marketing Communications* (September 1984): 19–23.

formats—from hypermarkets and warehouse stores to large convenience and specialty niche stores—have emerged to serve an increasingly heterogeneous consumer population. As a consequence, producers are under pressure to tailor their marketing programs by class of trade or according to the needs of individual key accounts. Manufacturers serving businesses such as grocery retailing, in which there are no truly national chains, where industry structure varies from region to region, and where decision making about product assortment and merchandising programs is increasingly decentralized, inevitably face demands for more local marketing.

These demands are a function of growing trade power. Concentration in many classes of trade is increasing, particularly when market shares are examined on a market-specific rather than a national basis. The sophistication of retail management is improving as retailers learn to exploit the information power afforded by sales data collected by scanner systems. Over 60% of grocery stores had scanning equipment in 1987,[5] and many other kinds of retail outlets are following suit. Decreased data processing costs are further encouraging retailers to use scanner data to gain a competitive advantage by tailoring assortments to the consumer needs in their specific trading areas. Unless they too customize marketing efforts, producers will find it harder to secure widespread acceptance of their products and merchandising programs.

Moreover, as trade power grows, retailers no longer merely respond to manufacturers' promotions but, increasingly, develop their own differentiated promotion programs and offer participation opportunities to manufacturers. For manufacturers' own promotion to attract trade attention, it must be geared to the local market and to individual accounts.

Media audience fragmentation, like trade-format proliferation, is a response to growing consumer heterogeneity. The prime time television audience commanded by the three networks fell from 92% in 1979 to 77% in 1989 in the face of expanding and improving cable and broadcast alternatives.[6] The rate advantages of national over local media advertising for equivalent exposures is diminishing, and spot ads can now be easily and cost-effectively incorporated into plans for brand promotions by purchasing them a year ahead through regional media-buying agencies. In the print media as well, local agencies aware of the trend toward local marketing are providing opportunities, attractive rates, and creative services to national brand advertisers. Not surprisingly, the growth rate of local-advertising expenditures is outpacing that of national advertising.[7]

---

5. Dwight J. Shelton, "Regional Marketing Works and Is Here to Stay," *Marketing News* (November 6, 1987): 1, 25.

6. Ibid.

7. Peter W. Barnes, "Forecaster Sees Local 1987 Ad Spending Strengthening, National Outlays Weaker," *Wall Street Journal*, June 18, 1987, p. 10.

The growing predominance of sales promotion (both trade and consumer promotion) over advertising in most brand budgets both reflects and reinforces the local marketing trend. Sales promotions can be more readily localized, right down to the store level; for example, in-store sampling and new-product coupon programs can be run in stores whose customers most closely match the manufacturer's target market. Sales promotion offers can be mailed to households identified through sophisticated geodemographic computer programs that match zip codes to target consumer profiles.[8] Offers in nationally distributed free-standing newspaper inserts can be customized by markets. In all these promotion areas, brand managers taking advantage of local marketing options discover that they make it difficult for national competitors to identify, match, and beat their advertising and promotion schedules.

AFFECTED PRODUCTS

Although these trends affect all consumer goods and service marketers, some nationally distributed products and services are especially suitable for local marketing. Certain products face significant differences in consumer behavior, product-line mix, or relative competitive position from one market area to another. Others, which are based on mature technologies, have limited or no superiority to other national brands or even to regional and store brands. For these goods, local promotion based on special prices or offers can have a greater influence on buying decisions than national marketing. Still other products are high-bulk-to-value goods, less subject to cross-market reselling, and can, therefore, be offered at different prices in different markets. Hence, there is more regional marketing of tuna and pasta than of health and beauty aids.

In addition, strong franchise brands are better candidates for local marketing, particularly for consumer promotions. They enjoy the dollar sales volume and margin structure needed to fund local programs and the additional managers for tailoring national programs to the locality. Ironically, weak franchise brands, which are more in need of the extra boost of local marketing, are less able to execute it.

COSTS AND RISKS

Many managers of consumer goods and service companies embrace local marketing without fully understanding its costs and risks. There are

---

8. Thomas W. Osborn, "Opportunity Marketing," *Marketing Communications* (September 1987): 49–54.

four key concerns to be kept in mind. First, the strategic implications of excessive local marketing must be recognized. The diversion of advertising and promotion funds to local marketing programs may dilute rather than reinforce national brand advantage, partly because field salespeople often have a shorter-term perspective than brand managers. For example, Frito Lay, the only nationally distributed U.S. snack food manufacturer, should not jeopardize this unique strength by overemphasizing local marketing to compete against Borden Inc.'s network of eight regional brands.[9] National brands can and must be defended in other ways besides local marketing; experience shows that they can boost market shares at the expense of less resource-rich regional brands and weaker national competitors by increasing either national marketing expenditures or new-product development.

Second, adapting national marketing programs to local needs costs time and effort that might be better directed toward developing innovative, differentiated product features that would contribute to long-term brand strength. In addition, local marketing demands additional management personnel in a slow-growth environment in which cost controls assume ever greater importance. Local marketing may also increase the costs of the market research and information systems needed to gather and process local market data and to evaluate local marketing efforts. Advertising costs may also rise if national buying cannot realize economies of scale. As with any segmentation scheme, managers must ask whether additional sales and/or higher margins will more than offset the extra costs.

A third concern is the practice of customizing trade deals and merchandising programs. When a brand's market share differs across markets, there is good reason to offer better rates to distributors and retailers in low-share markets. However, a retail chain with stores in several markets could buy its entire stock where the best deal is offered. Thus, local trade promotion programs can encourage forward buying and diversion, reduce the accuracy of sales forecasts, and add to production and logistics costs for additional capacity, emergency production runs, and extra inventory. Local marketing may thereby reinforce the power of large distributors and increase pressure on manufacturers to provide additional customized local marketing programs.

The fourth concern is a legal one. Under the Robinson-Patman Act, a manufacturer must offer equivalent trade discounts to all distributors in a particular market area. Although local marketing is perfectly legal, it encourages individual wholesalers and retailers to press claims for special treatment—more generous discounts or customized merchandising programs—that could result in manufacturers offering nonequivalent programs to trade customers.

---

9. Jennifer Lawrence, "Borden Snacks Focus on 'National Brands,'" *Advertising Age* (August 17, 1987): 3.

—— DEVELOPING A LOCAL MARKETING STRATEGY

Notwithstanding the costs and risks, environmental pressures for customizing the marketing mix to particular regions, classes of trade, or key trade accounts are strong. To develop an effective local marketing strategy, managers must first make three key decisions.

Deciding What to Localize   Using a framework such as *Exhibit 1,* managers can decide which elements of each product's marketing mix should be customized to consumer needs, trade demands, or competitive pressures. Local customization is more prevalent for such service- and price-related mix elements as trade and consumer promotion. On the other hand, we would expect more standardization on strategic and image-related dimensions such as brand name and product positioning. The Dechert-Hampe survey supports this contention, reporting that 80% of managers planned to regionalize trade promotion; 79%, consumer promotion; but only 52%, media advertising.[10]

Deciding How Far to Go   While some cost-conscious companies engage in token local marketing, merely as a defensive measure, others invest in it as an offensive strategy. A breakdown of marketing activities for a company following the latter strategy, as outlined in *Exhibit 2,* reveals a larger number of programs allocated to customized promotion on both geographic and trade

EXHIBIT 1
Customization of Marketing Program

	NATIONAL STANDARDIZATION	LOCAL CUSTOMIZATION
Product formulation		
Product positioning		
Packaging		
Brand name		
Product line		
Advertising		
Pricing		
Distribution		
Customer service		
Sales organization		
Consumer promotion		
Trade promotion		

10. Raffini, "Regional Marketing."

dimensions. A sampling (not necessarily representative) of the 1987 marketing budgets for four leading brands of packaged goods generated the average distribution of expenditures shown in *Exhibit 3*.

Marketing management should consider two further points related to the breakdown of marketing expenditures. The first suggests why local consumer promotion expenditures, although still lower than national spending, are growing at a faster rate. Usually production economics demand that consumer promotions involving a change in package size or content remain national in scope. But recently manufacturers have begun to see local couponing and sampling offers as a way to shift funds from purely price-oriented trade efforts

EXHIBIT 2
Allocation of Marketing Budget

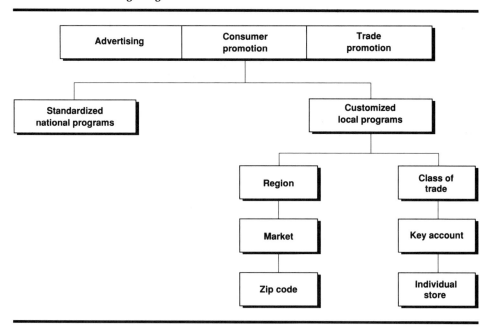

EXHIBIT 3
Average 1987 Budget Allocations for Four Brands

	NATIONAL	*LOCAL*
Advertising	23%	10%
Consumer promotion	8%	7%
Trade promotion	37%	14%

to those that deliver a brand-benefit message as well.[11] Retailer-initiated cooperative promotion and advertising are also fueling this trend and blurring traditional distinctions among advertising, consumer promotion, and trade promotion.

The second point is the fact that the ideal national/local mix for a brand varies across regions, depending on the unique demands of particular markets. Brand managers may nonetheless attempt to cluster markets and accounts in order to minimize the number of separate programs to be developed.

Deciding How Fast to Go   The speed with which a company moves toward local marketing is a function of three factors: (1) the strength of the environmental pressures outlined above, (2) constraints imposed by the firm's organizational structure, and (3) its recent financial performance. In 1987, for example, General Foods took a controlled experimental approach: it appointed a headquarters staff director for local marketing, tested a new local marketing strategy and organization in the Denver market, and injected more local marketing into its plans for new-product introductions.[12] Campbell Soup, by contrast, implemented a dramatic organizational change and appointed 22 new regional brand sales managers in an effort to position itself to the trade as a leader in regional marketing.[13]

AN INCREASED ROLE FOR THE SALES FORCE

Once these three strategic decisions are made, management will need to devise a marketing and sales structure to implement the local marketing strategy at three levels of organization: product, geography, and the trade. Traditionally, brand management represents the product dimension, while the field sales force is organized geographically. With local marketing, however, the increased decision-making responsibility of the sales force will reflect the relative importance of the geographic dimension. While brand managers are planning local coupon drops from headquarters by matching zip code profiles with targeted consumers, field salespeople will be developing new skills. Training programs will help regional sales managers learn to develop and coordinate special-event promotions with local distributors and retailers, use public relations to promote these events, and, perhaps, buy local advertising time and space. Greater organizational complexity is likely to result as companies explore

11. Judann Dagnoli, "Local Move: GF Prepares Regional Plan with Promo $," *Advertising Age* (February 9, 1987): 3.

12. Judann Dagnoli, "GF Tests Regional Tastes," *Advertising Age* (June 22, 1987): 3.

13. Christine Donahue, "Campbell Soup May Restructure in Favor of Regional Marketing," *Marketing Week* 28:22 (May 4, 1987): 1.

different combinations of direct salespeople, part-time employees, and brokers to maximize leverage in particular markets.

As a company embraces local programs of sales promotion, the marketing organization typically passes through three stages.

Stage 1   At this stage all decisions on sales promotions are made centrally by brand management, and all promotions are national in scope. There is minimal deviation from the promotion calendars planned by brand managers.

Stage 2   More local marketing programs are undertaken but are almost always directed from headquarters. Brand managers continue to make most sales promotion decisions and to evaluate sales force requests for additional or alternative promotion expenditures to meet unanticipated competition or opportunities in specific markets. Some regional and national promotions are planned and evaluated by assistant brand managers, particularly within larger brand groups. Sales merchandising managers are responsible for specific regions and for coordinating special requests and the promotion calendars of each product in their regions.

Stage 3   Brand managers set national and local sales promotion budgets, while regional sales managers have responsibility for allocating local brand budgets to meet agreed-upon sales goals. This approach has several important advantages. First, it enables the company to respond more quickly to retailers' offers to participate in vendor-support promotion programs. At the same time, it frees brand managers from the distraction of frequent requests from the field to approve unscheduled promotional spending. Moreover, increasing the decision-making responsibility of field people is very likely to improve their motivation. Finally, this devolution of responsibility eliminates the necessity for headquarters to examine the compliance of every promotion offer with the terms of the Robinson-Patman Act.

As a company moves to stage 3, it should consider basing its evaluations of district and regional sales managers on profit delivery and accurate sales forecasting—as reflected by the level of service to trade customers—as well as on sales volumes achieved. The company will probably need to hire a higher caliber of salespeople who possess marketing skills and/or provide extra training in these areas.

TRADE MARKETING

Traditionally, the marketing organizations of consumer goods manufacturers and service companies represent the interests of the trade in three ways: (1) by using separate sales forces for particular classes of trade; (2) by appointing proven salespeople as key account managers for major customers (and, where necessary, to coordinate the efforts of salespeople from different divisions of the company); and (3) by employing brokers with long-standing relationships in the trade whose frequent store visits can often achieve deeper account penetration than that attained by a direct sales force.

Given the increasing power and heterogeneity of the trade, however, these approaches may no longer be sufficient. Larger companies should also consider adding a headquarters function that focuses specifically on the strategic aspects of marketing to the trade—a parallel function to existing brand managers who concentrate primarily on product and consumer issues.[14] This new function may be created by retraining existing personnel or, in large organizations, by developing an entirely new department. Such a department would have the following responsibilities.

- Monitoring and analyzing trends in trade marketing and providing appropriate information to brand and sales managers.
- Developing business strategies for each class of trade and for certain key trade accounts; working with brand and sales managers to ensure their implementation.
- Evaluating the effectiveness of trade merchandising and devising measures, such as a store-development index (similar to brand- and category-development indices), to do so.
- Developing value-added services the sales force can offer to trade accounts. Such services might include assistance in allocating shelf space in a product category according to direct product profit and multiple- or single-brand turnkey promotion programs that field sales can take off the shelf as needed.[15]
- Serving as an information clearinghouse for creative promotion and merchandising programs developed in the field and for effective account-management strategies and tactics, to minimize reinvention of the wheel.
- Advising on the setting of terms of trade (e.g., quantity discounts, backhaul allowances) on the basis of cost analyses; working with the logistics and manufacturing departments to ensure that customer-service objectives are met.
- Developing training programs to give field salespeople and brokers the marketing skills necessary to distinguish themselves from competitors in the eyes of an increasingly sophisticated trade; improving the sales skills and trade sensitivity of brand managers.
- Providing information that encourages all employees to see the trade as a necessary partner in success.

---

14. Lee Nichols and Merle Wittenberg, "Trade Marketing: A Strategy for the Future," *DHC Viewpoint* (Winter 1987–88): 2–6.

15. Susan Zimmerman, "Study: Retail Direct Product Profit Use to Double in 4 Years," *Supermarket News* (February 16, 1987): 1.

After instituting such a trade-marketing function at headquarters, a company might also retrain existing sales managers and/or appoint tactically oriented trade-development managers at regional sales offices. These local trade developers can serve three principal functions. First, they can advise regional managers about field sales or broker requests for incremental trade promotions to respond to competitive activity or about retailer offers to participate in their own promotion programs. They can also develop an understanding of the merchandising strategies of key trade accounts in the region and develop custom promotion programs for them. Finally, they can coordinate the promotion calendars of the company's products and trade accounts in the region, minimizing the chances that competing products will initiate the same promotion at the same time in the same market.

These trade-development managers will need to possess an unusual combination of strategic ability and implementation skills and be able to merge the perspectives of field sales, brand management, and the trade. Not surprisingly, 75% of respondents to the Dechert-Hampe survey concluded that an entirely new breed of manager was needed to handle local marketing successfully.[16]

We have seen that local marketing will lead to increased responsibilities for the sales force and to the emergence of a new trade-marketing function. Most progressive brand managers will welcome these organizational changes. According to a 1987 survey, brand managers want to spend less time on time-consuming marketing tasks, such as sales promotion, that can be more effectively handled by local marketers, and more on such strategic activities as advertising-copy development, which will contribute to the long-term health of the national brand.[17]

Local marketing, however, means that both program costs and organizational complexity will increase. Marketers must determine whether the higher effectiveness stemming from customization (or the profit lost to more responsive competitors by *not* customizing) more than offsets the incremental costs. We believe that most consumer goods and service companies will decide to increase the proportion of their marketing expenditures assigned to local marketing programs. The best advice in most cases will be to "think nationally, act locally."

---

16. Raffini, "Regional Marketing."
17. John A. Quelch, Paul W. Farris, and James M. Oliver, "The Product Management Audit," *Harvard Business Review* (March–April, 1987).

── DISCUSSION QUESTIONS

1. There is a notable trend toward tailoring marketing programs to regional tastes. What benefits and opportunities does local marketing have over national marketing? In what instances would the national marketing strategy be a better choice? Explain.
2. Identify some of the problems and disadvantages of local marketing. Do its benefits always outweigh the drawbacks?
3. What differences would there be in formulating a local marketing strategy for industrial goods and consumer goods?
4. What kinds of industries benefit most from local marketing? What are some of the ways to assess the advisability of taking a local or a national approach?
5. The author advises, "Think national, act local." Is this contradictory? What does he mean?

10 Major Sales: Who *Really* Does the Buying?

THOMAS V. BONOMA

Effective buying and selling in the industrial arena is not simply a matter of offering a great product at the lowest price. Psychological and emotional factors figure strongly in buying and selling decisions, yet usually go unobserved. By overlooking these factors, a vendor can lose sales and not even understand why. This reading describes a procedure for identifying those who make the buying decisions and the factors that motivate them to purchase. Steps include identifying the actual decision makers, determining how they view their self-interests, and using that information to develop an effective sales strategy. The reading tells sellers how to apply the framework to specific situations.

You don't understand: Willy was a salesman. . . . He don't put a bolt to a nut. He don't tell you the law or give you medicine. He's a man way out there in the blue, riding on a smile and a shoeshine. And when they start not smiling back—that's an earthquake.
– Arthur Miller, *Death of a Salesman*

Many companies' selling efforts are models of marketing efficiency. Account plans are carefully drawn, key accounts receive special management attention, and substantial resources are devoted to the sales process, from prospect identification to postsale service. Even such well-planned and well-executed selling strategies often fail, though, because management has an incomplete understanding of buying psychology—the human side of selling. Consider the following two examples:

- A fast-growing maker and seller of sophisticated graphics computers had trouble selling to potentially major customers. Contrary to the industry practice of quoting high list prices and giving large discounts to users who bought in quantity, this company priced 10% to 15% lower than competitors and gave smaller quantity discounts. Even though its net price was often the lowest, the company met resistance from buyers. The reason, management later learned, was that purchasing agents measured themselves, and were measured by their superiors, less by the net price of the sophisticated computers they bought than by the amount deducted

140

from the price during negotiations. The discount had a significance to buyers that sound pricing logic could not predict.
- Several years ago, at AT&T's Long Lines Division, an account manager was competing against a vendor with possibly better technology who threatened to lure away a key account. Among the customer's executives who might make the final decision about whether to switch from Bell were a telecommunications manager who had once been a Bell employee, a vice president of data processing who was known as a "big-name system buster" in his previous job because he had replaced all the IBM computers with other vendors' machines, and an aggressive telecommunications division manager who seemed to be unreachable by the AT&T team.

AT&T's young national account manager was nearly paralyzed by the threat. His team had never seriously considered the power, motivations, or perceptions of the various executives in the customer company, which had been buying from AT&T for many years. Without such analysis, effective and coordinated action on short notice—the usual time available for response to sales threats—was impossible.

GETTING AT THE HUMAN FACTORS

How can psychology be used to improve sales effectiveness? My contention is that seller awareness of and attention to the human factors in purchasing will produce higher percentages of completed sales and fewer unpleasant surprises in the selling process.

It would be inaccurate to call the human side of selling an emerging sales concern; only the most advanced companies recognize the psychology of buying as a major factor in improving account selection and selling results. Yet in most industries, the bulk of a company's business comes from a small minority of its customers. Retaining these key accounts is becoming increasingly difficult as buyers constantly look not only for the best deal but also for the vendor that best understands them and their needs. It is this understanding and the targeted selling that results from it that can most benefit marketing managers.

BUYING A CORPORATE JET

The personal aspects and their complexities become apparent when one looks closely at an example of the buying process: the purchase of a business jet, which carries a price tag in excess of $3 million. The business-jet market splits obviously into two segments: those companies that already own or operate a corporate aircraft and those that do not.

In the owner market, the purchase process may be initiated by the chief executive officer, a board member (wishing to increase efficiency or security), the company's chief pilot, or through vendor efforts like advertising or a sales visit. The CEO will be central in deciding whether to buy the jet, but he or she will be heavily influenced by the company's pilot, financial officer, and perhaps the board itself.

Each party in the buying process has subtle roles and needs. The salesperson who tries to impress, for example, the CEO with depreciation schedules and the chief pilot with minimum runway statistics will almost certainly not sell a plane if he or she overlooks the psychological and emotional components of the buying decision. "For the chief executive," observes one salesperson, "you need all the numbers for support, but if you can't find the kid inside the CEO and excite him or her with the raw beauty of the new plane, you'll never sell the equipment. If you sell the excitement, you sell the jet."

The chief pilot, as an equipment expert, often has veto power over the purchase decisions and may be able to stop the purchase of one or another brand of jet by simply expressing a negative opinion about, say, the plane's bad-weather capabilities. In this sense, the pilot not only influences the decision but also serves as an information "gatekeeper" by advising management on the equipment to select. Though the corporate legal staff will formulate the purchase agreement and the purchasing department will acquire the jet, these parties may have little to say about whether or how the plane will be obtained, and which type. The users of the jet—middle and upper management of the buying company, important customers, and others—may have at least an indirect role in choosing the equipment.

The involvement of many people in the purchase decision creates a group dynamic that the selling company must factor into its sales planning. Who makes up the buying group? How will the parties interact? Who will dominate and who will submit? What priorities do the individuals have?

It takes about three months for those companies that already own or operate aircraft to reach a decision. Because even the most successful vendor will sell no more than 90 jets a year, every serious prospect is a key account. The nonowners, not surprisingly, represent an even more complex market, since no precedent or aviation specialists exist.

The buying process for other pieces of equipment and for services will be more or less similar, depending on the company, product, and people involved. The purchase of computer equipment, for example, parallels the jet decision, except that sales prospects are likely to include data processing and production executives, and the market is divided into small and large prospects rather than owners and nonowners. In other cases (such as upgrading the corporate communications network, making a fleet purchase, or launching a plant expansion), the buying process may be very different. Which common factors will reliably steer selling-company management toward those human considerations likely to improve selling effectiveness?

Different buying psychologies exist that make effective selling difficult. On the one hand, companies don't buy, people do. This knowledge drives the seller to analyze who the important buyers are and what they want. On the other hand, many individuals, some of whom may be unknown to the seller, are involved in most major purchases. Even if all the parties are identified, the outcome of their interaction may not be predictable from knowledge of them as individuals. Effective selling requires usefully combining the individual and group dynamics of buying to predict what the buying "decision-making unit" will do. For this combination to be practical, the selling company must answer four key questions.

——— WHO'S IN THE BUYING CENTER?

The set of roles, or social tasks, buyers can assume is the same regardless of the product or participants in the purchase decision. This set of roles can be thought of as a fixed set of behavioral pigeonholes into which different managers from different functions can be placed to aid understanding. Together, the buying managers who take on these roles can be thought of as a "buying center."[1]

Exhibit 1 shows six buying roles encountered in every selling situation. I have illustrated these roles using the purchase or upgrading of a telecommunications system as an example. Let's consider each triangle, representing a buying role, in turn.

The *initiator* of the purchase process, whether for a jet, paper towels, or communication services, recognizes that some company problem can be solved or avoided by acquiring a product or service. A company's turboprop aircraft may provide neither the speed nor the range to get top management quickly to and from scattered operations. The prospective buyer of communications equipment may want to take advantage of technological improvements or to reduce costs through owning instead of leasing.

One or more *gatekeepers* is involved in the purchase process. These individuals, who may have the title of buyer or purchasing manager, usually act as problem or product experts. They are paid to keep up with the range of vendor offerings. In the jet example, the chief pilot will ordinarily fill this role. In the telecommunications example given in *Exhibit 1*, corporate purchasing, the corporate telecommunications staff, or, increasingly, data processing experts may be consulted. By controlling (literally keeping the gate open or shut for) information and, sometimes, vendor access to corporate decision makers, the gatekeepers largely determine which vendors get the chance to sell. For some purchases the gatekeeping process is formalized through the use of an

---

1. The concept of the buying center was proposed in its present form by Frederick E. Webster, Jr., and Yoram Wind in *Organizational Buying Behavior* (Englewood Cliffs, N.J.: Prentice-Hall, 1972), pp. 75–87.

EXHIBIT 1
Members of the Buying Center and Their Roles

Initiator	Division general manager proposes to replace the company's telecommunications system
Decider	Vice president of administration selects, with influence from others, the vendor the company will deal with and the system it will buy
Influencers	Corporate telecommunications department and the vice president of data processing have important say about which system and vendor the company will deal with
Purchaser	Corporate purchasing department completes the purchase to specifications by negotiating or bidding
Gatekeepers	Corporate purchasing and corporate telecommunications departments analyze the company's needs and recommend likely matches with potential vendors
Users	All division employees who use the telecommunications equipment

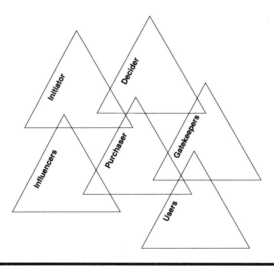

approved-vendors list, which constitutes a written statement of who can (and who, by absence, cannot) sell to the company.

Influencers are those who "have a say" in whether a purchase is made and about what is bought. The range of influencers becomes increasingly broad as major purchases are contemplated, because so many corporate resources are involved and so many people affected. In important decisions, board committees, stockholders of a public company, and even mechanics can become influencers. One mining-machinery company encountered difficulty selling a new type of machine to its underground-mining customers. It turned out that mine maintenance personnel, who influenced the buying decision, resisted the purchase because they would have to learn to fix the new machine and maintain another stock of spare parts.

The *deciders* are those who say yes or no to the contemplated purchase. Often with major purchases, many of a company's senior managers act together to carry out the decider role. Ordinarily, however, one of these will become champion or advocate of the contemplated purchase and move it to completion. Without such a champion, many purchases would never be made. It is important to point out that deciders often do not "sign off" on purchases, nor do they make them. That is left to others. Though signers often represent themselves as deciders, such representation can be deceptive. It is possible for a vendor with a poor feel for the buying center *never* to become aware of the real movers in the buying company.

The purchase of executive computer work stations clearly illustrates both the importance of the champion and the behind-the-scenes role of the decider. A high-level executive who has become interested in using computers at his or her job after reading a magazine article or after tinkering with a home computer might decide to try out microcomputers or time-sharing terminals. The executive might then ask the company's data processing group—which is likely to be quite resistant and averse to executive meddling—to evaluate available microcomputer equipment. When trial purchases are made, the high-level executive will quietly help steer the system through the proper channels leading to acceptance and further purchases. The vendor, dealing directly with the data processing people, may never be aware that this decider exists.

The *purchaser* and the *user* are those concerned, respectively, with obtaining and consuming the product or service. The corporate purchasing department usually fills the purchaser role. Who fills the user role depends on the product or service.

Remember that I am discussing social roles, not individuals or groups of individuals. Thus, the number of managers filling the buying roles varies from 1 to 35. In very trivial situations, such as a manager's purchase of a pocket calculator on a business trip, one person fills all six roles. The triangles in *Exhibit 1* would overlap: the manager initiates (perceives a need), gatekeeps (what brand did I forget at home?), influences himself or herself (this is more than I need, but it's only $39.95), decides, buys, and uses the equipment.

In more important buying situations, the number of managers assuming roles increases. In a study of 62 capital equipment and service acquisitions in 31 companies, Wesley J. Johnston and I quantified the buying center.[2] In the typical capital equipment purchase, an average of four departments (engineering and purchasing were always included), three levels of management hierarchy (for example, manager, regional manager, vice president), and seven different persons filled the six buying roles. For services, the corresponding numbers were four departments, two levels of management, and five managers. As might be expected, the more complex and involved the buying decision, the

    2. Wesley J. Johnston and Thomas V. Bonoma, "Purchase Process for Capital Equipment and Services," *Industrial Marketing Management* 10 (1981): 253.

larger the decision unit and the more careful its decisions. For example, when packing supplies were ordered, little vendor searching or postsale evaluation was involved. When a new boiler was bought, careful vendor comparisons and postsale audits were undertaken.

——— WHO ARE THE POWERFUL BUYERS?

As useful as the buying-center concept is, it is difficult to apply because managers do not wear tags that say "decision maker" or "unimportant person."[3] The powerful are often invisible, at least to vendor representatives.

Unfortunately, power does not correlate perfectly with organizational rank. As the case of the mine maintenance personnel illustrates, those with little formal power may be able to stop a purchase or hinder its completion. A purchasing manager who will not specify a disfavored vendor, or the secretary who screens one vendor's salespeople because of a real or imagined slight, also can dramatically change the purchasing outcome. Sales efforts cannot be directed through a simple reading of organizational charts; the selling company must identify the powerful buying-center members.

In *Exhibit 2*, I outline five major power bases in the corporation. In addition, I categorize them according to whether their influence is positive (champion power) or negative (veto power).

Reward power refers to a manager's ability to encourage purchases by providing others with monetary, social, political, or psychological benefits. In one small company, for instance, the marketing vice president hoped to improve marketing decisions by equipping the sales force with small data-entry computers. Anticipating objections that the terminals were unnecessary, she felt forced to offer the sales vice president a computer of his own. The purchase was made.

Coercive power refers to a manager's ability to impose punishment on others. Of course, threatening punishment is not the same thing as having the power to impose it. Those managers who wave sticks most vigorously are sometimes the least able to deliver anything beyond a gentle breeze.

Attraction power refers to a person's ability to charm or otherwise persuade people to go along with his or her preferences. Next to the ability to reward and punish, attraction is the most potent power base in managerial life. Even CEOs find it difficult to rebut a key customer with whom they have flown for ten years who says, "Joe, as your friend, I'm telling you that buying this plane would be a mistake."

---

3. Documentation for my assertions regarding psychological research can be found in Thomas V. Bonoma and Gerald Zaltman, *Management Psychology* (Boston: Kent Publishing Company, 1981). *See* Chapter 8 for the power literature and Chapter 3 for material on motivation.

EXHIBIT 2
Bases of Power

TYPE OF POWER	CHAMPION	or	VETO
Reward: Ability to provide monetary, social, political, or psychological rewards to others for compliance	■		
Coercive: Ability to provide monetary or other punishments for noncompliance	■		
Attraction: Ability to elicit compliance from others because they like you	■		■
Expert: Ability to elicit compliance because of technical expertise, either actual or reputed			■
Status: Compliance-gaining ability derived from a legitimate position of power in a company			■

Note: These five power bases were originally proposed by psychologists J. R. P. French, Jr., and Bertram Raven. *See* "The Bases of Social Power" in D. Cartwright, ed., *Studies in Social Power* (Ann Arbor: University of Michigan Press, 1959).

When a manager gets others to go along with his or her judgment because of real or perceived expertise in some area, *expert power* is being invoked. A telecommunications manager will find it difficult to argue with an acknowledged computer expert who contends that buying a particular telephone switching system is essential for the "office of the future"—or that not buying it now eventually will make effective communication impossible. With expert power, the skills need not be real, if by "real" we mean that the individual actually possesses what is attributed to him or her. It is enough that others believe that the expert has special skills or are willing to respect his or her opinion because of accomplishments in a totally unrelated field.

Status power comes from having a high position in the corporation. This notion of power is most akin to what is meant by the word *authority*. It refers to the kind of influence a president has over a first-line supervisor and is more restricted than the other power bases. At first glance, status power might be thought of as similar to reward or coercive power. But it differs in significant ways. First, the major influence activity of those positions of corporate authority is persuasion, not punishment or reward. They jawbone rather than dangle carrots and taunt with sticks because others in the company also have significant power which they could invoke in retaliation. Second, the high-status manager can exercise his or her status repeatedly only because subordinates allow it. In one heavy-manufacturing division, for example, the continual specification of favored suppliers by a plant manager (often at unfavorable prices) led to a "palace revolt" among other managers whose component cost evaluations were constantly made to look poor. Third, the power base of those in authority is very circumscribed, since authority tends to work only in a downward direction on the organization chart and is restricted to specific work-related requests. Status power is one of the weaker power bases.

Buying centers and individual managers usually display one dominant power base in purchasing decisions. In one small company, an important factor is whether the manager arguing a position is a member of the founding family—a kind of status power and attraction power rolled into one. In a large high-technology defense contractor, almost all decisions are made on the basis of real or reputed expertise. This is true even when the issue under consideration has nothing to do with hardware or engineering science.

The key to improved selling effectiveness is in observation and investigation to understand prospects' corporate power culture. The sales team must also learn the type of power key managers in the buying company have or aspire to. Discounts or offers of price reductions may not be especially meaningful to a young turk in the buying company who is most concerned with status power; a visit by senior selling-company management may prove much more effective for flattering the ego and making the sale. Similarly, sales management may wish to make more technical selling appeals to engineers or other buying-company staff who base their power on expertise.

The last two columns of *Exhibit 2* show that the type of power invoked may allow the manager to support or to oppose a proposal but not always both. I believe status and expert power are more often employed by their holders to veto decisions with which they do not agree. Because others are often "sold" on the contemplated purchase, vetoing it generally requires either the ability to perceive aspects not seen by the average manager because of special expertise or the broader view that high corporate status is said to provide. Reward and coercive power are more frequently used to push through purchases and the choice of favored vendors. Attraction power seems useful and is used by both champions and vetoers. The central point here is that for many buying-center members, power tends to be unidirectional.

SIX BEHAVIORAL CLUES

On the basis of the preceding analysis of power centers, I have distilled six behavioral clues for identifying the powerful:

1. Though power and formal authority often go together, the correlation between the two is not perfect. The selling company must take into account other clues about where the true buying power lies.
2. One way to identify buying-center powerholders is to observe communications in the buying company. Of course, the powerful

are not threatened by others, nor are they often promised rewards. Still, even the most powerful managers are likely to be influenced by others, especially by those whose power is based on attraction or expertise. Those with less power use persuasion and rational argument to try to influence the more powerful. Managers to whom others direct much attention but who receive few offers of rewards or threats of punishment usually possess substantial decision-making power.

3. Buying-center decision makers may be disliked by those with less power. Thus, when others express concern about one buying-center member's opinions along with their feelings of dislike or ambivalence, sellers have strong clues as to who the powerful buyer is.

4. High-power buyers tend to be one-way information centers, serving as focal points for information from others. The vice president who doesn't come to meetings but who receives copies of all correspondence about a buying matter is probably a central influencer or decider.

5. The most powerful buying-center members are probably not the most easily identified or the most talkative members of their groups. Indeed, the really powerful buying group members often send others to critical negotiations because they are confident that little of substance will be made final without their approval.

6. No correlation exists between the functional area of a manager and his or her power within a company. It is not possible to approach the data processing department blindly to find decision makers for a new computer system, as many sellers of mainframes have learned. Nor can one simply look to the CEO to find a decision maker for a corporate jet. There is no substitute for working hard to understand the dynamics of the buying company.

—— **WHAT DO THEY WANT?**

Diagnosing motivation accurately is one of the easiest management tasks to do poorly and one of the most difficult to do well. Most managers have lots of experience at diagnosing another's wants, but though the admission comes hard, most are just not very accurate when trying to figure out what another person wants and will do. A basic rule of motivation is as follows: all buyers (indeed, all people) act selfishly or try to be selfish but sometimes miscalculate and don't serve their own interests. Thus, buyers attempt to maximize their gains and minimize their losses from purchase situations. How do buyers choose their own self-interest? The following are insights into that decision-making process from research.

First, buyers act as if a complex product or service was decomposable into various benefits. Examples of benefits might include product features, price, reliability, and so on.

Second, buyers segment the potential benefits into various categories. The most common of these are financial, product-service, social-political, and personal. For some buyers, the financial benefits are paramount, while for others, the social-political ones—how others in the company will view the purchase—rank highest. Of course, the dimensions may be related, as when getting the lowest-cost product (financial) results in good performance evaluations and a promotion (social-political).

Finally, buyers ordinarily are not certain that purchasing the product will actually bring the desired benefit. For example, a control computer sold on its reliability and industrial-strength construction may or may not fulfill its promise. Because benefits have value only if they actually are delivered, the buyer must be confident that the selling company will keep its promises. Well-known vendors, like IBM or Xerox, may have some advantage over lesser-known companies in this respect.

As marketers know, not all promised benefits will be equally desired by all customers. All buyers have top-priority benefit classes, or "hot buttons." For example, a telecommunications manager weighing a choice between Bell and non-Bell equipment will find some benefits, like ownership, available only from non-Bell vendors. Other desired benefits, such as reputation for service and reliability, may be available to a much greater degree from Bell. The buyer who has financial priorities as a hot button may decide to risk possible service-reliability problems for the cost-reduction benefits available through ownership. Another manager—one primarily concerned with reducing the social-political risks that result from service problems— may reach a different decision. *Exhibit 3* schematically shows the four classes into which buyers divide benefits. The telecommunications example illustrates each class.

Outlining the buyer's motivation suggests several possible selling approaches. The vendor can try to focus the buyer's attention on benefits not a part of his or her thinking. A magazine ad sales representative, for instance, devised a questionnaire to help convince an uncertain client to buy advertising space. The questionnaire sought information about the preferred benefits—in terms of reach, audience composition, and cost per thousand readers. When the prospective buyer "played this silly game" and filled out the questionnaire, he convinced himself of the superior worth of the vendor's magazine on the very grounds he was seeking to devalue it.

Conversely, a vendor can de-emphasize the buyer's desire for benefits against which the vendor's offering stacks up poorly. For example, if a competing vendor's jet offers better fuel economy, the selling company might attempt to refocus the buyer's attention toward greater speed or lower maintenance costs.

The vendor can also try to increase the buyer's confidence that promised benefits will be realized. One software company selling legal administrative systems, for example, provides a consulting service that remote users can phone if they are having problems, backup copies of its main programs in case users

EXHIBIT 3
Dominant Motives for Buying a Telecommunications System

BENEFIT CLASS	(The benefits in bold type are more highly valued than the others and represent the company's "hot button.")		
Financial	Product or service	Social or political	Personal
Absolute cost savings	**Pre- and postsales service**	Will purchase enhance the buyer's standing with the buying team or top management?	Will purchase increase others' liking or respect for the buyer?
Cheaper than competitive offerings	**Specific features**		How does purchase fit with buyer's self-concept?
Will provide operating-cost reductions	**Space occupied by unit**		
Economics of leasing versus buying	**Availability**		

destroy the original, a complete set of input forms to encourage full data entry, and regular conferences to keep users current on system revisions. These services are designed to bolster the confidence of extremely conservative administrators and lawyers who are shopping for a system.

Finally, vendors often try to change what the buyer wants or which class of benefits he or she responds to most strongly. My view of motivation is that such an approach is almost always unsuccessful. Selling strategy needs to work with the buyer's motivations, not around them.

⸻ HOW DO THEY PERCEIVE US?

How buyers perceive the selling company, its products, and its personnel is very important to efficient selling. Powerful buyers invariably have a wide range of perceptions about a vending company. One buyer will have a friend at another company who has used a similar product and claims that "it very nearly ruined us." Another may have talked to someone with a similar product who claims that the vending company "even sent a guy out on a plane to Hawaii to fix the unit there quickly. These people really care."

One drug company representative relates the story of how the company was excluded from all the major metropolitan hospitals in one city because a single influential physician believed that one of the company's new offerings was implicated in a patient's death. This doctor not only generalized his impressions to include all the company's products but encouraged his friends to boycott the company.

A simple scheme for keeping tabs on how buyers perceive sellers is to ask sales officials to estimate how the important buyers judge the vending company and its actions. This judgment can be recorded on a continuum ranging from negative to positive. If a more detailed judgment is desired, the selling company can place its products and its people on two axes perpendicular to each other, like this:

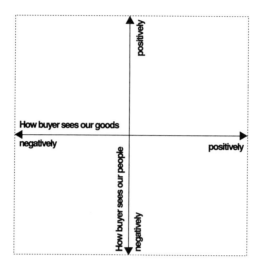

The scarcity of marketing dollars and the effectiveness of champions in the buying process argue strongly for focusing resources where they are likely to do the most good. Marketing efforts should aim at those in the buying company who like the selling company, since they are partially presold. While there is no denying the adage, "It's important to sell everybody," those who diffuse their efforts this way often sell no one.

GATHERING PSYCHOLOGICAL INTELLIGENCE

While I would like to claim that some new technique will put sound psychological analyses magically in your sales staff's hands, no such technique exists. But I have used the human-side approach in several companies to increase sales effectiveness, and there are only three guidelines needed to make it work well.

MAKE PRODUCTIVE SALES CALLS A NORM, NOT AN ODDITY

Because of concern about the rapidly rising cost of a sales call, managers are seeking alternative approaches to selling. Sales personnel often do not have

EXHIBIT 4
Matrix for Gathering Psychological Information

Who are in the buying center, and what is the base of their power?	Who are the powerful buyers, and what are their priorities?	What specific benefits does each important buyer want?	How do the important buyers see us?	Selling strategy
_____	_____	_____	_____	_____
_____	_____	_____	_____	_____
_____	_____	_____	_____	_____
_____	_____	_____	_____	_____

a good idea of why they are going on most calls, what they hope to find out, and which questions will give them the needed answers. Sales-call planning is a matter not only of minimizing miles traveled or courtesy calls on unimportant prospects but of determining what intelligence is needed about key buyers and what questions or requests are likely to produce that information.

I recently traveled with a major account representative of a duplication equipment company, accompanying him on the five calls he made during the day. None of the visits yielded even 10% of the potential psychological or other information that the representative could use on future calls, despite the fact that prospects made such information available repeatedly. At one company, for example, we learned from a talkative administrator that the CEO was a semirecluse who insisted on personally approving equipment requests; that one of the divisional managers had (without the agreement of the administrator) brought in a competitor's equipment to test; and that a new duplicator the vendor had sold to the company was more out of service than in. The salesperson pursued none of this freely offered information, nor thought any of it important enough to write down or pass on to the sales manager. The call was wasted because the salesperson didn't know what to look for or how to use what was offered.

Exhibit 4 shows a matrix that can be used to capture on a single sheet of paper essential psychological data about a customer. I gave some clues for filling in the matrix earlier in the article, but how sales representatives go about gathering the information depends on the industry, the product, and especially the customer. In all cases, however, key selling assessments involve (1) isolating the powerful buying-center members, (2) identifying what they want in terms of both their hot buttons and specific needs, and (3) assessing their perceptions of the situation. Additionally, gathering psychological information is more often a matter of listening carefully than of asking clever questions during the sales interview.

LISTEN TO THE SALES FORCE

Nothing discourages intelligence gathering as much as the sales force's conviction that management doesn't really want to hear what salespeople know about an account. Many companies require the sales force to file voluminous call reports and furnish other data—which vanish, never to be seen or even referred to again unless a sales representative is to be punished for one reason or another.

To counter this potentially fatal impediment, I recommend a sales audit. Evaluate all sales force control forms and call reports and discard any that have not been used by management for planning or control purposes in the last year. This approach has a marvelously uplifting effect all around; it frees the sales force from filling in forms it knows nobody uses, sales management from gathering forms it doesn't know what to do with, and data processing from processing reports no one ever requests. Instead, use a simple, clear, and accurate sales control form of the sort suggested in *Exhibit 4*—preferably on a single sheet of paper for a particular sales period. These recommendations may sound drastic, but where management credibility in gathering and using sales force intelligence is absent, drastic measures may be appropriate.

EMPHASIZE HOMEWORK AND DETAILS

Having techniques for acquiring sales intelligence and attending to reports is not enough. Sales management must stress that the company rewards careful fact gathering, tight analysis, and impeccable execution. This message is most meaningful when it comes from the top.

—— CAUTIONARY NOTES

The group that influences a purchase doesn't call itself a buying center. Nor do decision makers and influencers think of themselves in those terms. Managers must be careful not to mistake the analysis and ordering process for the buyers' actions themselves. In addition, gathering data such as I have recommended is a sensitive issue. For whatever reasons, it is considered less acceptable to make psychological estimates of buyers than economic ones. Computing the numbers without understanding the psychology, however, leads to lost sales. Finally, the notion implicit throughout this article has been that sellers must understand buying, just as buyers must understand selling. When that happens, psychology and marketing begin to come together usefully. Closed sales follow almost as an afterthought.

——— DISCUSSION QUESTIONS

1. The author points out that in developing an effective sales strategy it is important to identify the actual decision makers in an organization and the factors that motivate them to purchase. What is the strategic significance of this? How would you go about identifying the decision makers? What leverage do you think the buyer has who actually places the order with your salespeople?

2. The author also notes that there are people in a company who influence the decision makers, and they too should be identified. How can this knowledge contribute to the buying and selling activities? How would you go about identifying those with influence on decision makers?

3. The author contends that understanding the buying behavior of decision makers is key to successful industrial selling. In his view it is equally important to learn the physical and psychological factors that motivate buyers to purchase. How might these factors have an impact on purchasing behavior? Does having the best product on the market and the lowest possible price automatically negate any other influence in buying behavior?

4. Gathering the necessary human and emotional data to help you understand what motivates your customers' buying behavior presents some risks and problems. What are they, and what approach would you use to facilitate this sensitive undertaking?

5. How do companies benefit from an ability to forecast future sales? What must sales managers know in order to predict what buying decisions will be made by the decision makers? Think of a specific situation and show how you would apply your framework.

11   How to Segment
Industrial Markets

BENSON P. SHAPIRO AND THOMAS V. BONOMA

The difficulty of segmenting industrial markets has dissuaded many companies from trying, despite the benefits they could realize from skillful segmentation: The problem often lies in recognizing the criteria that would simplify the process. In this reading, the authors have identified a set of five criteria that managers can use to determine the best segmentation method for their company's capabilities. They present these criteria using a "nested" approach. The variables easiest to assess, such as demographics, form the outermost layer of the nest, while subtler, more complex variables, such as company and personal characteristics, form the innermost layers. The authors point out that a nested approach cannot be applied broadly but must be adapted to individual situations and circumstances. Once in place, however, the nested approach makes it easier to understand the total marketplace, including how and why customers buy—thus allowing management to develop strategies, plans, and programs that give the company a competitive edge and add to its profitability.

As difficult as segmenting consumer markets is, it is much simpler and easier than segmenting industrial markets. Often the same industrial products have multiple applications; likewise, several different products can be used in the same application. Customers differ greatly, and it is hard to discern which differences are important and which are trivial for developing a marketing strategy.

Little research has been done on industrial market segmentation. None of the ten articles in the *Journal of Marketing Research's* special August 1978 section, "Market Segmentation Research," for instance, dealt with industrial market segmentation in more than a passing manner. Our research indicates that most industrial marketers use segmentation as a way to explain results rather than as a way to plan.

In fact, industrial segmentation can assist companies in several areas:

- *Analysis of the market*—better understanding of the total marketplace, including how and why customers buy.
- *Selection of key markets*—rational choice of market segments that best fit the company's capabilities.
- *Management of marketing*—the development of strategies, plans, and programs to profitably meet the needs of different

market segments and to give the company a distinct competitive advantage.

In this reading, we integrate and build on previous schemes for segmenting industrial markets and offer a new approach that enables not only the simple grouping of customers and prospects but also the more complex grouping of purchase situations, events, and personalities. It thus serves as an important new analytical tool.

Consider the dilemma of one skilled and able industrial marketer who observed recently: "I can't see any basis on which to segment my market. We have 15% of the market for our type of plastics fabrication equipment. There are 11 competitors who serve a large and diverse set of customers, but there is no unifying theme to our customer set or to anyone else's."

His frustration is understandable, but he should not give up, for at least he knows that 15% of the market purchases one product, and that knowledge, in itself, is a basis for segmentation. Segments exist, even when the only apparent basis for differentiation is brand choice.

At other times, a marketer may be baffled by a profusion of segmentation criteria. Customer groups and even individual customers within these groups may differ in demographics (including industry and company size), operating differences (production technology is an example), purchasing organization, "culture," and personal characteristics. Usually, a marketer can group customers, prospects, and purchase situations in different ways depending on the variables used to segment the market. The problem is to identify relevant segmentation bases.

We have identified five general segmentation criteria (see *Exhibit 1*), which we have arranged as a *nested* hierarchy—like a set of boxes that fit one

EXHIBIT 1
Nested Approach

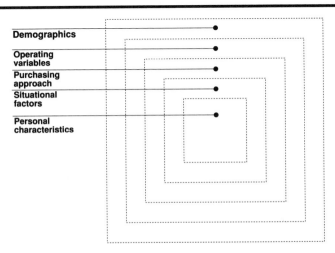

Demographics

Operating
variables

Purchasing
approach

Situational
factors

Personal
characteristics

into the other. Moving from the outer nest toward the inner, these criteria are: demographics, operating variables, customer purchasing approaches, situational factors, and personal characteristics of the buyers.

Exhibit 1 shows how the criteria relate to one another as nests. The segmentation criteria of the largest, outermost nest are demographics—general, easily observable characteristics about industries and companies; those of the smallest, innermost nest are personal characteristics—specific, subtle, hard-to-assess traits. The marketer moves from the more general, easily observable segmentation characteristics to the more specific, subtle ones. This approach will become clearer as we explain each criterion.

We should note at this point that it may not be necessary or even desirable for every industrial marketer to use every stage of the nested approach for every product. Although it is possible to skip irrelevant criteria, it is important that the marketer completely understand the approach before deciding on omissions and shortcuts.

—— DEMOGRAPHICS

The outermost nest contains the most general segmentation criteria, demographics. These variables give a broad description of the company and relate to general customer needs and usage patterns. They can be determined without visiting the customer and include industry, company size, and customer location.

The Industry Knowledge of the industry affords a broad understanding of customer needs and perceptions of purchase situations. Some companies, such as those selling paper, office equipment, business-oriented computers, and financial services, market to a wide range of industries. For these, industry is an important basis for market segmentation. Hospitals, for example, share some computer needs and yet differ markedly as a customer group from retail stores.

Marketers may wish to subdivide individual industries. For example, although financial services are in a sense a single industry, commercial banks, insurance companies, stockbrokerage houses, and savings and loan associations all differ dramatically. Their differences in terms of product and service needs, such as specialized peripherals and terminals, data handling, and software requirements, make a more detailed segmentation scheme necessary to sell computers to the financial services market.

Company Size The fact that large companies justify and require specialized programs affects market segmentation. It may be, for example, that a smaller supplier of industrial chemicals, after segmenting its prospective customers on the basis of company size, will choose not to approach large companies whose volume requirements exceed its own production capacity.

Customer Location   The third demographic factor, location, is an important variable in decisions related to deployment and organization of sales staff. A manufacturer of heavy-duty pumps for the petrochemical industry, for example, would want to provide good coverage in the Gulf Coast, where customers are concentrated, while putting little effort into New England. Customer location is especially important when proximity is a requirement for doing business, as in marketing products of low value-per-unit-weight or volume (such as corrugated boxes or prestressed concrete), or in situations where personal service is essential (as in job shop printing).

As noted, a marketer can determine all of these demographic variables easily. Industry-oriented and general directories are useful in developing lists of customers in terms of industry, size, and location. Government statistics, reports by market research companies, and industry and trade association publications provide a great deal of demographic data.

Many companies base their industrial marketing segmentation approach on demographic data alone. But while demographics are useful and easily obtained, they do not exhaust the possibilities of segmentation. They are often only a beginning.

——— OPERATING VARIABLES

The second segmentation nest contains a variety of segmentation criteria called "operating variables." Most of these enable more precise identification of existing and potential customers within demographic categories. Operating variables are generally stable and include technology, user/nonuser status (by product and brand), and customer capabilities (operating, technical, and financial).

Company Technology   A company's technology, involving either its manufacturing process or its product, goes a long way toward determining its buying needs. Soda ash, for example, can be produced by two methods that require different capital equipment and supplies. The production of Japanese color televisions is highly automated and uses a few large, integrated circuits. In the United States, on the other hand, color TV production once involved many discrete components, manual assembly, and fine tuning. In Europe, production techniques made use of a hybrid of integrated circuits and discrete components. The technology used affects companies' requirements for test gear, tooling, and components and, thus, helps determine a marketer's most appropriate marketing approach.

Product and Brand-Use Status   One of the easiest ways, and in some situations the only obvious way, to segment a market is by product and brand use. Users of a particular product or brand generally have some characteristics in common; at the very least, they have a common experience with a product or brand.

Manufacturers who replace metal gears with nylon gears in capital equipment probably share perceptions of risk, manufacturing process or cost structure, or marketing strategy. They probably have experienced similar sales presentations. Having used nylon gears, they share common experiences including, perhaps, similar changes in manufacturing approaches.

One supplier of nylon gears might argue that companies that have already committed themselves to replace metal gears with nylon gears are better customer prospects than those that have not yet done so, since it is usually easier to generate demand for a new brand than for a new product. But another supplier might reason that manufacturers that have not yet shifted to nylon are better prospects because they have not experienced its benefits and have not developed a working relationship with a supplier. A third marketer might choose to approach both users and nonusers with different strategies.

Current customers are a different segment from prospective customers using a similar product purchased elsewhere. Current customers are familiar with a company's product and service, and company managers know something about customer needs and purchasing approaches. Some companies' marketing approaches focus on increasing sales volume from existing customers, either by customer growth or by gaining a larger share of the customer's business, rather than on additional sales volume from new customers. In these cases, industrial sales managers often follow a two-step process: first they seek to gain an initial order on trial, and then they seek to increase the share of the customer's purchases. Banks are often more committed to raising the share of major customers' business than to generating new accounts.

Sometimes it is useful to segment customers not only on the basis of whether they buy from the company or from its competitors, but also, in the latter case, on the identity of competitors. This information can be useful in several ways. Sellers may find it easier to lure customers from competitors that are weak in certain respects. When Bethlehem Steel opened its state-of-the-art Burns Harbor plant in the Chicago area, for example, it went after the customers of one local competitor known to offer poor quality.

Customer Capabilities   Marketers might find companies with known operating, technical, or financial strengths and weaknesses to be an attractive market. For example, a company operating with tight materials inventories would greatly appreciate a supplier with a reliable delivery record. And customers unable to perform quality-control tests on incoming materials might be willing to pay for supplier quality checks. Some raw materials suppliers might choose to develop a thriving business among less sophisticated companies, for which lower-than-usual average discounts well compensate added services.

Technically weak customers in the chemical industry have traditionally depended on suppliers for formulation assistance and technical support. Some suppliers have been astute in identifying customers needing such support and in providing it in a highly effective manner.

Technical strength can also differentiate customers. Digital Equipment Corporation for many years specialized in selling its minicomputers to customers able to develop their own software, and Prime Computer sold computer systems to business users who did not need the intensive support and "hand holding" offered by IBM and other manufacturers. Both companies used segmentation for market selection.

Many operating variables are easily researched. In a quick drive around a soda ash plant, for example, a vendor might be able to identify the type of technology being used. Data on financial strength is at least partially available from credit-rating services. Customer personnel may provide other data, such as the name of current suppliers; "reverse engineering" (tearing down or disassembly) of a product may yield information on the type and even the producers of components, as may merely noting the names on delivery trucks entering the prospect's premises.

——— PURCHASING APPROACHES

One of the most neglected but valuable methods of segmenting an industrial market involves consumers' purchasing approaches and company philosophy. The factors in this middle segmentation nest include the formal organization of the purchasing function, the power structures, the nature of buyer-seller relationships, the general purchasing policies, and the purchasing criteria.

Purchasing Function Organization   The organization of the purchasing function to some extent determines the size and operation of a company's purchasing unit. A centralized approach may merge individual purchasing units into a single group, and vendors with decentralized manufacturing operations may find it difficult to meet centralized buying patterns.[1] To meet these different needs, some suppliers handle sales to centralized purchasers through so-called national account programs and those to companies with a decentralized approach through field-oriented sales forces.

Power Structures   These also vary widely among customers. The impact of influential organizational units varies and often affects purchasing approaches. The powerful financial analysis units at General Motors and Ford may, for example, have made these companies unusually price-oriented in their purchasing decisions. Or a company may have a powerful engineering department that strongly influences purchases; a supplier with strong technical skills

---

1. *See* E. Raymond Corey, "Should Companies Centralize Procurement?" *Harvard Business Review* (November–December 1978): 102.

would suit such a customer. A vendor might find it useful to adapt its marketing program to customer strengths, using one approach for customers with strong engineering operations and another for customers lacking these.

Buyer-Seller Relationships   A supplier probably has stronger ties with some customers than with others. The link may be clearly stated. A lawyer, commercial banker, or investment banker, for example, might define as an unattractive market segment all companies having as a board member the representative of a competitor.

General Purchasing Policies   A financially strong company that offers a lease program might want to identify prospective customers who prefer to lease capital equipment or who have meticulous asset management. When AT&T could lease but not sell equipment, this was an important segmentation criterion for it. Customers may prefer to do business with long-established companies or with small independent companies, or may have particularly potent affirmative action purchasing programs (minority-owned businesses were attracted by Polaroid's widely publicized social conscience program, for example). Or they may prefer to buy systems rather than individual components.

A prospective customer's approach to the purchasing process is important. Some purchasers require an agreement based on supplier cost, particularly the auto companies, the U.S. government, and the three large general merchandise chains—Sears, Roebuck; Montgomery Ward; and J. C. Penney. Other purchasers negotiate from a market-based price, and some use bids. Bidding is an important method for obtaining government and quasi-government business, but because it emphasizes price, bidding tends to favor suppliers that, perhaps because of a cost advantage, prefer to compete on price. Some vendors might view purchasers who choose suppliers via bidding as desirable, while others might avoid them.

Purchasing Criteria   The power structure, the nature of buyer-seller relationships, and general purchasing policies all affect purchasing criteria. Benefit segmentation in the consumer goods market is the process of segmenting a market in terms of the reasons why customers buy. It is, in fact, the most insightful form of consumer goods segmentation because it deals directly with customer needs. In the industrial market, consideration of the criteria used to make purchases and the application for these purchases, which we consider later, approximate the benefit segmentation approach.

SITUATIONAL FACTORS

Up to this point we have focused on the grouping of customer companies. Now we consider the role of the purchase situation, even single-line entries on the order form.

Situational factors resemble operating variables but are temporary and require a more detailed knowledge of the customer. They include the urgency of order fulfillment, product application, and the size of order.

Urgency of Order Fulfillment   It is worthwhile to differentiate between products to be used in routine replacement or for building a new plant and those for emergency replacement of existing parts. Some companies have found a degree of urgency useful for market selection and for developing a focused marketing-manufacturing approach leading to a "hot-order shop"—a factory that can supply small, urgent orders quickly.

A supplier of large-size, heavy-duty stainless steel pipe fittings, for example, defined its primary market as fast-order replacements. A chemical plant or paper mill needing to replace a fitting quickly is often willing to pay a premium price for a vendor's application engineering, for flexible manufacturing capacity, and for installation skills that would be unnecessary with routine replacement parts.

Product Application   The requirements for a 5-horsepower motor used in intermittent service in a refinery will differ from those of a 5-horsepower motor in continuous use. Requirements for an intermittent-service motor will vary depending on whether its reliability is critical to the operation or safety of the refinery. Product application can have a major impact on the purchase process and purchase criteria and thus on the choice of vendor.

Size of Order   Market selection can begin with the individual line entries on the order form. A company with highly automated equipment might segment the market so that it can concentrate only on items with large unit volumes. A nonautomated company, on the other hand, might want only small-quantity, short-run items. Ideal for these vendors would be an order that is split up into long-run and short-run items. In many industries, such as paper and pipe fittings, distributors break up orders in this way.

Marketers can differentiate individual orders in terms of product uses as well as users. The distinction is important; users may seek different suppliers for the same product under different circumstances. The pipe-fittings manufacturer that focused on urgent orders is a good example of a marketing approach based on these differences.

Situational factors can greatly affect purchasing approaches. General Motors, for example, makes a distinction between product purchases—that is, raw materials or components for a product being produced—and nonproduct purchases. Urgency of order fulfillment is so powerful that it can change both the purchase process and the criteria used. An urgent replacement is generally purchased on the basis of availability, not price.

The interaction between situational factors and purchasing approaches is an example of the permeability of segmentation nests. Factors in one nest affect those in other nests. Industry criteria, for instance, an outer-nest demographic description, influence but do not determine application, a middle-nest situational criterion. The nests are a useful mental construct but not a clean framework of independent units because in the complex reality of industrial markets, criteria are interrelated.

The nesting approach cannot be applied in a cookbook fashion but requires, instead, careful, intelligent judgment.

———— BUYERS' PERSONAL CHARACTERISTICS

People, not companies, make purchase decisions, although the or-ganizational framework in which they work and company policies and needs may constrain their choices. Marketers for industrial goods, like those for consumer products, can segment markets according to the individuals involved in a purchase in terms of buyer-seller similarity, buyer motivation, individual perceptions, and risk-management strategies.

Some buyers are risk averse, others risk receptive. The level of risk a buyer is willing to assume is related to other personality variables such as personal style, intolerance for ambiguity, and self-confidence. The amount of attention a purchasing agent will pay to cost factors depends not only on the degree of uncertainty about the consequences of the decision but also on whether credit or blame for these will accrue to him or her. Buyers who are risk averse are not good prospects for new products and concepts. Risk-averse buyers also tend to avoid untested vendors.

Some buyers are meticulous in their approach to buying—they shop around, look at a number of vendors, and then split their order to assure delivery. Others rely on old friends and past relationships and seldom make vendor comparisons.[2] Companies can segment a market in terms of these preferences.

Data on personal characteristics are expensive and difficult to gather. It is often worthwhile to develop good, formal sales information systems to ensure that salespeople transmit the data they gather to the marketing department for use in developing segmented marketing strategies. One chemical company attributes part of its sales success to its sales information system's routine collection of data on buyers. Such data-gathering efforts are most justified in the case of customers with large sales potential.

———— REASSEMBLING THE NEST

Marketers are interested in purchase decisions that depend on com-pany variables, situational factors, and the personal characteristics of the

---

2. For further discussion, *see* Thomas V. Bonoma, "Major Sales: Who *Really* Does the Buying?" *Harvard Business Review* (May–June 1982): 111, and Benson P. Shapiro and Ronald Posner, "Making the Major Sale," *Harvard Business Review* (March–April 1976): 68.

buyers. The three outer nests, as *Exhibit 2* shows, cover company variables; the fourth inner-middle nest, situational factors; and the innermost nest, personal characteristics.

Moving from the outer to the inner nests, the segmentation criteria change in terms of visibility, permanence, and intimacy. The data in the outer nests are generally highly visible (even to outsiders), are more or less permanent, and require little intimate knowledge of customers. But situational factors and personal characteristics are less visible, are more transient, and require extensive vendor research.

An industrial marketing executive can choose from a wide range of segmentation approaches other than the nested approach. In fact, the myriad of possibilities often has one of the four following outcomes:

- *No segmentation.* "The problem is too large to approach."
- *After-the-fact segmentation.* "Our market research shows that we have captured a high share of the distribution segment and low shares of the others; thus we must be doing something right for customers in high-share segments."
- *Superficial segmentation.* "While we know all banks are different, it's easier to organize marketing plans around banks because we can identify them and tell the salespeople whom to call on." This dangerous outcome gives a false sense of security.
- *Obtuse, convoluted, and disorganized segmentation.* "We have a 300-page report on market segmentation and customer buying patterns, but there is just too much information in there. So we have decided to focus on insurance companies and hospitals to avoid another two-day market planning meeting."

The hierarchical structure approach is easy to use. Marketers can, in most cases, work systematically from the outer nests to the inner nests. They can run through the whole set of criteria and identify important factors that otherwise might be neglected. And they can balance between reliance on the easily acquired data of the outer nests and the detailed analyses of the inner nests.

We suggest that a marketer begin at the outside nest and work inward because data are more available and definitions clearer in the outer nests. On the other hand, the situational and personal variables of the inner nests are often the most useful. In our experience, managers most frequently neglect situational criteria. In situations where knowledge and analysis exist, a marketer might decide to begin at a middle nest and work inward or, less probably, outward.

After several attempts at working completely through the process, companies will discover which segmentation criteria are likely to yield greater benefits than others and which cannot be considered carefully without better data. A warning is necessary, however. A company should not decide that an approach is *not* useful because data are lacking. The segmentation process requires that assessments of analytic promise and data availability be made

EXHIBIT 2
Classification of Nests

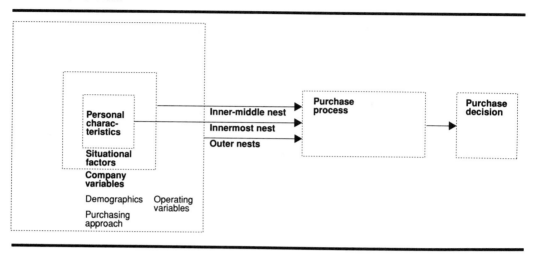

independently. The two steps should not be confused. When the necessary data are gathered, managers can weigh segmentation approaches.

A fine line exists between minimizing the cost and difficulty of segmentation by staying in the outer nests on the one hand and gaining the useful data of the inner nests at appreciable direct and indirect cost on the other. The outer-nest criteria are generally inadequate when used by themselves in all but the most simple or homogeneous markets because they ignore buying differences among customers. Overemphasis on the inner-nest factors, however, can be too expensive and time-consuming for small markets. We suggest achieving a sense of balance between the simplicity and low cost of the outer nests and the richness and expense of the inner ones by making the choices explicit and the process clear and disciplined.

▬▬▬ DISCUSSION QUESTIONS

1. Why is segmenting the industrial market much more complex than segmenting the consumer market? What issues make it more difficult? What variables complicate market analysis and selection?

2. The amount of investigation required to gather the voluminous and complex data necessary for industrial market segmentation is often discouraging to marketers. The authors present a unique approach for segmenting industrial markets. How does their approach facilitate the segmentation process? Will their approach work in every situation?

3. What kind of interaction may or may not take place between large and small companies? Between companies of varying proximity? Between marketers and individual industries?

4. To develop an effective sales strategy, say the authors, it is important to determine the personal characteristics of the buyers, but they caution that this can be a very complex and expensive undertaking. What factors complicate this procedure? What approaches would you use to gather this kind of sensitive information?

5. The authors acknowledge other approaches to market segmentation besides theirs but criticize them as faulty and ineffective. How do they justify this criticism? Do you agree?

PART FIVE

THE MARKETING MIX

The marketing mix is aptly named. It is the multifaceted blend of all the elements that comprise an organization's marketing operations. The approaches used by marketers are many and varied, and the subtle art of mixing, matching, and combining elements into a plan that works for a particular situation is the essence of marketing. The following readings review important concepts related to the marketing mix and summarize key relationships among the elements constituting the mix.

Concept of the Marketing Mix   12

NEIL H. BORDEN

Just what elements of the marketing program comprise an effective marketing mix? And what are the market forces that must be understood and adjusted to in a suitable mix? These and other questions dealing with the endless variations that can go into any marketing program are addressed in this brief reading. It provides a helpful approach to analyzing any marketing problem and to creating a mix that will achieve the company's goals.

In marketing operations the businessperson constantly searches for a marketing mix that will produce a profit for any product or line of products to be sold. Generally, in striving to maintain or improve profit position, he or she is an empiricist, trying changes on the procedures and policies that make up a marketing program. Success depends almost entirely on the marketer's understanding of market forces bearing on the product or product line and on his or her skill in devising a mix of methods that take advantage of these forces in such a way as to produce satisfactory net profits.

The marketing programs that have evolved under this empirical approach are as tremendously varied as company operating statements. Even in the same industry there is little uniformity among manufacturers; there is simply no standard expenditure for marketing. The same holds true among many retail and wholesale trades, where methods of operation otherwise tend to greater uniformity.

The ratios of sales devoted to the various functions of marketing are so widely diverse because, in large part, products, volume of sales, market covered, and other facts that govern operations tend to be unique to each company and not conducive to uniformity—except in companies whose product lines are subject to the same market forces. In general, however, the percentage of sales spent in any category of marketing expense covers wide ranges. The expense figure for advertising, for example, will vary among manufacturers from almost 0% to over 50%. The percentage of sales devoted to personal selling will cover a similarly wide range.

For example, manufacturers of over-the-counter proprietary medications often have no sales force. Advertising sells the product to consumers and literally pulls the product through the channels of distribution. At the retail level little or no effort is made to secure selling support. In contrast, manufacturers of, for example, heavy machinery put relatively little of the burden of selling on advertising and rely primarily on the push of personal selling by either their own sales force or those of distributors.

The role played in the marketing programs by distributors also varies markedly. Sometimes their close support and cooperation is actively sought (as in the case of heavy appliances). In other instances little effort is devoted to securing the involvement of the distributive trade (as in the proprietary medicine example). A similar lack of uniformity is evident in the employment of promotional devices and of retail point-of-purchase efforts.

Pricing and pricing policy also present wide variations. Whereas in some instances competition occurs largely in terms of price and margins are narrow, in other instances prices are set within wide margins and competition occurs on the basis of product quality, service, or advertising. For some goods resale prices are maintained; for others they are not.

In short, these and other elements of marketing programs can be combined in many ways. Or, stated another way, the marketing mixes for different types of products vary widely—and, even for the same class of product, competing companies may employ different mixes.

Moreover, a company may over time change its marketing mix for a given product, for in a dynamic world the marketer must adjust to changing market forces in search of a mix that will prove profitable. The various elements of the program have to be combined and recombined in a logically integrated program that takes account of market changes as they relate to the product.

Thus, the concept of the marketing mix refers to a schematic plan to guide analysis of marketing efforts by utilizing (a) a list of the forces emanating from the market that bear upon the marketing operations of an enterprise, and (b) a plan of the marketing procedures and policies to best achieve the objectives of the enterprise at a given time.

Just what elements of the marketing program comprise an effective marketing mix? What are the market forces that must be understood and adjusted to in a proper mix? The following outline incorporates all the important elements and forces that marketers need to analyze in formulating an appropriate marketing mix.

I. Market forces bearing upon the marketing mix
   A. Consumer attitudes and habits
      1. Motivation of users
      2. Buying habits and attitudes
      3. Import trends bearing on livings habits and attitudes
   B. Trade attitudes and methods
      1. Motivation of trade
      2. Trade structure
      3. Trade practices and attitudes
      4. Trends in trade procedures, methods, attitudes
   C. Competition
      1. Is competition on a price or nonprice basis?

2. What are the choices afforded consumers
    a. In products?
    b. In price?
    c. In service?
3. What is the relation of supply to demand?
4. What is your position in the market—size and strength relative to competitors?
    a. Number of firms
    b. Degree of concentration
5. What indirect competition *vs.* direct competition?
6. Competitors' plans—what new developments in products, pricing, or selling plans are impending?
7. Competitors' attitudes—behavior
8. What moves is the competition likely to make to actions taken by your firm?
D. Governmental controls
    1. Over product
    2. Over pricing
    3. Over competitive practices
    4. Over advertising and promotion

II. Elements of the marketing mix of manufacturers
    A. Merchandising—product planning
        1. Determination of product (or service) to be sold—qualities, design, etc.; to whom, when, where, and in what quantities?
        2. Determination of new product program—research and development, merger
        3. Determination of marketing research program
    B. Pricing
        1. Determination of level of prices
        2. Determination of psychological aspects of price, e.g., odd or even
        3. Determination of pricing policy, e.g., one price or varying price, use of price maintenance, etc.
        4. Determination of margins: freedom in setting?
    C. Branding
        1. Determination of brand policy, e.g., individualized brand or family brand
    D. Channels of distribution
        1. Determination of channels to use
            a. Direct sale to user
            b. Direct sale to retailers or users' sources of purchase, e.g., supply houses
            c. Sale through wholesalers
        2. Determination of degree of selectivity among dealers

3. Devising of programs to secure channel cooperation
E. Personal selling
   1. Determination of burden to be placed on personal selling and methods to be employed
      a. For manufacturer's organization
      b. For wholesalers
      c. For retailers
   2. Organization, selection, training, and guidance of sales force at various levels of distribution
F. Advertising
   1. Determination of appropriation—burden to be placed on advertising
   2. Determination of copy policy
   3. Determination of mix of advertising
      a. To trade
      b. To consumers
   4. Determination of media
G. Promotions
   1. Determination of burden to place on special selling plans or devices and formulation of promotions
      a. To trade
      b. To consumers
H. Packaging—determination of importance of packaging and formulation of packages
I. Display—determination of importance and devising of procedures
J. Servicing—determination of importance of service and devising of procedures to meet consumer needs and desires
K. Physical handling
   1. Warehousing
   2. Transportation
   3. Inventory policy
L. Fact-finding and analysis—marketing research

—— DISCUSSION QUESTIONS

1. The author makes the observation that there is no such thing as a "standard" marketing program among companies and manufacturers, even in the same industry. Why do you think concentration on the various elements of the marketing mix varies so much from company to company? How is it that different companies in the same business can reach the same level of success, yet show wide variation in their advertising expenditures, selling efforts, volume of sales, broadness of distribution, and so on?

2. In designing a "proper" marketing mix, a company is influenced by outside market forces and internal procedural elements. Describe important aspects of both and explain how they affect the formulation of a marketing program.

3. The author points out that the marketing operations of an organization are an ever-changing blend of elements designed to achieve different goals at different times. What challenges does this present to an organization as changes occur in the marketplace? How are goals affected? How are elements of the marketing mix affected?

4. How might the marketing mix for a consumer good differ from one for an industrial manufacturer's product? Contrast the two.

13   The Marketing Mix

BENSON P. SHAPIRO

This reading reviews the important concepts related to the marketing mix and summarizes the key relationships within the mix and between the mix and other aspects of the company's marketing approach. It suggests a number of analytical approaches companies can use to create a marketing mix that fits the market, company, and competitive situation.

One of the most striking aspects of marketing is the great variety of marketing approaches different companies use. Of course, the marketing approaches of companies that offer toothpaste differ greatly from those that offer coal-fed boilers for electric generation. Major differences in the cost of the product, size of the market, amount of labor required in making a choice, and the overall significance of the purchasing decision are reflected in the approaches.

More surprising are the variations among marketers of the same product categories. Cosmetics, for example, are sold in a myriad of ways. Avon has a direct sales force of several hundred thousand people who call on individual consumers. Charles of the Ritz and Estée Lauder use selective distribution through department stores. Cover Girl and Del Laboratories market their products in chain drugstores and other mass merchandisers. Cover Girl does a great deal of advertising, while Del emphasizes personal selling and promotions, and Redken sells exclusively through beauticians. Revlon's strategy encompasses a wide variety of approaches. How do we understand all these variations?

The purpose of this reading is to look at the marketing mix as an integrated whole, to provide tools that will explain why some programs prosper and others fail, and to improve readers' ability to predict, before the fact, which programs will succeed and which will not.

—— MARKETING PROGRAMS

A marketing program is made up of the various elements of the mix and the relationships among them. A useful way to look at each element and subelement separately, and in pairs, is the sales response curve. In its simplest

EXHIBIT
The Sales Response Curve

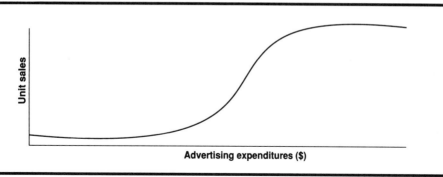

form, the curve shows the relationship between sales, usually measured in units but sometimes in dollars, and a marketing input measured in either physical or financial (e.g., dollars) terms, as shown in the *Exhibit*.

The same relationship can be represented by a mathematical function or a chart listing unit sales and advertising expenditures. The graphical representation of the sales response curve is more meaningful to most people.

A more sophisticated sales response curve will have two independent variables with one dependent variable—sales. One might, for example, picture a graph of the relationship between the number of sales calls and advertisements as the independent (input) variables and unit sales as the dependent (output) variable.

Sales response curves enable a marketer to study the relationship between a given level of expenditure in one or more marketing areas and the likely level of sales. Even more powerfully, however, it demonstrates how sales are affected by changes in expenditure. The *Exhibit*, for example, implies that as advertising expenditures increase, they have little impact initially, then a great deal of impact, and, finally, little impact again. Thus, the marketer can understand the dynamics of the relationships and interactions of the two elements.

The subject of interaction brings us naturally to the concept of the marketing mix itself, which emphasizes the fit of the various pieces and the quality and size of their interactions.

There are three degrees of interaction. The least demanding is consistency. Consistency is the lack of a poor fit between two or more elements in a mix. It would seem generally inconsistent, for example, to sell a high-quality product (product quality) through a low-quality retailer (distribution channels). Sometimes it is done successfully, but it is difficult to maintain such an apparent inconsistency over a long period of time.

The second level of positive relationship among elements of the mix is integration. While consistency is the lack of a poor fit, integration is the presence of a positive, harmonious interaction among the elements of the mix. For example, heavy advertising can sometimes be harmonious with a high price, because the added margin from the high price pays for the advertising and the high advertising creates the brand differentiation that justifies the high price. This does not mean, however, that heavy advertising and high price are always harmonious. Marketing is a very complex area, and each situation must be analyzed on its own merits.

The highest form of relationship is leverage, the situation in which each individual element of the mix is used to the best advantage in support of the total mix. A good example relates to the sales response curve introduced earlier. Even though it would not be sensible to invest additional advertising dollars in the flat part of the curve (upper end), it might be sensible to invest dollars in other elements of the mix at that time.

PROGRAM/MARKET FIT

The concept of program/market fit encompasses development of a program that fits the needs of the target-market segments. Such a program, in fact, builds solidly upon the concepts of consistency, integration, and leverage. Leverage, for example, involves choice of the most appropriate tools for a particular market segment over other, less efficient[1] tools. The price-sensitive but brand-insensitive consumer, for example, might be better approached with price promotions than with expensive advertising programs or packaging.

If the marketing program is to fit the market, the market must first be carefully and explicitly delineated. If the target has not been defined, it cannot be reached! One of the last steps before launching a program is a holistic analysis of the impact of each element and of the total mix on the people in the target market segment, emphasizing tests for consistency, integration, and leverage.

PROGRAM/COMPANY FIT

A good program/market fit and a consistent, integrated, and leveraged program are not enough for success. The program must also fit the company. When individuals with unique strengths and weaknesses work in formal organizations, the organizations themselves develop unique patterns of characteristics. These attributes relate to the human and cultural environment of the organization as well as to such material aspects as its financial strength and manufacturing prowess.

---

1. Efficiency, in this sense, corresponds to the engineering concept of output per unit of input. Thus, we might look at unit sales generated per dollar of advertising or personal selling to determine which is more efficient or what combination of the two is most efficient.

A marketing program must match the strengths of the company or organization that is implementing it. An organization with extensive mass advertising experience and expertise, for example, is more likely to be able to carry out a program that leans heavily on advertising than an organization less strong in that particular area. Over time, these behavioral or cultural attributes can change, but the rate of change is limited. It takes quite a while for a company that does not understand advertising to develop a strength in that area. The ability to identify and recruit experts from other companies takes time and, often, several trial-and-error cycles. One person, furthermore, generally cannot change a whole culture, particularly of a large organization. Clearly, the behavioral fit between the program and the company must be carefully considered.

Behavioral aspects go beyond just marketing, to the company at large; a marketing program must fit the company's broader capabilities. For example, a company that stresses efficient manufacturing and distribution and administrative austerity may very successfully carry out a price-oriented strategy but fail miserably with an account-oriented marketing program that calls for a customer-oriented culture with responsive operating and logistics people.

As we look beyond marketing, we must also consider the tangible effects of other corporate strengths and weaknesses. The large plant with facilities for long production runs, for example, is well suited to a marketing strategy based on a narrow product line and intense price orientation. By the same token, a company with a strong balance sheet and low cost of capital can much more easily accommodate a marketing program requiring generous credit terms than can its more financially limited competitor.

Market position can also help to determine the most sensible mix for a marketing program. The market-share leader, for example, gains when its astute marketing mix of national advertising, company-owned distribution, and heavy research and development encourages the industry to compete on a fixed-cost basis. Its position enables it to spread fixed costs over the larger unit volume and realize a lower cost per unit sold than smaller competitors.

Small unit-share competitors or niche marketers, on the other hand, need marketing programs that stress variable costs so that their cost per unit sold equals that of the largest competitors. Smaller companies, therefore, often emphasize intensive price promotions, a commission sales force, and independent distributors.

—— COMPETITOR/PROGRAM FIT

An effective marketing program must not only fit the company's own strengths and weaknesses, it must also take account of competitors' programs. Discussion of three topics can clarify questions about marketing-program design as they relate to the competition.

1. The concept of competitor/program fit
2. The "Why can't we emulate them?" question
3. The competitive-response matrix

Competitive/program fit can be defined as the characteristics of a marketing program that, while building on a company's strengths and shielding its weaknesses, protects it from competitors by capitalizing on *their* weaknesses, in the process creating a unique market personality and position. Accomplishing this set of tasks requires meticulous analysis and honest introspection. The most serious danger, other than that of neglecting the issue altogether, is underestimating both the strength of the competition and the weaknesses of one's own company.

Perhaps the height of disregard for the difference in situations is embodied in a question that is very frequently posed: "Why can't we emulate them?" The answer is twofold. First, the strengths of the leading competitor are almost certainly different from those of any other competitor. Second, in all likelihood, the leading competitor took command when the market was quite different. Most important, the market leader probably did not exist in its present form, nor was there another firm of equal stature and situation. Thus the leader expanded into a vacuum that no longer existed after it filled it. For these reasons, companies that blindly attempt to imitate the leader usually fail, often painfully.

The concept of the marketing mix can provide a powerful tool to view competitors as they compete with one another by emphasizing different elements and mixtures of those elements. A useful way to visualize alternative action/reaction patterns is the competitive-response matrix.[2] A simple matrix might include two companies and three subelements of the marketing mix, such as price, product quality, and advertising. The matrix would look like this:

		Company A		
		Price	*Quality*	*Advertising*
	Price	$C_{p,p}$	$C_{q,p}$	$C_{a,p}$
Company B	*Quality*	$C_{p,q}$	$C_{q,q}$	$C_{a,q}$
	Advertising	$C_{p,a}$	$C_{q,a}$	$C_{a,a}$

The coefficients (the Cs of the matrix) represent the probability of Company B responding to Company A's move. Thus the coefficient $C_{a,p}$ represents the probability of Company B responding with a price cut (top row of matrix) to Company A's increase in advertising (right-hand column of matrix). The diagonal ($C_{p,p}$, $C_{q,q}$, $C_{a,a}$) represents the likelihood of Company B responding to a move by Company A with the same marketing tool (e.g., meet a price cut

---

2. J. Lambin, *Advertising, Competition and Market Conduct in Oligopoly Over Time* (New York: American Elsevier, 1976).

with a price cut). The coefficients can be estimated by the study of past behavior and by management judgment.

The competitive response matrix is a flexible, analytical approach. For example, one can include many marketing tools and add more rows for delayed responses (e.g., will they cut price immediately or wait a month or a quarter?) and additional competitors.

The competitive response matrix can help develop a distinctive approach to the market by enabling a company to see how it can differentiate its program from the marketing program of competitors.

Such competitive analyses have proven useful to many companies and are particularly important for making major irreversible capital commitments. The essence of all these programs is role playing, in which executives and marketers take the parts of the major competitor or competitors. Some companies have even devised elaborate competitive games built around their industry, with one or several company executives representing each competitor. The response matrix can be usefully incorporated into programs of this kind.

⸻ THE EXPANDED MIX

Like most concepts, the marketing mix is an abstraction, and real marketing programs do not always fit perfectly the product, price, communication, and distribution paradigm. In fact, several parts of the mix—promotion, brand, and terms and conditions—fall at the interface of two elements.

Promotion, which is defined strictly as short-term price cuts to the trade and consumer incentives such as coupons, contests, and price allowances, actually shares characteristics with both price and communication.

Brand, which is often viewed as an aspect of product, is clearly also part of communications and can serve to help coordinate product policy and communication.

Terms and conditions relate to a myriad of contractual elements that, though closely related to price (payment terms, credit, leasing, delivery schedules, etc.), are so close to personal selling that they can be viewed as an interface between price and communications. Other elements such as service support, logistical arrangements, and so forth also relate to product policy. The important thing is to recognize their usefulness as marketing tools without worrying about categorizing them.

⸻ CONCLUSION

Implicit in this reading are several questions that, if answered through careful analysis, can help a company to focus on the most important aspects of the total marketing mix and their fit with the market, company, and competitive situation.

1. Are the elements of the marketing mix consistent with one another?
2. Do the elements add up to a harmonious, integrated whole?
3. Is each element being used to its best leverage?
4. Does the total program, as well as each element, meet the needs of the carefully and explicitly defined target market segment?
5. Does the marketing mix build on the organization's cultural and tangible strengths, and does it either avoid weaknesses or imply a clear program to correct them?
6. Does the marketing mix create a distinctive personality in the competitive marketplace and protect the company from the strongest competitors?

Copyright © 1984; revised 1991.

———— DISCUSSION QUESTIONS

1. What are the advantages of having the elements of the marketing mix closely integrated with one another? What are the disadvantages when the elements are not integrated?
2. What role does the marketing mix play in the competitive arena?
3. The author contends that a company that attempts to imitate its leading competitor usually fails. On what does he base this statement? Are there any instances where this premise could be proven wrong?
4. Assume your product is very similar to the product of your leading competitor. What are some of the considerations you would address in designing your marketing approach?
5. Why is it so important to define the market when planning a company's marketing approach? How does defining the market influence how the marketing mix is shaped?

PRODUCT DECISIONS

One of the most important elements of the marketing mix—and probably the most complicated one—is product policy. It is inextricably tied into a firm's marketing program; in fact, the organization's choice of products and services affects its entire marketing operation. Product policy depends on many variables, including market conditions, competition, pricing, distribution, communications, and, especially, the attributes of the product itself. For what is marketed to the consumer is not simply the product but a total concept—what the product means to the consumer and what benefits it brings with it.

The next readings attempt to shed light on this complex subject by focusing on the principal issues and criteria involved in product policy decisions.

Product Policy 14

JOHN A. QUELCH

Product policy decisions center around what goods and services a firm should offer for sale and what features they should incorporate. This reading focuses on these choices as they involve matching company resources and needs with market opportunities. Formulation of a successful product policy, therefore, requires a careful analysis of existing and potential products as they relate to the characteristics of both the market and the firm. Perhaps most important, the reading emphasizes the dynamic nature of the marketplace and the necessity of making product policy decisions flexible enough to adjust or reposition a product in response to changing forces.

The determination of product policy is central to an organization's marketing effort. A firm's choice of products influences all other elements of its marketing program and has significant implications for such other functional areas as finance, production and operations, and human resources management. So important is product policy that many firms structure their organizations around products, with individual product managers responsible for the marketing and profitability of each product or product line.

The word *product* connotes a physical good; however, in its marketing sense it also includes intangible services offered before, at, or after the time of sale. The entire package is sometimes referred to as the augmented product. The mix of tangibles and intangibles in the augmented product varies from one product or service to another. A manufacturer of canned vegetables is required to deliver few incremental services to the consumer beyond the physical product. On the other hand, a passenger airline's reason for being is the delivery of the service; its planes are tangible goods that permit it to do so and act as visual symbols of the service organization. Although this reading emphasizes product policy formulation from the standpoint of profitmaking private firms, nonprofit and government organizations are faced with similar decisions.

The following issues are typical of the varied product policy decisions faced by managements of different organizations.

- A major automobile producer considers dropping its line of large luxury sedans and broadening its small-car line.
- A well-known ski equipment firm debates purchase of a company that makes scuba and diving gear.

- A liberal arts college reviews the feasibility of adding a professional degree program to its curriculum.
- A manufacturer of high-quality electric motors considers developing an inexpensive utility model with lower performance characteristics.
- A manufacturer of private-label socks wonders whether to introduce its first branded line.
- A toy company evaluates whether to withdraw a recently introduced product after a safety hazard is uncovered.
- A manufacturer of health and beauty aids examines the implications of altering package sizes in its line of denture adhesives.

For many companies, appraising the need for changes in the product line is a continuing process, reflecting the dynamic nature of the marketplace as well as changes in the nature and resources of the firm itself. One objective should be to eliminate or modify products that no longer satisfy consumer needs or fail to contribute significantly (directly or indirectly) to the well-being of the firm. Another set of objectives relates to the addition of new products or product features that will better meet consumer needs, enhance the company's existing product line, or improve utilization of resources.

▬▬ PRODUCT DECISIONS

Most companies are multiproduct organizations, often producing a variety of different product lines. This means that policy decisions may be made at the level of individual products, product lines, or the company's entire product mix.

Individual product items have separate designations on the seller's list and include different flavors or colors, different forms of the same product, and different sizes.

Product lines are a group of different products that are related in the sense that they satisfy a particular class of need, are used together, and possess common physical or technical characteristics. They are sold to the same customer groups through the same channels, and fall within specific price ranges.

The product mix is the composite of products offered for sale by a firm. Although a particular product item—or even an entire product line—may not be profitable in itself, it may contribute to the well-being of the firm by enhancing the overall product mix, particularly among customers who wish to deal with a full-line supplier. Some large corporations produce several thousand product items, grouped into a wide variety of different product lines, which together constitute the firm's product mix.

Closely associated with these three levels of product decisions are the concepts of breadth, depth, and consistency of product mix. Breadth of product mix refers to the number of different product lines marketed by the company.

Depth of product mix designates the average number of items (e.g., sizes, weights, colors) offered in each product line. Consistency of product mix alludes to the degree of similarity between product lines in end use, technology and production techniques, distribution channels, and so forth.

Product-mix decisions tend to reflect not only the nature of the market and the resources of the firm, but also the underlying philosophy of company management. Most firms are faced with several options over time. Some pursue a policy of diversity, while others prefer to concentrate efforts on a narrow product mix, offered in a limited number of sizes and varieties.

A firm's choice of product strategy should be determined by management's long-run objectives for profit levels, sales stability, and growth, as modified by personal values and attitudes toward risk. Market opportunities for the firm's product mix determine the upper limits for potential corporate profitability, while the quality of the marketing program tends to determine the extent to which this potential is achieved.

While the ideal product mix is likely to vary from firm to firm and may be hard to define, certain situations suggest a suboptimal mix:

1. Chronic or seasonally recurring excess capacity in the firm's production, storage, or transportation facilities
2. A very high proportion of profits coming from a small percentage of product items
3. Inefficient use of the sales force's contacts and skills
4. Steadily declining profits or sales

When the product line is narrower than optimum, there is a loss in economies of scale. On the other hand, when the product line is broader than optimum, the firm suffers from excessive costs in manufacturing changeovers, order processing, and inventory management.

——— ADJUSTMENTS TO THE PRODUCT MIX

Changes in product policy designed to correct any of the above situations or otherwise enhance the firm's ability to meet established objectives can take one of three basic forms.

Product Abandonment   This step involves discontinuing either individual items or an entire line. Candidates for elimination include products for which demand is so low that uneconomically short production runs or uneconomically frequent price and inventory adjustments are required; products that absorb excessive management time relative to their profit contribution; and products that are out of date and, therefore, detract from the company's image.

Product Modification   Changes may involve either tangible or intangible product attributes and may be achieved by reformulation, redesign, changing unit sizes, and adding or removing features.

New-Product Introduction   Besides developing, test marketing, and commercializing new products or product lines, this might include an addition or extension to one of the company's existing product lines or a me-too imitation of a competitor's product line. In all cases, management must decide what brand name the new item(s) should carry. Frequently, there is a trade-off between the advertising economies of scale associated with extending an existing brand name and the higher costs of cannibalization—when new products "steal" sales from existing products.

THE NEW-PRODUCT DEVELOPMENT PROCESS

New-product development is widely viewed as a six-stage process:

1. Idea generation
2. Concept screening
3. Business analysis
4. Prototype development
5. Test marketing
6. Commercialization

The purpose at each stage is to increase the information available to management to reduce the risk of a wrong decision—to either continue or abandon a product. Note, however, that the process described here is highly stylized. In practice, steps overlap, are skipped or repeated, or are performed in a different order, depending on the realities of the situation, the urgency of the opportunity, competitive pressures, the judgment and whims of managers, and luck. In addition, the farther a new product moves through the process, the harder it is to cancel, because management develops a commitment to its success.

At the idea-generation stage, creativity is paramount, and the most frequent error is to generate too few ideas, not too many. Typical sources of new ideas are competitive products, implicit or explicit customer requests, ideas from salespeople and distributors, and special idea-generation meetings and committees including marketing, R&D, and manufacturing personnel. Once generated, ideas must be screened to reject clear losers. A set of screening criteria consistent with the company's goals must be established. It is important to identify the highest-priority projects and speed them through the process with special attention and extra resources.

Business analysis requires the development of a preliminary product description. The analysis should specify the target market, financial impact on existing items, opportunity for market development, likelihood of technical success, impact on manufacturing and service operations, and projected financial performance.

If prototype development is warranted, the concept must be carefully transferred from the marketing people to the technical developers. This is often a difficult transfer, as the cultural difference between the marketing department and the laboratory is often great. Each side must understand the other's role, perspective, and limitations.

The product emerges from the laboratory or engineering department as a prototype ready for test marketing. Consumer–packaged-goods test marketing is a precise art. The product is distributed in selected markets supported by the marketing program management expects to use in a national launch. Often, elements of the marketing program, such as the advertising and promotion budget, are the object of experimentation in the test markets. Because test marketing is expensive and broadcasts a company's intentions, a competitor may reach national distribution with an imitation product before an innovator has even finished analyzing its test-market data.

In the industrial arena, test marketing is different. Products are often shown to a few selected friendly customers for evaluation. These customers, known as beta test sites in electronics and related industries, report their experiences with the prototype. Good marketers send personnel to the test sites to monitor the units' performance and ensure that all relevant test data are carefully gathered and analyzed.

Toward the end of the test-market phase, a revised marketing program is developed. Volume and price forecasts are refined so that production and service capacity can be added.

Finally, the product is introduced into the commercial marketplace in a major national or international launch, a region-by-region rollout in the case of consumer goods, or a customer-by-customer or market-segment-by-market-segment rollout for industrial goods.

Few concepts that are generated in the first step of the process make it to prototype development. Fewer still reach commercialization, and even fewer succeed as established products.

The nature and length of the process and of each step and the relative importance of the steps vary by type of product, degree of newness, and the size of the company. A new flavor added to a line of food products may require more marketing investment than R&D effort and be executed within a year. Such a line extension is easily understood, fits into the established product line, and involves little risk. On the other hand, a new drug might require over a decade to be developed and to receive necessary government approval, and marketing costs would be much less than the R&D investment.

Such a discontinuous process of new-product development involves a great many risks: technological risk (Can we make a prototype?); marketing risk (If we can, will anyone buy it?); manufacturing and operating risk (Can we make it in volume?); and financial risk (Can we sell it at a price that will generate enough revenue to amortize the development process?).

Smaller companies with more limited resources tend to be more entrepreneurial and to commercialize an idea much more quickly than larger companies. In the latter, projects require many layers of executive approval in corporate cultures that generally discourage risk taking. Since the 1970s, large companies have attempted to foster more entrepreneurship and faster product development through new-product venture teams, while smaller companies have often been better funded because of the development of the venture capital marketplace. In addition, industries accustomed to rapid technological change tend to be more adept at managing the process. For example, electronics companies of all sizes innovate more quickly and easily than steel companies.

A good product-development process leads to successful products, while a poor one is unlikely to generate success. Unfortunately, the lag time between idea generation and commercialization is often so long that monitoring the process is a difficult task. Perhaps the best insurance a company can have is a portfolio of products at various stages of development. It is also worth noting that a process that produces few failures is probably too conservative and will not lead to major new-product successes. More than likely it will produce only safe but minor product modifications.

———— PRODUCT POSITIONING

Positioning is management's concept of where a product or service should stand in the marketplace relative to competitive products and services. An organization's ability to compete effectively in any given market is determined in large measure by its ability to position its product(s) appropriately relative to (1) the needs of specific market segments, and (2) the nature of competitive entries. Product positioning therefore requires a synthesis of consumer analysis and competitor analysis.

In developing a position for a new product, management first discovers the range of benefits or attributes consumers use to make choices in the product category. Second, it identifies key consumer segments within the overall market for the product. Third, management evaluates, on the basis of experience and/or market research data, the relative importance of each benefit to each segment.

In addition to this consumer analysis, management must consider how existing products perform in each area of interest to consumers. In choosing a position for a new product, management matches an appropriate package of benefits, clearly differentiated from competitive offerings on important dimensions, with a specific target segment whose needs are not fully satisfied by existing products. Positioning permits a firm to finesse the competition instead of competing head on.

Product positions often reflect not only intrinsic product characteristics but also the image created by promotional strategies, pricing decisions, and choice of distribution channels. Selective use of alternative brand names in multibrand companies may also help to achieve the desired image. For instance, the Mercury name, owned by Ford, carries different connotations for car buyers than does the Ford brand itself.

Effective positioning is essential to a product's success. If management does not consciously position a product, consumers will be confused, and competitive products that are precisely positioned will enjoy an advantage. At the same time, a product's positioning must be flexible enough to adjust to changes in competitive products and consumer needs.

——— REPOSITIONING

Instead of physically modifying an existing product, firms sometimes elect to reposition the product by revising such elements of the marketing mix as advertising and promotion, distribution strategy, pricing, or packaging. However, a revision of the entire mix, including product features, may also accompany a repositioning strategy.

Sometimes repositioning represents a deliberate attempt to attack another firm's product and eat into its market share. In other instances the objective is to avoid head-to-head competition by moving into alternative market segments with good potential whose needs are not presently well served.

Analysis of competitive offerings involves not only a review of product features and other marketing-mix strategies, but also an evaluation of competitive advertising content. The image generated by advertisements and the nature of the slogans employed may constitute a major positioning tool, especially for such image-intensive products as cosmetics, liquor, and apparel.

Repositioning along price and quality/functionality dimensions is generally referred to as "trading up" or "trading down." However, repositioning may also involve sideways moves in which price and quality remain basically similar but modifications are made to a product's tangible benefits or image to enhance its appeal to different types of consumers or for alternative end uses.

Examples of repositioning existing products include advertising a deodorant formerly promoted only to men as "the deodorant for all the family"; reducing the price of a felt-tip pen to take advantage of a perceived market need for a cheaper model; modifying the assortment at a supermarket chain to improve its appeal to family groups; and giving an airline a more exciting image through changes in aircraft color schemes and uniforms and addition of on-board service frills—then promoting these in a glamorous advertising campaign.

——— EVALUATING PRODUCT/COMPANY FIT

The fact that good opportunities exist in the marketplace for a new or repositioned product does not necessarily mean that the organization should proceed with such a product. Unless there is a good fit between the proposed product and the firm's needs and resources, the net result of a decision to proceed might be harmful, or at best, suboptimal.

Among the dimensions to consider when evaluating product/company fit are

1. Technological skills of labor and management
2. Size of work force
3. Financial resources
4. Production resources and capacity
5. Logistics facilities
6. Feasibility of using existing sales force and distribution channels
7. Needs and behavior of existing consumers
8. Impact on the market position of the firm's other products
9. Consistency with the organization's existing image
10. Seasonality of demand patterns for existing products. (Will the new product exaggerate existing fluctuations, or will it counter-balance them?)

If a proposed product is not consistent with one or more of the above dimensions, the company should not necessarily drop the idea. Companies in maturing markets, under pressure to diversify, often find that product options with a good product/company fit lack the necessary market-growth potential, and vice versa. In such cases, product/company fit may be sacrificed for the need to diversify. However, the poorer the fit, the larger the financial resources that may be needed either to purchase or to develop internally the requisite skills, production facilities, and market relationships.

——— CONCLUSION

Product policy determination as an on-going task reflects the changing nature of the marketplace. Because an organization's choice of products has such important implications for every facet of the business, it tends to be of great concern to top management.

Key considerations in the formulation of product policy are the skills, contacts, and other resources of the firm, its existing product mix, the corporate objectives established by management, the characteristics of existing and po-tential markets, and the nature of the competition. The process of evaluating product-policy decisions, therefore, involves all the analytical modes employed in marketing—namely, market, consumer, trade, competitive, and economic analyses.

──── DISCUSSION QUESTIONS

1. Deciding which market to serve is important; deciding which products to provide to that market—and when—is even more important. Consider, for example, a new product from one of your competitors that is gaining market share because of a new feature. How would you respond to the competitor's threat to your established market position? Would you change your planned schedule of new product introductions to counteract this threat?

2. Do you believe that product design and product introduction should be driven by the customer and by the competition? Should events in the market shape a company's product policy? Or can a company's product policy manage events in the market—what customers need and how, when, and whether to respond to those needs? Should a company's product policy be guided by management's view of market changes, product characteristics, and product introductions?

3. How does the product life cycle affect product policy decisions? Is it necessary to continually revise your product policy to match the current life-cycle stage of your product?

4. New products—especially in a market undergoing fast-moving technological change—are continually being improved through research and development advances. How would you manage the introduction of a new product that has more advanced features than its earlier version? Is the older product automatically relegated to the "obsolete" stage? Can it be salvaged through proper marketing? What problems does it create for the customer segment that purchased the older version?

5. Describe the dimensions of the relationship between product positioning and pricing policy.

6. Can the same elements of product policy that are applied to physical products also be applied to services?

15   Marketing Success Through Differentiation—of Anything

THEODORE LEVITT

This reading focuses on the importance of differentiating any product or service—even those that seem to differ only in price—from competitors' offerings. The author describes the product attributes that give marketers the opportunity to win customers from the competition and, having won them, to keep them. He further describes the alert, imaginative state of mind that characterizes good management of product differentiation, concluding that "the way in which the manager operates becomes an extension of product differentiation."

There is no such thing as a commodity. All goods and services are differentiable. Though the usual presumption is that this is more true of consumer goods than of industrial goods and services, the opposite is the actual case.

In the marketplace, differentiation is everywhere. Everybody—producer, fabricator, seller, broker, agent, merchant—tries constantly to distinguish his or her offering from all others. This is true even of those who produce and deal in primary metals, grains, chemicals, plastics, and money.

Fabricators of consumer and industrial goods seek competitive distinction via product features—some visually or measurably identifiable, some cosmetically implied, and some rhetorically claimed by reference to real or suggested hidden attributes that promise results or values different from those of competitors' products.

So too with consumer and industrial services—what I call, to be accurate, "intangibles." On the commodities exchanges, for example, dealers in metals, grains, and pork bellies trade in totally undifferentiated generic products. But what they "sell" is the claimed distinction of their execution—the efficiency of their transactions in their clients' behalf, their responsiveness to inquiries, the clarity and speed of their confirmations, and the like. In short, the *offered* product is differentiated, though the *generic* product is identical.

When the generic product is undifferentiated, the offered product makes the difference in getting customers and the delivered product in keeping them. When the knowledgeable senior partner of a well-known Chicago brokerage firm appeared at a New York City bank in a tight-fitting, lime green polyester suit and Gucci shoes to solicit business in financial instrument futures, the outcome was predictably poor. The unintended offering implied by his sartorial appearance contradicted the intended offering of his carefully prepared presentation. No wonder that Thomas Watson the elder insisted so uncompromisingly that his salespeople be attired in their famous IBM "uniforms." While clothes may not make the person, they may help make the sale.

The usual presumption about so-called undifferentiated commodities is that they are exceedingly price sensitive. A fractionally lower price gets the business. That is seldom true except in the imagined world of economics textbooks. In the actual world of markets, nothing is exempt from other considerations, even when price competition rages.

During periods of sustained surplus, excess capacity, and unrelieved price war, when the attention of all seems riveted on nothing save price, it is precisely because price is visible and measurable, and potentially devastating in its effects, that price deflects attention from the possibilities of extricating the product from ravaging price competition. These possibilities, even in the short run, are not confined simply to nonprice competition, such as harder personal selling, intensified advertising, or what's loosely called more or better "services."

To see fully what these possibilities are, it is useful first to examine what exactly a product is.

—— WHAT'S A PRODUCT?

Products are almost always combinations of the tangible and the intangible. An automobile is not simply a machine for movement visibly or measurably differentiated by design, size, color, options, horsepower, or miles per gallon. It is also a complex symbol denoting status, taste, rank, achievement, aspiration, and (these days) being "smart"—that is, buying fuel economy rather than display. But the customer buys even more than these attributes. The enormous efforts of the auto manufacturers to cut the time between placement and delivery of an order and to select, train, supervise, and motivate their dealerships suggest that these too are integral parts of the products people buy and are therefore ways by which products may be differentiated.

In the same way, a computer is not simply a machine for data storage and processing; it is also an operating system with special software protocols for use and promises of maintenance and repair. Carbon fibers are chemical additives that enhance flexuous stiffness, reduce weight, fight fatigue and corrosion, and cut fabrication costs when combined with certain other materials. But carbon fibers have no value for an inexperienced user without the design and applications help that only the experienced seller can provide.

In thousand-page contract proposals by government contractors or five-page consulting proposals to industrial clients, the product is a promise whose commercial substance resides as much in the proposer's carefully curried reputation (or "image") and in the proposal's meticulous packaging as it does in its physical content.

When the substantive content of the products of competing vendors is scarcely differentiable, sales power shifts to differentiating distinctions by which buyers may be influenced. In this regard, there is scant substantive difference among all that's done by Morgan Stanley & Co., Lockheed, Mc-Kinsey & Co., and Revlon. Though each will vigorously proclaim commanding generic distinctions vis-à-vis competitors, each is profoundly preoccupied with packaging—that is, with representing itself as unique. And, indeed, each may be unique, but its uniqueness resides most powerfully in things that transcend its generic offerings.

Take investment banking. Underwriters promise money to issuers and suggest similar promises to buyers. But how these promises are packaged profoundly influences both issuers and buyers. Consider this quotation from a close observer of the industry: "One eminent [U.S. investment banking] house has entrances on two streets, with different stationery printed for each entrance. One door is intended to be more exclusive than the other, and a visitor supposedly can tell the firm's assessment of his or her importance by the entrance indicated on the letterhead of the firm's stationery. . . ."[1] Obviously, the distinctions being made are selling devices based on the assumption that VIP treatment of certain visitors at reception will persuade them of VIP results later in actuality.

To the potential buyer, a product is a complex cluster of value satisfactions. The generic thing is not itself the product; it is merely, as in poker, table stakes—the minimum that is necessary at the outset to give its producer a chance to play the game. It is the playing that gets the results, and in business this means getting and keeping customers.

Customers attach value to a product in proportion to its perceived ability to help solve their problems or meet their needs. All else is derivative. As a specialist in industrial marketing has expressed it, "The 'product' . . . is the total package of benefits the customer receives when he or she buys."[2]

Consider the pragmatism of the Detroit auto manufacturers in buying sheet steel. Detroit buys to exceedingly tight technical specifications, but it specifies much more than the steel itself. It also demands certain delivery conditions and flexibilities, price and payment conditions, and reordering responsiveness. From year to year, the Detroit companies shift the proportions of steel they buy from their various suppliers on the basis of elaborate grading

1. Samuel L. Hayes III, "Investment Banking: Power Structure in Flux," *Harvard Business Review* (March–April 1971): 136.
2. E. Raymond Corey, "Key Options in Market Selection and Product Planning," *Harvard Business Review* (September–October 1975): 119. For an elaboration, see his *Industrial Marketing: Cases and Concepts* (Englewood Cliffs, N.J.: Prentice-Hall, 1976), pp. 40–41; also see Benson P. Shapiro, "Making Money Through Marketing," *Harvard Business Review* (July–August 1979): 136.

systems that measure each supplier's performance on the specified conditions, including the kind and quality of unsolicited help on such matters as new materials ideas, ideas for parts redesign, and even purchasing procedures.

Clearly, Detroit buys a bundle of value satisfactions of which the generic product is only a small portion. If, say, the delivery conditions and flexibilities are not fulfilled—or if they are fulfilled erratically, grudgingly, or only partially—the customer is not getting the product he or she expects. If, moreover, one supplier is more effectively active with new facilitating ideas, that supplier's "product" is better than the competition's. Detroit sees with supreme clarity that No. 302, 72-inch, hot-rolled strip carbon steel is not a commodity. It is a measurably differentiated product.

Customers never just buy the "generic" product like steel, or wheat, or subassemblies, or investment banking, or aspirin, or engineering consultancy, or golf balls, or industrial maintenance, or newsprint, or cosmetics, or even 99% pure isopropyl alcohol. They buy something that transcends these designations—and what that "something" is helps determine from whom they'll buy, what they'll pay, and whether, in the view of the seller, they're "loyal" or "fickle."

What that something is in its customer-getting and customer-satisfying entirety can be managed. To see how it can be managed, it is helpful to look at the process graphically. *Exhibit 1* does this, suggesting that a product consists of a range of possibilities, which I shall now describe.

THE GENERIC PRODUCT

The fundamental, but rudimentary, substantive "thing" that's the table stakes of business—what's needed for a chance to play the game of market participation—is the *generic product*. It is, for the steel producer, the steel itself—or, in the Detroit example, No. 302, 72-inch, hot-rolled strip, or somebody's technical equivalent. For a bank, it's loanable funds. For a realtor, it's for-sale properties. For a retailer, it's a store with a certain mix of vendables. For a lawyer, it's having passed the bar exam.

Not all generic products are the same. Having passed the New York bar exam is not the same as having passed the Colorado exam. Because of slight differences among automobile company manufacturing processes, one supplier's "302" may, in fact, be "better" than another's. One mill's 302 may take certain coatings more easily or quickly than another's. One supplier may fill orders from a single mill, and another from several. In the latter case, the sheen or hue of the generic product may vary slightly from mill to mill, which makes considerable difference in the case of stainless steel that is used for decorative trim.

In most cases, these differences are not salient. More important are the characteristics of the expected components of the product.

EXHIBIT 1
The Total Product Concept

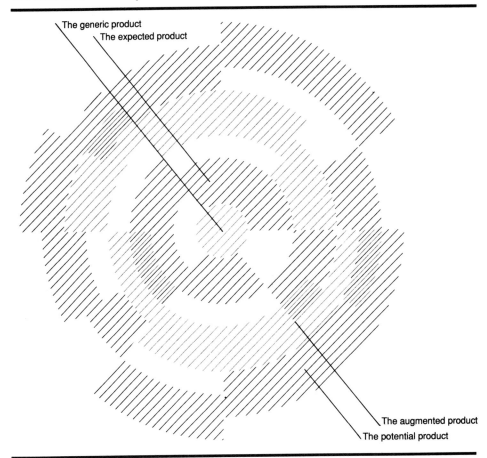

The generic product
The expected product
The augmented product
The potential product

THE EXPECTED PRODUCT

In *Exhibit 1* the *expected product* is everything within the outer and inner gray circles, including the generic product. It represents the customer's minimal purchase conditions. What, for example, does the customer consider absolutely essential in strip steel?

1. *Delivery.* At what plants? When? Not just on what day, but at what hours of each day, so as to minimize valuable space for backup stock and to reduce inventory costs? The supplier has to be "logistically even" with the buyer. The proper quantity and flexibility—that is, quick and hassle-free responsiveness to snags in delivery quantities and times—are also expected. Finally, preferential treatment may be specified in case of shortages.

2. **Terms**. Specific prices for specific quantities for specific lengths of time. In the case of a change in list prices, the terms contain negotiable parameters, perhaps linked to such indexes as moving price averages of scrap and other steel-making ingredients over specified periods. The terms may also be reflected in discount structures related to the promptness of payment and add-on provisions for extended payment periods.

3. **Support efforts**. Depending on what the uses of the product are, the purchaser may expect special applications advice and support.

4. **New ideas**. A normal expectation may include suppliers' ideas and suggestions for more efficient and cost-reducing ways of using the generic product in its various intended forms, such as fabrication, coating, and fastening.

All this may be well known, but the underlying principles encompass much more. The failure to fulfill certain more subtle expectations may reflect unfavorably on the generic product. A shabby brokerage office may cost a realtor access to customers for his or her properties. Even though the lawyer performed brilliantly in the bar exam and occupies offices of prudential elegance, his or her personality may clash with a potential client's. A manufacturer's competitively priced machine tools might have the most sophisticated of numerical controls tucked tightly behind an impressive panel, but certain customers may refuse to buy because output tolerances are more precise than necessary or usable. The customer may actually expect and want less.

The generic product can be sold only if the customer's wider expectations are met. Different means may be employed to meet those expectations. Hence differentiation follows expectation.

THE AUGMENTED PRODUCT

Differentiation is not limited to giving customers what they expect. What they expect may be augmented by things they have never thought about. When a computer manufacturer implants a diagnostic module that automatically locates the source of failure or breakdown inside his equipment (as some now do), the product goes beyond what was required or expected by the buyer. It has become an *augmented product*. When a securities brokerage firm includes with its customers' monthly statements a current balance sheet for each customer and an analysis of sources and disposition of funds, that firm has augmented its product beyond what was required or expected by the buyer. When a manufacturer of health and beauty aids offers warehouse management advice and training programs for the employees of its distributors, that company too has augmented its product beyond what was required or expected by the buyer.

These voluntary or unprompted augmentations to the expected product are shown in *Exhibit 1* by the irregular band that surrounds the expected product.

In every case, the supplier has exceeded the normal expectations of the buyer. In the steel example, it can be done by developing better ways of fabricating and coating the product or by reducing thickness to cut weight. The seller may provide other unexpected but moderately helpful aids, such as new delivery scheduling ideas, more "interesting" terms, different ways of delivering batches so as to reduce the buyer's handling problems and costs, and invoicing systems that give more information about the use patterns of the generic product by the buyer's various plants, divisions, or brands.

Not all customers for all products and under all circumstances, however, can be attracted by an ever-expanding bundle of differentiating value satisfactions. Some customers may prefer lower prices to product augmentation. Some cannot use the extra services offered. Steel users, for instance, once dependent on mills for applications help and engineering support, gradually grew sufficiently sophisticated to free themselves of that dependence—a freedom which, incidentally, led to the rapid growth of independent steel distribution centers in competition with the mills.

(Now the centers, which have distinguished themselves from the mills by faster delivery on standard grades and sizes, a wider item mix, and ability to handle small orders, have augmented *their* product by doing more minor fabricating and adding certain specialty steel application services.)

As a rule, the more a seller expands the market by teaching and helping customers to use his or her product, the more vulnerable that seller becomes to losing them. A customer who no longer needs help gains the flexibility to shop for things he or she values more—such as price.

At this point, it makes sense to embark on a systematic program of customer-benefiting, and therefore customer-keeping, product augmentation. The seller should also, of course, focus on cost and price reduction. And that's the irony of product maturity: precisely when price competition heightens, and therefore when cost reduction becomes more important, is when the seller is also likely to benefit by incurring the additional costs of new product augmentation.

The augmented product is a condition of a mature market or of relatively experienced or sophisticated customers. Not that they could not benefit from or would not respond to extra services; but when customers know or think they know everything and can do anything, the seller must test that assumption or be condemned to the purgatory of price competition alone. The best way to test a customer's assumption that he or she no longer needs or wants all or any part of the augmented product is to consider what's possible to offer that customer.

THE POTENTIAL PRODUCT

Everything that might be done to attract and hold customers is what can be called the *potential product*. For the steel user, the offering may include:

- Suggested technical changes, such as redesign of a component to reduce weight, add strength or durability, cut lateral flex, improve adhesion and desirability of coatings, or enhance safety.
- Market research findings regarding customers' attitudes toward, and their problems with, the various alternatives to steel (plastics and aluminum, for example).
- New methods and technologies for shaping, forming, and fastening steel to steel, steel to plastics, and the like.
- New ideas for lubricants, noise-reducing materials, buffers, and gaskets.
- Tested proposals for easier, faster, and cheaper assembly systems.
- New ideas for varying product characteristics for various user segments, such as commercial fleets, taxi fleets, and rental companies, each of which has its own buying criteria.
- Concrete, tested suggestions for combining materials like steel and fiberglass.

Only the budget and the imagination limit the possibilities. But what the budget is and ought to be is often a function of what is necessary to being competitive in all the dimensions of the potential product.

Offerings will vary with conditions—economic conditions and competitive conditions. Competition may be a function not simply of what other steel suppliers offer but also of what suppliers of substitute materials offer. Reordering responsiveness is not nearly as important to buyers in good times as in bad—except when a competitor strategically uses the good times (that is, when demand is high and supply short) to accommodate a large prospective customer in order to get a foot in the door.

Economic conditions, business strategies, customers' wishes, competitive conditions, and much more can determine what sensibly defines the product. Nor are the ingredients of the described classifications fixed. What's "augmented" for one customer may be "expected" by another; what's "augmented" under one circumstance may be "potential" in another; part of what's "generic" in periods of short supply may be "expected" in periods of oversupply.

As with most things in business, nothing is simple, static, or explained very reliably by textbook taxonomies. One thing is certain: there is no such thing as a commodity—or, at least from a competitive point of view, there need not be. Everything is differentiable, and, in fact, usually is differentiated. For example, consider the complexity of a generic product: durum wheat.

Durum is a variety of wheat produced in rather small quantities and almost exclusively in three counties in eastern North Dakota. Its main use is in pasta. Farmers generally deliver the durum in truckload quantities to country elevators, from which it is shipped to processors. In recent years, however, many large farm operations have built their own storage elevators. Using very large trailer trucks, they make direct shipments to the elevators of large users. Thus they not only avoid middleman storage discounts, but they also obtain access to premiums paid by the purchasers for high-quality wheat.

Similarly, country elevator operators in the Great Plains have increasingly organized to take advantage of unit-train shipments to the Gulf Coast and thereby qualify for substantial rail tariff discounts. These arrangements affect the quantities and schedules by which country elevators prefer to buy and take delivery from growers, which in turn affect how the growers manage their delivery capabilities and schedules.

The prices that elevator operators and processors pay vary substantially, even for identical grades of durum wheat. The elevator operators will pay premiums above, or take discounts from, prices currently quoted or prices previously agreed to with farmers, depending on the results of protein and moisture tests made on each delivery. Wheat users, like Prince Spaghetti Company, make additional tests for farina and gluten content. Premiums and discounts for quality differences in a particular year have been known to vary from the futures prices on commodity exchanges by amounts greater than the futures price fluctuations themselves during that year.

——— THE ROLE OF MANAGEMENT

The way a company manages its marketing can become the most powerful form of differentiation. Indeed, that may be how some companies in the same industry differ most from one another.

Brand management and product management are marketing tools that have demonstrable advantages over catchall, functional modes of management. The same is true of market management, a system widely employed when a particular tangible or intangible product is used in many different industries. Putting somebody in charge of a product that's used the same way by a large segment of the market (as in the case of packaged detergents sold through retail channels) or putting somebody in charge of a market for a product that's used differently in different industries (as in the case of isopropyl alcohol sold directly to manufacturers or indirectly to them via distributors) clearly focuses attention, responsibility, and effort. Companies that organize their marketing this way generally have a clear competitive advantage.

The list of highly differentiated consumer products that not long ago were sold as undifferentiated or minimally differentiated commodities is long: coffee, soap, flour, beer, salt, oatmeal, pickles, frankfurters, bananas, chickens, pineapples, and many more. Among consumer intangibles, in recent years brand or vendor differentiation has intensified in banking, insurance of all kinds, credit cards, stock brokerage, travel agencies, beauty parlors, entertainment parks, and small-loan companies. Among consumer hybrids, the same thing has occurred: theme restaurants, opticians, food retailers, and specialty retailers are burgeoning in a variety of categories—jewelry, sporting goods, books, health and beauty aids, pants and jeans, musical records and cassettes, auto supplies, and home improvement centers.

In each of these cases, especially that of consumer tangibles, the presumption among the less informed is that their competitive distinction resides largely in packaging and advertising. Even substantive differences in the generic products are thought to be so slight that what really counts are the ads and the packages.

This presumption is palpably wrong. It is not simply the heavy advertising or the clever packaging that accounts for the preeminence of so many General Foods and Procter & Gamble products. Nor is it their superior generic products that explain the successes of IBM, Xerox, ITT, and Texas Instruments. Their real distinction lies in how they manage—especially, in the cases of P&G, General Foods, IBM, and Xerox, in how they manage marketing. The amount of careful analysis, control, and field work that characterizes their management of marketing is masked by the visibility of their advertising or presumed generic product uniqueness.

The branded food products companies advertise heavily, and they work as hard and as closely with their wholesale and retail distributors as do the auto companies. Indeed, often these food companies work with distributors even harder because their distributors handle many competing brands, and the distribution channels are longer and more complex. Most grocery stores, of course, handle a number of more or less competing brands of the same generic (or functionally undifferentiated) product. There are more than two dozen national brands of powdered laundry detergent. The stores get them from a supermarket chain warehouse or from the warehouse of a cooperative wholesaler, a voluntary wholesaler, or an independent wholesaler. Each of these warehouses generally carries a full line of competing brands.

Though the national brands try via advertising and promotion to create consumer "pull," they also try to create retailer and wholesaler "push." At retail they regularly seek more advantageous shelf space and more advertising support from the retailer. At wholesale they do other things. Some years ago General Foods did a massive study of materials handling in distribution warehouses. Then the company made its results and recommendations available to the trade through a crew of specialists carefully trained to help implement those recommendations. The object, obviously, was to curry favor with the distributive trades for General Foods products.

The company did something similar for retailers: it undertook a major study of retail space profitability and then offered supermarket owners the opportunity to learn a new way of space-profitability accounting. By helping retailers manage their space better, General Foods presumably would gain retailers' favor for its products in their merchandising activities.

Another company, Pillsbury, devised a program to help convenience stores operate and compete more effectively. The object was, of course, to obtain preferential push treatment for Pillsbury products in these stores.

Similar examples abound in branded food marketing:

- The form in which goods are delivered—pallets, dollies, bulk—is often customized.
- When Heinz sells, delivers, and packages ketchup to institutional purveyors who supply hospitals, restaurants, hotels, prisons, schools, and nursing homes, it not only operates differently from the way it deals with cooperative wholesalers, but it also seeks to operate in some advantage-producing fashion different from the way Hunt Foods deals with the same purveyors.
- Some years ago the Institutional Food Service Division of General Foods provided elaborate theme-meal recipes for schools—"safari" meals that included such delectables as "groundnut soup Uganda" and "fish Mozambique." General Foods provided "decorations to help you go native" in the cafeteria, including travel posters, Congo face masks, pith helmets, lotus garlands, and paper monkeys.

THE CASE OF ISOPROPANOL

Four of the companies I have mentioned (General Foods, P&G, IBM, Xerox) are organized along product or brand-management lines for their major generic products. IBM and Xerox also have market managers and geographic managers. What differentiates them from others is how well they manage marketing, not merely what they market. It is the *process*, not just the product, that is differentiated.

To see the importance of the process, let's consider the lost opportunities of a company lacking the right process. Take the case of a large manufacturer of isopropyl alcohol, commonly called isopropanol. It is a moderately simple, totally undifferentiated generic product chemically synthesized via a well-known process from gas recovered in petroleum refining. It comes in two grades: crude, which is 9% water, and refined, which is 1% water. In 1970, 1.9 billion pounds were produced in the United States. Of that amount, 43% was bought as a feed stock to make acetone (principally a solvent), and most of the remainder was bought for use in chemicals, lacquers, and protective coatings.

With the introduction of the cumene process, isopropanol was no longer needed in the manufacturing of acetone. Hence in 1970 isopropanol was in vast oversupply. Prices were deeply depressed and expected to remain so for some five years until demand caught up with supply. One of the larger isopropanol companies employed a substantial proportion of its output to make acetone. In 1970 the company sold 310 million pounds of both products to the "merchant market"—that is, directly to manufacturers.

Although the prevailing prices per pound for both acetone and isopropanol were exceedingly low (as low as $.04 for acetone and $.067 for isopropanol), later analysis of this producer's invoices showed wide variations around these prices for sales made to different customers even on the same days. Two possible conclusions follow: (1) not all buyers were identically informed about what, indeed, were the "prevailing" prices on each of those days, and (2) not all buyers were equally price sensitive.

Analysis showed further that these price variations tended to cluster by industry category and customer size but not by geographical location. Another breakdown of industry categories revealed still other price segments: manufacturers of various kinds of coatings exhibited different clusterings of prices they had paid. Substantial differences in prices paid also showed up between agricultural chemical producers and biochemical producers. A category called "other" showed a great variety of price clusterings.

All this, however, is a matter of hindsight. No such analysis was made at the time. Had the marketing process been managed well, a product manager would have known these facts. The revealed differences in invoice prices and price clusterings would have led an intelligent and inquisitive product manager to ask:

1. Who are the least price-aware or price-sensitive among the industry users to whom we sell? What is their size distribution? Exactly which companies are they?
2. Who are the most and the least vendor-loyal—that is, who buys regularly from us, regardless of price fluctuations? Why? And who buys from us only occasionally, largely on considerations of price?
3. Who can use our applications help most? Who least?
4. Who would respond most to our offer of help?
5. Where and with whom could we selectively raise prices? Should we selectively hold prices?
6. How should we communicate all this to the sales organization and employ it in managing the sales forces?

Suppose that by astute management, the sales force had sold largely to the less informed or less price-sensitive industry sectors or customers. Suppose that each customer segment had yielded higher prices of as little as $.001, $.002, or $.005 per pound. What would have been the immediate cash contribution to the company? *Exhibit 2* gives an answer.

If only 10% of total sales had been made for only one-tenth of a penny more than they were, the pretax contribution would have risen $31,000. If 50% of sales had been raised by this minuscule amount, the yield would have been an extra $155,000; if 50% had been raised by two-tenths of a penny, the yield would have been $310,000 extra.

Given the analysis of markets and users that I outlined, such increases seem to have been well within reach. To achieve them, how much would it have been worth to expand the market analysis function into an on-the-spot, on-line differentiating activity guiding the sales organization? Obviously, a lot.

It is this and related kinds of attention to marketing details that characterize the work of product managers and market managers. Among producers of generically undifferentiated products—particularly products sold as ingredients to industrial customers—the management of the marketing process can itself be a powerful differentiating device. This device is constantly and

EXHIBIT 2
Presumed Results of Improved Sales Distribution

Industry and use	Millions of pounds	Additional cash contributions of incremental price points by price increments per pound		
		$ .001	$ .002	$ .005
Acetone	124	$ 124,000	$ 248,000	$ 620,000
Other intermediates	20	20,000	40,000	100,000
Agribiochemical	31	31,000	62,000	155,000
Coatings	86	86,000	172,000	430,000
Other	49	49,000	98,000	245,000
Total	310	$ 310,000	$ 620,000	$ 1,550,000
If 50% had been sold at the premiums		$ 155,000	$ 310,000	$ 775,000
If 10% had been sold at the premiums		$ 31,000	$ 62,000	$ 155,000

assiduously employed in the better-managed branded, packaged consumer goods companies.

It is a matter of staying aware of exactly what's going on in the market, of how people use, misuse, or modify their products, of how and where they buy, of who makes buying decisions and how these get modified, and the like. It is a matter of looking continuously for gaps in market coverage that the company can fill, of looking continuously at new ways of influencing buyers to choose one's product instead of a competitor's. In this unceasing effort of management, *the way in which the manager operates* becomes an extension of the idea of product differentiation itself.

Differentiation is most readily apparent in branded, packaged consumer goods; in the design, operating character, or composition of industrial goods; or in the features or "service" intensity of intangible products. However, differentiation consists as powerfully in how one operates the business. In the way the marketing process is managed may reside the opportunity for many companies, especially those that offer generically undifferentiated products and services, to escape the commodity trap.

━━━ DISCUSSION QUESTIONS

1. The author claims that there is no such thing as a commodity, that all goods and services are differentiable, and that industrial goods are even more differentiable than consumer goods. On what basis does he make these claims? Do you agree with his assertions?

2. What are some ways that even price-sensitive commodities can be effectively differentiated? What are some considerations in attracting and retaining customers for these products?

3. In the author's view, the sale of the generic product depends on how well the customer's wider expectations are met. What does this mean, and how does this add value to the generic product? What does the author mean by defining a product as a "combination of the tangible and the intangible"?

4. Can heavy advertising and unique packaging of generically similar products make a substantial difference in how each sells? Explain your view.

5. Consider the role of management in marketing. Does the way a company manages its marketing play a key role in differentiating its products? Give your views on the effectiveness or ineffectiveness of the role of management in differentiation.

16   Product Line Planning

BENSON P. SHAPIRO

This reading explains the difference between product line planning and product policy or product planning and focuses on the relationships between the various parts of a product line. It discusses three key aspects of product line planning: the general concept, the process, and the dynamics of managing the inevitable changes that occur within the product line.

To differentiate product line planning from simpler issues of product policy and product planning, we consider the relationships between the parts of a product line in terms of (1) the general concept of product line planning; (2) the product line planning process; and (3) the dynamics of product line planning.

THE CONCEPT OF PRODUCT LINE PLANNING

In this first section, we consider the concept of the product line in four different ways, beginning with a look at the vertical relationships among industry market strategy, product lines, and items. Next, we consider horizontal relationships among items in a given product line and among the separate segments of a product line. Third, we discuss product line planning as management of a capability; and, finally, as a connected set of consumer benefits.

VERTICAL RELATIONSHIPS

Product line planning considers the relationships among the various items in a product line and is closely involved in product policy, which operates at three strategic levels:

1. *Industry market strategy* refers to which markets the company will compete in. For example, will the company offer metalworking machine tools? Will it offer lathes?
2. *Product line strategy* focuses on how the company approaches each market. For example, will the company offer a complete line of lathes, parts, accessories, and service?

EXHIBIT 1
"Genealogy" of a Product Line

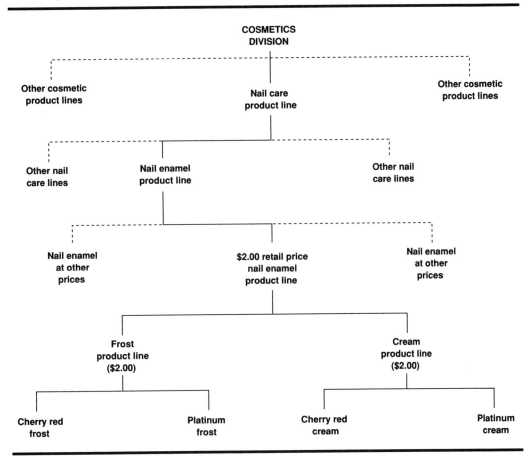

3. *Item strategy* refers to each individual element of the product line. For example, will the company offer a 20-foot bed, 10-horsepower metalworking lathe?

Industry market strategies[1] are at the interface between the study of marketing and the study of corporate strategy and business policy. But as an industry market strategy is in some sense a summation of all the decisions about product lines, it is sometimes difficult to distinguish between industry market strategies and product line strategies. Moreover, product lines often rest within broader product lines, and a company may have to revise its concept of a product line constantly.

For example, as shown in *Exhibit 1*, a marketer of cosmetics might offer colors of nail enamel, each of which can be grouped in many lines of cream

---

1. Robert J. Dolan, "Industry Market Strategy," Harvard Business School No. 9-585-107.

shades and frost shades. The manufacturer might offer several different product lines of creams and frosts at different prices or for different channels of distribution. And, the nail enamel line might be a product line in a broader array of nail-care products, which are, in turn, a subset of the total cosmetics offerings. Thus, four levels of product line fit between the industry market level (cosmetics) and the level of individual items ($2.00 cherry red frost).

- Nail care product line
- Nail enamel product line
- $2.00 retail price nail enamel product line
- $2.00 retail price frost/cream nail enamel product line

A more complex example might have even more subsets within a product line.

It is difficult to generalize about how the subsets of a product line fit together. There are different ways to view specific product lines and to fit the view to different situations. For some purposes, the nail enamel manufacturer might want to consider the total nail-care product line, while for other decisions the frost nail enamel product line might be the most appropriate unit of analysis and decision making.

This example also shows that in any given situation one cannot use the term *product line* loosely. It must be carefully defined; and the definition issue is not a meaningless theoretical one. Sometimes the definition of product lines determines the organizational jurisdictions and responsibilities of executives.

HORIZONTAL RELATIONSHIPS

Horizontal relationships exist among items in a product line, and among different product line segments in a larger product line. A basic way to view a product line is as a collection of items; the essence of product line planning is a recognition and management of the relationships among the items of the line.

The simplest view of relationships in a product line is that individual items are either complementary or competitive—that is, they either help to sell one another or they can be substituted for one another. Some products are clearly competitive with one another. To illustrate, a diner at a restaurant is unlikely to order two complete main dishes—for example, broiled salmon and filet mignon. But a diner *is* likely to order an appetizer, salad, soup, or dessert to complement the main dish. The filet mignon and the salmon are thus directly competitive but the other courses are complementary. In a food store, however, the salmon and filet mignon might be complementary, because customers who enjoy both beef and fish might buy both for variety or to satisfy the tastes of different members of the family.

Relationships among items in the product line become still more complex in industrial purchasing situations, where different forms or sizes of a given piece of equipment or supply might be needed for different applications or locations in the same buying unit. A company might purchase a simple direct-drive grinder for the maintenance shop and a large, complex, automated grinding machine for a production operation in the same factory.

Some products inevitably lead to the purchase of others in a fashion sometimes called "cascaded demand." Automobile sales lead to the sale of accessories such as air conditioning, parts, and service. In some businesses, the consumable supplies, parts, and service are much more important than the initial capital equipment in terms of revenue and profit generation.

The intricacy of the vertical and horizontal relationships in a product line make product line planning a complicated intellectual task. Before addressing some approaches to product line planning, there are two more views of the product line concept to consider.

PRODUCT LINE PLANNING AS MANAGEMENT OF A CAPABILITY

Product lines can consist of four different types of items:

1. Proprietary or catalog items standardized in certain configurations. These items are often sold from inventory and are thus produced in anticipation of orders.
2. Custom-built items usually offered as part of a standard set of basic units with accessories and options. For example, a lathe may be offered in several basic sizes, but with a variety of options (e.g., motor size, feeds, speeds, etc.), and with a range of accessories for different applications. Accessories may be mounted in the manufacturing plant, at the distributor or manufacturer field-branch level, or at the customer level.

    The most common example of a custom-built item is probably the automobile ordered from the factory. A consumer can order a specific automobile with air conditioning but not power steering or vice versa. But, the options are very carefully and completely specified, and can sometimes be ordered only in certain combinations or "packages."
3. Custom-designed items created to meet the desires of one (or sometimes a group of) customer(s). Sometimes these items are large one-of-a-kind units, such as a power plant, pipe line, machine-tool production line, and so on. At other times they are produced in large quantities, as in a weapons contract. In that situation, the product design may undergo several revisions during its lifetime. Custom-designed clothes or residential housing are examples of consumer products in this category.
4. Products completely tailored to the customer's specifications, for which no traditional manufacturing occurs at the seller's facility. Restaurants, law offices, and transportation companies are examples.

Each of these situations presents different problems, opportunities, and constraints in product line management. The differences also raise the question—How do we characterize the product line when there is no set product or products?

For example, consider a small manufacturer of equipment for automation. The company designs units to fit customer specifications and manufacturing processes, then manufactures the product, often as one of a kind. At most, it builds a few units costing in the $5-thousand to $50-thousand range. The company has two designers, two draftspeople who add details (bolt size, etc.) and turn the design into blueprints, and two versatile, highly competent machinists. Manufacturing equipment is limited to general-purpose metal-working machinery, such as a lathe and milling machine. The question of product policy in this situation cannot be viewed in traditional terms, for the company has no standard product line, no catalog in the sense of a description of specific products offered. Instead, it has a set of capabilities.

These capabilities are limited in terms of both size and applicability. The company could not accept an order that is very large; it has too little capacity. It could not accept an order involving advanced radiation technology because it does not have that capability. It must choose its prospects and sales situations carefully, so that it has a good chance of obtaining the order and almost certainty of filling it. This company must manage its "product line" in three stages.

First it must manage the capability it has available; this is the core of its product policy. Thus, if it increases its capacity by adding another designer, draftsperson, and machinist, it can accept larger jobs. Or it can add people and machines that give it capabilities in areas beyond its current competence.

It must also manage in terms of the assignments it seeks. Since, within its capabilities, it makes more money on some assignments than on others, it can manage its product line profitability by searching out lucrative assignments. In a sense, then, each order is an item in the product line.

Finally, it must manage the way in which it promotes its capabilities. While in strict marketing terminology promotion is part of the communications function within the marketing mix, in this situation it actually varies the "product line" by changing customers' views of assignments and capabilities it can handle. In some cases, if a company wants to penetrate a market segment or assignment type different from its current ones, it can simply vary the assignments it seeks and the way in which it promotes itself.

Having clarified the concept of product policy as the management of a capability, we can return to the four types of product lines and apply this concept to them.

In the case of proprietary or catalog items the capability is shown by the set of offerings in the product line. Product line decisions involve the choice of items to be added, deleted, or repositioned in the line. In many companies, producing the catalog forces product line decisions, which are essentially fixed for the life of the catalog (i.e., until another catalog or supplement is produced).

For custom-built items, the capability is again circumscribed by a list or catalog of offerings. The differences are that (1) the items are almost never inventoried as completed items, although they may be as subassemblies and components, and (2) a distributor or salesperson must "design" the product in partnership with the customer. Often, because of the variety of options and accessories offered, the number of possible combinations is very large, although many are never sold. The company is actually offering the customer a selection of building blocks with which to construct a product. As a consequence, product line decisions are less concerned with the end or completely finished product and more concerned with components, options, and accessories. Meanwhile, customers are more concerned with the finished product.

The category of custom-designed items leaves the realm of a specified, limited list of products and enters that of pure capability. In fact, not only is the product line described in terms of capabilities, but the customer purchases a capability that, eventually, is delivered as a finished unit. This is even more clear when the "product" (service) is designed specifically for the customer's need and there is no true physical product.

For obvious reasons, the capabilities view is most useful for planning product lines for service companies or companies in which service is a major part of the product line.

THE PRODUCT LINE AS A SET OF BENEFITS

The preceding discussion of vertical and horizontal relationships in product lines and product lines as collections of capabilities may tend to encourage marketers to look at the product line introspectively and to manipulate the items in the line in an internally focused and sometimes mechanical way. To counteract this tendency it is necessary to return to the customer—the key element in marketing—and reaffirm an orientation and devotion to the satisfaction of customer needs and desires.

Customers do not buy products, items or features—they buy benefits. The automobile purchaser does not want a couple of tons of metal and other material. He or she wants transportation, status, excitement, and other benefits. A useful way to look at the product line, therefore, is as a collection of customer benefits that the company provides through a "systems" approach. Sometimes, however, a company's manufacturing or operating capabilities set limits on its ability to meet a set of related customer needs.

The benefits approach fits well with the capabilities concept described above and helps focus product line planning on the most appropriate place—the customer.

——— THE PROCESS OF PRODUCT LINE PLANNING

Product lines tend to be developed in light of four factors:

1. Customer needs
2. Competitive offerings
3. Operating capabilities
4. Marketing strategy

Customer needs should be the primary determinant in planning a product line. Because different customers, and market segments, have different needs, the marketer must carefully select the target market segment before planning a product line. The target market segment may be defined in terms of certain kinds of customers, according to particular customer needs, or to fit with specific purchase occasions.

Competitive offerings are also an important influence on the development of a product line. A company might, for example, want to close "holes" in its product line to prevent competitive incursions. A capital-equipment supplier might offer related supplies and accessories to customers solely to prevent a competitor from building customer relationships through the sale of such day-to-day purchases. Some companies have introduced lower-priced "fighting brands" to protect the core of their line from cheaper competitive entries.

Manufacturing and other operating functions can limit a company's offerings of particular items or related product lines. A nail enamel manufacturer might, for example, choose not to offer nail-care implements such as clippers and files because it does not have a metal-working factory (alternatively it could, of course, purchase such items and resell them as part of the product line). A manufacturer of computers might choose not to offer repair service directly because it has too small an installed base to support a dedicated field service. In this situation the small computer company might make a formal arrangement with a service supplier for repair and maintenance, creating a joint "shared product line." Such arrangements are frequent among suppliers of complementary products.

Some items or segments in a product line are introduced to support a particular marketing strategy. For example, an apparel manufacturer might offer a few highly styled or faddish items to give the product line more of a fashion orientation. Or a farm equipment dealer might offer some products primarily to fill out its dealers' product lines in the hope that added dealer loyalty and support will lead to greater sales of existing items.

These examples show that different items serve different functions in a product line and present one of the great and continuing arguments in product line planning: Does each item in the line have to pull its own weight in terms of generating a minimum profit? (Profit, in this case, can be measured in dollars, contribution percent, return on investment, or whatever the company uses.) Some marketers believe that every item and every product line segment must be able to stand alone. While this view might seem shortsighted, it does ensure that product policy decisions are made on a disciplined basis. The opposing view—that some items should be in the line for purposes other than contributing to profit—can lead to some very "creative" justifications for low-profit products. There is no standard solution to the argument because each situation is different.

Once each item's role in the product line is determined, planners should examine the underlying theme of the total line. This is one of the most neglected aspects of product line planning, even though it provides the framework for making decisions on individual items.

There are two alternative evaluations for a product line: variety and value. Variety means offering a full line to meet the diverse needs of many prospects, customers, and market segments. The rationale is that because different customers have different priorities and needs, the company should offer a wide range of items. The costs of such an approach are high, due to the expense of short manufacturing runs, added inventory of parts and finished goods, extra engineering and development, and increased confusion and complexity for distributors, salespeople, and order-processing and logistics personnel.

The opposite approach emphasizes value. In this case, a company offers few items but prices them at such a favorable price/performance ratio that customers forgo their desires for diversity and customization and opt for value. The simplicity and focus of the value orientation carries through the entire company, encouraging efficient manufacturing and distribution functions (or operating function in a service company).

There is no simple, standard answer for this subtle choice—only the need for careful analysis. Once the variety-versus-value choice has been made, the item-level decisions become easier. The value orientation pushes a company toward a philosophy of retaining only those items that generate the minimum contribution required by the company. The variety orientation takes a more holistic view of the line, perhaps justifying items that have a purpose beyond direct contribution.

One other consideration in the value-versus-variety decision is whether to standardize products across national boundaries. Factors such as manufacturing and logistic economics, government regulations, and tradition make this a complex decision as well.

THE DYNAMICS OF PRODUCT LINE PLANNING

Product lines change over time and thus must be managed with a view toward these changes. Some changes relate to the product life cycle. Others relate to differences in the nature and pace of developments within the product line. Other changes result from the move from specialty to commodity. This section summarizes the dynamics of managing different types of product lines and examines the inevitable move from specialty to commodity.

Some product lines consist of many items and product-line segments that change frequently in relatively small ways. These product lines are managed by the day-to-day deletion, introduction, and repositioning of items. The major challenge in such a situation is to have a coherent long-term plan that governs these evolutionary changes and guides day-to-day activities. Without one, the product line will meander through a series of unrelated tactical moves that leave it constantly vulnerable to competitive attack, unresponsive to customer needs, and less profitable than it should be. Sometimes it is difficult to identify the need for long-term planning, for a constantly evolving product line often masks the need for it.

At the other extreme are product lines that consist of only a few items, which are changed infrequently. The commercial aircraft market is a good example. Boeing, with the most complete line in the industry, customizes each individual aircraft to the buyer's needs, and each item in the line (e.g., B-727) is slightly modified on a regular basis to respond to changing customer needs, competitive activity, technological opportunity, or environmental change. But, the introduction, deletion, or repositioning of an aircraft is a strategic decision of monumental proportion. The introduction of the B-747, for example, severely strained the financial and management resources of Boeing, a large company by any standard, for quite some time. Because these monumental decisions stand out more sharply than the evolutionary ones, they usually get the attention they need. But, they are still very difficult to make. Their sheer size and complexity create such trepidation that sometimes managers shrink from making the important decisions and accepting the high risks.

Most product lines consist of a mixture of constant evolutionary changes and a few cataclysmic decisions. Although it is hard for any group of individuals to make both kinds of life-cycle decisions well, it is clearly necessary.

Another dynamic affecting product line management is the fact that all products and product lines follow an inexorable path from specialty to commodity. When a genuinely new product is introduced, it is by definition substantially different from established products and is sold on the basis of unique attributes. If it offers important customer benefits in relation to cost, it succeeds. If it meets with substantial success, and if there are no overwhelming barriers to competitive entry, in a few years it meets with competition. Even products protected by patent—like the Xerox photocopier and the Polaroid camera—eventually meet with imitators. Imitation of a successful product is inevitable. The only questions are when will competitive products appear, how successfully will they imitate the original, and can the innovator make its product less vulnerable to competitive imitation.

As imitations become more numerous the whole focus of the industry changes. The customer has many similar alternatives, which are less and less significantly differentiated from each other. Companies move toward increasingly vicious head-to-head competition. The product moves gradually from being a specialty item endowed with unique attributes to being a partially (or perhaps totally) undifferentiated commodity. Companies in commodity busi-

EXHIBIT 2
The Role of Technological Excellence

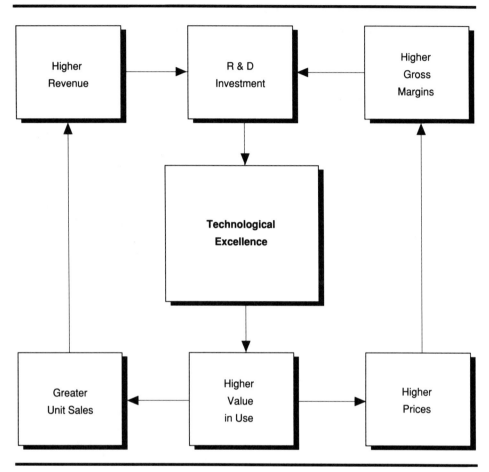

nesses seem to have only two choices. One is to compete effectively in head-to-head competition through meticulous cost control and aggressive use of capacity and price. The other is to create new specialty products by differentiating them from the competition through innovation in the physical products or in the way they are provided to customers. The market consists of constant movements—through imitation toward commodity status, and through innovation away from commodity status and toward a specialty orientation.

Technological excellence can lead to products that provide higher use values than those of competitors. Customers are willing to pay for added value and to buy the product in volume. The resulting high revenues and gross margins allow the company to reinvest in research and development, which in turn leads to more technological excellence, and the cycle continues (as shown in *Exhibit 2*).

Unfortunately, as time passes research and development in any area of technological endeavor meet the law of diminishing returns. It takes greater and greater investments to make smaller and smaller advances. Eventually the rate of innovation slows, and the rate of imitation surpasses it. Then the market and all the competing products move toward the commodity end of the spectrum. Once, long ago, even steel was an exciting and innovative product—before the inevitable move toward commodity status. Later, synthetic fibers went through the same transition: in the 1950s and 1960s the industry was replete with innovation, but by the late 1970s it was involved in a characteristically competitive commodity market. All markets and all products seem to move in that direction.

We have seen that product line planning is a complex effort with implications for product planning, overall marketing planning, and formulation of an industry marketing strategy. Every firm—whether a new venture or an established business, a manufacturer or a service company—needs to analyze carefully the opportunities, constraints, and problems of particular product lines and be prepared to adjust product line planning to heightened competition and the transition of products from specialty to commodity status.

━━ DISCUSSION QUESTIONS

1. How would you describe the difference between product policy and product line planning? Between vertical relationships and horizontal relationships among items in a product line? Does managing product policy differ from managing a product line? In what ways is it different? In what ways is it similar?

2. Some companies appoint individual product managers to be responsible for the marketing and profitability of each product in a product line. By encouraging competition among its products, how does a company benefit? Do the risks of this kind of competition within a company present a problem or an opportunity?

3. If you were a marketing manager in a company, would you prefer a central, unified approach to marketing all of the company's products? What are the advantages and disadvantages of this approach?

4. The author points out a controversial area in product line management. Some marketers believe that each individual item within a product line has to "pull its own weight" in profitability. The opposing view is that some items are included in the product line for reasons other than direct profit generation. Which view do you favor? Why? Could your view change with different product lines? Explain.

5. As a marketing manager, you are responsible for deciding which products and how many to include in a product line. You can choose to offer the broadest line possible, which will provide the greatest variety of products to satisfy more customers and more needs—although with more cost, inventory, confusion, and complexity. Or you can simplify the product line with a narrower offering that allows better value and pricing but sacrifices diversity and choice for the customer. How would you make your decision? What considerations would influence your choice?

17   The New Product Development Map

STEVEN C. WHEELWRIGHT AND W. EARL SASSER, JR.

One of the most invigorating business activities is new product development. If everything fits, the timing is right, and the competition is not underestimated, nothing quite matches the introduction of a new product. But the process cannot succeed unless everyone contributes: general managers, marketers, engineers, designers, and manufacturing executives. This reading describes a way to facilitate this cooperation: the "new product development map," which provides a guide that gives managers a better sense of where they are, how they came to be there, and how to get where they want to go. Once the goal and the purpose are understood by all and a map is provided so all can study the new terrain and share information, it becomes easier to follow the course and even plan alternative courses. In this reading, an illustrative product line is used to show how to construct a map and develop discussion around it.

No business activity is more heralded for its promise and approached with more justified optimism than the development and manufacture of new products. Whether in mature businesses like automobiles and electrical appliances, or more dynamic ones like computers, managers correctly view new products as a chance to get a jump on the competition.

Ideally, a successful new product can set industry standards—standards that become another company's barrier to entry—or open up crucial new markets. Think of the Sony Walkman. New products are good for the organization. They tend to exploit as yet untapped R&D discoveries and revitalize the engineering corps. New product campaigns offer top managers opportunities to reorganize and to get more out of a sales force, factory, or field service network, for example. New products capitalize on old investments.

Perhaps the most exciting benefit, though, is the most intangible: corporate renewal and redirection. The excitement, imagination, and growth associated with the introduction of a new product invigorate the company's best people and enhance the company's ability to recruit new forces. New products build confidence and momentum.

Unfortunately, these great promises of new product development are seldom fully realized. Products half make it; people burn out. To understand why, let's look at some of the more obvious pitfalls.

1. *The moving target.* Too often the basic product concept misses a shifting market. Or companies may make assumptions about channels of distribution that just don't hold up. Sometimes the project gets into trouble because of inconsistencies in focus; you start building a stripped-down version and wind up with a load of options. The project time lengthens, and longer projects invariably drift more and more from their initial target. Classic market misses include the Ford Edsel in the mid-1950s and Texas Instruments' home computer in the late 1970s. Even very successful products like Apple's Macintosh line of personal computers can have a rocky beginning.

2. *Lack of product distinctiveness.* This risk is high when designers fail to consider a full range of alternatives to meet customer needs. If the organization gets locked into a concept too quickly, it may not bring differing perspectives to the analysis. The market may dry up, or the critical technologies may be sufficiently widespread that imitators appear out of nowhere. Plus Development introduced Hardcard®, a hard disk that fits into a PC expansion slot, after a year and a half of development work. The company thought it had a unique product with at least a nine-month lead on competitors. But by the fifth day of the industry show where Hardcard® was introduced, a competitor was showing a prototype of a competing version. And within three months, the competitor was shipping its new product.

3. *Unexpected technical problems.* Delays and cost overruns can often be traced to overestimates of the company's technical capabilities or simply to its lack of depth and resources. Projects can suffer delays and stall midcourse if essential inventions are not completed and drawn into the designers' repertoire before the product development project starts. An industrial controls company we know encountered both problems: it changed a part from metal to plastic only to discover that its manufacturing processes could not hold the required tolerances and also that its supplier could not provide raw material of consistent quality.

4. *Mismatches between functions.* Often one part of the organization will have unrealistic or even impossible expectations of another. Engineering may design a product that the company's factories cannot produce, for example, or at least not consistently at low cost and with high quality. Similarly, engineering may design features into products that marketing's established distribution channels or selling approach cannot exploit. In planning its requirements, manufacturing may assume an unchanging mix of new products, while marketing mistakenly assumes that manufacturing can alter its mix dramatically on short notice. One of the most startling mismatches we've encountered was created by an aerospace company whose manufacturing group built an assembly plant too small to accommodate the wingspan of the plane it ultimately had to produce.

Thus new products often fail because companies misunderstand the most promising markets and channels of distribution and because they misapprehend their own technological strengths or the product's technological challenges. Nothing can eliminate all the risks, but clearly the most important thing to do early on when developing a new product is to get all contributors to the process communicating: marketing with manufacturing, R&D with both. Products fail from a lack of planning; planning fails from a lack of information.

Developing a new generation of products is a lot like taking a journey into the wilderness. Who would dream of setting off without a map? Of course, you would try to clarify the purpose of the journey and make sure that needed equipment is available and in order. But once committed to the trip, you need a map of the terrain, something everybody can study—the focus for discussion, the basis for planning alternative courses. Knowing where you've come from and where you are is essential to knowing how to get where you want to go.

──── MAPPING EXISTING PRODUCTS

We have often used this analogy of a map with corporate managers involved in product development, and gradually it has become clear to us that an actual map is needed, not just an analogy. Managers need a way to see the evolution of a company's product lines—the "where we are"—in order to expose the markets and technologies that have been driving the evolution—the "where we've come from." Such a map presents the evolution of current product lines in a summarized yet strikingly clear way so that all functional areas in the organization can respond to a common vision. The map provides a basis for sharing information. And by enabling managers to compare the assumptions underlying current product lines with the ideal assumptions of new research, it points to new market opportunities and technological challenges. Why, for example, should an organization build for department stores when specialty discount outlets are the emerging channels of distribution? Why bend metals when you can mold ceramics?

Exhibit 1 illustrates a generic map that indicates how the product offerings in one generation may be related to each other. These relations are the building blocks that allow us to track the evolution of product families from one generation to another.

The map categorizes product offerings (and the development efforts they entail) as "core" and "leveraged" products, and divides leveraged products into "enhanced," "customized," "cost reduced," and "hybrid." (These designations seem to cover most cases, but managers should feel free to add whatever other categories they need.) A core product, first in white for the engineering prototype, then in black, is the engineering platform, providing the basis for further enhancements. The core product is the initial, standard product introduced. It changes little from year to year and is often the benchmark against which consumers compare the rest of the product line.

Enhanced products, in gray, are developed from the core design; distinctive features are added for various, more discriminating markets. Enhanced

EXHIBIT 1
Generic Product Development Map

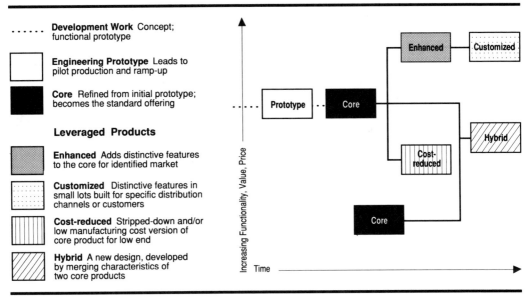

Development Work Concept; functional prototype

Engineering Prototype Leads to pilot production and ramp-up

Core Refined from initial prototype; becomes the standard offering

Leveraged Products

Enhanced Adds distinctive features to the core for identified market

Customized Distinctive features in small lots built for specific distribution channels or customers

Cost-reduced Stripped-down and/or low manufacturing cost version of core product for low end

Hybrid A new design, developed by merging characteristics of two core products

products are the first products leveraged from the capabilities put in place to produce the core, and the first aimed at new or extended market opportunities. Often companies even identify them as enhanced versions; for example, IBM's DisplayWrite 3.1 is an enhanced version of DisplayWrite 3. But a leveraged product isn't necessarily more costly; the idea is simply to get more out of a fixed process—more "bang for the buck." As companies leverage high-end products, they may customize them in smaller lots for specific channels or to give consumers more choice (shown as dotted). The cost-reduced model (shown with vertical lines) starts with essentially the same technology and design as the core product but is a stripped-down version, often with less expensive materials and lower factory costs, aimed at a price-sensitive market. (Think of the old Chevrolet Biscayne, which was many times the vehicle of choice for taxicabs and business fleets.)

Finally, there is the hybrid product (shown with diagonal lines), developed out of two cores. The initial two-stage thermostat products—accommodating a daytime and nighttime temperature setting—were hybrids of a traditional thermostat product and high-end, programmable thermostat lines.

On the generic map in *Exhibit 1,* from left to right is calendar time, and from bottom to top is lower to higher added value or functionality, which usually also means a shift from cheaper to more expensive products.

These distinctions—core, hybrid, and the others—are immediately useful because they give managers a way of thinking about their products more rigorously and less anecdotally. But the various turns on the product map—the various "leverage points"—also serve as crucial indicators of previous management assumptions about the corporate strengths and market forces shaping product evolutions.

A map that shows a proliferation of enhanced products toward the high end, for example, says something important about the market opportunities managers identified after they introduced the core. A map's configuration raises necessary questions about dominant channels of distribution—then and now. That products could have been leveraged in particular ways, moreover, says something important about in-house technological and manufacturing capabilities—capabilities that may still exist or may need changing. The map generates the right discussions. When managers know how and why they leveraged products in the past, they know better how to leverage the company in the present.

THE FIRST GENERATION

How can managers plan, develop, and position a set of products—that is, how do they build a dynamic map? With the generic map in mind, let us track offerings from generation to generation. (*Exhibit 2* shows the first generation.) Imagine a very simple line of vacuum cleaners, Coolidge Corporation's "Stratovac," introduced, say, in 1952. The core product, the Stratovac, was a canister-type appliance with a 2.5-horsepower motor. Constructed mainly from cut and stamped metals, it was distributed through department stores and hardware chains.

The following year, reaching for the somewhat more affluent suburban household, Coolidge brought out the "Stratovac Plus," an enhanced Stratovac delivered in a choice of three colors, with a 4-horsepower motor and a recoiling cord. In 1959, the company introduced the "Stratovac Deluxe"—a Stratovac Plus with a vacuum resistance sensor (which cut off the power when the bag was full) and a power head with a rotating brush for deep pile or shag carpeting. By 1959, the basic Stratovac cost $89, the Stratovac Plus, $109, and the Stratovac Deluxe, $159.

To reach the industrial market at $79, Coolidge had decided to offer the "Stratovac Workman," a stripped-down Plus model—one color, no recoiling cord. That was introduced in 1956. And when Deluxe sales rocketed, Coolidge offered Maybel's department store chain a customized version of it, the Stratovac "Maybel's Housekeeper." This came out in 1960, in Maybel's blue-gray, with the power head. The price was "only" $129. (Coolidge eventually customized the "Housekeeper Canadian" for the Simpton's chain in Canada, and the "Royal Housekeeper" for the Mid-Lakes chain in England.)

Again, this is a simple product line, but even so, the map raises interesting questions, especially for younger managers who came after this era. Why the Stratovac Plus? Why a proliferation of products toward the high end?

In fact, during the 1950s, most companies marketed home appliances through department stores with product families visibly shaped by the

EXHIBIT 2
Coolidge Vacuum Cleaner: First Generation 1952–1968

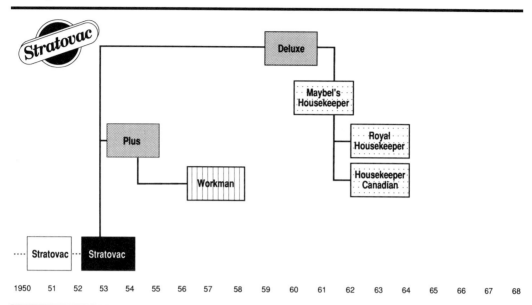

distribution channels. Products stood side by side in the stores, to be demonstrated by a salesperson. The markup was similar for each product on the floor.

What differentiated products in product families at the time was an appliance manufacturer's reach to satisfy more or less obvious customer segments—customers differentiated by factors like income and marital status. (In the 1950s, most vacuum cleaner purchasers were women, with more or less money, time, and patience.)

How Coolidge leveraged its products also points to certain fixed—and not especially unique—manufacturing capabilities. During the 1950s, company engineers designed appliances for manual assembly and traditional notions of economies of scale. By the end of the 1950s, Coolidge acquired new vacuum sensor innovations from the auto industry. It also learned certain flexible manufacturing techniques, making different colors and options possible.

By 1958, Coolidge had solved most of the technical problems of the Stratovac line and had recruited a number of ambitious design engineers to integrate vacuum sensor and power heads into the line. The life cycle of the products—including development time, which stretched back to 1949—was typical for core products of that time: 10 to 15 years. Demand for the Stratovac remained strong throughout the 1950s, and Coolidge sold to department stores in roughly the same proportion as its competition, except for companies organized around the door-to-door trade.

The company's increased (and not fully utilized) technical competence and the steadiness of its key distribution channels are crucial pieces of informa-

EXHIBIT 3
Coolidge Vacuum Cleaner (First Generation, with critical skills and distribution channels)

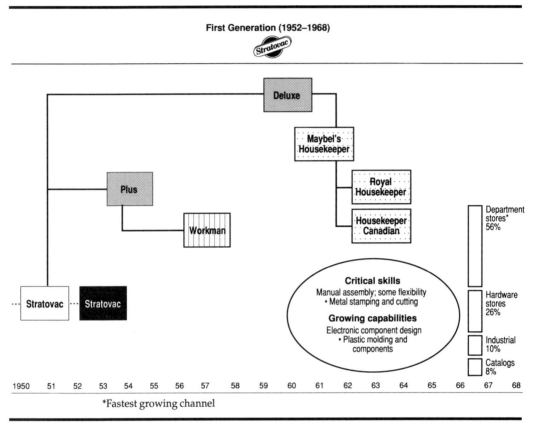

*Fastest growing channel

tion to add to the map (see *Exhibit 3*). The map summarizes technical competence in the oval beneath the product lines, and Coolidge's gross sales by distribution channel in the box graph.

──── THE SECOND GENERATION

With so much technical talent in-house, and a society growing increasingly affluent, Coolidge could not be expected to rest on the Stratovac's success indefinitely. Sales were steady, but by the mid-1960s customers assumed there would be some innovations. The age of plastics was dawning; the vanguard of the baby boom was taking apartments; it was the "new and improved" era.

Moreover, marketing people at Coolidge began to detect a new potential market at the low end. People who had relied on their Stratovacs for a decade were looking around for a second, lighter-weight appliance for quick cleanups or for the workroom or garage. Lighter-weight and cheaper naturally meant more reliance on plastic components.

In the early 1960s, Coolidge managers decided on two product families, each with its own core product (see *Exhibit 4* which juxtaposes the first two Stratovac generations). The design team that had brought out the old core Stratovac would handle the "Stratovac II," and company new hires would design a second line, the all-plastic, mass-produced "Handivac" ("any color, so long as it's beige").

The Stratovac II, introduced in 1968, was heavier and had a 4.3-horsepower motor, resulting in a slightly noisier operation ("jet noise"), which the marketing people reasoned would actually increase respect for its power. Half of the case was now plastic for a "streamlined" appearance. The core Stratovac II boasted a new dust-bag system, which virtually eliminated the need for handling dust. A retractable cord was also standard.

The Stratovac II "Sentry," an enhanced version of the core, included electronic controls for variable speed and came in many colors. The Stratovac II "Imperial," like the old Deluxe model, came with the power head. The Stratovac II Workman continued to sell steadily to the light industrial market, as did the Stratovac II Housekeeper line to the department store chains that still sold the vast majority of units.

Most notable about the Stratovac II was how little changed it was, certainly on the manufacturing end. Assembly was still chiefly manual, along the lines of the 1950s—no priority given to modularity, design for manufacturability, or any of the considerations that would drive designers later on. There was some outsourcing of components to Mexico and Taiwan but no real attention to automation. The only significant change in the Stratovac II came in 1973, when inflationary pressures pushed management to develop a fully plastic casing and critical plastic components—in effect, a hybrid developed by merging technologies of the high-end vacuum cleaner with the low-end Handivac.

Handivac, the second core product, introduced in 1969, was something of a disappointment—mostly because of the inexperience of the team managing its development. Reliability was a problem, given Handivac's almost complete dependence on plastic components, components subjected to higher than expected temperatures from an old, slightly updated 2.5-horsepower motor. Weight was also a problem: it was not as light as promised. Mass-production lines, which were partially automated, were considered a success when they were finally debugged.

Perhaps the greatest problem with the Handivac, however, was the fact that, like the Stratovac II, it was sold mainly through department stores and hardware chains, where markups were too large to permit it a significant price advantage over the more expensive core product. Handivac sold for $79, while the Stratovac II sold for $99. Handivac managers tried to cut costs by going to an overseas supplier for a lighter-weight, somewhat less powerful motor —over the vehement objections of Stratovac II designers, who had depended on Handivac's participation in their motor plant to keep their own costs in line.

EXHIBIT 4 Coolidge Vacuum Cleaner: First and Second Generation

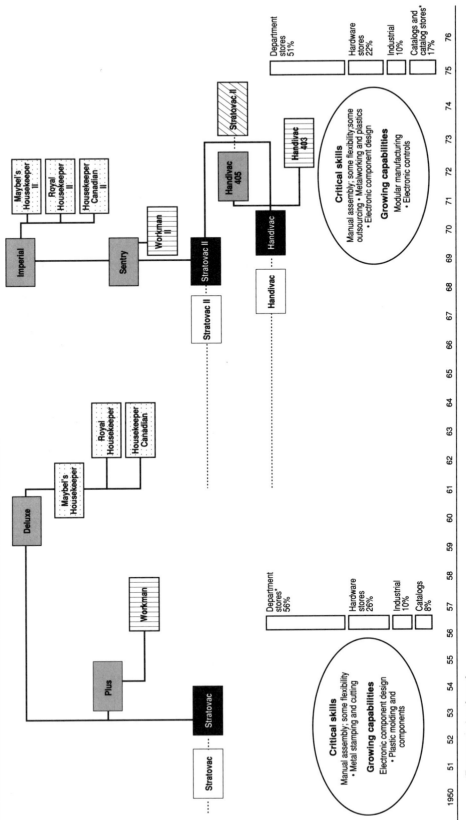

Eventually, Handivac introduced a cost-reduced "Handivac 403," which sold for $69, importing a 3.0-horsepower motor and cord subassembly from Japan. The enhanced "405" sold for $83. Handivac engineers began at this time to interact with Japanese manufacturing managers. But there were still no distribution channels where Handivac could enjoy the "price busting" opportunity it needed. The most promising channel, though hardly dominant, was the growing chains of catalog stores, which sold the Handivac 403 for $63, a 10% reduction from the department store price.

———— THE THIRD GENERATION

During 1976 and 1977, a number of external and internal pressures led to a redesign of the entire product line. Department stores were still the major source of revenue, but competitors were proliferating and the Stratovac II group felt the need to offer an increasing number of more enhanced and more customized products to maintain demand at the profitable high end. Consumers would pay a premium, marketing people believed, only if the company could produce so many versions that all customers felt they were getting the right color with the right options. Moreover, Coolidge had canvassed Stratovac II customers, who hadn't appreciated the "jet sound," as designers had assumed. Bulk was also a problem, as was the vacuum's unattractive look.

Inside the company, Coolidge's two design teams had become more cooperative, particularly as the advantages of molded plastic became obvious to everyone. The hybrid Stratovac II, which had been redesigned in plastic wherever possible, was something of a victory for the young Handivac designers over the more traditional group. Flexibility and cost were the keys to satisfying many markets, and plastics answered both needs. Eventually the more traditional designers also came to see the advantage of going to Japan for a smaller, lighter, more reliable motor—and for a number of subassemblies critical to the company's goal of offering arrays of options.

Concurrently in the mid-1970s, the Handivac designers were pressing for a complete merging of the design engineering teams and for studying Japanese manufacturing techniques. They argued that if flexibility, cost, and quality were going to be crucial, the manufacturing people would have to become more involved in product design. The young guard also believed that Coolidge could produce motors domestically—at required levels of quality—if it adopted certain innovations in machine tool and winding automation and instituted statistical process control at its existing motor plant.

Where the younger design group still lacked credibility, however, was on the bottom line. Top management was reluctant to give up on a two-track approach when the Handivac group had failed to deliver an appliance that made even as much as the Housekeeper line. The number of catalog stores was growing, and newer discount appliance chains were springing up in big cities, but the Handivac faced intense competition. Could the younger designers hope to come in with enough products, offering enough features, and at low enough costs to meet this competition?

In the end, Coolidge management decided to develop two core product families in its third generation (see *Exhibit 5*, showing all three product generations). The Stratovac II team redesigned the high-end vacuum cleaner in six models, the "Challenger 6000" series. All appliances in this series came with a power head and a new bag system. By steps —6001, 6002, and upward—consumers could buy increasingly sophisticated electronic controls. And they could order the 6004 and 6005 in an array of colors.

The 6000 series was constructed almost entirely of molded plastic. Manufacturing came up with an automated way of applying hot sealant to critical seams, and the Challenger's motor was quieter. Top management agreed with the younger engineers that a more advanced motor factory could be constructed in the United States. The design teams didn't merge, but they found themselves working more closely together and increasingly with manufacturing.

The traditional design group simultaneously came out with the "Pioneer 4000" series. This was a middle-range product, somewhat smaller than the Challenger 6000 and not offering a power head. The marketing people felt that department stores would want a cost-reduced model to compete with the proliferating "economy" products that discount chains were now offering. (The 4001, 4002, and 4003 were distinguished, again, by electronic controls.) The Pioneer 4000 series was leveraged largely from the Challenger 6000 as a cost-reduced version.

Since both series offered stripped-down models, Coolidge did not introduce a specific industrial product and eliminated the Workman. Coolidge executives also believed that it was no longer worthwhile to customize models for particular department stores where margins were shrinking, so they eliminated the Housekeeper line.

A year after they introduced the Challenger 6000, the Handivac team brought out its new series of products, the "Helpmate." With minor modifications, Helpmate was customized as "Helpmate SE," targeted at different low-end market segments—college students, apartment dwellers, do-it-yourselfers, and the industrial market. The cleaner was lightweight. Attachments varied, as did graphic design: the company expected a Spartan gray color and a longer hose to appeal to commercial customers, and bright pastels and different size brushes to appeal to college students.

The key to the Helpmate line, however, was its manufacturing. The motor was no longer outsourced, and designers worked with manufacturing engineers on modular components and subassemblies. Top management agreed to set aside manufacturing space in the assembly plants for cellular construction of the Helpmate so that the company could respond quickly to demand for particular models. And Helpmate came in at two-thirds the price of the Pioneer 4000.

There was still some debate among Helpmate's product development team members about most likely channels. Some saw it designed only for

EXHIBIT 5 Coolidge Vacuum Cleaner: First, Second, and Third Generations

First Generation (1952–1968)
- Product family evolved for department store segments
- Product cycle: 10 to 15 years
- Aggressive marketing

Stratovac

Second Generation (1967–1978)
- Product family extended ror discount channels
- Product cycle: 8 to 10 years
- Aggressive financial control

STRATOVAC II

Third Generation (1977–1985)
- Product family proliferated for all segments and channels
- Product cycle: 5 years and shortening
- Aggressive manufacturing

Challenger 6 0 0 0

Stratovac — Plus — Workman
Plus — Deluxe
Deluxe — Maybel's Housekeeper — Royal Housekeeper, Housekeeper Canadian

Imperial — Maybel's Housekeeper II — Royal Housekeeper II, Housekeeper Canadian II
Sentry — Workman II
Stratovac II — Stratovac II — Stratovac II
Handivac — Handivac — Handivac 405 — Stratovac II
Handivac 403

Challenger 6000 series — Challenger 6003, Challenger 6002, Challenger 6001, Challenger 6005, Challenger 6004
Pioneer 4003, Pioneer 4002, Pioneer 4001
Helpmate — Helpmate — Helpmate SE

Critical skills
Manual assembly; some flexibility
• Metal stamping and cutting

Growing capabilities
Electronic component design
• Plastic molding and components

Critical skills
Manual assembly; some flexibility; some outsourcing • Metalworking and plastics
• Electronic component design

Growing capabilities
Modular manufacturing
• Electronic controls

Critical skills
High productivity manual and automated assembly; cellular manufacturing •
Outsourcing • Plastics • Electronic controls

Growing capabilities
Computer-aided design and assembly
• Integration of design and manufacturing engineering • Quality: conformance to increasingly tight specifications

1950 — 1955 — 1960 — 1965 — 1970 — 1975 — 1980 — 1985

Department stores* 56%
Hardware stores 26%
Industrial 10%
Catalogs 8%

Department stores 51%
Hardware stores 22%
Industrial 10%
Catalogs and catalog stores* 17%

Department stores 48%
Hardware chains and stores 15%
Industrial 12%
Catalog and discount stores* 25%

*Fastest growing channel

discount chains and catalog stores, which by 1978 had pretty much eclipsed hardware stores. Others saw the Helpmate as a low-end product for department stores too. In the end, Helpmate was a smash in the discount stores and all but disappeared from department stores.

——— THE NEXT GENERATION?

Imagine that it is 1985 and Coolidge managers are gathered to consider the company's future. Their three-generation map (*Exhibit 5*) has simplified a great deal of information—information the managers might intuitively understand but could not have looked at so clearly before. Where can they go from here?

From their map, it's clear that Coolidge's product offerings are not appropriately matched to the new environment. They have aimed most of their products at department stores, and now discount chains are growing at a tremendous rate. They had devoted too much attention to figuring out how to leverage products at the high end, when the big battle was shaping up at the low end. Now Coolidge's managers wonder how long it will be before power options and accessories show up on cheaper, sturdier import lines distributed to high-volume outlets.

More growth in the company's manufacturing capabilities is obviously very important now. The map indicates the growing reciprocity between design and manufacturing engineers, owing largely to the initiatives of the younger design group. It would not be hard to imagine a merging of all engineering groups and the use of temporary dedicated development teams at this point. Product life cycles have obviously been shrinking; designers have to think fast now and cooperate across functional lines. To bring out a new line of inexpensive products that are both reliable and varied in options, Coolidge will need automated, flexible manufacturing systems. This development means bringing all parts of the company together—designers with marketing, and manufacturing with both. It means, interestingly enough, a need for even clearer, more complete new product development maps.

The finished product development map presented here may appear elementary, but managers who have mapped their products' evolution have experienced substantial payoff in several areas. First, the map can be extremely useful to product development efforts. It helps focus development projects and limit their scope, making them more manageable. The map helps set specifications and targets for individual projects, provides a context for relating concurrent projects to one another, and indicates how the sequence of projects capitalizes on the company's previous investments. These benefits do much to minimize the likelihood of encountering two of the pitfalls we identified at the outset of this article: the moving target and the lack of product distinctiveness.

A second important benefit is the motivation the map provides the various functional groups—all with a stake in effective product development—

to develop their own complementary strategies. As illustrated in the Coolidge Corporation example, the product development map raises a number of issues regarding distribution channels, product technology, and manufacturing approaches that must be answered in all parts of the company if the map is to represent the organization's agreed-on direction.

This point brings up the need for submaps in each functional area. In the Coolidge case, the first couple of product generations may not have shown the need for a more careful distribution channel map, but by the third the need is painfully clear. Capturing other strategic marketing variables in, say, a price map, a competitive product positioning map, and a customer map would enable the marketing function to identify and present important trends in the marketplace, define targets for future product offerings, and provide guidance for developing and committing sales and marketing resources.

Equally apparent by the third generation is the need for supporting maps in design engineering. A set of design engineering submaps can produce a clearer sense of the mix of engineering talent the company requires, how it should be organized and focused, and the rate at which the company should bring new technologies into future product generations. These maps would not only help managers integrate design resources with product development efforts but would also ensure that they hire and train new employees in a timely and effective manner and that they focus new project tools (such as computer-aided engineering) on pressing product development needs. The key is achieving technical agreement in advance of product development.

Toward the end of the third generation at Coolidge, the map reveals the need for more detailed manufacturing functional maps to bring out issues raised in the "critical skills" oval. Such maps would focus on strategic issues relating to manufacturing facilities, vendor relationships, and automation technology.

Again, the development of such functional submaps not only benefits manufacturing but also helps the company maximize the return on new product development resources. The most interesting and useful benefits will come out of debates about what to put in the submaps.

Submaps capture the essence of the functional strategies and, when integrated with the new product development map, serve to tie those functional strategies together and provide both a foundation and a process for achieving a company's business strategy. The whole process facilitates the cross-functional discussion and resolution of strategic issues. How often have well-intentioned functional managers met to discuss their various substrategies only to have those from other functions tune out within the first two minutes, as the discussion becomes too technical, too detailed, or simply too parochial to comprehend?

Mapping provides a process for planning that avoids too much detail (like budgeting) and too much parochialism (like traditional functional strategy sessions). Managers will inevitably develop linkages across the organization by going through the steps of selecting the resources or factors to develop into a map, identifying the key dimensions to capture in the map, reviewing historical data to understand the relationships of those dimensions, and examining what is likely to drive future versions of the map. Functions can share their maps to communicate, refine, and agree on important product strategy choices. It is the sharing of functional capabilities—capabilities applied in a systematic, repetitive fashion to product development opportunities—that will become the company's competitive advantage.

——— DISCUSSION QUESTIONS

1. One of the best ways to revitalize a company is to put out a new product. The authors claim that the product development process should involve everyone—from general manager to engineers, designers, manufacturing executives, and marketers. How can having so many participants result in advantages? What are some of these advantages? Or can "too many cooks spoil the broth," causing dissension, confusion, delays, and added costs?

2. Assume that the product development process were to exclude marketing representatives. Would their absence help the process? Or could it create important risks? If so, what are they?

3. Do you believe the designers of a product should work with manufacturing? Are there advantages to this kind of cooperation? Are there potential problems in their collaboration?

4. Who on the product development team is best equipped to decide on the product's eventual channels of distribution? What are some important considerations that would influence this decision?

5. The authors propose a "map" to guide development of a new product—including the areas of pricing, competitive positioning, changing customer trends in the marketplace, and so on. Why are these factors important for product development?

The New New Product Development Game

18

HIROTAKA TAKEUCHI AND IKUJIRO NONAKA

In the fast-paced, competitive world of commercial new product development, the old, sequential approach to developing new products will not get the job done. This reading describes the features of a holistic method for developing new products—built-in instability, self-organizing project teams, overlapping development phases, "multilearning," subtle control, and organizational transfer of learning. In addition to providing speed and flexibility, this approach can act as a change agent, introducing creative, market-driven ideas and processes into rigid organizations.

The rules of the game in new product development are changing. Many companies have discovered that it takes more than the accepted basics of high quality, low cost, and differentiation to excel in today's competitive market. It also takes speed and flexibility.

This change is reflected in the emphasis companies are placing on new products as a source of new sales and profits. At 3M, for example, products less than five years old account for 25% of sales. A 1981 survey of 700 U.S. companies indicated that new products would account for one-third of all profits in the 1980s, an increase from one-fifth in the 1970s.[1]

This new emphasis on speed and flexibility calls for a different approach for managing new product development. The traditional sequential or "relay race" approach to product development—exemplified by the National Aeronautics and Space Administration's phased program planning (PPP) system—may conflict with the goals of maximum speed and flexibility. Instead, a holistic or "rugby" approach—where a team tries to go the distance as a unit, passing the ball back and forth—may better serve today's competitive requirements.

Under the old approach, a product development process moved like a relay race, with one group of functional specialists passing the baton to the next group. The project went sequentially from phase to phase: concept development, feasibility testing, product design, development process, pilot produc-

---

1. Booz Allen & Hamilton survey reported in Susan Fraker, "High-Speed Management for the High-Tech Age," *Fortune,* March 5, 1984, p. 38.

EXHIBIT 1
Sequential (A) vs. Overlapping (B and C) Phases of Development

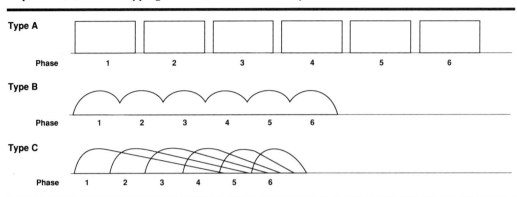

tion, and final production. Under this method, functions were specialized and segmented: the marketing people examined customer needs and perceptions in developing product concepts; the R&D engineers selected the appropriate design; the production engineers put it into shape; and other functional specialists carried the baton at different stages of the race.

Under the rugby approach, the product development process emerges from the constant interaction of a hand-picked, multidisciplinary team whose members work together from start to finish. Rather than moving in defined, highly structured stages, the process is born out of the team members' interplay (see *Exhibit 1*). A group of engineers, for example, may start to design the product (phase three) before all the results of the feasibility tests (phase two) are in. Or the team may be forced to reconsider a decision as a result of later information. The team does not stop then, but engages in iterative experimentation. This goes on in even the latest phases of the development process.

Exhibit 1 illustrates the difference between the traditional, linear approach to product development and the rugby approach. The sequential approach, labeled type A, is typified by the NASA-type PPP system. The overlap approach is represented by type B, where the overlapping occurs only at the border of adjacent phases, and type C, where the overlap extends across several phases. We observed a type B overlap at Fuji-Xerox and a type C overlapping at Honda and Canon.

This approach is essential for companies seeking to develop new products quickly and flexibly. The shift from a linear to an integrated approach encourages trial and error and challenges the status quo. It stimulates new kinds of learning and thinking within the organization at different levels and functions. Just as important, this strategy for product development can act as an agent of change for the larger organization. The energy and motivation the effort produces can spread throughout the big company and begin to break down some of the rigidities that have set in over time.

In this reading, we highlight companies both in Japan and in the United States that have taken a new approach to managing the product development process. We examined such multinational companies as Fuji-Xerox, Canon, Honda, NEC, Epson, Brother, 3M, Xerox, and Hewlett-Packard. We then analyzed the development process of six specific products:

- FX-3500 medium-sized copier (introduced by Fuji-Xerox in 1978)
- PC-10 personal-use copier (Canon, 1982)
- City car with 1200-cc engine (Honda, 1981)
- PC 8000 personal computer (NEC, 1979)
- AE-1 single-lens reflex camera (Canon, 1976)
- Auto Boy lens shutter camera, known as the Sure Shot in the United States (Canon, 1979)

We selected each product on the basis of its impact, its visibility within the company as part of a "breakthrough" development process, the novelty of the product features at the time, the market success of the product, and the access to and availability of data on each product.

MOVING THE SCRUM DOWNFIELD

From interviews with organization members from the CEO to young engineers, we learned that leading companies show six characteristics in managing their new product development processes:

1. Built-in instability
2. Self-organizing project teams
3. Overlapping development phases
4. "Multilearning"
5. Subtle control
6. Organizational transfer of learning

These characteristics are like pieces of a jigsaw puzzle. Each element, by itself, does not bring about speed and flexibility. But taken as a whole, the characteristics can produce a powerful new set of dynamics that will make a difference.

BUILT-IN INSTABILITY

Top management kicks off the development process by signaling a broad goal or a general strategic direction. It rarely hands out a clear-cut new product concept or a specific work plan. But it offers a project team a wide measure of freedom and also establishes extremely challenging goals. For example, Fuji-Xerox's top management asked for a radically different copier and gave the FX-3500 project team two years to come up with a machine that could be produced at half the cost of its high-end line and still perform as well.

Top management creates an element of tension in the project team by giving it great freedom to carry out a project of strategic importance to the company and by setting very challenging requirements. An executive in charge of development at Honda remarked, "It's like putting the team members on the second floor, removing the ladder, and telling them to jump or else. I believe creativity is born by pushing people against the wall and pressuring them almost to the extreme."

SELF-ORGANIZING PROJECT TEAMS

A project team takes on a self-organizing character as it is driven to a state of "zero information"—where prior knowledge does not apply. Ambiguity and fluctuation abound in this state. Left to stew, the process begins to create its own dynamic order.[2] The project team begins to operate like a start-up company—it takes initiatives and risks, and develops an independent agenda. At some point, the team begins to create its own concept.

A group possesses a self-organizing capability when it exhibits three conditions: autonomy, self-transcendence, and cross-fertilization. In our study of the various new product development teams, we found all three conditions.

Autonomy Headquarters' involvement is limited to providing guidance, money, and moral support at the outset. On a day-to-day basis, top management seldom intervenes; the team is free to set its own direction. In a way, top management acts as a venture capitalist. Or as one executive said, "We open up our purse but keep our mouth closed."

This kind of autonomy was evident when IBM developed its personal computer. A small group of engineers began working on the machine in a converted warehouse in remote Boca Raton, Florida. Except for quarterly corporate reviews, headquarters in Armonk, New York, allowed the Boca Raton group to operate on its own. The group got the go-ahead to take unconventional steps such as selecting outside suppliers for its microprocessor and software package.

We observed other examples of autonomy in our case studies:

- The Honda City project team, whose members' average age was 27, had these instructions from management: to develop "the kind

2. *See*, for example, Ilya Prigozine, *From Being to Becoming* (San Francisco, Calif.: Freeman, 1980); Eric Jantsch, "Unifying Principles of Evolution," in Eric Jantsch, ed., *The Evolutionary Vision* (Boulder, Colorado: Westview Press, 1981); and Devendra Sahal, "A Unified Theory of Self-Organization," *Journal of Cybernetics* (April–June, 1979): 127. *See also* Todao Kagono, Ikujiro Nonaka, Kiyonari Sakakibara, and Akihiro Okumura, *Strategic vs. Evolutionary Management: A U.S.–Japan Comparison of Strategy and Organization* (Amsterdam: North-Holland, 1985).

of car that the youth segment would like to drive." An engineer said, "It's incredible how the company called in young engineers like ourselves to design a car with a totally new concept and gave us the freedom to do it our way."

- A small group of sales engineers who originally sold microprocessors built the PC 8000 at NEC. The group started with no knowledge about personal computers. "We were given the go-ahead from top management to proceed with the project, provided we would develop the product by ourselves and also be responsible for manufacturing, selling, and servicing it on our own," remarked the project's head.

Self-transcendence   The project teams appear to be absorbed in a never-ending quest for "the limit." Starting with the guidelines set forth by top management, they begin to establish their own goals and keep on elevating them throughout the development process. By pursuing what appear at first to be contradictory goals, they devise ways to override the status quo and make the big discovery.

We observed many examples of self-transcendence in our field work. The Canon AE-1 project team came up with new ideas to meet the challenging parameters set forth by top management. The company asked the team to develop a high-quality, automatic exposure camera that had to be compact, lightweight, easy to use, and priced 30% lower than the prevailing price of single-lens cameras. To reach this ambitious target, the project team achieved several firsts in camera design and production: an electronic brain consisting of integrated circuits custom-made by Texas Instruments; modularized production, which made automation and mass production possible; and reduction in the number of parts by 30% to 40%. "It was a struggle because we had to deny our traditional way of thinking," recalled the head of the AE-1 team. "But we do that every day in the ongoing parts of our business," responded another Canon executive. The entire organization makes daily, incremental improvements to strengthen what the president calls "the fundamentals": R&D, production technology, selling prowess, and corporate culture.

The Honda City project team also achieved a breakthrough by transcending the status quo. The team was asked to develop a car with two competitive features for the youth segment: efficiency in resources and fuel, and uncompromising quality at a low price. The team's natural instinct was to develop a scaled-down version of Honda's best-selling Civic model. But after much debate, the team decided to develop a car with a totally new concept. It challenged the prevailing idea that a car should be long and low and designed a "short and tall" car. Convinced that an evolution toward a "machine minimum, human maximum" concept was inevitable, the team was willing to risk going against the industry norm.

Cross-fertilization   A project team consisting of members with varying functional specializations, thought processes, and behavior patterns carries out new product development. The Honda team, for example, consisted of hand-picked members from R&D, production, and sales. The company went a step further by placing a wide variety of personalities on the team. Such diversity fostered new ideas and concepts.

While selecting a diverse team is crucial, it isn't until the members start to interact that cross-fertilization actually takes place. Fuji-Xerox located the multifunctional team building the FX-3500—consisting of members from the planning, design, production, sales, distribution, and evaluation departments—in one large room. A project member gave the following rationale for this step: "When all the team members are located in one large room, someone's information becomes yours, without even trying. You then start thinking in terms of what's best or second best for the group at large and not only about where you stand. If everyone understands the other person's position, then each of us is more willing to give in, or at least to try to talk to each other. Initiatives emerge as a result."

OVERLAPPING DEVELOPMENT PHASES

The self-organizing character of the team produces a unique dynamic or rhythm. Although the team members start the project with different time horizons—with R&D people having the longest time horizon and production people the shortest—they all must work toward synchronizing their pace to meet deadlines. Also, while the project team starts from "zero information," each member soon begins to share knowledge about the marketplace and the technical community. As a result, the team begins to work as a unit. At some point, the individual and the whole become inseparable. The individual's rhythm and the group's rhythm begin to overlap, creating a whole new pulse. This pulse serves as the driving force and moves the team forward.

But the quickness of the pulse varies in different phases of development. The beat seems to be most vigorous in the early phases and tapers off toward the end. A member of Canon's PC-10 development team described this rhythm as follows: "When we are debating about what kind of concept to create, our minds go off in different directions and list alternatives. But when we are trying to come to grips with achieving both low cost and high reliability, our minds work to integrate the various points of view. Conflict tends to occur when some are trying to differentiate and others are trying to integrate. The knack lies in creating this rhythm and knowing when to move from one state to the other."

Under the sequential or relay race approach, a project goes through several phases in a step-by-step fashion, moving from one phase to the next only after all the requirements of the preceding phase are satisfied. These checkpoints control risk. But at the same time, this approach leaves little room for integration. A bottleneck in one phase can slow or even halt the entire development process.

Under the holistic or rugby approach, the phases overlap considerably, which enables the group to absorb the vibration or "noise" generated

EXHIBIT 2
Fuji-Xerox's Product Development Schedule

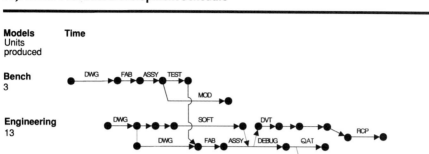

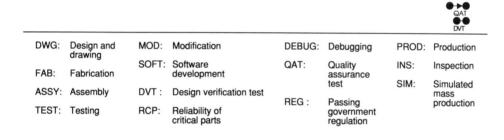

DWG:	Design and drawing	MOD:	Modification	DEBUG:	Debugging	PROD:	Production
		SOFT:	Software development	QAT:	Quality assurance test	INS:	Inspection
FAB:	Fabrication					SIM:	Simulated mass production
ASSY:	Assembly	DVT:	Design verification test				
TEST:	Testing	RCP:	Reliability of critical parts	REG:	Passing government regulation		

throughout the development process. When a bottleneck appears, the level of noise obviously increases. But the process does not come to a sudden halt; the team manages to push itself forward.

Fuji-Xerox inherited the PPP system (see type A in *Exhibit 1*) from its parent company, but revised it in two ways. First, it reduced the number of phases from six to four by redefining some of the phases and aggregating them differently. Second, it changed the linear, sequential system into the so-called "sashimi" system shown in *Exhibit 2*. (Sashimi is slices of raw fish arranged on a plate, one slice overlapping the other.)

The sashimi system requires extensive interaction not only among project members but also with suppliers. The FX-3500 team invited them to join the project at the very start (they eventually produced 90% of the parts for the model). Each side regularly visited the other's plants and kept the information channel open at all times. This kind of exchange and openness—both within the project team and with suppliers—increases speed and flexibility. Fuji-Xerox shortened the development time from 38 months for an earlier model to 29 months for the FX-3500.

If sashimi defines the Fuji-Xerox approach, then rugby describes the overlapping at Honda. Like a rugby team, the core project members at Honda stay intact from beginning to end and are responsible for combining all of the phases.

In the relay-like PPP system, the crucial problems tend to occur at the points where one group passes the project to the next. The rugby approach smooths out this problem by maintaining continuity across phases.

The Auto Boy project proceeded with much overlapping across phases as well. Canon's design engineers stayed alert throughout the process to make sure their design was being converted into what they had in mind. The production people intruded onto the design engineers' turf to make sure that the design was in accord with production scale economies.

The overlapping approach has both merits and demerits. Greater speed and increased flexibility are the "hard" merits. But the approach also has a set of "soft" merits relating to human resource management. The overlap approach enhances shared responsibility and cooperation, stimulates involvement and commitment, sharpens a problem-solving focus, encourages initiative taking, develops diversified skills, and heightens sensitivity toward market conditions.

The more obvious demerits result from having to manage an intensive process. Problems include communicating with the entire project team, maintaining close contact with suppliers, preparing several contingency plans, and handling surprises. This approach also creates more tension and conflict in the group. As one project member aptly put it, "If someone from development thinks that 1 out of 100 is good, that's a clear sign for going ahead. But if someone from production thinks that 1 out of 100 is not good, we've got to start all over. This gap in perception creates conflict."

The overlapping of phases also does away with traditional notions about division of labor. Division of labor works well in a type A system, where management clearly delineates tasks, expects all project members to know their responsibilities, and evaluates each on an individual basis. Under a type B or C system, the company accomplishes the tasks through what we call "shared division of labor," where each team member feels responsible for—and is able to work on—any aspect of the project.

MULTILEARNING

Because members of the project team stay in close touch with outside sources of information, they can respond quickly to changing market conditions. Team members engage in a continual process of trial and error to narrow down the number of alternatives that they must consider. They also acquire broad knowledge and diverse skills, which help them create a versatile team capable of solving an array of problems fast.

Such learning by doing manifests itself along two dimensions: across multiple levels (individual, group, and corporate) and across multiple functions. We refer to these two dimensions of learning as "multilearning."

Multilevel Learning   Learning at the individual level takes place in a number of ways. 3M, for example, encourages engineers to devote 15% of their company time to pursuing their "dream." Canon utilizes peer pressure to foster individual learning. A design engineer for the PC-10 project explained, "My senior managers and some of my colleagues really study hard. There is no way I can compete with them in the number of books they read. So whenever I have time, I go to a department store and spend several hours in the toy department. I observe what's selling and check out the new gadgets being used in the toys. They may give me a hint or two later on."

Learning is pursued emphatically at the group level as well. Honda, for example, dispatched several members of the City project team to Europe for three weeks when the project reached a dead end at the concept development phase. They were told simply to "look around at what's happening in Europe." There they encountered the Mini-Cooper—a small car developed decades ago in the United Kingdom—which had a big impact on their design philosophy.

While it was developing the PC-10 copier, Canon team members left the project offices to hold a number of meetings in nearby hotels. In one of the early meetings, the entire project team broke up into subgroups, each with a representative from the design team and the production team. Each subgroup was told to calculate the cost of a key part and figure out ways of reducing that cost by one-third. "Since every subgroup faced the same mandate and the same deadline, we had no choice," recalled one project member. Learning took place in a hurry.

Learning at the corporate level is best achieved by establishing a company-wide movement or program. Fuji-Xerox, for example, used the total quality control (TQC) movement as a basis for changing the corporate mentality. TQC was designed to heighten the entire organization's sensitivity toward simultaneous quality and productivity improvement, market orientation, cost reduction, and work simplification. To achieve these goals, everyone in the organization had to learn the basics of techniques like statistical quality control and value engineering.

Hewlett-Packard embarked on a four-phased training program in marketing as part of the corporation's aim to become more market oriented. The company now brings in top academics and business consultants to spread the marketing message. It also applies techniques borrowed from the consumer packaged goods industry, such as focus group interviews, quantitative market research, and test marketing. Further, the company has created a corporate marketing division to accelerate what one insider calls "the transition from a company run by engineers for engineers to one with a stronger marketing focus."

Multifunctional Learning   Experts are encouraged to accumulate experience in areas other than their own. For instance:

- All the project members who developed Epson's first miniprinter were mechanical engineers who knew little about electronics at the start. So the leader of the project team, also a mechanical engineer, returned to his alma mater as a researcher and studied electrical engineering for two years. He did this while the project was under way. By the time they had completed the miniprinter project, all the engineers were knowledgeable about electronics. "I tell my people to be well-versed in two technological fields and in two functional areas, like design and marketing," the leader said. "Even in an engineering-oriented company like ours, you can't get ahead without the ability to foresee developments in the market."
- The team working on NEC's PC 8000 consisted of sales engineers from the Electronic Devices Division. They acquired much of the know-how to develop the company's first personal computer by putting together TK 80, a computer kit, and introducing it on the market two years in advance of the PC 8000, and by stationing themselves for about a year, even on weekends, at BIT-IN, an NEC service center in the middle of Akihabara, talking with hobbyists and learning the user's viewpoint.

These examples show the important role that multilearning plays in the company's overall human resource management program. It fosters initiative and learning by doing on the part of the employees and helps keep them up to date with the latest developments. It also serves as a basis for creating a climate that can bring about organizational transition.

SUBTLE CONTROL

Although project teams are largely on their own, they are not uncontrolled. Management establishes enough checkpoints to prevent instability, ambiguity, and tension from turning into chaos. At the same time, management avoids the kind of rigid control that impairs creativity and spontaneity. Instead, the emphasis is on "self-control," "control through peer pressure," and "control by love," which collectively we call "subtle control."

Subtle control is exercised in the new product development process in seven ways:

1. Selecting the right people for the project team while monitoring shifts in group dynamics and adding or dropping members when necessary. "We would add an older and more conservative member to the team should the balance shift too much toward radicalism,"

said a Honda executive. "We carefully pick the project members after long deliberation. We analyze the different personalities to see if they would get along. Most people do get along, thanks to our common set of values."

2. Creating an open work environment, as in the case of Fuji-Xerox.

3. Encouraging engineers to go out into the field and listen to what customers and dealers have to say. "A design engineer may be tempted to take the easy way out at times, but may reflect on what the customer had to say and try to find some way of meeting that requirement," noted an engineer from Fuji-Xerox.

4. Establishing an evaluation and reward system based on group performance. Canon, for example, applied for patents for products from the PC-10 project on a group basis.

5. Managing the differences in rhythm throughout the development process. As mentioned earlier, the rhythm is most vigorous in the early phases and tapers off toward the end.

6. Tolerating and anticipating mistakes. Engineers at Honda are fond of saying that "a 1% success rate is supported by mistakes made 99% of the time." A Brother executive in charge of R&D said, "It's natural for young engineers to make a lot of mistakes. The key lies in finding the mistakes early and taking steps to correct them immediately. We've taken steps to expedite the trial production cycle for that reason." A 3M executive noted, "I believe we learn more from mistakes than from successes. That's not to say we should make mistakes easily. But if we do make mistakes, we ought to make them creatively."

7. Encouraging suppliers to become self-organizing. Involving them early during design is a step in the right direction. But the project team should refrain from telling suppliers what to do. As Xerox found out, suppliers produce better results when they have the problem explained to them and are allowed to decide how to furnish the parts.

TRANSFER OF LEARNING

The drive to accumulate knowledge across levels and functions is only one aspect of learning. We observed an equally strong drive on the part of the project members to transfer their learning to others outside the group.

Transfer of learning to subsequent new product development projects or to other divisions in the organization takes place regularly. In several of the companies we studied, the transfer took place through "osmosis"—by assigning key individuals to subsequent projects. A Honda executive explained, "If the factory is up and running and the early-period claims are resolved, we dismantle the project team, leaving only a few people to follow through. Since we have only a limited number of unusually able people, we turn them loose on another key project immediately."

Knowledge is also transmitted in the organization by converting project activities to standard practice. At Canon, for example, the Auto Boy project produced a format for conducting reviews that was used in later projects. One team member recalled, "We used to meet once a month or so to exchange notes on individual subprojects in progress and once in three months or so to discuss the project from a larger perspective. This pattern later became institutionalized into the monthly and quarterly progress reviews adopted from the PC-10 minicopier project."

Naturally, companies try to institutionalize the lessons derived from their successes. IBM is trying to emulate the personal computer development project—which was completed in 13 months with outside help—throughout the company.

At Hewlett-Packard, the personal computer group is reprogramming the way the entire company develops and sells new products. In the past, the company was famous for designing a machine for a particular customer and charging a premium price. But it later engineered its ThinkJet—a quiet inkjet printer—for low-cost mass production and priced it low. Within six months of its introduction, the printer captured 10% of the low-end market. Hewlett-Packard began to apply what it had learned from designing and pricing ThinkJet to its minicomputer line. Within months of putting ThinkJet on the market, the company introduced a minicomputer system for a broad corporate audience at a modest price.

But institutionalization, when carried too far, can create its own danger. Passing down words of wisdom from the past or establishing standard practices based on success stories works well when the external environment is stable. Changes in the environment, however, can quickly make such lessons impractical.

Several companies have tried to unlearn old lessons. Unlearning helps keep the development team in tune with the realities of the outside environment. It also acts as a springboard for making more incremental improvements.

Much of the unlearning is triggered by changes in the environment. But some companies consciously pursue unlearning. Consider these examples:

- Epson's target is to have the next-generation model in development stages as a new model is being introduced on the market. The company tells its project teams that the next-generation model must be at least 40% better than the existing one.
- When Honda was building the third-generation Civic model, its project team opted to scrap all the old parts and start anew. When the car made its debut before the public, all the new parts were displayed right next to the car at the request of the project members. The car won the 1984 Car of the Year Award in Japan.
- Fuji-Xerox has refined its sashimi approach, first adopted for the FX-3500. Compared with that effort, a new product today requires one-half of the original total manpower. Fuji-Xerox has also reduced the product development cycle from 4 years to 24 months.

——— SOME LIMITATIONS

Some words of caution are in order. The holistic approach to product development may not work in all situations. It has some built-in limitations:

- It requires extraordinary effort on the part of all project members throughout the span of the development process. Sometimes, team members record monthly overtime of 100 hours during the peak and 60 hours during the rest of the project.
- It may not apply to breakthrough projects that require a revolutionary innovation. This limitation may be particularly true in biotechnology or chemistry.
- It may not apply to mammoth projects like those in the aerospace business, where the sheer project scale limits extensive face-to-face discussions.
- It may not apply to organizations where product development is masterminded by a genius who makes the invention and hands down a well-defined set of specifications for people below to follow.

Some limitations also stem from the scope of our research. Our sample size was limited to a handful of companies, and our findings were drawn, for the most part, from observing how the development process was managed in Japan. General conclusions, therefore, must be made with some caution. But as new approaches to product development gain acceptance in the United States, the difference between the two countries may not be so much a difference of kind as a difference of degree.

——— MANAGERIAL IMPLICATIONS

Changes in the environment—intensified competition, a splintered mass market, shortened product life cycles, and advanced technology and automation—are forcing managements to reconsider the traditional ways of creating products. A product that arrives a few months late can easily lose several months of payback. A product designed by an engineer afflicted with the "next bench" syndrome—the habit of designing a product by asking the coworker on the next bench what kind of a product he or she would like—may not meet the flexible requirements of the marketplace.

To achieve speed and flexibility, companies must manage the product development process differently. Three kinds of changes should be considered.

First, companies need to adopt a management style that can promote the process. Executives must recognize at the outset that product development seldom proceeds in a linear and static manner. It involves an iterative and dynamic process of trial and error. To manage such a process, companies must maintain a highly adaptive style.

Because projects do not proceed in a totally rational and consistent manner, adaptability is particularly important. Consider, for example, situations where:

- Top management encourages trial and error by purposely keeping goals broad and by tolerating ambiguity. But at the same time, it sets challenging goals and creates tension within the group and within the organization.
- The process by which variety is amplified (differentiation) and reduced (integration) takes place throughout the overlapping phases of the development cycle. Differentiation, however, tends to dominate the concept development phase of the cycle, and integration begins to take over the subsequent phases.
- Operational decisions are made incrementally, but important strategic decisions are delayed as much as possible in order to allow a more flexible response to last-minute feedback from the marketplace.

Because management exercises subtle forms of control throughout the development process, these seemingly contradictory goals do not create total confusion. Subtle control is also consistent with the self-organizing character of the project teams.

Second, a different kind of learning is required. Under the traditional approach, a highly competent group of specialists undertakes new product development. An elite group of technical experts does most of the learning, accumulating knowledge on an individual basis, within a narrow area of focus—what we call learning in depth.

In contrast, under the new approach (in its extreme form) nonexperts undertake product development. They are encouraged to acquire the necessary knowledge and skills on the job. Unlike the experts, who cannot tolerate mistakes even 1% of the time, the nonexperts are willing to challenge the status quo. But to do so, they must accumulate knowledge from across all areas of management, across different levels of the organization, functional specializations, and even organizational boundaries. Such learning in breadth serves as the necessary condition for shared division of labor to function effectively.

Third, management should assign a different mission to new product development. Most companies have treated it primarily as a generator of future revenue streams. But in some companies, new product development also acts as a catalyst to bring about change in the organization. The personal computer project, for example, is said to have changed the way IBM thinks. Projects coming out of Hewlett-Packard's personal computer group, including ThinkJet, have changed its engineering-driven culture.

No company finds it easy to mobilize itself for change, especially in noncrisis situations. But the self-transcendent nature of the project teams and the hectic pace at which the team members work help to trigger a sense of crisis or urgency throughout the organization. A development project of strategic importance to the company, therefore, can create a wartime working environment even during times of peace.

Changes affecting the entire organization are also difficult to carry out within highly structured companies, especially seniority-based companies like the ones commonly found in Japan. But unconventional moves, which may be difficult to pull off during times of peace, can be legitimized during times of war. Thus management can uproot a competent manager or assign a very young engineer to the project without encountering much resistance.

Once the project team is formed, it begins to rise in stature because of its visibility ("we've been hand-picked"), its legitimate power ("we have unconditional support from the top to create something new"), and its sense of mission ("we're working to solve a crisis"). It serves as a motor for corporate change as project members from a variety of functional areas begin to take strategic initiatives that sometimes go beyond the company's conventional domain and as their knowledge gets transferred to subsequent projects.

The environment in which any multinational company—from the United States or Japan—operates has changed dramatically in recent years. The rules of the game for competing effectively in today's world market have changed accordingly. Multinationals must achieve speed and flexibility in developing products; to do so requires the use of a dynamic process involving much reliance on trial and error and learning by doing. What we need today is constant innovation in a world of constant change.

——— DISCUSSION QUESTIONS

1. The authors present an unorthodox approach to developing new products that, they claim, is faster and more flexible in meeting today's fast-paced, competitive market demands. They advocate commissioning a cross-functional team spanning all departments in the company with a specific idea and goal, setting a price limit and deadline, and giving them the freedom to work without interference from top management. What are the benefits of this holistic approach? How does this differ from the traditional approach?

2. In a company that has successfully used conventional approaches to product development, how does unlearning the old way present a problem? What risks are created when the pressure of a new approach is applied?

3. Does the authors' team concept have limitations? Under what circumstances? How would you assess its limitations?

4. The authors point out that a bottleneck can develop at some points in both their approach and in the traditional method. They claim, however, that a bottleneck occurring in the old, sequential approach slows everything down and holds up the next phase, while

the same bottleneck in the new approach does not slow the process. What in their opinion causes the difference? Do you agree?

5. The authors admit that pursuing their method of new product development can result in "instability, ambiguity, and tension" that can turn into chaos. Input from nonexperts, however, results in unconventional, trial-and-error efforts that can have powerful results. How can the problems of the team approach be managed to get positive results?

PRICING DECISIONS

The following section focuses on the fundamental pricing principles from the marketer's point of view. How the marketer arrives at the value of a product, idea, or service is a complex process indeed. Understanding consumer behavior and understanding the competition's strategy are just two of the many considerations. These readings address specific concepts: how pricing new products differs from pricing established products; applying proactive pricing to industrial products; and pricing to maintain or increase profits. All of these strategies require a skillful assessment of outside factors and careful analysis and management of the customer base.

Pricing: The Strategy and Process

19

E. RAYMOND COREY

"All of marketing comes to focus in the pricing decision," maintains the author of this reading. This comprehensive overview outlines six factors that affect pricing strategy: product costs, value to the customer, competition, government influences, management's sense of fairness, and pricing objectives. It also explains how the pricing process adjusts to market value, competition, supply and demand, and cost-factor changes and reviews the procedures consumer- and industrial-goods manufacturers use to set prices.

A price is an expression of value. The value rests in the product's usefulness and quality, in the image conveyed through advertising and promotion, in the product's availability through wholesale and retail distribution systems, and in the service that goes with it. A price is the seller's estimate of what all of this is worth to potential buyers, recognizing the other options buyers have for filling the need the product is intended to satisfy. As long as the product or service finds markets and is profitable at given price levels, it provides a viable economic base for building and maintaining a business.

In the competitive milieu, pricing is game playing. The struggle for market share focuses critically on price. Pricing strategies of competing firms, therefore, are highly interdependent. The price one competitor sets is a function not only of what the market will pay but also of what other firms charge. Individual firms set prices in response to the competition, often with the intention of influencing competitors' pricing behavior in return. Pricing is an art, a game played for high stakes; and for marketing strategists, it is the "moment of truth." All of marketing comes to focus in the pricing decision.

This reading explores pricing strategy—including the considerations that bear on pricing decisions—and it examines the pricing process. The final section delineates certain pricing conventions, or forms, commonly used when pricing consumer and industrial goods and services. For most of us, who see pricing from the buying end of transactions, the marketer's perspective is both fascinating and revealing.

——— PRICING STRATEGY

Price should be set somewhere between what the product costs to make and sell and its value to the customer. If a price exceeds the perceived value of the product to potential purchasers, it has no market. If it is below what the product costs to produce, the business cannot survive for long. Just where a price should be set between cost and customer value is a strategic decision. The factors that influence this decision are competitors' product/price strategies, governmentally imposed constraints, and the seller's and buyer's sense of what's fair. Finally, the most important determinant of price is the marketer's objective—what is the firm trying to do?

We examine each of these areas in the discussion of pricing strategy that follows, and conclude by viewing pricing as a dynamic process.

PRODUCT COSTS

Costs may be classified as *variable* (or out-of-pocket), *fixed,* and *semifixed.* An airline considers the annual depreciation on an aircraft as a fixed cost. Taking the plane off the ground to fly from one city to another incurs certain semifixed costs such as fuel, wages of flight personnel, and airport takeoff and landing fees. These costs are approximately the same for any given flight whether the plane is empty, half-loaded, or completely full of passengers.

The variable costs of the flight include primarily the costs of food and beverages. They vary directly with the number of passengers.

In a manufacturing plant making glass bottles, the fixed costs include the depreciation on plant and capital equipment such as furnaces and forklift trucks. The variable costs are what the glass manufacturer pays for energy to fuel the furnaces, sand and limestone to make the glass, and labor. All are a direct function of the level of output.

If fixed and semifixed costs make up a large portion of total costs, as in the airline example, pricing to attain maximum capacity is crucial. Until the seller covers fixed costs, money is lost. After fixed costs are covered, each incremental sale contributes proportionally larger amounts to profit.

If variable costs are a relatively high percentage of total costs, as they might be for the glassmaker, pricing to maximize unit contribution—that is, the difference between unit variable cost and price—on each bottle produced will be critical to profitability. Under these cost conditions, the manufacturer would work to maximize unit prices and to reduce variable costs.

The objective of the airline's pricing strategy will be to generate enough total revenue to cover its fixed costs, and above that to operate at maximum capacity to make profits. The glass company will set a price to cover its high variable costs per unit and to contribute enough to amortize fixed costs and make a profit.

Under certain conditions companies may elect to price at less than full cost. In conditions of capacity underutilization, for instance, firms with high fixed costs may take business at prices that cover variable costs and make some incremental contribution to fixed costs (or overheads). The hope is to get through bad times, keep the plants running, and hold some critical nucleus of managers, skilled technicians, and laborers.

Pricing temporarily at less than full cost may also be used as a strategy to win a particularly large order. The expectation is that by taking in the new business, the firm may be able to reduce its unit costs and later to raise its prices so as to make a profit on subsequent orders. Taking business below cost with the hope of offsetting near-term losses with longer-term profits is a risky tactic, for there is no assurance that the losses can be made up.

A firm may also set a price near or below cost to gain a large market share—a strategy called *penetration pricing* (on which more will be said later). Generally, pricing low to preempt market share is predicated on the assumption that unit costs will decrease significantly as volume increases. This may happen as the company gains manufacturing experience. In fact, many businesses use an experience (or learning) curve to calculate the effect of volume growth on unit costs.

Learning-curve experience helps reduce the variable-cost component of unit costs. Labor gains in efficiency and purchases of materials and parts in larger volumes result in lower prices, and manufacturing-process improvements produce cost savings.

Moreover, the fixed-cost component of unit costs may come down with volume increases, for larger plants may be more cost efficient. Large-scale selling and advertising programs may also be more cost efficient. If product sales are particularly sensitive to heavy advertising, or if the product requires widespread distribution or extensive field service support, fixed marketing expenditures for these purposes must usually be high.

These scale economies occur in certain cost categories, depending on the product, the processes used to manufacture it, and the level of marketing spending required to be competitive. If significant scale economies are achievable, some competitors may be willing to price low enough to gain volume, thus preventing other competitors from employing the learning curve and emerging as low-cost producers with dominant market shares.

Product cost, then, is not a simple, hard number but rather for pricing purposes, a matter of managerial judgment. It may be construed as full cost or as out-of-pocket cost. It may be the cost levels then in place or experience-curve estimates of future costs. The interpreting of cost factors for pricing depends greatly on product/market objectives (a topic also treated later).

CUSTOMER VALUE

Some business managers set prices simply by adding a percentage over costs to yield an acceptable profit. That approach has two advantages. The price is simple to calculate, and if a firm is a low-cost producer (relative to competitors), "cost-plus" pricing may provide some protection from competitive attack.

The trade-off for simplicity and security, however, may be lost profits. In theory the amount of profit sacrificed is the difference between what customers actually paid and what they would have been willing to pay.

Compared with cost-plus pricing, pricing according to the value of the product to the customer is more difficult and conjectural. How does a manufacturer determine the value of the product in the customer's mind?

First, it helps to distinguish between perceived value and potential value. Perceived value is what the buyer presently recognizes. Potential value is what he or she can be educated to see in the product. That is a task of marketing and may be accomplished through advertising, personal selling, and getting the buyer to try the product.

Second, different customer groups or market segments may perceive product value differently. Different segments may place different values on the several elements that make up the set of product attributes. (*Product*, here, is used in the broadest sense to include the product or service itself, its brand image, its availability, and the service the seller provides.) Businesspeople traveling by air will place little or no value on the free parking at their hotel, but it may be an important consideration for a family vacationing by car. A large firm may place little value on the technical service a supplier offers if the firm has comparable or superior technical resources of its own. But a small company dependent on the supplier's technical service will place high value on them in making purchasing decisions.

A third factor to consider when establishing customer value is the potential buyer's options. Clearly, if one source offers a product at a lower price than another, the lower price sets the upper limit in the marketplace. A corollary, however, is that for buyers to have effective options, they must know about them.

The options of different customers may vary widely. For example, a manufacturer of shower heads may have a choice between using chrome-plated brass or a high-performance plastic. Given this choice and the exceedingly high cost of brass, the plumbing manufacturer is likely to put a high value on the plastic alternative. But a toymaker choosing between a plastic molded part and a steel stamping may not value the plastic as highly.

Another option for customers may be to forgo the product and make do with what they have. Customers may make the buy–not buy decision by comparing the outcome of one course of action with the other. A family may choose, for example, between keeping its old, gas-guzzling automobile and suffering the increasing costs of maintenance and fuel or buying a new, fuel-efficient car. An industrial company may choose between keeping an old machine in operation or buying new, more efficient equipment.

These choices are quantifiable. One may calculate the operating savings in either instance and relate them to the cost of investing in the new car or new machine tool. The anticipated savings may be expressed as a percentage *return on investment* (ROI). Thus, the amount of realizable savings establishes the value of a product to the customer. Buyers can establish their purchasing priorities by calculating ROI measures for each possible use of available funds.

Of course, expected savings may not always quantify the choice between buying or not buying. Part of the value of a new car may be psychic or a more comfortable ride. The buyer of a new television set can hardly establish its clarity of image and its better color rendition as a savings when comparing it against the performance of the old set. But these elements are, nevertheless, real and important considerations.

Finally, the potential customer often regards the seller's price as the supplier's estimate of the worth of the product. If the seller does not value the product highly, it is not likely that the buyer will. Therefore, pricing a product significantly below what the buyer might pay for its functional equivalent can be self-defeating. The buyer may infer that value is, in fact, connoted by price and choose the higher-priced option.

Value, then, for a given product tends to be a function of (1) the utility of its several attributes to the prospective buyer, (2) the options the buyer has and is aware of (i.e., the offerings of competing suppliers and the option of simply not buying at all), and (3) the extent to which the buyer perceives price itself as a measure of product value.

Price Discrimination   If the seller were truly value-pricing, then it would price the product differently for different customer groups. Like the proverbial rug merchant in the Persian bazaar, the seller would negotiate each sale at a price that was mutually acceptable to the seller and the customer. For physical goods, however, that may be an impractical strategy unless the product's form can be altered so as to persuade customers that the product sold in one market segment is different from that sold in others. A manufacturer of a heavy-duty cleaner could, for example, use different brand names and different kinds of containers for in-home applications, industrial uses, and the hobby (say, boating) market and charge three different prices for the same chemical formulation. Price discrimination of this sort works only as long as (1) the products sold in one market are not, for all practical purposes, available to buyers in other segments, and (2) buyers in different markets are not aware that they can buy the same product under a different brand name at a different price. Price differences, however, that reflect variations in the design or formulation of the product to adapt it to the needs of different market segments are more sustainable.

On the other hand, marketers of services commonly practice price discrimination among different classes of buyers. An airline may charge one fare for adults, another for children, another for spouses, another for standby passengers, and a different rate for service personnel. Rates may vary between weekdays and weekends, summer and winter, day and evening. Hotels have similar pricing strategies. Another example is a computer-based information service, which may have one rate for peak-hour usage and one for off-peak, another for libraries, and still another for business firms.

Price discrimination is possible for services because they have high time utility. A room in the Waldorf-Astoria unoccupied on a Sunday night cannot be saved and sold Monday, or shipped to Chicago, put in inventory, and sold during the busy fall months. The same is true of an airline seat on any given flight, a 30-second spot television commercial, and a seat at a Red Sox–Yankees baseball game. If each of these services is not sold at the time it is available, the selling opportunity is lost forever.

Price Sensitivity   The buyer's sensitivity to price is a relevant consideration when linking price to product value. Price sensitivity will vary considerably among purchasers and, for the same purchaser, it will vary from one time and one set of circumstances to another. Buyers who can pass on the cost of the purchase are less sensitive to price than those who cannot. A businessperson with an expense account is less price sensitive to travel costs than a family vacationer.

Price sensitivity also relates to the performance standards by which the purchaser is measured. An engineer buying process equipment for a new chemical plant will be less sensitive to price than to other factors, such as on-time delivery, a trouble-free start-up, and good service. What the equipment costs is less important to the engineer's performance measures than how it performs. Consequently, he or she may be willing to pay a premium price to a supplier who has a reputation for high-quality standards and exceptional service.

For the manager who has to make the decision and be judged for it, performance measures effectively establish the relative worth of different product attributes. For example, industrial purchasing managers are characteristically more price sensitive than engineers because each employee's performance is measured along different dimensions.

A factor in price sensitivity is the uncertainty that attends switching from one supplier to a lower-priced source. Modest price differences are often insufficient to overcome the purchaser's uncertainties about an untried supplier's product quality, reliability, and service. Moreover, there is often concern about being locked in to a new sourcing arrangement and becoming vulnerable to subsequent price increases. Thus, price differences between the "in" supplier and the "outs" may have to be significant to get the buyer to switch from a known and comfortable buyer-seller relationship to a relatively unknown source of supply.

COMPETITION

Competitive market price levels usually impose a tight discipline on value pricing. They reflect not so much what the product is worth to the customer in some absolute sense as the availability of supply relative to demand. The greater the supply relative to demand, the lower the price.

For *commodities*—that is, virtually undifferentiated products—all competitors generally charge identical prices. If one goes above the market price, its sales will drop off sharply; if one goes below, all others are likely to follow or risk losing market share.

How much any individual firm is constrained by competitors' prices, therefore, depends largely on how differentiated its product is. A product may command a price premium if it stands out from other market offerings in ways that have value to customers—for example, functional design, appearance, brand image, and the supplier's reputation for service and availability. IBM, for instance, has typically priced its computers above its competitors' prices for comparable equipment. IBM persuades its customers that it offers superior systems design and field service and is in the forefront of computer technology.

In some circumstances, however, firms will price above competitive levels even though the price differences are not really justified by superior product quality and service. For example, a company may consciously elect not to meet competitive prices in a strategy of "milking" the business—that is, yielding market share and gradually withdrawing from the market. It may continue to sell profitably for some time to loyal customers, in the meantime cutting back gradually on selling and promotional expenses until it eventually phases out of the market.

Some companies choose not to price competitively because to do so would mean selling below cost. These marginal firms eventually go out of business.

Some large companies may not elect to meet the low price of a smaller competitor because to do so might mean giving up unit profits on a large sales base. It may be less costly in the short run to hold prices and give up a small percentage of market share. In the long run, however, the smaller competitor will encroach increasingly on the market positions of major competitors until it too becomes a major factor.

Under shortage conditions some firms may price opportunistically above prevailing market levels, knowing that demand far exceeds available supply and that some buyers will pay the high price.

Finally, some firms may unknowingly be underpriced by competitors on some of their products. These products may be part of a broad line and a reporting system that does not allow the company to monitor the profit performance of each item on the list. Thus it may be losing sales and market position because of price and never realize, until too late, that the business has gone to more aggressive competitors.

Generally, however, pricing strategies must be shaped with regard for present and future competition. In this respect there is significant pricing interdependency among firms in an industry, with each being heavily influenced by the others' strategies and tactics. Some firms follow price trends; others—the larger ones—seek to lead them. Accordingly, the marketing manager contemplating price changes will often try to anticipate competitive responses: "If we do this, what will they do?" Price leaders, moreover, will plan their moves to elicit certain anticipated responses from competitors.

Price Leadership   What is a price leader and what are the qualifications for filling that role? A price leader is the dominant influence on market prices for a class of products. By initiating price increases or decreases the leader may give direction to market price patterns. Moreover, a company may lead without moving at all. If, for example, others seek to raise prices and the leader does not follow, the upward move falters.

This is not to say that firms other than the leader do not influence price levels. On the contrary, it is often the smaller firms in an industry that undermine the prevailing price level by shading prices in a series of transactions.

Thus price leaders' ability to enforce discipline on market prices is limited; the general price level tends strongly to reflect supply–demand forces. The leader does act, however, as the dominant, or reference-point, firm among competing sellers of a product line.

Price leadership is a phenomenon observed primarily in oligopolistic industries. The leader generally has the largest (or a large) market share, is a low-cost producer, has strong distribution, and is often in the technical forefront of product and process development. In particular, the leader earns and holds its position by initiating price moves that are followed by competitors and accepted by customers. False moves, of course, tend to destroy the leader's credibility among its competitors.

The industry may acknowledge a price leader by tacit recognition that the dominant firm's low-cost position and resulting high margins give it the resources to fund new-product development, market development, and extensive promotional programs. Competitors also recognize the leader as having superior financial resources and hence superior capacity for withstanding economic reverses. Finally, there is the implicit assumption that, because of its large market share, the leader will act in the overall industry's best interest.

An effective leadership role is contingent on several factors. First, it is essential that the leader have a superior market-information system as the basis for understanding the market and reacting in a timely way. Another condition of effective leadership is a strong strategic sense. A third is long-term (more than one year) measures of managerial performance. Managers in leadership firms may be required to act in ways that, in the short term, adversely affect market share or profitability; a strategic plan in which price is a key factor may take two to three years to yield a profitable outcome.

Finally, price leaders must want to lead. They must be willing to take responsibility and to act responsibly. They must have a broad concern for the health of their industries that goes beyond selfish interests.

Pricing Strategies   What are some of the characteristic pricing strategies of leader firms? In oligopolistic industries, the leader tends to behave in a way that preserves short-run, market-share stability. An aggressive bid to increase market share will have the opposite effect and invite sharp competitive price reactions and a resultant reduction in overall industry profits.

In an effort to preserve sales volume, industry leaders may even yield market share to smaller, weaker competitors to forestall their price cutting. There is a general tendency for individual firms in oligopolistic industries to seek a share of market that approximates its share of industry capacity. Because of this tendency, market prices in conditions of general underutilization of capacity tend to be set by the firm that has the least-favorable ratio of market share to share of industry capacity. It seeks to redress the balance by reducing prices to improve volume, and all competitors are forced to follow. A way for the leader to preserve price levels during economic downturns, then, may be to yield market share, if possible, to competitors whose market share/plant capacity ratio is such as otherwise to lead them to cut prices. The leader may then take share back on the economic upturn by lagging slightly behind the rising price trend.[1]

Because price leaders are often technical leaders as well, their strategies also take into account the relationship between the prices of new products and present offerings. New products, superior in performance to the ones they will replace, are usually priced at a premium over the old ones commensurate with the increased value to customers. This premium tends to preserve price levels and margins in the old lines and give competitors less incentive to cut prices to preserve volume. The strategy is a reinforcing one; the higher margins on new products provide overhead funding to support continued product development and a strengthened leadership position.

GOVERNMENT INFLUENCES

Government agencies also exert strong influence over prices. In regulated industries such as utilities, airlines, and railroads, state and federal commissions can approve or reject price changes. The motive is both to protect consumer interests and allow the regulated company enough profit to expand capacity as demand grows and a reasonable return on its investment.

---

1. For a detailed study of competitive behavior in the heavy electrical equipment industry, *see* Ralph G. M. Sultan, *Pricing in the Electrical Oligopoly*, Volume 1, *Competition or Collusion* (Boston: Division of Research, Harvard Business School, 1974).

Unregulated industries are also subjected to government influence on pricing. Some agencies can set price guidelines based, usually, on inflation factors; monitor announced price changes; and, often, force firms to roll back increases that exceed the guidelines. In 1978, for example, the President's Council on Wage-Price Stability successfully took action against Sears, Roebuck to get the large retailer to roll back the prices in its 1978 catalog. Given a long history of periodic government efforts to hold down prices, business managements are increasingly loath to reduce prices in an economic downturn for fear of lowering the baseline against which subsequent price increases will be measured.

Other sources of government influence on prices are such legislative actions as the Sherman Act and the Robinson-Patman Act. In general the Sherman Antitrust Act seeks to preserve competition by proscribing predatory pricing (i.e., pricing that has the intent or effect of driving firms out of business). The Robinson-Patman Act makes it illegal to sell the same product at different prices to different customers who are, themselves, in competition with each other. Granting one customer a lower price than is being charged to its competitors, however, is permissible if (1) a low price to one customer meets the equally low price being offered to that firm by a competitor, or (2) the reduced price passes on a cost savings that results from lowered manufacturing, transportation, or marketing costs associated with the sale.[2]

A SENSE OF FAIRNESS

In the absence of government restraints in periods of shortages, a natural tendency for those who control the supply of a product is to raise prices to reflect the supply/demand imbalance. Public pressures, however, such as those brought to bear by citizen groups in the gasoline shortages of 1978 and 1979, may often be powerful restraints. Moreover, business managers often exercise such restraint voluntarily because of their sense of what is fair. Fairness has a high value in the relationship between buyer and seller. If buyers feel that they were gouged when market conditions gave the seller the upper hand, the seller's long-term customer relationships and market base may be damaged.

PRICING OBJECTIVES

Pricing is a key element in strategy, and to make strategic pricing decisions it is important to know what objectives are being served. The range

---

2. *See* John F. Cady, "Note on Legal Issues in the Pricing Process," Harvard Business School No. 9-578-205, for an in-depth treatment of the regulation of pricing practices under the Sherman Act and Robinson-Patman Act.

of possibilities is quite large. One may seek to gain market share or to yield it opportunistically with little concern for future consequences (i.e., "milk" the business). A seller may price to discourage some competitors and to forestall others from entering the market. Or a seller may hold prices high (constructing a "price umbrella") to avoid driving out less efficient competitors and possibly risking antitrust charges. Last, a seller may seek to maximize short-run profits or to "buy in" with the hopes of making profits in the long run.

One may price low to meet a competitive attack, to gain a new customer, or to acquire experience in designing and making certain products. A seller might also price a product to break even or even to sustain losses on some products in the line in order to offer customers a full line. Alternatively, a company may price a new product high to minimize impact on the sales of old products in the line (avoid "cannibalization"). Whatever the objective, it is important that it be determined explicitly. Otherwise pricing decisions become aimless responses to the moves of others.

Skimming and Penetration Pricing Market entry situations and the development of new markets raise particular questions of pricing objectives and strategies. Marketers often face the choice in the early stages of the product life cycle of pricing high (skimming) to maximize short-term unit contribution, or pricing low (penetration) to maximize unit volume and preempt competition.

A skimming strategy has the advantage of permitting an early-stage focus on those customers for whom the product has the highest value and who will pay the most. Theoretically, as the price comes down, new market segments open up, in order of declining product value to different customer sets. A strategy of reducing price gradually to broaden the potential market, in principle, maximizes total profits. It may also serve long-run market development by establishing a prestige image in the introductory phases. Polaroid, for example, first introduced the Land camera in 1948 at over $200, gradually bringing out new models until, in 1965, it brought out the Swinger, priced at under $20.

A skimming strategy on the part of the innovator, however, may be an open invitation to competitors to enter the market and exploit the new product at lower price levels. This is typical, for example, in high-fashion merchandise. New styles introduced to a selected clientele in Paris at prices only the wealthy can afford find their way quickly to New York shops at a fraction of the original price and then to the bargain basements of big department stores. The originator may be content to take the cream off the top and leave the mass market to copiers—or may have no choice in the matter.

Penetration pricing, in contrast, incurs high risks but offers potentially high rewards. There are several conditions that must prevail if the gamble is to pay off. First, the product should be free of any possible defects; otherwise the seller runs the risk of generating high demand by its low prices and facing extensive field-service costs or product recalls.

Second, potential customers should be able to adopt the product quickly without long periods of testing so that competitors do not have time to execute their own market programs. Third, sufficient plant capacity and distribution channels should be in place to fill market demand quickly. Success in penetration pricing hinges critically on timing and on leaving competitors no opportunity to react.

Examples of successful penetration pricing are Bic's takeover of the lion's share of the ballpoint pen market and Texas Instrument's rise to dominance in the hand-held calculator market in the 1970s. Both aggressively cut prices and emerged as market leaders. According to industry sources, TI "priced ahead of the experience curve" in the early stages of market development, willingly sustaining losses and eventually becoming profitable as many smaller competitors dropped out.

These examples suggest another precondition for penetration pricing: a vast potential demand to be tapped at lower price levels. A penetration-price strategy is unlikely to be effective in mature, slow-growth industries dominated by entrenched competitors. Their ability to fight off the invader by reducing prices to variable-cost levels would hardly make the game "worth the candle" for the new entrant. Penetration pricing is also unlikely to be effective in new fields if the product, even though priced close to cost, is still too expensive for most potential purchasers.

Demand Elasticity   The consideration of penetration pricing brings up the matter of demand elasticity as it relates to pricing strategy. In economic theory, the lower the price the greater the demand for a product. In developing a pricing strategy, however, marketers must recognize some modifications of the theory. The demand for many goods, particularly in the industrial sector, is "derived" demand; the demand for truck motors, for example, depends directly on the demand for trucks. Price reductions on this component are not likely to increase truck sales volumes.

Furthermore, price reductions in the early stages of market development for a product that customers must be educated to use are not likely to stimulate sales. It takes more than low prices at this stage to overcome customers' inherent caution.

Price elasticity for any product usually reflects users' shifts from one product or service to another as significant price differences occur among substitutable products. When gasoline prices rise relative to the cost of public transportation, more people travel by air, train, or bus instead of by car. When ballpoint pen prices drop, sales of pencils decline.

In setting pricing objectives, therefore, it is important to ask a range of questions: What is "do-able"? Where will sales volume come from? How will competitors react? What will be the impact of the pricing strategy for one product on other products in the line? How will potential customers react? But the most important question of all is "What are we trying to do?"

THE PRICING PROCESS

In economic theory, prices are set at the intersections of supply and demand curves. But for the individual firm this notion offers little help. Supply/demand analysis may be broadly relevant for an entire class of products such as wheat or nylon fiber or beef or television sets. But unless the product of one supplier is unique and has no direct competition (as in a monopoly), a single firm's price is necessarily a function of market price levels for that class of products, adjusted for any differentiation between that firm's products and those of reference-point competitors—as customers perceive the difference.

Pricing Objectives   The first objective of the pricing process, then, is to establish the market value of the firm's differentiated product relative to the competitor's product. A second purpose may be to probe and adjust for any shifts in supply/demand conditions and to test the willingness of competitors to follow. A third purpose is to adjust price to reflect cost-factor changes and to prevent cost escalation from eroding margins.

The pricing process is a reiterative exercise. Like game playing, each decision is usefully perceived as one in a series of moves. Effective pricing strategies can be carried out effectively if

- Pricing decisions are based on extensive current market information.
- Competitive and customer responses to price changes are carefully monitored and recorded.
- Pricing decisions are made centrally and not delegated to field representatives. (Centralized control is critical for formulating and implementing price strategies.)
- Pricing moves are planned responses to market conditions and competitive behavior.

Announcing Price Changes   An essential part of the process is the implementation of price decisions. It is not enough to decide what the price should be; customers and competitors must be prepared to accept it. Consumers as well as industrial procurement managers must understand and, often, explain to others (the family unit or the business) the reasons for significant price changes. Competitors will have to decide whether they will follow.

The great bulk of price increases are publicly explained as adjustments for cost escalations; others are said to reflect product improvements. In either case, customers must be persuaded that increases are justified by changes in cost economics or product value. How the seller announces the price increase is therefore a critical part of the pricing process.

——— PRICING MODES

As prices for consumer and industrial products are expressed in various forms, it is important for marketers to know the range of practices. In addition, the way a price is stated often has strategic implications for the seller or buyer or for both. We will look first at consumer goods pricing conventions and then turn to the industrial side.

PRICING CONSUMER PRODUCTS

Consumer goods sold through wholesalers and retailers are priced to reflect the margins accruing to these resellers. Margins, unless otherwise stated, are expressed as percentages off the list price to the consumer. An item selling for $1, for example, might be priced to provide the retailer a 40% margin and the wholesaler a 10% margin. These margins are taken successively. Thus,

Manufacturer's suggested retail price (MSRP)	$1.00
Less: retail gross margin (RGM) at 40%	–.40
Wholesaler's price to retailer	.60
Less: wholesale margin at 10%	–.06
Manufacturer's selling price (MSP)	$.54

In the above example the manufacturer sells to the wholesaler at 40% + 10% (a total of 46%) off MSRP or $.54, and the wholesaler sells to the retailer at 40% off list price or $.60. Thus, the wholesale margin is $.06 (10% of $.60).

The fact that the manufacturer may suggest a retail price, however, in no way binds the retailer to sell at that price. But if the retailer sells below that price, any difference must come out of the margin it would receive if it had, in fact, sold at the MSRP.

Some manufacturers that sell through wholesalers simultaneously sell directly to large retail accounts such as supermarket chains. In this situation the manufacturer has a choice. It may sell to wholesalers and to large retail accounts at the same price, on the theory that the large retailer is actually performing both wholesale and retail functions. Or it may protect its wholesalers by selling to retail accounts at the same price the wholesaler would charge retailers. Usually the choice depends on the importance of wholesalers in the manufacturer's overall marketing strategy. If they are important and account for a high percentage of the manufacturer's sales, the manufacturer will not want to risk its good relations with wholesalers by undercutting them in their markets.

The manufacturer's selling price often varies with the quantity purchased. The larger the order, the lower the unit price. Here, for example, is one manufacturer's discount schedule for furniture polish sold in cases of 24 one-quart cans.

Cases to Wholesalers

1–99	47½%
100–400	47½ + 2.5%
401–900	47½ + 4.0%
901–above	47½ + 6.5%

Cases to Retailers

1–5	30%
6–above	30 + 10%

In addition to volume discounts, other percentage discounts may be taken off the manufacturer's prices to wholesalers and retailers. For example, the manufacturer may give a cooperative advertising allowance of 5% of sales as an inducement to resellers to advertise its products. Thus, the manufacturer reimburses the reseller for half the cost of local advertising up to a maximum of 5% of the reseller's purchases.

Often manufacturers and/or wholesalers also offer customers percentage discounts for prompt payment. The bill, for example, might include a statement such as "terms—2%, 10 days, net 30 days." That means that if the buyer pays within a 10-day period, it may deduct 2% from the total bill but that the full amount is due in 30 days.

Some manufacturers also sell on consignment, a type of selling in which title to the goods remains with the manufacturer until they are sold by the reseller; at that time, payment is due. Consignment selling relieves the reseller of investing in inventory and puts that burden back on the manufacturer.

An important consideration in consignment selling is that the manufacturer may legally specify the retail selling price because it owns the goods until they are sold to the ultimate purchaser.[3] The reseller, in fact, acts as the manufacturer's agent. Manufacturers may offer consignment arrangements to resellers both to persuade the reseller to carry the goods and to control the retail price.

PRICING INDUSTRIAL PRODUCTS

Many of the conventions used in consumer goods pricing are also practiced in industrial marketing, although they may take a slightly different form. An industrial counterpart of the furniture polish pricing schedule, for example, is shown in the *Exhibit*. Different prices for grinding wheels are quoted for different purchase quantities and for two different classes of purchasers: distributors and end users. Prices are expressed as percentages of a list price.

---

3. The legality of using consignment arrangements as a way of fixing resale prices has been tested in the courts over a long period of time and is still unclear.

Another pricing convention used in pricing both industrial and consumer goods involves freight costs from the point of shipment to destination. Typically the price quotation specifies whether these charges are paid by the seller or the buyer. If the price is specified as *f.o.b.* (freight on board) *plant*, the buyer pays the freight charges. If *f.o.b. destination* is stipulated, transportation costs are paid by the seller.

In industrial goods marketing, freight charges and who pays them may have considerable competitive significance. For products such as cement and steel, transportation costs are relatively high compared with the value of the product itself. High shipping costs, naturally, serve to limit the area within which a manufacturing plant can effectively compete. To extend their markets geographically, producers of products having high weight or bulk relative to value may use *basing-point pricing* (also called freight equalization). In this system, the transportation cost component of a quoted price is the freight to the buyer's plant from the nearest source of supply, often the plant of a competitor. Although basing-point pricing is a way of competing for distant customers, it also means that by absorbing freight costs the seller earns lower revenues from these customers than from those closer to its plant.

Much industrial buying is done by competitive bidding. In the sealed bid method all bids must be submitted before a given time on a specified date. They are opened publicly at the announced time and the lowest qualified bid is awarded the contract. "Qualified" means that the seller's bid meets the specifications issued by the buyer in the RFQ (request for quotation).

A negotiated bidding procedure differs from sealed bidding in two respects. Bids are not necessarily made public, and buyers may continue to negotiate with the one or two lowest bidders rather than accept the lowest initial offer.

Prices specified in purchase contracts may be fixed-fee, cost-plus, or target-incentive. In contracts negotiated as cost-plus arrangements, the buyer agrees to pay the seller certain costs of fulfilling the contract plus an amount to

EXHIBIT
User-Customer and Distributor Multipliers

QUANTITY GROUP	NO. OF UNITS	USER-CUSTOMER MULTIPLIERS	DISTRIBUTOR MULTIPLIERS
<A	1–9	1.027	0.822
A	10	0.689	0.551
B	20	0.585	0.476
C	50	0.503	0.418
D	100	0.447	0.393
E	250	0.394	0.355
F	750	0.379	0.341
G	1,250	0.365	0.328

Source: Norton Company

cover fixed overheads and profit. Typically, costs paid directly include labor and material. Overheads-plus-profit may be charged on a per-labor-hour basis. In addition, any capital investments needed to do the work may be amortized as part of the unit price until they are completely written off.

In a cost-plus contract the buyer usually negotiates audit privileges with the seller. That is, the buyer has the right to inspect the contractor's cost records.

Some contracts also provide for cost-factor escalation. These provisions allow for price adjustments as certain specified costs (e.g., labor and materials) increase. Contracts specifying cost escalation must stipulate what particular price indices will be used to determine the amounts of price adjustments. Often these indices are those published by the U.S. Bureau of Labor Statistics or issued by trade associations.

Finally, some contractual arrangements are intended to provide cost-efficiency incentives to the contractor. These target-incentive contracts specify a target cost, a ceiling price, and a profit-sharing formula. If the contractor beats the target cost, the contractor splits the savings with the customer in a prescribed ratio. If the target cost is exceeded, the contractor pays part of the difference and the customer pays the rest. The customer is obligated, however, to pay no more than the ceiling price.

A brief review of pricing conventions cannot be all-inclusive. The range of possible arrangements is limited only by the ingenuity of buyers and sellers negotiating with each other in the marketplace. They reflect the strategic objectives of the latter shaped in recognition of the needs and concerns of the former. What we have presented here, however, are among the most widely used and recognized pricing practices.

—— DISCUSSION QUESTIONS

1. Putting a price on a product or service involves many options; it is more than a process—it is a strategy. What are some of the considerations that mold pricing strategy? What factors influence the pricing decision?
2. Define what "value added" to a product or service means to you. Choose a product or service and explain how you would go about "adding value" to it.
3. The author relates that "some business managers set prices simply by adding a percentage over costs to provide an acceptable profit." This sounds simple and fair. Does this pricing strategy have drawbacks?
4. Compare pricing strategy for consumer products with that for industrial products. What are the similarities? What are the differences?

20   Pricing Policies for New Products

JOEL DEAN

This reading, first published in the Harvard Business Review *in 1950, is a practical guide to the problems involved in pricing new products. It outlines the possible price strategies for each stage of a product's life cycle, including the unpredictable period after rollout, and the various grounds for making a choice. Although some of the references and examples go back many years, the fundamental principles of new-product pricing policies are still as sound today as when first written. The version presented here includes the author's retrospective commentary, written twenty-five years later, in which he amplifies his earlier article with insights from the intervening years, providing the reader with a historical perspective on pricing issues.*

How to price a new product is a top management puzzle that is too often solved by cost-theology and hunch. This article suggests a pricing policy geared to the dynamic nature of a new product's competitive status. Today's high rate of innovation makes the economic evolution of a new product a strategic guide to practical pricing.

New products have a protected distinctiveness which is doomed to progressive degeneration from competitive inroads. The invention of a new marketable specialty is usually followed by a period of patent protection when markets are still hesitant and unexplored and when product design is fluid. Then comes a period of rapid expansion of sales as market acceptance is gained.

Next the product becomes a target for competitive encroachment. New competitors enter the field, and innovations narrow the gap of distinctiveness between the product and its substitutes. The seller's zone of pricing discretion narrows as his or her distinctive "specialty" fades into a pedestrian "commodity" which is so little differentiated from other products that the seller has limited independence in pricing, even if rivals are few.

Throughout the cycle, continual changes occur in promotional and price elasticity and in costs of production and distribution. These changes call for adjustments in price policy.

Appropriate pricing over the cycle depends on the development of three different aspects of maturity, which usually move in almost parallel time paths:

1. Technical maturity, indicated by declining rate of product development, increasing standardization among brands, and increasing stability of manufacturing processes and knowledge about them.

2. Market maturity, indicated by consumer acceptance of the basic service idea, by widespread belief that the products of most manufacturers will perform satisfactorily, and by enough familiarity and sophistication to permit consumers to compare brands competently.
3. Competitive maturity, indicated by increasing stability of market shares and price structures.

Of course, interaction among these components tends to make them move together. That is, intrusion by new competitors helps to develop the market, but entrance is most tempting when the new product appears to be establishing market acceptance.

The rate at which the cycle of degeneration progresses varies widely among products. What are the factors that set its pace? An overriding determinant is technical—the extent to which the economic environment must be reorganized to use the innovation effectively. The scale of plant investment and technical research called forth by the telephone, electric power, the automobile, or air transport makes for a long gestation period, as compared with even such major innovations as cellophane or frozen foods.

Development comes fastest when the new gadget fills a new vacuum made to order for it. Electric stoves, as one example, rose to 50% market saturation in the fast-growing Pacific Northwest, where electric power had become the lowest-cost energy.

Products still in early developmental stages also provide rich opportunities for product differentiation, which with heavy research costs holds off competitive degeneration.

But aside from technical factors, the rate of degeneration is controlled by economic forces that can be subsumed under rate of market acceptance and ease of competitive entry.

Market acceptance means the extent to which buyers consider the product a serious alternative to other ways of performing the same service. Market acceptance is a frictional factor. The effect of cultural lags may endure for some time after quality and costs make products technically useful. The slow catch-on of the garbage-disposal unit is an example.

On the other hand, the attitude of acceptance may exist long before any workable model can be developed; then the final appearance of the product will produce an explosive growth curve in sales. The antihistamine cold tablet, a spectacular example, reflected the national faith in chemistry's ability to vanquish the common cold. And, of course, low unit price may speed market acceptance of an innovation; ball-point pens and all-steel houses started at about the same time, but look at the difference in their sales curves.

Ease of competitive entry is a major determinant of the speed of degeneration of a specialty. An illustration is found in the washing machine business before the war, where with little basic patent protection the Maytag position was quickly eroded by small manufacturers who performed essentially an assembly operation. The ball-point pen cascaded from a $12 novelty to a 49-cent "price football," partly because entry barriers of patents and techniques were ineffective. Frozen orange juice, which started as a protected specialty of Minute Maid, sped through its competitive cycle, with competing brands crowding into the market.

At the outset innovators can control the rate of competitive deterioration to an important degree by nonprice as well as by price strategies. Through successful research in product improvement innovators can protect their specialty position both by extending the life of their basic patents and by keeping ahead of competitors in product development. The record of IBM punch-card equipment is one illustration. Ease of entry is also affected by a policy of stay-out pricing (so low as to make the prospects look uninviting), which under some circumstances may slow down the process of competitive encroachment.

───── STEPS IN PIONEER PRICING

Pricing problems start when a company finds a product that is a radical departure from existing ways of performing a service and that is temporarily protected from competition by patents, secrets of production, control at the point of a scarce resource, or by other barriers. The seller here has a wide range of pricing discretion resulting from extreme product differentiation.

A good example of pricing latitude conferred by protected superiority of product was provided by the McGraw Electric Company's "Toastmaster," which, both initially and over a period of years, was able to command a very substantial price premium over competitive toasters. Apparently this advantage resulted from (1) a good product that was distinctive and superior and (2) substantial and skillful sales promotion.

Similarly, Sunbeam priced its electric iron $2 above comparable models of major firms with considerable success. And Sunbeam courageously priced its new metal coffeemaker at $32, much above competitive makes of glass coffeemakers, but it was highly successful.

To get a picture of how a manufacturer should go about setting a price in the pioneer stage, let me describe the main steps of the process (of course the classification is arbitrary and the steps are interrelated): (1) estimate of demand, (2) decision on market targets, (3) design of promotional strategy, and (4) choice of distribution channels.

ESTIMATE OF DEMAND

The problem at the pioneer stage differs from that in a relatively stable monopoly because the product is beyond the experience of buyers and because the perishability of its distinctiveness must be reckoned with. How can demand for new products be explored? How can we find out how much people will pay for a product that has never before been seen or used? There are several levels of refinement to this analysis.

The initial problem of estimating demand for a new product can be broken into a series of subproblems: (1) whether the product will go at all (assuming price is in a competitive range), (2) what range of price will make the product economically attractive to buyers, (3) what sales volumes can be expected at various points in this price range, and (4) what reaction will price produce in manufacturers and sellers of displaced substitutes.

The first step is an exploration of the *preferences and educability of consumers,* always, of course, in the light of the technical feasibility of the new product. How many potential buyers are there? Is the product a practical device for meeting their needs? How can it be improved to meet their needs better? What proportion of the potential buyers would prefer, or could be induced to prefer, this product to already existing products (prices being equal)?

Sometimes it is feasible to start with the assumption that all vulnerable substitutes will be fully displaced. For example, to get some idea of the maximum limits of demand for a new type of reflecting-sign material, a company started with estimates of the aggregate number and area of auto license plates, highway markers, railroad operational signs, and name signs for streets and homes. Next, the proportion of each category needing night-light reflection was guessed. For example, it was assumed that only rural and suburban homes could benefit by this kind of name sign, and the estimate of need in this category was made accordingly.

It is not uncommon and possibly not unrealistic for a manufacturer to make the blithe assumption at this stage that the product price will be "within a competitive range" without having much idea of what that range is. For example, in developing a new type of camera equipment, one of the electrical companies judged its acceptability to professional photographers by technical performance without making any inquiry into its economic value. When the equipment was later placed in an economic setting, the indications were that sales would be negligible.

The second step is marking out this *competitive range of price.* Vicarious pricing experience can be secured by interviewing selected distributors who have enough comparative knowledge of customers' alternatives and preferences to judge what price range would make the new product "a good value." Direct discussions with representative experienced industrial users have produced reliable estimates of the "practical" range of prices. Manufacturers of electrical equipment often explore the economic as well as the technical feasibility of a new product by sending engineers with blueprints and models to see customers, such as technical and operating executives.

In guessing the price range of a radically new consumers' product of small unit value, the concept of barter equivalent can be a useful research guide. For example, a manufacturer of paper specialties tested a dramatic new product in the following fashion: A wide variety of consumer products totally unlike the new product were purchased and spread out on a big table. Consumers selected the products they would swap for the new product. By finding out whether the product would trade evenly for a dish pan, a towel, or a hairpin, the executives got a rough idea of what range of prices might strike the typical consumer as reasonable in the light of the values received for his or her money in totally different kinds of expenditures.

But asking prospective consumers how much they think they would be willing to pay for a new product, even by such indirect or disguised methods, may often fail to give a reliable indication of the demand schedule. Most times people just do not know what they would pay. It depends partly on their income and on future alternatives. Early in the postwar period a manufacturer of television sets tried this method and got highly erratic and obviously unreliable results because the distortion of war shortages kept prospects from fully visualizing the multiple ways of spending their money.

Another deficiency, which may, however, be less serious than it appears, is that responses are biased by the consumer's confused notion that he or she is bargaining for a good price. Not until techniques of depth interviewing are more refined than they are now can this crude and direct method of exploring a new product's demand schedule hold much promise of being accurate.

One appliance manufacturer tried out new products on a sample of employees by selling to them at deep discounts, with the stipulation that they could if they wished return the products at the end of the experiment period and get a refund of their low purchase price. Demand for foreign orange juice was tested by placing it in several markets at three different prices, ranging around the price of fresh fruit; the result showed rather low price elasticity.

While inquiries of this sort are often much too short-run to give any real indication of consumer tastes, the relevant point here is that even such rough probing often yields broad impressions of price elasticity, particularly in relation to product variations such as styling, placing of controls, and use of automatic features. It may show, for example, that $5 of cost put into streamlining or chromium stripping can add $50 to the price.

The third step, a more definite inquiry into the *probable sales from several possible prices*, starts with an investigation of the prices of substitutes. Usually the buyer has a choice of existing ways of having the same service performed; an analysis of the costs of these choices serves as a guide in setting the price for a new way.

Comparisons are easy and significant for industrial customers who have a costing system to tell them the exact value, say, of a forklift truck in terms of warehouse labor saved. Indeed, chemical companies setting up a research project to displace an existing material often know from the start the top price that can be charged for the new substitute in terms of cost of the present material.

But in most cases the comparison is obfuscated by the presence of quality differences that may be important bases for price premiums. This is most true of household appliances, where the alternative is an unknown amount of labor of a mysterious value. In pricing a cargo parachute the choices are: (1) free fall in a padded box from a plane flown close to the ground, (2) landing the plane, (3) back shipment by land from the next air terminal, or (4) land shipment all the way. These options differ widely in their service value and are not very useful pricing guides.

Thus it is particularly hard to know how much good will be done by making the new product cheaper than the old by various amounts, or how much the market will be restricted by making the new product more expensive. The answers usually come from experiment or research.

The fourth step in estimating demand is to consider the *possibility of retaliation by manufacturers of displaced substitutes* in the form of price cutting. This development may not occur at all if the new product displaces only a small market segment. If old industries do fight it out, however, their incremental costs provide a floor to the resulting price competition and should be brought into price plans.

For example, a manufacturer of black-and-white sensitized paper studied the possibility that lowering its price would displace blueprint paper substantially. Not only did the manufacturer investigate the prices of blueprint paper, but it also felt it necessary to estimate the out-of-pocket cost of making blueprint paper because of the probability that manufacturers already in the market would fight back by reducing prices toward the level of their incremental costs.

DECISION ON MARKET TARGETS

When the company has developed some idea of the range of demand and the range of prices that are feasible for the new product, it is in a position to make some basic strategic decisions on market targets and promotional plans. To decide on market objectives requires answers to several questions: What ultimate market share is wanted for the new product? How does it fit into the present product line? What about production methods? What are the possible distribution channels?

These are questions of joint costs in production and distribution, of plant expansion outlays, and of potential competition. If entry is easy, the company may not be eager to disrupt its present production and selling operations to capture and hold a large slice of the new market. But if the prospective profits shape up to a substantial new income source, it will be worthwhile to make the capital expenditures on plant needed to reap the full harvest.

A basic factor in answering all these questions is the expected behavior of production and distribution costs. The relevant data here are all the production outlays that will be made after the decision day—the capital expenditures as well as the variable costs. A go-ahead decision will hardly be made without some assurance that these costs can be recovered before the product becomes a football in the market. Many different projections of costs will be made, depending on the alternative scales of output, rate of market expansion, threats of potential competition, and measures to meet that competition that are under consideration. But these factors and the decision that is made on promotional strategy are interdependent. The fact is that this is a circular problem that in theory can only be solved by simultaneous equations.

Fortunately, it is possible to make some approximations that can break the circle: scale economies become significantly different only with broad changes in the size of plant and the type of production methods. This narrows the range of cost projections to workable proportions. The effects of using different distribution channels can be guessed fairly well without meshing the choices in with all the production and selling possibilities. The most vulnerable point of the circle is probably the decision on promotional strategy. The choices here are broad and produce a variety of results. The next step in the pricing process is therefore a plan for promotion.

DESIGN OF PROMOTIONAL STRATEGY

Initial promotion outlays are an investment in the product that cannot be recovered until some kind of market has been established. The innovator shoulders the burden of creating a market—educating consumers to the existence and uses of the product. Later imitators will never have to do this job; so if the innovator does not want to be simply a benefactor to future competitors, he or she must make pricing plans to recover initial outlays before his or her pricing discretion evaporates.

The innovator's basic strategic problem is to find the right mixture of price and promotion to maximize long-run profits. He or she can choose a relatively high price in pioneering stages, together with extravagant advertising and dealer discounts, and plan to recover promotion costs early; or he or she can use low prices and lean margins from the very outset in order to discourage potential competition when the barriers of patents, distribution channels, or production techniques become inadequate. This question is discussed further later on.

CHOICE OF DISTRIBUTION CHANNELS

Estimation of the costs of moving the new product through the channels of distribution to the final consumer must enter into the pricing procedure, since these costs govern the factory price that will result in a specified consumer price and since it is the consumer price that matters for volume. Distributive margins are partly pure promotional costs and partly physical distribution costs. Margins must at least cover the distributors' costs of warehousing, handling, and order taking. These costs are similar to factory production costs in being related to physical capacity and its utilization, i.e., fluctuations in production or sales volume.

Hence these set a floor to trade-channel discounts. But distributors usually also contribute promotional effort—in point-of-sale pushing, local advertising, and display—when it is made worth their while.

These pure promotional costs are more optional. Unlike physical handling costs they have no necessary functional relation to sales volume. An added layer of margin in trade discounts to produce this localized sales effort (with retail price fixed) is an optional way for manufacturers to spend their prospecting money in putting over a new product.

In establishing promotional costs, manufacturers must decide on the extent to which the selling effort will be delegated to members of the distribution chain. Indeed, some distribution channels, such as house-to-house selling and retail store selling supplemented by home demonstrators, represent a substantial delegation of the manufacturers' promotional efforts, and these usually involve much higher distribution-channel costs than do conventional methods.

Rich distributor margins are an appropriate use of promotion funds only when the producer thinks a high price plus promotion is a better expansion policy in the specialty than low price by itself. Thus there is an intimate interaction between the pricing of a new product and the costs and the problems of floating it down the distribution channels to the final consumer.

——— POLICIES FOR PIONEER PRICING

The strategic decision in pricing a new product is the choice between (1) a policy of high initial prices that skim the cream of demand and (2) a policy of low prices from the outset serving as an active agent for market penetration. Although the actual range of choice is much wider than this, a sharp dichotomy clarifies the issues for consideration.

SKIMMING PRICE

For products that represent a drastic departure from accepted ways of performing a service, a policy of relatively high prices coupled with heavy promotional expenditures in the early stages of market development (and lower prices at later stages) has proved successful for many products. There are several reasons for the success of this policy:

1. Demand is likely to be more inelastic with respect to price in the early stages than it is when the product is full grown. This is particularly true for consumers' goods. A novel product, such as the electric blanket when it first came out, was not accepted early on as a part of the expenditure pattern. Consumers remained ignorant about its value compared with the value of conventional

alternatives. Moreover, at least in the early stages, the product had so few close rivals that cross-elasticity of demand was low.

Promotional elasticity is, on the other hand, quite high, particularly for products with high unit prices such as television sets. Since it is difficult for customers to value the service of the product in a way to price it intelligently, they are by default principally interested in how well it will work.

2. Launching a new product with a high price is an efficient device for breaking the market up into segments that differ in price elasticity of demand. The initial high price serves to skim the cream of the market that is relatively insensitive to price. Subsequent price reductions tap successively more elastic sectors of the market. This pricing strategy is exemplified by the systematic succession of editions of a book, starting with a very expensive limited personal edition and ending up with a much lower-priced paperback.

3. This policy is safer, or at least appears so. Facing an unknown elasticity of demand, a high initial price serves as a "refusal" price during the stage of exploration. It is difficult to predict how much costs can be reduced as the market expands and as the design of the product is improved by increasing production efficiency with new techniques. When an electrical company introduced a new lamp bulb at a comparatively high initial price, it made the announcement that the price would be reduced as the company found ways of cutting its costs.

4. Many companies are not in a position to finance the product flotation out of distant future revenues. High cash outlays in the early stages result from heavy costs of production and distributor organizing, in addition to the promotional investment in the pioneer product. High prices are a reasonable financing technique for shouldering these burdens in the light of the many uncertainties about the future.

PENETRATION PRICE

The alternative policy is to use low prices as the principal instrument for penetrating mass markets early. This policy is the reverse of the skimming policy in which the price is lowered only as short-run competition forces it.

The passive skimming policy has the virtue of safeguarding some profits at every stage of market penetration. But it prevents quick sales to the many buyers who are at the lower end of the income scale or the lower end of the preference scale and who therefore are unwilling to pay any substantial premium for product or reputation superiority. The active approach in probing possibilities for market expansion by early penetration pricing requires research, forecasting, and courage.

A decision to price for market expansion can be reached at various stages in a product's life cycle: before birth, at birth, in childhood, in adulthood, or in senescence. The chances for large-volume sales should at least be explored in the early stages of product development research, even before the pilot stage, perhaps with a more definitive exploration when the product goes into production and the price and distribution plans are decided upon. And the question of pricing to expand the market, if not answered earlier, will probably arise once more after the product has established an elite market.

Quite a few products have been rescued from premature senescence by being priced low enough to tap new markets. The reissues of important books as lower-priced paperbacks illustrate this point particularly well. These have produced not only commercial but intellectual renascence as well to many authors. The patterns of sales growth of a product that had reached stability in a high-price market have undergone sharp changes when it was suddenly priced low enough to tap new markets.

A contrasting illustration of passive policy is the pricing experience of the airlines. Although safety considerations and differences in equipment and service cloud the picture, it is pretty clear that the bargain-rate coach fares of scheduled airlines were adopted in reaction to the cut rates of nonscheduled airlines. This competitive response has apparently established a new pattern of traffic growth for the scheduled airlines.

An example of penetration pricing at the initial stage of the product's market life—again from the book field—occurred when Simon & Schuster adopted the policy of bringing out new titles in a low-priced, paper-bound edition simultaneously with the conventional higher-priced, cloth-bound edition.

What conditions warrant aggressive pricing for market penetration? This question cannot be answered categorically, but it may be helpful to generalize that the following conditions indicate the desirability of an early low-price policy:

- A high price-elasticity of demand in the short run, i.e., a high degree of responsiveness of sales to reductions in price.
- Substantial savings in production costs as the result of greater volume—not a necessary condition, however, since if elasticity of demand is high enough, pricing for market expansion may be profitable without realizing production economies.
- Product characteristics such that it will not seem bizarre when it is first fitted into the consumers' expenditure pattern.
- A strong threat of potential competition.

This threat of potential competition is a highly persuasive reason for penetration pricing. One of the major objectives of most low-pricing policies in the pioneering stages of market development is to raise entry barriers to prospective competitors. This is appropriate when entrants must make large-scale investments to reach minimum costs and they cannot slip into an established market by selling at substantial discounts.

In many industries, however, the important potential competitor is a large, multiple-product firm operating as well in other fields than that represented by the product in question. For a firm, the most important consideration for entry is not existing margins but the prospect of large and growing volume of sales. Present margins over costs are not the dominant consideration because such firms are normally confident that they can get their costs down as low as competitors' costs if the volume of production is large.

Therefore, when total industry sales are not expected to amount to much, a high-margin policy can be followed because entry is improbable in view of the expectation of low volume and because it does not matter too much to potential competitors if the new product is introduced.

The fact remains that for products whose market potential appears big, a policy of stayout pricing from the outset makes much more sense. When a leading soap manufacturer developed an additive that whitened clothes and enhanced the brilliance of colors, the company chose to take its gains in a larger share of the market rather than in a temporary price premium. Such a decision was sound, since the company's competitors could be expected to match or better the product improvement fairly promptly. Under these circumstances, the price premium would have been short-lived, whereas the gains in market share were more likely to be retained.

Of course, any decision to start out with lower prices must take into account the fact that if the new product calls for capital recovery over a long period, the risk may be great that later entrants will be able to exploit new production techniques which can undercut the pioneer's original cost structure. In such cases, the low-price pattern should be adopted with a view to long-run rather than to short-run profits, with recognition that it usually takes time to attain the volume potentialities of the market.

It is sound to calculate profits in dollar terms rather than in percentage margins, and to think in terms of percentage return on the investment required to produce and sell the expanded volume rather than in terms of percentage markup. Profit calculation should also recognize the contributions that market-development pricing can make to the sale of other products and to the long-run future of the company. Often a decision to use development pricing will turn on these considerations of long-term impacts upon the firm's total operation strategy rather than on the profits directly attributable to the individual product.

An example of market-expansion pricing is found in the experience of a producer of asbestos shingles, which had a limited sale in the high-price house market. The company wanted to broaden the market in order to compete effectively with other roofing products for the inexpensive home. It tried to find the price of asphalt shingles that would make the annual cost per unit of roof over a period of years as low as the cheaper roofing that was currently commanding the mass market. Indications were that the price would have to be at least this low before volume sales would come.

Next, the company explored the relationship between production costs and volume, far beyond the range of its own volume experience. Variable costs and overhead costs were estimated separately, and the possibilities of a different organization of production were explored. Calculating in terms of anticipated dollars of profit rather than in terms of percentage margin, the company reduced the price of asbestos shingles and brought the annual cost down close to the cost of the cheapest asphalt roof. This reduction produced a greatly expanded volume and secured a substantial share of the mass market.

PRICING IN MATURITY

To determine what pricing policies are appropriate for later stages in the cycle of market and competitive maturity, the manufacturer must be able to tell when a product is approaching maturity. Some of the symptoms of degeneration of competitive status toward the commodity level are:

- *Weakening in brand preference.* This may be evidenced by a higher cross-elasticity of demand among leading products, the leading brand not being able to continue demanding as much price premium as initially without losing position.
- *Narrowing physical variation among products as the best designs are developed and standardized.* This has been dramatically demonstrated in automobiles and is still in process in television receivers.
- *The entry in force of private-label competitors.* This is exemplified by the mail-order houses' sale of own-label refrigerators and paint sprayers.
- *Market saturation.* The ratio of replacement sales to new equipment sales serves as an indicator of the competitive degeneration of durable goods, but in general it must be kept in mind that both market size and degree of saturation are hard to define (e.g., saturation of the radio market, which was initially thought to be one radio per home and later had to be expanded to one radio per room).
- *The stabilization of production methods.* A dramatic innovation that slashes costs (e.g., prefabricated houses) may disrupt what appears to be a well-stabilized oligopoly market.

The first step for the manufacturer whose specialty is about to slip into the commodity category is to reduce real prices promptly as soon as symptoms of deterioration appear. This step is essential if the manufacturer is to forestall the entry of private-label competitors. Examples of failure to make such a reduction are abundant.

By and large, private-label competition has speeded up the inevitable evolution of high specialties into commodities and has tended to force margins down by making price reductions more open and more universal than they would otherwise be. From one standpoint, the rapid growth of the private-label share in the market is a symptom of unwise pricing on the part of the national-brand sector of the industry.

This does not mean that manufacturers should declare open price war in the industry. When they move into mature competitive stages they enter oligopoly relationships where price slashing is peculiarly dangerous and unpopular. But, with active competition in prices precluded, competitive efforts may move in other directions, particularly toward product improvement and market segmentation.

Product improvement at this stage, where most of the important developments have been put into all brands, practically amounts to market segmentation. For it means adding refinements and quality extras that put the brand in the elite category, with an appeal only to the top-income brackets. This is a common tactic in food marketing, and in the tire industry it was the response of the General Tire Company to the competitive conditions of the 1930s.

As the product matures and as its distinctiveness narrows, a choice must sometimes be made by the company concerning the rung of the competitive price ladder it should occupy—roughly, the choice between a low and a not-so-low relative price.

A price at the low end of the array of the industry's real prices is usually associated with a product mixture showing a lean element of services and reputation (the product being physically similar to competitive brands, however) and a company having a lower gross margin than the other industry members (although not necessarily a lower net margin). The choice of such a low-price policy may be dictated by technical or market inferiorities of the product, or it may be adopted because the company has faith in the long-run price elasticity of demand and the ability of low prices to penetrate an important segment of the market not tapped by higher prices. The classic example is Henry Ford's pricing decision in the 1920s.

—— IN SUMMARY

In pricing products of perishable distinctiveness, a company must study the cycle of competitive degeneration in order to determine its major causes, its probable speed, and the chances of slowing it down. Pricing in the pioneering stage of the cycle involves difficult problems of projecting potential demand and of guessing the relation of price to sales.

The first step in this process is to explore consumer preferences and to establish the feasibility of the product, in order to get a rough idea of whether demand will warrant further exploration. The second step is to mark out a range of prices that will make the product economically attractive to buyers. The third step is to estimate the probable sales that will result from alternative prices.

If these initial explorations are encouraging, the next move is to make decisions on promotional strategy and distribution channels. The policy of relatively high prices in the pioneering stage has much to commend it, particularly when sales seem to be comparatively unresponsive to price but quite responsive to educational promotion.

On the other hand, the policy of relatively low prices in the pioneering stage, in anticipation of the cost savings resulting from an expanding market, has been strikingly successful under the right conditions. Low prices look to long-run rather than short-run profits and discourage potential competitors.

Pricing in the mature stages of a product's life cycle requires a technique for recognizing when a product is approaching maturity. Pricing problems in this stage border closely on those of oligopoly.

* * *

Twenty-five years after publication of this article, the author added the following commentary in which he amplifies his earlier article with insights from intervening years and in light of such developments as inflation.

——— RETROSPECTIVE COMMENTARY

Twenty-five years have brought important changes and have taught us much, but the basics of pricing pioneer products are the same, only clearer. New product pricing, if the product is truly novel, is in essence monopoly pricing—modified only because the monopoly power of the new product is (1) restricted because buyers have alternatives, (2) ephemeral because it is subject to inevitable erosion as competitors equal or better it, and (3) controllable because actions of the seller can affect the amount and the durability of the new product's market power.

In pricing, the buyers' viewpoint should be controlling. For example, buyer's-rate-of-return pricing of new capital equipment looks at your price through the eyes of the customer. It recognizes that the upper limit is the price that will produce the minimum acceptable rate of return on the investment of a sufficiently large number of prospects. This return has a broad range for two reasons. First, the added profits obtainable from the use of your equipment will differ among customers and among applications for the same customer. Second, prospective customers also differ in the minimum rate of return that will induce them to invest in your product.

This capital-budgeting approach opens a new kind of demand analysis, which involves inquiry into: (1) the costs of buyers from displaceable alternative ways of doing the job, (2) the cost-saving and profit-producing capability of your equipment, and (3) the capital management policies of your customers, particularly their cost of capital and cutoff criteria.

ROLE OF COST

Cost should play a role in new product pricing quite different from that in traditional cost-plus pricing. To use cost wisely requires answers to some questions of theory: Whose cost? Which cost? What role?

As to whose cost, three persons are important: prospective buyers, existent and potential competitors, and the producer of the new product. For each of the three, cost should play a different role, and the concept of cost should differ accordingly.

The role of prospective *buyers'* costs is to forecast their response to alternative prices by determining what your product will do to the costs of your buyers. Rate-of-return pricing of capital goods illustrates this buyer's-cost approach, which is applicable in principle to all new products.

Cost is usually the crucial estimate in appraising *competitors'* capabilities. Two kinds of competitor costs need to be forecasted. The first is for products already in the marketplace. One purpose is to predict staying power; for this the cost concept is competitors' long-run incremental cost. Another purpose may be to guess the floor of retaliation pricing; for this we need competitors' short-run incremental cost.

The second kind is the cost of a competitive product that is unborn but that could eventually displace yours. Time-spotted prediction of the performance characteristics, the costs, and the probable prices of future new products is both essential and possible. Such a prediction is essential because it determines the economic life expectancy of your product and the shape of its competitiveness cycle.

This prediction is possible, first, because the pace of technical advance in product design is persistent and can usually be determined by statistical study of past progress. It is possible, second, because the rate at which competitors' cost will slide down the cost compression curve that results from cost-saving investments in manufacturing equipment, methods, and worker learning is usually a logarithmic function of cumulative output. Thus this rate can be ascertained and projected.

The *producer's* cost should play several different roles in pricing a new product, depending on the decision involved. The first decision concerns capital control. A new product must be priced before any significant investment is made in research and must be periodically repriced when more money is invested as its development progresses toward market. The concept of cost that is relevant for this decision is the predicted full cost, which should include imputed cost of capital on intangible investment over the whole life cycle of the new product. Its profitability and investment return are meaningless for any shorter period.

A second decision is "birth control." The commercialization decision calls for a similar concept of cost and discounted cash-flow investment analysis, but one that is confined to incremental investment beyond product birth.

Another role of cost is to establish a price floor that is also the threshold for selecting from candidate prices those that will maximize return on a new product investment at different stages of its life. The relevant concept here is future short-run incremental cost.

SEGMENTATION PRICING

Particularly for new products, an important tactic is differential pricing for separated market segments. To enhance profits, we split the market into sectors that differ in price sensitivity, charging higher prices to those who are impervious and lower prices to the more sensitive souls.

One requisite is the ability to identify and seal off groups of prospects who differ in sensitivity of sales to price or differ in the effectiveness of competition (cross-elasticity of demand). Another is that leakage from the low price segment must be small and costs of segregation low enough to make it worthwhile.

One device is time segmentation: a skimming price strategy at the outset followed by penetration pricing as the product matures. Another device is price-shaped modification of a basic product to enhance traits for which one group of customers will pay dearly (e.g., reliability for the military).

A similar device is product-configuration differentials (notably extras: the roof of the Stanley Steamer was an extra when it was a new product). Another is afterlife pricing (e.g., repair parts, expendable components, and auxiliary services). Also, trade channel discounts commonly achieve profitable price discrimination (as with original equipment discounts).

COST COMPRESSION CURVE

Cost forecasting for pricing new products should be based on the cost compression curve, which relates real manufacturing cost per unit of value added to the cumulative quantity produced. This cost function (sometimes labeled "learning curve" or "experience curve") is mainly the consequence of cost cutting investments (largely intangible) to discover and achieve internal substitutions, automation, worker learning, scale economies, and technological advances. Usually these move together as a logarithmic function of accumulated output.

Cost compression curve pricing of technically advanced products (for example, a microprocessor) epitomizes penetration pricing. It condenses the time span of the process of cutting prices *ahead* of forecasted cost savings in order to beat competitors to the bigger market and the resulting manufacturing economies that are opened up because of creative pricing.

This cost compression curve pricing strategy, which took two decades for the Model T's life span, is condensed into a few months for the integrated circuit. But though the speed and the sources of saving are different, the principle is the same: a steep cost compression curve suggests penetration pricing of a new product. Such pricing is most attractive when the product superiority over rivals is small and ephemeral and when entry and expansion by competitors is easy and probable.

IMPACTS OF INFLATION

Continuous high-speed inflation has important impacts on new product pricing. It changes the goal. It renders obsolete accounted earnings per share as the corporation's overriding goal—replacing it with maximization of the present worth (discounted at the corporation's cost of capital) of the future stream of real purchasing power dividends (including a terminal dividend or capital gain). Real earnings in terms of cash-flow buying power alone determine the power to pay real dividends.

Inflation raises the buyers' benchmark costs of the new products' competitive alternatives. Thus it lifts the buyer benefits obtainable from the new products' protected distinctiveness (for example, it saves more wage dollars).

It raises the seller's required return on the investment to create and to launch the new product. Why? Because the cost of equity capital and of debt capital will be made higher to compensate for anticipated inflation. For the same reason, inflation raises the customer's cutoff point of minimum acceptable return. It also intensifies the rivalry for scarce investment dollars among the seller's new product candidates. Hence it probably tends to increase stillbirths, but may lower subsequent infant mortality. For these reasons, perennial inflation will make an economic attack on the problem of pricing new products even more compelling.

Pricing of new products remains an art. But the experienced judgment required to price and reprice the product over its life cycle to fit its changing competitive environment may be improved by considering seven pricing precepts suggested by this analysis.

1. Pricing a new product is an occasion for rethinking the overriding corporate goal. This goal should be to maximize the present worth, discounted at the corporation's cost of capital, of the future stream of real (purchasing-power) dividends, including a terminal dividend or capital gain. The Wall Street traditional objective— maximizing the size or the growth of book earnings per share—is an inferior master goal that is made obsolete by inflation.
2. The unit for making decisions and for measuring return on investment is the entire economic life of the new product. Reported

annual profits on a new product have little economic significance. The pricing implications of the new product's changing competitive status as it passes through its life cycle from birth to obsolescence are intricate but compelling.

3. Pricing of a new product should begin long before its birth, and repricing should continue over its life cycle. Prospective prices coupled with forecasted costs should control the decision to invest in its development, the determination to launch it commercially, and the decision to kill it.

4. A new product should be viewed through the eyes of the buyer. Rate of return on customers' investment should be the main consideration in pricing a pioneering capital good: the buyers' savings (and added earnings), expressed as return on their investment in the new product, are the key to both estimating price sensitivity of demand and pricing profitably.

5. Costs can supply useful guidance in new product pricing, but not by the conventional wisdom of cost-plus pricing. Costs of three persons are pertinent: the buyer, the competitor, and the producer. The role of cost differs among the three, as does the concept of cost that is pertinent to that role: different costs for different decisions.

6. A strategy of price skimming can be distinguished from a strategy of penetration pricing. Skimming is appropriate at the outset for some pioneering products, particularly when followed by penetration pricing (for example, the price cascade of a new book). In contrast, a policy of penetration pricing from the outset, in anticipation of the cost compression curve for manufacturing costs, is usually best when this curve falls steeply and projectably, and is buttressed by economies of scale and of advancing technology, and when demand is price sensitive and invasion is threatened.

7. Penetration and skimming pricing can be used at the same time in different sectors of the market. Creating opportunities to split the market into segments that differ in price sensitivity and in competitiveness, so as to simultaneously charge higher prices in insensitive segments and price low to elastic sectors, can produce extra profits and faster cost-compression for a new product. Devices are legion.

——— DISCUSSION QUESTIONS

1. Marketing managers often use a different pricing strategy for new products than they do for established products. Explain why the pricing strategies might differ. What role does cost play in pricing? What other factors influence the new product price?

2. What are some of the product-related problems at the pioneer stage? How does this unpredictable period after product introduction affect pricing policy?

3. What steps can be taken to help determine the price a new product will command in the market?

4. Two pricing strategies can be used to launch a new product: pricing low to gain wider market penetration or pricing high to skim bigger profits in the early stages. What are the advantages of each strategy? What are the disadvantages? How does customer diversity influence the marketer's choice of strategy?

5. How do pricing strategies differ for each stage of a product's life cycle? Describe the various stages and tell how adjustments in pricing become necessary. Can you imagine circumstances in which price might not follow the general pattern?

Making Money with Proactive Pricing

21

ELLIOT B. ROSS

The pricing decision, one of the most important in business, is also one of the least understood. Many industrial companies habitually set prices on the basis of simple criteria—to recover costs, to maintain or gain market share, to match competitors. This reading shows that some companies have discovered the benefits of thinking more shrewdly about pricing. The rewards of a better understanding of pricing strategy and tactics can be substantial. By carefully studying pertinent information about customers, competitors, and industry economics and by selectively applying appropriate techniques, "proactive pricers" can enjoy high profitability that might otherwise be lost.

Some of today's most profitable industrial companies are by no means the lowest-cost competitors in their industries. By and large, operational efficiency and work force productivity are adequate but not outstanding in these companies. Where these companies really shine is in skillful pricing strategy and tactics. Year in and year out, they manage to outmaneuver their competitors on price. They leave less money on the table in competitive bid situations, they have mastered the art of shaving prices to gain volume without provoking competitive retaliation, and they know when they can quote a higher price without risking the loss of an order or a long-term relationship. By understanding the competitive dynamics of pricing in their industries and the purchasing approaches of their customers, these companies have turned pricing into a potent competitive weapon.

This approach—call it proactive pricing for want of a better label—has in most cases taken shape under the impact of forces that are putting ever-increasing pressures on industrial companies. Across a spectrum of industries ranging from lighting equipment to computer software, customers are gaining power at the expense of suppliers. Competitive intensity is increasing, causing specialty products to evolve into near-commodities. Computerized information systems enable the purchaser to compare price and performance factors with unprecedented ease and accuracy. Improved communications and increased use of telemarketing and computer-aided selling have opened up many markets to additional competitors. In this environment, the penalties for maladroit pricing practices are fast becoming prohibitive.

Take the case of a midwestern electromechanical components manufacturer, which recently found itself in a tough spot. With market share stagnant and industry prices edging downward, the company's margins were taking a terrible beating, and there was no relief in sight. In an effort to gain share and restore income levels, the marketing vice president ordered prices to be cut by an average of 7%. Within three weeks, however, the move had provoked severe price cuts from the company's major competitors and set off a full-scale price war. Prices swiftly declined in a kind of death spiral that soon had everyone in the industry doing business at a loss.

What the initiator of this downward spiral had failed to realize was that conditions in the industry—a high-fixed-cost, high-contribution-margin business—were ripe for a price war: there was substantial excess capacity at the time, and the major competitors were desperate to hold their own share positions. Ironically, the unfortunate executive who had started it all by failing to anticipate her competitors' reaction to her ill-fated initiative, saw her company as the victim of an unprovoked attack. This misapprehension was natural enough; all the information the company had about current price levels in the industry was what it had gleaned from the bids on orders lost to competitors. Where pricing was concerned, the company had weighed its options with all the weights on one side of the scale.

Because the consequences of a rash pricing initiative can be so disastrous, most managers are disposed to play it safe and price defensively, keeping a close eye on their competitors and parrying as best they can any pricing moves that could cost them orders or threaten their position with marginal accounts. By adopting a reactive pricing posture, they escape the pitfalls of reckless price leadership. But over time they may also pay a heavy penalty in forgone profits—money left on the table on hundreds or even thousands of orders.

Today's more sophisticated industrial marketers realize that they need not put up with either the risks of rash price pioneering or the invisible costs associated with a reactive pricing posture. Some increasingly popular proactive pricing techniques enable aggressive companies to reap the rewards of intelligent pricing initiatives while minimizing the risks of competitive retaliation.

To see how they attain this objective, let us explore some frequently overlooked aspects of pricing in the industrial environment. We shall then look at the major elements of pricing strategy and tactics as practiced by these companies and conclude with some observations on building a system for effective pricing.

——— THE DYNAMICS OF PRICING

The secret of improving pricing performance without the risk of damaging market repercussions lies in understanding how pricing works in an industry and particularly how customers perceive prices (see *Exhibit 1* for a simple diagnostic test of pricing policies). In general, in comparing suppliers'

EXHIBIT 1
Are You a Proactive Pricer?

The 20 questions below provide a simple diagnostic test of your pricing strategy and tactics. If you can answer no to the first 10 and yes to the second 10, you are a shrewd pricer. If the results are otherwise, it may be rewarding to reconsider how you set prices.

1. Is your market share constant or declining while prices are falling in real terms?

2. Do you have a nagging suspicion—but no real evidence—that you are regularly bidding too high for contracts?

3. Do your salespeople keep complaining that your prices are several percentage points too high although your share is holding steady?

4. Do your contribution margins for the same product vary widely from customer to customer?

5. Are you unsure who is the industry price leader?

6. Do your pricing approval levels seem to be functioning more as a volume discount device than as a control mechanism?

7. Would you have trouble describing your competitors' pricing strategies?

8. Do you find that too many pricing decisions seem aimed at gaining volume, despite an overall nonvolume strategy?

9. Are most of your prices set at minimum approval levels?

10. Do your competitors seem to anticipate your pricing actions with ease, while theirs often take you by surprise?

11. Do you have a planned method of communicating price changes to customers and distributors?

12. Do you know how long to wait before following a competitor's price change?

13. Are your prices set to reflect such customer-specific costs as transportation, set-up charges, design costs, warranty, sales commissions, and inventory?

14. Do you know how long it takes each of your major competitors to follow one of your price moves?

15. Do you know the economic value of your product to your customers?

16. Do you use the industry's price/volume curve as an analytic aid to price setting?

17. Do you know whether you would be better off making a single large price change or several small changes?

18. Do you know how to go about establishing price leadership in your industry?

19. Are your prices based strictly on your own costs?

20. Do you have a consistent and effective policy for intracompany pricing?

---

offerings, a customer will measure purchase prices against the relative value of the performance it expects from each product and the service it expects from the product's supplier. Of the three factors—performance, service, price—price seems to be the least subjective. What could be less ambiguous than a number?

As the customer perceives it, however, price is in fact a relatively subjective thing. The dollars-and-cents price level is only one element in perceived price. Equally important, in many cases, is the way the price is structured. For example, some industrial companies quote setup costs as a separate charge to maintain the appearance of low unit prices. Volume discounts, year-end rebates, credit terms, and inclusion of transportation costs are other methods of structuring and communicating prices to influence the customer's perception.

The timing of price changes is another factor influencing the customer's perception. For example, customers may perceive a company that follows its competitor's price increase announcements by two or three weeks as a low-price supplier, even though the price changes both companies announce may take effect on the same day.

Inadequate information compounds the difficulty of making the right decisions on price level, structure, and timing. Lacking precise internal cost data, a clear market-price reference point, or the value customers place on the product, manufacturers have to rely on guesswork in setting price level; and if they don't understand the thinking that goes into customers' purchase decisions, they are likely to structure and communicate prices in a counterproductive way. Finally, uncertainty about such things as future rates of inflation, changes in costs, competitors' actions, and customers' reactions complicates the correct timing of price changes.

In the perfect markets that theoretical economists envision, of course, pricing freedom doesn't exist: the point where the demand curve intersects the supply curve reflects the collective costs and capacities of all suppliers and determines the price. However, successful industrial marketers have understood and exploited the fact that a multitude of imperfections in the marketplace affect the dynamics of supply and demand in the real world of industrial products. These imperfections determine the degree of pricing freedom and open the door to significant profit improvement through proactive pricing.

THE PRICE BAND

When a large number of individual orders for a particular industrial product in a particular market are plotted on a graph against price, something close to a normal frequency distribution curve is likely to emerge. Because of differences in prevailing practices with respect to list prices, automatic discount points, and so on, the shape of the curve varies from industry to industry, but a spread of 10 percentage points on either side of an average industry price level is not uncommon (see *Exhibit 2*).

Regardless of its shape, the existence of this price band in virtually every industrial market results from variations or imperfections in both demand and supply factors. On the demand side, customer inertia—the tendency to stick with an established supplier—often contributes greatly to the spread of prices. In some industries, getting a new customer's business is rarely possible without a substantial price inducement. Sometimes inducements are needed because the customer is averse to the business and personal risks involved in changing to a new supplier whose quality and reliability are untested; sometimes inducements are a matter of straight economics. (One supplier of plastic resins, for

EXHIBIT 2
Typical Distribution of Orders for a Product

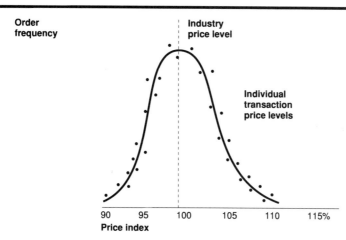

Source: McKinsey & Company

example, reports that a 3% to a 5% price break is usually needed to persuade a typical customer to change suppliers, simply because it would cost the customer about $75,000 to clean out its system and put in a new product.) And even within an industry, customers differ in their buying practices, in the importance they attach to price, in their willingness to pay extra for product quality, performance, or delivery, and in their responsiveness to terms and discounts.

Price visibility is another factor that influences the width of the price band. In commodity-type industries, where every customer knows what its competitors are paying for the same product, there is little if any price variation. In contrast, in industries where price visibility is low, the price band is usually wide. Finally, customer purchasing power is often reflected in the width of the price band. A massive purchaser like Ford or Procter & Gamble tends to limit the supplier's freedom to raise prices, while fragmentation of market power among a host of small customers tends to enhance it.

On the supply side, differences among competitors—such as in run lengths and transportation costs; in product quality, features, and performance; in service; in pricing terms and conditions; or in sales efficiency and effectiveness—contribute to price variations. The level of competitive intensity in an industry further affects price variation and hence the degree of freedom available to the proactive pricer; the higher the ratio of customers to suppliers, the wider the price band.

The ice cream industry provides a simple illustration of how the price band can vary between market segments (see *Exhibit 3*). In the case of the generic product, the equivalent of a commodity, the consumer price band is very narrow—plus or minus 2 cents a serving. But in the specialty segments, the price band broadens to plus or minus 10 cents per serving. This range of prices

EXHIBIT 3
The Price Band in Ice Cream

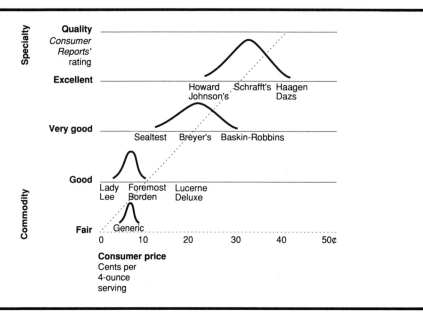

depends partly on the way customers perceive the relative value of different brands of ice cream that are sold in that segment and partly on the competitive intensity in each segment.

PRICING STRATEGY AND TACTICS

In light of the complex ways in which each variable influences a company's latitude for action, some of the most adroit industrial pricing practitioners are careful to distinguish between pricing strategy and pricing tactics. Moves aimed at shifting the company's position within the existing price band of the industry are seen as pricing tactics. A supplier normally takes its market share from a portion of the price band: it may opt for high volume at a low price or for lower volume at the high-price end of the band to earn higher total profit dollars. (In practice, many companies are more preoccupied with volume than with profit share and give little thought to this degree of freedom.)

Pricing strategy, in contrast, aims at shifting the price band and the company's relative competitive position. Such shifting may entail changing the product, the customer group, the distribution channels, or the sales strategy—all with the objective of bringing about a movement of the industry price level.

The degree of strategic pricing freedom open to any supplier depends on both the product's perceived value to the customer and the competitive intensity of the business, as defined in terms of either the uniqueness of the product or the number of suppliers bidding on a typical order. At one extreme of the competitive intensity scale is the specialty manufacturer of a patented product with unique performance characteristics. This sole supplier has tremendous latitude with respect to price; it can virtually set a price at any level it wishes and in effect choose a position on the demand curve. At the other end of the spectrum, where several suppliers are fighting for every order and where the laws of supply and demand dictate prices, management has no real strategic pricing freedom. At best, a company can try to anticipate how specific changes in capacity and cost position on its own part or that of its competitors will affect the price level.

The second determinant of a supplier's strategic pricing freedom, the product's perceived value to the customer, can be defined as the benefits the customer expects to achieve from its purchase relative to an alternative product or to no purchase at all. At one end of the scale stands the product that uniquely fills a vital need, such as the CAT scanner. (In these cases, the value is sufficiently high to allow the supplier to raise prices.) At the other end are products that can be differentiated from substitutes only on the basis of net price, such as the corn syrup sold to soft drink manufacturers when it is cheaper than cane sugar. In between lie the industrial products in which the supplier has room to cut its production costs—though not, as a rule, to raise its prices.

THE PRICING FRAMEWORK

In combination, these two variables—competitive intensity and perceived value—provide a useful framework for thinking about pricing (see *Exhibit 4*). Any business can be assigned to one of four categories within this framework. In the upper left-hand quadrant are specialty products such as prescription drugs, wire-line services in the oil field, and water-treatment chemicals—businesses characterized by high perceived value and low competitive intensity. Pricing is a high-leverage independent variable in such businesses. In the lower right-hand quadrant are products like steel, PVC, caustic soda, aluminum, and standard fasteners—commodity businesses characterized by low economic value and high competitive intensity. Here, pricing is a dependent variable based on the intersection of supply and demand curves. In the lower left-hand quadrant are businesses like xerography back in 1955, Polavision in 1975, and genetic engineering in 1984—unique products whose economic value to the customer is unknown. In these businesses, competitive intensity is very low, and pricing, though subject to certain constraints, can be considered a largely independent variable. Finally, in the upper right-hand quadrant are engineered commodities like cathode-ray tubes, jet engines, steam

EXHIBIT 4
Price Bands in the Pricing Framework

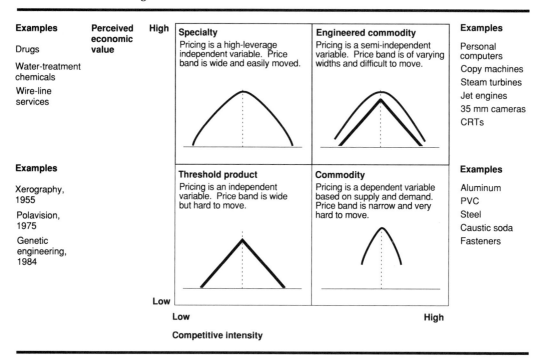

Examples	Perceived economic value	High	Specialty	Engineered commodity	Examples
Drugs			Pricing is a high-leverage independent variable. Price band is wide and easily moved.	Pricing is a semi-independent variable. Price band is of varying widths and difficult to move.	Personal computers
Water-treatment chemicals					Copy machines
Wire-line services					Steam turbines
					Jet engines
					35 mm cameras
					CRTs
Examples			Threshold product	Commodity	Examples
Xerography, 1955			Pricing is an independent variable. Price band is wide but hard to move.	Pricing is a dependent variable based on supply and demand. Price band is narrow and very hard to move.	Aluminum
Polavision, 1975					PVC
Genetic engineering, 1984					Steel
					Caustic soda
					Fasteners
		Low			

Low   High

Competitive intensity

turbines, personal computers, and copying machines, characterized by both high economic value and high competitive intensity. For these manufacturers, pricing is a semi-independent variable, limited mainly by the competitive intensity factor.

The available latitude for proactive pricing in an industrial market can easily be seen when the pricing framework is coupled with the concept of the price band. In the specialty quadrant, the price band is usually both wide and easy to shift. Customarily, a threshold product has a wide band that is difficult to move until the market begins to recognize the value of the product. In the engineered commodity segment, the band may vary in width but is almost always immovable. In the commodity segment, the band is both narrow and fixed.

—— PROACTIVE PRICING STRATEGY

Marketers who understand where their products or businesses fit in the pricing framework can easily take advantage of pricing opportunities. In seeking to capitalize on these opportunities, they tend to focus on four questions: (1) Is the price accurately keyed to the value to the customer? (2) Will the price help the purchasing decision makers look good? (3) How will prices change over time? (4) How will competitors respond?

PRICING TO REFLECT PERCEIVED VALUE

On the principle that effective product pricing must be based on customer economics, successful industrial marketers, when calculating how much financial incentive their prices should reflect, give careful consideration to the cost and the risk the customer may incur in purchasing their products.

Consider the example of a numerically controlled machine tool that not only offers the customer lower start-up and operating costs but works to closer tolerances than the best available alternative. Altogether, these benefits may be worth an extra $30,000 to the customer. But there may be certain risks as well: the union may object, the maintenance staff may not be qualified to service the new device, and/or customers may not want to pay much extra for better finish. Extensive discussions with customers may lead the supplier to conclude that these costs and risks probably reduce the $30,000 benefit by $12,000 and that a further $2,500 will be needed to induce customers to switch. The manufacturer would then set the price premium for its new product at $15,500 ($30,000 − [$12,000 + $2,500]).

Some successful marketers routinely apply this kind of analysis before they make any major commitment to a new industrial product. After having used the results to assess the likely returns from the new product and the switching cost (and hence the amount of the required customer inducement) likely to be involved, these marketers find that they can decide much more confidently whether to proceed with a major resource commitment.

TARGETING THE PURCHASING DECISION MAKER

In approaching any important decision, proactive pricers take care to ensure that the price is sensitive to the requirements of the individuals in the customer's organization who will influence the buying decision. It is important to give the buyer a price that will help him or her to look good. In many cases, this task is anything but a simple matter, because it must take into account the distinctive buying processes that, with innumerable individual variations, characterize customers in a particular industry.

Consider the case of the specialty chemical industry. Here the purchasing decision is the culmination of three distinct stages: (1) product testing and demonstration, (2) product specification, and (3) ongoing purchase. At the first stage, the typical decision maker is an R&D manager; at the second, R&D shares responsibility with other management; at the final stage, the purchasing department makes the ongoing buying decisions subject to the approval of top management. At each stage, price is a factor in the decision, and an understanding of the needs and motivations of the decision makers along the way is basic to successful pricing.

When a new product is under consideration, the supplier needs to demonstrate to the decision maker—usually an R&D scientist with a tight budget and an outsize workload—that the product promises the company some benefit. If this benefit is substantial enough in relation to the price, the decision maker will be inclined to pass the product ahead to the specification stage. Here price tends to become a central issue. Besides providing a clear inducement to buy, the price must be thoughtfully structured and communicated. For example, managers who are judged on their contributions to longer-term profitability may benefit from life-cycle pricing, which takes into account the various costs of a component over its useful life.

Success in securing repeat orders often depends on the timing of price increases. Many purchasing people, for example, are evaluated on the basis of material variance against standard costs that increase annually to account for expected inflation. Accordingly, they routinely compare product cost increases with several different inflation indices. A supplier who attempts to raise prices ahead of inflation can expect to be passed over. Proactive pricers who try to hold their increase below the inflation rate can make the purchasing manager look like a hero. Often, by doing so, proactive suppliers succeed in cementing a sole-source position.

Skillful use of discounts, payment terms, financing, spare-parts prices, consigned stock, warranties, and other techniques affords these suppliers the flexibility to communicate price in a way that is sensitive to the needs of the customer decision makers. Consider, for example, a situation in which an initial equipment purchase locks in a number of subsequent expenditures (e.g., for spare parts) and the purchasing manager is evaluated on initial expenditures. Here, shrewd suppliers price the original equipment relatively low and the spare parts relatively high. This is a common practice in aerospace components, where the original supplier is virtually guaranteed a 20-year stream of spare-parts orders. (This tactic can, however, be overdone, as some Defense Department suppliers have discovered.) Again, where the performance of the purchasing decision maker is assessed on the basis of unit costs rather than on his or her contributions to long-term profitability, it makes better sense to structure the price as a low piece rate plus an initial set-up charge than to prorate the set-up charge as part of the piece rate.

Beyond securing the initial sale, some suppliers use discounts to induce sales in large quantities or at times that optimize their manufacturing or distribution costs. In process industries, seasonal discounts help to smooth out the demand patterns. One bulk chemicals supplier offers a 3% discount during the first 10 days of each quarter, solely to counter the sales representatives' tendency to relax at the beginning of a bonus period. Other manufacturers are beginning to experiment with similar approaches.

CHANGING THE PRICE

The issues of when, how often, and how much to change prices are complicated by inflation, which drives costs up, and the experience curve, which—especially in the case of new products—tends to bring them down. In some industries, as a manufacturer doubles its cumulative volume, it can expect its costs to go down by 20% to 30% because of improved direct labor productivity, scale economies, technological improvements, and the like. Sophisticated marketers take inflation and the experience curve carefully into account as they approach the risky initial pricing decision for a new product or prepare to enter a new customer segment. Over time, cost changes and competitive actions will create a need for price changes. Starting too low makes it hard to raise prices to achieve an acceptable return, while starting (and staying) too high may frustrate the company's efforts to achieve the volume necessary for the new product's survival. Or if, despite unduly high prices, attractive volume should develop, competitors will inevitably be attracted into the market and prices will go down.

Inflation obliges every supplier to monitor its costs so as to ensure continuing profitability. Fortunately, cost reductions resulting from the experience-curve phenomenon may partly or wholly offset the impact of inflation. An understanding of this process—which, again, is an industry-specific phenomenon—enables proactive pricers to forecast with reasonable accuracy when and by how much they must adjust prices to maintain their margins.

Proactive pricers realize, however, that the timing of change in price level or structure and the way they communicate such change strongly affect how new customers and competitors see them. These pricers know too that customers, especially those for whom the product represents a major item of cost, value the consistency and predictability of price changes. Leadership in raising prices can help build attractive margins but may be costly in terms of customer perception since the first to announce an increase is often seen as the high-price supplier. Proactive pricers, however, often take the lead in introducing new pricing structures or communications methods as a means of gaining competitive differentiation.

Proactive suppliers usually time price changes to the anticipated reactions of customers and competitors rather than to the results of their own analysis of costs. They know that accounting-driven cost and price changes are normally predictable and that both competitors and customers can exploit these changes to the supplier's disadvantage.

CALCULATING COMPETITORS' RESPONSES

The need for an industrial marketer to consider its competitors' probable responses in planning its own price moves is obvious. In relatively stable commodity or near-commodity industries, the price behavior of established competitors tends to be predictable, so that the price leader seldom has to worry about what to expect. Nearer the specialty-product end of the industrial spectrum, however, the exercise of prediction becomes both more complex, because perceived product value is a function of having many variables, and more speculative, because competitive behavior is more volatile.

Still, sophisticated industrial marketers in these industries succeed surprisingly well in anticipating the reactions of their principal competitors to major price moves. In most cases, the secret seems to be nothing more mysterious than patient gathering, collation, and analysis of bits and pieces of information about key competitors—their costs, the details of their business systems, their approaches to technology, product design, marketing and distribution, and any other key functions. Some notably successful proactive pricers have their most knowledgeable managers act out the roles of key competitors to help predict likely reactions to a proposed price initiative or probable bids on a major order. The pricing question that should be asked in such cases is not "What price will it take to win this order?" but "Do we want this order, given the price our competitors are likely to quote?"

Legitimate sources of competitive intelligence range from advertising and product literature to trade gossip picked up by salespeople. Companies that have tried thoroughly debriefing their sales forces about particular competitors have often been astonished at the sheer volume of information that collectively surfaces and at the usefulness of the insights that can emerge once this information is fitted together.

Because an understanding of each competitor's pricing process can provide important clues to its responses, some sophisticated marketers routinely instruct their salespeople to note and report the prices quoted by specific competitors in various marketing situations, with the aim of assembling a statistically valid sample. Supplemented by insights into competitors' organizations, the caliber of their people, and the share and margin pressures they face, the resulting statistical picture enables these marketers to predict with reasonable confidence whether a given price move will secure the intended competitive advantage.

━━━ FROM STRATEGY TO TACTICS

The value of the tools and concepts that today's proactive pricers use is not confined to major decisions on the level, structuring, and timing of product prices. Day-by-day attention to the pricing of individual orders, based on the same principles, has enabled many companies to improve their positions in the industry price band (and hence, over the long run, their profitability) without provoking serious competitive reactions.

EXHIBIT 5
Guidelines for Tactical Pricing

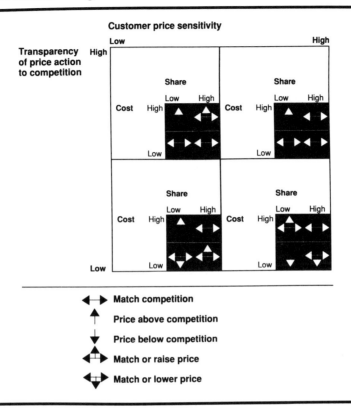

Match competition

Price above competition

Price below competition

Match or raise price

Match or lower price

SETTING THE PRICE LEVEL

A marketing manager can evaluate the profit opportunities inherent in day-to-day tactical pricing by looking at the money left on the table for orders the company has won. One U.S. industrial manufacturer decided to spot-check five out of several dozen orders for an engineered commodity that his sales-people had won over a one-month period. He discovered that his winning prices had averaged fully 5% below those of the next lowest bidder.

Because salespeople are normally eager to report competitors' prices on the orders that they have lost but not on those they have won, unwary executives can easily get the impression that competitors always have the lowest prices in the industry and may pass up the opportunity to put through price increases that could stick.

Proactive pricers are not so credulous. They provide each price decision maker with explicit guidelines that indicate whether—because of the company's cost position and the customer's circumstances and characteristics— the price quoted on a given order should be equal to, lower than, or higher than the competition's. As illustrated in *Exhibit 5*, the guidelines one well-managed

EXHIBIT 6
How to Time Pricing Moves

		Cost relative to competition in the segment	
		Lower	**Higher**
Share position in the segment	**Strong**	Meet price drops quickly — 3 weeks	Meet price drops quickly to protect share — 1 week Follow price increases quickly — 1 week
	Weak	Follow price increases grudgingly — 3 months	Meet price drops grudgingly — 2 months Follow price increases quickly — 1 week

industrial company uses can be keyed to two customer-specific factors: the price sensitivity and the price transparency (how well-informed competitors are likely to be about the price quoted on a given order). When the customer's price sensitivity is high, it makes good sense to match or underprice competitors; the reverse is true if it is low. For a highly "transparent" customer—one who will show every competitor every other competitor's price—it usually is best, even at the risk of losing some orders, to price high, encouraging competitors to think that the industry price level is higher than it actually is. With a relatively "opaque" customer, on the other hand, this manufacturer tends to price low— particularly where the cost to serve the account in question is low—as a means of safely gaining volume without provoking the competition to respond in kind.

——— TIMING PRICE CHANGES

Nimble, but by no means hasty, response to competitors' price moves is a hallmark of today's best-managed industrial marketing organizations. These companies are thoughtful price tacticians as well as skilled strategists. How quickly should the company follow a competitor's price cut? How long, if at all, should the company put off following a price increase? One business has based its guidelines on two key variables: (1) its share strength in the market segment involved, and (2) its cost relative to that of the competition (see *Exhibit 6*).

Some sophisticated marketers who consistently practice price-following have mastered the art of building customer loyalty and even attracting new business by playing the role of the low-cost supplier who never initiates a price increase and follows competitors' increases only reluctantly. Success in this role owes much to careful calculation of the time interval between competitive price move and corporate response. Too short a lag, and the policy may not register with customers; too long, and money will be left on the table. In one case in which customer interviews indicated that a six-week time lag following a competitor's price increase would suffice to reinforce the low-cost supplier image, the company discovered that it was actually lagging behind competitors by two to eight months because of its own internal delays in changing prices. A clear-cut timing plan for putting price changes into effect and streamlining the decision process corrected this problem.

Successful proponents of proactive pricing often outmaneuver their competitors by cleverly adapting the price structure to the customer's purchasing procedures and criteria. The approach that a big manufacturer of power distribution equipment follows illustrates the point. The manufacturer's electrical utility customers buy on an annual basis, asking for bids once a year and subsequently ordering monthly installments of the total order placed at the beginning of the year. Suppliers to this industry structure their prices in different ways: some quote fixed prices for the full year; others give firm prices for the first two quarters, with monthly escalation thereafter; still others quote firm prices for one quarter, again with monthly escalation thereafter; and a fourth group includes an escalation clause taking effect from the end of the first month.

The supplier in question took the trouble to find out how all the customers in its market evaluated suppliers' bids. Fully a third of the customers, it discovered, ranked bids on the basis of year-end prices alone, while one in four examined prices in January without regard to escalation clauses. The manufacturer, whose policy had been to price for a single quarter with monthly escalation thereafter, switched to quoting a fixed inclusive price to the first group of customers, and monthly escalation over the whole year to the second group. The effect on its winning-bids ratio and its margins was dramatic. Now competitors have belatedly begun to follow suit.

——— A PRICING SYSTEM FOR PROFITS

Proactive pricing approaches are more likely to succeed if they are supported by sound pricing systems. Such systems are not always easy to develop, and their effective implementation takes time and perseverance. The elements of a successful pricing system include the following:

1. Marketers must gather a great deal of information about market and customer characteristics, competitor capabilities and actions, and internal capabilities and costs. After thorough and imaginative analysis, marketers can use this information to draw up pricing

policies and guidelines that can then be translated into customer-specific pricing tactics.

2. Collection and analysis of price data for each product must begin early in the development process and continue throughout the product's life. Sources of customer and competitor data are the sales force, targeted customer interviews, competitor sales literature, trade publications, security analysts' reports, and former employees of customers and competitors. Proactive pricers use information gathered from these sources—data on competitors' product performance, cost structure, current and expected capacities, and pricing strategies as well as on customer product expectations and buying processes—to stay a jump ahead of the rest of their industry in pricing skill and sophistication. Good market, competitive, and internal data give top management a vital edge in developing pricing strategy and put a potent competitive weapon in the hands of the middle managers and salespeople who will be making the day-to-day pricing decisions.

3. Successful companies are structured to take advantage of the data needed to support effective pricing. Because this information must be up-to-the-minute and must be drawn from a wide variety of sources, organizing to collect and use it is always something of a challenge. Responsibility for this effort is normally lodged in the marketing function, usually not with marketing research staffers but with product or market managers so as to capitalize on their closeness to the customers and daily involvement with competition.

4. Flexible and responsive systems for collecting and using pricing data are characteristic of the most successful pricing practitioners. Many companies have developed special incentives to encourage salespeople to bring in good customer and competitive data, especially prices on both won and lost orders. Most also provide their pricing decision makers with on-line linkages to the product cost systems and with quick access to current customer-specific costs. One company reports a very high payoff from an approval and tracking system that links each pricing decision to an individual and provides those concerned (and their immediate superiors) with feedback on their performance, in terms of their "win" rates and actual profitability.

5. Successful pricers usually assign more and better people than their competitors to jobs involving collecting, analyzing, and using price information. Aware that poor pricing performance is often more a reflection of overworked and underqualified staff than of ineffective pricing strategies or tactics, proactive companies fill these positions with people who combine quantitative skills with a sense for competitive dynamics.

6. Effective control and feedback on results are essential to the success of a proactive pricing system. Management must have a reliable way of tracking and evaluating the pricing decisions made by each individual with pricing responsibilities in the organization so that it will know, among other things, if consistently specified approval levels are being observed in day-to-day practice.

The value of a superior pricing information system can often be measured in hard cash. One company, determined to improve its pricing information, started by revising its accounting data to reflect fixed and variable costs accurately by product and by market. By surveying the sales force, it created a pricing history by customer and product type of each key competitor as well as a profile of the buying process of each major customer. Finally, it provided each pricing decision maker with a personal microcomputer, access to three data bases (cost, competitor, and customer), guidelines on pricing strategy, and feedback on individual performance. In less than a year (and at a time of declining market demand), its margins improved by several percentage points, representing almost $25 million in added profits.

In most industrial companies major pricing opportunities are waiting to be realized. They exist for a number of reasons. For one, most managers are unaware of the latitude that the price band affords and hence of the opportunity costs of passive, purely reactive pricing policies. For another, not many companies really understand their customers' economics and buying behavior. Taking advantage of proactive pricing opportunities, if done intelligently, entails little risk. Improvements in pricing, moreover, are possible in many situations without provoking competitive retaliation, and they are often sustainable because the competitors cannot readily detect them.

A final attraction of proactive pricing is that the approach itself carries such a low price tag. Installing a proactive pricing system entails limited investment, minimal added expense, and minor organizational adjustments. But the payoff is usually both substantial and quick in coming. Given a solid understanding of the dynamics of price level, structure, and timing; knowledge of the customer; an up-to-date data base; and consistency in execution, any industrial company can successfully use pricing proactively as a tool for building and sustaining profits.

——— DISCUSSION QUESTIONS

1. Increasing customer diversity has spawned new pricing techniques. The author says that the most powerful industrial companies
   are successful not because they have the lowest costs but because
   they outmaneuver their competitors on price. Do you agree that
   this is a viable approach? How would this work?
2. The reading presents a different technique for designing a price
   strategy for industrial products. With "proactive pricing," says the
   author, profits can be much higher than with the conventional
   pricing methods. How does proactive pricing compare with the
   traditional cost-based "passive" pricing strategy?
3. The author calls proactive pricing a powerful competitive weapon
   for industrial companies. What information does the industrial
   marketer need to have in order to design a proactive pricing system?
4. Are there risks to the proactive pricing approach?

Manage Customers for Profits (Not Just Sales) 22

BENSON P. SHAPIRO, V. KASTURI RANGAN,
ROWLAND T. MORIARTY, AND ELLIOT B. ROSS

Raising prices or giving volume discounts to increase sales is not the automatic answer to increasing profits. The costs incurred by these actions often determine the amount of profit generated—and the results are sometimes surprising. Much depends on geography, order size, and extra attention to keep the account. If companies want profits and not just sales, say these authors, they must start by understanding the differences among their customers. Some customers cost more to serve; others will pay any price to get a certain product. The authors describe four customer categories—the carriage trade, bargain basement customers, passive customers, and aggressive customers—that companies can use to analyze customers and steer themselves into more profitable markets.

High sales volume does not necessarily mean high income, as many companies have found to their sorrow. In fact, profits (as a percentage of sales) are often much higher on some orders than on others, for reasons managers sometimes do not well understand. If prices are appropriate, why is there such striking variation? Let's look at two examples of selling and pricing anomalies:

1. A plumbing fixtures manufacturer raised prices to discourage the "worthless" small custom orders that were disrupting the factory. But a series of price hikes failed to reduce unit sales volume. A study of operations two years later revealed that the most profitable orders were these custom orders. The new high prices more than compensated for costs; customers weren't changing suppliers because of high switching expenses; and competitors had shied from short runs because of the conventional wisdom in the industry.
2. A prominent producer of capital equipment, realizing it was losing big sales potential in its largest accounts, started a national account program. It included heavy sales support with experienced account managers; participation by high-level executives; special support like applications engineering, custom design services, unusual

maintenance work, and expedited delivery; and a national purchase agreement with a hefty graduated volume discount.

Customers, however, viewed the program as merely a dog-and-pony show, having no substance. To convince the skeptics, top executives personally offered greater sales and service support and even more generous discounts.

Sales finally turned upward, and this "success" justified even higher levels of support. But profit margins soon began to erode; the big national accounts, the company discovered, were generating losses that were large enough to offset the rise in volume and the profitability of smaller, allegedly less attractive accounts.

Clearly these two companies discovered that it costs more to fill some orders than others. The plumbing fixtures executives raised prices precisely because they knew it was costing them more to fill small custom orders. The capital equipment company willingly took on extra costs in the hope of winning more sales. Management in both companies recognized that their price tags would vary, the first from boosted prices on custom orders, the other because of volume discounts. But executives in both companies failed to see that the cost and price variations would cause profound differences in the profitability of individual accounts and orders.

Many companies make this mistake. Managers pay little attention to account profitability, selection, and management. They seldom consider the magnitude, origins, and managerial implications of profit dispersion. Here we examine three central aspects of this important factor: costs to suppliers, customer behavior, and management of customers.

—— COSTS TO SUPPLIERS

Profit, of course, is the difference between the net price and the actual cost to serve. In terms of individual accounts and orders, there can be dramatic differences in both price and cost.

Despite legal constraints that encourage uniformity in pricing, customers usually pay quite different prices in practice. Some buyers can negotiate or take advantage of differential discounts because of their size or the functions they can perform themselves, like in-house maintenance or technical support. And some customers exploit deals and promotions more than others. Moreover, the costs of serving customers and filling orders can vary significantly.

Presale costs vary greatly from order to order and account to account. Geography matters: some customers and prospects are located far from the salesperson's home base or normal route. Some customers require seemingly endless sales calls, while others place their orders over the telephone. Some must be courted with top-level executives backed up by sophisticated account management techniques, while others need little special effort. Such variations in cost reflect differences in customers' buying processes or the nature of their buying teams. (Some teams are large and geographically and functionally dispersed; others are small and concentrated by location or function.) Finally, some customers demand intensive presale service, like applications engineering and custom design support, while others accept standard designs.

Production costs also vary by customer and by order. Order size influences cost, as do setup time, scrap rate, custom designs, special features and functions, unusual packaging, and even order timing. Off-peak orders cost less than those made when demand is heavy. Fast delivery costs more. Some orders call on more resources than others. A company that inventories products in anticipation of orders, however, will have difficulty tracing production costs to particular orders and customers. Accounting policies and conventions, furthermore, often cloud the distinctions in product costs.

Distribution costs naturally vary with the customer's location. It also costs more to ship via a preferred transportation mode, to drop ship to a separate receiving location, to find no back-haul opportunity, or to extend special logistics support like a field inventory.

Postsale service costs also differ. Sometimes customer training, installation, technical support, and repair and maintenance are profit-making operations, but businesses often bundle such services into the product price, and the buyer pays "nothing extra" for them. For some items, including capital equipment, postsale costs are heavy.

Thus there are variations among customers in each of the four components of cost: before-the-sale expenses, production, distribution, and after-the-sale service. Moreover, if prices and costs do not correlate, the distribution of gross income will have a dispersion that is the sum of the individual price and cost dispersions and thus much greater than either. Of course, prices and costs are often viewed as correlated, but our research suggests that they usually aren't—which produces a broad dispersion of account profitability.

With real cost-plus pricing, profitability could be uniform across customers despite wide variations in both costs and prices. But there is evidence that prices seldom reflect the actual costs in serving customers (though they may be somewhat related to production costs). In many businesses, the difference between the highest and lowest prices realized in similar transactions for the same product is as much as 30%, not including quantity discounts.[1] Consider, for example, the relationship between prices and total costs in one month's orders for a manufacturer of pipe resin (see *Exhibit 1*). The diagonal line indicates a price level equal to costs. If gross margin were the same on all orders, the orders would all lie along a line parallel to the diagonal line. Instead,

---

1. *See* Elliot B. Ross, "Making Money with Proactive Pricing," *Harvard Business Review* (November–December 1984): 145.

EXHIBIT 1
Wide Gross Margin Dispersion for a Pipe Resin Manufacturer for One Month

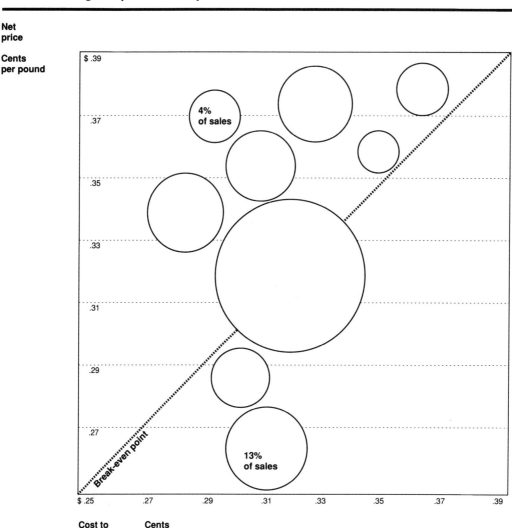

they are widely dispersed. Nearly 13% of sales volume resulted in losses of about a nickel a pound, while about 4% of volume generated an eight-cent profit. The rest fell somewhere between.

This pattern is not unusual. In a wide variety of situations, we have consistently observed a lack of correlation between price and the cost to serve. Some orders and customers generate losses, and in general the dispersion of profitability is wide.

——— CUSTOMER BEHAVIOR

It is useful to think of customers in terms of two dimensions: net price realized and cost to serve. To show graphically the dynamics of the interplay between seller and buyer, we have devised a simple matrix (see *Exhibit 2*). The vertical axis is net price, low to high, and the horizontal axis is cost to serve, low to high. This categorization is useful for any marketer. The *carriage trade* costs a great deal to serve but is willing to pay top dollar. (This category would include the customers of our introductory example, who placed small orders for high-cost custom plumbing fixtures.) At the opposite extreme are *bargain basement* customers—sensitive to price and relatively insensitive to service and quality. They can be served more cheaply than the carriage trade.

Serving *passive* customers costs less too, but they are willing to accept high prices. These accounts generate highly profitable orders. There are various reasons for their attitude. In some cases the product is too insignificant to warrant a tough negotiating stance over price. Other customers are insensitive to price because the product is crucial to their operation. Still others stay with their current supplier, more or less regardless of price, because of the prohibitive cost of switching. As an example from another industry, many major aircraft components cannot be changed without recertifying the entire aircraft. And in some cases vendor capability is so well matched to buyer needs that cost to serve is low though the customer is receiving (and paying for) fine service and quality.

EXHIBIT 2
Customer Classification Matrix

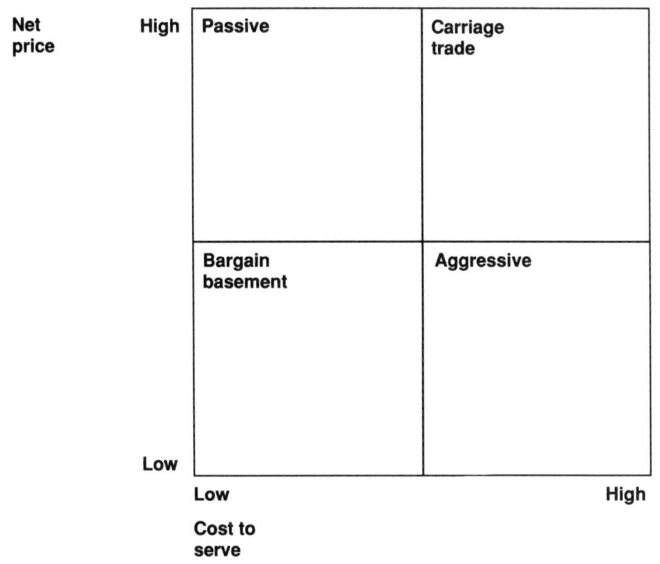

Net price	High	Passive	Carriage trade
		Bargain basement	Aggressive
	Low		
		Low	High
		Cost to serve	

Aggressive customers, on the other hand, demand (and often receive) the highest product quality, the best service, and low prices. Procter & Gamble, boasting an efficient procurement function, has a reputation among its suppliers for paying the least and getting the most. Aggressive buyers are usually powerful; their practice of buying in large quantities gives them leverage with suppliers in seeking price deals and more service. The national accounts described in the second example at the beginning of this reading drove hard bargains with the capital equipment supplier.

Marketing managers often assume a strong correlation between net price and cost to serve; they reason that price-sensitive customers will accept lower quality and service, and demanding customers will pay more for better quality and service. Thinking in terms of service and quality demands unfortunately deflects attention from the critical issue of cost to serve. In addition, weak cost accounting practices that average costs over products, orders, and customers often support the high-cost, high-price myth. But as we have seen, costs and prices are not closely correlated.

A supplier of industrial packaging materials analyzed the profitability of its large national accounts. For each one it calculated approximate indicators of net price and cost to serve, based on averages of the aggregate values of a year's transactions. Top officers expected to find most of its customers in the carriage trade quadrant and the rest in the bargain basement. They were

EXHIBIT 3
Customer Matrix of an Industrial Packaging Materials Supplier

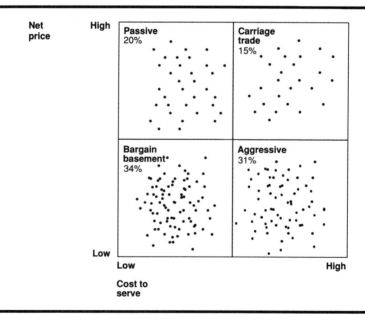

shocked when the results put about half of the 164 large customers in the passive and aggressive quadrants (see *Exhibit 3*).

We believe this pattern is more common than is generally recognized. Among the various factors influencing buying behavior, the most important are the customer's situation and migration patterns.

CUSTOMER'S SITUATION

Four aspects of the customer's nature and position affect profitability: customer economics, power, the nature of the decision-making unit, and the institutional relationship between the buyer and seller.

As we all know, fundamental economics helps determine a buyer's price and service sensitivity. Customers are more sensitive to price when the product is a big part of their purchases, more sensitive to service when it has a big impact on their operations. Independent of economics, buying power, of course, is a major determinant of the buyer's ability to extract price concessions and service support from vendors. The power of big customers shows in their ability to handle many aspects of service support in-house—like breaking bulk—for which they demand price adjustments. Sometimes small customers also wield considerable power. A technological innovator that influences industry standards commands the eyes and ears of suppliers. Thus the relationship of cost to serve and customer size in this industry is not clear without careful measurement.

In respect to the decision-making unit, the purchase staff is generally sensitive to price, while engineering and production personnel are sensitive to service. The roles will affect decisions, depending on who most influences vendor choice and management.

Naturally, this element is bound up with any relationships that have built up between the buyer and seller. Long-standing friendships, long histories of satisfactory performance, and appreciation for any special help or favors all tend to make customers reluctant to pressure suppliers for price and service concessions. Procter & Gamble rotates the responsibilities of its purchasing department members to discourage the development of strong personal relationships with vendors.

MIGRATION PATTERNS

Changes in organizational buying behavior and competitive activity can produce predictable patterns of change in customer profitability. Often a relationship begins in the carriage trade category. Customers need extensive sales and service support, insist on high product quality, and do not worry much about price if the product is new to them. They need the functionality and will pay for it.

Over time, however, as the customers gain experience with the product, they grow confident in dealing with the vendor and operating with less sales and service support or even without any. The cost of serving them is likely to decline, and they are likely to become more price sensitive. In addition, the buying influence of the customer's procurement department often grows, while the role of engineering and operating personnel diminishes. This shift, of course, reinforces the tendency toward price sensitivity and away from service concerns. Finally, through rival product offerings (often at lower prices), customers gain knowledge that improves their competence with the product and thus their ability to demand price concessions and lessen their dependence on the vendor's support efforts.

If the customer perceives the product as trivial (as in the case of office supplies) and therefore does not seek it avidly, price sensitivity will not necessarily increase as service needs abate. In terms of the matrix in *Exhibit 2*, migration will be toward the passive and bargain basement areas. If the buyer values the product and it is complex or service sensitive (like CAD/CAM equipment), the buyer may pressure the supplier for price reductions even while service requirements remain high. The migration tends to be downward from the carriage trade toward the aggressive quadrant, as in the case of electrical generation equipment for utilities. In commodities like pipe resin, a combination of customer experience, expanding influence of the purchasing staff, and increasing competitive imitation often leads customers into the bargain basement category.

—— MANAGEMENT OF CUSTOMERS

The shifts toward the bargain basement and aggressive quadrants are part of the general tendency of products to evolve from high-margin specialties to low-margin commodities. The dispersion of customer profitability we have observed can be managed. We suggest a five-step action program: pinpoint your costs, know your profitability dispersion, focus your strategy, provide support systems, and analyze repeatedly.

Pinpoint Your Costs   Manufacturers can usually measure their factory costs better than they can costs incurred by the sales, applications engineering, logistics, and service functions. For instance, few companies have a sense of the cost of unscheduled executive effort to handle the demands of aggressive customers. So it seems likely that customer profitability varies more widely in businesses where a large percentage of the total expenditure is incurred outside the factory. This would be the case in many high-tech companies that have low manufacturing costs but spend a great deal on sales, design engineering, applications engineering, and systems integration.

Because many specialty products are custom designed and manufactured and carry heavy nonfactory costs, the cost dispersion for these products is greater than for commodities. But as we pointed out in our pipe resin example, profit dispersion can be high even in a commodity product.

Costs incurred at different times in the order cycle have different effects on the true cost to serve the customer or order. In major sales with long order cycles and long lead times, the presale effort may begin several years ahead, and service under warranty may extend several years after installation and billing. If the cost of capital is 15%, a dollar spent two years before the billing of the customer is worth $1.32, and a dollar spent three years after billing is worth only 61 cents at the time of delivery. Companies with long lead times and order cycles, such as sellers of power generation equipment and commercial airliners, with long-term, substantial service liabilities, evidently have cost dispersions much larger than average, except where progress payments balance out cost flows. These companies need particularly good control systems and management judgment to measure costs and act accordingly.

Companies with poor cost accounting systems have no way to determine order, customer, product, or market segment profitability. Consequently, their cost control and management systems will be weak, and the result is likely to be above-average dispersion of costs. The sales manager of a large office equipment supplier who lacked adequate cost information described his situation thus: "It's management by anecdote. Salespeople regularly make passionate pleas for price relief on specific orders. When I press them for reasons, they say 'threat of competitive entry.' When I ask them if a cutback in service would be acceptable to make up for the price decrease, they give me a resounding no! What choice do you have in the absence of cost data, except to go by your judgment of the salesperson's credibility! I've wrongly accepted as many bad price relief requests as I've rejected."

An effective cost accounting system records data by product, order, and account, and records costs beyond the factory, including selling, transportation, applications or design engineering, and even unusual, unprogrammed activities like investments of blocks of corporate management time. Presale, production, distribution, and postsale service costs should all be recorded, analyzed, and related to orders and accounts.

Of course, there are enormous difficulties in creating and maintaining such a system. But even a system that estimates such costs only approximately can help a great deal. Twice a year, for example, one industrial company calculates the cost of serving three sizes of customers (large, medium, and small) and two sizes of orders (truckload and less-than-truckload) for a representative sample of accounts and orders. During the following six months, sales managers use these numbers to guide their decisions on price-relief requests.

Know Your Profitability Dispersion   Once costs are known, the company can plot them against realized prices to show the dispersion of account profitability, as in *Exhibit 2*. Clearly the framework must be adapted to the characteristics of the business. Similarly, the price axis should be defined in a meaningful way. Since list prices are often misleading, use some sort of net price.

However, discounts should not be double-counted under costs as well. The ultimate objective is a measure of net profit by customer and order. Tracking cost and price data by order is an essential first step in building an account profitability matrix.

Companies that know their costs and use cost-plus pricing schemes will find most of their accounts in the bargain basement or carriage trade quadrants of the matrix. Though this pattern is perfectly reasonable, sales management should try to develop accounts in the passive quadrant. Many such customers will accept higher prices because they like the product so much. The cost to them of negotiating a lower price (or better service) outweighs the extra benefits they would get. The passive quadrant represents a region of maximum value for both the seller and the buyer.

A dispersion of profits is no bad thing; only not knowing it exists is. The best-managed companies know their costs well and set prices on the basis of product value to customers rather than cost to serve. So they have some accounts in the passive categories. In fact, their profit dispersion will be greater than that of companies pricing on a cost-plus basis. The worst-managed companies, ignorant of their costs and setting prices mainly in response to customer demands, are likely to have a large number of accounts in the aggressive category, with, obviously, pessimistic implications for profitability.

Focus Your Strategy   The next step is to use your knowledge of cost, price, and profit dispersion to define a strategy for managing your accounts. Here the company defines its personality. The low-cost, low-service, low-price provider is in the lower left of a profitability matrix, while the company that offers differentiated and augmented products, intensive service, and customization—and, therefore, more value added—is in the upper right quadrant. Because any company's capability is necessarily limited, it cannot span the entire dimension. If it tries to, the poor focus will leave the company vulnerable to competition. This will allow rivals to jump into the aggressive quadrant with high service and low prices, drawing customers away from both the bargain basement and carriage trade quadrants. The result for the stretched-out company is reduced profitability.

The company has two strategy decisions to make. One is to locate the center of gravity or core of the company's business along the axis. The other is to define the range along the axis it will cover.

The fundamental choice to be made is the selection of customers, for companies that reside in a given quadrant will *generally* produce orders in that quadrant. Customers in each quadrant of the profitability matrix behave in a distinctive manner. The supplier has to decide which behavior is most consistent with its strengths. For instance, in an industry with high transport costs, like cement or sand, a customer located at the maximum practical distance from your plant is likely to be in one of the right-hand quadrants—for you. For a competitor whose plant is located near the customer, that account will probably be in a left-hand quadrant. Unless you can form a carriage-trade relationship with that customer—realizing high prices because of the value of your services—you would do better to concede the account to your competitor.

Provide Support Systems   Unless it wants to follow a policy of cost-plus pricing, the company needs to develop processes and systems that will help it manage the profitability dispersion. The company's information system should produce reports based on order, customer, and segment profitability, not just on sales. Management must be oriented toward lateral cooperation among functions. A procedure that simply rewards salespeople for high unit sales and manufacturing personnel for low-cost production is unlikely to lead to the most profitable order mix.

Price setting rates special attention. Companies that operate in the bargain basement and aggressive quadrants of the profitability matrix must often set up centralized offices to price large orders and screen customers' demands for services. A "special bids" group is often the only way to give the quick replies and careful analyses such orders require. Such a group can best balance financial implications, production and operating capacity, and customer needs, without giving away the store. Since carriage trade customers value the supplier's extra services, a cost-plus pricing policy may be appropriate for them. Finally, pricing for the trade in the passive quadrant has to be based on the value the customer places on the product.

The analysis, strategy, and customer negotiation functions must be kept separate. A men's and boys' coat manufacturer we know of is a good example of what happens when this rule is ignored. The owner's three sons headed divisions serving the department store, discount store, and export markets, while the owner himself managed the private-label business. He called on the three big general merchandise chains (Sears, Ward, and Penney), one of which gave him almost all of his business. The sons' divisions were very profitable, but the private-label unit was a big money loser.

Why was this so? Before a son went out to negotiate an order, the owner stressed the need to get high prices, keep costs reasonable, and secure orders that fit the company's abilities. The father analyzed large orders for profitability. But when the father went to talk to his biggest customer, no one pressured him to keep profits up. He consistently caved in to demands for lower prices, higher service, and better quality. His sons felt powerless to analyze his orders for profitability. The lesson: the same person should not set profit goals and negotiate with customers.

The more services a company provides, the more coordination is necessary among the engineers, field-service staff, and other functionaries in delivering the product and service. Likewise, the more a company increases its cost to serve, the more important interfunctional coordination becomes. Low-cost, low-price, low-service bargain basement operators don't need and can't afford elaborate logistics, field service, and other coordinating mechanisms. Carriage trade customers can't operate without them.

Deciding what strategic choices to make requires maintaining market research, pricing analysis, and cost-accounting functions. While these are high-leverage operations in which small investments can yield high returns, in hard times companies often view them as nonessential overhead expenses. This short-sighted attitude can be very damaging.

Repeat Analysis Regularly   A one-shot profit dispersion and strategy analysis is of little use. Buying behavior and migration patterns, like markets and competitors, are dynamic. Migration patterns gradually dilute a company's account selection and management policies.

Cumberland Metals (a disguised name) made pollution control components for the Big Three auto companies in the mid-1970s. Margins were very good, reflecting the high value the auto companies placed on the product, their lack of experience with pollution control, and the absence of competition. The entry of competitors in the early 1980s and, on the customers' part, a shift in influence from engineering to procurement staff signaled a fundamental migration in their buying behavior, but Cumberland management ignored the warning signs. This inattention caused long-standing customer relations problems and a prolonged earnings slump.

Cumberland Metals is unusual because it had only three large accounts. The loss of accounts and orders from the carriage trade quadrant is normally a matter of erosion.

How often a company should analyze profit dispersion and strategy depends on the rate of change in the market and in technology. In many cases, a once-a-year analysis integrated with the annual marketing plan makes sense. In high technology or other rapidly changing industries, a more frequent review may be better. In any case, the main difficulty lies in setting up good systems to track costs, prices, and profits; once the supporting information is available, the analysis is not difficult to perform.

——— MANAGE THE DISPERSION

A custom fabricator of industrial equipment, though operating at capacity, was losing money. The obvious problem was low price levels for the industry. Investigation, however, pointed to a mixture of poor pricing, poor cost estimating, and a lack of knowledge of profitability dispersion. Some bids were too aggressively priced: after winning contracts, the company then lost money on them. Executives had structured other bids to "make good money," basing them on inflated cost estimates. Astute competitors costed these bids better, handled the price negotiations more skillfully, and won the contracts. So the fabricator was winning only unprofitable bids.

The electrical products division of a large corporation, on the other hand, understood the importance of profitability analysis. It carefully analyzed its costs, developed a proactive pricing approach, and meticulously selected orders, products, and customers that fit its production competence and capacity. After a thorough before-and-after review, the financial analysis department at headquarters declared that the division had gone from a 5% loss to a 10% profit on sales in a glutted, static commodity market.

When meticulous analysis, a sensible strategy, and effective implementation are combined, a company can manage its profitability dispersion to generate profits, not just sales.

──── DISCUSSION QUESTIONS

1. To meet the challenges of customer diversity, the authors have developed a pricing system that takes into account product value and cost to serve. How does this system differ from the traditional methods for increasing profits?

2. How does understanding the differences among their customers help companies to gain bigger profits without having to raise prices or increase sales volume? How is this accomplished and what factors must be considered?

3. The authors state that some customers cost more to serve than others. From your own experience, give an example of what this means. How does this difference in cost affect pricing policy?

4. Assuming that some customers will pay any price to get a product, how can this factor be integrated into pricing policy? Will this policy remain effective throughout the stages of a product's life cycle?

5. What factors need to be monitored continually in order to produce a predictable pattern of change in customer profitability?

DISTRIBUTION DECISIONS

The readings in this section discuss some of the fundamental aspects of developing and managing appropriate channels of distribution. How does a product get to the customer? The channels of distribution are many: Some are direct to the customer; others involve one or more intermediaries; still others, especially now in the 1990s, require a mix of various marketing methods to reach different customer segments. Such a hybrid approach uses more than one channel, adds new channels when needed, devises new methods of communication—and in short creates a customized marketing system.

Selecting and designing a distribution channel to meet the goals of the manufacturer or service provider requires a thorough knowledge of customer buying and usage behavior, proper segmentation of the market according to these and other dimensions, and full cognizance of the strengths and weaknesses of the competition. Once it is in place, managing the channel becomes an even more complex and time-consuming enterprise in which establishing controls, motivating channel members, and nurturing their goodwill are vital. A mix-and-match marketing system is extremely difficult to manage, but the rewards of doing so are increased coverage and lower costs.

Strategic Issues in Distribution   23

HIROTAKA J. TAKEUCHI

This detailed reading provides an overview and in-depth discussion of chan-nels of distribution from the perspective of the manufacturer. The first section addresses the strategic issues related to designing and modifying an effective channel. The second section deals with channel management—motivating members, controlling the channel, and maintaining communications within the system.

The selection and management of a distribution channel is one of the most critical strategic marketing issues for two reasons: (1) it intimately affects every other element of a manufacturer's marketing strategy; and (2) it commits the manufacturer to relatively long-term, complex relationships with other independent parties.

Although channel decisions do not necessarily precede other decisions, they do exert substantial influence on other elements of a marketing strategy. A company's pricing structure, for example, may depend on whether it seeks a limited number of high-markup dealers or mass distribution. Its promotion strategy too depends on whether it sells directly to consumers, through manufacturers' representatives, or through retailers. In some instances, even the product strategy hinges on whether the product will be sold through a prestigious department store or a discount chain.

Moreover, changing a company's channel strategy is usually very difficult because of the long time required to build effective working relationships with dealers and wholesalers. If, for instance, a franchisor such as Dunkin' Donuts signs up an independent businessperson to open a franchised outlet, it cannot easily replace the franchisee with a company-owned store. When a brand of high-quality luggage carried only in selected retail outlets was placed on sale in a Boston discount chain, buyers at the specialty stores that sold it besieged the manufacturer with threats to cancel future orders. (It turned out that the discount chain had obtained the luggage from a local company that had purchased "seconds" directly from the manufacturer for a sales promotion that was later canceled.)

The critical importance of decisions about the distribution channel can be appreciated by considering the situation of a hypothetical company contemplating major changes in its channel system.

Yankee Shoe, a manufacturer of men's work shoes with production facilities in New England, distributes its products to customers scattered throughout the country. In the past the company sold its brand of work shoes, known for comfort and long wear, directly to customers. Police officers in Manhattan, for example, bought the plain black model from George Pine, an authorized salesperson for Yankee, who stopped by the precincts periodically, took orders, and delivered the shoes by mail.

But as the customer base expanded in both number and geographical spread, the company added other channels of distribution. It is currently utilizing six channels to reach its customers.

1. *Direct selling.* The company retains thousands of authorized full-time and part-time salespeople paid on commission. They sell the shoes primarily at job locations, such as gas stations, factories, and construction sites. They send orders to the company, which ships orders directly to customers. About two-thirds of the orders are shipped prepaid; a third are sent C.O.D.

2. *Direct mail.* Every quarter Yankee mails out about a million fliers to direct-mail customers; orders are received from about 2% of the customers solicited. These orders are recorded in the company's computer system, which maintains each customer's past order record. When the record indicates that a customer has not purchased shoes for more than two years, he or she is listed as "inactive."

3. *"Shoemobiles."* The company sells its steel-tipped safety shoes to large industrial accounts through 20 shoemobiles. These vans visit industrial concerns (mostly factories) and provide on-site fittings. Since the shoemobile carries a limited inventory, most orders are written up by the salesperson and shipped either prepaid or C.O.D.

4. *Retail stores.* The company owns more than 100 free-standing retail stores in major U.S. cities. They sell the company's shoes, principally for cash, with about a third of sales billed through major credit cards. The stores carry a large inventory of various styles and sizes and receive shipments from the company warehouse every few weeks.

5. *Franchised stores.* The company also operates about 50 franchised stores in smaller market areas. They are independently owned, often by former direct salespersons or retail store managers. Franchisees pay a one-time franchise fee and a continuing monthly fee or royalty (a percentage of total gross sales). Local owners set their own prices and store hours.

6. *Sears.* Yankee supplies work shoes to Sears through a private-label program. The department store specifies production quantities and inventory levels to be maintained at each stockkeeping unit (SKU). The contract provides that Sears pay full standard production costs plus a negotiated amount to cover overhead and profit.

In addition, the company has recently been offered the opportunity to lease the men's shoe departments of a discount chain planning to open some 30 stores in New England. As is the case with Sears, all shoes would be sold under the chain's brand name. Yankee would be responsible for managing inventory and staffing the leased departments; it would pay a percentage of total gross sales to the chain as rent.

CHANNEL DESIGN

The Yankee example illustrates three critical decisions about channel selection faced by every producer. They are

- Determining the vertical length of the distribution channel
- Deciding on the optimum breadth or intensity of distribution coverage
- Dealing with decisions to modify the channel to meet new market opportunities

DETERMINING THE VERTICAL LENGTH OF THE CHANNEL

The length of the distribution channel refers to the numbers of channel intermediaries (or "middlemen") who participate in the process of moving the product from manufacturer to ultimate user. They are the wholesalers and retailers located at various points along the channel. In the Yankee Shoe example, the shortest channel consists of direct selling through company salespersons and direct mail. The other channels involve one intermediary each, for company-owned stores and even shoemobiles are retail intermediaries.[1]

A manufacturer's initial decision is thus a choice between selling directly to customers or selling through one or more intermediaries. Manufacturers who decide to sell directly through their own sales forces (a more common choice among industrial-goods manufacturers than consumer-goods producers) cite several advantages.[2] First, if the manufacturer has a large enough volume base, the use of a field sales force may be a cost-effective means of reaching the customer. Second, the manufacturer can exert better control over the distribution function than if it is handled by independent wholesalers and retailers. Third, the manufacturer may be better able to satisfy customers' needs, for example, for technical services. Fourth, direct contact with customers enables the manufacturer to acquire up-to-date information on market trends and conditions.

---

1. The shoe example also demonstrates several vertical channels—such as an integrated system (i.e., the manufacturer selling its own products in company-owned stores) and a franchising system—which we will discuss in more detail later.

2. For a more detailed description, *see* E. Raymond Corey, *Industrial Marketing: Cases & Concepts* (Englewood Cliffs, N.J.: Prentice-Hall, 1976), pp. 266–72.

Manufacturers that decide *not* to sell directly to customers can choose from three basic options. (1) They can construct a corporate system, in which the manufacturer owns and operates its own, vertically integrated channel system. (2) They may employ a contractual system, by negotiating contracts with independent intermediaries. (3) They can sell through a conventional system, utilizing independent intermediaries to move products to final consumers.

Corporate Systems   Companies marketing a great diversity of products—from men's clothing, to gasoline, to doughnuts—employ vertically integrated distribution systems. By virtue of ownership a company can exercise tight control over its marketing activities. For example, a corporate system can permit a clothing manufacturer to set and maintain its list prices, oil companies to control the quality of the gasoline pumped at their service stations, or a chain of doughnut shops to achieve better coordination of its promotional campaigns.

Vertically integrated companies can also achieve operating economies through standardizing, automating, and streamlining channel operations.[3] In addition they may be able to offer better in-store services to customers (e.g., performing alterations on men's suits or serving doughnuts baked on the premises).

Although a corporate system has distinct advantages, there are also risks. First, large investments in financial and human resources are required to take over the functions otherwise performed by independent wholesalers and retailers. Second, a vertically integrated company may not be able to adapt freely to new market opportunities. In the early 1970s Sherwin-Williams, which operates its own retail paint stores, could not capitalize on the increase in sales at do-it-yourself home centers and discount stores. Du Pont, which sold its Lucite paint through a conventional system, was in a strong position to take advantage of the trend. Third, certain legal risks are associated with corporate integration, particularly when it is accomplished through vertical merger or acquisition. Section 7 of the Clayton Antitrust Act forbids any vertical merger or acquisition that may substantially lessen competition or tend to create a monopoly by raising barriers to entry or disadvantaging unintegrated or partially integrated firms.

Contractual Systems   Although contractual integration can take various forms, franchising is the most common. By 1985, retail sales of all firms associated with a franchise system reached approximately $529 billion, accounting for about a third of all U.S. retail sales. In that year over 5.6 million people were employed in the franchise sector.[4]

---

3. Louis W. Stern and Adel I. El-Ansary, *Marketing Channels* (Englewood Cliffs, N.J.: Prentice-Hall, 1982), p. 424.

4. The data utilized in this section are from U.S. Department of Commerce, *Franchising in the Economy, 1983–1985* (Washington, D. C.: U.S. Government Printing Office, 1985).

Broadly speaking, there are two types of franchising arrangements: product trade-name franchising and business-format franchising. The former consists primarily of product-distribution arrangements in which the franchisee acquires the right to market a franchisor's product within a designated market area, using the franchisor's trade name. These arrangements are found among automobile and truck dealers, gasoline service stations, and soft drink bottlers. Business-format franchising is a more integrated system in which the franchisee buys the right to utilize the business knowhow of the franchisor (i.e., operating manuals and standards, quality control and information systems, and marketing plans) as well as the right to offer the franchisor's product or service in a particular market. This is a typical arrangement for operating fast food restaurants, motels and hotels, personnel services, and real estate agencies, among others. The list is growing as more and more service businesses turn to franchising.

For both independent franchise owners and franchisors, the arrangement offers obvious advantages. To franchise owners it provides the opportunity to be their own bosses, fulfilling the American dream of the "small guy making it big." It permits individuals with no prior experience to get started in business by providing an entire pre-packaged business that includes, besides a well-recognized trade name, (1) assistance in site selection, store layout, and equipment procurement; (2) training in basic business management skills; and (3) continuing support through new-product development, promotional activities, and operational management.

The franchisor, on the other hand, gains the ability to exercise control and coordination over marketing policy while expanding the business with someone else's time and money. (Franchise owners are typically highly motivated people willing to devote time and energy as well as the necessary start-up capital.) Once a chain reaches a certain size the franchisor can realize economies of scale in procurement and promotional expenses.

Conventional Systems   Manufacturers participating in conventional systems employ independent intermediaries to perform specific marketing tasks on their behalf. *Newsweek*, for example, employs independent wholesalers and retailers to distribute its weekly magazine to millions of newsstand readers. Local wholesalers deliver the magazines to individual retailers, reclaim unsold copies, maintain sales and return records, collect from retailers, and prepare the magazines for display. Some 85,000 U.S. retail outlets (supermarkets, drugstores, newsstands, etc.) sell the newsweekly to consumers. Many industrial-goods manufacturers also employ independent distributors. The latter typically maintain warehouses, carry inventories of goods for sale, deliver them, extend credit to customers, and feed market information back to manufacturers.

Producers utilize conventional systems partly in the belief that independent wholesalers and retailers can perform certain marketing tasks more efficiently than they can themselves. Moreover, they may opt for such a system because they cannot afford the substantial up-front investments in financial and human resources needed to establish corporate and contractual systems. In addition, they can reduce their exposure by having other members of the channel take title to the products. Finally, conventional systems permit the manufacturer to respond quickly to changes in market conditions by altering or terminating existing arrangements. They thus offer low barriers to entry, low risk, and high flexibility relative to other systems.

Of course, conventional systems too have offsetting drawbacks. Because channel members are independent and not bound by contracts, manufacturers may have to achieve channel coordination and set the terms of sale through hard bargaining and aggressive negotiation. In addition, they may not realize systemic economies if some intermediaries are so preoccupied with their own advantage that they ignore the needs of the channel as a whole. The system also tends to instability because of the low index of member loyalty and the ease of entry and exit. Manufacturers thus trade off some control, systemic economies, and stabilities for low investment and high flexibility.

To overcome these disadvantages, companies sometimes use either a "carrot" or a "stick" approach to try to achieve system control and economies in a conventional system. Some employ administered programs, providing intermediaries with merchandising assistance, inventory management, advertising support, or sales training. Other manufacturers try to reach the same goals by requiring channel members to sign agreements specifying sales terms and mutual obligations. One U.S. manufacturer of high-quality sound equipment, for example, had dealers sign a seven-page agreement binding them to practices that would assure maintenance of sales and technical standards and protect the good name and reputation of the company. Both methods are attempts by manufacturers to play the role of "channel captain." The more successful the effort, the more closely the conventional system will resemble corporate and contractual systems.

DETERMINING THE BREADTH OF THE CHANNEL SYSTEM

Decisions about the breadth of the channel or relative intensity of distribution coverage involve the number and kind of retail outlets through which the product is offered to customers and the number of intermediaries who will distribute to these outlets. At the retail level products can be sold through a wide variety of outlets (i.e., intensive distribution), through selected subsets of these outlets (i.e., selective distribution), or through only one outlet per defined market area (i.e., exclusive distribution).

Manufacturers of soft drinks, for example, actively pursue an intensive distribution strategy. The list of retail outlets selling soft drinks in the United States is almost endless; it includes supermarkets, convenience stores, liquor stores, restaurants, gasoline service stations, drugstore chains, sports stadiums, taverns, hotels and motels, and countless vending machines.

The reasons for using an intensive approach for frequently purchased products seems clear: the more intensive the products' distribution the higher the sales potential. Consumers are most likely to make purchases of commodity items with low unit value at the most conveniently located outlets. Often, share of distribution translates directly into share of market.

Apparel manufacturers, on the other hand, often distribute their products selectively. A $75-plus tennis shirt sold to fashionable enthusiasts as the brand worn by the current Wimbledon champion might be found in only a few upscale pro shops or departmentalized specialty stores like Neiman-Marcus or Saks. By imposing a high minimum-order size and limiting outlets to a few prestigious stores, the manufacturer tries to (1) maintain the high-fashion image of its products, (2) make the full line of its apparel available to customers, and (3) exercise control over retail prices.

Levi Strauss & Co. is an example of an apparel manufacturer that originally adhered to a policy of selective distribution but has gradually broadened its distribution channel. For many years Levi Strauss preferred to distribute its products only in outlets that harmonized with the tough, plain, quality image of the working cowboy. They were often barebones dry goods stores or dealers of work clothes and specialty outdoor apparel with highly knowledgeable sales assistants. The company believed its products should be sold through retailers with good local reputations and stable financial structures who specialized in selling a few high-quality lines.

In the 1960s and 1970s, however, Levi Strauss expanded into many youth-oriented specialty stores, traditional department stores, and departmentalized specialty stores; by the end of the 1970s the firm had approximately 30,000 outlets. It now also sells through mass merchandisers like Sears, and Levis can be found in many retail clothing outlets and catalogs.

The choice between intensive and selective distribution strategies depends on several factors:

- Product characteristics
- Buyer behavior
- Degree of manufacturer control
- Competitive strategies

Product Characteristics   Products that consumers purchase frequently without much thought (convenience goods) tend to be intensively distributed. Goods for which customers shop carefully and comparatively before making the final purchase (shopping or specialty goods) are likely to be selectively distributed.

Buying Behavior   Selective distribution is a good choice if the perceived risk associated with a buying decision is high. In buying a compact disc player, for example, consumers rely on the technical advice of specialty store salespeople, as well as on assurances of postpurchase service. Where knowledgeable salespeople are required to complete the sale (as in microcomputers) or where retail costs are high (as in furniture), selective distribution is almost always indicated. In general, goods for which frequency of purchase is low and brand loyalty is high are strong candidates for selective distribution.

Conversely, intensive distribution is a good choice if frequency of purchase is high and perceived risk, brand loyalty, and retail sales costs are all low.

Competitive Strategies   The choice between an intensive and selective strategy may depend on what strategies are being employed by major competitors. For example, noting that branded hosiery was sold selectively through department stores and specialty shops, L'eggs decided to sell its products intensively—through supermarkets and drugstores—and others soon followed suit. Hartmann luggage, on the other hand, chose not to pursue an intensive distribution strategy, partly to differentiate itself from such competitors as Samsonite and American Tourister, which were selling their products through catalog showrooms and general merchandise chains.

Whatever decision is made, the choice between intensive and selective strategy should never be seen as permanent. Many products, like Levis, move from selective to intensive distribution during their life cycle. Another good example is hand-held calculators, first sold only in college bookstores and office equipment stores because customers needed information about using them from sales personnel. When consumers became more knowledgeable and the perceived risks associated with purchase declined, the need for shopping convenience prevailed, and they are now distributed intensively.

MODIFYING THE CHANNEL

Manufacturers need to do more than design and select an appropriate channel system. Every so often they must reevaluate the appropriateness of the channel system and make necessary modifications to meet new market opportunities.

As with channel selection, major modification schemes involve shifts in the breadth and length of the channel. A change in the breadth of the channel may mean no more than adding or dropping particular types of channel intermediaries at the wholesale or retail level (i.e., horizontal shift). Changing the length of the channel, however, may require reformulating the whole vertical arrangement by adding or eliminating a level of channel intermediary or by developing an entirely new way to distribute the product. A manufacturer may decide to replace its independent distributors with its own direct sales force, thereby eliminating the wholesale level within the vertical chain. Or it may decide to add new vertical channels, as Yankee Shoe did. The company that started by selling work shoes directly to the customer added a corporate system by operating company-owned stores, a contractual system by establishing franchised outlets, and a conventional system by selling to Sears.

The most difficult of the channel-modification decisions, however, involves revising the overall distribution system. When Yankee considered the discount chain's offer to run its shoe departments it faced the question of whether it could continue to supply Sears, which competes directly with the discount chain. Such revisions typically require trade-offs between the advantages of new opportunities and the risks of disturbing existing relationships. They frequently necessitate a reformulation of the elements of the marketing strategy and may require sizable financial commitments.

A manufacturer may decide to develop a new channel system for several reasons. It may be forced into change by competitive pressures. In 1972, for example, Toro, a manufacturer of lawn and snow-removal equipment, surprised its 65 independent distributors by announcing that large retailers could buy lawn mowers directly from the company, reducing distributors' margins from 40% to 12%. This decision, which Toro knew would upset many distributors, was based on its belief that under the old system competition from Sears and discount chains would continue to eat away Toro's share of the market. The company doubled its advertising budget for that year to help distributors make the transition.[5]

A manufacturer may also add a channel system to serve a new customer segment or geographical region. For example, a foreign automobile producer that sells through wholly owned retail outlets has added its own sales force to sell directly to car rental and leasing companies. An industrial parts manufacturer in Chicago uses its sales force to sell to industries in and around Chicago. The market is large and concentrated, so that a salesperson can make up to a dozen calls a day and write up large orders. To sell to customers outside the city, however, the manufacturer uses independent agents. It argues that the customer base outside Chicago is presently too thin to support a full-time salesperson.

Often, operating dual-channel systems (e.g., selling both directly and through intermediaries) increases the flexibility of the company's distribution policy. It sets up a system tailor-made to particular customer segments and easily adaptable to changes in market density. Nonetheless, the manufacturer should be mindful that such an arrangement can become a major source of interchannel conflict and must be managed carefully.[6]

The difficulty and danger associated with carrying out a channel-modification decision reaffirms the importance of making the right channel selection in the first place. When a modification becomes necessary for strategic reasons (i.e., to capitalize on new market opportunities or adapt to market changes), the manufacturer must evaluate the impact of the decision from all angles—from the perspective of the total channel system as well as from that of

---

5. Adapted from James L. Heskett, *Marketing* (New York: Macmillan, 1976), pp. 331–32.
6. R. T. Moriarty and Ursula Moran, "Managing Hybrid Marketing Systems," *Harvard Business Review* (November–December 1990): 146–55.

individual retailers and wholesalers. How a manufacturer implements a change may be as important as the action itself. As one distributor for Toro put it, "I don't blame Toro for putting in the new program. The other big brands already had them. Toro had to compete. But it didn't consult us beforehand."[7]

─────── CHANNEL MANAGEMENT

The discussion has thus far centered on the importance of channel selection and design. Equally important, and certainly more time consuming, is the task of maintaining and controlling it once the system is in place. Channel goodwill can flow when the manufacturer takes the leadership role, motivating channel members, communicating with them, and constructing a sense of belonging, even among independent distributors. Channel control can emerge when the manufacturer assumes responsibility for a sound interchannel information system, establishes equitable and clearcut performance standards, and puts evaluation programs into action. The range and number of such managerial tasks extend far beyond the partial listing provided above, but one thing seems clear: maintaining a good channel relationship requires extensive and detailed planning.

One of the first questions the manufacturer engaged in a conventional system must ask is whether or not it should assert itself as the channel leader. It is generally a good idea for the manufacturer to take on this role if it possesses the following:

- A unique product with strong consumer demand and loyalty
- The ability to influence the ultimate buying decision, either through a strong point-of-purchase program or brand advertising
- Economic power resulting from its relative size, financial resources, and ability to test and develop a series of new products

In addition, the manufacturer needs to assess carefully whether the benefits that could accrue from channel leadership (e.g., stronger loyalty from channel members and smoother implementation of marketing programs) will compensate for the costs and efforts of administering and coordinating the channel. In other words, are the potential returns worth it?

The tasks of channel management, whether carried out by the manufacturer or another member, are complex, and seemingly paradoxical. On the one hand, channel members are independent entities. On the other, they are interdependent components of a network of relationships. Moreover, although no explicit rules govern relations among channel members, adequate performance of the system depends on members behaving as others expect them to behave. Even though each channel member has individual goals, it must also work

---

7. Ibid., p. 332.

toward broader, collective goals. In short, even where there is no formal chain of command and communication, channel members rely heavily on an unspoken, informal system.

One way of coping with these ambiguities is to establish a formal system that clearly defines the roles, goals, and chains of command and communication. Franchising is one such formal system. Stating the rules of the game in writing can also be an effective mechanism for coordination and control. It does not, however, replace the need for continued channel management.

What happens if a franchisor leaves the system unattended? What if no one takes on the tasks of channel management within a conventional system? Almost certainly such a situation will lead to one or more types of conflict within the channel.

Role Conflict This occurs when members of the channel deviate from agreed-upon or expected roles. For example, conflict arose between a sound equipment manufacturer and one of its dealers when it was discovered that the dealer was employing a sales tactic specifically proscribed by the dealership agreement. In another case, a large food franchisor confronted role conflict with a franchisee whose scores on cleanliness, product freshness, and other criteria were consistently substandard.

Goal Conflict The goal of one channel member may be directly opposed to those of another member or the channel as a whole. For example, while a large manufacturer may want volume growth, small retailers may be satisfied with stability or earning high profits from a limited number of products. Or a soft drink manufacturer may want controlled territorial allocation, while its bottlers want growth opportunities. Differences over goals often create the most serious conflicts.

Communication Failure Conflict is very likely when relevant information, both formal and informal, is not disseminated throughout the channel. In the early 1970s, Levi Strauss let its European inventories of obsolete goods climb high when it failed to keep pace with swift changes in continental fashions. Such a situation could not have happened in the United States, where Levi Strauss receives up-to-date information from its retailers.

Although some students of human behavior contend that a certain degree of conflict is creative because it discourages complacency and encourages innovation, many conflicts end up being disruptive, expensive, and time consuming. Those that go to court often take a long time to resolve and may result in long-term damage to or destruction of the channel.

The best method of dealing with conflict is prevention, and the best preventive may simply be good management and effective communications. In general, managerial techniques that are effective within a company will work equally well in an interorganizational context. Among other tasks, the manufacturer needs to motivate channel members, communicate with them, and establish appropriate controls within the channel system.

MOTIVATING CHANNEL MEMBERS

Channel members can be motivated to work on behalf of the manufacturer in numerous ways. The basic level of motivation is already built into the terms of trade established between the manufacturer and its channel partners. All things being equal, a broker or a commission wholesaler will be motivated to work hard for a manufacturer that offers a high commission. Similarly, a retailer will be motivated to work for a manufacturer, or a manufacturer's representative, that offers better credit terms, higher gross margins, better promotional allowances, or better return policies than other manufacturers. Besides favorable fundamental terms, a manufacturer can offer temporary financial incentives such as coupon programs, free point-of-sale displays, and special trade promotions.

A manufacturer may also stimulate greater efforts from channel members by using nonfinancial incentives: sales contests, high-performance awards, Caribbean cruises, even dinner with a celebrity or free use of a Rolls Royce for a month! All of these schemes have similar goals—either a pat on the back for work well done or a morale booster for work to be done.

Sometimes manufacturers with substantial market power resort to using the stick instead of the carrot. The wisdom of such an approach, however, is questionable. Philip Kotler describes how some large toy manufacturers make retailers take slow-moving items in order to get a supply of popular, fast-moving toys; and the way certain large soap companies use their market power to get the best shelf space, rather than offering dealers trade allowances or other incentives. "These policies," he notes, "can breed ill will in the channels and someday come back to haunt the manufacturer."[8] Although there may be times when the stick approach is necessary, it is not a viable solution in the long run.

COMMUNICATING WITH CHANNEL MEMBERS

The basic task of maintaining good communications is simply to supply intermediaries with accurate, timely, and relevant information. Any changes in the marketing mix that affect other channel members should be communicated immediately, through newsletters, verbal messages by the sales force, or information sessions. Some companies even invite distributors or dealers (and their spouses) to a "seminar" held at an exotic resort.

---

8. Philip Kotler, *Marketing Management: Analysis, Planning, and Control* (Englewood Cliffs, N.J.: Prentice-Hall, 1976), p. 298.

It is often to the manufacturer's interest to share the results of market and consumer research studies with its intermediaries. Information about overall market trends, changes in consumer buying patterns, or changes in the demographic composition of a target segment may be instrumental in convincing the trade of the existence of an untapped market for the product.

Ideally, communication is a two-way street. A manufacturer who can tap relevant information from retailers and wholesalers will be in a better strategic position to plan the next move. When Levi Strauss linked its computers with those of the retailers it not only enhanced its capacity to forecast fashion trends, it also improved inventory turns and reduced markdowns.

ESTABLISHING CONTROLS

As noted in the discussion of channel selection and design, the desire for control is one of the key determinants of channel choice. Manufacturers that desire maximum control and coordination with the channel generally opt for direct selling or wholly owned retail outlets. Companies seeking control but unable or unwilling to make large financial investments have found in franchising a happy medium. Even within a conventional system, manufacturers have sought control by creating a selective distribution strategy or by sponsoring various administered programs.

Once the selection has been made, control is built into the channel system through performance standards and sanctions. Much grief can be avoided if channel members agree upon these standards in the beginning. The areas posing the greatest need for explicit agreement include (1) territorial coverage, (2) exclusive-dealer contracts, (3) participation in manufacturer-initiated promotional programs, and (4) treatment of damaged and lost goods. Since the first three areas also pose the greatest threat from antitrust litigation, the terms of the agreements must conform to the law.

Once initial agreements are made, an important managerial task is enforcing standards within the channel. Franchisors like Dunkin' Donuts often conduct periodic inspections, which may take two to three hours to complete and include a long checklist of items about food freshness and color, cleanliness, and quality of service. Some manufacturers send a company employee to the store as a disguised shopper. He or she interacts with store personnel and later prepares a report on the salesperson's and store's attitudes and comments about the product, displays, and other pertinent matters.

Manufacturers can resort to techniques other than direct inspection to enforce control standards. It may, like L'eggs, sell the product on consignment to prevent price cutting; or, like automobile manufacturers, issue periodic sales quotas to define performance standards for dealers. Some manufacturers have even circulated the sales figures of dealers to others in the area—the intent being to give positive reinforcement to stronger performers while motivating those at the bottom to do a better job. Such a scheme, which combines motivation, communication, and controls into one consistent program, is an effective managerial tool.

Although there are no simple answers to good channel management, the following advice given by an executive of a large, successful West Coast consumer goods company seems appropriate:

> You basically go back to the marketing concept and apply it twice. First of all, you try to satisfy the wants and needs of the consumer with no *ifs, ands,* or *buts.* Unless there is a strong pull for your product from the consumer, why bother to involve other people in the channel for a losing cause?
>
> Second, you try to satisfy the wants and needs of the middlemen *if* doing so is going to help the system at large. Over the years I've come to realize how interdependent we are with each other. We sink or swim together in our business.

———— DISCUSSION QUESTIONS

1. In meeting the distribution goals of a manufacturer or service provider, how can the choice of proper channels result in increased coverage and lower costs? What basic information does the marketer need to know to select and design the most rewarding distribution system?
2. How complex an undertaking is it to design an effective channel distribution system? How does a manufacturer determine the channel length and breadth and whether to modify the existing channel system? Explain the specifics of these requirements and the design options for each.
3. How does buyer behavior impact channel design?
4. Designing a channel system is one challenge; managing it is another. What assessments need to be made before a plan of action can be formulated? What are the vital areas that need to be managed?

Customer-driven Distribution Systems

24

LOUIS W. STERN AND FREDERICK D. STURDIVANT

This reading describes an eight-step process for designing a distribution system that reaches specific customer groups. It calls for in-depth study of what services and conveniences the company's customers value, followed by segmentation of the market according to those values. At several crucial stages, the process requires getting outside checks and hard data for market segments, company objectives, and the projected costs of distribution outlets. The climax of the process is an off-site meeting at which top management tests its prejudices against the evidence researchers have gathered.

Too often, distribution is the neglected side of marketing. Automobile companies, savvy in many aspects of strategy, have lost huge shares of the parts and service markets to NAPA, Midas, and Goodyear because they resist making changes in their dealer franchise networks. A great many other American companies—Tupperware springs to mind—are reaching their markets in similarly outmoded ways. It is hardly seemly for Tupperware to continue with its "parties" when more than half of American women are working outside their homes.

In contrast, a number of companies have outstripped their competition with imaginative strategies for getting products to their customers—and marketing executives can learn from them. The Federal Express system is so innovative and formidable that it might be considered a model even beyond the small-package delivery industry. American Hospital Supply has gained the edge over its competition by linking up to hospitals and clinics with a sophisticated system of data processing, while Steelcase has set a standard for delivering complex office furniture installations, complete and on time.

Although American companies have been ignoring the ways in which they deliver products and services, their customers are increasingly inclined to demand higher standards of performance. Customers want companies to value their time and trouble.

And so important opportunities for gaining a competitive advantage through distribution remain, and given the new technology, some companies may, as Federal Express has, achieve a breakthrough. Will the management of American companies (deregulated telecommunications companies included) make use of these opportunities or even recognize them for what they are? Just what process should a company use to select or structure the best possible distribution channels for its products?

We suggest eight steps to design a distribution system that really performs. The word *process* is key here because whatever the result of taking these steps, management will gain by clarifying what its customers want and how to serve them. Managers are always saying that they want their company to be "market driven." In following these steps, they can give substance to what is too often merely corporate rhetoric.

STEP 1: FIND OUT WHAT YOUR CUSTOMERS WANT

Of all marketing decisions, the ones regarding distribution are the most far-reaching. A company can easily change its prices or its advertising. It can hire or fire a market research agency, revamp its sales promotion program, even modify its product line. But once a company sets up its distribution channels, it will generally find changing them to be difficult.

Thus, the first step calls for researching what customers want from the buying process and then using their preferences to group customers into market segments. Managers conducting the research concentrate on learning what their ultimate customers—the end users—want in the way of service. It is these people, of course, who actually benefit from the products a company makes.

It is important for the researchers to emphasize that the product's quality is not an issue. Nor should there be any question at this stage of what may or may not be most practical for the company, whether it be a service company, a manufacturer, or a middleman. Rather, respondents should be encouraged to consider the delivery of the service, the convenience of shopping for the product, and the kind of add-ons that are sold along with either.

There is, of course, no such thing as a truly homogeneous market, in which all customers view the company's offerings in exactly the same way. Yet managers who routinely try to ascertain what market segments are worth preparing for when they design a product rarely try this when they make decisions about how to distribute it. This is a crucial mistake.

The preliminary research is meant to generate an inventory of customers' desires, but it is important to exclude ideas too grand or trivial for consideration. Without restrictions of any kind, who wouldn't ask for the moon? Needless to say, an overarching consideration is price: respondents should be made to realize that for every service (or lack of one) there will be a correspondingly higher or lower price. Equally important, however, respondents must be forced to weigh their preferences not only in relation to price but also in relation to one another.

Consider personal computers. The delivery of service might include such things as a demonstration of the product before sale or the provision of long-term warranties and flexible financing. After the sale, there might be training programs for using the equipment and a program to install and repair it. Customers might appreciate "loaners" while their equipment is being repaired or technical advice over a telephone hot line. They should be prepared to make trade-offs among these inducements.

Services, we've found, usually fall into five categories:

1. *Lot size.* Do customers want to buy in units of one or in multiple units?
2. *Market decentralization.* Do customers value around-the-corner convenience, or are they willing to deal across great distances, say via an 800 number?
3. *Waiting time.* Do customers want immediate delivery, or are they more concerned about the assurance of delivery?
4. *Product variety.* Do customers value having the choice of many related products, or do they prefer the store to specialize?
5. *Service backup.* Do customers want immediate, in-house repair and technical help, or can they wait and choose their own local repair services?

Once customers have traded off, say, demands for convenient location against product variety or variety against expert sales assistance, researchers can group these preferences into market segments and look for links between the segments suggested by the survey and the segments that may be generated by analysis of independent demographic or other marketing data.

We suspect, for example, that a segment of small businesses would be much more concerned about one-stop shopping than large businesses; big companies have purchasing specialists with the time to choose complementary products from different sources and to secure the lowest prices within various quality ranges. If a company sells to people who want one-stop shopping, it might want to know whether this segment coincides with self-employed accountants, for example. This small market segment is likely to be substantial, and it has needs quite different from those of a segment consisting of start-up scientific research companies.

A number of marketing research techniques are available to researchers at this step in the process, among them conjoint analysis, hybrid modeling, and constant-sum scales.[1] Unfortunately, most of these techniques have been developed to elicit choices among the tangible properties of product design: gas mileage versus size of car, size versus model, and so on. The things people want from a distribution system tend to be less tangible and more difficult to visualize and make judgments about (convenience of location versus depth of assortment, for example). Survey instruments ought to be designed with this challenge in mind.

---

1. *See* Paul E. Green, "Hybrid Models of Conjoint Analysis: An Expository Review," *Journal of Marketing Research* (May 1984): 155.

——— STEP 2: DECIDE ON APPROPRIATE OUTLETS

At this stage researchers focus on the relation between market segments—defined as clusters of demands for service—and the outlets where services are normally delivered. Suppose, for example, that customers for a home computer indicate a desire for self-service, a somewhat narrow assortment of merchandise, limited after-sale service, and a relatively Spartan atmosphere—so long as the prices are low. Clearly, this segment consists of people who would put up with a discount store operation—a 47th St. Photo, for instance—and trade off the amenities of upscale service or nearby location.

The fame of a store such as 47th St. Photo can be an asset in the analysis. Using the names of such well-known existing outlets or suggesting a hybrid of two or more kinds of such outlets, researchers can label potential clusters of service attributes. Respondents are asked about the service outlets they visualize, and researchers label the clusters constituting a segment precisely and vividly. On the other hand, labels are merely points of reference. They suggest existing kinds of retail outlets without limiting the possibilities.

For clusters suggesting no existing kinds of outlets, short descriptions of hypothetical outlets may be of help. Researchers may coin new names and, in analyzing the data, position the various segments along a wide continuum. The chemical industry, for example, may have no analog to a discount store or a rack jobber. But if many respondents indicate that they would like to see something along these lines, then the research team might, in the course of the survey, develop an appropriate option, describe it, think of a label for it, and present it to new respondents for consideration.

Venturesome financial institutions such as Merrill Lynch, Bank One, and GE Credit have scored impressive gains with just such distribution ideas. How else did we get to "financial supermarkets" and "discount brokerage"? In contrast, many marketing strategists in the personal computer industry have failed to predict the significance of value-added resellers or retail outlets with multiple but highly focused assortments. Obviously, they did not start by conceiving their distribution channels according to the shopping needs of potential customers.

Do not be hamstrung by industry experience. The more creative researchers are with their labels, the better step 2 will work.

——— STEP 3: FIND OUT ABOUT THE COSTS

Up to this point, the customer is sovereign: the process aims to determine what customers perceive to be optional shopping conditions among the many pertaining to distribution and related services. In the first part of step 3, however, it is essential to obtain an impartial assessment of whether the things that customers want (more precisely, the "clusters" of things they want) are feasible for the company. This is the first reality check, one that is made before management as a whole gets involved in the process.

It may be made by selected members of the corporation's staff, assuming they are professionals who can be objective about the company's line operations. Otherwise, the company must turn to executives from unaffected wholesaling or retailing enterprises or to academic authorities.

Researchers have already asked customers to trade off their demands for service against price, so utterly implausible combinations of shopping conditions—outlets combining small-lot purchases and low unit prices, for example—have been eliminated from further consideration. But less obviously implausible combinations may remain. Suppose a group of customers for personal computers claim they are willing to pay any price for a hypothetical shopping outlet combining custom tailoring with quick delivery. Are these two shopping conditions ever practical in combination?

The second part of step 3 aims to determine what kind of support will be needed from suppliers or other "up-channel" participants for any hypothetical outlet suggested by the data. Distribution outlets do not operate in isolation; there is always a distribution system backing them up.

For example, if an attribute cluster suggests a "limited line, full function, vertically oriented industrial distributor," the question would be this: What backup system ensures that this kind of distribution will satisfy customers as well as possible? The answers should be concrete: high-technology distribution centers, training programs, catalog expertise. Sometimes existing distribution systems enjoy the necessary support, sometimes not. If not, the division of labor among suppliers will have to be restructured so that what customers desire may be delivered by the most capable up-channel participant.

Step 3 is a good time to get insights from people out in the distributive trades. It is also the time to tap in-house knowledge, the opinions of salespersons and others who stay in contact with customers.

The third and final part of step 3 is to project the cost of support systems feasible for each outlet type, on the assumption that the company may be able to contract with third parties to perform the outlet functions. Researchers cost out the new support systems on an incremental basis, starting with the company's existing distribution system. Costing requires informed guesswork; any change in one element of a distribution system has ramifications for another. But if, for example, the data suggest that customers want rapid delivery, local inventories will have to be maintained. Distribution centers may have to be constructed to support the local inventories. Cost accountants familiar with distribution may provide estimates, although they may have trouble dealing with the more theoretical scenarios. In the end, the question to be answered is this: What increase in market share is required to offset the added costs of the new distribution alternatives?

It is important to collect these cost estimates during step 3 because they are backup material for step 4. The figures may well reveal that certain systems of distribution are prohibitively expensive and should be removed from further consideration. We know one manufacturer of specialty medical supplies and equipment that was losing sales to competitors selling via mail order. But the added cost of establishing a competing catalog system did not make sense, so the company abandoned the option at this stage.

─── STEP 4: BOUND THE "IDEAL"

At this point the researchers have come as close as they can to discerning an ideal market-driven system. Top management has been obliged to keep its hands off. Researchers have had a chance to find out, perhaps for the first time, what it really takes to please customers.

Step 4 gives a cross section of the company's executives an opportunity to subject the research findings to their own hard tests. Researchers invite these executives to investigate how any existing or hypothetical channel of distribution would affect company efficiency (costs, revenues, and profits), effectiveness (especially market share), and adaptability (fluidity of capital invested, ability to accept new products or adjust to new technologies). At the same time, executives give their impressions of what distribution is or is not doing. Though this part of the process is meant to generate reliable numbers, discussions with managers should be open-ended. They may even bring up their pet peeves.

Finally, researchers develop a list of company objectives for distribution based on their conversations with top management. They turn this list into a survey instrument and send it to every executive in the company who has a stake in distribution matters. Executives trade off objectives in the same way that customers trade off their requirements for outlet design. The result is a list of weighted objectives that are the constraints bounding the system.

Inevitably, at this stage, some executives want to impose constraints on the distribution design, which they justify not so much by numbers as by industrial tradition. There are rigidities and prejudices in most industries, some of which are reinforced by law, some of which are perceived to have the force of law.

The faltering car dealer system has not been altered since the mid-1920s, in part because of peculiarities in the legal structure of auto distribution (franchise laws, dealer-day-in-court laws). But there is also an industry folklore that gets in the way of change, even though auto companies face a shift in power to consolidating dealers. How much longer before the executives of Chrysler, GM, Toyota, and other companies will be forced to compare their old objectives with new options?

The Coca-Cola Company and PepsiCo, in contrast, are consolidating their traditionally independent franchise bottler networks into distribution systems with greater maneuverability. At IBM, distribution by means of a direct sales force had been a sacred principle essentially until the company started making personal computers. It finally began to use third parties but only after great internal strain, after which the personal computer division was accorded the status of an independent business unit.

—— STEP 5: COMPARE YOUR OPTIONS

With the completion of step 4, company researchers will have a weighted list of management's objectives and constraints on the one hand and on the other a roster of the various ideal, market-driven distribution systems generated earlier in the process. Step 5 requires them to compare these two sets of data with each other and also with the system of distribution already in place. The researchers will, of course, consult with distribution managers about the company's present system: structure, functions performed by various channel participants, costs, discounts, and the like. It may be necessary for researchers to undertake an analysis of volume flows by channels as well as by margins, functions, and value-added at each level. A reasonably detailed map of this type can be very illuminating.

One of three conclusions will emerge from these comparisons. First, the existing system, the management-bounded system, and the ideal system may closely resemble each other. If this is the case, then management knows for sure that the existing system is about as good as it can get. If customer satisfaction is mediocre nevertheless, the message should be clear: the fault lies not in the design of the system but in its implementation.

Second, the existing and management-bounded systems may be similar to each other but substantially different from the ideal. This outcome may mean that the objectives and constraints adopted by management are causing the gap. Such a finding calls for a careful investigation of management's perceptions, the purpose of step 6.

Third and especially sobering, all three systems may be substantially different. Assuming that the management-bounded system is positioned somewhere between the existing and the ideal, it may be possible to improve customer satisfaction without relaxing management's objectives. This is the time to ask if relaxation of certain management constraints might not produce even greater benefits.

By 1980, IBM's direct sales force and sales branches had formed the core of the distribution network for its existing line—mainframe and word processors. These channels could not, however, be cost-effective in delivering personal computers to the small business market—not, in any case, at the standard for customer satisfaction that IBM's executives considered their company's hallmark.

The ideal would have been a network of highly decentralized, service-intensive specialty stores carrying an assortment of personal computer brands and models as well as other types of office equipment. Because some IBM executives were convinced that the company could not maintain control over the quality of service without ownership, the company opened its own retail outlets to sell IBM equipment alone. IBM product centers offered the consumer a variety of equipment, but comparison shopping within them was impossible. In 1986, IBM sold off its product center network to NYNEX. (Interestingly enough, IBM has since come to realize that the small business market is so heterogeneous that it consists of multiple segments.)

And so the ideal system acts as a stake in the ground. If the management-bounded options are not reasonably similar to the ideal, then researchers will ultimately have to confront managers with the fact that the company has been sacrificing customer satisfaction to other objectives.

In the long run, some of these other objectives may be critical and may even supersede the effort to satisfy customers via distribution. When management decides on any new strategy, it will simultaneously establish a hurdle rate—a minimum projected return on investment that justifies going ahead. Managers may, of course, set hurdles incorrectly, not only because they miscalculate costs but because they acquire a prejudice for or against particular channels of distribution. In any case, distribution strategies that do not clear their hurdles should be dropped from consideration in step 5.

───── STEP 6: REVIEW YOUR PET ASSUMPTIONS

This step is meant to help distinguish a serious constraint from an ordinary prejudice. It entails bringing in outsiders—lawyers, political consultants, distribution experts from other industries—who will call management's assumptions into question. Management often protects the status quo, for example, by claiming that changes might violate the law or encourage shadowy activities. Outsiders can look at the relevant laws and ask if they are what they seem. Can't they be changed? Does holding to one value force the company to sacrifice another?

The automobile industry has clung steadfastly to the dealer franchise system, in part out of fear of legal tangles. Porsche's attempt to implement a more consumer-responsive approach to distribution in the early 1980s turned into a fiasco largely because Porsche's dealers made clear that it would keep the company tied up in the courts for a generation. Alas, Porsche was on the right track.

But the impulse to stand pat does not always stem from anxiety about the law. The use of authorized third-party outlets for personal computers is an example: it often portends gray market activities. Some time ago, top managers at IBM indicated that they had been worried about the price cutting and "footballing" that would result if they authorized third-party outlets—a concern that proved justified. Had they let this serious concern paralyze them, their personal computer division would never have expanded as quickly as it did.

And so during step 6, outside authorities should be called on to check whether legal and other constraints exist and, if they do, whether they can be overcome. Of course reliance on outside experts can be risky. Who is to say top management doesn't know what it is talking about? Who can tell what course a lawsuit will take or what laws Congress and state legislatures will enact?

Business decisions are based on judgments, not certainties. Merrill Lynch would never have launched its highly successful cash management account program if it had not altered its assumptions about how the SEC would enforce federal banking laws. What are other companies missing?

—— STEP 7: CONFRONT THE GAP

This is the climax of the process. It requires top management to confront the gap between its practices or objectives and the ideal. For the first and only time, managers conducting the research bring together all executives responsible for distribution to determine the shape of a new system. To underline its significance, the company holds the meeting somewhere offsite.

The researchers get things going by presenting the ideal distribution system. Then they share the results of steps 4 and 5. In the course of this discussion, researchers outline for top management the objectives and constraints that were used to bound the ideal and show their effect, if any, in limiting what customers really desire. Next, researchers present the data and expert opinions challenging the validity of management's objectives and constraints—what was gained from step 6.

All this information serves as background for what usually proves to be a provocative discussion. We have found that researchers can prompt openness to it if they use computers to readjust weightings or other data and display the results instantaneously. This session brings top management face-to-face with the folklore restricting its thinking. Executives compare alternatives, weigh opportunity costs in relation to risk and exposure, and consider a host of other quantitative and subjective variables that are all too easily buried under day-to-day affairs. Most important, they make decisions in a new context—one in which an attainable ideal has been delineated, the intervening distance between the ideal and the reality has been measured, and the obstacles to closing the gap have been made explicit.

Such was the case for a personal care products company, whose ideal suggested the elimination of one level in its system—the brokers. It was a big step for managers to contemplate. When the company's brand lacked visibility and strong consumer demand, brokers had played a key role in providing access to the retail trade. Management felt a strong sense of loyalty and indebtedness to them. Over the years the brand had emerged as the best seller in its category; now the brokers contributed little to volume. Indeed, a growing price sensitivity on the part of consumers, coupled with the inefficiency of the broker system, placed the manufacturer in a vulnerable position.

It's not important to know this company's final decision. What is important is how the process teased out the lines of a crucial choice. Apple Computer, for example, would not likely have experimented with mail order channels in its early history had it followed this line of investigation to its conclusion. It would have found that the amount of hand-holding required to make a personal computer plus a software sale is extremely high. Similarly, IBM would not have been so surprised to find that dealers with outbound sales forces have greater staying power than those who simply rely on inbound retail sales. IBM retail showrooms cannot provide the kind of in-depth analysis and training that visits to a customer's premises can.

——— STEP 8: PREPARE TO IMPLEMENT

The final step in the process modifies the ideal distribution system emerging from step 3 according to the final objectives and constraints established in step 7. What managers are left with is a good system—not ideal, perhaps, but optimal.

This should be the subject of intensive implementation planning. And it is important for senior managers to help implement the system, if for no other reason than to give them a personal stake in the outcome. Besides, having confronted the ideal and having tested it against the other options, management has a full understanding of the trade-offs as well as the obstacles to implementation.

When it comes time to change the existing distribution system or to scrap it entirely, managers should test modifications on a small scale before committing resources to them. The major problem is that word will spread quickly. The gossip network among dealers and distributors is one of the busiest around.

The process we lay out in this article is not a simple one. Managers are required to focus on something as insubstantial as quality, or the ideal system, and then to come up with hard numbers to project a reasonable ratio of return to expense. They must even anticipate how adaptable their ideal might be to changes in the law or the political environment. Clearly, there is as much art here as science.

Still, none of the eight steps we outline should be skipped in the interest of apparent expediency. Managerial sophistication will speed things along, but sophistication alone will be no substitute for going through the entire process. With all the effort reevaluating the system requires, readers may assume that the process always justifies itself by the constructive changes it brings about. In fact, its real value is in the clarity it brings to a critical aspect of doing business.

A specialty grocery products manufacturer discovered that it was getting its products onto supermarket shelves in ways that on the surface looked Rube Goldbergian. It was using an array of third-party players, including food brokers, grocery wholesalers, and health food distributors, some of whom carried out a remarkable range of functions between the manufacturing and the retail level of the distribution chain. When the company drew a structural diagram, it looked like a bowl of spaghetti. Nevertheless, further analysis revealed that the system met all the criteria of an ideal.

The recommendation? "Don't mess with it! Don't touch a thing!" Sometimes the eight-step process explains precisely why you should do nothing to change the distribution system you already have.

——— DISCUSSION QUESTIONS

1. How powerful an influence does customer diversity have on a manufacturer's choice of distribution system? Does it warrant customizing distribution systems to reach specific customer groups? Does this approach have advantages? Disadvantages? Explain.

2. The authors present an approach to customizing the distribution system that matches customer segments. Do you believe this approach will replace the one based on convenient logistical arrangements? How would you characterize the differences in the two approaches? What steps would you take to accomplish customer segmentation?

3. The authors say that there are several crucial stages in the process of designing a distribution system that require getting outside checks and hard data for market segments, company objectives, and the projected costs of distribution outlets. Why would outside checks be advisable? Would you rely on outside advice? Doesn't top management know its own business better than outsiders?

4. The authors advise, "Think of the 'ideal' distribution system. Then introduce reality." What do you think they mean? How is this step crucial to shaping a more effective distribution system?

5. Assume that your existing distribution system is unorthodox but works very well. Can anything be gained by redesigning it? Or should you leave well enough alone? Are there ways to tell when "hands off" is advisable? Or when improvements can be made?

25 Turn Your Industrial Distributors into Partners

JAMES A. NARUS AND JAMES C. ANDERSON

This reading focuses on the advantages of creating and nurturing a working partnership between manufacturers and distributors. The manufacturer should understand the needs of a distributor and actively manage those needs, from supplying incentives and increasing the distributor's ROI to providing demonstrations to train distributors in the use and service of the product.

When the president of a small chemical distributor phoned a major chemical producer to request expedited delivery of a specialty chemical for an important customer, the manufacturer's inside salesperson did not recognize her and said that a credit check would have to be run first. "Our company's dealt with this manufacturer for over 50 years, and they don't even know my name, our credit history, or how important this kind of order is to our business," the distributor lamented afterwards. "And they wonder why my salespeople don't go all out to sell their chemicals."

A veteran distributor sales manager for a major fastener manufacturer called on an industrial supply distributor only to discover it had a new president. "Here we go again," the sales manager said to himself. In the past five years, almost half the principal owners of his company's distributors had sold out, died, or retired. "It seems as though we have to start from scratch when one of our distributors changes management," he said. "For years, I'd visit this guy's dad every six months to see how things were going. To gain his cooperation, all we had to do was give competitive discounts, keep him well stocked, and run an occasional sales incentive program. But his son insists on knowing what we're doing to improve his company's ROI, how we plan to help him develop a new market, and what computer software his company should be using. I wonder if we're losing touch with our distributors."

A bushing manufacturer's sales rep called on a distributor for the first time in a year. The sales rep's prime concern was to learn why the distributor's sales of the manufacturer's product had remained flat during that period. The question was particularly vexing to the rep because her company had given the distributor a new and costly set of merchandising aids "proven" to boost sales. The sales rep found the materials unused—stacked up in a remote corner of the distributor's warehouse. When asked about them, the distributor responded that they were very elaborate and too technical. More important, he said, no one from the sales rep's company had taken the time to demonstrate to the distributor how to use them in a sales presentation.

These situations show that for manufacturers to effectively plan and implement industrial distributor programs, they must

- Gain a deep understanding of distributor requirements.
- Build working partnerships with distributors.
- Actively manage these partnerships.

Building working partnerships has become a priority for many manufacturers because of industrial distributors' expanded role in the U.S. economy. In 1982, sales by all wholesaler-distributors topped $1.1 trillion. Of this total, $20 billion was accounted for by industrial supply distributors that sell primarily to maintenance, repair, and operating supply accounts; another $314 billion can be attributed to other types of distributors that sell the majority of their products to industrial and commercial businesses.[1]

A 1983 Arthur Andersen & Company study projected wholesaler-distributor sales to grow in real terms at a rate faster than the economy well into the 1990s.[2] And a 1985 McGraw-Hill survey found that only 24% of all industrial marketers sell their products directly to end users exclusively; the remaining 76% use some type of intermediary, of which industrial distributors are the most prominent.[3]

—— UNDERSTANDING DISTRIBUTOR NEEDS

How can manufacturers, especially those unfamiliar with distribution, determine their distributors' most important needs? The key appears to be in continuous, routine information collection. Here are some common practices:

Monitor distributors. The best way to learn about distributor requirements is to get out into the field periodically and listen carefully to what they have to say. It is the field salespeople who must perform this important task on a continuing basis. Timken Corporation, the leading manufacturer of tapered roller bearings, requires all its outside sales representatives to make calls on various officials of each of their distribution companies, including general managers, purchasing managers, and inside and outside salespeople.

Each contact contributes bits of information about the distributor's current opportunities, problems, and changing needs. Timken sales reps also

1. Calculated from "Preliminary Report," *1982 Census of Wholesale Trade* (Washington, D.C.: U.S. Department of Commerce, May 1984).

2. Arthur Andersen & Company, Inc., *Future Trends in Wholesale Distribution* (Washington, D.C.: Distribution Research and Education Foundation, 1983), p. 7.

3. "Industry Markets Goods Through Dual Channels, Says McGraw-Hill Study," *Industrial Distribution* (April 1985): 15.

call on end users and other individuals connected with the industry to learn about market trends and competitive actions that may affect distributors. Based on their observations, Timken sales reps recommend program changes to their national sales manager that are designed to improve distributor effectiveness.

One way that Square D, a leading manufacturer of circuit breakers, switchboards, transformers, and controller equipment, keeps in touch with its distributors' and customers' needs is through its "counter days" program, whereby Square D field salespeople spend a day at the distributor's location "working the counter"—answering customer questions and demonstrating Square D products. The counter days program is an excellent way to learn about distributor needs and reinforces to both distributors and customers Square D's commitment to a working partnership.

Learn from companywide experiences. Du Pont has established a distributor marketing steering committee, consisting of 35 divisional distributor marketing managers, to discuss common distribution problems, share market information on trends affecting the function, and ponder changing distributor requirements. Committee meetings often include presentations by market research analysts, consultants, and the distributor marketing managers of non-competing companies.

Conduct market research studies. Parker Hannifin Corporation, a major fluid power products manufacturer, has developed two comprehensive research programs to monitor distributor needs. The first is an annual mail survey that asks distributors to rate each Parker division on key performance dimensions and recommend program improvements.

The second program uses the Parker distributor agreement, which requires each distributor to forward to Parker's market research division a photocopy of every invoice for the sale of a Parker product. The invoices are sorted and analyzed by industry, product, and customer to enable Parker to develop distributor programs that mirror changing market conditions. One such program produces a series of market research reports tailored to each distributor. The reports analyze the distributor's sales and recommend customers that should be targeted for greater sales effort, products that should be promoted to various potential customers, and types of marketing techniques the distributor should use.

Establish a distributor council. Although some executives believe that distributor councils are little more than banquets and tennis or golf outings for a manufacturer's best distributors, this need not be the case. Dayco Corporation, a manufacturer and distributor of engineered plastic and rubber products, uses its council to keep up with its industrial distributors' changing needs. Selected to represent the entire network, about 10% of Dayco's distributors comprise the council and serve on a rotating basis.

Prior to the annual four-day meeting, Dayco asks council members to write suggestions for improving policies and programs; Dayco uses the responses to draft an agenda for the meeting. The council sessions are then largely taken up with discussion of proposed policy changes and new programs, distributor problems and concerns, the competition, and other pressing issues. Within one month of the council meetings, Dayco sends its distributors a written report outlining the suggested policies and programs that will be implemented. Historically, Dayco puts about 75% of distributor proposals into effect.

⸻ BUILDING WORKING PARTNERSHIPS

Building effective partnerships usually takes two to three years because they must be earned, not merely declared. The manufacturer's distributor programs are the basic implementation tools. These programs should be designed to meet distributor requirements and furnish benefits that surpass those of the competition.

Companies seeking to initiate or resuscitate distributor relationships can take any of three approaches to develop distributor programs:

1. Get the benefit of industry experience. Several years ago, a Du Pont division decided to start selling Tyvek, a spun-bonded olefin that can be used for home insulation, through building products distributors. Rather than assume that the division had all the answers on steps to take, management obtained from a building products distributor association the name of a consultant who had been a distributor for many years. The consultant helped Du Pont draft a distributor marketing plan, select the distributors, and implement initial programs. The division has been pleased with the results.

2. Establish a position in the distribution marketplace. In the early 1980s, Cherry Electrical Products, a manufacturer of electrical switches and electronic keyboards, displays, and components, noticed a dramatic rise in sales through electronics distributors, while its own sales through distributors plateaued. Determined to improve its productivity, Cherry hired a new distributor marketing manager and charged him with revamping its distribution network.

   He set to work by calling on end users, distributors, and manufacturers' reps. He gathered information on how distributors marketed electronic components, distributor requirements, and on what programs competitors were using. Thereupon the new manager rewrote company policies, revised the distributor discount system, and devised a set of marketing programs. These efforts created Cherry's reputation not only as a manufacturer of quality products and first-rate services but also as a company committed to its distributors. Cherry maintains its position by making every effort to meet changing distributor needs and by offering an array of superior distributor programs.

3. Devise a formal distributor marketing plan. This plan should be written for the whole network and then broken down individually. The plan should include the following: a situation analysis, describing the network's makeup and activities; an opportunities and

threats section, identifying the business situations the company should capitalize on or avoid; an objectives section, detailing sales quotas, products, and markets to receive special attention; a basic requirements analysis, spelling out the kinds of support distributors will need in the coming year to meet objectives and seize market opportunities; a distributor programs section, describing all the manufacturer's marketing actions for the coming year designed to meet distributor requirements; and, finally, a control section, charting a timetable for program implementation and assigning responsibilities for execution.

If the manufacturer takes the time to obtain distributors' input for the plan, the distributors will be likely to perceive it as their plan and work hard to implement it.

DEVELOPING SOUND COMMUNICATION

An essential ingredient for successful partnerships is sound, two-way communication between a manufacturer and its distributors that occurs at multiple levels and uses a variety of communication means. Communication between the manufacturer's order center or inside salesperson and the distributor's purchasing manager is extremely important since these individuals deal with each other more often than any others in the partnership. The manufacturer's order center personnel or inside salespeople, therefore, should be well qualified and trained.

These employees must take distributors' orders accurately and cheerfully, comprehend and work to resolve their problems, respond quickly to distributors' requests, know the names of their counterparts, be familiar with the distributors' history, and use their contacts to gather market information. Cherry Electrical Products assigns each distributor to a pair of inside salespeople. Although one person has primary responsibility for the distributor's orders, both are familiar with the distributor and can take orders and respond to problems.

Contacts between the manufacturer's outside salesperson and the distributor's top officers, purchasing managers, and salespeople should be nurtured. When visiting a distributor, the outside salesperson should help explain policy changes, gather distributor suggestions and market information, demonstrate products and merchandising tools, solve problems, train distributor sales and technical people on proper procedures and product applications, and conduct joint sales calls.

Because outside salespeople often get promoted, change territories, or quit, the distributor marketing manager should make periodic calls on the president or CEO of each distributorship. The manager should explain major policy changes, review mutual performance, plan joint marketing programs, and generally reinforce the working partnership. Dayco takes this approach one step further. Each year, all its distributor marketing managers, the president, and even the chairman of the board make selected calls on distributors to demonstrate the importance of each distributor to Dayco.

While face-to-face contacts have the greatest impact on distributors, they are obviously the most expensive communication option. They should be used mainly to resolve differences, explain new products or policy changes, or review performance. Timken, for instance, makes a point of announcing all of its major policy and program changes to the distributor in person to permit full explanation and full responses to questions.

Quite a few manufacturers (Du Pont and Dayco are two examples) use newsletters to inform distributors about new products and applications, personnel changes, distribution news, and human interest stories. Finally, with the boom in VCR sales, many manufacturers such as Parker Hannifin are communicating via videotape. The cassettes can contain messages to distributors from the manufacturer's senior management, training programs, and promotional information (such as new product application stories).

SIGNALING COMMITMENT

To gain the benefits of a productive working partnership, manufacturers must demonstrate that they are committed to distributors for the long term. Companies boasting successful distributor partnerships usually have the most competent and best-trained field sales forces in their industries (signaling by this that they expect the best from their distributors).

Lincoln Electric, a manufacturer of arc-welding equipment and supplies, hires graduate engineers for its field sales positions. As part of their eight-month training program, they attend welding school and become certified welders. Before promotion to a field sales position, each trainee also must do what generations of sales trainees have done: demonstrate his or her ability to find a welding-related potential cost reduction at the company's production facility. When placed in the field, these knowledgeable salespeople are a useful resource to Lincoln Electric's distributors and customers on efficient welding technology and applications.

Another way to communicate confidence in distributors is to refer all customer inquiries and requests to them. Timken, for instance, encourages customers to seek technical assistance on minor difficulties from distributors. Timken handles only major problems. Du Pont's Chemicals and Pigments Division does not publish a less-than-truckload (LTL) price list; LTL quantities are sold exclusively by distributors. Du Pont refers callers asking for an LTL price quote to distributors, thereby demonstrating that the company will not take business away from them.

Finally, manufacturers that limit the number of distributors per trading area are indicating that they want their distributor partners to be successful. When selective distribution is used, authorized distributors gain status and an enhanced local reputation, which can motivate them to sell aggressively.

Square D and Parker Hannifin are just two examples of manufacturers whose distributors prominently display their authorized distributorship signs and strive to perform up to the manufacturers' reputations. Of course, multiple distributors are justified when a trading area's potential sales are extremely large; similarly, different types of distributors may have to be used when a market contains radically different types of customers. The key for the manufacturer is to be aware of the level of sales potential per trading area.

PASSING THE CRITICAL INCIDENT TEST

Incidents in which the distributor critically needs the manufacturer's assistance eventually come up in all relationships. For a working partnership to evolve, the manufacturer must respond decisively and meet this critical need so as to reinforce the importance and quality of the partnership in the distributor's mind.

Manufacturers excelling in marketing through distributors can usually cite stories of situations in which they came through in the clutch. Dayco provides an excellent example. Several years ago, an industrial distributor needed to place an emergency order but could not get through to Dayco's order center. He was, however, able to phone Dayco's chairman of the board because the chairman makes a point of being accessible to all the distributors.

Rather than turn the distributor over to a subordinate, the chairman listened carefully to him, worked up a three-page order, and later made sure that the order had been filled. This story sent a loud and clear message to everyone in Dayco's organization and distribution system. To be able to deal with critical incidents, a manufacturer must train its personnel, especially sales and order center people, to be sensitive to distributors' key concerns, including product delivery, pricing, and credit.

────── MANAGING THESE PARTNERSHIPS

What action can manufacturers take to improve the productivity of their distributor partnerships? The main short-run task is to ensure that operational promises are kept. Distributors want delivery within stated lead times, quality products that are not defective, adequate promotional and merchandising support, and rapid technical problem-solving assistance. Manufacturers must coordinate sales activities with those of the transportation and manufacturing people so that delivery promises will be kept. To facilitate problem solving, Cherry Electrical Products has a policy of rapid, in-kind response (for example, if distributors call, Cherry responds by phone).

Over time, a manufacturer must develop a reputation for equitable policies that are consistently and uniformly implemented. Policies that are grounded in marketplace realities, that are in tune with distributor requirements, and that are well publicized will accomplish this. To underscore its consistent and uniform dealings with all its distributors, Square D in the mid-1960s published portions of its distributor policies in full-page advertisements in *Electrical Wholesaling*.

Manufacturers must be able to defuse the occasional disputes that inevitably arise. The key to turning problems into opportunities is launching an immediate resolution attempt. If after investigation you determine that the distributor has caused the problem, present its executives with your conclusions supported by the facts. If the problem is your fault, tell the distributor what you plan to do to resolve it. Be sure also to check whether the problem is widespread, and if it is, determine how to solve it systemwide. Inform all distributors of any policy or program changes needed to resolve the issue.

Look at how Lincoln Electric works with its distributors to meet the challenges of a changing marketplace. To deal with intense price competition, the company has devised what it calls the "Guaranteed Cost Reduction Program" for its distributors; whenever a customer requests that a distributor lower its prices on Lincoln supplies and equipment to meet those of competitive manufacturers, the company and the particular distributor guarantee in writing that they will find cost reductions in the customer's plant during the coming year that meet or exceed the price difference between Lincoln's products and the competition's. The Lincoln sales rep and distributor counterpart together survey the customer's operations, identify possible cost reductions, and help to implement them.

At the end of the year, the customer independently audits performance. If the cost savings do not match those promised, Lincoln Electric and the distributor pay the customer the difference (Lincoln contributes 70%). All the customer has to do is continue buying Lincoln Electric products from the distributor. To date, individual customers have reaped up to $100,000 in annual cost savings and, more important, Lincoln has reinforced its relationships with its distributors.

Finally, in sustaining long-term working partnerships, manufacturers should plan for the future. Dayco uses an intriguing program, called "Aftermarket 2000," to accomplish long-term continuity in its partnerships. Each year, Dayco sponsors a week-long retreat for 20 young distributor executives and 20 young Dayco executives that features notable speakers, seminars on future economic and market trends, and, most important, plenty of time to interact. In this way, the future senior executives of Dayco and its distributors have an opportunity to get to know each other and develop over time the mutual trust and understanding that will be critical to the continued success of Dayco and its distributors. Such a program can help to alleviate the problem of starting all over again when managements change.

Building productive partnerships with industrial distributors takes years of effort. When the effort is successful, the partnership can be expected to yield the following results:

1. Motivation for superior effort and performance from both parties
2. An atmosphere of goodwill that produces a willingness to overlook inevitable mistakes

3. A reduction in the distributor turnover rate and a consequent lowering of the manufacturer's costs of bringing new distributors into the network

4. Coordinated performance in the marketplace, with satisfied end users who are loyal to both the manufacturer and the distributor

Clearly, building sound partnerships is worth the effort.

▬ DISCUSSION QUESTIONS

1. The authors' advice to manufacturers is to "turn your industrial distributors into partners." In building a sound partnership between manufacturer and distributor, who gains the most—the manufacturer or the distributor? What advantages does this approach bring to the manufacturer? To the distributor?

2. How long does it take a manufacturer to build a working partnership with distributors? What are some of the steps and requirements necessary before the manufacturer can cement this relationship? Should end users be involved? Can the process be improved?

3. Would it be more advantageous to the manufacturer to "go it alone" by putting all its resources into its own sales force and letting them deal directly with the end user? Are distributors considered "competitors" of the manufacturer, since their profits come at the manufacturer's expense?

4. Assume a dispute occurs between the manufacturer and its distributor. What is management's role in resolving differences? What are some of the areas that need management consideration? How can management play a role in improving its own productivity and that of its distributors?

Managing Hybrid Marketing Systems 26

ROWLAND T. MORIARTY AND URSULA MORAN

The drive to reach new customers while reducing costs has led to new, customized approaches to marketing that are becoming more dominant in the 1990s. Companies are creating new hybrid marketing systems that employ several different approaches under different circumstances. These new systems may require breaking with tradition by adding new channels to existing ones and by using new communications methods directed toward reaching specific targeted customers. Companies can enjoy substantial rewards by customizing their marketing approaches, but managing these hybrid systems can be difficult. Inevitably, problems of conflict and control arise. This reading describes how managers can make the task easier by using a "hybrid grid"—a map that illustrates the combination of channels and tasks that will optimize cost and coverage.

There was a time when most companies went to market only one way—through a direct sales force, for instance, or through distributors. But to defend their turf, expand market coverage, and control costs, companies today are increasingly adopting arsenals of new marketing weapons to use with different customer segments and under different circumstances. In recent years, as managers have sought to cut costs and increase market coverage, companies have added new channels to existing ones; they use direct sales as well as distributors, retail sales as well as direct mail, direct mail as well as direct sales. As they add channels and communications methods, companies create hybrid marketing systems.

Look at IBM. For years, IBM computers were available from only one supplier, the company's sales force. But when the market for small, low-cost computers exploded, IBM management realized that its single distribution channel was no longer sufficient. In the late 1970s, it started expanding into new channels, among them dealers, value-added resellers, catalog operations, direct mail, and telemarketing. IBM had built and maintained its vaunted 5,000-person sales force for 70 years. In less than 10 years, it nearly doubled that number and added 18 new channels to communicate with customers.

Apple Computer also started out with a clear and simple channel strategy. It distributed its inexpensive personal computers through an independent dealer network. But when the company began to sell more sophisticated systems to large companies, it had to change. Apple hired 70 national account managers as part of a new direct sales operation.

In adding these new channels and communications methods, IBM and Apple created hybrid marketing systems. Powerful forces lie behind the appearance of such hybrid systems; all signs indicate that they will be the dominant design of marketing systems in the 1990s. At the same time, smart managers recognize the high risks of operating hybrid systems. Whether the migration is from direct to indirect channels (such as IBM) or from indirect to direct (like Apple), the result is the same—a hybrid that can be hard to manage.

The appearance of new channels and methods inevitably raises problems of conflict and control—conflict because more marketing units compete for customers and revenues; control because indirect channels are less subject to management authority than direct channels are. As difficult as they are to manage, however, hybrid marketing systems can offer substantial rewards. A company that can capture the benefits of a hybrid system—increased coverage, lower costs, and customized approaches—will enjoy a significant competitive advantage over rivals that cling to traditional ways.

Examples of hybrid marketing systems extend beyond high-tech businesses such as computers to older industries such as textiles, metal fabrication, and office supplies and to service industries such as insurance. Many of the examples in this article are high-tech companies because the accelerated pace of high-tech industries foreshadows trends that tend to occur more slowly in other industries. The trend to hybrid systems, however, appears to be accelerating in many industries. According to a senior manager survey conducted in the late 1980s, 53% of the respondents indicated that their companies intended to use hybrid systems by 1992—a dramatic increase over the 33% that used those systems at the time of the survey.

Two fundamental reasons explain this boost in the move to hybrids: the drive to increase market coverage and the need to contain costs. To sustain growth, a company generally must reach new customers or segments. Along the way, it usually supplements existing channels and methods with new ones designed to attract and develop new customers. This addition of new channels and methods creates a hybrid marketing system.

The need to contain costs is another powerful force behind the spread of hybrid systems, as companies look for ways to reach customers that are more efficient than direct selling. In 1990, the loaded cost of face-to-face selling time for national account managers reached $500 per hour; for direct sales representatives, the average was about $300 per hour. Selling and administrative costs often represent 20% to 40% of a company's cost structure and thus have a direct effect on competitive advantage and profitability. For instance, Digital Equipment's selling and administrative costs in 1989 were 31% of revenues; for Sun Microsystems, the figure was only about 24%.

Given such economics, many companies are pursuing techniques such as telemarketing, which costs about $17 per hour, or direct mail, which runs about $1 per customer contact. A marketing strategy built on such low-cost communications methods can yield impressive results. Tessco, a distributor of supplies and equipment for cellular communications, emerged as one of the industry's fastest growing competitors by relying on low-cost communications methods. Tessco generates leads through direct mail and catalog operations; it uses telemarketing to qualify sales leads, make its sales pitch, answer questions, and close the sale. It then follows up each sale with service telemarketing and maintains accounts through an automatic reordering process. The result: Tessco enjoys significantly lower costs than most of its competitors, which continue to rely on traditional methods such as direct sales.

——— WRIGHT LINE'S PROBLEMS

Despite the proliferation of marketing methods, few companies pay sufficient attention to the design of marketing systems or seek to manage them in ways that optimize coverage and costs. Indeed, most companies decide to add new channels and methods without a clear and realistic vision of an ultimate "go to market" architecture. These decisions are usually made separately and independently—and often swiftly as well. As a consequence, companies can find themselves stumbling over their hastily constructed, overlapping hybrid system.

Consider how an ill-conceived and mismanaged hybrid system contributed to the 1989 hostile takeover of Barry Wright Corporation. Many factors made the Massachusetts-based company vulnerable, but a principal cause of its troubles was the performance of a major subsidiary, Wright Line, Inc. A leading supplier of accessories used to store, protect, and provide access to computer tapes, diskettes, and other media, Wright Line was struggling vainly to halt the erosion of its market position.

Wright Line's troubles stemmed from a decision made in the early 1980s to reorganize its marketing and sales functions. Previously, the company had sold its products exclusively through a direct sales force. Although the company had been growing rapidly and adding new sales reps every year, Wright Line's management was alarmed by several trends: inability to increase market penetration, declining sales productivity, high turnover of sales reps, and what appeared to be a fundamental shift in the market away from the company's traditional stronghold in large, central computer installations.

After analyzing these trends, Wright Line supplemented its direct sales force with additional marketing channels and communications methods.[1] The company formed two new units: a direct marketing operation to handle midsize

---

1. Channels are either direct or indirect. Methods are the communications options companies can use to reach potential customers; they may also be direct or indirect. For example, through a direct channel, a company may use account managers, a sales force, or telemarketing. The same methods may also be used singly or in combination through indirect channels.

accounts through direct catalog and telephone sales, and a unit to serve small accounts and to attract nonusers through indirect channels. Management's goal was to combine the advantages of high-quality personal selling to major accounts with lower cost, increased coverage of smaller accounts.

Signs of trouble appeared almost immediately. By 1985, the reorganization had yielded declining growth rates, diminishing market share, and plummeting profits. Inside the company, strife over account ownership was rampant, and turnover among the direct sales reps reached an all-time high. Worst of all, Wright Line's customers grew confused and angry after encountering different sales offerings of the same products under widely disparate terms and conditions. Wright Line's best customers became alienated, and its margins shrank as major accounts ordered the company's products from discount suppliers.

By the time new leadership tried to untangle the mess, it was already too late. Its stock weakened by Wright Line's rapidly eroding market position and declining profitability, Barry Wright Corporation was taken over in 1989.

The Barry Wright story is an extreme example of an increasingly evident problem. Fewer and fewer major industrial or service companies go to market through a single channel or a "purebred" channel strategy that matches a specific product or service to an exclusive segment. Rather than designing an ideal distribution strategy, companies tend to add channels and methods incrementally in the quest to extend market coverage or cut selling costs. Unfortunately, such actions typically result in conflict and morale problems inside the marketing organization and confusion and anger among distributors, dealers, and customers on the outside.

——— MAPPING THE HYBRID

At the heart of the problem of designing and managing hybrid systems is the fundamental question of what mix of channels or communication methods can best accomplish the assortment of tasks required to identify, sell, and manage customers. The trick to designing and managing hybrid systems is to disaggregate demand-generation tasks both within and across a marketing system—recognizing that channels are *not* the basic building blocks of a marketing system; marketing tasks are. This analysis of tasks and channels will identify the hybrid's basic components and permit managers to design and manage the system effectively.

A map of tasks and channels—what we call a hybrid grid—can help managers make sense of their hybrid system (see *Exhibit 1*). A hybrid grid, for example, can be used to illustrate graphically what happened at Wright Line and what might have happened differently.

Before its reorganization, Wright Line used direct sales for all demand-generation tasks and all customers (see *Exhibit 2*). When it reorganized in 1982, Wright Line wanted the direct sales force (unit 1) to perform all demand-generation tasks for big customers; the new direct response unit (unit 2) to

EXHIBIT 1
The Hybrid Grid: The Elements of a Hybrid Marketing System

		Demand-Generation Tasks						
		Lead generation	Qualifying sales	Presales	Close of sale	Postsales service	Account management	
Marketing Channels and Methods — VENDOR	National account management							CUSTOMER
	Direct sales							
	Telemarketing							
	Direct mail							
	Retail stores							
	Distributors							
	Dealers and value-added resellers							

Note: A simple graphic captures the elements of a hybrid marketing system. Along the top are the basic marketing tasks required to obtain and maintain customers: generation of leads; qualification of these leads; presales activities, such as sales calls to woo specific customers; closing the sale; provision of postsales service; and ongoing management of the account.

Along the side of the grid are the various marketing channels and methods used to reach customers, ranging from elaborate direct to elaborate indirect options. The shaded areas represent one possible approach through a direct channel: direct mail to generate leads, telemarketing to qualify leads and manage presales and postsales activities, and a direct sales force to close deals and manage the account on an ongoing basis.

The hybrid grid can be a useful diagnostic tool to identify points of overlap and conflict in a marketing system. It can also aid in the design of a new marketing system tailored to the needs of specific customers. As a marketing map, the grid depicts the situation at a particular moment and needs to be updated as changes occur.

EXHIBIT 2
Wright Line's Marketing System: What It Had

		Demand-Generation Tasks						
		Lead generation	Qualifying sales	Presales	Close of sale	Postsales service	Account management	
Marketing Channels and Methods — VENDOR	National account management							CUSTOMER
	Direct sales	ALL CUSTOMERS						
	Telemarketing							
	Direct mail							
	Retail stores							
	Distributors							
	Dealers and value-added resellers							

EXHIBIT 3
Wright Line's Marketing System: What It Wanted

Marketing Channels and Methods (VENDOR)	Demand-Generation Tasks						CUSTOMER
	Lead generation	Qualifying sales	Presales	Close of sale	Postsales service	Account management	
National account management							
Direct sales	B I G C U S T O M E R S						
Telemarketing		M I D S I Z E C U S T O M E R S					
Direct mail							
Retail stores							
Distributors	S M A L L C U S T O M E R S A N D N O N C U S T O M E R S						
Dealers and value-added resellers							

concentrate exclusively on midsize customers (using catalogs and telemarketing); and the new third party and resale unit (unit 3) to market to small customers and nonusers through indirect channels (see *Exhibit 3*).

Instead, Wright Line wound up with a marketing system that was neither what it wanted nor what it needed (see *Exhibit 4*). The three marketing units were performing all of the demand-generation tasks for many different types of customers. Units 1 and 2 bickered constantly over account ownership. To avoid losing accounts, for example, some sales reps improperly classified accounts to hide them from the direct response marketing division. Those who complied were frustrated by guidelines that prohibited them from calling on smaller and midsize accounts in their territories and growing with them. The activities of unit 3 added fuel to the fire. Among major customers, purchasing managers who read catalogs and received visits from the sales reps of office supply vendors found that Wright Line products were available at a substantial discount off the direct sales price.

In many respects, Wright Line's experience was typical, both in terms of the problems the company faced and its approach to solving them. Management's effort focused on identifying new channels that could be added to or substituted for all of the marketing tasks performed by the existing direct sales force channel. But this approach incorrectly assumes that each channel must perform and control all demand-generation tasks. The hybrid grid forces managers to consider various combinations of channels and tasks that will optimize both cost and coverage.

In addition, the company assumed that certain channels could best serve all the needs of certain customer segments. Hence, units 1, 2, and 3 were

EXHIBIT 4
Wright Line's Marketing System: What It Got

		Demand-Generation Tasks						
		Lead generation	Qualifying sales	Presales	Close of sale	Postsales service	Account management	
Marketing Channels and Methods — VENDOR	National account management							CUSTOMER
	Direct sales	BIG, MIDSIZE, AND SMALL CUSTOMERS						
	Telemarketing		BIG, MIDSIZE, AND SMALL CUSTOMERS					
	Direct mail							
	Retail stores							
	Distributors	BIG, MIDSIZE, AND SMALL CUSTOMERS						
	Dealers and value-added resellers							

aligned with big, midsize, and small customers. The process of aligning high-cost channels—that is, the direct sales force—with big customers and low-cost channels with small customers is very logical, if that is the way customers buy. In Wright Line's case, however, customers bought from multiple sales channels. The attempt to use a single channel to reach a single customer group resulted in severe channel conflicts, along with customer confusion.

The design of an effective hybrid system depends not only on a thorough understanding of channel costs but also on a thorough understanding of buying behavior. When a new channel is added to service a particular customer segment, the segmentation scheme must clearly reflect the customer's buying behavior—not just the channel costs of the company. The design of an effective hybrid system requires balancing the natural tension between minimizing costs and maximizing customer satisfaction. In Wright Line's situation, the hybrid design was driven by costs, without regard for buying behavior.

Wright Line's fatal flaw was basing its marketing strategy on what was best for the company, not what was best for its customers. In focusing its costliest marketing resources on the targets with the highest potential payoff and devoting less expensive resources to less promising accounts, it ignored the buying behavior of its customers. Too late, Wright Line discovered that its customers could not be segmented so neatly, nor would they conform docilely to the company's perception of its most efficient channel structure. Its hybrid system was intended to lower costs and increase coverage. Instead, Wright Line lost control of both its channels and its customers.

The hybrid grid illustrates how Wright Line might have successfully

EXHIBIT 5
Wright Line's Marketing System: What It Needed

Marketing Channels and Methods		Demand-Generation Tasks						
		Lead generation	Qualifying sales	Presales	Close of sale	Postsales service	Account management	
VENDOR	National account management			BIG	BIG		BIG	CUSTOMER
	Direct sales							
	Telemarketing		BIG AND MIDSIZE	MIDSIZE		ALL MIDSIZE		
	Direct mail	ALL		SMALL			SMALL	
	Retail stores							
	Distributors							
	Dealers and value-added resellers							

designed and managed its hybrid system (see *Exhibit 5*). The company could have used direct mail and response cards to generate leads among potential customers of all sizes and to perform most other tasks for small accounts. It could have used telemarketing to qualify leads among big and midsize prospects and determine approximate order size. It could have routed qualified prospects interested in buying a certain amount of equipment to direct sales reps. (Qualified prospects that turn out to be current national accounts would be turned over to the appropriate national account managers.) To midsize customers, it could have made phone calls to close sales and handle accounts; a direct sales rep or a national account manager could have performed these tasks for larger customers. For all customers, telemarketing could have been used for postsales tasks like reordering.

This version assigns demand-generation tasks to various channels, balancing both cost and customer buying behavior. Distributors were a principal part of Wright Line's setup. But this approach avoids using indirect channels, thereby allowing the company to maintain broad coverage without sacrificing control of pricing and product policy. (Of course, indirect channels are appropriate and necessary in many situations.) By establishing boundaries around genuine segments and building bridges across tasks, Wright Line might have gained the advantages of expanded market coverage and cost-effective marketing management without losing control of its marketing system and its customers.

———— MANAGING CONFLICT IN HYBRID SYSTEMS

Conflict is an inevitable part of every hybrid system. When a company adds a channel or substitutes a new communication method within a channel, existing stakeholders—sales reps, distributors, telemarketers—invariably resist. And why not: each faces a potential loss of revenue as well as competition for ownership of customers. In seeking to build and manage a hybrid system, therefore, companies must recognize and communicate the existence of conflict as the first and most important step.

The next step is to assess the magnitude of the conflict, asking some simple but penetrating questions: How much revenue does the company have in conflict? (Revenue is in conflict whenever two or more channels simultaneously attempt to sell the same product to the same customer.) Where is this conflict? How do channels and customers react to it? How much management time is devoted to dealing with the conflict?

The answers to these questions will vary by industry and by company, but some generalizations are possible. Clearly, a company with no revenue in conflict may be sacrificing coverage, failing to attract new customers by focusing too narrowly on a particular segment. Indeed, a certain amount of conflict in a hybrid marketing system is not only inevitable but also healthy. On the other hand, as the Wright Line story illustrates, conflict that is pervasive across channels is debilitating and potentially destructive.

Of course, the concept of having revenue in conflict is alien to many CEOs and senior managers, particularly those who are accustomed to using only a single channel. They should seek a point of balance where conflict is neither too little nor too much. Although the location of this point depends on many variables—as a rule of thumb, destructive behavior occurs when 10% to 30% of revenues are in conflict—managers can estimate it by monitoring feedback from customers and marketing personnel. When phone calls and letters become angry, or when a significant portion of management time is absorbed in mediating internal disputes or dealing with customer complaints, warning bells should go off.

———— BOUNDING THE CONFLICT

After they determine the amount and location of conflict, managers can establish clear and communicable boundaries and specific and enforceable guidelines that spell out which customers to serve through which methods.

Most companies observe some natural boundaries in the marketplace—areas defined by the interaction between buyer behavior and channel costs. Typically, companies target the largest and most profitable customers for some form of direct personal selling and serve smaller, less profitable accounts through less expensive methods. The problems arise with those customers residing somewhere in the middle: midsize accounts or markets with fuzzy boundaries, such as large national accounts that use a combination of centralized and decentralized purchasing practices that vary by product, location, or order size.

In this no-man's-land, neither the customer's buying behavior nor the company's transaction economics indicates definitively which method is the most effective way to serve the customer. Because no single method is clearly superior or appropriate, several may compete with each other—an example of a situation where clear boundaries will not work. These no-man's-land customer segments should be identified and clearly communicated to all marketing units so they know they will have intracompany competition.

Once the "jump ball" selling situations are identified, it is easier to construct barriers where natural segments exist. Boundaries between classes of customers are frequently couched in terms of sales, but effective boundary design involves much more than spelling out who makes which sale. It should instead indicate who owns and who doesn't own certain customers. Boundary mechanisms that help achieve this goal are generally based on customer characteristics, geography, and products.

Customer Characteristics. Customer size is a familiar boundary criterion. One large computer manufacturer specifies that, for its banking customers, its value-added resellers (VARs) should sell to small community financial institutions with less than $250 million in assets. For larger institutions, the manufacturer should sell through its direct sales force or some combination of that group and a third-party software supplier.

Order size provides another standard for drawing boundaries. A leading maker of PCs, for example, specifies that orders for more than 25 units must go through its direct sales force and orders of less than 5 units through independent dealers. Either direct or indirect channels may handle orders in the no-man's-land between 5 and 25 units.

Customers can also be classified by decision-making process or decision-making unit. A manufacturer of specialty and commodity chemicals uses a direct sales force to sell specialty chemicals because the purchasing process for these products is complex and requires several engineers to develop specifications and participate in supplier selection. The company's commodity products, however, are most often bought by a purchasing agent, and price is the key consideration. Hence, commodity chemicals are handled by distributors.

Finally, customers can be categorized by industry, particularly when there are genuine differences both in the product, price, and service package and in the expertise demanded of salespeople. The paper industry is a good example of differences in end use or applications. A different channel serves each of the four major end-use groups—newsprint, magazines, office products, and business forms.

Geographic Boundaries. Bounding by geography is clear and easy to enforce. A major manufacturer of computer-aided design/computer-aided manufacture (CAD/CAM) systems sells its offerings in the United States and Europe through a direct sales force; in Japan, it uses an exclusive distributor.

The company has little difficulty preventing major conflict (except in global accounts) because the channels are physically separated. Many companies serve large, urban markets through some form of direct sales and use distributors or reps to cover less densely populated areas.

Product Boundaries. Xerox used product boundaries when it entered the personal copier market. It sells midrange and high-end machines through a combination of direct sales and dealer distribution; it sells low-end machines exclusively through retail channels. Electronics and appliance stores, mass merchants, department stores, and an American Express direct mail program are all sources of Xerox personal copiers. The company has tried to avoid excessive conflict among these different retail channels by producing distinct models for each. The basic model 5008 personal copier was designed in three different versions so retailers would not compete with one another over an identical product.

Boundary mechanisms will help contain and control conflict when it arises, but they do not—and should not—eliminate it. It is impossible to hermetically seal each segment or customer group. Astute marketers identify and communicate to their channels not only those areas where clear boundaries exist but also those where they are either impossible or impractical.

MANAGING CHANNEL ADDITIONS

Maintaining order in a hybrid marketing system is a complex administrative challenge. The addition of new channels and methods inevitably requires modifications to existing reporting relationships, organization structure, and management policies with respect to motivation, evaluation, and compensation. The stakes are high since organizational moves issue a strong signal about the direction of change and top management's commitment to it. In the 1980s, for example, Wang Laboratories struggled through three separate attempts to create an indirect sales organization to supplement direct sales of its products. Each new attempt foundered after meeting entrenched resistance inside the company. Indeed, Wang's inability to solve this problem is a hidden cause of its much-publicized troubles in recent years.

Although each hybrid system presents unique challenges to managers, two general administrative guidelines may be helpful. First, decisions about structure and support policies should conform to the overall goals of the marketing system. Each potential configuration should be measured against the obvious tests: Will it satisfy customers in the most cost-effective manner? Will it maximize the prospect of achieving greater coverage and control throughout the system? Will it limit destructive conflict inside the organization?

Second, the timing of changes in structure and policies should reflect a realistic assessment of revenue flows through various channels and methods over time. In a large company, for example, it is extremely unlikely that a new channel or method will account for a significant fraction of total revenues in its first year. A new indirect channel added to a system dominated by a direct channel may account for 3% to 5% of revenues in the first year and perhaps 20% by the fifth. During such a transition, management should weight its policies heavily in favor of the new channel to ensure its success.

Management sends the most powerful and immediate signals through the compensation system. Companies with hybrid systems rely heavily on compensation policies to reinforce new boundaries and routinely subsidize new activities during transition periods. The most common approach involves paying personnel in the older units to allow personnel in the newer units to make the sale. An example reveals the reasoning behind such a tactic. A large computer company was struggling with the familiar problem of adding low-cost direct methods and indirect channels to supplement its direct sales force. In seeking to motivate the direct sales reps to relinquish revenue responsibilities, the company considered three options: a penalty, a modest incentive, and a strong incentive.

In weighing the penalty option, the company reasoned that requiring direct sales reps to forfeit commissions on each sale that should be made elsewhere would discourage them from stealing sales from new units. The risks of such an approach, however, seemed overwhelming: the company saw that conflict and petty rivalries were bound to erupt throughout the marketing organization as soon as it instituted the policy.

The modest incentive option would entail paying direct sales reps a portion of their normal commission when the new units made a sale. On reflection, this solution appeared too cumbersome: it would be difficult to determine appropriate compensation levels and to define and enforce a policy that would avoid sending mixed signals.

In the end, the company chose the strong incentive option—and eventually implemented it successfully. After a thorough analysis of long-term costs and benefits, the company paid the direct sales reps their normal commission for every sale regardless of whether they were responsible. Once the new units became established, the company phased out this system of double pay.

——— ORCHESTRATING A HYBRID SYSTEM

Once a hybrid system is up and running, its smooth functioning depends not only on management of conflict but also on coordination across the channels and across each selling task within the channels. Each unit involved in bridging the gap between the company and the customer must "hand off" all relevant information concerning the customer and the progress of the sale to the next appropriate unit.

A recent technical tool called a marketing and sales productivity (MSP) system can be an invaluable aid in coordinating customer handoffs.[2] Beyond this, an MSP system can help a company combine and manage distinct marketing approaches to produce customized hybrid channels. An MSP system helps serve customers by identifying and coordinating the marketing methods best suited to each customer's needs. In other words, it allows the development of customized channels and service for specific customer segments.

An MSP system consists of a central marketing database containing essential information on customers, prospects, products, marketing programs, and methods. All marketing units regularly update the database. At any point, it is possible to determine previous customer contacts, prices quoted, special customer characteristics or needs, and other information. These systems can significantly lower marketing costs and increase marketing effectiveness by acting as a central nervous system that coordinates the channels and marketing tasks within a hybrid system. With a fully integrated MSP system, it is now possible to know how much it costs to acquire and maintain a customer—essential data in understanding a company's marketing productivity.

Data Translation, a small manufacturer of computer peripherals, installed an in-house MSP system to manage its hybrid marketing organization. At the outset, the company could not afford to hire sales reps but instead generated leads through trade advertising that featured an 800 number. Interested prospects received the company's catalog; they were also encouraged to call and speak to an inside sales representative about products. All contacts with prospects were tracked by the MSP system. Inside sales reps were supported by a group of technical engineers who handled customer inquiries. When Data Translation later added a direct sales force, it continued to rely on its MSP system to coordinate various marketing tasks, including generating leads and dealing with customer calls.

Coordinating the handoffs within its hybrid system and knowing the cost of acquiring and maintaining its customers gives Data Translation significantly lower marketing costs than its competitors. These lower costs translate directly into competitive advantage and bigger margins.

—— CAPTURING THE BENEFITS

Staples, a Massachusetts-based office supplies company, is achieving outstanding growth through clever allocation of marketing tasks based on what it has learned about customer behavior. At its birth in the mid-1980s, Staples's founders decided to offer discounted office supplies in a retail superstore format, targeting white-collar companies with up to 100 employees.

---

2. For an analysis of these systems, *see* Rowland T. Moriarty and Gordon S. Swartz, "Automation to Boost Sales and Marketing," *Harvard Business Review* (January–February 1989): 100.

Staples encouraged customers to accept a free savings card that granted additional discounts and, more important, allowed the company to track purchases and to build up a customer database.

Armed with this information, management discovered that its penetration of businesses with 2 to 10 employees was good, those with 10 to 20 not so good, and those with more than 20 quite weak. Customers in the latter two segments wanted more service. In response, Staples started accepting phone orders and added a delivery service. It has also used direct mail, telemarketing, and catalogs and has considered adding a direct sales force to handle large accounts. An MSP system orchestrates and monitors the entire hybrid system and provides management with performance and productivity information on each marketing element. Staples credits much of its success to the design and implementation of its hybrid system.

Many signs indicate that hybrid systems will be the dominant design for going to market throughout the 1990s. How a company manages its system will help determine its fate in the marketplace. A company that designs and manages its system strategically will achieve a powerful advantage over rivals that add channels and methods in an opportunistic and incremental manner. A company that makes its hybrid system work will have achieved a balance between its customers' buying behavior and its own selling economics. A well-managed hybrid system enables a marketer to enjoy the benefits of increased coverage and lower costs without losing control of the marketing system. Further, it enables a company to customize its marketing system to meet the needs of specific customers and segments.

In sum, a company with a successful hybrid marketing system will accomplish the following:

- It will recognize that the design and management of its marketing system is a powerful weapon in an increasingly competitive and continually shifting battle for customers.
- It will construct its marketing system using marketing tasks, not entire marketing channels, as the fundamental building blocks.
- It will anticipate, recognize, communicate, and contain conflicts inherent in the marketing system.
- In designing boundaries between customer segments, it will strike a balance between too loose and too strict limits.
- It will form policies and an organizational structure that allow new channels to grow, minimize internal conflict, and reinforce segment boundaries.
- It will exploit information technology and other managerial tools to coordinate handoffs of customers and accounts from one channel or method to another and eventually develop customized marketing systems for each important customer or segment.

————— DISCUSSION QUESTIONS

1. According to the authors, a new hybrid marketing system promises to become the dominant marketing design in the next decade. They contend that the hybrid system is a more efficient way to reach customers than direct selling, with increased sales and decreased costs. Do you think hybrid systems will ever replace the direct sales force or diminish its role? Does direct selling have any role in a hybrid system?

2. Do you see potential conflict in managing these hybrid systems? As companies add new channels to existing ones, are they not also introducing competition within the system, causing some loss of revenue within each channel? Is there a way to manage this without sacrificing coverage?

3. The authors go so far as to say that conflict within a hybrid system is not only inevitable but also may be healthy. How is this possible? What happened in the Wright Line case as related by the authors? How can conflict that is so debilitating and destructive also be healthy?

4. How can a well-managed hybrid system bring to the marketer increased coverage? Lower costs? Strategic advantages over rivals? How difficult is it to customize a marketing system to meet the needs of specific customers and segments in a rapidly changing market?

5. Can channels be added one by one as the need arises? Why or why not?

COMMUNICATIONS DECISIONS

Personal communications? Mass communications? Direct or indirect communications? What means? What media? How are they used to sell goods, services, ideas? To reach targeted customers?

The choices and combinations are many and are determined by a company's goals, budget, product, customers, and distribution methods. Each choice to employ personal selling, direct mail, mass media advertising, catalogs, trade show demonstrations, telemarketing, or publicity plays a specific role in meeting the marketer's objectives. And the methods used for consumer goods differ from those used for industrial goods.

The readings in this section focus on the various methods of communications and the role they play in marketing decision making.

Communications Policy   27

STEVEN H. STAR

No matter how excellent the product, its success in the marketplace can be achieved only when its benefits are effectively communicated to potential customers. This introductory reading on communications policy focuses on six aspects of developing a communications program: setting program objectives, selecting target market segments, delineating the message, deciding on the appropriate intensity of communications, choosing the medium or media mix, and calculating the economics of the program. Throughout it emphasizes the need for program integration and consistency among all elements of communications policy.

Communications policy is a critical ingredient in virtually all marketing programs. Even a well-designed product or service intended to satisfy a pressing consumer need will have scant opportunity to do so if target consumers are unaware of its existence, do not understand what it can do for them, and have no idea of where to obtain it. Although communications policies frequently have far more complex objectives than providing this information, any marketing program must accomplish at least this minimum goal.

To develop an effective communications program for a product or products, the marketer must consider six interrelated issues:

1. Objectives of the communications program,
2. Market segments to be targeted,
3. Message to be communicated,
4. Necessary intensity of communication,
5. Choice of media,
6. Economics of the proposed communications program.

——— PROGRAM OBJECTIVES

Management's first task is to specify clearly its communications objectives. These are often summarized as changing customer attitudes toward a product in terms of one or more elements of the awareness→knowledge→preference→trial→repurchase continuum known as the *hierarchy of effects.* The goal of a communications program might, for example, be to increase brand-name awareness from 40% to 70% of households or to increase the rate of brand trial from 10% to 25% of households. Though this hierarchy of effects may not be an appropriate model for all products, it encourages marketers to examine in detail the effects of their programs in order to focus future efforts on the appropriate elements in the hierarchy.[1]

A second dimension of specifying communications objectives centers on the audience to be reached. The marketers may need, for example, to raise brand awareness only among nonusers if the purchaser is not the user. To specify communications objectives clearly, therefore, management must understand the decision-making process for a product: who initiates the search, who influences the decision, who makes the purchase, and who uses the product.

A third dimension to the specification of communications objectives centers on the type of demand the firm is seeking to stimulate. As well as increasing selective demand for its own products, a company with a dominant market share in a particular product category may aim to increase demand for the category as a whole, knowing that it will reap a large portion of the incremental business.

A variety of other objectives may also be assigned to marketing communications programs. An advertising campaign by an airline, for example, may be designed to raise the morale and performance of service personnel, as well as to attract more travelers. So-called corporate advertising campaigns may be designed to raise the company's profile among the investment community, while advocacy advertising campaigns can be designed to present a political point of view often only indirectly related to sale of the company's products.

There is, however, always the danger that too many objectives will be assigned to a communications program. In general, it is preferable to have a limited set of objectives set forth in sufficiently specific detail to permit performance measurement.

——— TARGET MARKET SEGMENTS

A market segment is a subgroup of consumers who share some common characteristic(s). These consumers may have the same demographic profile, (e.g., age, sex, and class distribution), live in the same region of a country, share a similar lifestyle, or be heavy users of a particular product or brand. The basic assumption underlying market segmentation is that consumers are heterogeneous and that different groups will respond to particular products and communications programs in different ways. The art of market segmentation is to identify the dimensions or the criteria on which it is most useful to segment actual and potential customers for the purposes of marketing. To be of value to

---

1. Some scholars suggest an alternative model in which a low-risk product trial *precedes* attitude change. *See* Krugman, Herbert E., "The Impact of Television Advertising: Learning Without Involvement," *Public Opinion Quarterly* (Fall 1965): 349–56.

management, a segment must be large enough in market potential to make tailoring a distinct marketing program economically worthwhile. Moreover, there should be enough media-audience information available to make media purchases cost effective.

Determining the appropriate audiences for a specific communications program generally depends on the target market segment(s) of the overall marketing program and the nature of the purchase-decision process in these market segments. Based on the understanding of their firms' marketing strategy, marketing managers select both the households or organizations to be reached and the individuals in those households or organizations who either make or strongly influence the purchase decision. Marketing managers will sometimes communicate a different message to each of several target segments at the same time.

One segmentation approach of special value in developing communications policy is benefit segmentation. Different segments are identified according to the varying importance they attach to different product benefits. This benefit analysis can guide the communications messages to be targeted at different segments. For example, a manufacturer of printing presses found that book publishers are especially sensitive to production quality and consistency but not especially concerned about machine downtime; newspapers, on the other hand, are less concerned about quality but extremely time sensitive and very concerned about machine reliability and avoidance of downtime. The manufacturer developed different products and communications programs to address these two benefit segments.

Consider a second example, that of a specialized manufacturer of industrial instant adhesives used to bond metal and plastic surfaces. In selecting the appropriate audiences for its communications program, such a manufacturer might usefully develop a complete listing of all users of industrial adhesive in the United States, categorized by geographic location, capacity, size and nature of the firm, and (possibly) current purchasing behavior. Using these data, the adhesive manufacturer could determine which segment or segments of this market it should target with its overall marketing strategy and what priorities to assign to each market segment, or even to each potential customer.

Having decided which organizations are to be the targets of its marketing program, the marketing manager would then determine which individuals or positions in those target firms play significant roles in the purchase-decision process for adhesives. In this case, he or she might determine that purchasing agents play the decisive role but that production foremen have strong views regarding the ostensible advantages of competitive brands of adhesives and that senior executives regularly review supply arrangements for items such as adhesives in order to assure guaranteed availability during strikes or shortages. Under these circumstances, the adhesive manufacturer might decide that all these members of the purchase decision-making unit (DMU) should receive communications—to different degrees and with different messages.

Defining target audiences for consumer goods is also complex. The manufacturer of a new children's breakfast cereal, for example, might define new target segments in various ways: as households with children; as households with two or more children below the age of twelve; as households with two or more children below the age of twelve who currently are or are not heavy users of children's breakfast cereals; or even as households that are currently heavy users of a competitive brand. After selecting one or more of these segments, the cereal manufacturer would then determine who makes or influences the decision to buy breakfast cereals. The purchase may be made by an adult member of the household, but young children, or their older brothers and sisters, may contribute to the decision process. Like the adhesive manufacturer, the cereal manufacturer might usefully include several members of the DMU in its communications program.

Demographics may not, however, always be an adequate basis for segmentation. A health and beauty aid manufacturer, for example, found that all demographic groups in all regions of the country were equally likely to use a particular product. In addition, a group of heavy users with outdoor lifestyles was identified; they were more price conscious and less brand loyal than lighter users and tended to buy larger sizes in discount stores, whereas lighter users usually purchased smaller sizes in drug stores. Further investigation revealed that heavy users were more frequent viewers of televised sports, which enabled the marketing manager to develop one communications campaign for light users and one for heavy users of the product—employing different media and focusing on different product uses.

——— MESSAGE DELINEATION

Having identified the specific individuals to be reached through its communications policy, the company's next task is determining what message or messages it wishes to communicate to each of its audience segments. At a conceptual level, such messages may be viewed as satisfying each audience segment's need or desire for information relevant to the purchasing process. Once the message content is determined, the marketer can turn his or her attention to *how* to communicate it. An audience segment's need for information may generally be ascertained by answering such questions as

- At what life-cycle stage is the product or service?
- At what stage is the audience segment along the awareness→ trial→repurchase continuum?
- What is the product or service intended to do for members of the audience segment?
- How does it compare with available alternatives?
- What role does this audience segment play in the household or organizational purchase-decision process?

The position of the product in its life cycle often determines what information should be communicated. For a totally new product category (e.g., an optical scanner to be used in automated typesetting), the initial communications task may simply be to create awareness that it is now possible to do something not previously feasible. For a new entry in an existing product category (e.g., a new type of potato chip), however, it may be necessary not only to announce that the new product is available, but also to describe its benefits relative to alternatives. In either case, the marketer developing a message strategy needs to distinguish between what consumers already know and what they need to know, since the frequent repetition of well-known facts may eventually generate a negative reaction rather than a positive reinforcement.

Once the target audience is aware of a new product or service and knows, in general terms, what it is supposed to do, the next communications objective is often to encourage a trial or a closer look. For frequently purchased consumer goods (e.g., toothpaste or potato chips), it is generally enough to communicate convincing reasons why the customer should deviate from a well-established purchasing pattern. For infrequently purchased durable or capital goods (e.g., furniture or word processors), the most appropriate communications objective might be to convince members of the target audience to consider the product or service the next time they enter the market and to explain how to learn more about the product and locate a dealer.

Once the target audience has been directly exposed to the new product or service—whether through actual trial or, say, a supermarket or trade show demonstration—the marketer's communications objective may shift. At this point, he or she will try to ensure that the target audience is fully aware of the various uses and advantages of the product or service. At this stage in the communications cycle the differing information needs of individual members of the DMU are especially significant. In the case of the optical scanner, for example, it may initially be critical to inform members of the target DMU that the new product exists, that it is made by the XYZ Company, that they can now get further information and observe the equipment in operation, and so on. Once these communications objectives have been accomplished, however, it is frequently necessary to convey different messages to potential customers' top management, technical staffs, production people, and procurement personnel.

In designing messages for specific audience segments, it is generally useful to know what the product or service will do for the intended recipient of the message. While it may be noteworthy that the instant adhesive described earlier is baked at an exceptionally high temperature and allowed to cool slowly, the relevance of this aspect of the production process is probably not immediately apparent to the firm's target audiences. However, the manufacturing process *may* be highly relevant to the purchasing agent, if it is related to fewer rejects at the time of delivery, or to the shop foreman, if it indicates high quality consistency and, therefore, fewer process problems.

In a similar vein, a consumer-products manufacturer will generally find it useful to focus on what its product will do for individual members of its target audience. A children's good-tasting nutritious cereal may, for example, provide a parent with a convenient way of preparing a quick, wholesome breakfast during the morning rush or simply with something a three-year-old will eat rather than throw on the floor. For children, however, the salient message may be that the cereal tastes good, is fun to eat, or makes them feel like a big-game hunter, secure against childhood fantasies of rampaging lions and tigers.

——— INTENSITY OF COMMUNICATION

Given the target audiences and the clearly delineated messages to be communicated to these audiences, what level of communications effort will achieve the desired impact? To a considerable extent, the appropriate intensity of a communications program will be a function of

- The nature of the message to be communicated,
- The number of targets to be reached,
- The receptivity of the audience to the message,
- The intensity of competitive communications activities,
- The amount of funds available for the communications effort.

Some messages simply require more time and effort to communicate than others. A new entry in an existing product category (e.g., a new flavor in an established line of soft drinks) requires no major behavioral change of the target consumer and generally calls for only a low level of communications intensity. In effect, all that is necessary is to inform the target consumer that the new flavor is available and is worthy of trial. At the other extreme, a complex industrial new product, such as the optical scanner cited earlier, may perform a new function in such a way as to necessitate major changes in the production process in which it is applied; it is therefore likely to require a very intensive communications effort to educate and convince customers about the new technology.

In general, a more intense communications effort is required when a product is introduced than later in its life cycle. At the time of introduction, it is often necessary to inform customers about the existence of a new product; its function, features, benefits, and costs; and where or how to buy it. As an increasing percentage of the target audience becomes aware of the product's existence and major attributes, it may only be necessary to remind them of these facts or to stress particular benefits.

The number, heterogeneity, and receptivity of members of the target audience have a significant influence on the necessary intensity of communications effort. In general, a greater level of effort is needed to reach a lot of people than to reach a few people, or to reach separate audiences with different messages than to reach a single audience with a single message. Similarly, it often requires less effort to communicate a message when the audience is actively seeking information of the kind being communicated (e.g., gasoline mileage data in the 1990s) than to communicate the same message to a relatively passive audience (e.g., gasoline mileage data in 1965). In general, a higher level of communications intensity is required for mundane, unimportant products than for those which more readily engage a customer. Nonetheless, marketers should remember that the importance of a product category varies from customer to customer and may be heightened by, for example, the introduction of new products.

In situations where the purpose of a communications program is to convince potential customers to purchase one brand rather than another that promises similar benefits, the intensity of competitive communications efforts will often establish a minimum threshold that must be surpassed if a communications program is to achieve its desired effects. If, for example, one brand of analgesic communicates to target consumers the importance of "getting rapidly into the bloodstream" ten times per week, it is unlikely that the message of a competitive analgesic emphasizing "gentleness to your stomach" will have much impact if it reaches the target only once a week. Similarly, even an exceptional salesperson will find the going tough if a buyer he or she visits twice a year has weekly lunches with the competition.

Ultimately, however, the intensity of a communications program depends largely on the extent of the target audience's need for information and the willingness of the purchaser to pay for the information. In the competition between private-label or generic grocery and advertised brands, for example, the higher price necessitated by the advertised brand's communications program will be paid only if the target consumer finds the information communicated worth the difference in price. Not surprisingly, private labels tend to do least well in product categories that present consumers with considerable perceived risk or in which it is difficult for them to determine the respective merits of competitive brands. Similarly, consumers who have the least confidence in their own purchasing ability are most likely to purchase more expensive, advertised brands, even at income levels that would most benefit from the savings from buying generic goods.

Although every company has limits to its communications budget, the prime determinant should be the nature of the communications task rather than the spending level of the firm's principal competitor or the firm's historical advertising-to-sales ratio. There is usually no reason to believe that the competitor's budget-setting process is superior and, therefore, worthy of imitation. Moreover, the advertising-to-sales ratio approach is based on circular reasoning; it makes advertising a function of sales rather than sales a result of advertising.

In addition to setting the absolute level of the communications budget, management must also decide on its allocation. This allocation may occur along several dimensions, according to products in the line, in which new products may receive proportionately more funds than mature products; target groups, in which current users who need merely to be reinforced will probably receive less emphasis than nonusers who need to be made aware of the product and induced to prefer it; and geographic regions, where low-share development markets may receive proportionately more funds than high-share markets. Communications expenditures must also be allocated among media types and specific vehicles. In addition, management must decide how to allocate funds over the planning cycle—for example, whether to have a constant level of media spending or periodic "blitzes." Finally, communications expenditures are sometimes allocated between the manufacturer and its channel intermediaries on a cooperative basis, particularly when consumers are as concerned about the quality of the distributors from which they buy the product as they are about the brands they select.

——— CHOICE OF MEDIA

Marketers can choose from a wide range of communications media to convey their messages to target audiences. They can employ, for example, such mass media as outdoor billboards, television, mass-circulation magazines, and newspapers; more selective media such as FM radio, specialized magazines, or the *Wall Street Journal*; point-of-purchase advertising; direct mail; or personal selling. Moreover, the diversity of the communications mix available to consumer-goods and industrial marketers has increased greatly in recent years, partly in response to rapid escalation in the costs of network television advertising and the personal sales call. More and more often, consumer marketers are supplementing advertising efforts with point-of-sale merchandising and in-store sales promotions, particularly for products that are seen as impulse purchases. Even industrial marketers are supplementing the efforts of their salespeople with telemarketing and direct mail. As such new technologies as interactive videotex emerge, selecting the appropriate communications mix will become even more complicated.

In virtually all cases, personal selling is considerably more expensive than the various types of media and nonmedia advertising. In the 1980s the typical industrial sales call cost almost $200. By contrast, the estimated cost of 20 minutes spent by a retail salesperson explaining the features of a major appliance to a consumer was about $5.00; a high-quality direct mail piece cost between $2.00 and $3.00 (including the cost of the mailing list); the selective media cost between 10¢ and 15¢ per impression; and the mass media cost as little as 1¢ per impression.

However, personal selling offers two principal compensatory advantages over advertising. First, communications can be precisely tailored to individual customer needs in a two-way process. The audience's attention can be held longer, and more complex messages can be more easily delivered. Second, salespeople provide valuable feedback to headquarters on new sales prospects, product performance, and competitive activity.

Before discussing media selection criteria further, it is important to stress three points. First, all elements of the marketing mix, intentionally or unintentionally, perform a communications function. The price at which a product is offered and the channels through which it is distributed tell the consumer as much about it as the advertising copy. Second, many communications about a product are outside the control of the marketer: word-of-mouth and friends' recommendations are highly valued as information sources, especially in the case of such high-risk purchases as automobiles and microcomputers. Third, only rarely will there be a single best medium to which all communications dollars should be allocated. Selecting a mix of media, however, requires the marketer to define carefully the role of each element and to send a consistent message across all media.

In choosing among communications media, a number of considerations are especially significant. First, it is necessary to ensure that the medium chosen will actually reach the target audience. Second, it is essential that it be appropriate for the message conveyed. Finally, because the relative costs of alternative communications media vary widely, cost differences must be taken into account in establishing an effective communications mix.

Generally, the marketer of a complex technical product (e.g., the optical scanner described earlier) has no choice but to rely principally on personal selling, despite its costs. Personal selling makes certain that the relevant decision makers and influencers are exposed to the message, allows for custom tailoring to the information needs of each customer, and gives the communicator the opportunity to respond to questions and objections and to convey feedback to the manufacturer. Even so, the salesperson's task can often be simplified—and sometimes made possible—by a media advertising campaign that establishes credibility and stimulates a need for information.

In the case of infrequently purchased, high-ticket goods for which the consumer shops around (e.g., major appliances, furniture), the bulk of the target audience's information needs will generally be satisfied in the retail store, through visual inspection, descriptive tickets and price tags, and personal selling. Under these circumstances, the marketer's media efforts will generally emphasize retailer "push" rather than direct consumer "pull." Even in these circumstances, however, media advertising may be used to stimulate primary demand, presell desirable product features, or draw consumers to outlets that carry a particular brand.

At the opposite extreme, marketers of frequently purchased, low-ticket convenience goods rely mostly on impersonal communications through print or electronic media. Package copy and in-store displays may communicate part of the message and reinforce or supplement media communications.

Depending on the targets of the communications program, the marketer may find it more economical to use mass media (intended to reach everybody) or selective media (intended to reach targets with specified characteristics). In making the choice of media, the marketer should consider the probability that a particular message will reach its target. This assessment requires an appreciation of (1) where target consumers expect, on the basis of experience, to obtain information about a particular product category; (2) the appropriateness of particular media for specific communications objectives (e.g., advertising to build awareness); and (3) the degree to which competitive advertising already dominates particular media. An additional critical factor is the comparative economics of reaching the target audience through different means. A marketer of disposable diapers, for example, may pay less per impression (cost per thousand readers or viewers) for a mass medium that reaches both mothers with infants and a lot of other people, or more per impression for a selective medium that reaches a higher concentration of mothers with infants.

The nature of the medium is also relevant to the selection of media. Certain products (e.g., food preparation gadgets), which require visual demonstration as part of their communication programs, are good candidates for television advertising. Other products (e.g., compact disk players) require a good deal more detailed descriptive copy, which makes magazine advertising the best medium. Supermarkets, which seek to communicate reduced prices on specific items for limited periods, find newspapers to be the appropriate vehicle because of their low-cost, mass audiences, large formats, and precisely timed impact on readers.

———— THE ECONOMICS OF COMMUNICATIONS

With few exceptions, the types of communications efforts described here require the expenditure of funds and other scarce resources. Such expenditures can vary from a few hundred dollars for a small retailer who simply wishes to announce its existence, to many millions of dollars for firms with large sales forces or extensive advertising programs. Whatever the size of a firm's communications budget, however, its costs must ultimately be paid by the purchasers of the firm's products or services.

Alternative communications media differ significantly in the timing with which expenditures take place. A new product introduced with a pull advertising campaign, for example, requires a sizable up-front investment in communications that (it is hoped) will be recovered through subsequent purchases. Marketers employing a push strategy, conversely, can often compensate distribution channels for their communications efforts through extra discounts and pay salespeople on a commission basis for a—in effect—pay-as-you-go method of covering communications costs. Partly for this reason, push strategies are often favored by small companies with limited resources.

Whatever the timing of communications costs, they can be justified economically only if they lead to either a higher price (and unit contribution) or a greater unit volume than would occur without them. In either case, the product of incremental unit contribution (if any) multiplied by incremental volume (if any) must exceed the expenditure on communications. The appropriate time frame in which communications costs are to be recovered will, of course, depend largely on the objectives of the communications effort.

——— MANAGEMENT OF MARKETING COMMUNICATIONS

The complexities of communications policy are such that many producers seek the assistance of outside specialist firms, most often advertising agencies. Though companies usually develop their own advertising objectives and strategy, they often leave the execution to the agency. Some companies use a similar approach to personal selling, hiring independent representatives, who sell their products on a commission basis, along with the products of other, noncompeting companies. Manufacturers with sufficiently broad product lines and the necessary resources generally prefer to have the control and leverage that comes from working through their own sales forces.

Five functions are involved in the management of a sales force. First, the appropriate type of salesperson, which varies according to the communications task, must be recruited. The selling skills required to make door-to-door cold calls selling encyclopedias are different from those required to solve information-processing problems and sell computer systems to a large account.

Second, salespeople must be trained, not only in general selling skills but also in the technicalities of their product lines and in how the products they are selling can benefit different types of customers.

Third, salespeople must be deployed, that is, they must be assigned to particular territories, products, or customer accounts. Relationships with an organization's larger customers, which may buy nationwide rather than in a single sales territory, are frequently handled by national account managers. These managers not only sell but work with customers to solve problems and provide feedback to the vendor's headquarters, which may lead to the development of new or improved products or services.

Fourth, salespeople must be motivated and compensated in a manner consistent with the tasks defined for them. A salesperson whose responsibilities include solving customer problems is likely to be compensated on a straight salary basis. Conversely, a salesperson handling noncomplex products and acting primarily as an order taker is more likely to work on commission.

Fifth, a sales organization must be developed to manage these various tasks and to evaluate the performance of both individual salespeople and the entire sales force. As in the case of advertising, it is essential to set specific, quantifiable objectives against which performance can be evaluated.

Other communications activities, such as advertising, require similar careful management. However, because it involves fewer people, who usually work in a centralized setting, as opposed to the dispersion of the sales force, advertising management tends to be less complex.

——— CONCLUSION

Communications policy is critical to the success of any marketing program. An excellent product can never be successful in the marketplace if its benefits are not communicated effectively to target consumers. In the 1980s, an increasing diversity of communications approaches was available to marketers to reach end consumers, channel intermediaries, and other constituencies. In the 1990s, the formulation and implementation of communications policy promises to become even more complex and challenging.

A final note—We have presented the steps in the development of a communications policy in a fixed sequence, as if it were always appropriate for the marketer to begin with step 1 and proceed serially through to step 6. In actual practice, however, it is generally more fruitful to consider all six steps more or less simultaneously, adjusting the various elements in the communications policy as the program is developed. In this way, consistency—the primary requisite of an effective communications program—can be achieved by integrating objectives, target, message, intensity, media, and economics.

——— DISCUSSION QUESTIONS

1. Advertising, personal selling, and sales promotion are only a few of the traditional communications approaches available to marketers of consumer and industrial goods. But before deciding on which approach to use, the author tells us, "management's first task is to specify clearly its communications objectives." These are often stated in terms of one or more elements of the "hierarchy-of-effects" process: first, awareness; then knowledge, preference, trial, and repurchase. How do you view the validity of this sequence for a product such as automobiles? For a product such as lemons? Do you see benefits or disadvantages from this process?

2. Can a communications program have too many objectives?

3. Why is it critical for the marketer to understand the needs of the decision-making unit before developing a communications program? How would the DMU's differing needs affect the marketer's message?

4. Assume you are planning an advertising campaign. Before committing the funds, you conduct an extensive field test and gather a considerable amount of data. Can these results be interpreted accurately enough to design an advertising program around them? In your view, how effective is research methodology? What pitfalls do you think exist in advertising research?

5. Some companies maintain their own sales forces, while others hire independent representatives to sell their products on a commission

basis. Compare these two approaches, and explain the advantages and disadvantages of each. Why would a company choose to use a sales force of any kind when other methods, such as advertising, involve fewer people, less expense, and less management attention?

6. In measuring the performance of your sales force, which elements do you think contribute more—the quality of the salesperson or the nature of the territory?

28   New Ways to Reach
Your Customers

BENSON P. SHAPIRO AND JOHN WYMAN

Cost pressures and the need for greater flexibility in devising marketing programs have led to new approaches for communicating with potential and existing customers: national account management, demonstration centers, telemarketing, and improved catalog selling. This reading offers guidelines for incorporating these techniques into marketing programs. The authors describe a four-step approach for developing an effective marketing program by showing how to analyze communications costs, specify communications needs, formulate a creative, coherent program, and monitor the total system.

From farther back than any of us can remember, personal selling, advertising, and sales promotion have been the essential marketing approaches. But these tested and proved methods for reaching customers also have their limitations, particularly in light of two significant changes that took place in the business picture in the 1970s.

1. The costs of communication climbed radically. Media costs skyrocketed. And the cost of a sales call, as estimated by McGraw-Hill, rose from $49 in 1969 to $137 in 1979.
2. A new set of options evolved, giving marketers a wider array of communications tools.

These developments mean that the marketing manager can make the best use of the newer methods, as well as the older ones, to respond to increasing top management demand for efficient and effective communication. In particular, the evolving options offer opportunities to improve the precision and impact of the marketing program, sometimes at great cost savings over the traditional methods.

There is no need for us to belabor the all too familiar change in communications costs. On the other hand, little note has been made of the newer options, so in the first section of this reading we will focus on them. Then, in the second section, we will provide a four-step approach for developing a marketing program that makes the best use of both the newer and the older communications tools.

——— EVOLVING OPTIONS

In the past, the marketer's primary communications tools were media advertising, direct mail advertising, telephone selling, trade shows, and face-to-face selling. These traditional methods differed in impact and cost per message, with media advertising at the low end and personal selling at the high end. Telephone and personal selling offered flexibility in tailoring the message to the target prospect and in having two-way contact—but at a substantial cost, particularly for the field sales force. Trade shows added the excitement and impact of product demonstration but were competitive and temporary in nature.

Whereas the opportunities to "mix and match" the five traditional approaches into a coherent, synergistic marketing program were limited in the past, we believe that the increase in the number of available tools gives the marketing manager the ability to develop a more integrated, tailored, and cost-effective communications program than was previously possible.

The newer tools include national account management, demonstration centers, industrial stores, telemarketing, and new forms of catalog selling. These tools, used together and with the traditional methods, are leading to a new economics of selling. Let us look first at these five evolving options individually and then at the opportunities they offer when combined with the traditional methods.

NATIONAL ACCOUNT MANAGEMENT

A few large accounts comprise a disproportionately large percentage of almost any company's sales (industrial as well as consumer goods and services). National account management can often be applied (1) if these large accounts are geographically or organizationally dispersed, (2) if the selling company has many interactions with the buying company's operating units, and (3) if the product and selling processes are complex. National account management is thus an extension, improvement, and outgrowth of personal selling. In essence, this method is the ultimate form of both personal selling and management of the personal selling process.

National account management responds to the needs of the customer for a coordinated communications approach while giving the seller a method of coordinating the costs, activities, and objectives of the sales function for its most important accounts. It is expensive, but the value to customer and seller alike is high if the situation is appropriate and the concept well executed.

Many people and companies use other names for this approach. Banks (as well as some other companies) call it *relationship management* because it draws attention to the primary objective of creating and developing an enduring relationship between the selling and buying companies. Others call it *corporate account management* because the accounts are managed at the corporate level, although the customers buy from several divisions in a multidivisional corporation. Yet others prefer the term *international account management* because the relationships transcend national boundaries. We prefer to use *national account management* because it appears to be the most popular and descriptive term.

National account management programs share certain characteristics, depending on the sales situation:

1. The accounts managed are large relative to the rest of the company's accounts, sometimes generating more than $50 million each.
2. The national account manager is often responsible for coordinating people who work in other divisions of the selling company or in other functional areas. (This raises a great many issues of conflicting objectives and priorities.)
3. The national account manager often has responsibility for a team that includes support and operations people.
4. The manager calls on many people in the buying company (e.g., engineering, manufacturing, finance) in addition to those in the formal buying function and often gets involved in highly conceptual, financially oriented systems sales.

The first issue that confronts companies considering national account management is how many accounts to involve. At this point the marketing managers need to understand the difference between "special handling" for a few select accounts and a real national account management program. Almost any company can develop a way to give special attention to a few accounts. But a full-blown national account management program requires fundamental changes in selling philosophy, sales management, and sales organization. Often the special handling of a few select accounts by top-level sales and marketing managers will lead to a formal program because the managers involved cannot find enough time for both the accounts and their regular duties.

Once the program begins, the selection of national accounts is an important phase. American Can Co., for example, found that careful account selection helped to define the nature of the program and to ease its implementation. Many companies, including IBM, separate their programs into different account categories depending on size, geographical dispersion, and servicing needs.

National accounts need special support, as do the managers responsible for them. All of the standard issues of sales management arise: selection, training, supervision, and compensation. The job requires people with both selling and administrative skills. Training and supervision must be keyed to the need for both depth and breadth in skills. And compensation—both amount and form (salary, commission, or both)—becomes important.

But often the most sensitive matter is how to organize. Some companies organize their national account managers with line authority over a large, dispersed sales and support team. Some go so far as to create separate manufacturing operations for each account, and the account team becomes a profit center. Other companies prefer to view the national account managers as coordinators of salespeople who report to different profit centers or divisions. There is a myriad of choices between these two extremes.

DEMONSTRATION CENTERS

Specially designed showrooms, or demonstration centers, allow customers to observe and usually try out complex industrial equipment. The approach supplements personal selling and works best when the equipment being demonstrated is complex and not portable. Demonstration centers have been used in many industries, including telecommunications, data processing, electronic test gear, and machine tools. A variant of the approach is a traveling demonstration center in which the equipment (or process) for sale is mounted in a trailer truck or bus. Rank Xerox, for example, once used a railroad train to demonstrate its equipment all over Europe.

The demonstration center also supplements trade shows, with three major differences between them:

1. The demonstration center is permanent and thus can more easily be fitted in a company's marketing and sales schedule. Trade shows, on the other hand, are temporary and are not scheduled for the convenience of any single company.
2. The company can determine the location of the demonstration center, which it cannot do with trade shows.
3. Demonstration centers are designed to provide a competition-free environment for the selling process. Trade shows, of course, are filled with competitors.

But the primary benefit to the seller comes from demonstration—often to high-level executives who are unavailable for standard sales presentations. Demonstration centers in some situations, furthermore, replace months of regular field selling. The economic trade-off then becomes partially a comparison of the cost of the center with the cost of traveling salespeople. Demonstrating equipment or processes often has more impact than describing them. The most effective demonstration centers relate directly to the customer's needs and include a custom-designed demonstration.

An outstanding example of the concept is the trailer-mounted, demonstration-sized versions of Union Carbide's UNOX wastewater treatment system used by the company's Linde division in the early 1970s. Linde used these models (costing $100,000 each) to demonstrate that its system could handle the wastewater of an industrial plant or even a particular municipality.

Linde had available to it all of the traditional communications approaches. UNOX sales, however, had been slow and difficult. After carefully considering the time and effort involved in selling, Linde executives decided that the demonstration units would speed sales, generate some sales that otherwise would be lost, and save the substantial expense of traditional approaches. And the demonstration units in fact accomplished all these objectives.

INDUSTRIAL STORES

This approach also involves a demonstration of equipment or a process with the emphasis generally on cost reduction, not the creation of seller benefits. Stores are permanent, but the same concept is used by companies that present customer seminars and demonstrations in hotels, trade shows, or other temporary facilities. Here too the idea is to bring the customer to the salesperson. Boeing Computer Services, for example, has used hotel room demonstrations effectively in selling structural analysis computer time-sharing services to engineering firms. The store approach works well under these conditions:

- The sale is too small to justify sales calls. A substantial percentage (often as high as two-thirds) of industrial salespeople's time is spent traveling and waiting to see customers. If the sale is small, personal selling is not economical. One way around the problem is to ask the prospect to do the traveling. Thus, the customer comes to the salesperson's location, not vice versa.
- The product or process is complex and lends itself to demonstration.
- The company does not sell many products to the same customer. (If, on the other hand, the company has a large, active account with the same customer, the cost of a sales call can be amortized over the sale of many products.)

The store approach has been successful in the small business computer industry, where Digital Equipment has more than 20 stores in operation and development. IBM uses a similar approach but promotes it differently, using office space instead of retail space and encouraging appointments instead of drop-ins. In 1980, however, IBM announced a commitment to develop stores more along the evolving concept used by Digital and other competitors. Xerox has made stores a major part of its marketing strategy.

Industrial stores vary widely according to product lines offered and approach used to attract people to visit. Xerox carries a wide variety of items, including many not made by Xerox; other stores offer limited lines produced only by the owners. Some, especially those in prime retail locations, can generate walk-in traffic. Others are in more office-oriented settings. For management, the stores certainly raise retail-oriented questions—location, fixtures, sales staffing—concerning their operations. In addition to display and sales service, stores can also provide physical distribution and service facilities to customers.

Economics has played a large part in the development of the store concept. As selling and travel costs escalate, the use of stores will become even more popular.

TELEMARKETING

Telephone marketing is an important emerging trend that companies can exploit in five ways—as a less costly substitute for personal selling, as a supplement to personal selling, as a higher-impact substitute for direct-mail and media advertising, as a supplement to direct mail and other media, and as a replacement for other slower, less convenient communications techniques.

Cost savings: Telephone selling has traditionally provided a highly customized means of two-way communication. Greater sophistication in tele-communications equipment and services, new marketing approaches, and broader applications have turned telephone selling into telemarketing. It still does not provide the quality of a personal visit but is much cheaper. While a commercial or industrial salesperson might average perhaps 5 or 6 fast personal sales calls per day, he or she can average perhaps 30 long telephone calls. The costs are much lower because of the lack of travel. In 1980 personal sales calls cost upward of one hundred dollars each, while normal-length telephone sales calls cost generally under ten dollars each.

The cost advantage makes telemarketing a good substitute for visits to small accounts. Fieldcrest, for example, has been using telemarketing in conjunction with catalogs to introduce and sell bed and bath fashions to stores in sparsely settled areas.

Supplement to personal visits: Some selling situations require periodic sales visits. Often the cost of the required call frequency is greater than the sales volume justifies and, in these cases, telephone calls can supplement personal visits. The visits might be made two to four times per year and the telephone calls eight to ten times per year for a total frequency of one per month—but at a cost substantially lower than twelve visits. Personal visits would be used for the opening presentation of, say, a new line of apparel or furniture or the sale of equipment, while telephone calls would be used for fill-in orders or supply sales.

Substitute for direct mail: Some insurance salespeople who wish to keep in touch with their customers have switched from using direct mail to the telephone, which gives greater impact—at an admittedly higher cost. For the economics to work well, the person called must be either an existing customer or a good prospect, not just a random name from the phone book. Telemarketing has been successful in selling subscription renewals and other continuity sales and could also aid sales of large consumer durables such as automobiles, swimming pools, and appliances. A Cadillac salesperson might, for example, telephone owners of Lincoln Continentals or Mercedes that are a few years old.

Supplement to direct mail and other media: Telemarketing can add to as well as replace direct mail and media advertising. Many companies have effectively used the 800 telephone numbers in direct mail, television, and print media advertising. Such a program has three advantages over mail replies: (1) the prospect can make an immediate commitment to purchase while the idea is fresh and the desire for action greatest—and, perhaps more important, he or she can get an immediate reply; (2) it is easier for most people to telephone than to fill in a coupon and mail it; and (3) the selling company can become actively involved in supplying product information to aid the customer's decision making, and the customer can also express concerns to be responded to by the telephone salespeople in future media communication or even in later product development.

The combined media/telemarketing approach has been successful for a variety of products, including specialty coffees, smokeless tobacco, books, and records. AT&T uses the approach to sell many of its products and services. An additional advantage is the quick generation of data about media effectiveness. Within a few days a company or its advertising agency can determine the effectiveness of a new advertising campaign. With mail response, the time lag slows the analysis so that a campaign is generally run longer before review.

Customer–company coordination: Finally, the telephone can be used as a part of a communications program to tie companies to their constituencies. The responsiveness and convenience of the telephone, combined with its two-way message content, make it particularly appropriate for this use. A dissatisfied customer, for example, can get a quick response to a problem.[1]

Confused customers who need product information can get it when they need it most, thus preventing product misuse and abuse. O. M. Scott & Sons Co. uses this approach to good advantage in its lawn and garden care business. Problems with the product or its distribution become clear to the seller and can be rectified quickly without much loss of the expensive time of dealers and salespeople. A manufacturer can use the telephone to gather information from salespeople or dealers to find, for example, whether a new product is selling well or whether competitors met a price increase.

The use of the telephone in marketing can create junk phone calls much like junk mail in direct mail advertising. For both economic and customer relations reasons, we advocate the use of selective telemarketing, showing good judgment and good taste. Otherwise, the attention-getting quality of the telephone in uncontrolled situations can irritate consumers.

The telephone's particular mix of benefits and its growing cost-effectiveness versus other media make it an increasingly important part of the communications mix. Ongoing telephone contact with customers or prospects can produce important information through close communication. And once the line is open, there are ever-increasing opportunities to creatively cross-sell complementary products and services.

CATALOG SELLING

An old approach in the consumer goods market, catalog selling is an evolving method in industrial and commercial markets. Companies active in the office- and computer-supply businesses have found catalogs to be an

---

1. For an example of this application, *see* "Good Listener: At Procter & Gamble Success Is Largely Due to Heeding Customer," *Wall Street Journal*, April 29, 1980.

efficient way of generating the relatively small dollar sales typical of their businesses. The Drawing Board, an office supply company in Dallas, apparently relies solely on its catalog for communication with customers.

Wright Line, Inc., a $50 million vendor of computer-related supplies and capital equipment for computer rooms, programmers and analysts, and small businesses, has developed an elaborate communications system that includes personal selling, telemarketing, and catalogs. The 140-person sales force makes visits for the larger capital equipment sales and for developing systems sales. The quarterly catalog generates both fill-in sales of capital equipment and supplies for already-sold systems, as well as orders from customers whose size would not justify a personal call. Customers can place orders by mail, through the salespeople, or by telephone. Most orders come in by telephone and mail. The catalog—a new approach at Wright Line—has improved sales volume more than Wright Line executives had expected.

Wright Line's integrated approach developed through a combination of careful analysis and trial-and-error testing. Management has been willing and able to try new approaches, carefully analyze the results, and commit resources to the successful experiments.

Other industries have also used catalogs, particularly in conjunction with telephone order centers or telemarketing centers. Sigma Chemical Co., for example, uses a catalog to sell enzymes for laboratory use, although competitors generally use sales forces. Other catalog applications include electronic components and industrial supplies. The approach is highly cost-effective in transmitting a great deal of information to selected prospects and customers in a usable, inexpensive format.

It is interesting to relate the development of the five evolving options to the more traditional approaches. Personal selling led to national account management; demonstration centers and industrial stores are variations on the trade show; telemarketing developed from telephone selling and the early inside order desks of industrial distributors; and industrial stores and catalog selling are based on retail stores and consumer catalogs, such as those used by Sears, Roebuck and Co., that date from the nineteenth century.

Economics and technology are driving the evolution, and the need for more precise communications programs is encouraging it.

CREATING A PROGRAM

The newer ways of selling, when combined with the traditional communications approaches, enable marketers to make precise choices in developing their communications programs. Four major steps are necessary for developing an effective program:

- Analyze the communications costs.
- Specify the communications needs.
- Formulate a coherent program.
- Monitor the total system.

ANALYZE CURRENT COSTS

The basic device for understanding marketing costs is a marketing-oriented income statement that divides all costs into three primary categories—manufacturing, physical distribution, and communication—and two generally smaller categories—nondivisible overhead and profit (see *Exhibit 1*).

This income statement differs from the company's income statement. To be useful, it should begin with the price the customer pays. Distributor discounts are allocated to communications cost (the value of the retail and wholesale salespeople, display, advertising, trade show attendance) and physical distribution cost (order processing, inventory carrying, transportation). If the distributor customizes the product in the field (e.g., adds accessories, cuts to shape, or mixes), the cost of doing so should be allocated to the manufacturing task.

The well-designed marketing-oriented income statement helps marketers determine the role of each set of costs (manufacturing, distribution, and communication) in their businesses. Marketers can then ask questions such as:

- Where should I concentrate my cost-cutting activities?
- What do I get and, more important perhaps, what does my customer get from each of the three functions?
- Do the benefits provided by each function justify the costs?

Marketing executives can thus categorize their businesses as communications intensive, distribution intensive, or manufacturing intensive and can then analyze competitors from the same viewpoints. Avon Products, for example, trades off higher physical distribution costs (sending its cosmetics and toiletries in small packages to its several hundred thousand salespeople) against the higher communications costs of its competitors, which place more emphasis on advertising but use more efficient distribution methods (large sales to supermarket and drug chains that depend on the customer to pick up the order and transport it home).

The marketing-oriented income statement helps to analyze communications costs at a strategic, but not a tactical, level. We cannot consider the detailed costs without first specifying marketers' communications needs or objectives.

SPECIFY NEEDS

Marketing executives must state precisely the objectives of the communications program and also understand the costs of achieving each objective. There are many different types of communication between a company and its marketing constituencies. Companies may wish to strive for four major goals in specifying their needs:

1. *Persuasive impact.* Two-way communication is more effective than one-way communication. Media advertising by itself, for

EXHIBIT 1
A Marketing-Oriented Income Statement

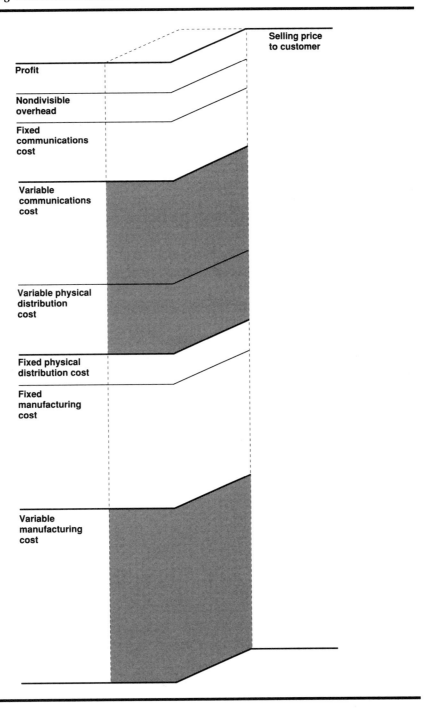

Selling price
to customer

Profit

Nondivisible
overhead

Fixed
communications
cost

Variable
communications
cost

Variable physical
distribution
cost

Fixed physical
distribution cost

Fixed
manufacturing
cost

Variable
manufacturing
cost

example, tends to be one way—from the seller to the buyer—while methods such as telemarketing allow a two-way dialogue.

2. *Customization.* Different people, even within the same buying unit, desire different information, and opportunities for customization vary. Two-way communication, of course, enables the seller to tailor a message to the precise needs of a specific customer at a given moment.

3. *Speed.* Some types of information are much more time sensitive than others. An order to a commodities broker, for example, is urgent. And because we live in an era that stresses instant gratification, many customers want to obtain the product as soon as possible after making their choice, even if they have labored over that choice for weeks, months, or even years.

4. *Convenience.* Almost everybody, from a professional purchasing agent to a child buying a stick of bubble gum, wants convenience in making purchases.

FORMULATE A PROGRAM

Marketers can create the most effective communications program only with a complete understanding of the relationships among both the old and the evolving options. Perhaps even more important than the media on their own is their potential for integration into a synergistic system that uses each medium to its best advantage. *Exhibit 2* shows the evolving and traditional options and their varying impact and cost per message.

Combinations are especially powerful because each medium has a different mix of benefits and economics. It is easy to envision a communications system that uses all 10 of the media and combinations listed in *Exhibit 2.* For example, media advertising gives broad coverage at a low cost. Direct mail delivers a somewhat focused message to a specific group of people at a very reasonable cost. Catalog selling provides a great deal of information, particularly for a wide product assortment, to a focused audience. Telemarketing increases the cost relative to options below it but adds a two-way personalized message, convenience, speed, and the best timing.

The combination of catalogs and telemarketing mixes good economics, much information transmittal, and the advantages of the telephone. Industrial stores and trade shows offer the benefits of personal selling with the cost advantages of a stationary sales force. Of course, customer convenience suffers.

Again, personal selling provides important advantages at a high cost. The addition of a demonstration center increases the cost but provides important benefits in major sales. And, finally, national account management provides the ultimate communications medium at the highest cost.

Different approaches can be used for different customers, products, situations, and communications needs. Companies that market many products to many different types of customers will generally need a wider variety of

EXHIBIT 2
Comparing the Evolving and Traditional Options

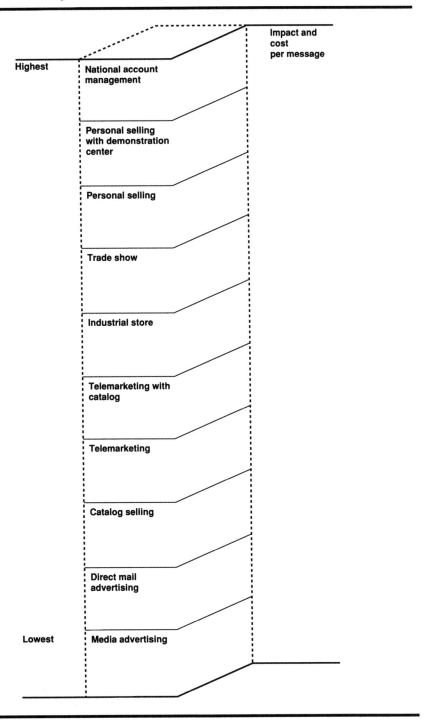

communications modes than companies having a narrower product and customer mix. It should be no surprise that companies such as Digital Equipment and AT&T, with their many products, many types of customers, and new technologies to sell, have been at the forefront of the new approaches. They had little choice.

Time is an important dimension in the development of a synergistic communications program for three major reasons:

1. Marketers must plan each communications program with regard to the events of the product's life cycle. The planned introduction of a variation in a product, for example, might require an equally carefully planned change in the communications mix—perhaps to emphasize a new use or a new set of users. Customer knowledge moves through its own life cycle. At some points in a product's life, developing brand awareness among prospects might be particularly important, while at other times the primary emphasis would be on reassuring existing customers.

2. Communications programs take a long time to implement. The progression from initial start-up to effective operation of a national account program, for example, can take four to five years. The same is true, but to a lesser extent, of the other media shown in *Exhibit 2*. It can take a year to develop, test, and carefully execute a good media advertising or catalog sales program. In general, the communications methods with greater impact and higher cost per message in *Exhibit 2* require more time to implement than those lower in the hierarchy.

3. Careful planning over time involves the raison d'être of all marketing activities—the customer. Customers remember. Thus, frequently changing communications programs is ineffective, inefficient, and confusing. Customers used to sales calls will not immediately embrace an industrial store or a telemarketing program. All communications programs must reflect a concern for the customer's memory.

The mix-and-match process of developing a program from a set of communications media alternatives has four integral dimensions: market segments, products, media, and time. A lack of concern for any of these elements weakens the whole program.

MONITOR THE TOTAL SYSTEM

In some communications-intensive companies the cost of communication can be upward of one-fourth of total sales. Obviously, such expenditures warrant careful control.

Wherever possible, managers should gather and analyze all the data related to the communications process. Executives who use industrial stores will have to think as retailers do about such things as traffic (flow of people into the store) and accessibility.

For example, they should monitor the number of visitors to an industrial store, the source of their initial communication, the percentage of "qualified" prospects, and the percentage of sales. Catalog marketers and telemarketers, of course, can monitor such factors as the average size of an order by customer type, the types of products purchased, and frequency of order.

—— EFFECTIVENESS AND EFFICIENCY

This article began by discussing reasons for the evolution of newer communications options which, in essence, developed because of cost pressures and the need to accomplish new tasks. The evolving options save costs in three ways:

1. *Greater impact.* A demonstration center, for example, replaces a great deal of traditional personal selling effort. The concept that a smaller amount of high-impact media is more effective than a larger amount of low-impact media is behind a good deal of the evolving options.
2. *Time saving.* Marketers can save time either through the use of the medium with the greatest impact (as in the demonstration center) or through less travel (as in the case of industrial stores, telemarketing, or catalogs).
3. *Greater coordination and closer control.* Marketers can also eliminate waste through greater coordination, as in national account management, or through the closer control possible in industrial stores, telemarketing centers, and catalog operations than in a traditional field sales force.

In summary, then, careful cost analysis, precise needs specification, creative program formulation, and meticulous monitoring will lead to more effective and efficient communication with greater customer impact and lower costs.

——— DISCUSSION QUESTIONS

1. The reading offers new approaches to reaching customers. Would you say these new ways are an improvement over the traditional methods? Are the authors saying that traditional methods are no longer adequate?

2. How did these new methods evolve? Why do you think they have come into usage? What are their advantages and disadvantages?

3. Are there instances when one of these approaches can bring satisfaction to some customers and dissatisfaction to others? Give an example.

4. As a marketing manager, how would you resolve or minimize the problem set forth in question 3?

Aspects of Sales Management: Key Themes

29

FRANK V. CESPEDES

This reading considers sales management in terms of the representative's role in implementing a company's marketing strategy. It is not an overview of the techniques of selling nor of the sales function. Instead it explores some salient issues to consider in managing sales resources.

After a brief review of the research on selling behaviors, it discusses the unique "boundary role" the salesperson typically plays between the organizations of seller and buyer. Next it looks at various types of selling to focus attention on the nature of the sales task and the appropriate selling behaviors for particular situations. Finally, it presents a framework for thinking about how these factors (and others) interact and influence the nature of sales tasks and sales management requirements facing the firm.

For some decades, marketing textbooks and professors have distinguished carefully between *sales* and *marketing*. The best statement of the difference emphasizes that "selling is preoccupied with the seller's need to convert his product into cash; marketing with the idea of satisfying the needs of the customer by means of the product and the whole cluster of things associated with creating, delivering, and finally consuming it."[1] Nonetheless, whatever else marketing encompasses, it certainly includes selling—the getting and keeping of customers and the revenues they represent. As the old saying goes, "In most companies, sales is the only revenue-generating function; everything else is a cost center." Sales' importance as a source of revenue tends to loom large in defining the form and substance of companies' marketing programs—for both good (e.g., close attention to buying processes at specific accounts) and ill (e.g., confusion between "sales" and "marketing").

In most companies, moreover, the sales force is the major vehicle for implementing marketing strategy. As a result, sales-management policies and procedures for managing customer encounters are core dimensions of the marketing effort.

---

1. Theodore Levitt, "Marketing Myopia," *Harvard Business Review* (July–August 1960).

——— THE SALES REPRESENTATIVE

What is a salesperson? What does it "take" to be good in sales? For generations, researchers and sales managers have asked these questions. Research conducted on sales effectiveness has produced, at best, ambiguous results. It generally focused on uncovering salesperson behaviors, personality traits, and capabilities related to performance.[2] One stream of research examined different types of messages delivered by salespeople. While some have found that a "good presentation" is generally more effective than a "poor presentation"—(especially when the audience for the presentation is more "technically oriented")—these studies have generally found no significant differences in effectiveness between

1. A product-oriented message and a personal-oriented message (academic terminology for getting at the sales manager's distinction between "selling a product" versus "selling yourself" to the prospective customer)
2. "Hard sell" emotional appeals versus "soft sell" rational appeals (in response to the manager's question, "How should we talk to customers?")
3. Different personality traits, such as "forcefulness" or "sociability" (in line with managerial curiosity when considering "what kind of person should we hire for a sales position?")

A second stream of research has examined the link between a salesperson's performance (e.g., meeting or exceeding sales goals) and specific traits presumably related to one's ability to "persuade" another person to buy something. These studies indicated that sales effectiveness *is* related to the salesperson's ability to develop accurate impressions of the customer's beliefs about product functions and the ability to articulate these beliefs (qualities that some researchers call "empathy"). But depending upon the product and/or market situation, the links between sales performance and salesperson traits such as age, education, sales experience, product knowledge, training, intelligence, and empathy are very inconsistent and, for many of these traits, even contradictory. That is, even those variables that can be assessed with high accuracy and reliability (e.g., age, education, and sales experience) are related to performance in some studies and unrelated (or negatively related) in others.

What can a manager take away from such studies? First, the fact that academic studies in these areas are statistically inconsistent and inconclusive

---

2. For good reviews of academic research on sales effectiveness, *see* Barton A. Weitz, "Effectiveness in Sales Interactions: A Contingency Framework," *Journal of Marketing* 45 (Winter 1985): 85–103; David M. Szymanski, "Determinants of Selling Effectiveness: The Importance of Declarative Knowledge," *Journal of Marketing* 52 (January 1988): 64–77; and Thomas W. Leigh and Patrick F. McGraw, "Mapping the Procedural Knowledge of Industrial Sales Personnel," *Journal of Marketing* 53 (January 1989): 16–34. Several chapters in Gilbert A. Churchill, Jr., Neil M. Ford, and Orville C. Walker, Jr., eds., *Sales Force Management*, 3rd ed. (Homewood, Ill.: Irwin, 1990) discuss the research on various issues in sales management.

does *not* mean that these links are nonexistent or unimportant. Clearly, depending upon the sales situation, many of these traits will be vitally important and, conversely, it will be very difficult for a manager to train and motivate poorly selected people to effective sales performance. Many experienced sales managers, reflecting on what it takes to sell effectively in a given situation, can legitimately claim that "I know it when I see it."

Second, the inconsistent results generated by these studies are themselves significant. They strongly suggest that a search for universal selling rules, guidelines, or personalities is probably misguided. So much depends on specific sales conditions that a contingency, or situation-specific, approach is necessary. Simply stated, they suggest that the common stereotype of a good salesperson (loud voice, forceful personality, deep inventory of stories, and a pleasing demeanor) is precisely that—a stereotype, or a conventional, hackneyed mental image that obscures the realities of a situation. Selling jobs vary greatly depending on the kind of product or service sold, the number of customers encountered, and the ancillary requirements (e.g., relative extent of travel, technical knowledge, number and types of people contacted during the sales calls, and the pertinence of customer entertaining). As one observer argues, "Selling is a demanding job, but a great personality is not one of the demands."[3]

Third, the differing results attained, looking at the same factor in different product or market contexts, should remind both researchers and managers that the characteristics of the customer, as well as those of the salesperson, must be considered. The starting point for analyzing sales effectiveness, performance, and requirements should be the specific nature of the sales task; and the nature of the task depends as much on the customer's buying process as on the seller's marketing strategy.

─── THE BOUNDARY ROLE

What does it take to be good in sales? The answer is that different things are important, depending on the specific industry, marketing strategy, and buying situation. But in most companies, the salesperson is at the heart of the company's encounter with customers and therefore plays what some call a "boundary role." Working at the boundary of two different organizations, he or she is required to manage and respond to the often-conflicting rules, procedures, and task requirements of both organizations. (The boundary role of the sales representative is illustrated in *Exhibit 1.*)

Salespeople represent the buyers' organizations in the seller's organization and vice versa. As a result they must interact with many more people than most personnel: internally with sales managers, marketing people, product managers, production and engineering managers, credit personnel,

3. Benson P. Shapiro, *Sales Program Management* (New York: McGraw-Hill, 1977), p. 9.

EXHIBIT 1
The Boundary Role Person

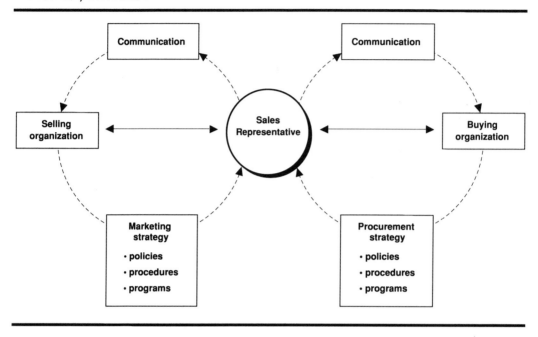

and so on; externally, at their client companies, they must deal with purchasing managers and, depending on the product and buying process, a host of other people.

In performing this boundary role, moreover, field sales representatives are often placed in situations that, in turn, help to define the sales manager's goals, problems, and opportunities. For example, most sales jobs require travel, some "cold calls" (i.e., calling on prospects who do not know the salesperson), time spent in nonselling activities, and bringing back to the selling organization the concerns, complaints, and requirements of different customers. The sales representative, therefore, is often the focus of conflict and controversy within the selling organization and, due to the boundary role he or she performs, is likely to feel a certain psychological as well as physical distance from the organization. Indeed, some have argued that boundary-role personnel are often distrusted by members of their own organizations and that, consequently, many sales policies and procedures can be viewed as attempts to "keep the sales rep under control."[4]

More generally, however, this view of the sales representative empha-

---

4. *See* J. S. Adams, "The Structure and Dynamics of Behavior in Organizational Boundary Roles," in *Handbook of Industrial and Organizational Psychology,* M. Dunnette, ed. (Chicago: Rand McNally, 1976); and Robert E. Spekman, "Organizational Boundary Behavior: A Conceptual Framework for Investigating the Industrial Salesperson," in *Sales Management: New Developments from Behavioral and Decision Model Research,* R. P. Bagozzi, ed. (Cambridge, Mass.: Marketing Science Institute, 1978).

sizes that *the prime objectives of sales management are to aid, focus, and evaluate the effective performance of a boundary role.* It focuses attention on how sales policies, procedures, and programs do—or do not—encourage the kinds of behavior required to perform the boundary role effectively in a given sales job. In turn, this means paying attention to important differences among sales jobs and considering the implications for the kinds of people, training, motivation, and evaluation policies relevant to the activities that a sales representative must perform.

———— A CLASSIFICATION OF SALES JOBS

Can sales tasks be classified in a meaningful, orderly scheme? Again, research in this area has generated diverse, sometimes conflicting results.[5] Moreover, common sense suggests that the range of sales tasks is not likely to remain constant in a competitive economy. Nonetheless, the basis for one influential categorization of sales jobs was provided some years ago by Robert McMurray, who classified salespeople into five categories, briefly described below:[6]

Missionary A missionary salesperson attempts to build goodwill and/or educate the potential user about the company's product line. This salesperson may never book an order personally; instead, the focus is on building sales volume by persuading end users to order from the firm's wholesalers or other channels of distribution. (Example: a sales representative for a pharmaceuticals firm, a soft-drink company, or a distillery who calls on a doctor, restaurant, or bar, respectively, even though the customers in each instance buy from a pharmacy, bottler, or distributor rather than directly from the salesperson.)

Delivery A delivery salesperson's primary responsibility is to increase business from current customers by providing good service (especially order-delivery service) and perhaps promotional assistance. This salesperson often calls on "the trade" (retail or wholesale intermediaries) rather than end users; a common distinction emphasizes that the goal here is to perform tasks aimed at "selling through" the channel rather than "selling to" user customers. This sales emphasis is especially common for consumer goods such as furniture, apparel,

---

5. For a review of various classifications of sales tasks and a suggested taxonomy, *see* William C. Moncrief, "Five Types of Industrial Sales Jobs," *Industrial Marketing Management* 17 (1988): 161–67.

6. Robert N. McMurray, "The Mystique of Super-Salesmanship," *Harvard Business Review* (March–April 1961): 113–22. Another influential classification is by Derek A. Newton, "Get the Most Out of Your Sales Force," *Harvard Business Review* (September–October 1969). Newton delineates four kinds of selling: new-business selling (similar to McMurray's demand-creation category), trade selling (similar to McMurray's delivery selling but with more emphasis on promotional/merchandising assistance), and—identical with McMurray's scheme—missionary selling and technical selling.

textiles, and food; and it is the focus for salespeople in that very substantial part of most economies known as wholesalers.

Order Taker   The order taker is a salesperson who may also call on the trade but does little in the way of service support, merchandising assistance, or "creative selling." The sales process tends to focus on rebuys of familiar, frequently purchased goods. Salespeople for some consumer goods companies often deal with store personnel on this basis; similarly, salespeople at many industrial distributors often tend to interact with customer purchasing personnel on the basis of price and in-stock availability of the goods listed on a purchase order.

Technical Sales   The technical salesperson attempts to increase business, usually from current customers, by providing them with technical assistance in the form of engineering support, applications development, user training, documentation, or perhaps advice and help in setting specifications. The technical salesperson, unlike the missionary or delivery salesperson, usually sells directly to end users. Many industrial salespeople in industries such as chemicals, computers, office products, and heavy machinery are examples of this sales category.

Demand Creation   This final category refers to the salesperson whose primary responsibility is to obtain new accounts for the company through extensive cold calling (or, in the lingo of some industries, "canvassing" or "bird-dogging"). In this sense, the sales task is to create demand for a product by persuading a potential customer who is unfamiliar with the company's product to switch from their existing vendor or to make a new purchase that was never previously considered. Like technical selling, this sales task tends to focus on the users of a product (e.g., the end user, in many product categories, or a key intermediary, such as a building contractor, for many electrical, houseware, and other goods); and it often requires the salesperson to provide a good deal of information about the product to the customer. But, unlike technical selling, "customer education" is secondary to qualities such as sheer persistence, aggressiveness, frequent calls, and the ability to withstand feelings of rejection in the face of many nonpurchase sales visits.

These five categories are not, of course, mutually exclusive. The same salesperson calling on the same account may perform a number of these roles during the sales process and account-management cycle. Further, depending on the seller's marketing strategy and sales-management system, the sales job may differ significantly from company to company, even among those employing similar kinds of sales personnel in the same industry or product category. Thus, applying any classification scheme requires more than a few grains of salt. The virtue of such a scheme, however, is that it focuses attention on a key dimension of the salesperson's boundary role: the nature of the sales task to be accomplished in a given situation and the kinds of behaviors and skills to be encouraged, discouraged, or developed. This is an essential starting point in establishing or changing a sales management system.

—— MANAGING SALES TASKS

Whatever the sales position, the nature of the sales task depends upon an accurate analysis of market conditions and customer behavior in important segments or accounts. Beginning with this analysis, marketing managers attempt to fit their available resources to the opportunities and constraints presented by the environment. This "fit" is essential to developing a coherent marketing strategy: defining the marketing objectives, a plan for achieving those objectives, and making decisions concerning the resources to be allocated among the product categories, markets, and channels in which the company competes. Conversely, if a company has a marketing strategy (as opposed to an abstract set of objectives), then that strategy should have specific implications for the kind of behavior desired among the company's sales personnel.

Thus, a core issue facing sales managers is, how to encourage that desired behavior among sales personnel? As *Exhibit 2* indicates, several factors

EXHIBIT 2
Factors Influencing the Behavior of Sales Personnel

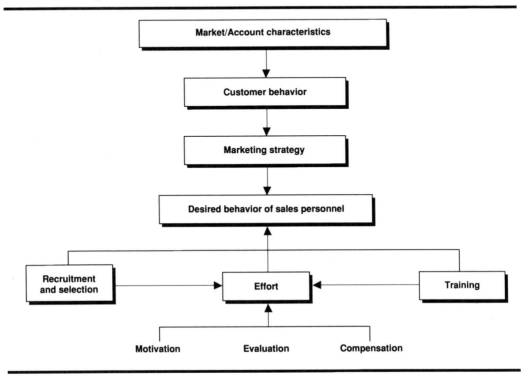

EXHIBIT 3
Linkages Among Motivation, Evaluation, and Compensation

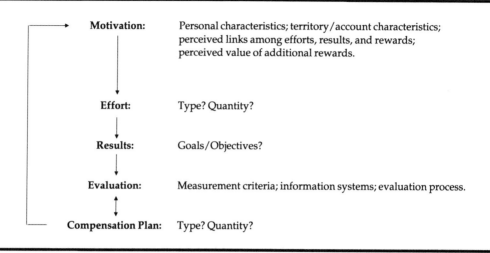

influence the behavior of sales personnel: recruitment and selection policies; the kinds of training provided them; and the components of effort among sales-people.

At one level, then, managing customer encounters means achieving sales performance that is consistent with marketing strategy by guiding field marketing efforts toward desired behavior. This view has two important implications. The first is that, despite the importance and salience of individual abilities in sales, the sales representative is ultimately not an "individual contributor" within the organization; he or she should be viewed as an agent of the firm's marketing strategy and the components of that boundary role influenced accordingly. The second is that recruitment, training, and the factors affecting sales effort should be linked coherently in the policies established to manage sales tasks. Otherwise, the actual performance of these tasks is likely to vary from the behavior required by the firm's marketing strategy.

One way to think about the important linkages among motivation, effort, evaluation, and compensation is suggested by *Exhibit 3.*

Motivation is a core function of management. "How do I get other people to do as much as possible of the right kind of work?" may lack the elegance of current business school terminology, but it is a question at the heart of most managerial responsibilities. In sales, motivation will involve many factors.

One factor is the individual salesperson's personal characteristics, including knowledge, skills, and attitudes. Some people work harder than others, and some are smarter than others. Recruitment criteria and training policies can take these differences into account and attempt to mitigate them. But in most sales organizations, a range of personal abilities must be developed and managed. Another factor is the salesperson's territory or account characteristics, which define the opportunity available to the salesperson and often provide a direction for the salesperson's efforts. In some situations, for example, certain territories and accounts seem to have an inherently higher "yield rate" for sales efforts, independent of the salesperson assigned to that territory or account. Another factor affecting motivation is the salesperson's perceptions of the causal connections among effort, results, and rewards. In some instances, working harder or smarter may *not* translate into better sales results—because of factors such as the firm's product policy, pricing, or competitive situation. In other instances, increased effort by the salesperson may indeed lead to better sales results, but these results are not necessarily acknowledged by the firm's compensation and recognition systems.

Finally, motivation is also influenced by the perceived value of additional rewards. Effort, results, and rewards may be linked, but the amount of effort required may be perceived as disproportionately high relative to compensation received. Many sales incentive systems, for example, pay salespeople for incremental volume increases over the previous year's results, the intention being to motivate field salespeople to develop new business. But in many selling situations, the effort required to develop new business is perceived as "not worth it" by the sales representative who already has a base of mature but steady accounts in his or her territory.

An important outcome of motivation is effort. In a sales organization, effort has *two* important dimensions: type and quantity. Type of effort refers to such factors as the sales force's focus on account development versus account maintenance, the relative emphasis on new versus established products, or (in some situations) an emphasis on selling products that generate revenue and manufacturing volume rather than products that may have higher margins but lower unit sales. Quantity of effort refers to the sheer amount of effort expended by salespeople, as measured by factors such as call frequency, number of accounts, orders booked, or other measures of output. Compensation plans play a role in influencing both types of effort.

Effort presumably leads to results of one kind or another. The issue in sales management is, What goals or objectives should be established in an attempt to guide efforts toward desired results?[7]

While sales volume is probably the most common goal used for sales incentive systems, there are many other possible performance measures applicable to a business. For example:

- *Product mix.* Especially important in a company that sells different items, such as equipment and related supplies used as a system by its customers;

---

7. Some important choices in goal setting and rewarding efforts are discussed in F. V. Cespedes, "Deployment, Focus, and Measuring Effectiveness," Harvard Business School No. 9-590-044.

- *Pricing.* Important when negotiations are an important part of the sales task and the salesperson can exercise control or discretion over price-exception requests by customers;
- *Bad debt/returned goods.* In many companies, such as service merchandisers, this is a major component of selling expenses and of firm profitability or unprofitability in a given quarter;
- *Type of sale.* For example, outright sale versus rental, which often has a major impact on cash flow, the nature of the company's installed base, and future after-market revenues available to the firm;
- *Training.* In some industries, such as computers or corporate software, training is both an important aspect of the sales task and a major source of gross profits.

Having established goals, results must be measured, raising issues concerning the appropriate (or feasible) measurement criteria, the information systems needed to provide the data for such measurements, and the process by which evaluations of effort and results are conducted. There are many possible criteria for evaluating sales performance. Often, however, the company's information systems may not gather the relevant data; or sales force call reports (an important source of sales data in most companies) may be "noisy" or unreliable. Equally important, but often overlooked, is the process by which the evaluation is administered. Even when a salesperson receives a tangible, significant monetary reward for the results of his or her efforts, the process of providing this compensation (i.e., how the compensation plan is administered and implemented via specific performance evaluations of individual salespeople) may be at odds with the company's formal performance evaluation of that person. The result is demotivation or, perhaps worse, motivation to perform the wrong type of sales effort. Many managers assert that they "pay for product, not process"; but if they ignore process in a sales environment, they often don't get what they have paid for.

Finally, the mechanics of the compensation plan must be considered. Here, the important decisions are, again, type and quantity. Type relates to issues such as the relative emphasis on base salary versus incentive pay, while quantity refers both to the total amount of compensation provided relative to industry norms and, within a sales organization, the amount of compensation provided for performing a given sales task.[8]

The important point to emphasize here, however, is the inevitable links (intended or unintended) among sales compensation, evaluation, and motivation. Faced with these links, the framework sketched in *Exhibit 3* provides the following advice: start with the engine—the motivational objectives relevant to the sales situation—and *then* build the transmission—the specific evaluation

---

8. Both these topics are examined in F. V. Cespedes, "Managing Selling and the Salesperson," Harvard Business School No. 9-590-043.

and compensation policies aimed at encouraging specific efforts and behaviors to be adopted by the sales force.

——— A SALES MANAGEMENT SYSTEM

More than most aspects of business, effective sales management requires the ability to recognize the interaction among a set of complex factors while also being able to translate that conceptual understanding into specific action plans that *can* be implemented by the company's field personnel. Because, by their very nature, sales-management decisions directly affect a company's revenue stream and interactions with customers, marketing managers must above all understand the consequences of field selling decisions on many other parts of the organization. The emphasis in sales-management policies and practices will affect the quantity and kinds of orders received by manufacturing, the cash-flow profile of the business managed by finance, the recruitment and training needs facing marketing and personnel, and the daily organizational interactions between sales and all of these other functional areas.

Exhibit 4 serves two purposes: first, it suggests a framework that helps to place in context some of the topics discussed in this reading, such as the nature of the salesperson's boundary role, the central importance of an analysis of sales tasks, and the different roles played by elements of sales management in influencing the sales force toward appropriate selling behaviors. Second, it can also help to remind us, at the outset of our investigations into field marketing requirements, of other aspects of sales management that were *not* discussed in this introductory overview but that are nonetheless important in analyzing sales situations.

In *Exhibit 4*, the box labeled "Sales Force Control Systems" refers to aspects of sales management that are relatively quantitative and measurable in nature, susceptible to "management-by-objectives" or policy direction on the part of sales management. This includes attention in a given situation to the impact on sales personnel of the performance-measurement, evaluation, compensation, and training systems in place at a company. By contrast, "Sales Force Environment" refers to more qualitative issues concerning the impact of human resource patterns (e.g., amount of turnover in the sales force), communication patterns (amount and types of communications among sales personnel), interaction patterns (e.g., how conflicts are managed), and management patterns (e.g., how goals are set and results rewarded). The policy (quantitative aspects of control systems) and the process (qualitative aspects of the sales force environment) affect each other. That is, what a company measures and rewards, for example, will affect process in its sales force; conversely, how salespeople interact should affect what a company decides to measure, train, and reward. In turn, both the control systems and the environment will affect the focus of the company's sales personnel, their selling behaviors, and their performance of required sales tasks.

EXHIBIT 4
A Sales Management Framework

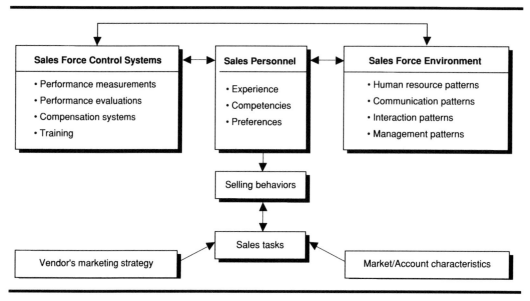

Using the framework in *Exhibit 4*, consider the following questions as you analyze a sales organization:

1. What is the vendor's marketing strategy for its product(s) or service(s), and what does this strategy imply for the role of personal selling activities at the company?

2. What do specific market-segment conditions, or account characteristics, imply for the kinds of tasks that must be performed effectively by the company's field sales personnel?

3. Who *are* the salespeople at the company (both the formal sales force and other personnel responsible for customer encounters)? What is the nature of their experience, skills, competencies, and selling preferences?

4. What control systems are used by management to influence sales force behavior? To what extent are sales force productivity measurements, performance evaluations of individual salespeople, the emphasis in the compensation system, or the nature of current sales training programs in line with your analysis of the requirements of the sales task?

5. How well or poorly are these control systems being implemented? What is the effect of human resource, communication, or interaction patterns between sales rep and sales manager on sales force behavior?

6. Finally, what gaps exist between the requirements of sales tasks and current selling behaviors, and what should the company do to address these gaps?

The basic idea behind this perspective is that a sales management system must integrate three factors internal to the sales organization—the people involved, the systems established to try to influence their behaviors (sales force control systems), and how those systems are applied or misapplied in the sales organization (sales force environment)—with two sets of factors external to the sales organization: the vendor's marketing strategy (e.g., "push" versus "pull" emphasis and the consequent impact on the role of sales personnel) and key market/account characteristics (e.g., buying processes and market structure). The latter, external factors largely determine what sales tasks will be required; the former, internal factors have the objective of influencing selling behaviors so that these sales tasks are performed in a way that is consistent with strategic goals.

When there is coherent integration among these factors, the company is focusing on customer encounters and "selling" has traveled a long way toward effective "marketing."

Copyright © 1989; revised 1991.

DISCUSSION QUESTIONS

1. Locate a recent feature article from the business press (e.g., *Business Week, Fortune, Sales and Marketing Management*) about a company that employs salespeople. Use the information in the article to describe the role of personal selling in that company's marketing strategy. What does the company's strategy—and the developments in its industry—imply for the key boundary-role requirements facing its salespeople?

2. The author cites a common five-category classification of sales jobs: (1) Missionary, (2) Delivery, (3) Order Taker, (4) Technical Sales, and (5) Create Demand. What are the important differences in key responsibilities among these generic types of sales jobs? What kinds of challenges and problems would you expect each type of salesperson to encounter? What kinds of skills become important to build and maintain in training programs for each type of sales job?

3. Consider how one or more of the following factors will affect selling and sales-management requirements during the next decade: (1) increased use of resellers and multiple channels of distribution; (2) more multinational and global accounts with multiple, geographically dispersed buying locations and buying influences; (3) shorter product life cycles; (4) the development of flexible manufacturing systems that enable companies to add options and customize products at relatively low incremental costs; and (5) the continuing diffusion of on-line electronic links between suppliers and buyers in many industries.

4. "Selling is preoccupied with the seller's need to convert a product into cash; marketing is preoccupied with the idea of satisfying the needs of the customer by means of the product and the whole cluster of things associated with creating, delivering, and finally consuming it." Do you agree? What do these descriptions of "selling" and "marketing" imply for the proper relationship between the sales and marketing functions in a company? What issues are likely to arise between those responsible for each set of sales and marketing activities?

After the Sale Is Over . . . 30

THEODORE LEVITT

As our economy becomes more service and technology oriented, marketers must shift their focus from simply making the sale to ensuring customer satisfaction after the purchase. As the author points out in this reading, buyers no longer purchase products and services but sets of expectations as well. Thus, the buyer-seller relationship often intensifies once the sale has been made, and this helps determine the buyer's choice the next time around. To keep buyers happy, vendors must maintain constructive interaction with purchasers—which includes responding to their complaints and anticipating their future needs. This reading offers suggestions for doing the best job possible of nurturing buyer-seller relationships.

The relationship between a seller and a buyer seldom ends when a sale is made. Increasingly, the relationship intensifies after the sale and helps determine the buyer's choice the next time around. Such dynamics are found particularly with services and products dealt in a stream of transactions between seller and buyer—financial services, consulting, general contracting, military and space equipment, and capital goods.

The sale, then, merely consummates the courtship, at which point the marriage begins. How good the marriage is depends on how well the seller manages the relationship. The quality of the marriage determines whether there will be continued or expanded business, or troubles and divorce. In some cases divorce is impossible, as when a major construction or installation project is under way. If the marriage that remains is burdened, it tarnishes the seller's reputation.

Companies can avoid such troubles by recognizing at the outset the necessity of managing their relationships with customers. This takes special attention to an often ignored aspect of relationships: time.

The theory of supply and demand presumes that the work of the economic system is time-discrete and bare of human interaction—that an instantaneous, disembodied sales transaction clears the market at the intersection of supply and demand. This was never completely accurate and has become less so as product complexity and interdependencies have intensified. Buyers of automated machinery, unlike buyers at a flea market, do not walk home with their purchases and take their chances. They expect installation services, application aids, parts, postpurchase repair and maintenance, retrofitted enhancements,

EXHIBIT 1
Purchase Cycles and Assurances

ITEM	PURCHASE CYCLE (in years)	ITEM	PREVIOUS ASSURANCE	PRESENT ASSURANCE
Oil field installation	15 to 20	Tankers	Spot	Charter
		Apartments	Rental	Cooperative
Chemical plant	10 to 15	Auto warranties	10,000 miles	100,000 miles
EDP system	5 to 10	Technology	Buy	Lease
Weapons system	20 to 30	Labor	Hire	Contracts
Major components of steel plant	5 to 10	Supplies	Shopping	Contracting
		Equipment	Repair	Maintenance
Paper supply contract	5			

and vendor R&D to keep the products effective and up to date for as long as possible and to help the company stay competitive.

The buyer of a continuous stream of transactions, like a frozen-food manufacturer that buys its cartons from a packaging company and its cash-management services from a bank, is concerned not only with completing transactions but also with maintaining the process. Due to the growing complexity of military equipment, even the Department of Defense makes most of its purchases in units of less than a hundred and therefore has to repeat transactions often.

Because the purchase cycles of products and major components are increasingly stretched, the needs that must be tended to have changed. Consider the purchase cycles and the changing assurances backing purchases (see *Exhibit 1*). Under these conditions, a purchase decision is not a decision to buy an item (to have a casual affair) but a decision to enter a bonded relationship (to get married). This requires of the would-be seller a new orientation and a new strategy.

Selling by itself is no longer enough. Consider the compelling differences between the old and the new selling arrangements *Exhibit 2* illustrates. In the selling scheme the seller is located at a distance from buyers and reaches out with a sales department to unload products on them. This is the basis for the notion that a salesperson needs charisma, because it is charisma rather than the product's qualities that makes the sale.

Consider, by contrast, marketing. Here the seller, being physically close to buyers, penetrates their domain to learn about their needs, desires, and fears and then designs and supplies the product with those considerations in mind. Instead of trying to get buyers to want what the seller has, the seller tries to have

EXHIBIT 2
The Change from Selling to Marketing

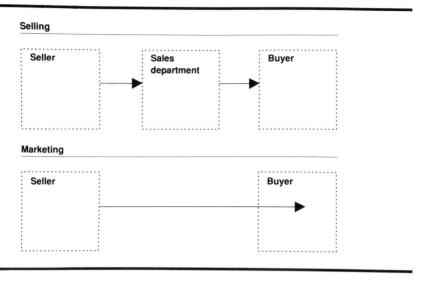

Selling

| Seller | → | Sales department | → | Buyer |

Marketing

| Seller | ————————→ | Buyer |

what they want. The "product" is no longer merely an item but a whole bundle of values that satisfy buyers—an "augmented" product.[1]

Thanks to increasing interdependence, more and more of the world's economic work gets done through long-term relationships between sellers and buyers. It is not a matter of just getting and then holding on to customers. It is more a matter of giving the buyers what they want. Buyers want vendors who keep promises, who'll keep supplying and standing behind what they promised. The era of the one-night stand is gone. Marriage is both necessary and more convenient. Products are too complicated, repeat negotiations too much of a hassle and too costly. Under these conditions, success in marketing is transformed into the inescapability of a relationship. Interface becomes interdependence.

Under these circumstances, being a good marketer in the conventional sense is not enough. When it takes five years of intensive work between seller and buyer to "deliver" an operating chemical plant or a telecommunications system, much more is required than the kind of marketing that simply 'lands the contract. The buyer needs assurance at the outset that the two parties can work well together during the long period in which the purchase gets transformed into delivery.

The seller and the buyer have different capital structures, competitive conditions, costs, and incentives driving the commitments they make to each

---

1. *See* Theodore Levitt, "Marketing Success Through Differentiation—of Anything," *Harvard Business Review* (January–February 1980): 83.

EXHIBIT 3
Perceptions of Product Values

CATEGORY	PAST	PRESENT	FUTURE
Item	Product	Augmented product	System contracts
Sale	Unit	System	System over time
Value	Feature advantages	Technology advantages	System advantages
Leadtime	Short	Long	Lengthy
Service	Modest	Important	Vital
Delivery place	Local	National	Global
Delivery phase	Once	Often	Continually
Strategy	Sales	Marketing	Relationship

other. The seller has made a sale that is expected to yield a profit. The buyer has bought a tool with which to produce things to yield a profit. For the seller it is the end of the process; for the buyer, only the beginning. Yet their interdependence is inescapable and profound. To make these differently motivated dependencies work, the selling company must understand the relationship and plan its management in advance of the wedding. It can't get out the marriage manual only after trouble has begun.

────── THE PRODUCT'S CHANGING NATURE

The future will be marked by intense business relationships in all areas of marketing, including frequently purchased consumer goods. Procter & Gamble, copying General Mills's Betty Crocker advisory service, has found that the installation of a consumer hot line to give advice on its products and their uses has cemented customer brand loyalty.

In the industrial setting we have only to review changing perceptions of various aspects of product characteristics to appreciate the new emphasis on relationships (see *Exhibit 3*). The common characteristic of the terms in the "future" column of this exhibit is time. What is labeled "item" in the first column was in the past simply a product, something that was bought for its own value. More recently that simple product has not been enough. Instead, buyers have bought augmented products.

During the era we are entering the emphasis will be on systems contracts, and buyer-seller relationships will be characterized by continuous contact and evolving relationships to effect the systems. The "sale" will be not just a system but a system over time. The value at stake will be the advantages of that total system over time. As the customer gains experience, the technology will decline in importance relative to the system that enables the buyer to realize the benefits of the technology. Services, delivery, reliability, responsiveness, and the quality of the human and organizational interactions between seller and buyer will be more important than the technology itself.

The more complex the system and the more "software" (including operating procedures and protocols, management routines, and service components) it requires, the greater the customer's anxieties and expectations. People buy expectations, not things. They buy the expectations of benefits promised by the vendor. When it takes a long time to fulfill the promise (to deliver a new custom-made automated workstation, for example) or when fulfillment is continual over a long period (as it is in banking services, fuel deliveries, or shipments of components for assembly operations), the buyer's anxieties build up after the purchase decision is made. Will the delivery be prompt? Will it be smooth and regular? Did we select the best vendor?

DIFFERING EXPECTATIONS

When downstream realities loom larger than up-front promises, what do you do before, during, and after the sale? Who should be responsible for what?

To answer these questions it helps to understand how the promises and behavior of the vendor, before the sale is made, shape the customer's expectations. It is reasonable for a customer who has been promised the moon to expect it to be delivered. But if those who make the promises are paid commissions before the customer gets everything he or she bargained for, they're not likely to feel compelled to ensure that the customer gets fully satisfied later. After the sale, they'll rush off to pursue other prey. If marketing plans the sale, sales makes it, manufacturing fulfills it, and service services it, who's in charge and who takes responsibility for the whole process?

Problems arise not only because those who do the selling, the marketing, the manufacturing, and the servicing have varying incentives and views of the customer but also because organizations are one-dimensional. With the exception of those who work in sales or marketing, people seldom see beyond their company's walls. For those inside those walls, inside is where the work gets done, where the penalties and incentives are doled out, where the budgets and plans get made, where engineering and manufacturing are done, where performance is measured, where one's friends and associates gather, where things are managed and manageable. Outside "has nothing to do with me" and is where "you can't change things."

Many disjunctions exist between seller and buyer at various stages of the sales process. These may be simply illustrated, as in *Exhibit 4*.

AFTER THE FACT

The fact of buying changes the dynamics of the relationship. The buyer expects the seller to remember the purchase as having been a favor bestowed, not as something earned by the seller. Hence it is wrong to assume that getting an account gives you an advantage because you've got a foot in the door. The opposite is more often the case. The buyer who views the sale as a favor conferred on the seller in effect debits the seller's account. The seller owes the buyer one and is in the position of having to rebuild the relationship from a deficit stance.

In the absence of good management, the relationship deteriorates because both organizations tend naturally to face inward rather than outward toward each other. The natural tendency of relationships, whether in marriage or in business, is toward erosion of sensitivity and attentiveness. Inward orientation by the selling organization leads to insensitivity and unresponsiveness in customer relations. At best the company substitutes bureaucratic formalities for authentic interaction.

A healthy relationship maintains, and preferably expands, the equity and the possibilities that were created during courtship. A healthy relationship requires a conscious and constant fight against the forces of decline. It becomes important for sellers regularly and seriously to consider whether the relationship is improving or deteriorating, whether their promises are being completely fulfilled, whether they are neglecting anything, and how they stand

EXHIBIT 4
Varying Reactions and Perceptions Before and During Sale Process

WHEN THE SALE IS FIRST MADE

Seller	*Buyer*
Objective achieved	Judgment postponed; applies test of time
Selling stops	Shopping continues
Focus goes elsewhere	Focus on purchase; wants affirmation that expectations have been met
Tension released	Tension increased
Relationship reduced or ended	Commitment made; relationship intensified

THROUGHOUT THE PROCESS

Stage of Sale	*Seller*	*Buyer*
1 Before	Real hope	Vague need
2 Romance	Hot and heavy	Testing and hopeful
3 Sale	Fantasy: bed	Fantasy: board
4 After	Looks elsewhere for next sale	"You don't care"
5 Long after	Indifferent	"Can't this be made better?"
6 Next sale	"How about a new one?"	"Really?"

EXHIBIT 5
Actions That Affect Relationships

POSITIVE ACTIONS	NEGATIVE ACTIONS
Initiate positive phone calls	Make only callbacks
Make recommendations	Make justifications
Use candid language	Use accommodative language
Use phone	Use correspondence
Show appreciation	Wait for misunderstandings
Make service suggestions	Wait for service requests
Use "we" problem-solving language	Use "owe us" legal language
Get to problems	Respond only to problems
Use jargon or shorthand	Use long-winded communications
Air personality problems	Hide personality problems
Talk of "our future together"	Talk about making good on the past
Routinize responses	Fire drill/emergency responsiveness
Accept responsibility	Shift blame
Plan the future	Rehash the past

vis-à-vis their competitors. *Exhibit 5* compares actions that affect—for better or worse—relationships with buyers.

BUILDING DEPENDENCIES

One of the surest signs of a bad or declining relationship is the absence of complaints from the customer. Nobody is ever *that* satisfied, especially not over an extended period of time. The customer is either not being candid or not being contacted—probably both. The absence of candor reflects the decline of trust and the deterioration of the relationship. Bad things accumulate. Impaired communication is both a symptom and a cause of trouble. Things fester inside. When they finally erupt, it's usually too late or too costly to correct the situation.

We can invest in relationships, and we can borrow from them. We all do both, but we seldom account for our actions and almost never manage them. Yet a company's most precious asset is its relationships with its customers. What matters is not whom you know but how you are known to them.

Not all relationships can or need be of the same duration or at the same level of intimacy. These factors depend on the extent of the actual or felt dependency between the buyer and the seller. And of course those dependencies can be extended or contracted through various direct links that can be established between the two parties. Thus, when Bergen Brunswig, the booming drug and health care products distributor, puts computer terminals in its customers' offices to enable them to order directly and get instant feedback regarding their sales and inventory, it creates a new link that helps tie the customer to the vendor.

At the same time, however, the seller can become dependent on the buyer in important ways. Most obvious is vendor reliance on the buyer for a certain percentage of its sales. More subtle is reliance on the buyer for important information, including how the buyer's business will change, how changes will affect future purchases, and what competitors are offering in the way of substitute products or materials, at what prices, and including which services. The buyer can also answer questions like these for the vendor. How well is the vendor fulfilling the customer's needs? Is performance up to promises from headquarters? To what new uses is the customer putting the product?

The seller's ability to forecast the buyer's intentions rests on the quality of the overall relationship. In a good relationship the buyer shares plans and expectations with the vendor, or at least makes available relevant information. With that information the vendor can better serve the buyer. Surprises and bad forecasts are symptoms of bad relationships. In such instances, everybody— even the buyer—loses.

Thus, a system of reciprocal dependencies develops. It is up to the seller to nurture the relationship beyond its simple dollar value. In a proper relationship both the buyer and the seller will benefit or the relationship will not last.

Moreover, both parties should understand that the seller's expenses rarely end with acquisition costs. This means that the vendor should work at convincing the customer of the importance of maintaining the vendor's long-term profitability at a comfortable level instead of squeezing to get rock-bottom delivered prices. Unless the costs of the expected postpurchase services are reflected in the price, the buyer will end up paying extra in money, in delays, and in aggravation. The smart relationship manager in the selling company will help the buyer do long-term life-cycle costing to assess the vendor's offering.

BONDS THAT LAST

Professional partnerships—in law, medicine, architecture, consulting, investment banking, and advertising—rate and reward associates by their client relationships. Like any other assets, these relationships can appreciate or depreciate. Their maintenance and enhancement depend not so much on good manners, public relations, tact, charm, window dressing, or manipulation as they do on management. Relationship management requires companywide maintenance, investment, improvement, and even replacement programs. The results can be spectacular.

Examine the case of the North Sea oil and gas fields. Norway and Britain urged and facilitated exploration and development of those resources. They were eager and even generous hosts to the oil companies. The companies, though they spent hundred of millions of dollars to do the work, didn't fully

EXHIBIT 6
Cumulative Cash Flow History of an Account

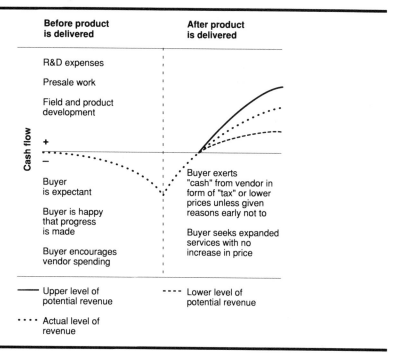

nurture their relationships. When oil and gas suddenly started to flow, the host countries levied taxes exceeding 90% of the market prices. No one was more surprised than the companies. Why should they have been surprised? Had they built sound relationships with the governments, the politicians, and the voters—by whatever means—so as to have created a sense of mutuality and partnership, they might have moderated the size of the taxes. What would it have been worth?

This is not an isolated occurrence. The same problem crops up in similar circumstances where vendors are required to make heavy expenditures to get accounts and develop products. *Exhibit 6* depicts cash flows to a vendor of this type during the life of the account. During the customer-getting and development period, cash flows are negative and the customer eagerly encourages the expenditures. When the product is delivered or the joint venture becomes operative, cumulative cash flows turn up and finally become positive. In the case of the North Sea, the surprising new high taxes represent the difference between what revenues to the oil companies might have been (the upper level of potential revenue) and what they actually became. With worse relationships they might, of course, have fallen to an even lower level of potential revenue.

Consider also the case of Gillette North America. It has four separate sales forces and special programs for major accounts to ensure Gillette's rapid and smooth response to customers' requirements. Gillette also has a vice president of business relations who counts among his major duties cultivation of relationships with major retailers and distributors. This VP carries out that responsibility via a vast array of ceremonial activities ranging from entertainment at trade association conventions to organization of special events for major accounts in connection with the annual All-Star baseball game, the World Series, the Superbowl, and the NCAA playoffs. These activities establish bonds and affirm reciprocal obligations and benefits.

Some companies now require engineering and manufacturing people to spend time with customers and users in the field—not just to get product and design ideas or feedback regarding present products but also to get to know and to respond to customers in deep and abiding ways so as to build relationships and bonds that last. The Sperry Corporation's much-advertised "listening" campaign has included training employees to listen and communicate effectively with each other and with customers.

All too often company officials take action instead of spending time. It is all too easy to act first and later try to fix the relationship, instead of the other way around. It is all too simple to say, "We'll look into it and call you back" or "Let's get together for lunch sometime." These are tactics of diversion and delay, not of relationship building.

When a purchase cycle is long—as when a beer-making plant contracts with a can-making vendor to build a factory next door, or when the U.S. Air Force commits itself to buying a jet engine with a life of 20 to 30 years—the people in the vendor organization who did the selling and those in the customer organization who did the buying will be replaced over the course of those relationships. So, in all likelihood, will the entire upper levels of management on both sides. What must the seller do to ensure continuity of good relations? What is expected of the customer when people who did the buying are changed and gone? Clearly the idea is to build bonds that last no matter who comes and goes.

MAKING IT HAPPEN

To effectively manage relationships, managers must meet four requirements:

1. *Awareness.* Understand both the problem and the opportunity areas.
2. *Assessment.* Determine where the company now stands, especially in terms of what's necessary to achieve the desired results.
3. *Accountability.* Establish regular reporting on individual relationships, and then on group relationships, so that these can be weighed against other measures of performance.
4. *Actions.* Make decisions and allocations and establish routines and communications on the basis of their impact on the targeted relationships. Constantly reinforce awareness and actions.

Relationship management can be institutionalized, but in the process it must also be humanized. One company has regular sensitivity sessions and role-playing seminars in which sales officials assume the buyer role. It also conducts debriefings on meetings with customers. And it requires its customer-contact people (including those who make deliveries and handle receivables) to regularly ask of various accounts the seminal questions: How are we doing in the relationship? Is it going up or down? Are we talking with the right people about the right issues? What have we *not* done lately?

The emphasis on "lately" is not incidental. It reflects the recognition that relationships naturally degrade and have to be reinvigorated. If I owe you a favor, I forget—but you don't. And when I've done you a favor, you feel obligated—but not for long. You ask, "What have you done for me lately?" A relationship credit must be cashed in or it expires, and it must be used soon or it depreciates.

Another way companies can institutionalize relationship management is by establishing routines that ensure the right kinds of customer contacts. A well-known Wall Street investment firm requires its security analysts and salespeople to make regular constructive contacts with their institutional customers. *Constructive* is defined as conveying useful information to them. The firm has set up a regular Monday-morning investment strategy "commentary" that analysts and salespeople can convey by telephone to their customers. In addition, each analyst must develop periodic industry commentaries and updates, to be mailed or telephoned to customers. Analysts and salespeople are required to keep logs of these contacts, which are compiled, counted, and communicated to all in a weekly companywide report. Those salespeople and analysts making the fewest contacts have to explain their inaction to supervisors.

The firm allocates end-of-year bonuses on the basis of not only commissions earned from the various institutions but also the number and types of contacts initiated and maintained. Meanwhile, the firm conducts regular sensitivity-training sessions to enhance the contacts and the quality of the relationships. The results, which show that the efforts have been highly successful, are analyzed and made known to all, thus reinforcing the importance of the process.

Relationship management is a special field all its own, and is as important to preserving and enhancing the intangible asset commonly known as "goodwill" as is the management of hard assets. The fact that it is probably more difficult makes hard work at it that much more important.

──── DISCUSSION QUESTIONS

1. The author states that buyers no longer purchase products and services but sets of expectations. What does he mean by this? How does this translate from the customer's point of view? From the vendor's point of view?

2. Do all products and services require the same degree of relationship cultivation? Assume you have a sought-after product. Is there any reason to nurture a relationship with the buyer once the sale is consummated? For what reasons? Is it just a matter of getting and then holding on to the customer? Or do the expectations of each party differ?

3. Explain the difference between selling and marketing. What can happen when the vendor completes a sale, considers the transaction closed, and feels free to move on to the next prospect, while the buyer expects the seller "to remember the purchase as having been a favor bestowed"? How should good management resolve these two opposing attitudes?

4. The author claims that the absence of complaints from a customer is a sure sign of a bad relationship and a dissatisfied customer. How can this be? Do you agree?

5. Certain links established between vendor and buyer can serve to nurture and strengthen their relationship. The closer their relationship becomes, the stronger their dependency on each other. Are there any disadvantages to this relationship? What does the vendor—and the buyer—gain from this interdependency?

Close Encounters of the Four Kinds: Managing Customers in a Rapidly Changing Environment

31

BENSON P. SHAPIRO

This reading* first describes four approaches to selling and explains the advantages, disadvantages, and risks of each. Next, it compares the four approaches and offers some guidelines for segmenting a company's customer base to the most appropriate—and cost-effective—approach for each.

Finally, it discusses in depth the relationship approaches to selling—in particular strategic-account relationships—which are responses to more complex customer demands as well as to a vendor's own technology and applications needs and competitive position. These new selling relationships, which embody importance, intimacy, and longevity for both vending and buying companies, are not simply better sales techniques. They are a wholly different philosophical approach based on continuity, trust, and mutual advantage. They offer great opportunities, rewards, and risks in the limited number of selling situations for which they are appropriate.

Get close to your customers and do what they want—be customer oriented!

Don't give away the store!

Selling is dead; there was respect, and courtship, and gratitude in it. Today it's all cut and dried, and there's no chance for bringing friendship to bear or personality.[1]

Customer relationships are more important than they have ever before been!

**The author gratefully acknowledges the help of colleagues Thomas V. Bonoma, Rosabeth M. Kanter, Thomas J. Kosnik, Rowland T. Moriarty, Jr., Roy D. Shapiro, and Richard S. Tedlow in preparing this reading, as well as Michele Marram of Harvard's Baker Library.*

1. Arthur Miller, *Death of a Salesman* (New York: The Viking Press, 1949), p. 81 (speech by Willy Loman).

There are many different ways to think about the role of selling and customer relations in a complex world. Perhaps the truest statement about relationships between buyers and sellers appears in *Death of a Salesman* by Arthur Miller. But, it wasn't made by Willy Loman, the salesman. It was made by his devoted wife, Linda: "It's changing, Willy, I can feel it changing."[2]

The management of account relationships, particularly those between organizations such as businesses or between businesses and major institutions such as governments, *has* changed; it has grown more varied and more difficult. We need new ways to look at selling and serving customers.

The discussion begins by examining four distinct ways to sell, emphasizing the differences among them and their relative strengths and weaknesses. The last half of the paper focuses on a new form of selling—the strategic-account relationship, a very complex approach that is replete with traps and expenses. It does not receive this attention because it is a panacea or even an appropriate choice for every vendor. It is not! The best way to understand its usefulness is to compare it with simpler, yet very serviceable approaches.

—— FOUR APPROACHES TO SELLING

For many years, indeed, back to the days of open markets and caravan traders, personal selling was a fairly simple activity, consisting of a single exchange or a series of exchanges. We can call this type of selling *transaction selling*. During the last few decades we have seen the introduction and development of three more sophisticated forms: *systems sales, major-account management,* and *strategic-account relationships.*

TRANSACTION SELLING

In transaction selling the exchange is generally quite discrete, with a product or service moving from seller to buyer and money moving in the other direction after a period of negotiation and information transfer. This approach is still useful for selling fairly simple products—ranging from office furniture to standard electronic products to raw materials—in a one-time exchange or a continuing series of exchanges. The product is usually purchased on the basis of physical attributes, availability, convenience, or price. The seller views each sales transaction as the outcome of immediately preceding efforts and as one of a series of transactions separated by "down time" for servicing the account.

---

2. Ibid., p. 74.

SYSTEMS SALES

The advent of complex businesses required that the transaction approach be supplemented by heightened concern for customer benefits and integration of system components. A system consists of separate pieces, including capital equipment, parts, supplies, and services. Office and factory automation systems are typical examples, but petrochemical complexes and textile mills also fit the systems description. The systems sale necessitated the introduction and development of new sales techniques such as team selling, in which several departments or functional areas (applications engineering, design, field service, etc.) of the vendor are involved in the sales process.[3]

Systems sales are also used when the system is not a product but a program. In consumer packaged goods, for example, the system may be a promotional program involving several different product lines, national advertising, cooperative advertising, and in-store promotions. The system can also be a related set of services, such as a cash-management service sold to a company with many locations and bank accounts.

Thus the systems sale differs in size and complexity from the transaction sale as well as in the ratio of service time to actual selling time. Nonetheless, the heart of the activity remains the sales transaction, and there is still a tendency to view the time between sales as down time. The approach is more sophisticated but the fundamental philosophy is not.

MAJOR-ACCOUNT MANAGEMENT

The increasing size and complexity of sales and the development of purchasing approaches like national contracts and master purchasing agreements has led to more intimacy and permanence in buyer-seller relations. Instead of buying a product or service, or even a set of products and services (as in the systems purchase), the customer literally purchases a relationship with a vendor. Major-account management, or national-account management, developed because customers transcend regional sales boundaries. Major-account management, still evolving and growing in popularity, is becoming the crème de la crème of personal selling.[4] Its core is an account manager who quarterbacks the approach to the customer and employs the vendor's resources for the customer's benefit. Primary issues in national-account programs include organizational structure and the quality of support provided by functional

3. Benson P. Shapiro and Ronald S. Posner, "Making the Major Sale," *Harvard Business Review* (March–April 1979).

4. Benson P. Shapiro and John Wyman, "New Ways to Reach Your Customers," *Harvard Business Review* (July–August 1981); Benson P. Shapiro and Rowland T. Moriarty, Jr., *National Account Management*, and *National Account Management: Emerging Insights* (Cambridge, Mass.: Marketing Science Institute, 1980, 1982).

EXHIBIT 1
Four Selling Approaches

TRANSACTION ORIENTATION	*RELATIONSHIP ORIENTATION*
1. Transaction Selling	3. Major-Account Management
2. Systems Sales	4. Strategic-Account Relationships

groups other than the sales operation.[5] Its essence is an on-going relationship with a major vendor based on intense, well-coordinated service support.

Account management also signals a change in sales philosophy. Actual sales transactions "are seen as the punctuation marks of a larger relationship. Sales are 'natural fallout.' "[6] The whole concept of selling has changed. In essence, it has shifted from a transaction orientation to a relationship orientation (see *Exhibit 1*). Whereas the systems sale is simply a more important and more complex transaction, major-account management is a fundamental change in conception. *Exhibit 2* highlights the differences between transaction selling and relationship creation.

Account management is expensive and difficult. It can be used only for major customers. And, to be effective, it must be seen as a philosophy of customer commitment, not as a collection of advanced persuasion techniques. Its essence is superior customer responsiveness based on outstanding support systems. It goes beyond selling. Moreover, it has laid the foundation for strategic-account relationships; for, in spite of its opportunities and rewards, as well as its significant investments and costs, even major- or national-account management cannot completely satisfy the evolving needs for closer, more permanent vendor-customer relationships. Joint product, service, and infrastructure developments have led to even more intimate buyer-seller relations. Strategic-account relationships are one of several types of coalitions formed between companies that may be related as competitors, buyers and sellers, or sharers of technology or resources.[7]

STRATEGIC-ACCOUNT RELATIONSHIPS

Because strategic-account relationships are a new and specialized approach, there are few publicly documented examples. Furthermore, several are proprietary and thus beyond discussion here. It is instructive, however, to look at several examples.

---

5. Benson P. Shapiro and Rowland T. Moriarty, Jr., *Organizing the National Account Force,* and *Support Systems for National Account Management Programs* (Cambridge, Mass.: Marketing Science Institute, 1983).

6. Quoting from a speech by Professor Thomas V. Bonoma of the Harvard Business School.

7. For other types of coalitions, *see,* for example, Michael E. Porter, *Competitive Advantage* (New York: Free Press, 1985), pp. 191–93, for a discussion of licensing; and Joseph L. Bower and Eric A. Rhenman, "Benevolent Cartels," *Harvard Business Review* (July–August 1985).

EXHIBIT 2
Transactions and Relationships

TRANSACTION SELLING	RELATIONSHIP CREATION
1. Selling dominates learning.	1. Learning about the customer is intense and dominates selling.
2. Talking dominates listening.	2. Listening dominates talking.
3. Persuading the customer is product-driven and benefits-focused.	3. Teaching the customer is need-driven and problem-focused.
4. The goal is to build buyers and sales through persuasion, price, presence, and terms.	4. The goal is to build relationships through credibility, responsiveness, and trust.

Source: This exhibit is based on a chart by Thomas V. Bonoma.

The first is the Hartford Component Company, the disguised name of a manufacturer of a specialized component of measuring instruments. In the past Hartford competed directly with several companies that use the same technology and with others whose components are based on a competing technology. One of Hartford's primary customers, New Haven Instrument (N.H.I.), made measuring instruments for chemical analysis and medical diagnosis; several of its products were based on the Hartford component. After several months of negotiation—and following years of successful vendor-supplier relations—the companies agreed to a joint-development effort. Hartford management understood that to develop its technology further it needed more knowledge of product use, additional technical expertise in several related engineering disciplines, and an assured outlet for a new product whose development would require substantial investments in time and funds. N.H.I., for its part, faced intense international competition and needed a technological "leg up" to improve its market position. It lacked the ability to develop the component technology and wanted to leverage its strong customer relationships, applications knowledge, and skill in related technologies. The companies—each of which had sales of $50 million to $200 million—did not wish to merge; but each needed a more important, intimate, and permanent connection than their preferred vendor–major customer relation.

Their strategic partnership involved a joint-development project, information exchange, and a carefully developed sales agreement that gave N.H.I. a temporary exclusive right to purchase components and Hartford an assured source of sales. Despite the high cost, substantial required level of organizational cooperation and integration, and considerable loss of autonomy for each, both companies saw the arrangement as worthwhile. Because they managed the relationship well and had carefully defined expectations, both companies gained.

This example demonstrates three attributes upon which strategic-account relationships must always be based.

1. Mutual importance
2. Intimacy
3. Longevity

Importance usually involves three forms of interdependence: financial, technological and/or design, and strategic. One company must be exceedingly important to the other financially; sometimes, as in the Hartford–New Haven case, the companies are financially important to each other. Technological and/or design cooperation is at the heart of most strategic partnerships and is the element that most clearly separates companies that will profit most from strategic-account relationships from those better suited to a traditional relationship. Strategic importance is usually based on the technological/design dependence and is supplemented by the financial importance of one firm to the other.

Intimacy and longevity flow from the nature of the joint effort, which requires sharing intimate technological, design, and operating information. Trust is a critical ingredient in the relationship because it enables intimacy to develop, while longevity protects the intimacy and allows the partners to reap the financial rewards from long-term investments with, they hope, high payouts.

Another strategic-account relationship is that between the EDS (Electronic Data Systems) division of General Motors and what was formerly the Information Systems portion of AT&T. EDS had substantial skills in integrating computers, telecommunications gear, and software to customer systems. AT&T IS sold telecommunciations equipment, computers, and related equipment, but it did not have sufficient systems-integration skills to satisfy all its customers. EDS and AT&T IS signed a systems-integrator agreement under which EDS's integration skills made it considerably more important than a major distributor.

In another strategic relationship, Fujitsu Fanuc Ltd., a Japanese robot vendor, established a joint venture with General Motors. The joint venture gave Fanuc a better "window" on factory technology and robot application than it could have gained as an ordinary vendor. The joint venture, which sold robots and related factory-automation equipment to GMC and other customers, also enabled GMC to better understand and capitalize on the rapidly evolving robot technology. Moreover, GMC gained financially because it shared the returns from sales to other customers.

—— COMPARISONS AND APPLICATIONS

Exhibit 3 compares the four types of sales approaches. On the far left is the transaction approach, with systems selling, major-account management, and strategic-account relationships each representing further evolutions in sophistication and horsepower. Most important are the differences in goal and essence. The transaction and systems approaches emphasize sales, while the

EXHIBIT 3
The Four Types of Sales Approaches

	TRANSACTION	SYSTEMS	MAJOR-ACCOUNT MANAGEMENT	STRATEGIC-ACCOUNT RELATIONSHIP
Goal	Sales and satisfied customers	System sales and satisfied customers	The position as preferred supplier	An enduring, intimate relationship
Essence	Product sales because of performance, price, and effective selling	Integration benefits from good support and team selling	Intense service through account management	Company-to-company bonding with an institutional relationship leading to a shared destiny
Impact on buyer	Lowest			Highest
Impact on seller	Lowest			Highest
Organizational level and size of buying team	Lowest			Highest
Organizational level and size of selling team	Lowest			Highest
Length of relationship	Shortest			Longest
Relative amount of vendor effort	Lowest			Highest
Information needs at all levels of vendor	Lowest			Highest
Vendor management integration needs	Limited			Highest
Sales force goals	Narrow—sell products			Broad—manage the partnership
Number of customers appropriate for each approach	Most or some	Most or some	Not many	Very few

Note: In some industries such as electronics the transaction sales are called "box" or "piece part" sales to contrast them to systems sales.

major-account and strategic-relationship approaches emphasize the mutuality of a long marriage. As we move from left to right we see that the impact of the sale and the approach increase for both buyer and seller. Thus, organization level and the size of the buying and selling teams increase, as does the length of the relationship.

However, the relative amount of vendor effort also increases; integration and information flow within the vendor organization expand in response to the increased effort and because of the degree of customer responsiveness and service required. As we move from left to right on the chart, the relative amount of account work done by the sales force decreases and the amount done by supporting functional units such as manufacturing, field service, and logistics increases. More and more of the salesperson's time is spent on internal coordination and service support and less in customer persuasion. The best relationship managers have just as strong an internal focus as they do an external focus—a paradox to most traditional salespeople. Salespeople have broad account-related goals instead of narrow sales-related ones.

Because of the effort involved, a vendor can support only a few strategic-account relationships. Most customers will remain systems or transaction customers, and some will be major accounts. Since transaction selling is the easiest and cheapest, it should be used wherever possible. When products become complex and sophisticated, however, companies will need to shift to the systems approach. Many firms need go no further.

When, however, the importance of individual customers grows and they need intensive service because of their buying process and dependencies, the seller must switch to major-account management and relationship selling. The shift must be understood as a commitment to customer service and responsiveness and not merely as use of an improved selling technique. Major-account management is, indeed, a powerful tool, but it is expensive, in terms of support and integration, cost, and effort. It is an efficient competitive weapon only when it is justified.

Finally, for the few situations in which customer importance (financial, technological and/or design, and strategic), intimacy, and longevity are high, the company should use the most potent weapon: strategic-account relationships. It is the most expensive because of support and integration demands and loss of autonomy, but it is justified where the relationship must be long and intimate and where the rewards are strategic.

Simply put, the message is: use the cheapest tool (left column, *Exhibit 3*) wherever possible. Escalate (to the right) only when necessary and justified.

WHY GET CLOSER?

If transaction selling is so much cheaper and easier than the three other types, why do we need systems selling, major-account management, and strategic-account relationships? When are they justified?

Systems selling evolved because of product changes and the resulting changes in customers' buying processes. Some products became more complex, with more separate parts and services. And, the pieces had to fit together. The added complexity meant that other people and departments had to become involved in the purchase. When machine tools, for example, were relatively simple, the engineer at the customer company could give a clear specification to the purchasing agent, who could negotiate for a good price. Although there might be a few conversations between the engineer and purchasing agent, the communication was generally simple and the coordination needs limited.

As machine tools were replaced by complex multipurpose machining centers, the whole buying process changed. What had been a simple stand-alone machine purchase became a complex systems purchase. Process engineers, product-design engineers, manufacturing management, logistical personnel, procurement executives, and financial specialists got involved. The machining center affected the way various departments operated: the role of inventory and product variety (bringing in product and marketing managers); the whole concept of coordinated engineering, manufacturing, and logistics; and the risks of down time. Service and support became complicated. New types of suppliers were needed.

Successful vendors developed better sales techniques to match this more complicated buying process and product configuration. Systems selling integrated these techniques into a new sales approach.

Later, additional, broader changes in the environment forced a "quantum leap" to major-account management. Mergers, acquisitions, bankruptcies, and differential growth lead to a smaller, more concentrated account base in many industries. In some, such as the market for commercial jet engines and aircraft, as few as a dozen customers control the market. For the manufacturer these became do-or-die customers. Economic concentration brought added changes to the buying and selling organizations. Buying, receiving, using, producing, inventorying, shipping, and selling locations multiplied. Sales calls had to be made to more customer locations from more sales locations. And sales efforts had to be coordinated with more numerous support (manufacturing, inventorying, etc.) locations. Communication and coordination systems could no longer confine their activities to one or a few systems or to one or a few large, complex transactions; they were embedded in a total vendor-customer relationship. And, to make matters worse, the dispersion was not simply geographical. It involved many buying and selling organizational jurisdictions; the problems of internal coordination at the vendor became as important as vendor-customer coordination.

At the same time, the impact of the vendor, not simply the product choice, increased substantially. The experiences, good and bad, of computer buyers in particular influenced views of vendor importance. Because computers of different manufacturers could not talk to one another in the 1960s, 1970s, and early 1980s, choice of a product was a long-term commitment to a vendor and to a technological approach. It was perhaps to be expected that a computer vendor, IBM, would lead in the development of major- and national-account marketing.

Individual transactions and annual vendor-to-customer sales increased dramatically in size. Bonds between vendor and customer became more intimate. Coordination became difficult; the risk of a poor choice soared; and major- and national-account management became a fad. Those who thought it was a collection of advanced sales techniques failed. Those who saw it as a new philosophy of vendor-customer cooperation and internal vendor coordination, and who were able to make it work despite organizational inertia, complexity, and jurisdictional warfare, succeeded. The difference between success and failure was clear and involved many functions. Better customer relationships enabled vendor engineers, for example, to do a better job of developing new products; and the new products improved the relationship. As the better major-account marketer drew farther ahead of the disorganized, disoriented competitor, the better sales approach led to greater business success.

In some businesses, vendor-customer relationships grew even closer. Joint technological work was the cause in many but not all situations. An interesting marketing-oriented situation developed at NutraSweet, where a patented sweetener made the company a primary supplier to Coca-Cola and Pepsi-Cola. NutraSweet's "branded ingredient strategy" linked its marketing strategy inextricably to its customers, and the transactions were large and the dollar volume very great. But, more important, NutraSweet and Coke, and NutraSweet and Pepsi, developed long-term interests in promoting NutraSweet-branded diet soft drinks. In cases like these, joint marketing, operating, and/or technological dependencies can lead to strategic-account relationships.

The evolution of the four sales approaches is really the history of more complex responses to more demanding customer purchasing initiatives. System selling arose because of buyer demands beyond those that could be filled with the traditional transaction approach. Major-account management represented a still more powerful approach to greater customer opportunity. And, the antecedents for the strategic-account relationship approach lie in original equipment manufacturer (OEM) industrial marketing and franchised distributor arrangements. Suppliers of complex, important components to OEMs have found it necessary to undertake joint-development and engineering work, and the proprietary nature of the products and interfaces developed led to long-term relationships. A manufacturer of numerically controlled machine tools, for example, is typically locked in to a computer-control vendor for a five-year or so generation of controls.

Franchised distributors in the industrial, commercial, and consumer sphere (e.g., McDonald's and Dunkin' Donuts) have intimate, long-term relationships with the franchisor who supplies a mixture of branded marketing and advertising, technical support, capital equipment, and merchandise. The relationship of the franchisor and franchisee is a strategic-account relationship with a very specific legal definition.

Because the four different sales approaches offer such different rewards and involve such different costs, they must be applied to the right situations. Transaction selling will be ineffective where major-account management is needed, and strategic-account relationships will be wasted where major-account management will do. Thus, accounts and prospects must be segmented for different approaches.

—— SEGMENTING ACCOUNTS AND PROSPECTS

Given the differences in cost and impact among the four different sales approaches, it is appropriate to consider which accounts and prospects might be appropriate for each approach. Although much has been written about market segmentation, the approach here differs in being focused primarily on segmenting an existing customer base.[8]

SEGMENTING BY SIZE

The easiest way to segment customers is by size; typically, there are more small customers than large ones. If they are visualized as a pyramid (*Exhibit 4*) and are ranked by size from largest at the top to smallest at the bottom, the increasing width of the base indicates the larger number of smaller sales. This simple approach is a useful beginning.

Account volume can also be visualized in a pyramid or triangle (middle triangle, *Exhibit 5*), but this one is upside-down with a large base at the top. That is because the few large accounts typically comprise a disproportionate amount of volume. The point at the bottom represents the many accounts that represent a small percentage of total volume.

The largest accounts also often demand and perhaps justify more service and customization per dollar or unit of volume. This is reflected in the right-hand triangle in *Exhibit 5*, which has a wider top than the middle triangle.

A simple approach is to apply the transaction sales approach to the smallest accounts (labeled *micro* in *Exhibit 4*), the systems approach to the next, and so on up to the strategic-account relationship approach at the very top for the few largest mega accounts. This method is mechanistic and heavy-handed but better than a

---

8. For more on commercial/industrial market segmentation, *see* Thomas V. Bonoma and Benson P. Shapiro, *Segmenting the Industrial Market* (Lexington, Mass.: Lexington Books, 1983); Benson P. Shapiro and Thomas V. Bonoma, "How to Segment Industrial Markets," *Harvard Business Review* (July–August 1984); and Thomas V. Bonoma and Benson P. Shapiro, "Evaluating Market Segmentation Approaches," *Industrial Marketing Management* (October 1984).

random approach. However, it neglects customer potential, account profitability, customer needs, and vendor rewards other than sales volume and profits.

SEGMENTING BY POTENTIAL AND PROFITABILITY

Potential is easy to add to the process. The simplest way is to use the pyramids and triangles to represent realizable potential instead of current sales volume. The same general shape is likely to appear, but the approach

EXHIBIT 4
The Customer Pyramid

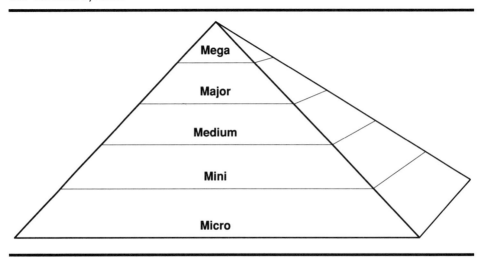

EXHIBIT 5
Customer Potential and Customer Demands

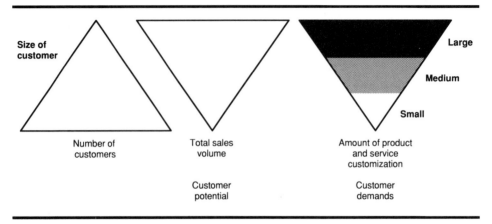

EXHIBIT 6
The Customer/Order Profitability Matrix

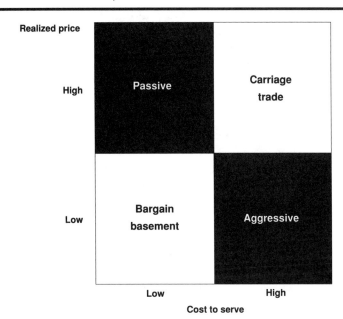

is more future-oriented. Specifying potential requires some careful analysis of each account and is a good place to begin effective account planning.

Account profitability can be added by using the account profitability matrix (*Exhibit 6*), which separates accounts (and orders) by realized price and cost to serve. Passive accounts, which pay high realized prices and are inexpensive to serve, are more attractive than aggressive accounts, which pay low realized prices and are expensive to serve.[9] This approach requires an account-profitability analysis system and fairly well-developed account plans to determine which accounts will provide incremental profitable business. Such pro forma analysis is important because the cost of serving an account with the strategic-account relationship approach is much higher than with the transaction and systems sales approaches or even major-account management.

There is no reason to use a more expensive approach when customer needs and prospective vendor rewards do not justify it. Wherever possible the least expensive, easiest approach (to the left on *Exhibit 3*) should be chosen. Only a few customers will justify the strategic-account relationship approach. And, a fairly small number of most vendors' customers, relative to the account base, will even justify major-account management.

---

9. Benson P. Shapiro, V. Kasturi Rangan, Rowland T. Moriarty, and Elliot B. Ross, "Manage Customers for Profits (Not Just Sales)," *Harvard Business Review* (September–October 1987).

CANDIDATES FOR RELATIONSHIP SELLING

The accounts and prospects most likely to demand advanced approaches are also usually the accounts most sensitive to vendor quality and performance as opposed to price, product quality and performance, rapid availability, and convenience. Commodity markets are characterized by buyers who emphasize price. Specialty markets are made up of buyers who want either rapid availability, convenience, product quality and performance, or vendor quality and performance.[10] Those specialty buyers who are sensitive to vendor quality and performance are most appropriate candidates for the advanced sales approaches.

Finally, some accounts have special attributes that make them appropriate for special-account relationships. An account providing an entry into a new marketplace or familiarity with new technologies or manufacturing processes may be attractive far beyond its current sales volume and profitability or future potential for volume or profitability. A good example of such an account is a mid-sized account identified for strategic-account treatment by a high-technology material supplier. The account was a consistent technological leader in the supplier's most important market and was viewed, because of this technical prowess, as the "account of the future." The materials supplier decided that being close to the technological cutting edge was more important than current volume.

Other accounts can help the vendor manage product mix in a strategic sense. Such an account might, in a strategic relationship, for example, accept "rejected" product that is not up to specification for other customers but is much better than scrap. This arrangement can have a major impact on operations and profitability.

Other attributes which make an account appropriate for development of a strategic-account relationship include industry visibility and image, and compatibility. When we confront implementation, we will give more attention to this latter consideration.

To summarize, if we define strategic accounts as those appropriate for the development of strategic-account relationships, we would look for accounts that satisfy the following criteria:

1. Current sales volume
2. Future sales potential
3. Current profitability
4. Future profitability
5. Strong customer-service needs
6. Strong customer interest in vendor quality and performance
7. Entry into a new market, technology, or manufacturing process

---

10. For more on these distinctions, see Benson P. Shapiro, "Specialties vs. Commodities: The Battle for Profit Margins," Harvard Business School No. 9-587-120.

    8. Impact on product mix
    9. Industry visibility and image
   10. Ability to work with, or compatibility

Ideally, a strategic account will rank high on all criteria; but often one or even several criteria will have to be sacrificed. The list indicates the need to analyze more than current volume and even current profitability. Myopia is dangerous when planning for the long term. Perhaps only one trap is more dangerous—selecting too many strategic accounts so that none gets the attention it needs.

——— SPECIAL SERVICES FOR THE FEW

The relations between the amount of special sales and service attention provided and the number of strategic accounts can be visualized as a graph (see *Exhibit 7*). The vertical dimension is the number or percentage of accounts receiving special effort, and the horizontal dimension is the amount of that effort. In *Exhibit 8* on the upper right, a few customers get major special attention. In the lower left, many customers get little differentiation. The line between the two (lower left to upper right) can be a constant-cost line. The choice of giving a great deal of special effort to each of a few customers versus less special effort to each of a larger group is indeed strategic.

If the account base is concentrated (few customers and prospects comprise a large percentage of potential) and accounts are interested in special services, then the upper right-hand corner of intensively nurturing a few accounts with the strategic-account relationship approach will pay off. A more dispersed account and prospect potential and/or less responsiveness to special services suggests that less differentiation for a larger group of accounts would be a better strategy. Unfortunately, *Exhibit 7* is somewhat unidimensional and does not allow us to look at the total account and prospect base to better determine what number of customers should get each type of sales treatment.

Having examined the four different sales approaches and seen that most vendors will use a mixture of the four, we turn to a deeper analysis of strategic-account relationships, first reiterating that these complex relationships are not appropriate to every vendor nor to every customer of any vendor.

WHAT DO STRATEGIC ACCOUNT RELATIONSHIPS PROVIDE TO CUSTOMERS?

The essence of strategic-account relationships is provision of a special set of efforts by the vendor that provide the customer with a long-term competitive advantage. The customer hopes to receive some mixture of technological, operational, and strategic benefits from the approach.

EXHIBIT 7
Amount of Special Attention vs. Number of Strategic Accounts

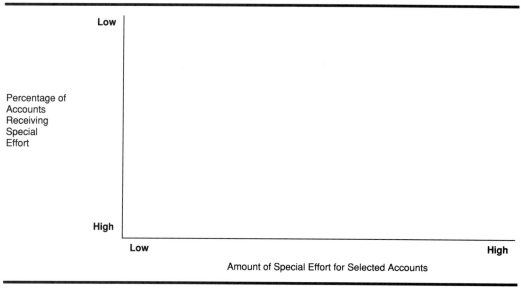

Most strategic-account relationships are fostered by intense and rapid technological development. The need for technological specialization and integration has forced customers to look beyond their boundaries for the requisite skills and resources. Often the partners must integrate their technologies and design products cooperatively and, because technology needs are so pressing and the integration is so complex, the level of sharing must be high. Design and development often requires a good deal of "cutting and fitting."

Many customers and prospects also seek operational rewards from the strategic-account vendor. Sometimes these result naturally from the technological integration; at other times they are the primary benefit.

Evolving approaches to manufacturing often force intimate operational coordination. Because components, equipment, and systems exchanged in a strategic partnership are often customized—with no second source and no other prospective customers—the operational integration system has fewer safety valves and alternatives for the vendor than more traditional approaches. Thus, sales forecasting and capacity planning must be jointly executed. The higher the levels of technological and design integration, the higher the need for operational integration.

The relationship between NutraSweet and its primary customers is an example of operational benefits focused on joint marketing interests. Consumer franchisor-franchisee relationships such as McDonald's and Dunkin' Donuts also demonstrate the marketing benefits of the relationship.

By their nature, strategic-account relationships work only when the relationship is strategically important to both companies. The cost and effort

EXHIBIT 8
Special Services for the Few

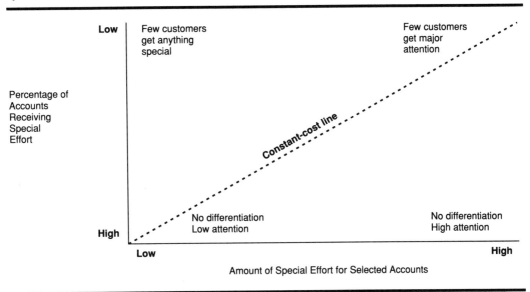

involved in making the partnership work can be justified only if there is a strategic need. They are not justified and will not be provided unless the need is clear to the relevant, and powerful, managers on both sides as well as to the lower-level people who must carry out the work. General Motors needed Fanuc's factory-automation skills to survive and prosper in a hostile competitive environment; Fanuc needed a large, worldwide base of leading-edge, high-volume customers, advanced applications knowledge, and factory involvement to develop its dominant position in robots. Each company needed the other to prosper.

HOW ARE STRATEGIC ACCOUNT RELATIONSHIPS NURTURED?

We have shown that strategic-account relationships require importance, intimacy, and longevity and that intimacy sets the tone for the relationship. Technological, operational, and strategic integration lead naturally to a necessarily high level of organizational integration—a degree of integration beyond that developed in the 1970s and early 1980s as part of major-account management.

Organizational integration extends to virtually every part of the vendor's and customer's organizations: engineers talk to engineers; production people talk to one another; and, top management must get together as well.

Old-fashioned arm's-length organizational relationships are not enough. In many cases, the success of people in one company is more dependent on their personal relationships in the partner organization than with anyone in their own firm. Designers, for example, must work together very closely, often merging different technologies and philosophies.

Sometimes the seller's employees must work at the customer's facilities, or even operate equipment there. In the chemical industry, some vendors have found it advantageous, even necessary, to operate leased equipment at a customer site. This raises a raft of issues about integration—everything from union contracts to cafeteria and parking privileges.

Successful organizational and personal integration can take place only between a vendor and a customer who share business values and culture. It sometimes seems that the greatest strategic and technological rewards would come from the partnership of two quite disparate companies, but the likelihood of success tends to go down in such a situation. Strong management support on both sides and unusual organizational arrangements may help, but some disparities cannot be bridged regardless of goodwill, effort, and potential reward.

Finally, there is financial integration. The strategic bond here is so great that the typical financial relationship is often too weak to reflect it. Some strategic-account relationships work on a typical "I make it, I sell it, you buy it, and you pay for it" basis. But other arrangements better reflect the closeness of the relationship. Outright acquisition is one approach; formal joint ventures, such as GM-Fanuc, are much more likely. Other approaches include development contracts, supply contracts, licensing, and very strong informal relationships. Seldom does the buyer ask for bids for a specified product. Instead, the development is joint, and the financial relationship attempts to reflect the sharing of risk, contribution, and reward.[11]

Sometimes the integration of a strategic partnership must extend beyond the two partners to the vendor's suppliers and the customer's customers. System tasks may be so complex that other levels in the supply chain or distribution channel are needed to provide strategic, technological, operational, and financial horsepower.

Finally, integration within each of the partner firms must be stronger than in a normal company. Roy Shapiro argues that the purchasing, engineering, and production functions in the customer company must themselves become more integrated in order to deal successfully with suppliers in strategic-account relationships.[12] The vendor organization must also be well integrated; everyone must sell and service the strategic partner. If the engineering

---

11. For more on these new types of relationships, *see* Roy D. Shapiro, "Toward Effective Supplier Management: International Comparisons," Harvard Business School Working Paper No. 9-785-062.

12. Ibid.

and sales functions cannot operate well together, it is hard to believe that they will be able to sustain an intimate relationship with customers.

——— THE REWARDS

All this integration must be justified by substantial rewards. Strategic-account relationships offer the selling company the opportunity to leverage its skills and resources, develop long-term customers, and build strong competitive positions. Companies in a wide variety of industries have understood the rewards and opportunities. Some have realized them successfully; others have not.

Strategic-account relationships are not necessarily a way station between acquisition—in a sense the ultimate form of strategic partnership—and more arm's-length forms of buyer-seller relations. They can be very special continuing vendor-customer connections that offer rewards to both parties. At the core of many strategic-account relationships is the exchange of knowledge, "soft" management skills as well as "hard" technological capabilities. The seller learns how its product is used and develops unique applications approaches; the customer is willing to share such knowledge with an outsider because it too can gain knowledge and unique support for new activities.

If the partnership is with a distributor, a manufacturer gains commitment of the distributor's resources to its product line and to developing capabilities applicable only to the company's products. For example, a distributor's salespeople may spend substantial amounts of time learning about the benefits of the products, their competitive position, and the best ways of selling them. Distributor engineers will learn the details of how the vendor's product can interface with customers' products and systems; and the distributor's service people will develop skill in maintaining and repairing the equipment. The distributor is willing to make these commitments because of the permanence and intimacy of the relationship. In the distribution realm, the strategic-account relationship differs more in degree than in nature from a solid, close, but typical major or national distributor–vendor arrangement.

The permanency of the relationship and the knowledge exchange can produce a stronger competitive position. Sometimes, in fact, a vendor cannot afford to invest in a major new product without the long-term assurance of a customer to ensure profitability, or at least limit the financial risk.

——— TRAPS

The astute choice and efficient management of strategic-account relationships are critical determinants of success. The process of developing them, however, presents some major traps, which can be divided into four groups:

1. Attempting to develop too many strategic relationships
2. Picking unsuitable partners
3. Allocating too few resources to the relationship
4. Losing sight of the importance of cultural compatibility

Because they are so intensive and extensive, a company can adequately maintain only a few strategic-account relationships. Some companies have a very concentrated customer and prospect list; that is, they have few existing and potential accounts and even fewer with high sales potential. These companies, obviously, can develop only a few—perhaps only one—strategic-account relationships. But even companies with very extensive prospect and customer lists cannot manage more than a few such relationships, given their high demands on resources and time.

Strategic accounts almost always demand, for example, at least a degree of product and service customization, which affects the vendor's whole organization and product line. If the customization is major and the vendor has too many strategic accounts, it can be torn apart as each account pressures the company to give priority to its needs. If there are too many conflicting pulls, the vendor will be able to satisfy none of them well. Even worse, it will probably lose its internal coherence and end up with a poorly integrated product line.

If the vendor can have only a few relationships, and if the relationships are strategic, it is clear that the choice of the accounts is critical. A poor choice leads to wasted resources, but that is not its major cost. The highest cost is usually the loss of the opportunity to develop an effective strategic-account relationship with another customer. Instead, a competitor may move in and reap long-term rewards. The choice of accounts is particularly difficult when it is impossible to have strategic relationships with two accounts that compete intensively.

Therefore, the criteria for choice, and their priority, must be set out very carefully indeed. They should include the following:

1. A leading-edge technical and/or operational capability
2. A willingness to share in joint technical and/or operational development
3. A willingness to make the vendor an important part of the customer's business activities, including frequent meetings with a wide variety of functional units within the customer organization
4. Substantial sales potential
5. Long-term profit potential
6. An existing relationship as a basis for the partnership
7. Good cultural fit

The technical and/or operational capability and development in criteria 1 and 2 must relate to activities of clear strategic importance to the vendor. The capability may be "hard," like a scientific or engineering expertise, or "soft," like a particular operational competency (e.g., marketing, service, or manufacturing).

Some companies have attempted to develop strategic accounts without devoting enough resources to them. In some cases they have tried to develop too many account relationships, or have chosen strategic-account relationships that are not justified by other criteria. Sometimes, they have simply underestimated the cost and commitment needed. Four forms of resource starvation are particularly common:

1. Not assigning enough top management skill and power, or enough technical and functional expertise, to the relationships. Strategic accounts justify and require the best staffing and attention.
2. Using a sales-oriented approach when more engineering, production, service, and financial skills are needed. (This is not a standard sale; it is a long-term, intimate partnership.)
3. An unwillingness to customize products and services for each strategic account. The customized nature of such partnerships is one of the limiting factors of the number that can be developed. If each relationship needs a separate product line, and the base business needs to maintain its own product line, the engineering, production, service, and logistics functions must be adequate to handle the total diversity.
4. If personal relationships are to develop, people must spend time together. Travel and telephone budgets must be extensive enough to support the development of trust. And managers and experts working on the accounts must have adequate time to do their jobs. Some may have to move to the partner's location for an extended, but temporary, period. The drain of international partnerships, with their attendant travel costs—and jet lag is a real cost!—is very high indeed.

Patience is another important part of nurturing strategic-account relationships. The life cycle of the relationship dictates that, as in most situations, an investment in time must be made before rewards can be reaped. Major-account management takes a long time, and strategic-account relationship development takes even longer. Many months are needed to build a good personal relationship and even longer to build the deep institutional bonds of the relationship. Patience is particularly necessary when joint projects involve major technological development or when the customer is a mature, cyclical company. Although the down cycle is often the best time to build strategic relationships, the more visible benefits, such as sales increases, will often not accrue until the up cycle.

Another particularly good time to build strategic-account relationships is when the supplier industry is oversold and customers are in desperate need of support. Short-term optimization of profits by such maneuvers as price-gouging or allocating scarce products to new customers instead of established ones can cost dearly over the long term and make it impossible to establish the deep trust needed for this type of relationship.

Finally, some companies have failed to understand the delicate mating of cultures that leads to successful relationships. Some pairs of cultures are difficult to integrate; some are impossible. Partnerships require compromise and constant joint nurturing to succeed.

——— IMPLEMENTATION: BUILDING INSTITUTIONAL RELATIONSHIPS

Although strategic-account relationships are fairly new, it is possible to suggest some guidelines for success. Some are similar to those for acquisitions, an even more intimate and permanent relationship. The critical issue is always the human management of the relationship, which must build something closer than the typical buyer-seller relationship but less internally integrated than an acquisition. To do this and avoid the traps, management should

1. Develop only a few strategic partnerships. In most businesses some customers will be transactional customers, some systems customers, a limited number major or national accounts, and a very small number strategic-account relationships. If the number of the latter is not countable on the fingers, the relationships will not be truly strategic.

2. Choose accounts that meet the explicit chosen criteria and share a long-term vision of the future. Only long-term relationships can really be strategic; they must last long enough to generate profits after the expensive, initial investment period. They should be seen as long-term company-to-company relationships, not as limited to one product or technology or—worst of all—one deal.

3. Allocate adequate resources to the relationship. If the resource allocation is parsimonious, the relationship is doomed.

4. Understand that these relationships involve a substantial loss of autonomy. Decisions will be based on the needs and desires of both partners. This loss of autonomy is one of the primary costs of strategic-account relationships, and the loss will be most severe in the areas closest to the heart of the relationship—often product design and technology choice.

5. Develop a financial relationship that reflects the long-term needs and interests of both parties; that is flexible enough to adjust to changing conditions (in a long-term relationship, conditions will surely change); and that is explicit enough to avoid arguments about interpretation. It helps to identify, discuss, and clarify beforehand issues that are likely to create problems in the future. The relationship should be so intimate and pervasive that troublesome parts of it cannot be swept under the carpet in hopes that they will not be noticed. If they are, they will fester until the infection destroys the relationship. There are many financial forms the venture can take; all the relevant ones—from supply contracts to joint ventures—should be explored to find the optimum mix of flexibility and explicitness.

Finally, we turn to the management of the relationship. To succeed the partnership must be institutionalized; that is, it must supersede the relationship between any two individuals and become a relationship between organizations.

Most major-account relationships depend ultimately upon one person, an able account manager who can mobilize internal resources to support the

EXHIBIT 9
The Communications Network

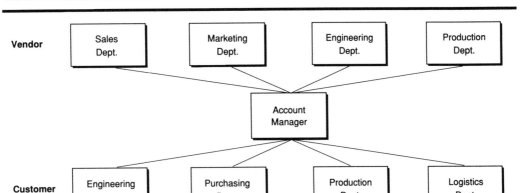

account and call on many people at the account with confidence and competence. He or she becomes the primary node in the communications network (as shown in *Exhibit 9*).

A true strategic-account relationship cannot, however, operate with one primary node. There must be intense communication among many vendor and customer functions (as illustrated in *Exhibit 10*). The obvious problem with this scheme is that the communication can easily become unmanageable, uncoordinated, and, hence, inefficient. One solution is to manage the venture through a partnership team consisting of two senior executives—one from each company—and a group of top-level functional executives. This structure imitates the joint-venture board of directors in a more informal and day-to-day way.

The senior partnership team should not replace or limit other, direct communications, but manage and coordinate the relationship by nurturing cross-company integration and communication at all levels in all functions. If the engineers do not talk to one another, for example, the benefits of the partnership will not accrue, though the costs will.

National-account management has been described as a case of making and keeping promises to customers.[13] This view is appropriate in all four sales approaches, even transaction selling. It is especially relevant to the relationship-building activities that are central to major-account management and strategic-account relationships. Because of the long-term nature of the activities and results, yesterday's promises must be kept tomorrow; when they are not kept,

---

13. Benson P. Shapiro and Rowland T. Moriarty, Jr., *Support Systems for National Account Management Programs: Promises Made, Promises Kept* (Cambridge, Mass.: Marketing Science Institute, 1983).

EXHIBIT 10
Communication Between Vendor and Customer

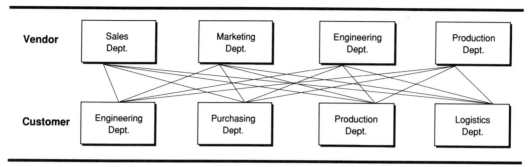

the present relationship suffers, which can have long-term impacts. Moreover, the great upside opportunity of strategic-account relationships puts a premium on unmade promises as well, for the unmade promise is, in essence, a lost opportunity. It sacrifices long-term return, just as unkept promises hurt the present situation.

We have seen that strategic-account relationships are a response to the need to develop and manage more complex and more permanent partnerships between suppliers and customers. They are expensive and difficult, but they offer great benefits when used selectively and implemented effectively. Undoubtedly some companies will view them as a panacea. They are not. In fact, in most industries they will supplement and enhance only a small part of the company's sales and marketing efforts. They differ in intensity and degree—but not truly in nature—from major- and national-account management. They differ in fundamental nature from transaction and systems selling. There are four kinds of close encounters in selling, but one is closer than the others.

———— DISCUSSION QUESTIONS

1. The author presents four approaches to selling that are quite different. The first one is transaction selling, the same kind of selling that took place in the early days of open markets and caravan traders. Is this type of selling still useful in today's economy? Does it have advantages? Limitations?

2. How do the other three approaches compare with transaction selling? When is each approach justified over the others? Compare their costs, their complications, and their advantages.

3. The author gives high marks to strategic-account relationships if they are carefully nurtured. He does, however, point out several traps that can render them ineffective and in some cases even debilitate the vendor company. What are those traps, and how can they be avoided or managed properly to produce the rewards that should accrue to both partners in the strategic relationship?

PART SIX

MARKETING IMPLEMENTATION AND CONTROL

No matter how well a company has planned its marketing strategy, its program cannot succeed without effective implementation. Skillful implementation will reinforce a good marketing strategy and compensate for a weak one. Indeed, the ability to turn drawing-board plans into marketplace reality is the true measure of marketing leadership. The readings that follow offer perspectives on the challenges that inevitably arise in implementing a marketing program—for example, how to solve the organizational, structural, and human conflicts that impede effective action and how to distinguish between marketing effectiveness and sales effectiveness.

Making Your Marketing Strategy Work

32

THOMAS V. BONOMA

Too often a seemingly effective marketing strategy fails to do what it is supposed to do, and marketing executives immediately assume that the strategy is at fault. In this reading, based on a study of 35 companies, the author argues that more often than not faulty implementation of the strategy is to blame. Implementation troubles can result from a variety of organizational and structural problems as well as from inadequate personal skills. The reading offers guidelines for identifying the most common difficulties as well as suggestions for remedying them.

The marketing literature is replete with research and analysis to help managers devise marketing strategies tailored to the marketplace. Yet when it comes to implementing those strategies, the literature is silent and the self-help books ring hollow. What top management needs is not new answers to questions about strategy but increased attention to marketing practice, to the signposts of good marketing management that direct clever strategies toward successful marketplace results.

The purposes of this article are to explain and help in diagnosing and solving marketing implementation problems, to catalog common problems of translating marketing strategies into management acts, and to recommend tactics for increasing the effectiveness of marketing practices. The examples and conclusions are drawn from a three-year clinical research program I conducted to initiate a course on marketing implementation at the Harvard Business School.

It is invariably easier to think up clever marketing strategies than it is to make them work under company, competitor, and customer constraints. Consider a pipe company that invented a new kind of triangular pipe 180% more efficient than the existing line, needing only two-thirds as much material. On the basis of value to users, the new marketing vice president wanted to price the new pipe high. He feared, however, that lack of support from other top managers, the company's marketing systems, and the sales force would hamper his strategy. "Everything three generations of managers have learned about doing business in this market, everything the company *is*," he complained, "seems to conspire against my being able to introduce this innovation properly."

What to do—the marketing strategy—is clear to this vice president: price according to value, encourage cannibalization of existing lines, and reap the profits. *How* to accomplish the strategy—the marketing implementation—is problematic.

This family-owned company customarily produced pipe in large quantities and sold it in a nongrowing market at low margins. The company started every year with high margins, but because of competitive pressure and the need to keep its plants at capacity, it wound up cost cutting in the heat of the selling season. Plant managers were paid on the basis of pipe produced per minute. The sales force thought in terms of cutting list prices to stimulate orders and ensure commissions.

Top management encouraged this commodity-oriented culture by setting budgets with high fixed costs and maintaining a measurement system designed to track the selling price of each unit of raw material rather than of the pipe itself. The vice president rightly worried that simply declaring a high price on the new pipe by fiat or even constructing a marketing program for the innovation would be ineffective in combating the entrenched and commodity-focused way of doing business.

As this example suggests, problems in marketing practice have two components: structural and human. The structural one includes the company's marketing functions, like pricing and selling, as well as any program based on these functions, any control systems, and policy directives. The second component is the people themselves, the managers charged with getting the marketing job done.

━━━ STRATEGY OR IMPLEMENTATION?

Marketing strategy and implementation affect each other. While strategy obviously affects actions, execution also affects marketing strategies, especially over time. Despite the fuzzy boundary between strategy and execution, it is not hard to diagnose marketing implementation problems and to distinguish them from strategy shortfalls. When a 50-person computer terminal sales force sells only 39 of the company's new line of "smart" microcomputers during a sales blitz—in which sales of more than 500 units were forecast—is the problem with sales force management or with the strategy move to the smart machines? The question is answerable.

Intense competition is eroding margins on sales of its old "dumb" terminals. Additionally, the smart terminals category is expected to grow by over 500% over the next five years. The new product, a portable microcomputer with built-in printer and memory, has many benefits that the target market values. But because sales representatives already earn an average of more than $50,000 a year, they have little incentive to struggle with an unfamiliar new product. Management also inexplicably set sales incentive compensation on the new machines lower than on older ones. Finally, the old terminals have a selling cycle half as long as the new ones and require no

EXHIBIT
Marketing Strategy and Implementation Problem Diagnosis

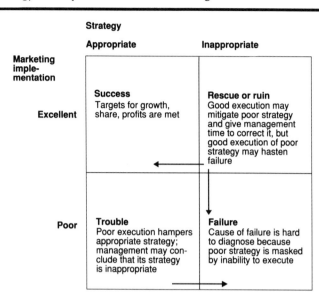

software knowledge or support. Here is a case where poor execution stifles good strategy.

The *Exhibit* shows how marketing strategy and implementation affect each other. The computer example falls in the lower left cell of the matrix and illustrates an important rule about strategy and implementation: poor implementation can disguise good strategy. As the *Exhibit* indicates, when both strategy and implementation are on target, the company has done all it can to ensure success. Similarly, when strategy is inappropriate and implementation poor, implementation shortcomings may mask problems with the strategy; not only is failure the probable result, but such failures will be especially intractable because of the difficulty in identifying the cause of the problem.

When strategy is appropriate but implementation is poor, or vice versa, diagnosis becomes tricky. Poor marketing execution may cause management to doubt even sound strategies because they are masked by implementation inadequacies (the lower left cell of the *Exhibit*). As the foregoing computer company example suggests, management may hasten marketplace failure if it then changes its strategy. I have labeled such a situation the "trouble" cell on the matrix because poor execution hampers confirmation of the strategy's rightness and can provoke unnecessary change.

When strategy is inappropriate and execution excellent (the upper right cell), management usually winds up with time to recognize and fix its strategic mistakes. Good branch office heads, for instance, have been known to modify potentially disastrous headquarters directives. Indeed, some companies that are noted for excellent marketing execution, like Frito-Lay, expect such modifications from their managers. But at other times, good execution of bad strategy acts as the engine on a plane in a nosedive—it hastens the crash. Because it is hard to predict the result of inappropriate strategy coupled with good execution, I label this cell "rescue or ruin."

From this analysis two points stand out to help managers diagnose marketing implementation problems. First, poor execution tends to mask both the appropriateness and the inappropriateness of strategy. Therefore, when unsure of the causes of poor marketing performance, managers should look to marketing *practices* before making strategic adjustments. A careful examination of the *how* questions, those dealing with implementation, often can identify an execution culprit responsible for problems that are seemingly strategic.

STRUCTURAL PROBLEMS OF MARKETING PRACTICE

In his book *Zen and the Art of Motorcycle Maintenance*, Robert Pirsig proposes a catalog of traps that can sap the mechanic's resolve to do quality work. He tells, for instance, how a five-cent screw holding an access cover in place can, if stuck, render a $4,000 motorcycle worthless and the mechanic a frustrated wreck headed for truly grave mistakes. Like mechanics, managers need a catalog of the traps in marketing practice.

In the following sections I take up the problems and pitfalls of each level, or "place," in the structural hierarchy of marketing practice: functions, programs, systems, and policy directives. I then discuss the implementation skills required of those who are doing the marketing.

FUNCTIONS: THE FUNDAMENTALS

Marketing functions include selling, trade promotion, and distributor management. These low-level tasks are the fundamentals, the "blocking and tackling" of the marketer's job. Yet I have observed that most companies and their managers have great difficulty with these tasks. Often the difficulty stems from a failure to pursue marketing's fundamentals in any determined way, as when one CEO doubted that the company's trade show expenditure was a good marketing communications device but continued to authorize $1 million every year thinking the company had to be there.

Although the pitfalls peculiar to each function are worthy of a separate article, there are some management problems common to all.

Problems with marketing functions generally outnumber problems at the marketing program, systems, and policy levels. Managers most often have trouble with sales force management, distributor management, or pricing moves. When functions go awry, it is often because headquarters simply assumes that the function in question will get executed well by someone else, somewhere else, and thus ignores it until a crisis intervenes.

In one company, for instance, management decided to offer low list prices with correspondingly low discounts from list prices. In making what it thought was a sound pricing move for its line of graphics computers, however, management failed to take into account how pricing got implemented. The pricing scheme that resulted satisfied no one because, as it turned out, buyers in many companies proved their effectiveness not by the list price they paid but by the size of the discounts they received.

Thus, implementation problems at the functions level are caused primarily by faulty managerial assumptions or, as they say in the sports world, by not keeping your eye on the ball. As might be expected, this "disease" is more prevalent in large operating units, where administrators have functional specialists to rely on, than in small ones.

A second cause of marketing function problems is structural contradiction. A highly promising start-up business with $600,000 in revenues decided after careful deliberation to expand its domestic distribution network by setting up—at great expense—its own sales offices. The purpose was to control its distribution channels. For international distribution, though, management was torn between its need for control and its unfamiliarity with international markets. The conflict was heightened when a potential foreign partner said it would guarantee $30 million in sales.

Management was stumped. Its policy dictated that it should own foreign channels, but implementation was beyond its capabilities. Cash flow needs eventually seduced the company into deciding on indirect foreign distribution, with a different partner and arrangement in each country. The overall result was a complicated patchwork of direct and indirect distribution, which the thin ranks of executives could not handle. Management's attempts to balance the contradiction between desired control policies and functional-level distribution structure were ineffective and led to conflicts among company executives and foreign distributors.

A third cause of problems is when the head office fails to pick one marketing function for special concentration and competence and instead takes satisfaction in doing an adequate job with each—what I call "global mediocrity." Officials thereby spread resources and administrative talent democratically but ineffectively. Typically, the pricing, advertising, promotion, and distribution functions are satisfactory, but no one function is outstanding.

The best companies have a facility for handling one or two marketing functions and are competent in the remainder. No marketers are good at everything, but the most able concentrate on doing an outstanding job at a few marketing functions. Frito-Lay is an example of a company that has refined two functional skills—selling and distribution—to such heights that they serve as the company's marketing basis. Gillette's Personal Care Division makes a science of advertising. Both these companies allocate resources, often un-equally, to maintain competitive preeminence in the "showcase" functions.

PROGRAMS: THE RIGHT COMBINATION

A marketing program is a combination of marketing and nonmarketing functions, such as sales promotion and production, for a certain product or market. Marketing programs are a basic reference point for marketing practice analyses; from them, it is possible to look down at the functions comprising the programs or up at the systems and policies directing the programs' execution.

At the program level, management seeks to blend marketing and non-marketing functions in an attempt to sell a particular product line or penetrate a target segment. Managing all aspects of the Silkience hair conditioner line is an example of a marketing program; so is managing a company's key accounts and their special needs. If functions are the blocking and tackling of execution, marketing programs are the playbook showing how customers will be courted and the competition confounded.

A computer vendor, for example, wished to install a national account program to better serve its small but growing number of key accounts. The vendor recruited a highly regarded national account manager from another company and issued a presidential mandate to put a key account program together.

Exactly how was this to be done? Perhaps the manager should try to create a headquarters-based, dedicated national account sales force despite the attendant risks that competition with the sales vice president implied. Or would it be better to work in a dotted-line capacity through the company's sales managers, attempting no sales or service coordination beyond simple inter-functional persuasion, and running different risks with the customer base? The art of blending functions into programs is a poorly understood one at best, often left to on-the-job learning by trial and error.

One common program problem stems from what I call "empty prom-ises" marketing, which results from instituting programs that either are con-tradicted by the company's identity or are beyond its functional capabilities. The computer graphics company mentioned previously made a generalized piece of computer equipment that served all the industry's segments, but most purchasers were small single-site users. Indeed, with the exception of its national account manager, every implementation action and policy directive geared the company to small customers. Unlike many businesses that obtain 80% of revenues from the largest 20% of customers, this company received only 30% of its revenues from its large accounts. In short, the business's national account program ran counter to what the company was set up to do in marketing. The program was an empty promise internally and to the market-place.

In another case, the country's largest producer of private-label light bulbs decided it had to give its bulbs a brand name and place them on the grocery shelves to preempt others from an attack on its profitable main business. The company, which specialized in industrial lighting products, had no experience in consumer marketing or advertising and only a little in important retailing areas like trade promotion. Nonetheless, it created "Project Shopping Cart." After spending several million dollars for the design of a new display and packaging for the bulbs and even more to sponsor athletic events and recruit a host of brokers to place the bulbs, management accrued a .3% share of the market in two years. The marketing functions in this industrially and generically oriented company were unable to supply the retail blocking and tackling that headquarters simply assumed would be there to implement its well-conceived program.

A second program-level execution error is one I term "bunny marketing." It arises not from a functional inability to execute program plans but from a lack of direction in top management's execution policies. One heavy manufacturing company was continually frustrated because it came out late with new products in an industry in which spare parts inventories and operator loyalties give the first-in vendor a significant advantage. One of its products, a machine for special mining conditions, came out almost two years after the competition's entry. Headquarters had kept its thin developmental engineering staff busy with a torrent of engineering projects, some to rework machines already in the field, one to come up with an automatic machine prototype under government grant, and another to design the new machine. In short, the profusion of programs lacked focus because it stemmed from a poor sense of what the company was and what it did.

The presence of many clever marketing programs—a great playbook— is often associated with implementation problems. This is so because when a strong sense of marketing identity and direction are absent, programs tend to go off in all directions. Such bunny marketing results in diffusion of effort and random results.

SYSTEMS: BUREAUCRATIC OBSTACLES

Marketing systems include the formal organization, monitoring, budgeting, and other "overlays" that foster or inhibit good marketing practice. Systems can be as simple as voice telecommunications or as complex as profit accounting.

Of the systems at lower organizational levels, the most problematic is sales force reporting and control. Of the pervasive systems, those concerned with the allocation of marketing resources and those that help management monitor results are bugbears in all but a few companies. Especially in smaller companies, allocation systems cause many problems; in larger ones, control systems do more damage. Other kinds of systems as well as personnel and the formal organizational structure can also be problematic, but managers usually can get around these obstacles by exercising their execution skills.

Three problems that commonly occur at the systems level are errors of ritual, politicization, and unavailability. Errors of ritual arise when the company's systems drive it down habitual pathways, even when good judgment dictates a different course. At one concrete producer, the marketing control system relied on a plant backlog measure. When backlogs were low, the sales force beat the bushes for jobs no matter how marginal, the estimators (who control pricing in construction companies) shaved the margins, and everyone from the CEO on down got nervous. When backlogs were high, reactions were the opposite. As a consequence, the low-margin business taken in bad times hindered the company when it sought high-margin business in better times. When the president accepted suggestions for a new sales control system to remedy the problem, he instituted new forms and reports but refused either to modify backlog management or to approach profitability by job as a means toward more effective segmentation and selling.

The problem of politicization is never more evident than when observing sales force reporting and control systems and, in particular, call reports. Sales managers often weed out their call reports to fit their preconceptions. Even more dangerous, call reports can lose their intelligence function altogether and become instead a device with which to punish sales representatives who submit "inappropriate" ones.

The politicization of systems is in no way limited to sales controls, however. In one case, division management in an equipment rental company chose to report to headquarters that its new pricing scheme would increase unit revenues by 11% and margins by 13%. It neglected to note, unfortunately, that the rental equipment would be obsolete a year sooner than headquarters had planned.

The final, and most pervasive, systems problem is unavailability. That is, some systems designed to make line officers' lives easier just don't do so. In all but a handful of the companies I studied, for example, the financial accounting and sales accounting systems can only be called perverse in failing to meet marketing's requests.

One would expect that in today's data-oriented companies managers could make projections based on detailed analysis of results. Few executives, however, have any idea of profitability by segment, to name one element. Rarer still are good numbers on profitability by product, and only once have I seen a system that allowed profitability to be computed by individual account. Instead, managers either are treated to incomprehensible, foot-thick printouts of unaggregated data or are told in response to their requests that "accounting won't give it to us that way." The inevitable result is a kind of bell-jar environment in which it is impossible to make sound decisions.

POLICIES: SPOKEN AND UNSPOKEN

At the broadest structural level of marketing practice are policy directives. While policies cover the spectrum of administrative activity, I focus here on two especially important marketing implementation policies: identity policies—those relating to what the company is—and direction policies—those concerning what it does. By policies I do not mean only verbal or written statements; indeed, some of the policies most central to good marketing practice are unspoken.

Identity problems are the most common policy difficulties and, paradoxically, occur more often in mature than in young business units. *Marketing theme* and *marketing culture* are two terms I use to capture the powerful but often unspoken feeling of common purpose that the best implementers have and others do not. Theme and culture transmit the company's identity policies.

Marketing theme is a fuzzy but significant term that refers to management's shared understanding of marketing's purpose. In one company, some executives perceived themselves as heading a commodity vendor with the only hope for the future being blue-sky R&D projects. Others believed that the company's key attribute was in differentiating its basic lines. The managers consistently functioned according to their different understandings, and the result was a confused and ineffective marketing effort—a sales force that thought headquarters gave it contradictory signals, a divisive trade, and unhappy customers.

By contrast, another company's management and entire 10,000-person sales force could recite (with conviction): "We are the premier vendor of snack foods in this country. Our products are great. But we have only two seconds to reach the supermarket shopper, so we live or die on service." Management's shared understanding and continual reinforcement of this theme (through compensation, training, and the like), simple though it sounds, promoted exceptionally effective sales performance and consistent customer reactions.

It is tempting to dismiss the notion of fostering a common understanding of the company's marketing theme as a vague and insignificant idea. A test of your company executives' perceptions of that theme may stir up some concern. To conduct this test, write a single sentence describing your company's marketing essence. Then have your key people do so as well. The results are usually as instructive as they are shocking.

Marketing culture is a broader notion than marketing theme. Whereas themes often can be verbalized, culture is the underlying and usually unspoken "social web" of management. It subtly but powerfully channels managers' behavior into comfortable ruts. Culture can be observed clearly from such things as lunchroom conversations and mottoes management puts on the walls.

For example, when I asked managers in one company why they were planning a $700-million plant addition to support a new product line that market research suggested would require only half that capacity, the marketing vice president responded, "We don't see much sense around here in chinning ourselves on the curb."

Direction policies refer to both marketing strategy and leadership. While marketing strategy is outside the realm of this article, leadership deserves attention as a key aspect of implementation. It has become fashionable in corporations to blame shortcomings in practice on culture. It is undeniably true, however, that some top marketing managers are top-notch leaders and others are not. The former inspire us with their eagerness to get out into the field; they are clever at designing simple and effective monitoring methods, and their understanding of customers is powerful. Others are much less effective as leaders, being immersed in complex conceptualizing or unwilling to leave their leather chairs for the marketplace; they are inspirational only as models of what their juniors hope not to become.

The quality of marketing leadership has a far-reaching effect on the quality of marketing practice. Indeed, of the business units I observed that had low-caliber leaders, not one had high-quality marketing practices overall.

Whether a strong theme and culture are brought about by the charisma of the person on top or orchestrated through memoranda is irrelevant. The critical question is whether these intangibles of identity, or "who we are," and direction, or "what we are about," exist as powerful though unquantifiable forces that impose themselves on an observer in the same way they permeate the company.

——— GAP BRIDGING: EXECUTION SKILLS

Up to this point I have analyzed the motorcycle without much attention to the mechanic. Indeed, the primary reason good marketing practice occurs is that managers often use their personal skills to supplant, support, and sometimes quietly overthrow inadequate practice structures. I call this substitution of personal skills for weak structure a "subversion toward quality." Poorly functioning formal marketing systems are frequently "patched up" when the managers using them exercise informal organizing skills. Similarly, informal monitoring schemes often are created to get data the control system can't, and budget "reallocations" often are designed to subvert formal policy constraints. Managers bring four execution skills to the marketing job: interacting, allocating, monitoring, and organizing.

Interacting. The marketing job by its nature is one of influencing others inside and outside the corporation. Inside, there is a regular parade of peers over which the marketer has no power to impose preferences; instead he or she has to strike horse trades. Outside, the marketer deals with a plethora of helpers, including ad agencies, consultants, manufacturers' reps, and the like, each with an agenda and an ax to grind. I observed that those managers who show empathy, that is, the ability to understand how others feel, and have good bargaining skills are the best implementers.

Allocating. The implementer must parcel out everyone's time, assignments, and other resources among the marketing jobs to be done. Able managers have no false sense of egalitarianism or charity but are tough and fair in putting people and dollars where they will be most effective. The less able ones routinely allocate too many dollars and people to mature programs and too few to riskier and amorphous programs.

Monitoring. It is by using monitoring skills that a manager can do the most to reconstruct degraded corporate information and control systems. Good implementers struggle and wrestle with their markets and businesses until they can simply and powerfully express the "back-of-the-envelope" ratios necessary to run the business, regardless of formal control system inadequacies. Poor implementers either wallow blissfully in industry clichés or get mired in awesome and often quantitative complexity that no one understands. The general manager of a company with 38 plants and 300,000 customers, for instance, ran everything he considered crucial according to notations on two three-by-five-inch index cards. By contrast, the sales manager of a company about a hundredth that size generated hand-truckfuls of computer printouts monthly in his monitoring zeal, then let them age like cheese.

Organizing. Good implementers have an almost uncanny ability to create afresh an informal organization, or network, to match each problem with which they are confronted. They "know somebody" in every part of the organization (and outside too) who, by virtue of mutual respect, attraction, or some other tie, can and will help with each problem. That is, these managers reconstruct the organization to suit the marketing job that needs to be done. They customize their informal organization to facilitate good execution. Often, their organization and the formal one have little in common.

GOOD PRACTICE IN MARKETING

The administration of marketing is problematic in all but a few companies, and management's adeptness often is restricted to a few functions or programs within the marketing discipline. Yet some of the businesses in my sample showed truly excellent marketing implementation, and it is from them that some simple but important characteristics that differentiate good marketing practice emerge:

- In the best companies, a strong sense of identity and of direction in marketing policies exists. There is no confusion and little disagreement among managers over "who they are." Further, the leaders are strong and able. There is, indeed, clarity of theme and vision.
- The best implementers continually appeal to the customers, including the trade or distributors, in several unusual ways. Customer concern is an ingrained part of the culture and is always prominent in the theme of the best implementers. Interestingly, the

distributors are also viewed as customers, and management has as a main objective the maintenance of a partnership with both distributors and end users. I call this behavior "profit partnership with wide definition."

I did not find that the good implementers are less profit oriented than the poor ones; quite the opposite. Yet managers best at execution take special care to see that the end users also profit in terms of true value for the money they spend. The trade profits in more traditional ways, with dollar margins, but also benefits from having good implementers consider them as key accounts. The companies less competent at implementation never form a partnership with these two key marketing constituencies or, worse, lose a focus they once had.

- In the best organizations, management is able and willing to substitute its own skills for shortcomings in the formal structure. At United Parcel Service, the story is told with some pride of the regional manager who took it on himself to untangle a misdirected shipment of Christmas presents by hiring an entire train and diverting two UPS-owned 727s from their flight plans.[1] When top management learned of his actions, it praised and rewarded him. The culture supported the manager's substitution of skill for structure, but the regional manager was also "combat ready" to defend his judgment.

- Finally, in the companies that handle execution best, top management has a distinctly different view of both the marketing structure and the managers than do bosses in other companies. In the best companies, without exception, the importance of the executives dominates the importance of the execution structure. That is to say, marketing (and other) managers are top management's "key accounts" and are treated with a latitude not found in other corporations. Top executives in companies that are good at marketing encourage their followers to challenge and question them because it is not always possible for those at the top to be right. Those who are poor at following continually thwart the tendency for policies and structure to become religion, which causes management to lose its flexibility in times of change.[2] This process can be characterized as a "good leaders, poor followers" common theme.

Top managers in the best companies also view the marketing structure differently. They tend to foster a philosophy of "allocation extravagance with program pickiness" in marketing investments. It is not always easy to get new programs approved by these managers, but the plans that are endorsed are staffed,

---

1. "Behind the UPS Mystique: Puritanism and Productivity," *Business Week*, June 6, 1983, p. 66.

2. *See* Thomas V. Bonoma, "Market Success Can Breed 'Marketing Inertia,'" *Harvard Business Review* (September–October 1981).

funded, and otherwise fully supported to maximize their chances of success.

The full endorsement of fewer, sounder marketing programs seems to give these officers the critical mass they need to make the programs work in good times and bad and limits the risk to the company. This approach worked well for one business-jet distributor I studied, which weathered the recession of the early 1980s in much better shape than its more programmatically prolific peers.

Again, in the best companies, management concentrates on one or a few marketing functions that it fosters and nurtures into a competitive distinction through expertise. When strong theme and culture, program pickiness, and functions-level concentration are combined, the conclusion that emerges is that the businesses best at marketing execution encourage soundness at the top (policies) and at the bottom (functions) rather than flashiness in the middle (programs).

When all is said and done, quality in marketing practice is not a guarantee of good marketplace results. There's just too much luck, competitive jockeying, and downright customer perverseness involved to hope for that sort of predictive accuracy. Rather, good marketing practice means using skill artfully to cope with the inevitable execution crises that blur the strategies for managing customers and middlemen. Individually, such threats are not much to fear. Taken collectively, they are strategy killers.

—— DISCUSSION QUESTIONS

1. Can a good marketing strategy succeed without good implementation? The author argues that implementation is more likely to fail than strategy. Is there merit to this thinking? Is it possible to have a very good strategy and see it stifled by poor execution? Provide an example.

2. What are the difficulties that can prevent effective implementation? How can these be remedied?

3. Do you agree with the author that "it is invariably easier to think up clever marketing strategies than it is to make them work under company, competitor, and customer constraints"? Don't both affect each other? Where and how do you draw the line? Give an example of how strategy is shaped by existing constraints. Are there instances when strategy can override and/or reshape the constraints?

33　From Sales Obsession to Marketing Effectiveness

PHILIP KOTLER

This reading points out the problems that arise when companies confuse marketing effectiveness with sales effectiveness. According to the author, executives can determine how well an organization understands and practices marketing by conducting a marketing effectiveness audit. The audit rates effectiveness in five major functions: customer philosophy, integrated marketing organization, adequate marketing information, strategic orientation, and operational efficiency. The resulting score tells where the organization falls on a scale ranging from superior marketing effectiveness to none at all. The reading further shows top management how to respond to a low or mediocre score by injecting more marketing thinking into the division or company.

The president of a major industrial equipment company with annual sales of over \$1 billion was unhappy with his company's performance. Overall sales were at a standstill; market shares were under attack in several key divisions; profits were low and showing no signs of improvement. Yet the divisions prepared annual marketing plans and employed marketing executives and marketing services. Also, the sales force was well-trained and motivated.

The president called in the corporate vice president of marketing and said:

> I would like to know how each division rates from a marketing point of view. I don't mean current sales performance. I mean whether it exhibits a dynamic marketing orientation. I want a marketing score for each division. For each deficient division, I want a plan for improving its marketing effectiveness over the next few years. I want evidence next year that each division is making progress.

The corporate vice president left feeling uncomfortable about this assignment. Marketing effectiveness is a complex subject. What key indicators are involved? How can they be scaled? How can they be combined into an index? How reliable would this index be?

The vice president got little help from the marketing literature. Some articles described "the marketing concept" in philosophical terms. A few articles featured instruments to rate the "marketing-orientedness" of companies or divisions. However, these instruments were oversimplified.

The marketing vice president had to create a marketing effectiveness auditing system. The system had to be based on a sound philosophical concept of the role of marketing in the modern corporation. It had to have credibility. It had to yield clear directions on steps that the corporation could take to improve marketing effectiveness where it was lacking. It had to be available for periodic application to measure progress toward greater marketing effectiveness.

—— SALES/MARKETING CONFUSION

Marketing is one of the most misunderstood functions of the modern corporation. Of the *Fortune* 500 corporations, it seems to me that only a handful—such as Procter & Gamble, Eastman Kodak, Avon, McDonald's, IBM, Xerox, General Electric, and Caterpillar—really understand and practice sophisticated marketing. Most of the other companies are only under the illusion they practice sophisticated marketing. A chief executive in one of the world's largest automobile companies once said: "I thought we were doing marketing. We have a corporate vice president of marketing, a top-notch sales force, a skilled advertising department, and elaborate marketing planning procedures. These fooled us. When the crunch came, I realized that we weren't producing the cars that people wanted. We weren't responding to new needs. Our marketing operation was nothing more than a glorified sales department."

In industrial goods companies, too, management often confuses sales and marketing. Sales and distribution are the major elements of the marketing mix, with advertising playing a very minor role. Most if not all of the marketing talent in the company comes from the sales organization. These people are not counterbalanced often enough with "brand management" personnel, who think in terms of long-run product strategy and its financial implications.

CONTRASTS IN THINKING

Yet the thinking of sales executives is very different from the thinking of marketing executives. One marketing executive recently complained: "It takes me about five years to train sales people to think marketing. And in many cases I never succeed."

Sales executives tend to think in the following terms:

- *Sales volume rather than profits.* They aim to increase current sales to meet quota commitments and to achieve good commissions and bonuses. They are usually not attentive to profit differences among different products or customer classes unless these are reflected in compensation.

- *Short-run rather than long-run terms.* They are oriented toward today's products, markets, customers, and strategies. They don't tend to think about product/market expansion strategies over the next five years.
- *Individual customers rather than market segment classes.* They are knowledgeable about individual accounts and the factors bearing on a specific sales transaction. They are less interested in developing strategies for market segments.
- *Field work rather than desk work.* They prefer to try to sell to customers instead of developing plans and strategies and working out methods of implementation.

In contrast, marketing executives think in these terms:

- *Profit planning.* They plan sales volume around profits. Their aim is to plan product mixes, customer mixes, and marketing mixes to achieve profitable volume and market shares at levels of risk that are acceptable.
- *Long-run trends, threats, and opportunities.* They study how the company can translate these into new products, markets, and marketing strategies that will assure long-term growth.
- *Customer types and segment differences.* They hope to figure out ways to offer superior value to the most profitable segments.
- *Good systems for market analysis, planning, and control.* They are comfortable with numbers and with working out the financial implications of marketing plans.

A COMMON DILEMMA

Once the management of a company recognizes such differences between sales and marketing thinking, it may decide to establish a high-level marketing position. Here it faces a dilemma. No one in the company is a trained marketing manager. The whole industry may be devoid of trained marketing managers. Yet trained marketers outside the industry are not knowledgeable about the industry's products and customers' buying patterns.

The company typically resolves the problem by promoting a top sales manager to a new title—vice president of marketing. However, the new marketing executive continues to think like a sales executive. Instead of taking time to analyze environmental changes, new consumer needs, competitive challenges, and new strategies for company growth, he or she worries about the disappointing sales in Kansas City last week or the price cut initiated by a rival corporation yesterday. The marketing executive probably spends almost as much time putting out new fires as when he or she was a sales executive.

Moreover, former sales executives heading the marketing operation often lack a balanced view of the effectiveness of different marketing tools. They continue to favor the sales force in the marketing mix. They are reluctant to take dollars out of the sales force budget to help increase new-product development, advertising, sales promotion, or marketing research. They underestimate the cost-effectiveness or non-sales-force marketing expenditures in increasing customer awareness, interest, conviction, and purchase.

The sales executive dressed in a marketing vice president's clothing often fails to appreciate the negative impact of aggressive sales action on a company's bottom line. In one company where the marketing vice president is extremely strong, short-run sales-oriented promotions are constantly disrupting production planning and cash flow requirements. One of the company's plants, for example, operates at 50% capacity much of the time and at 150% the rest of the time. Sales-oriented marketing managers are in the saddle and give little heed to the adverse impact of their actions on manufacturing costs or working capital costs.

JOB OF THE MARKETING EXECUTIVE

What is the proper conception of the job of a high-level marketing executive? The answer has gone through three stages of thinking.

The earliest and most popular view is that the marketing executive is an expert at *demand stimulation*. He or she is someone who knows how to combine the tools of marketing to create an efficient impact on chosen markets. The marketing executive understands buyers' wants, buying influences, channels, and competition, and is able to use product features, personal selling, advertising, sales promotion, price, and service to stimulate purchasing behavior.

More recently, a broader conception of the marketing executive has been proposed: he or she should be an expert in *demand management*. The marketing executive works with a varied and changing set of demand problems. Sometimes demand is too low and must be stimulated; sometimes demand is too irregular and must be evened out, or "smoothed"; sometimes demand is temporarily too high (as in a shortage period) and must be reduced with "demarketing."[1]

The increasingly volatile state of the economy is one reason that the marketing executive needs broad skills in demand management rather than abilities only in demand stimulation. The varying fortunes of different company divisions is another reason. Every multidivision company has certain divisions whose low sales growth, market share, or profitability may call for a strategic

---

1. *See* Philip Kotler and Sidney J. Levy, "Demarketing, Yes, Demarketing," *Harvard Business Review* (November–December 1971).

objective other than growth. The strategic objective might be to maintain, "harvest," or terminate sales. Hence the marketing executive must be skilled at more tasks than simply stimulating demand.

Even the conception of the marketing executive as an expert in demand management may be too limited. The newest view is that he or she should be effective at *systems management*. The executive who focuses only on attaining a certain demand level may cause undue costs in engineering, purchasing, manufacturing, servicing, or finance. The marketing executive should be able to develop marketing strategies and plans that are profitable. These plans should strike a balance between the needs of the marketing mix (sales force effort, advertising, product quality, service), business functions (manufacturing, finance, marketing), and the external system (customers, distributors, suppliers) from the vantage point of profit.

Where is this person to come from? The ideal marketing manager should have general management experience, not just sales and marketing experience. To deal effectively with manufacturing, research and development, finance and control, advertising, the sales force, and marketing research, the marketing executive should have moved through these departments on the way up. He or she should understand the problems of these other departments; and they should know that the marketing executive knows all about their problems.

────── AUDITING EFFECTIVENESS

Many top managers believe that a division's performance in terms of sales growth, market share, and profitability reveals the quality of its marketing leadership. The high-performing divisions have good marketing leadership; the poor-performing divisions have deficient marketing leadership. Marketing executives in the high-performing divisions are rewarded; the others are replaced.

Actually, marketing effectiveness is not so simple. Good results may be due to a division's being in the right place at the right time rather than the consequence of effective management. Improvements in market planning might boost results from good to excellent. At the same time, another division might have poor results in spite of the best strategic marketing planning. Replacing the present marketing leaders might only make things worse.

In my view, the marketing effectiveness of a company, division, or product line depends largely on a combination of five activities:

1. *Customer philosophy.* Does management acknowledge the primacy of the marketplace and of customer needs and wants in shaping company plans and operations?

2. *Integrated marketing organization.* Is the organization staffed so that it will be able to carry out marketing analysis, planning, and implementation and control?

3. *Adequate marketing information.* Does management receive the kind and quality of information needed to conduct effective marketing?

4. *Strategic orientation.* Does marketing management generate innovative strategies and plans for long-run growth and profitability?

5. *Operational efficiency.* Are marketing plans implemented in a cost-effective manner, and are the results monitored for rapid corrective action?

The *Exhibit* at the end of this reading presents the questions that should be asked in auditing the marketing effectiveness of business. This audit has been helpful to a number of companies and divisions. In the next few sections I will elaborate on each main part of the marketing audit.

CUSTOMER PHILOSOPHY

The first requirement for effective marketing is that key managers recognize the primacy of studying the market, distinguishing the many opportunities, selecting the best parts of the market to serve, and gearing up to offer superior value to the chosen customers in terms of their needs and wants. This requirement seems elementary, yet many executives never grasp it.

Some managements are product oriented. They think the trick is to make a good product and go out and sell it. Some are technology oriented. They are fascinated with the challenge of new technologies and pay little attention to the size and requirements of the market. Still others are sales oriented. They think anything can be sold with sufficient sales effort.

If a company starts with the marketplace when it is designing the organization's structure, plans, and controls, it is well on the way to effective marketing.

INTEGRATED ORGANIZATION

The organizational structure of the company or division must reflect a marketing philosophy. The major marketing functions must be integrated and controlled by a high-level marketing executive. Various marketing positions must be designed to serve the needs of important market segments, territories, and product lines. Marketing management must be effective in working with other departments and earning their respect and cooperation. Finally, the organization must reflect a well-defined system for developing, evaluating, testing, and launching new products because they constitute the heart of the business's future.

ADEQUATE INFORMATION

Effective marketing calls for the executives to have adequate information for planning and allocating resources properly to different markets, products, territories, and marketing tools. A telltale sign of the quality of information is whether management possesses recent studies of customers' perceptions, preferences, and buying habits. Many marketing managers operate primarily on what they learned as sales managers in a particular industry 20 years earlier. They don't want to spend money for marketing research because "we already know the market." They spend little to monitor direct and indirect competition.

Another sign is the presence of good information regarding the sales potential and profitability of different market segments, customers, territories, products, channels, and order sizes. The controller must work closely with marketing and provide a responsive accounting system that gives profit information by line item. Finally, skillful marketers need information to evaluate the results of their marketing expenditures.

STRATEGY AND OPERATIONS

Marketing effectiveness depends also on whether management can design a profitable strategy out of its philosophy, organization, and information resources. First, this requires a formal system for annual and long-range marketing planning. Second, the system should lead to a core strategy that is clear, innovative, and data-based. Third, management should look ahead toward contingent actions that might be required by new developments in the marketplace.

And last, marketing plans do not bear fruit unless they are efficiently carried out at various levels of the organization. The interests of the customers must be of paramount concern to employees throughout the organization. Marketing management must have the right amount of resources to do the job. It also must have systems that enable it to react quickly and intelligently to on-the-spot developments.

——— IMPROVING POOR PERFORMANCE

The auditing instrument enables management to identify marketing weaknesses in a company or division. But diagnosis is not enough. Management should follow up by forming a marketing committee staffed with top executives of the company or division and a suitable complement of functional managers.

The task of the committee is to review the results of the audit and prepare a marketing improvement plan. The plan should deal with these needs:

1. Training of officers, through seminars, for example, to provide a better understanding of modern marketing.
2. Hiring of consultants to bring into the company specific marketing improvements that are needed.
3. Creation of new positions in the marketing organization.
4. Personnel transfers where necessary.
5. Increased investment—or sometimes just more efficient investment—in marketing research.
6. Installment of improved formal planning procedures.

Suppose these steps are not pursued vigorously. This situation is not unlikely in an organization with poor marketing ability; the managers prefer to think exclusively in terms of production, sales, or research.

CHOOSING AN EFFECTIVE APPROACH

To visualize what top management can do, consider the following case.

One division of a large company was headed by a general manager with the vice presidents of manufacturing, finance, and sales reporting to her. This division had enjoyed steady growth of sales and profit during the past decade. However, during the preceding two years there had been a sales decline. Managers thought the decline reflected the maturing of the industry and the slowing down of the national economy. The sales vice president's answer was to increase the sales force and push harder.

The corporate marketing vice president applied the marketing audit to the division and found that it scored very poorly. The division's executives did not have a marketing philosophy; there was no high-level marketing position; marketing information was poor; and there was little strategic thinking.

The corporate marketing vice president expressed his concern to the general manager. Together, they agreed on the need to infuse modern marketing thinking into the division, but in a way that did not alienate those in power, especially the vice president of sales.

They considered three different strategies for bringing marketing thinking into the division.

The first called for convincing the sales vice president to add a marketing person to her staff. This person would handle such activities as marketing research, problem solving, and planning. The hoped-for result was that the sales vice president would gradually come to develop a better appreciation of marketing thinking.

The corporate marketing vice president and the general manager realized, however, that the first approach might fail. The sales vice president might choose not to hire anyone, or to hire a person but give him or her little responsibility, or to hire an incompetent person and prove that marketing planning is a waste. Many marketing staff people who report to sales vice presidents complain that their bosses do not pay attention to plans and recommendations. Therefore the two executives decided to consider a possible second approach.

This second approach was to hire a marketing vice president from the outside and place the incumbent sales vice president (whose title might be changed to general sales manager) under him or her. In addition, advertising, customer service, and other marketing functions would be placed under the new marketing vice president. The message would come across loud and clear that sales was only one, albeit the most important, of several elements in a coordinated marketing planning system.

The danger of this solution was that the sales vice president and her sales force could become angry and sabotage the new vice president. Therefore, the corporate vice president and the general manager considered still another approach.

The third approach fell between the two extremes and called for the general manager to appoint a marketing director to her staff. The marketing director would not have control or responsibility for field sales. He or she would prepare studies of new products, markets, and marketing strategies; estimate the profitability and cost-effectiveness of different marketing activities; conduct studies of customer perceptions, preferences, and buying habits; and supervise the preparation of marketing plans. The general manager could then decide to give this person the title of corporate marketing director, marketing planner, or planning director.

The third approach had the most to recommend it. The new marketing director would not be under the thumb of the sales vice president; nor would he or she be appointed over the sales vice president, with all the problems that this move might create. Over time, the marketing director might be promoted to marketing vice president to run all the marketing activities, including sales. But this would be done only after he or she developed a record of accomplishment and proved able to work harmoniously with the sales vice president, sales managers, and other key people.

—— CONCLUSION

We tend to confuse marketing effectiveness with sales effectiveness. This is our big mistake—and in the end it hurts sales as well as marketing. A company or division may have a top-notch sales force that could not perform better. But if the salespeople don't have the right products to sell, know the best customers, and have the best values to offer, their energy counts for little.

One way to view the difference between marketing and sales is in terms of the difference between seeding a field and harvesting the crops. Good marketing work is tantamount to planting seeds; without planting, there will be no future crops. Good sales work is equivalent to efficiently harvesting the crops. In the short run, the harvest may be good and sales will take the credit. But if there is no reseeding by marketing, heavy sales effort will be for naught.

This is not to say that top marketing executives are supposed to keep their heads in the clouds and stay out of the daily storms beating the field. They must do both. They are responsible for this year's profits as well as long-run profitability. If they spend all their time slugging it out with competitors to reap today's profits, they make their job harder tomorrow. If they only consider tomorrow, they may be lashed for today's inadequate profits. They have no choice but to balance their time between both objectives.

Marketing thinking is not easy to introduce into an organization. It tends to be misunderstood or, once understood, easily forgotten in the wake of success. Marketing is characterized by a law of slow learning and rapid forgetting.

The corporation, and particularly the corporate vice president of marketing, has the responsibility of assessing marketing effectiveness in each division. An audit of the type described in this article can be a useful tool. Using it, the top executive can work constructively with general managers of divisions that have a low score, apprising them of the factors that make up marketing effectiveness. This plan may include attending marketing seminars, reading the marketing literature, hiring inside experts or outside consultants, carrying out fresh research, and improving strategy and planning.

In some divisions, as I have pointed out, top management may need to intervene. It may need to hire a marketing-trained person to work for the sales vice president, a marketing director to work for the general manager, or a marketing vice president to head all sales and marketing activity.

The results of trying to improve the division's marketing effectiveness can be evaluated each year. The amount of progress can be measured by using the audit.[1] If progress has been good, the division will be encouraged to develop a new plan for further progress. If progress has been poor, top management will have to consider the need for more drastic steps to protect the interests of the corporation against the marketing division with poor marketing skills.

---

1. *See* the *Exhibit* on the next page.

EXHIBIT
Outline for Marketing Effectiveness (Check one answer for each question.)

CUSTOMER PHILOSOPHY

A. Does management recognize the importance of designing the company to serve the needs and wants of chosen markets?

Score

0   ☐   Management primarily thinks in terms of selling current and new products to whoever will buy them.
1   ☐   Management thinks in terms of serving a wide range of markets and needs with equal effectiveness.
2   ☐   Management thinks in terms of serving the needs and wants of well-defined markets chosen for their long-run growth and profit potential for the company.

B. Does management develop different offerings and marketing plans for different segments of the market?

0   ☐   No.
1   ☐   Somewhat.
2   ☐   To a good extent.

C. Does management take a whole marketing system view (suppliers, channels, competitors, customers, environment) in planning its business?

0   ☐   No. Management concentrates on selling and servicing its immediate customers.
1   ☐   Somewhat. Management takes a long view of its channels although the bulk of its effort goes to selling and servicing the immediate customers.
2   ☐   Yes. Management takes a whole marketing systems view recognizing the threats and opportunities created for the company by changes in any part of the system.

INTEGRATED MARKETING ORGANIZATION

D. Is there high-level marketing integration and control of the major marketing functions?

0   ☐   No. Sales and other marketing functions are not integrated at the top and there is some unproductive conflict.
1   ☐   Somewhat. There is formal integration and control of the major marketing functions but less than satisfactory coordination and cooperation.
2   ☐   Yes. The major marketing functions are effectively integrated.

E. Does marketing management work well with management in research, manufacturing, purchasing, physical distribution, and finance?

0   ☐   No. There are complaints that marketing is unreasonable in the demands and costs it places on other departments.
1   ☐   Somewhat. The relations are amicable although each department pretty much acts to serve its own power interests.
2   ☐   Yes. The departments cooperate effectively and resolve issues in the best interest of the company as a whole.

F. How well-organized is the new product development process?

0   ☐   The system is ill-defined and poorly handled.
1   ☐   The system formally exists but lacks sophistication.
2   ☐   The system is well-structured and professionally staffed.

EXHIBIT
Outline for Marketing Effectiveness (Continued)

ADEQUATE MARKETING INFORMATION

    G. When were the latest marketing research studies of customers, buying influences, channels, and competitors conducted?

0 ☐ Several years ago.
1 ☐ A few years ago.
2 ☐ Recently.

    H. How well does management know the sales potential and profitability of different market segments, customers, territories, products, channels, and order sizes?

0 ☐ Not at all.
1 ☐ Somewhat.
2 ☐ Very well.

    I. What effort is expended to measure the cost-effectiveness of different marketing expenditures?

0 ☐ Little or no effort.
1 ☐ Some effort.
2 ☐ Substantial effort.

STRATEGIC ORIENTATION

    J. What is the extent of formal marketing planning?

0 ☐ Management does little or no formal marketing planning.
1 ☐ Management develops an annual marketing plan.
2 ☐ Management develops a detailed annual marketing plan and a careful long-range plan that is updated annually.

    K. What is the quality of the current marketing strategy?

0 ☐ The current strategy is not clear.
1 ☐ The current strategy is clear and represents a continuation of traditional strategy.
2 ☐ The current strategy is clear, innovative, data-based, and well-reasoned.

    L. What is the extent of contingency thinking and planning?

0 ☐ Management does little or no contingency thinking.
1 ☐ Management does some contingency thinking although little formal contingency planning.
2 ☐ Management formally identifies the most important contingencies and develops contingency plans.

OPERATIONAL EFFICIENCY

    M. How well is the marketing thinking at the top communicated and implemented down the line?

0 ☐ Poorly.
1 ☐ Fairly.
2 ☐ Successfully.

    N. Is management doing an effective job with the marketing resources?

0 ☐ No. The marketing resources are inadequate for the job to be done.
1 ☐ Somewhat. The marketing resources are adequate but they are not employed optimally.
2 ☐ Yes. The marketing resources are adequate and are deployed efficiently.

EXHIBIT
Outline for Marketing Effectiveness (Continued)

O. **Does management show a good capacity to react quickly and effectively to on-the-spot developments?**

0 ☐ No. Sales and market information is not very current and management reaction time is slow.

1 ☐ Somewhat. Management receives fairly up-to-date sales and market information; management reaction time varies.

2 ☐ Yes. Management has installed systems yielding highly current information and fast reaction time.

TOTAL SCORE

Rating marketing effectiveness

The auditing outline can be used in this way. The auditor collects information as it bears on the 15 questions. The appropriate answer is checked for each question. The scores are added with the total somewhere between 0 and 30. The following scale shows the equivalent in marketing effectiveness:

0–5	None
6–10	Poor
11–15	Fair
16–20	Good
21–25	Very good
26–30	Superior

To illustrate, 15 senior managers in a large building materials company were invited to rate their company using the auditing instrument in this exhibit. The resulting overall marketing effectiveness scores ranged from a low of 6 to a high of 15. The median score was 11, with three-fourths of the scores between 9 and 13. Therefore, most of the managers thought their company was at best "fair" at marketing.

Several divisions were also rated. Their media scores ranged from a low of 3 to a high of 19. The higher scoring divisions tended to have higher profitability. However, some of the lower scoring divisions were also profitable. An examination of the latter showed that these divisions were in industries where their competition also operated at a low level of marketing effectiveness. The managers feared that these divisions would be vulnerable as soon as competition began to learn to market more successfully.

An interesting question to speculate on is the distribution of median marketing effectiveness scores for *Fortune* 500 companies. My suspicion is that very few companies in that roster would score above 20 ("very good" or "superior") in marketing effectiveness. Although marketing theory and practice have received their fullest expression in the United States, the great majority of U.S. companies probably fail to meet the highest standards.

────── DISCUSSION QUESTIONS

1. The difference between being sales-minded and marketing-minded is a subtle one. Most sales executives, says the author, are unable to detect that difference. Explain the difference in their thinking from that of marketing executives. Would you ever promote a top-notch sales executive into a marketing management position? Why or why not?

2. In the author's view, sales executives need to learn to think in terms of marketing. Explain his philosophy. Do you agree? Doesn't each function contribute substantially to a company's health?

3. Marketing strategy needs good implementation to be effective. How can management assess successful implementation? Assume that your company's marketing department has implemented a program and is now waiting for the results. Sales volume is disappointing. Is this a reliable indicator that the program itself was not a good one? What are some of the elements that should be targeted in measuring the success of a program?

PART SEVEN

ISSUES FOR THE 1990s

As we approach the twenty-first century, we recognize that social and economic change inevitably influences the marketplace—and marketing management must respond accordingly. Are certain marketing methods becoming obsolete as certain areas shift in importance? How do such phenomena as the emergence of a service economy, the growth of multinational firms, greater awareness of ethical and legal issues, and the development of high technology shape the way managers plan and execute marketing programs? This group of readings explores the problems and opportunities for marketers in the 1990s as they strive to reach and influence customers in new and creative ways.

SECTION A

SERVICES

Strategies used to market services differ from those used to market manufactured products. Both need essential market information and segmentation, but a service company is more dependent on knowing who its customers are, what those customers want most from a service provider, and how to give them what they expect in an efficient, economical way. Since service is not a tangible product, effective service marketing entails not only meeting customers' needs but also their expectations. No matter what the service—health care, transportation, lodging, food, or retail—quality, in fact and perception, is the important commodity to deliver to customers. The following readings explore such issues as ensuring service quality and identifying and segmenting customers.

Lessons in the Service Sector   34

JAMES L. HESKETT

Whatever your business, services have something to teach, argues the author. "[They] display some common themes and practices [that] yield lessons for managers in any sector of business." According to the author, a company can greatly enhance the delivery of a service to customers if all its employees cooperate in the effort. In this reading, he illustrates this principle in action, describing how marketing and operating managers at the Hartford Steam Boiler Inspection and Insurance Company worked together to develop and implement a strategic service vision. He focuses on identification of a target market segment, development of a service concept to address the targeted customers' needs, construction of an operating strategy to support the service concept, and design of a delivery system to make the operating strategy effective. The author also shows how involvement of the employees who actually deliver the service enables companies to benefit from shared values, peer-group control, incentive programs, and close customer relationships.

A large food and lodging company creates and staffs more general management jobs than any ten manufacturers of comparable size. This company, like many others dispensing high customer-contact services, has eliminated functional lines of responsibility between operations and marketing. In its planning the company routinely combines operations and marketing with what I call a strategic service vision.

The most profitable large American company daily assumes the task of managing a work force of window washers, cooks, and maintenance personnel. An almost single-minded concentration on people—their jobs, their equipment, their personal development—accounts for much of its success.

The quality control process in a decentralized oil-field services business involves careful selection, development, assignment, and compensation of employees working under varying conditions and in widespread locations where close supervision is impossible. In this prosperous company, the process builds shared values and bonds people together.

An international airline, by paying more attention to market economies than to production scale economies, reduces the average size of its aircraft and increases its net income.

Products introduced since 1982 by a well-known financial service generated 10% of its revenues in 1985. The raw material for these products is data already existing in other forms in the company's vast data base.

These examples give a glimpse of forward-looking management practice. When examined closely, they offer insights into the ideas on which successful competitive strategies have been fashioned in the much-maligned and little-understood service sector.

It's no coincidence that dominant industries have cutting-edge management practices. Some U.S. railroads in the nineteenth century pioneered in divisionalized management of their far-flung systems and in good procurement procedures to support their sizable construction and operational needs. At the turn of the century, basic industries led the way in experimenting with scientific management. Then the rise of the large consumer goods manufacturer, epitomized by the auto industry, spawned concepts of decentralization and a full product line aimed at carefully segmented markets.

Today service industries have assumed the mantle of economic leadership. These industries—encompassing trade, communications, transportation, food and lodging, financial and medical services, education, government, and technical services to industry—account for about 70% of the national income and three-fourths of the nonfarm jobs in the United States. In generating 44 million new jobs in the past 30 years, they have absorbed most of the influx of women and minorities into the work force, softened the effects of every post–World War II recession, and fueled every recent economic recovery.

In view of this leadership role, now is a good time to look at the exemplars in the service sector for insights into ways of boosting productivity and altering competitive strategies. Despite their diversity, leading companies in many service industries display some common themes and practices. And they yield lessons for managers in any sector of business. Let's look first at the way the best service companies are structured.

—— INTEGRATED FUNCTIONS

Most goods-producing businesses follow the traditional organizational pattern of separate and equally important marketing and manufacturing functions, with coordinating authority at high levels. Some service businesses do the same thing, but the pattern is much less common in service companies where contact with customers is close, as in retailing, passenger transport, and food and lodging. In these businesses, service is marketed and produced at the same place and time, and often by the same person. Naturally, close coordination between marketing and operations management in these cases, regardless of reporting relationships, is essential.

Integration of marketing and operations is often found at very low levels in these organizations. In fact, in a survey of field managers in four multisite service companies, more than 90% claimed responsibility for operations, personnel, and marketing. They could not say which was most important, and paid great attention to each.[1]

Even where operations are buffered from marketing activities in organizations offering little customer-contact service, there are ways to break down the traditional functional barriers. Several years ago, the Chase Manhattan Bank launched an effort to upgrade its nonloan products, improve its external communications and customer service, and make its back-office (production) operations more market based. A weak spot was Chase's international business. In the highly visible "product" of international money transfer, differences of viewpoint between marketing—embodied in the account relations manager in the field—and the back office in New York had frustrated communication. Errors were frequent, a large backlog of inquiries about balances and transactions had piled up, and morale in the operations group was poor.

A study ordered by the executive put in charge showed that headquarters accounted for operational errors in only about one-third of all the inquiries and that the marketing people had little idea what operations could offer the bank's customers. The executive traced the backlogged errors to their sources, often a correspondent bank, and resolved them. He launched a campaign to improve operations staff morale around the theme "We make it happen" and formed a new group, the customer mobile unit, consisting of the bank's most experienced international operations people. The unit visited Chase customers at their businesses to help resolve problems and smooth operations. The executive brought the marketing and back-office people together to talk about ways to improve the flow of information. Perhaps most important, the bank revised reporting relationships so that operations units serving specific market segments reported to both the customer relationship manager and the head of operations—a move that improved functional coordination.[2]

The product manager's job was created in many manufacturing organizations to address the problem of coordinating manufacturing and marketing. But in most cases, product managers have had profit responsibility without the authority to coordinate. Assignment to these positions has been regarded as temporary, which encourages decisions with a short-term orientation.

Because of their importance, the high-contact service company makes a point of developing numbers of marketing-operations managers, often carrying the title of store or branch manager. At hand, therefore, is a large

1. Christopher H. Lovelock, Eric Langeard, John E. G. Bateson, and Pierre Eiglier, "Some Organizational Problems Facing Marketing in the Service Sector," in *Marketing of Services*, eds. James H. Donnelly and William R. George (Chicago, Ill.: American Marketing Association, 1981), p. 168.

2. James F. Loud, "Organizing for Customer Service," *The Bankers Magazine* (November–December 1980): 41.

cadre of talent from which the company can draw senior managers already trained for administrative responsibilities.

——— STRATEGIC SERVICE VISION

The need of most service organizations to plan as well as direct marketing and operations as one function has led to the formation in leading companies of what I call a strategic service vision. It consists of identification of a target market segment, development of a service concept to address targeted customers' needs, codification of an operating strategy to support the service concept, and design of a service delivery system to support the operating strategy. (These basic elements appear in labeled columns in *Exhibit 1.*)

A company naturally tries to position itself in relation to both the target market and the competition. The links between the service concept and the operating strategies are those policies and procedures by which the company seeks to maximize the difference between the value of the service to customers (the service concept) and the cost of providing it. This difference, of course, is a primary determinant of profit. And the link between the operating strategy and the service delivery system is the integration achieved in the design of both. (These integrative links appear in labeled columns in *Exhibit 1.*)

To see how the strategic service vision works, examine the Hartford Steam Boiler Inspection & Insurance Company. For many years, HSB has been in the business of insuring industrial and institutional equipment. Its market targets are organizations using boilers and related pieces of equipment with high operating risk. It offers the same risk reduction as many other insurance companies but positions itself against the competition by emphasizing cost reduction as well.

HSB concentrates on a few types of equipment and has built a large data base on their operating and performance characteristics. (Manufacturers of the equipment often turn to HSB for wear and maintenance data.) The information furnishes the actuarial base on which HSB prices its insurance. The company's engineers, who inspect customers' equipment before and after it is insured, are also qualified to give advice on preventing problems and improving utilization rates, and through many years of association they often get very close to their customers. As a service manager of one HSB client told me, "If I tried to replace that insurance contract, my operating people in the plant would let me know about it."

This practice enhances the perceived value of the service to the customer at little extra cost to HSB. Of course, by reducing the risk to the customer HSB can improve its own loss ratio.

HSB has a larger cadre of engineers than any of its competitors. These engineers, in tandem with the big data base, make up a service delivery system that capitalizes on the knowledge of marketing and operating managers at all levels of the organization.

EXHIBIT 1 Externally Oriented Strategic Service Vision

BASIC ELEMENT	INTEGRATIVE ELEMENT	BASIC ELEMENT	INTEGRATIVE ELEMENT	BASIC ELEMENT	INTEGRATIVE ELEMENT	BASIC ELEMENT
Target Market Segments	*Positioning*	*Service Concept*	*Value-Cost Leveraging*	*Operating Strategy*	*Strategy-Systems Integration*	*Service Delivery System*
What are common characteristics of important market segments?	How does the service concept propose to meet customer needs?	What are important elements of the service to be provided, stated in terms of results produced for customers?	To what extent are differences between perceived value and cost of service maximized by:	What are important elements of the strategy?	To what extent are the strategy and delivery system internally consistent?	What are important features of the service delivery system, including:
What dimensions can be used to segment the market?	How do competitors meet these needs?	How are these elements supposed to be perceived by the target segment? By the market in general? By employees as a whole?	Standardization of certain elements?	Operations?	Can needs of the strategy be met by the delivery system?	The role of people?
Demographic?	How is the proposed service differentiated from competition?		Customization of certain elements?	Financing?	If not, what changes must be made in:	Technology?
Psychographic?	How important are these differences?		Emphasizing easily leveraged services?	Marketing?		Equipment?
How important are various segments?			Management of supply and demand?	Organization?	The operating strategy?	Layout?
What needs does each have?	What is good service?	How do customers perceive the service concept?	Control of quality through—	Human resources?	The service delivery system?	Procedures?
How well are these needs being served?	Does the proposed service concept provide it?	What efforts does this suggest in terms of the manner in which the service is:	Rewards?	Control?	To what extent does the coordination of operating strategy and service delivery system ensure:	What capacity does it provide?
In what manner?	What efforts are required to bring customer expectations and service capabilities into alignment?	Designed?	Appeal to pride?	On which will the most effort be concentrated?		Normally?
By whom?		Delivered?	Visibility and supervision?	Where will investments be made?	High quality?	At peak levels?
		Marketed?	Peer group control?	How will quality and cost be controlled?	High productivity?	To what extent does it:
			Involving the customer?	Measured?	Low cost?	Help ensure quality standards?
			Effective use of data?	Incentives?	High morale and loyalty of servers?	Differentiate the service from competition?
			To what extent does this effort create barriers to entry by potential competition?	Rewards?	To what extent does this integration provide barriers to entry to competition?	Provide barriers to entry by competitors?
				What results will be expected versus competition in terms of:		
				Quality of service?		
				Cost profile?		
				Productivity?		
				Morale and loyalty of servers?		

The net result is a strategic service vision (though HSB doesn't use the term) that is highly valued by its customers and very profitable for its provider. It addresses implementation issues as part of the strategic plan, and it requires agreement and coordination among marketing and operating managers throughout the organization.

—— INNER-DIRECTED VISION

High-performance service companies have gained their status in large measure by turning the strategic service vision inward: by targeting important groups of employees as well as customers. In the head offices of these organizations, questions such as those listed in *Exhibit 2* are heard often. The questions parallel those in *Exhibit 1;* but in asking them about employees, management shows it's aware that the health of the enterprise depends on the degree to which core groups of employees subscribe to and share a common set of values and are served by the company's activities.

The basic elements (columns are labeled as in *Exhibit 1*) start with the service concept designed with employees' needs in mind. The operating strategy is set to meet these needs in a superior fashion at the lowest cost, a result often achieved through the design of the service delivery system. The integrative elements, shaded lighter, include positioning of a service concept, which, it is hoped, will lead to low turnover, low training costs, and the opportunity to develop shared goals and values. High-performance service organizations invariably have operating strategies designed to maximize differences between operating costs and value perceived by employees in their relations with the company. And delivery systems designed with the operating strategy in mind can form the foundation for remarkable gains in productivity.

A case in point is the ServiceMaster Company, based in Downers Grove, Illinois, which manages support services for hospitals, schools, and industrial companies. It supervises the employees of customers' organizations engaged in housekeeping, food service, and equipment maintenance. These are services that are peripheral to the customers' businesses and therefore receive little management attention.

Many of the people whom ServiceMaster oversees are functionally illiterate. To them, as well as its own managers, ServiceMaster directs a service concept centered around the philosophy stated by its CEO: "Before asking someone to do something, you have to help them be something." ServiceMaster provides educational and motivational programs to help these employees "be something."

To its own supervisors the company offers training that leads to an ambitious "master's" program taught in part by the chief executive. New responsibilities and opportunities present themselves via the rapid growth of the company, approximating 20% per year, nearly all of it from expansion of

EXHIBIT 2 Internally Orientated Strategic Service Vision

BASIC ELEMENT	INTEGRATIVE ELEMENT	BASIC ELEMENT	INTEGRATIVE ELEMENT	BASIC ELEMENT	INTEGRATIVE ELEMENT	BASIC ELEMENT
Target Employee Group	*Positioning*	*Service Concept*	*Value-Cost Leveraging*	*Operating Strategy*	*Strategy-Systems Integration*	*Service-Delivery System*
What are common characteristics of important employee groups?	How does the service concept propose to meet such needs?	What are important elements of the service to be provided, stated in terms of results produced for employees and the company?	To what extent are differences between returns to employees and the level of effort they put forth maximized by:	How important is direct human contact in the provision of the service?	To what extent are the strategy and the delivery system for serving important employee groups internally consistent?	What are important features of the service delivery system, including: The role of people? Technology? Equipment? Layout? Procedures?
What dimensions can be used to describe these employee groups? Demographic? Psychographic?	How do competitors meet such needs? How are relationships with employees differentiated from those between competitors and their employees?	How are these elements supposed to be perceived by the targeted employee group?	The design of the service concept? The design of the elements of the operating strategy? Job design?	To what extent have employees been involved in the design of the service concept and operating strategy?	To what extent does the integration of operating strategy and service delivery system ensure: High quality? High productivity? Low cost? High morale and "bonding" of the target employee group?	What does it require of target employee groups? Normally? At peak periods of activity?
How important are each of these groups to the delivery of the service?	How important are these differences?	How are these elements perceived?	The leveraging of scarce skills with a support system? The management of supply and demand?	How desirable is it to: Increase employee satisfaction? Increase employee productivity?		To what extent does it help employees: Meet quality standards?
What needs does each group have?	What is "good service" to employees? Does the proposed service concept provide it?	What further efforts does this suggest in terms of the manner in which the service is: Designed? Delivered?	Control of quality through— Rewards? Appeal to pride? Visibility? Supervision? Peer group control?	What incentives are provided for: Quality? Productivity? Cost?		Differentiate their service from competitors? Achieve expectations about the quality of their work life?
How well are these needs being served? In what manner? By whom?	What efforts are required to bring employee expectations and service capabilities into alignment?		Involving the customer in the delivery of the service? Effective use of data?	How does the strategy address employee needs for: Selection? Assignment? Development? Evaluation? Compensation? Association?		

existing operations rather than acquisition. Elaborate training aids and a laboratory for developing new equipment and materials enhance the employee-
managers' "be something" feeling.

For customers' employees ServiceMaster tries to build the "be something" attitude and improve their productivity by redesigning their jobs and by
developing equipment and pictorial, color-coded instructional materials. In
most cases it is the first time that anyone has paid attention to the service of
which these employees are a part. ServiceMaster also holds weekly sessions to
exchange ideas and offers educational programs to, among other things, develop literacy. ServiceMaster also recruits up to 20% of its own managers from
the ranks in jobs it handles. The service concept clearly is improved self-respect,
self-development, personal satisfaction, and upward mobility.

Another company slogan, repeated often, is "to help people grow."
When a hospital served by the company decided to hire a deaf person,
ServiceMaster's local head didn't object but instead authorized three supervi-
sors to take a course in sign language.

It should be no surprise that the turnover rate among ServiceMaster's
7,000 employees is low. Further, the turnover rate in organizations it services is
much lower than the averages for their industries. And when ServiceMaster
takes a job, the productivity achieved by supervised support workers invariably
rises dramatically.

Now a billion-dollar company, ServiceMaster had a return on equity
from 1973 through 1985 that was the highest of all the largest service or
industrial companies in the United States, averaging more than 30% after taxes.
It oversees the support service employees for 15 hospitals in Japan, which
probably makes it the largest exporter of managerial talent to Japan. According
to one ServiceMaster executive, "The Japanese immediately recognize and
identify with what we do and how we do it." This company turns its strategic
service vision inward with dramatic results.

━━━ THE VISION APPLIED

In addition to building a strategic service vision, the best service companies apply it to customers and to those who deliver the service and oversee
its delivery—in new or different ways. From my study of organizations like
Hartford Steam Boiler and ServiceMaster, I've gathered a series of lessons useful
for service providers to consider. These lessons can furnish food for thought for
goods producers too.

RETHINK QUALITY CONTROL

Executives whose careers have spanned service as well as manufacturing agree that reaching a consistently high quality level is tougher in services.

In high-contact (so-called high-encounter) services, the interaction between two or more people varies with each transaction. In low-contact services, people many miles from the customer have to rely on their own judgment in handling orders and other transactions and in fielding complaints.

Those who have tried to solve the quality control problem by adding more supervision have found that it limits effectiveness. A service transaction cannot be halted, examined, and recycled like a product.

The most effective approaches to the problem include restructuring of incentives to emphasize quality, designing jobs to give service providers higher visibility in dealing with customers, and building a peer group to foster team-work and instill a sense of pride.

One incentive that is often effective in organizations ranging from rapid transit companies to hotels is the employee-of-the-month award—especially if based on customer feedback. Both monetary and nonmonetary incentives have been used successfully. What's more, the cost is low.

Making the person who delivers the service more visible is another technique. In England, at the Lex Service Group's luxury auto dealerships, the customer is encouraged to go directly to the mechanic working on the car. The Shouldice Hospital near Toronto, Canada, specializes in the repair of hernias using only local anesthetic—a practice that allows the doctor to talk with the patient during the operation. Defective work is referred to the doctor responsi-ble. The remission rate for hernias performed at Shouldice is less than one-tenth that of the average North American hospital. At Benihana, the U.S. chain of Japanese-style steak houses, the chef cooks at a grill in front of the restaurant guests. The chef's visibility and proximity to customers promote a consistently high quality of service and a consistently high level of tips.

Incentives and visibility may be insufficient for those tasks performed without supervision and out of view of the customer. In these cases, some companies rely on careful selection and thorough training of employees and the development of programs to build both a sense of pride in the service and a sense of identification with the company. This bonding process can be hard for rivals to emulate and can thereby contribute to competitive advantage.

Schlumberger's wire-line service has roughly 2,000 geological engi-neers, each responsible for a mobile rig equipped with more than $1 million worth of computers and electronic gear that help predict the outcome of petroleum producers' drilling efforts. Each year the company recruits those it considers the brightest of the crop of college engineering graduates, spends months teaching them how to use the equipment, and goes to great lengths to make them feel a part of a special tradition. As one engineer put it, "Indoctrination is just as important as technical training." This is all in preparation for an assignment to represent Schlumberger in the field, with-out direct supervision, often in a remote part of the world. Two measures of the success of this program are Schlumberger's dominant share of the world's wire-line business and the profit-to-sales ratios for this company, which consis-tently exceed others in its industry in good times and bad.

Often effective in achieving and maintaining quality is peer group control, supported by incentives, training, job design, and service delivery system design. In cases where professional standards have been established for a task, they reinforce peer group control.

In an architectural firm, the mere existence of a policy requiring partners' review of every piece of work can keep partners and associates on their toes. Surgeons are sometimes assigned in teams to foster the learning process and encourage peer group control. A partner of a leading real estate development company told me, "There are three things I'm most concerned about in my work. In this order, they are not to embarrass my colleagues, not to cast a bad light on the company by inadequately serving my clients, and making money." It's not surprising that this company has a strong sense of shared values, reinforced by a policy of encouraging partners to invest in the projects that they propose and carry out.

Recent research suggests that the internal strategic service vision, quality control, and success are connected, especially in those providers of high-encounter service requiring judgment in delivery (shown as the "quality wheel" in *Exhibit 3*). Studies directly link customer satisfaction and the resulting sales volume to the satisfaction derived by the person serving the customer.[3] Naturally, the more motivated the employee, the better the service.

The selection and development of employees, care in assignment, and the layout and equipment of the facility (in a high-contact environment) are all integral elements of the design of the service encounter, which in turn is based on the company's assessment of customer needs. Preconditioning of the customer may also be a part of the design of the service encounter. Review and redesign of the encounter go on continually as the organization assesses how well it is meeting those needs.

A part of the internal service vision is the design of policies and performance measures that further the fulfillment of customers' needs. For example, the server's well-being in the job apparently depends, at least in part, on the extent to which his or her superiors emphasize the solution of problems for customers rather than strict adherence to a set of policies and procedures.[4]

Driving the self-reinforcing elements of the quality wheel takes a great deal of executive time and requires an honest interest in people across the organization. The senior vice president for finance of Delta Airlines, an organization well regarded for its service and its employee programs, remarked, "I

---

3. Benjamin Schneider and David E. Bowen, "New Services Design Development, and Implementation and the Employee," in *New Services*, eds. William R. George and Claudia Marshall (Chicago, Ill.: American Marketing Association, 1985), p. 82; and Eugene M. Johnson and Daniel T. Seymour, "The Impact of Cross Selling on the Service Encounter in Retail Banking," in *The Service Encounter*, eds. John A. Czepiel, Michael R. Soloman, and Carol F. Surprenant (Lexington, Mass.: D. C. Heath, 1985), p. 243.

4. This is the implication of John J. Parkington and Benjamin Schneider in "Some Correlates of Experienced Job Stress: A Boundary Role Study," *Academy of Management Journal* (June 1979): 270.

EXHIBIT 3
How Success Builds High-Contact Services

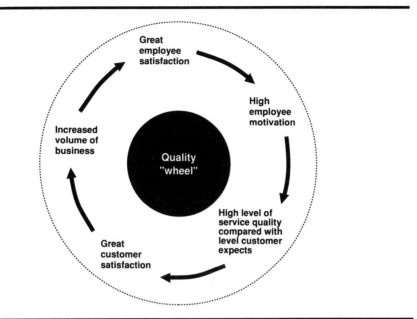

would guess that 25% of the time of the finance department officers is spent listening to people problems."

For most service companies, people obviously are more important than machines in the control of quality. But even where the machines employed carry an unusually high value, as in Schlumberger and Delta, developing and building the dedication of people takes precedence.

REASSESS THE EFFECTS OF SCALE

In service organizations, scale economies are often much more important at the company level than at the operating unit level. This is particularly true for companies that have many units over wide areas connected by a common identity. Such scale gives McDonald's and Hertz great purchasing clout and General Cinema the advantage of selling soft drinks of its own manufacture.

Large scale at the company level is important for exploiting network effects, a phenomenon much more important in the service than in the manufacturing sector. To a point, the addition of new network links augments volume for those parts already in place, thus building average network capacity utilization. The addition of service to Las Vegas from its Memphis hub gave Federal Express more volume on the Memphis–New

York link. When Visa adds a large retailer to its network of card-accepting establishments, it increases the attractiveness of its credit card to present and potential cardholders and the potential volume to be realized by retailers already accepting the card.

Bigger is not better in those service industries in which the factory must be taken into the marketplace to sell a more accessible, visible, and convenient product that meets customers' needs. Factories operated by the Hyatt and Marriott organizations (called hotels) have not, on average, grown in size for years. These companies have settled on a range of hotel dimensions that can be designed, located, and operated effectively to achieve the capacity utilization, quality of service, and financial performance they want. The range describes sizes at which diseconomies resulting from poor supervision and inflexibility tend to outweigh advantages of larger scale. In the design and siting of hotels, Hyatt and Marriott give the less quantifiable advantages of market flexibility weight equal to operating economies of scale.

At the unit operating level, many service companies have found that the loss of flexibility and greater difficulty in supervising those delivering the service far outweigh any savings realized in operating costs as unit size grows. In the rush to cut costs per seat-mile, for example, many of the world's airlines bought large, wide-bodied aircraft like the Airbus 300 and McDonnell DC-10. While these planes performed admirably, their effective utilization required funneling large numbers of passengers into the airline's hub. Moreover, because business travelers, who represent the most attractive market segment, are prone to choose an airline on the basis of times and frequency of flights, the load and schedule consolidation necessary for effective employment of wide-bodied aircraft worked against the goal of building traffic.

When Jon Carlzon became CEO of Scandinavian Airlines System in 1980, wide-bodied aircraft were used extensively between the airline's hub at Copenhagen and major cities like London and Paris. With smaller DC-9s, SAS funneled travelers between the hub and other Scandinavian cities. To reclaim the business travelers SAS had lost, Carlzon relegated most of the wide-bodies to charter work and offered nonstop flights using DC-9s between Scandinavian and principal European cities.

A size question confronts nearly every power utility in the United States today. For years it was industry gospel that the more power-generating capacity concentrated in one place, the greater the economies of scale. This was the case until the 1970s, when ever-larger units began encountering reliability problems. Furthermore, construction schedule stretchouts, at times fomented by environmental groups' agitation against big plants, caused the expected power-generating economies to vanish. Finally, an improved capability for transmitting excess energy from one market to another made it possible to buy energy for less than the big units could offer to charge. Thus, many utilities today are meeting the needs of smaller markets' fluctuating demands more economically through new means.

REPLACE AND CREATE ASSETS WITH INFORMATION

For decades, manufacturers have sought ways of substituting information for assets. Foremost among these are forecasting and inventory control techniques. For many service operations, information offers creative new ways to substitute for assets.

Heating oil dealers, by maintaining data on the capacity of their customers' tanks, on habitual consumption rates, and on weather, program fuel oil deliveries to provide 100% availability while reducing delivery times and the number of trucks and drivers. These companies substitute information for assets.

The Rural/Metro Fire Department extends effective fire protection at a fraction of the cost of most municipally run fire departments. This Scottsdale, Arizona-based company analyzes data on past fires and uses much smaller, less expensive trucks staffed with smaller crews and equipped with a large-diameter hose that can shoot a lot of water on a fire very fast. On the way to a fire, a truck crew can learn the floor plan of the building to which it is going. While speeding through the streets, the crew examines a microfiche of the layout on a screen. Rural/Metro substitutes information for assets.

Many service industries are information driven, beginning with familiarity between the server and the served. In many (not all), assets have never been allowed to become dominant, perhaps because of limited capital. But with the development of new technologies for processing and communicating information, companies in these industries have advanced far beyond the use of information as a substitute for assets. They are instead using the information they have collected in one business as the basis for new services.

Companies servicing manufactured goods, for example, have built data bases on the types, wear rates, and failure rates of various parts of a furnace, appliance, or automobile. A company can use this information for sending timely service reminders to customers and also to manage parts inventories to reflect the age and condition of the particular machine serviced. In the process, the data have taken on great value for the producers of the goods—and they're willing to pay for the information.

A credit card service builds expenditure profiles for its customers; broken patterns may signal a problem like stolen cards. Theft is sometimes suspected when a large expenditure is made far from the cardholder's address. Instead of outright disallowance of a retailer's request for a big charge, one major travel card issuer tries to determine whether the cardholder is indeed traveling in the retailer's area. Information collected for this service yields person-specific data about travel patterns that often are valuable to airlines and hotel chains (to name two businesses). But the company limits the use of such information to ways that benefit its cardholders.

Dun & Bradstreet's $2.7 billion enterprise is centered on its data base, a file of credit information describing businesses in 30 countries. Through development and acquisition, the file steadily grows. D&B has consistently realized about 10% of its revenues from business that did not exist three years before. Nearly all of these services use the same data base but package the information in different ways. A potential competitor would have to spend an estimated $1 billion—nearly half D&B's net asset value—to duplicate the data base.

Though a data base may constitute a service provider's most important asset, it doesn't appear on the balance sheet and can't be depreciated. But the degree to which many such companies rely on an accumulation of knowledge as their chief competitive weapon and source of new business development suggests opportunities for their counterparts in the manufacturing sector.

Harlan Cleveland has pointed out that information, unlike most manufactured products, is often infinitely expandable (as it is used), compressible, substitutable (for capital, labor, or physical materials), transportable, diffusive (hard to keep secret), and sharable (as opposed to exchangeable).[5] If it is infinitely expandable, those who possess it are limited only by their imagination in creating new ideas, revenue sources, and job opportunities. As the demand for creative exploitation of information grows, so will job creation in the service sector.

——— THE SERVICE ECONOMY

Many successful service providers have strategies in common that offer lessons to other companies. Among these are:

- Close coordination of the marketing–operations relationship
- A strategy built around elements of a strategic service vision
- An ability to redirect the strategic service inward to focus on vital employee groups
- A stress on the control of quality based on a set of shared values, peer group status, generous incentives, and, where possible, a close relationship with the customer
- A cool appraisal of the effects of scale on both efficiency and effectiveness
- The substitution of information for other assets
- The exploitation of information to generate new business

Why these particular lessons among all I might cite? For one reason, they feature characteristics that distinguish many service industries from goods-producing industries; notice the emphasis on people, ideas, and information instead of things. For another, they promise twin benefits as part of a business strategy. Each can provide further differentiation of the service product as well as lower costs.

---

5. Harlan Cleveland, "Information as a Resource," *The Futurist* (December 1982): 37.

These lessons have significance for the economy too. While the service economy has wrought a gigantic social restucturing of the United States, it has come in for unwarranted criticism for its low rate of productivity gains. Companies like those I have described, however, have created new jobs while raising productivity. If other companies learn these lessons, job opportunities in the service sector will continue to expand and productivity continue to rise. These developments will ease the pressures for the inflation of service prices, sharpen the already respected competitiveness abroad of U.S.-based services, and contribute to the partnership between services and manufacturing that is crucial to a healthy, balanced national business base.

——— DISCUSSION QUESTIONS

1. Since service is an intangible product, it requires a different marketing strategy than that used in manufacturing. But both intangible and tangible products need to meet customers' expectations as well as their needs. How would you resolve the implications of these statements for marketing strategy?
2. To maximize their offerings and minimize costs, would service companies be better served by standardizing their offerings or customizing them?
3. Service industries play a dominant role in the economy, accounting for more revenue and employment than manufacturing. How and why do you think service industries have become economically dominant? What are the lessons to be learned from their success? Can these be applied to manufacturing? In what respects?
4. How important a role does internal employee satisfaction and employee productivity play in satisfying the needs and expectations of customers? In what ways? How would this shape your marketing strategy?

35   Service Companies: Focus or Falter

WILLIAM H. DAVIDOW AND BRO UTTAL

Good service marketing means focusing on a particular market segment and designing services that meet the needs of that segment. Exceeding customers' expectations is even better, especially when it disadvantages the competition, but it must be done with caution, lest customers come to expect too much. Using a variety of examples, this reading argues that to gain an edge in service marketing, a company must develop a strategy that enables it to meet customer needs that are not met by its competitors—and to do it without raising expectations that it is unable to fulfill. As the authors acknowledge, managing expectations is not easy, but by identifying customers' needs and striking a smart balance in meeting them, companies can avoid delivering excessive service that is diffused and ineffective.

In an industry bedeviled by rising costs, Shouldice Hospital near Toronto, Canada, is a model of cost-bashing productivity. Surgery patients stay at Shouldice for 3½ days compared with 5 to 8 days at most hospitals. Its doctors perform many more operations a year than doctors elsewhere, yet they are paid less than they would make in private practice; nurses attend to several times as many patients as they would in most other hospitals. Patients care for themselves; they get to the operating room under their own steam, walk to the recovery room, and take their meals in a common dining room.

Does this sound like a low-quality, uncaring production line? It's just the opposite. Measured by how often patients need treatment for the same problem, Shouldice is ten times more effective than other hospitals. Ex-patients are so delighted with the Shouldice experience that they hold an annual reunion to commemorate it. The January 1988 jamboree at the Royal York Hotel in Toronto attracted some 1,500 "alumni."

There's something else unusual about this picture of great service: most sick people couldn't get admitted to Shouldice. If you have a broken bone, gallstones, or clogged arteries, apply elsewhere. Shouldice accepts only one type of patient—people whose single complaint is a hernia. Even then, the hospital will reject hernia victims who have histories of heart trouble or who have undergone surgery in the last 12 months or who weigh more than Shouldice recommends.

A tightly focused service strategy is the key to Shouldice's performance. By segmenting the market of sick people according to their complaints, then concentrating on one segment that is inexpensive to serve, Shouldice has optimized its operations, fulfilled its mission—and enjoyed a handsome return.

After doing hundreds of hernia repairs a year using a special technique, Shouldice's doctors have become highly proficient and productive. The hospital usually can avoid using general anesthesia because local anesthesia, which is safer and cheaper, works well for hernia repair. Patients recover from surgery faster if they're up and about, so Shouldice avoids paying for a fleet of wheelchairs and gurneys, armies of aides to push them, and banks of wide elevators. Instead, it gives patients hallways with comfortable carpeting, staircases with low risers, and acres of well-groomed grounds on which to stroll. The central location of television sets and toilets encourages patients to walk around even as it saves the hospital money.

Concentration on hernias enables Shouldice to produce a highly competitive core service. But that's not the main reason for Shouldice's success. Other organizations, notably the Lichtenstein Hernia Institute of Los Angeles, do low-cost repairs that work at least as well. Consumers, most of whom have medical insurance, are somewhat insensitive to health care costs. And those who have personal physicians tend to follow their advice, which normally is to get a hernia fixed at a hometown hospital.

No, people flock to Shouldice mainly because they hear from former patients that being there is a great experience. The hospital earns this enthusiastic word of mouth because it adds significant (though intangible) value to its core service. Most people can't accurately judge the quality of a hospital's core service. What they can and do appraise, at least when they're not very sick, are experiences like the welcome received at check-in, the behavior of fellow patients, and the attentiveness and perceived competence of doctors and nurses.

Could Shouldice produce outstanding customer service absent its clear strategy? Probably not without completely redesigning its physical and social systems and sending its rates sky high. Shouldice is ill-suited for treating people with broken legs or weak hearts, those who can't walk much or who have had major surgery and need intravenous feeding, or patients recovering from plastic surgery (they seldom want to socialize). Shouldice managers have thought about undertaking minor eye surgery and repairing varicose veins and hemorrhoids—procedures fairly similar to hernia repair in their demands on facilities. But "fairly similar" isn't close enough. Shouldice has decided to stick with the segment it knows best and serves most effectively.[1]

In contrast, fuzzy or conflicting strategies make good customer service impossible. Look at People Express. In 1981, it focused tightly on budget travelers—students, backpackers, vacationers, and others willing to sacrifice convenient schedules and airport gates for low fares. Customers actually

1. *See* James L. Heskett, *Managing in the Service Economy* (Boston: Harvard Business School Press, 1986).

enjoyed the airline's widely advertised "no-frills" service, which gave them the options of bringing their own food or paying extra for a snack in flight, of carrying their luggage or paying $3 a bag to check it, and of buying a ticket on board instead of in advance. In five years, People Express's fleet grew from 3 airplanes to 117, and its revenues soared from $38 million to nearly $1 billion.

But People had overexpanded. Every day, the airline had thousands of seats available, but its steady customers wanted to fly mainly on weekends and during the summer and other vacation times. The glut of empty seats produced a $3.7 million loss in 1984. So People scrambled to get more revenue from its fleet. It scheduled each plane for as many flights as possible and it grossly overbooked to compensate for customers who made reservations but didn't show up. The airline also went after business travelers, whose demand is heaviest Monday through Friday and nicely complements the weekend demand pattern of budget fliers. To attract executives, the airline pitched its luxurious first-class service, complete with leather seats.

Nearly everything People Express had done to serve the budget-minded conflicted with this new strategy. Businesspeople intensely dislike inconvenient schedules and gates, paying extra for checked baggage and for meals, and waiting until the last minute to buy tickets. People's tight scheduling meant that many flights were late, and overbooking meant that it often turned away customers who had reserved seats. The carrier earned a new name, "People Distress."

Business travelers stayed away, and the airline racked up a $300 million net loss in 1986, when Texas Air took it over. If it had continued to focus tightly on budget fliers and had sold off or leased planes to cut capacity, People Express might still be around. But it broadened, and irrecoverably blurred, its original winning strategy.

—— MARKETS AND MARKET SEGMENTS

To some managers, developing a strategy for customer service may sound like a waste of time. How much strategy do you need to send out a repairperson or to adjust an erroneous bill? Yet even those seemingly simple activities won't do much for customer satisfaction or corporate profits unless they are part of a considered strategy. Without one, you don't know who your customers are, how much they value different aspects of service, how much you must spend to satisfy them, and how big the payoffs are likely to be. Without a strategy, you can't develop a concept of service to rally employees or catch conflicts between corporate strategy and customer service or come up with ways to measure service performance and perceived quality. In short, without a strategy you can't get to first base.

Developing a service strategy is an essential step toward choosing an optimal mix and level of service for different customer sets. Provide too little service, or the wrong kind, and customers will leave; provide too much, even the right kind, and your company will go broke or price itself out of the market.

Proof of that assertion comes from a General Electric experiment that varied the levels of repair service for out-of-warranty appliances over a two-year period. GE discovered that repair service is very sensitive to the law of diminishing returns. At a certain point, each incremental investment in service starts to yield lower returns than the previous investment. The only way to find that point is to segment customers, find out how much they value different levels of service, and estimate the costs and benefits of serving them well.

Simply charging ahead with extraordinary service doesn't guarantee a high return, as Service Supply Corporation of Indianapolis, the "house of a million screws," should know. If Service Supply had a cogent customer service strategy, it would stratify its 15,000 customers according to their sensitivity to stockouts of difference classes of fasteners, then adjust its inventory levels and prices to address those tiers with the highest potential returns. As it is, Service Supply gives outstanding service to *all* its customers, regardless of what service they need or their willingness to pay, and it can't charge enough on average to bring profits up to industry norms.

The essence of any customer service strategy is to segment the customers to be served. As with classic market segmentation, the goal is to isolate a reasonably homogeneous set of customers that can be served at a profit. But customer service segments differ from the usual market segments in significant ways. For one thing, they tend to be narrower. While many different kinds of customers may be happy to buy the same product, they're less likely to feel that their expectations have been met or exceeded if the service they receive is standardized and routinized. Service expectations, after all, are highly personal.

Moreover, marketing segmentation focuses on what people and organizations *need*, while customer service segmentation focuses on what they *expect*. Marketers tend to use immediate sales to judge whether a segment is valid. Since purchasing decisions look binary—the sale is made or it isn't—the validity of marketing segments seems easy to assess.

Occasionally, marketing segments and customer service segments are the same, especially for service companies that have well-focused, comprehensive marketing strategies. Those strategies can meet a broad range of service expectations. Federal Express's strategy, for example, is to meet expectations for all the actions and reactions that customers perceive they have purchased, including not only pickup and delivery but also documentation and information about shipments.

More often, though, defining customer service segments means rethinking overly broad market segments and the ways in which they impede superior service. Intelligent segmentation can transform the productivity and profitability of customer service operations, as Shouldice's strategy shows.

It's hard to get big productivity gains by substituting capital and technology for labor, since high-touch customer service by definition means lots of flexible, warm, human contact. So managers often seek to substitute low-touch service for the high-touch kind—offering, for instance, automatic checkout from the hotel instead of the usual front-desk checkout.

The problem is that some customers welcome low-touch substitutes while others view them as cost-cutting measures that seriously reduce the quality of service. Compared with business travelers, tourists staying at a grand hotel have a far less favorable view of automatic checkout. They may see it as a jarring, impersonal note in their hotel experience. Veteran users of large home appliances may prefer getting repair instructions over the telephone, while novices expect a human repair expert to show up. Only after a company has segmented its customers and chosen which ones to serve can it figure out where to substitute low touch for high, thus improving productivity without imperiling customer satisfaction.

Segmentation also is key to solving one of the thorniest problems in customer service—matching supply and demand. Manufacturers with over-capacity will produce for inventory or shut down machines and lay off workers. When demand exceeds supply, they draw down inventory, run their factories continuously, hire extra shifts, and call on the capacity of other suppliers.

Service providers have fewer options. Service can't be stored in inventory. Seldom can you substitute another company's service for your own and keep meeting customer expectations, since those expectations refer to a unique experience, not an interchangeable product. A sudden addition to or reduction in capacity (people, mainly) ensures shoddy quality, or even a breakdown of the service "factory," as anyone can attest who has stayed at a large hotel when it's hosting a convention. Since demand for customer service isn't homogeneous—every customer demands somewhat different versions of excellent service—service organizations need idle capacity for adapting their product to mixed demand. By some estimates, service quality drops off sharply when demand exceeds as little as 75% of theoretical capacity.[2]

Until it segments, a hotel or field force of computer engineers may see huge and apparently random fluctuations in demand. But segmenting usually shows that the overall pattern is made up of several smaller, more predictable, and therefore more manageable patterns. For instance, convention visitors, ordinary business travelers, foreign tourists, and vacationing families all contribute to variations in demand for hotel service. The distinctive patterns of their demands can be forecast.

Segmenting may even reveal that some kinds of demand are undesirable and should be finessed, like the demand on a bank to make a change for noncustomers and the demand on a fire department to rescue cats from trees.[3] But simply ignoring demand is nearly always dangerous. Disgruntled noncustomers, like the grandmother whose cat is up a tree, can spread as

2. Ibid., p. 38.
3. The cats come courtesy of Christopher H. Lovelock, *Services Marketing* (Englewood Cliffs, N.J.: Prentice-Hall, 1984).

much bad word about a company as genuine customers can. Better than ignoring inappropriate demand is lowering the expectations of noncustomers, say by broadcasting to cat owners how busy the fire department is fighting fires or by creating disincentives like a $20 charge for restoring arboreal cats to earth.

Among the most powerful ways to vary service capacity with demand is to expand the role of customers in producing service, in effect making them coproducers. To some degree, the customer always helps produce service, by reading a manual, returning an appliance for repair, filling out an air bill, or participating in the service ritual at a fancy restaurant. Finding opportunities to expand the customer's role and move toward self-service often depends on savvy segmentation.

Automated teller machines, for example, increase the role of customers in producing some banking services and thus represent highly flexible capacity. The greater the demand on the machines, the greater the capacity customers provide (at least until the waiting line gets too long). But targeting the right kinds of customers for ATMs is crucial. Retirees and other older people, especially in smaller towns, tend to resist the machines. So do many of the very wealthy, who expect the attention of human beings in return for their lucrative business.

Carving out segments is a matter of life and death for some companies. A good example is banking, whose core services are close to being pure commodities. Pundits have forecast the death of the small-town bank ever since the early 1980s, when deregulation started opening local markets to more efficient regional and money-center banks. Many local banks have in fact closed their doors or disappeared into the maws of acquisition-hungry superregionals.

Some local banks, though, have prospered despite the competition by focusing on certain customer segments whose service expectations the big boys don't satisfy. University National Bank & Trust of Palo Alto, California, has just one office. The bank discourages small depositors by setting a high monthly fee for checking accounts, $20, and waiving it only for average monthly balances of at least $3,000. Deadbeats need not apply: the bank accepts new customers only with a referral or after a credit check. Bounce two checks and UNBT will close your account.

Yet UNBT keeps gaining market share and consistently earns a return on assets more than twice the average for California banks. Like its mammoth competitors Wells Fargo, First Interstate, and Bank of America, UNBT has targeted individuals with high net worth, generally more than $500,000. Unlike its competitors, UNBT serves *only* those customers, and it serves them with an array of services that includes free traveler's checks, cashier's checks, and stop-payment orders; streamlined approval of large loans; free shoe shines on visits to the bank; and a sack of sweet onions gratis every July. UNBT successfully targeted the people in the community who wanted lots of hands-on service.

More important than any of these features, however, says CEO Carl J. Schmitt, "was the concept of keeping the ½ of 1% of customers who are bad guys out of the bank's customer base. It is that ½ of 1% that causes the large banks to create the arbitrary rules that in turn create the hassle experienced in the large bank."

The "two bad checks and you're out" policy improves the bank's service in an interesting way. For one thing, local merchants know all UNBT checks are good, so they honor them as if they were cash. For another, tellers don't have to spend time checking the customer's credit. In almost all cases, the bank cashes customer checks without inquiring whether they have money in their accounts. This reduces lines at the teller windows. So the bad-checks policy leads to better credit outside and faster service inside the bank.

If you can carve out a niche by offering platinum service, can you also carve out a niche by offering virtually no service? Sure, if you spot the niche and handle it right. One market segment that is too "cheap" to pay for service is the college population. The East Lansing State Bank has prospered mightily by taking on Michigan State students with no-minimum-balance, all-ATM checking accounts. The students get five checks a month for a monthly service charge of $1, and they pay 50 cents for each window transaction. The bank knows where it wants the students—and it isn't at the teller windows clogging up service to its regular customers.

———— CLASSIFYING CUSTOMERS

In reality, most companies can't segment their customers as sharply as Shouldice Hospital and University National Bank & Trust do; the set of existing customers is usually too diverse to be stuffed into a single pigeonhole. The problem is most difficult, of course, for manufacturers because they usually sell to a wide range of buyers and use distribution channels that insulate them from direct knowledge about their customers.

Nonetheless, any company can carve out useful segments, rank their attractiveness, and develop a focused service strategy by examining a few key characteristics of its customers and its business. The traits to look at first are obvious financial ones. How do the typical size of a sale and the likelihood of repeat sales vary among customers? What are the costs of giving superior service to different types of customers? Approximating the answers produces a rough segmentation and working notion of the benefits and costs of different service strategies.

In any well-run business, service levels normally correlate closely with size of sale. For a $150 suit off the rack at a discount store, you won't get free alterations, let alone any advice from a salesperson about fashion trends, the fit of the suit, or appropriate accessories. But in keeping your appointment with Bijan, which sells $1,500 suits behind barred storefronts on Rodeo Drive in Beverly Hills and on Fifth Avenue in New York, you can expect head-to-toe fashion advice, any alteration you care to name, and a phone call after the sale to make sure that everything fits as well as you thought it would.

Note that people who buy discount suits don't necessarily get worse service. They do get less of it, but whether they perceive that consequence as low-quality service depends on their expectations.

When automotive analyst Martin Stein examined 26 auto service programs and their impact on customer satisfaction, he was not surprised to find that the more expensive the car, the more elaborate the service. The manufacturers of Mercedes and Acura take the "open pocketbook" approach: whatever customers want, they get, including 24-hour roadside assistance.

The companies with the worst service quality and the lowest customer satisfaction weren't those making the lowest priced cars or offering the lowest absolute levels of service, but those lacking a service strategy and failing to match service levels with the size of sale. Except in the case of Cadillac, General Motors took a cosmetic approach: it sent service managers through a training program where they learned to refuse requests for service politely, and it used 800 numbers to field complaints. "This approach backfires," according to Stein. "Customers say that General Motors is 'supercilious' and that 'they are overly courteous but don't want to fix your car.' Polite evasion antagonizes people more than if you just say you can't do it. Tactically, there's nothing wrong with 800 numbers, but given GM's lack of a service strategy, its managers don't see any positive change in customer satisfaction."

When their product permits it, sophisticated companies look for customer segments that are less costly to serve. Part of Shouldice's secret is that basically well people cost less to serve than the seriously ill. Older, more conservative car owners who live in the suburbs are less costly to serve than people in their twenties who live in urban and rural areas, a fact that canny auto dealers and insurance companies appreciate. Companies with strong central-purchasing offices tend to be less expensive to serve than those that let each branch or division make its own buying decisions.

Besides traits like health, age, and geographical location, some segments have other characteristics that cut the costs of serving them. Many customers are happy to share the burdens of service, like shoppers at self-service stores and industrial buyers who order parts and supplies through computers linked directly to their suppliers. Other customers are willing to adjust their demand for service to accommodate the supplier, like the budget-minded who accepted People Express's no-frills tack, like Shouldice patients who shave their own groins and abdomens before surgery, and like utility customers who limit their electrical usage during peak demand hours.

The cost of service also is affected by customers' knowledgeability and by their ability and willingness to cooperate in getting service. Buyers of semiconductor chips expect the products to meet their specifications, and living up to specs is a crucial aspect of the service that chip makers offer. But unless the buyer adjusts its automated test equipment to perform the same way the chip maker's does, the buyer will reject batch after batch of chips for being out of spec, even though, according to the chip maker's test equipment, the parts were fine when they left the factory.

Competent customers are what Network Equipment Technologies seeks for its communications multiplexers. The California manufacturer focuses on large companies with sophisticated communication needs and able communication management teams. Its equipment is designed with diagnostic features that make it easy for NET to diagnose failures remotely. With telephone support, most customers can fix the equipment themselves. As a result, service engineers stay at home; the company needs to dispatch them on a customer call in only about 240 of every 1,000 incidents. NET can extend service to competent customers cheaply, and on top of that, customers get their equipment up and working again faster. That makes for happier customers.

Classification of customers by the value they place on service and by their service expectations often generates a rough idea of the cost of satisfying them. But which customers are the best targets? Those who are the most valuable compared with the likely costs of serving them. While, as we suggested, size and frequency of purchase are good indicators of value, there are many others, such as customers whose demand is likely to grow faster than average; influential customers, who will generate powerful word of mouth; and loyal customers. Buyers who are especially demanding, sophisticated, or technologically advanced often go to the top of the list because serving them gives a supplier insight into the needs of more ordinary customers.

Ranking customers by their value is essential for any service operation that must live with big swings in aggregate demand and can't adjust capacity quickly to meet those swings. Ranks or tiers are the key to allocation. When capacity is short, smart suppliers give top-tier customers first claim on service and cut back on service to lower-value customers. That's what popular restaurants do at peak dining times by finding tables for regulars and keeping newcomers waiting, and it's what American and Japanese semiconductor makers do when capacity is short and they fill the orders of long-term customers first.

Without assigning its customers to tiers, a company that serves numbers of segments has difficulty getting the most out of its service capacity. Stretching and straining to satisfy every segment, it may end up giving low-quality service to all customers, not just to the less desirable ones in lower tiers.

Service companies have discovered through painful experience that using the same organization to serve different market segments, or to provide very different services to the same segment, seldom works. Frito-Lay, the PepsiCo subsidiary that leads the potato chip business, is famous for its customer service. A corps of 10,000 route drivers visits most stores, many of them small grocers, two or three times weekly to ensure that the stock is fresh—and prominently displayed. At one point, the company decided to add packaged cookies that they would deliver in the same way and at the same time.

The attempt failed. Frito-Lay's service infrastructure, very efficient for potato chips, was too specialized to handle cookies well. As Leo Kiely, senior vice president for sales and marketing, explains it: "On the surface it looked easy, but there were underlying problems. Our other products turn over in about seven days, which is very rapid. Cookies have a much slower turn, with a 60- to 90-day shelf life. That's a different inventory problem for our drivers, so our regular visit two to three times a week proved inefficient for cookies."

While handling many customer segments piles on complexities, few companies can afford the luxury of addressing just one segment. The challenge of exploiting service capacity forces them to diversify at least a little, as airlines do in targeting both business and vacation travelers. Moreover, the same customer is often a different type of customer at different times. Business executives go on vacation. New bank customers, who value location and convenience most, quickly become established bank customers and start giving the highest rankings to different criteria, like operational accuracy, dependability, and friendliness.

The best practice is to pick segments that are as similar as possible and to keep your priorities straight. People Express failed to do that.

——— WHAT DO CUSTOMERS EXPECT?

After segmenting your market so that you can target your customers, the next step is to find out what they want and expect. This takes research and analysis.

The payoffs for good analysis are tangible sales and profits. In Norway, where customers are particularly sensitive to service, Toyota used to think of cars as simply products. Then the company began looking into the total car experience and asking what kinds of service customers expected. Discovering that they were concerned not just about reliability and performance but also about the difficulties of buying cars and car insurance and about the anxieties of repair, Toyota used its large customer base to bargain for very competitive financing and insurance services, and it started offering free diagnostic service. In 1985 and 1986, Toyota's sales in Norway rose more than 30% and its earnings went from the equivalent of $12 million to $22 million.

It's tempting to forgo analysis because you assume you know what customers expect. But assumptions don't make effective customer service strategies. Inward-looking companies that are guided by industry norms and their own past practices end up with inappropriate strategies, lower market shares, and anemic profits. Time after time, studies have shown large differences between the ways that customers define service and rank the importance of different service activities and the ways that suppliers do.[4]

---

4. *See*, for example, Norman E. Marr, "Do Managers Really Know What Service Their Customers Require?" *International Journal of Physical Distribution and Materials Management*, 10 (no. 7, 1980): 433.

Numbers of companies have triumphed by filling the gap between what customers see as good service and what competitors think it is. Tom Ford, founder and head of the Ford Land Company, perceived that most developers of office buildings see their business as financial plays where return on assets is paramount. Most commercial tenants, he noted, are convinced that their landlords are trying to squeeze the last penny of return from their properties.

So Ford decided to stress tenant service in the 34 office and industrial buildings he put up and operates on the peninsula south of San Francisco. He doesn't charge for extras like installing electrical outlets, laying computer cable, or changing names on doors and building directories. When remodeling creates a racket that disturbs neighboring tenants, Ford brings the neighbors wine and flowers to show he's at least aware of the problem.

The result? Since 1977, Ford's properties have been 100% leased, a remarkable record in an area where vacancy rates have been running between 10% and 30%. A competitor who opened an office building next to Ford's flagship property in Menlo Park tried to draw away Ford's tenants by offering months of free or reduced rent. None of the tenants would bite, and the new building was only 50% occupied 15 months after opening.

Good service has nothing to do with what the provider believes it is; it has to do only with what the customer believes is true. Good service results when the provider meets or exceeds the customer's expectations. Do less than the customer expects and the service is bad. Do what is expected and the service is good. Exceed by a great amount what is anticipated, as Tom Ford does, and the service will be superior. This is why the providers of good service have to be extremely careful to set the customer's expectations at the proper level.

Levels of expectation are why two organizations in the same business can offer far different levels of service and still keep customers happy. It is why McDonald's can extend excellent industrialized service with few employees per customer and why an expensive restaurant with many tuxedoed waiters may be unable to do as well from the customer's point of view. It is why diners like the folksy service at New York City's upscale steak house, Christ Cella, and would perhaps be disappointed with the same type of service at a fancy French restaurant.

Setting customer expectations at the right level can be a very tough job even for service experts. Consider Nordstrom, the most service-oriented large fashion retailer in the United States. Nordstrom's reputation for good service has gotten out of control. Stories about heroic service deeds of Nordstrom employees, fueled by the word of mouth spread by enthusiastic customers, are threatening to ruin Nordstrom's service. Why? Because customers enter the store with unrealistically high expectations.

In an effort to rein in expectations, Nordstrom has stopped talking about service to the press. Too much publicity about a company's good service can be bad. Likewise, fire departments should stress their expertise in fighting fires, and keep mum about rescuing animals, if they want to lower the expectations of owners of tree-climbing cats.

There are severe limits to any company's ability to set expectations. The strictest one is reality. Few patrons of a high-priced hotel can be led to expect anything other than luxury service, and few people who have experienced bad service can be persuaded to expect anything else. As Martin Stein, the auto-industry analyst observes, "General Motors's advertising campaign for Mr. Goodwrench, the GM dealer's mythical service expert, doesn't work because people doubt that the quality of service being advertised will be available. They may be looking for Mr. Goodwrench, but they aren't finding him." Trying to set expectations that vary widely from the realities customers perceive is futile.

Expectations are formed by many uncontrollable factors, from the experience of customers with other companies and their advertising to a customer's psychological state at the time of service delivery. Strictly speaking, what customers expect is as diverse as their education, values, and experience. The same advertisement that shouts "personal service" to one person tells another that the advertiser has promised more than it possibly can deliver.

Yet some straightforward tactics can help bring expectations into line with the service strategy. The job is basically the same as positioning a company or product in the marketplace. Service positioning starts with four givens: the segments targeted, the expectations of those segments, the strategy for exceeding those expectations, and the positions of competitors, that is, the images they have created for their companies in customers' minds.

A winning service position meets two criteria. It uniquely distinguishes a company from the competition, and it leads customers to expect slightly less service than a company can deliver. That's what Avis did years ago by positioning itself as the second-place car rental company that has to try harder, and it's what Avis is doing today by portraying itself as the rent-a-car outfit that tries harder because the employees own the company. Maytag has done the same, positioning its washing machines as so reliable that the Maytag repairperson is bored to death.

The tools used to position customer service operations are the same communication tools any marketer uses—advertising, promotion, public relations, and everything else that affects the all-important word of mouth. But sending messages about service is different from most forms of marketing communication. Since service is intangible, advertising has a special mission to dramatize service in ways that make the benefits clear and real.

All forms of communication should be tightly focused on the target segment because customers' expectations about service are affected strongly by the other kinds of customers they see. Reaching the wrong segments can be a disaster. A business traveler checking into a budget motel radically revises any expectations if he or she sees a drunk asleep in the lobby.

Positioning customer service differs from normal positioning in other ways as well. Customers are hypersensitive to tangible service clues like uniforms, repair trucks, brochures, and hotel lobbies. Often they can't tell that a service has been performed without some additional evidence like the elaborate receipts car mechanics make out or the strip of paper hotels wrap around toilet seats to let guests know the toilet has been cleaned. Customers' expectations of service rise and fall markedly because of seemingly minor clues or tip-offs like these.

The key to successful positioning of customer service is not to create expectations greater than the service your company can deliver. The whole organization must be together on this. Network Equipment Technologies, for one, disciplines salespeople who overpromise. NET realizes that keeping expectations at just the right level—slightly below perceived performance—is a constant challenge.

────── THREE STEPS TO TAKE

Great service providers inform customers about what to expect and then exceed the promise. Not all customers want or deserve high levels of service, but they are entitled to what they have been promised, explicitly or implicitly.

The strategy of great service providers has a rather familiar ring. Almost all of these companies have taken the same three steps:

1. They segmented the market carefully and designed core products and core services to meet the needs of the customer base. They realized that not all customers who bought the same product or service had the same service needs.
2. They realized that only the customer knew what he or she wanted. Therefore, they researched the needs of the customer base thoroughly, both with formal programs and by paying close attention to what the customer was saying.
3. They were careful to set the customer's expectations at the right level. They underpromised and overdelivered.

Providing good service is a towering challenge. There are many reasons businesses and professions fail in the endeavor, even when they have a perfect strategy. Without a focused service strategy, however, meeting the challenge becomes impossible.

──── DISCUSSION QUESTIONS

1. What are the elements of good customer service? As a marketing manager, how important would it be for you to identify the difference between your perception of good customer service and your customers' perception?

2. Do you need a customer service strategy at all? Is there anything that could take its place?

3. How do you identify your customers? What considerations do you use to rank them and what is their order of importance?

4. Should the way your competition ranks its customers influence your strategy?

5. Is it possible to disadvantage yourself by exceeding the needs of your customers and giving them too much service? Wouldn't this strategy help to disadvantage your competition? Is there a better strategy?

6. What are the advantages—and disadvantages—of a tightly focused service strategy?

MULTINATIONAL MARKETING

Should global marketing be standardized or customized? What degree of standardization or adaptation is appropriate? Will producing globally standardized products result in economies of scale in production, distribution, marketing, and management? Or should management distinguish between those products that will benefit from the efficiencies of standardization and those that will not overcome the cultural barriers that vary from country to country? The upcoming section covers both points of view as well as the issues of when to go international and how to meet global competition at home and abroad.

The Globalization of Markets 36

THEODORE LEVITT

Companies must learn to operate as if the world were one large market—ignoring superficial regional and national differences, asserts the author in this reading. Technology, he claims, has proletarianized communication, transport, and travel and driven the world toward a converging commonality. Well-managed companies, he demonstrates, have moved from emphasis on customizing products to offering globally standardized products that are advanced, functional, reliable, and low priced to enjoy economies of scale in production, distribution, marketing, and management. Multinationals that continue to develop products that cater to idiosyncratic consumer preferences, he asserts, will be left behind, as consumer goals worldwide become more and more alike. The author shows how and why companies that concentrate on what everyone wants rather than worrying about the details of what everyone thinks they might like will achieve long-term success.

A powerful force drives the world toward a converging commonality, and that force is technology. It has proletarianized communication, transport, and travel. It has made isolated places and impoverished peoples eager for modernity's allurements. Almost everyone everywhere wants all the things they have heard about, seen, or experienced via the new technologies.

The result is a new commercial reality—the emergence of global markets for standardized consumer products on a previously unimagined scale of magnitude. Corporations geared to this new reality benefit from enormous economies of scale in production, distribution, marketing, and management. By translating these benefits into reduced world prices, they can decimate competitors that still live in the disabling grip of old assumptions about how the world works.

Gone are accustomed differences in national or regional preference. Gone are the days when a company could sell last year's models—or lesser versions of advanced products—in the less-developed world. And gone are the days when prices, margins, and profits abroad were generally higher than at home.

The globalization of markets is at hand. With that, the multinational commercial world nears its end, and so does the multinational corporation.

The multinational and the global corporation are not the same thing. The multinational corporation operates in a number of countries, and adjusts its products and practices in each—at high relative costs. The global corporation operates with resolute constancy—at low relative cost—as if the entire world (or major regions of it) were a single entity; it sells the same things in the same way everywhere.

Which strategy is better is not a matter of opinion but of necessity. Worldwide communications carry everywhere the constant drumbeat of modern possibilities to lighten and enhance work, raise living standards, divert, and entertain. The same countries that ask the world to recognize and respect the individuality of their cultures insist on the wholesale transfer to them of modern goods, services, and technologies. Modernity is not just a wish but also a widespread practice among those who cling, with unyielding passion or religious fervor, to ancient attitudes and heritages.

Who can forget the televised scenes during the 1979 Iranian uprisings of young men in fashionable French-cut trousers and silky body shirts thirsting for blood with raised modern weapons in the name of Islamic fundamentalism?

In Brazil, thousands swarm daily from preindustrial Bahian darkness into exploding coastal cities, there quickly to install television sets in crowded corrugated huts and, next to battered Volkswagens, make sacrificial offerings of fruit and fresh-killed chickens to Macumban spirits by candlelight.

During Biafra's fratricidal war against the Ibos, daily televised reports showed soldiers carrying bloodstained swords and listening to transistor radios while drinking Coca-Cola.

In the isolated Siberian city of Krasnoyarsk, with no paved streets and censored news, occasional Western travelers are stealthily propositioned for cigarettes, digital watches, and even the clothes off their backs.

The organized smuggling of electronic equipment, used automobiles, western clothing, cosmetics, and pirated movies into primitive places exceeds even the thriving underground trade in modern weapons and their military mercenaries.

A thousand suggestive ways attest to the ubiquity of the desire for the most advanced things that the world makes and sells—goods of the best quality and reliability at the lowest price. The world's needs and desires have been irrevocably homogenized. This makes the multinational corporation obsolete and the global corporation absolute.

—— LIVING IN THE REPUBLIC OF TECHNOLOGY

Daniel J. Boorstin, author of the monumental trilogy *The Americans*, characterized our age as driven by "the Republic of Technology [whose] supreme law . . . is convergence, the tendency for everything to become more like everything else."

In business, this trend has pushed markets toward global commonality. Corporations sell standardized products in the same way everywhere—autos, steel, chemicals, petroleum, cement, agricultural commodities and equipment, industrial and commercial construction, banking and insurance

services, computers, semiconductors, transport, electronic instruments, pharmaceuticals, and telecommunications, to mention some of the obvious.

Nor is the sweeping gale of globalization confined to these raw material
or high-tech products, where the universal language of customers and users
facilitates standardization. The transforming winds whipped up by the prole-
tarianization of communication and travel enter every crevice of life.

Commercially, nothing confirms this as much as the success of
McDonald's from the Champs Elysées to the Ginza, of Coca-Cola in Bahrain
and Pepsi-Cola in Moscow, and of rock music, Greek salad, Hollywood movies,
Revlon cosmetics, Sony televisions, and Levi jeans everywhere. "High-touch"
products are as ubiquitous as high-tech.

Starting from opposing sides, the high-tech and the high-touch ends of
the commercial spectrum gradually consume the undistributed middle in their
cosmopolitan orbit. No one is exempt and nothing can stop the process. Everywhere everything gets more and more like everything else as the world's
preference structure is relentlessly homogenized.

Consider the cases of Coca-Cola and Pepsi-Cola, which are globally
standardized products sold everywhere and welcomed by everyone. Both
successfully cross multitudes of national, regional, and ethnic taste buds
trained to a variety of deeply ingrained local preferences of taste, flavor,
consistency, effervescence, and aftertaste. Everywhere both sell well. Cigarettes, too, especially American-made, make year-to-year global inroads on
territories previously held in the firm grip of other, mostly local, blends.

These are not exceptional examples. (Indeed their global reach would
be even greater were it not for artificial trade barriers.) They exemplify a general
drift toward the homogenization of the world and how companies distribute,
finance, and price products.[1] Nothing is exempt. The products and methods of
the industrialized world play a single tune for all the world, and all the world
eagerly dances to it.

Ancient differences in national tastes or modes of doing business disappear. The commonality of preference leads inescapably to the standardization
of products, manufacturing, and the institutions of trade and commerce. Small
nation-based markets transmogrify and expand. Success in world competition
turns on efficiency in production, distribution, marketing, and management,
and inevitably becomes focused on price.

The most effective world competitors incorporate superior quality and
reliability into their cost structures. They sell in all national markets the same
kind of products sold at home or in their largest export market. They compete
on the basis of appropriate value—the best combinations of price, quality,

1. In a landmark article, Robert D. Buzzel pointed out the rapidity with which barriers to
standardization were falling. In all cases they succumbed to more advanced and cheaper ways of doing
things. See "Can You Standardize Multinational Marketing?" *Harvard Business Review* (November–
December 1968).

reliability, and delivery for products that are globally identical with respect to design, function, and even fashion.

That, and little else, explains the surging success of Japanese companies dealing worldwide in a vast variety of products—both tangible products like steel, cars, motorcycles, hi-fi equipment, farm machinery, robots, microprocessors, carbon fibers, and now even textiles, and intangibles like banking, shipping, general contracting, and soon computer software. Nor are high-quality and low-cost operations incompatible, as a host of consulting organizations and data engineers argue with vigorous vacuity. The reported data are incomplete, wrongly analyzed, and contradictory. The truth is that low-cost operations are the hallmark of corporate cultures that require and produce quality in all that they do. High quality and low costs are not opposing postures. They are compatible, twin identities of superior practice.[2]

To say that Japan's companies are not global because they export cars with left-side drives to the United States and the European continent, while those in Japan have right-side drives, or because they sell office machines through distributors in the United States but directly at home, or speak Portuguese in Brazil is to mistake a difference for a distinction. The same is true of Safeway and Southland retail chains operating effectively in the Middle East, and to not only native but also imported populations from Korea, the Philippines, Pakistan, India, Thailand, Britain, and the United States. National rules of the road differ, and so do distribution channels and languages. Japan's distinction is its unrelenting push for economy and value enhancement. That translates into a drive for standardization at high quality levels.

VINDICATION OF THE MODEL T

If a company forces costs and prices down and pushes quality and reliability up—while maintaining reasonable concern for suitability—customers will prefer its world-standardized products. The theory holds at this stage in the evolution of globalization—no matter what conventional market research and even common sense may suggest about different national and regional tastes, preferences, needs, and institutions. The Japanese have repeatedly vindicated this theory, as did Henry Ford with the Model T. Most important, so have their imitators, including companies from South Korea (television sets and heavy construction), Malaysia (personal calculators and microcomputers), Brazil (auto parts and tools), Colombia (apparel), Singapore (optical equipment), and, yes, even the United States (office copiers, computers, bicycles, castings),

---

2. There is powerful new evidence for this, even though the opposite has been urged by analysts of PIMS data for years. *See* "Product Quality: Cost Production and Business Performance—A Test of Some Key Hypotheses" by Lynn W. Phillips, Dae Chang, and Robert D. Buzzell, Harvard Business School Working Paper No. 83-13.

Western Europe (automatic washing machines), Rumania (housewares), Hungary (apparel), Yugoslavia (furniture), and Israel (pagination equipment).

Of course, large companies operating in a single nation or even a single city don't standardize everything they make, sell, or do. They have product lines instead of a single product version, and multiple distribution channels. There are neighborhood, local, regional, ethnic, and institutional differences, even within metropolitan areas. But although companies customize products for particular market segments, they know that success in a world with homogenized demand requires a search for sales opportunities in similar segments across the globe in order to achieve the economies of scale necessary to compete.

Such a search works because a market segment in one country is seldom unique; it has close cousins everywhere precisely because technology has homogenized the globe. Even small local segments have their global equivalents everywhere and become subject to global competition, especially on price.

The global competitor will seek constantly to standardize its offering everywhere. It will digress from this standardization only after exhausting all possibilities to retain it, and will push for reinstatement of standardization whenever digression and divergence have occurred. It will never assume that the customer is a king who knows his own wishes.

Trouble increasingly stalks companies that lack clarified global focus and remain inattentive to the economics of simplicity and standardization. The most endangered companies in the rapidly evolving world tend to be those that dominate rather small domestic markets with high value-added products for which there are smaller markets elsewhere. With transportation costs proportionately low, distant competitors will enter the now-sheltered markets of those companies with goods produced more cheaply under scale-efficient conditions. Global competition spells the end of domestic territoriality, no matter how diminutive the territory may be.

When the global producer offers its lower costs internationally, its patronage expands exponentially. It not only reaches into distant markets, but also attracts customers who previously held to local preferences and now capitulate to the attractions of lower prices. The strategy of standardization not only responds to worldwide homogenized markets but also expands those markets with aggressive low pricing. The new technological juggernaut taps an ancient motivation—to make one's money go as far as possible. This is universal—not simply a motivation but actually a need.

——— THE HEDGEHOG KNOWS

The difference between the hedgehog and the fox, wrote Sir Isaiah Berlin in distinguishing between Dostoevski and Tolstoy, is that the fox knows a lot about a great many things, but the hedgehog knows everything about one great thing. The multinational corporation knows a lot about a great many countries and congenially adapts to supposed differences. It willingly accepts vestigial national differences, not questioning the possibility of their transformation, not recognizing how the world is ready and eager for the benefit of modernity, especially when the price is right. The multinational corporation's accommodating mode to visible national differences is medieval.

By contrast, the global corporation knows everything about one great thing. It knows about the absolute need to be competitive on a worldwide basis as well as nationally and seeks constantly to drive down prices by standardizing what it sells and how it operates. It treats the world as composed of few standardized markets rather than many customized markets. It actively seeks and vigorously works toward global convergence. Its mission is modernity and its mode is price competition, even when it sells top-of-the-line, high-end products. It knows about the one great thing all nations and people have in common: scarcity.

Nobody takes scarcity lying down; everyone wants more. This in part explains division of labor and specialization of production. They enable people and nations to optimize their conditions through trade. The median is usually money.

Experience teaches that money has three special qualities: scarcity, difficulty of acquisition, and transience. People understandably treat it with respect. Everyone in the increasingly homogenized world market wants products and features that everybody else wants. If the price is low enough, they will take highly standardized world products, even if these aren't exactly what one's parents said was suitable, what immemorial custom decreed was right, or what market-research fabulists asserted was preferred.

The implacable truth of all modern production—whether of tangible or intangible goods—is that large-scale production of standardized items is generally cheaper within a wide range of volume than small-scale production. Some argue that computer-aided design and manufacturing (CAD/CAM) will allow companies to manufacture customized products on a small scale—but cheaply. But the argument misses the point. (For a more detailed discussion, see *Exhibit 1*.) If a company treats the world as one or two distinctive product markets, it can serve the world more economically than if it treats it as three, four, or five product markets.

WHY REMAINING DIFFERENCES?

Different cultural preferences, national tastes and standards, and business institutions are vestiges of the past. Some inheritances die gradually; others prosper and expand into mainstream global preferences. So-called ethnic markets are a good example. Chinese food, pita bread, country and western music, pizza, and jazz are everywhere. They are market segments that exist in worldwide proportions. They don't deny or contradict global homogenization but confirm it.

Many of today's differences among nations as to products and their features actually reflect the respectful accommodation of multinational corporations to what they believe are fixed local preferences. They *believe* preferences are fixed, not because they are but because of rigid habits of thinking about what actually is. Most executives in multinational corporations are thoughtlessly accommodating. They falsely presume that marketing means giving customers what they say they want rather than trying to understand exactly what they would like. So the corporations persist with high-cost, customized multinational products and practices instead of pressing hard and pressing properly for global standardization.

I do not advocate the systematic disregard of local or national differences. But a company's sensitivity to such differences does not require that it ignore the possibilities of doing things differently or better.

There are, for example, enormous differences among Middle Eastern countries. Some are socialist, some monarchies, some republics. Some take their legal heritage from the Napoleonic Code, some from the Ottoman Empire, and some from British common law; except for Israel, all are influenced by Islam. Doing business means personalizing the business relationship in an obsessively intimate fashion. During the month of Ramadan, business discussions can start only after 10 o'clock at night, when people are tired and full of food after a day of fasting. A company must almost certainly have a local partner; a local lawyer is required (as, say, in New York), and irrevocable letters of credit are essential. Yet, as Coca-Cola's senior vice president Sam Ayoub noted, "Arabs are much more capable of making distinctions between cultural and religious purposes on the one hand and economic realities on the other than is generally assumed. Islam is compatible with science and modern times."

EXHIBIT 1
Economies of Scope

One argument that opposes globalization says that flexible factory automation will enable plants of massive size to change products and product features quickly, without stopping the manufacturing process. These factories of the future could thus produce broad lines of customized products without sacrificing the scale economies that come from long production runs of standardized items. CAD/CAM, combined with robotics, will create a new equipment and process technology(EPT) that will make small plants located close to their markets as efficient as large ones located distantly. Economies of scale will not dominate, but rather economies of scope—the ability of either large or small plants to produce great varieties of relatively customized products at remarkably low costs. If that happens, the customers will have no need to abandon special preferences.

I will not deny the power of these possibilities. But possibilities do not make probabilities. There is no conceivable way in which flexible factory automation can achieve the scale economies of a modernized plant dedicated to mass production of standardized lines. The new digitized equipment and process technologies are available to all. Manufacturers with minimal customization and narrow product-line breadth will have costs far below those with more customization and wider lines.

Barriers to globalization are not confined to the Middle East. The free transfer of technology and data across the boundaries of the European Common Market countries are hampered by legal and financial impediments. And there is resistance to radio and television interference ("pollution") among neighboring European countries.

But the past is a good guide to the future. With persistence and appropriate means, barriers against superior technologies and economics have always fallen. There is no recorded exception where reasonable effort has been made to overcome them. It is very much a matter of time and effort.

—— A FAILURE IN GLOBAL IMAGINATION

Many companies have tried to standardize world practice by exporting domestic products and processes without accommodation or change—and have failed miserably. Their deficiencies have been seized on as evidence of bovine stupidity in the face of abject impossibility. Advocates of global standardization see them as examples of failures in execution.

In fact, poor execution is often an important cause. More important, however, is failure of nerve—failure of imagination.

Consider the case for the introduction of fully automatic home laundry equipment in Western Europe at a time when few homes had even semiautomatic machines. Hoover, Ltd., whose parent company was headquartered in North Canton, Ohio, had a prominent presence in Britain as a producer of vacuum cleaners and washing machines. Due to insufficient demand in the home market and low exports to the European continent, the large washing machine plant in England operated far below capacity. The company needed to sell more of its semiautomatic or automatic machines.

Because it had a "proper" marketing orientation, Hoover conducted consumer preference studies in Britain and each major continental country. The results showed feature preferences clearly enough among several countries (see *Exhibit 2*).

The incremental unit variable costs (in pounds sterling) of customizing to meet just a few of the national preferences were:

	£	s.	d.
Stainless steel vs. enamel drum	1	0	0
Porthole window		10	0
Spin speed of 800 rpm vs. 700 rpm		15	0
Water heater	2	15	0
6 vs. 5 kilos capacity	1	10	0
	£6	10s	0d

$18.20 at the exchange rate of that time.

Considerable plant investment was needed to meet other preferences.

EXHIBIT 2
Consumer Preferences as to Automatic Washing Machine Features in the 1960s

FEATURES	GREAT BRITAIN	ITALY	WEST GERMANY	FRANCE	SWEDEN
Shell Dimensions*	34" and narrow	Low and narrow	34" and wide	34" and narrrow	34" and wide
Drum Material	Enamel	Enamel	Stainless steel	Enamel	Stainless steel
Loading	Top	Front	Front	Front	Front
Front Porthole	Yes/no	Yes	Yes	Yes	Yes
Capacity	5 kilos	4 kilos	6 kilos	5 kilos	6 kilos
Spin Speed	700 rpm	400 rpm	850 rpm	600 rpm	800 rpm
Water-heating System	No[†]	Yes	Yes[††]	Yes	No[†]
Washing Action	Agitator	Tumble	Tumble	Agitator	Tumble
Styling Features	Inconspic-uous ap-pearance	Brightly colored	Indestruc-tible appear-ance	Elegant appearance	Strong appearance

* 34" height was in the process of being adopted as a standard work-surface height in Europe.

[†] Most British and Swedish homes had centrally heated hot water.

[††] West Germans preferred to launder at temperatures higher than generally provided centrally.

The lowest retail prices (in pounds sterling) of leading locally produced brands in the various countries were approximately:

U.K.	£110
France	114
West Germany	113
Sweden	134
Italy	57

Product customization in each country would have put Hoover in a poor competitive position on the basis of price, mostly due to the higher manufacturing costs incurred by short production runs for separate features. Because Common Market tariff reduction programs were then incomplete, Hoover also paid tariff duties in each continental country.

HOW TO MAKE A CREATIVE ANALYSIS

In the Hoover case, an imaginative analysis of automatic washing machine sales in each country would have revealed that

1. Italian automatics, small in capacity and size, low-powered, without built-in heaters, with porcelain enamel tubs, were priced aggressively low and were gaining large market shares in all countries, including West Germany.
2. The best-selling automatics in West Germany were heavily advertised (three times more than the next most promoted brand), were ideally suited to national tastes, and were also by far the highest-priced machines available in that country.
3. Italy, with the lowest penetration of washing machines of any kind (manual, semiautomatic, or automatic), was rapidly going directly to automatics, skipping the pattern of first buying hand-wringer, manually assisted machines and then semiautomatics.
4. Detergent manufacturers were just beginning to promote the technique of cold-water and tepid-water laundering then used in the United States.

The growing success of small, low-powered, low-speed, low-capacity, low-priced Italian machines, even against the preferred but highly priced and highly promoted brand in West Germany, was significant. It contained a powerful message that was lost on managers confidently wedded to a distorted version of the marketing concept according to which you give customers what they say they want. In fact, the customers *said* they wanted certain features, but their behavior demonstrated they'd take other features provided the price and the promotion were right.

In this case, it was obvious that, under prevailing conditions, people preferred a low-priced automatic over any kind of manual or semiautomatic machine and certainly over higher-priced automatics, even though the low-priced automatics failed to fulfill all their expressed preferences. The supposedly meticulous and demanding German consumers violated all expectations by buying the simple, low-priced Italian machines.

It was equally clear that people were profoundly influenced by promotions of automatic washers; in West Germany, the most heavily promoted ideal machine also had the largest market share despite its high price. Two things clearly influenced customers to buy: low price regardless of feature preferences, and heavy promotion regardless of price. Both factors helped customers get what they most wanted—the superior benefits bestowed by fully automatic machines.

Hoover should have aggressively sold a simple, standardized high-quality machine at a low price (afforded by the 17% variable cost reduction that the elimination of £6–10-0 worth of extra features made possible). The suggested retail prices could have been somewhat less than £100. The extra funds "saved" by avoiding unnecessary plant modifications would have supported an extended service network and aggressive media promotions.

Hoover's media message should have been: *this* is the machine that you, the homemaker, *deserve* to have to reduce the repetitive, heavy daily household burdens, so that *you* may have more constructive time to spend with your children and your husband. The promotion should also have targeted the husband to give him, preferably in the presence of his wife, a sense of obligation to provide an automatic washer for her even before he bought an automobile for himself. An aggressively low price, combined with heavy promotion of this kind, would have overcome previously expressed preferences for particular features.

The Hoover case illustrates how the perverse practice of the marketing concept and the absence of any kind of marketing imagination let multinational attitudes survive when customers actually want the benefits of global standardization. The whole project got off on the wrong foot. It asked people what features they wanted in a washing machine rather than what they wanted out of life. Selling a line of products individually tailored to each nation is thoughtless. Managers who took pride in practicing the marketing concept to the fullest did not, in fact, practice it at all. Hoover asked the wrong questions, then applied neither thought nor imagination to the answers. Such companies are like the ethnocentricists in the Middle Ages who saw with everyday clarity the sun revolving around the earth and offered it as Truth. With no additional data but a more searching mind, Copernicus, like the hedgehog, interpreted a more compelling and accurate reality. Data do not yield information except with the intervention of the mind. Information does not yield meaning except with the intervention of imagination.

ACCEPTING THE INEVITABLE

The global corporation accepts for better or for worse that technology drives consumers relentlessly toward the same common goals—alleviation of life's burdens and the expansion of discretionary time and spending power. Its role is profoundly different from what it has been for the ordinary corporation during its brief, turbulent, and remarkably protean history. It orchestrates the twin vectors of technology and globalization for the world's benefit. Neither fate, nor nature, nor God but rather the necessity of commerce created this role.

In the United States, two industries became global long before they were consciously aware of it. After over a generation of persistent and acrimonious labor shutdowns, the United Steelworkers of America had not called an industrywide strike since 1959; the United Auto Workers had not shut down General Motors since 1970. Both unions realize that they have become global; shutting down all or most of U.S. manufacturing would not shut out U.S. customers. Overseas suppliers are there to supply the market.

CRACKING THE CODE OF WESTERN MARKETS

Since the theory of the marketing concept emerged a quarter of a century ago, the more managerially advanced corporations have been eager to offer what customers clearly wanted rather than what was merely convenient.

They have created marketing departments supported by professional market researchers of awesome and often costly proportions. And they have proliferated extraordinary numbers of operations and product lines—highly tailored products and delivery systems for many different markets, market segments, and nations.

Significantly, Japanese companies operate almost entirely without marketing departments or market research of the kind so prevalent in the West. Yet in the colorful words of General Electric's chairman John E. Welch, Jr., the Japanese, coming from a small cluster of resource-poor islands, with an entirely alien culture and an almost impenetrably complex language, have cracked the code of Western markets. They have done it not by looking with mechanistic thoroughness at the way markets are different but rather by searching for meaning with a deeper wisdom. They have discovered the one great thing all markets have in common—an overwhelming desire for dependable, world-standard modernity in all things, at aggressively low prices. In response, they deliver irresistible value everywhere, attracting people with products that market-research technocrats described with superficial certainty as being unsuitable and uncompetitive.

The wider a company's global reach, the greater the number of regional and national preferences it will encounter for certain product features, distribution systems, or promotional media. There will always need to be some accommodation to differences. But the widely prevailing and often unthinking belief in the immutability of these differences is generally mistaken. Evidence of business failure because of lack of accommodation is often evidence of other shortcomings.

Take the case of Revlon in Japan. The company unnecessarily alienated retailers and confused customers by selling world-standardized cosmetics only in elite outlets; then it tried to recover with low-priced, world-standardized products in broader distribution, followed by a change in the company president and cutbacks in distribution as costs rose faster than sales. The problem was not that Revlon didn't understand the Japanese market; it didn't do the job right, wavered in its programs, and was impatient to boot.

By contrast, the Outboard Marine Corporation, with imagination, push, and persistence, collapsed long-established three-tiered distribution channels in Europe into a more focused and controllable two-step system—and did so despite the vociferous warnings of local trade groups. It also reduced the number and types of retail outlets. The result was greater improvement in credit and product-installation service to customers, major cost reductions, and sales advances.

In its highly successful introduction of Contac 600 (the timed-release decongestant) into Japan, SmithKline Corporation used 35 wholesalers instead of the 1,000-plus that established practice required. Daily contacts with the wholesalers and key retailers, also in violation of established practice, supplemented the plan, and it worked.

Denied access to established distribution institutions in the United States, Komatsu, the Japanese manufacturer of lightweight farm machinery, entered the market through over-the-road construction equipment dealers in rural areas of the Sunbelt, where farms are smaller, the soil sandier and easier to work. Here inexperienced distributors were able to attract customers on the basis of Komatsu's product and price appropriateness.

In cases of successful challenge to prevailing institutions and practices, a combination of product reliability and quality, strong and sustained support systems, aggressively low prices, and sales-compensation packages, as well as audacity and implacability, circumvented, shattered, and transformed very different distribution systems. Instead of resentment, there was admiration.

Still, some differences between nations are unyielding, even in a world of microprocessors. In the United States almost all manufacturers of microprocessors check them for reliability through a so-called parallel system of testing. Japan prefers the totally different sequential testing system. So Teradyne Corporation, the world's largest producer of microprocessor test equipment, makes one line for the United States and one for Japan. That's easy.

What's not so easy for Teradyne is to know how best to organize and manage, in this instance, its marketing effort. Companies can organize by product, region, function, or by using some combination of these. A company can have separate marketing organizations for Japan and for the United States, or it can have separate product groups, one working largely in Japan and the other in the United States. A single manufacturing facility or marketing operation might service both markets, or a company might use separate marketing operations for each.

Questions arise if the company organizes by product. In the case of Teradyne, should the group handling the parallel system, whose major market is the United States, sell in Japan and compete with the group focused on the Japanese market? If the company organizes regionally, how do regional groups divide their efforts between promoting the parallel versus the sequential system? If the company organizes in terms of function, how does it get commitment in marketing, for example, for one line instead of the other?

There is no one reliably right answer—no one formula by which to get it. There isn't even a satisfactory contingent answer.[3] What works well for one company or one place may fail for another in precisely the same place, depending on the capabilities, histories, reputations, resources, and even the cultures of both.

3. For a discussion of multinational reorganization, *see* Christopher A. Bartlett, "MNCs: Get Off the Reorganization Merry-Go-Round," *Harvard Business Review* (March–April 1983).

——— THE EARTH IS FLAT

The differences that persist throughout the world despite its globalization affirm an ancient dictum of economics—that things are driven by what happens at the margin, not at the core. Thus, in ordinary competitive analysis, what's important is not the average price but the marginal price; what happens not in the usual case but at the interface of newly erupting conditions. What counts in commercial affairs is what happens at the cutting edge. What is most striking today is the underlying similarities of what is happening now to national preferences at the margin. These similarities at the cutting edge cumulatively form an overwhelming, predominant commonality everywhere.

To refer to the persistence of economic nationalism (protective and subsidized trade practices, special tax aids, or restrictions for home market producers) as a barrier to the globalization of markets is to make a valid point. Economic nationalism does have a powerful persistence. But, as with the present almost totally smooth internationalization of investment capital, the past alone does not shape or predict the future. (For reflections on the internationalization of capital, see *Exhibit 3*.)

Reality is not a fixed paradigm, dominated by immemorial customs and derived attitudes, heedless of powerful and abundant new forces. The world is becoming increasingly informed about the liberating and enhancing possibilities of modernity. The persistence of the inherited varieties of national prefer-

EXHIBIT 3
The Shortening of Japanese Horizons

One of the most powerful yet least celebrated forces driving commerce toward global standardization is the monetary system, along with the international investment process. Today money is simply electronic implulses. With the speed of light it moves effortlessly between distant centers (and even lesser places). A change of 10 basis points in the price of a bond causes an instant and massive shift of money from London to Tokyo. The system has a profound impact on the way companies operate throughout the world.

Take Japan, where high debt-to-equity balance sheets are "guaranteed" by various societal presumptions about the virtue of "a long view," or by government policy in other ways. Even here, upward shifts in interest rates in other parts of the world attract capital out of the country in powerful proportions. In recent years more and more Japanese global corporations have gone to the world's equity markets for funds. Debt is too remunerative in high-yielding countries to keep capital at home to feed the Japanese need. As interest rates rise, equity becomes a more attractive option for the issuer.

The long-term impact on Japanese enterprise will be transforming. As the equity proportion of Japanese corporate capitalization rises, companies will respond to the shorter-term investment horizons of the equity markets. Thus the much-vaunted Japanese corporate practice to taking the long view will gradually disappear.

ences rests uneasily on increasing evidence of, and restlessness regarding, their inefficiency, costliness, and confinement. The historic past, and the national differences respecting commerce and industry it spawned and fostered everywhere, is now subject to relatively easy transformation.

Cosmopolitanism is no longer the monopoly of the intellectual and leisure classes; it is becoming the established property and defining characteristic of all sectors everywhere in the world. Gradually and irresistibly it breaks down the walls of economic insularity, nationalism, and chauvinism. What we see today as escalating commercial nationalism is simply the last violent death rattle of an obsolete institution.

Companies that adapt to and capitalize on economic convergence can still make distinctions and adjustments in different markets. Persistent differences in the world are consistent with fundamental underlying commonalities; they often complement rather than oppose each other—in business as they do in physics. There is, in physics, matter and antimatter simultaneously working in symbiotic harmony.

The earth is round, but for most purposes it's sensible to treat it as flat. Space is curved, but not much for everyday life here on earth.

Divergence from established practice happens all the time. But the multinational mind, warped into circumspection and timidity by years of stumbles and transnational troubles, now rarely challenges existing overseas practices. More often it considers any departure from inherited domestic routines as mindless, disrespectful, or impossible. It is the mind of a bygone day.

The successful global corporation does not abjure customization or differentiation for the requirements of markets that differ in product preferences, spending patterns, shopping preferences, and institutional or legal arrangements. But the global corporation accepts and adjusts to these differences only reluctantly, only after relentlessly testing their immutability, after trying in various ways to circumvent and reshape them, as we saw in the cases of Outboard Marine in Europe, SmithKline in Japan, and Komatsu in the United States.

There is only one significant respect in which a company's activities around the world are important, and this is in what it produces and how it sells. Everything else derives from, and is subsidiary to, these activities.

The purpose of business is to get and keep a customer. Or, to use Peter Drucker's more refined construction, to *create* and keep a customer. A company must be wedded to the ideal of innovation—offering better or more preferred products in such combinations of ways, means, places, and at such prices that prospects *prefer* doing business with the company rather than with others.

Preferences are constantly shaped and reshaped. Within our global commonality, enormous variety constantly asserts itself and thrives, as can be seen within the world's single largest domestic market, the United States. But in the process of world homogenization, modern markets expand to reach cost-reducing global proportions. With better and cheaper communication and transport, even small local market segments hitherto protected from distant competitors now feel the pressure of their presence. Nobody is safe from global reach and the irresistible economies of scale.

Two vectors shape the world—technology and globalization. The first helps determine human preferences; the second, economic realities. Regardless of how much preferences evolve and diverge, they also gradually converge and form markets where economies of scale lead to reduction of costs and prices.

The modern global corporation contrasts powerfully with the aging multinational corporation. Instead of adapting to superficial and even entrenched differences within and between nations, it will seek sensibly to force suitably standardized products and practices on the entire globe. They are exactly what the world will take, if they come also with low prices, high quality, and blessed reliability. The global company will operate, in this regard, precisely as Henry Kissinger wrote in *Years of Upheaval* about the continuing Japanese economic success: "voracious in its collection of information, impervious to pressure, and implacable in execution."

Given what is everywhere the purpose of commerce, the global company will shape the vectors of technology and globalization into its great strategic fecundity. It will systematically push these vectors toward their own convergence, offering everyone simultaneously high-quality, more or less standardized products at optimally low prices, thereby achieving for itself vastly expanded markets and profits. Companies that do not adapt to the new global realities will become victims of those that do.

Copyright © 1983; revised 1991.

━━━ DISCUSSION QUESTIONS

1. Give your views on standardizing global marketing in today's global environment. What are the advantages of standardization? The disadvantages?
2. The author states that technology today is standardizing everything from communication to transport and travel. Because of this, he says, the world is converging in common needs and preferences. Do you agree with this view? Try to think of examples that support or contradict the author's argument.
3. Can people's needs and expectations be shaped by the availability of functional, reliable, and low-priced products? Is this how the Japanese have penetrated world markets so successfully? Does this conflict with the premise that customers' needs and expectations are the forces that shape the ultimate product offered by a supplier?
4. What is the difference between multinational operations and global operations? How does this difference affect marketing strategy?

Customizing Global Marketing 37

JOHN A. QUELCH AND EDWARD J. HOFF

According to this reading, the issue for most companies today is not "whether to go global but how to tailor the global marketing concept to fit each business." In determining the appropriate degree of standardization or adaptation, managers should consider their companies' overall business strategy, which products will benefit from the economies or efficiencies of standardization, which products won't fight cultural barriers, what trade-offs will result from standardizing various elements of the marketing mix, and how standardization will vary from country to country. This reading offers guidance on how to answer these questions and how to manage the transition to global marketing.

In the best of all possible worlds, marketers would only have to come up with a great product and a convincing marketing program to have a worldwide winner. But despite the obvious economies and efficiencies they could gain with a standard product and program, many managers fear that global marketing, as popularly defined, is too extreme to be practical. Because customers and competitive conditions differ across countries, or because powerful local managers will not stand for centralized decision making, they argue, global marketing just won't work.

Of course, global marketing has its pitfalls, but it can also yield impressive advantages. Standardizing products can lower operating costs. Even more important, effective coordination can exploit a company's best product and marketing ideas.

Too often, executives view global marketing as an either/or proposition—either full standardization or local control. But when a global approach can fall anywhere on a spectrum from tight worldwide coordination on programming details to loose agreement on a product idea, why the extreme view? In applying the global marketing concept and making it work, flexibility is essential. Managers need to tailor the approach they use to each element of the business system and marketing program. For example, a manufacturer might market the same product under different brand names in different countries or market the same brands using different product formulas.

The big issue today is not whether to go global but how to tailor the global marketing concept to fit each business and how to make it work. In this reading, we'll first provide a framework to help managers think about how they should structure the different areas of the marketing function as the business shifts to a global approach. We will then show how companies we have studied are tackling the implementation challenges of global marketing.

HOW FAR TO GO

How far a company can move toward global marketing depends a lot on its evolution and traditions. Consider these two examples:

- Although the Coca-Cola Company had conducted some international business before 1940, it gained true global recognition during World War II, as Coke bottling plants followed the march of U.S. troops around the world. Management in Atlanta made all strategic decisions then—and still does now, as Coca-Cola applies global marketing principles, for example, to the worldwide introduction of Diet Coke. The brand name, concentrate formula, positioning, and advertising theme are virtually standard worldwide, but the artificial sweetener and packaging differ across countries. Local managers are responsible for sales and distribution programs, which they run in conjunction with local bottlers.
- The Nestlé approach also has its roots in history. To avoid distribution disruptions caused by wars in Europe, to ease rapid worldwide expansion, and to respond to local consumer needs, Nestlé granted its local managers considerable autonomy from the outset. While the local managers still retain much of that decision-making power today, Nestlé headquarters in Vevey, Switzerland, has grown in importance. Nestlé has transferred to its central marketing staff many former local managers who had succeeded in their Nestlé businesses and who now influence country executives to accept standard new product and marketing ideas. The trend seems to be toward tighter marketing coordination.

To conclude that Coca-Cola is a global marketer and Nestlé is not would be simplistic. In *Exhibit 1,* we assess program adaptation or standardization levels for each company's business functions, products, marketing mix elements, and countries. Each company has tailored its individual approach. Furthermore, as *Exhibit 1* can't show, the situations aren't static. Readers can evaluate their own *current* and *desired* levels of program adaptation or standardization on these four dimensions. The gap between the two levels is the implementation challenge. The size of the gap—and the urgency with which it must be closed—will depend on a company's strategy and financial performance, competitive pressures, technological change, and converging consumer values.

EXHIBIT 1 Global Marketing Planning Matrix: How Far to Go

		Adaptation		Standardization	
		Full	**Partial**	**Partial**	**Full**
Business functions	Research and development			Nestlé	Coca-Cola
	Finance and accounting			Nestlé	Coca-Cola
	Manufacturing		Nestlé	Coca-Cola	
	Procurement	Nestlé		Coca-Cola	
	Marketing		Nestlé		Coca-Cola
Products	Low cultural grounding / High economies or efficiencies				Coca-Cola
	Low cultural grounding / Low economies or efficiencies				
	High cultural grounding / High economies or efficiencies		Nestlé		
	High cultural grounding / Low economies or efficiencies				
Marketing mix elements	Product design			Nestlé	Coca-Cola
	Brand name			Nestlé	Coca-Cola
	Product positioning		Nestlé		Coca-Cola
	Packaging			Coca-Cola	
	Advertising theme		Nestlé		Coca-Cola
	Pricing		Nestlé	Coca-Cola	
	Advertising copy	Nestlé			Coca-Cola
	Distribution	Nestlé	Coca-Cola		
	Sales promotion	Nestlé	Coca-Cola		
	Customer service	Nestlé	Coca-Cola		
Countries Region 1	Country A			Nestlé	Coca-Cola
	Country B			Nestlé	Coca-Cola
Region 2	Country C		Nestlé		Coca-Cola
	Country D		Nestlé		Coca-Cola
	Country E	Nestlé			Coca-Cola

Legend: ☐ Nestlé ■ Coca-Cola

FOUR DIMENSIONS OF GLOBAL MARKETING

Now let's look at the issues that arise when executives consider the four dimensions shown in *Exhibit 1* in light of the degree of standardization or adaptation that is appropriate.

Business Functions   A company's approach to global marketing depends, first, on its overall business strategy. In many multinationals, some functional areas have greater program standardization than others. Headquarters often controls manufacturing, finance, and R&D, while the local managers make the marketing decisions. Marketing is usually one of the last functions to be centrally directed. Partly because product quality and accounting data are easier to measure than marketing effectiveness, standardization can be greater in production and finance.

Products   Products that enjoy high scale economies or efficiencies and are not highly culture-bound are easier to market globally than others.

1. *Economies or efficiencies.* Manufacturing and R&D scale economies can result in a price spread between the global and the local product that is too great for even the most culture-bound consumer to resist. In addition, management often has neither the time nor the R&D resources to adapt products to each country. The markets for high-tech products like computers are not only very competitive but also affected by rapid technological change.

   Most packaged consumer goods are less susceptible than durable goods (like televisions and cars) to manufacturing or even R&D economies. Coca-Cola's global policy and Nestlé's interest in tighter marketing coordination are driven largely by a desire to capitalize on the marketing ideas their managers around the world generate rather than by potential scale economies. Nestlé, for example, manufactures its packaged soups in dozens of locally managed plants around the world, with some transference of engineering know-how through a headquarters staff. Products and marketing programs are also locally managed, but new ideas are aggressively transferred, with local managers encouraged—or even prodded—to adapt and use them in their own markets. For Nestlé, global marketing does not so much yield high manufacturing economies as high efficiency in using scarce new ideas.

2. *Cultural grounding.* Consumer products used in the home—like Nestlé's soups and frozen foods—are often more culture-bound than products used outside the home such as automobiles and credit cards, and industrial products are inherently less culture-bound than consumer products. (Products like personal computers, for example, are often marketed on the basis of performance benefits that share a common technical language worldwide.) Experience also suggests that products will be less culture-bound if they are

used by young people whose cultural norms are not ingrained, people who travel in different countries, and ego-driven consumers who can be appealed to through myths and fantasies shared across cultures.

Exhibit 1 lists four combinations of the scale economy and cultural grounding variables in order of their susceptibility to global marketing. Managers shouldn't be bound by any matrix, however; they should find creative ways to prepare a product for global marketing. If a manufacturer develops a new version of a seemingly culture-bound product that is based on new capital-intensive technology and generates superior performance benefits, it may well be possible to introduce it on a standard basis worldwide. Procter & Gamble developed Pampers disposable diapers as a global brand in a product category that intuition would say was culture-bound.

Marketing Mix Elements   Few consumer goods companies go so far as to market the same products using the same marketing program worldwide. And those that do, like Lego, the Danish manufacturer of construction toys, often distribute their products through sales companies rather than full-fledged marketing subsidiaries.

For most products, the appropriate degree of standardization varies from one element of the marketing mix to another. Strategic elements like product positioning are more easily standardized than execution-sensitive elements like sales promotion. In addition, when headquarters believes it has identified a superior marketing idea, whether it be a package design, a brand name, or an advertising copy concept, the pressure to standardize increases.

Marketing can usually contribute to scale economies most significantly by creating a standard product design that will sell worldwide, permitting savings through globalized production. In addition, scale economies in marketing programming can be achieved through standard commercial executions and copy concepts. McCann-Erickson claims to have saved $90 million in production costs over 20 years by producing worldwide Coca-Cola commercials. To ensure that they have enough attention-getting power to overcome their foreign origins, however, marketers often have to make worldwide commercials expensive productions.

To compensate local management for having to accept a standard product and to fit the core product to each local market, some companies allow local managers to adapt those marketing mix elements that aren't subject to significant scale economies. On the other hand, local managers are more likely to accept a standard concept for those elements of the marketing mix that are less important and, ironically, often not susceptible to scale economies. Overall, then, the driving factor in moving toward global marketing should be the efficient worldwide use of good marketing ideas rather than any scale economies from standardization.

In judging how far to go in standardizing elements of the marketing mix, managers must also be mindful of the interactions among them. For example, when a product with the same brand name is sold in different countries, it can be difficult and sometimes impossible to sell it at different prices.

Countries How far a decentralized multinational wishes to pursue global marketing will often vary from one country to another. Naturally, headquarters is likely to become more involved in marketing decisions in countries where performance is poor. But performance aside, small markets depend more on headquarters assistance than large markets do. Because a standard marketing program is superior in quality to what local executives, even with the benefit of local market knowledge, could develop themselves, they may welcome it.

Large markets with strong local managements are less willing to accept global programs. Yet these are the markets that often account for most of the company's investment. To secure their acceptance, headquarters should make standard marketing programs reflect the needs of large rather than small markets. Small markets, being more tolerant of deviations from what would be locally appropriate, are less likely to resist a standard program.

As we've seen, Coca-Cola takes the same approach in all markets. Nestlé varies its approach in different countries depending on the strength of its market presence and each country's need for assistance. In completing the *Exhibit 1* planning matrix, management may decide that it can sensibly group countries by region or by stage of market development.

────── TOO FAR TOO FAST

Once managers have decided how global they want their marketing program to be, they must make the transition. Debates over the size of the gap between present and desired positions and the speed with which it must be closed will often pit the field against headquarters. Such conflict is most likely to arise in companies where the reason for change is not apparent or the country managers have had a lot of autonomy. Casualties can occur on both sides:

- Because Black & Decker dominated the European consumer power tool market, many of the company's European managers could not see that a more centrally directed global marketing approach was needed as a defense against imminent Japanese competition. To make the point, the CEO had to replace several key European executives.
- In 1982, the Parker Pen Company, forced by competition and a weakening financial position to lower costs, more than halved its number of plants and pen styles worldwide. Parker's overseas subsidiary managers accepted these changes but, when pressed to

implement standardized advertising and packaging, they dug in their heels. In 1985, Parker ended its much heralded global marketing campaign. Several senior headquarters managers left the company.

If management is not careful, moving too far too fast toward global marketing can trigger painful consequences. First, subsidiary managers who joined the company because of its apparent commitment to local autonomy and to adapting its products to the local environment may become disenchanted. When poorly implemented, global marketing can make the local country manager's job less strategic. Second, disenchantment may reinforce not-invented-here attitudes that lead to game playing. For instance, some local managers may try bargaining with headquarters, trading the speed with which they will accept and implement the standard programs for additional budget assistance. In addition, local managers competing for resources and autonomy may devote too much attention to second-guessing headquarters' "hot buttons." Eventually the good managers may leave, and less competent people who lack the initiative of their predecessors may replace them.

A vicious circle can develop. Feeling compelled to review local performance more closely, headquarters may tighten its controls and reduce resources without adjusting its expectations of local managers. Meanwhile, local managers trying to gain approval of applications for deviations from standard marketing programs are being frustrated. The expanding headquarters bureaucracy and associated overhead costs reduce the speed with which the locals can respond to local opportunities and competitive actions. Slow response time is an especially serious problem with products for which barriers to entry for local competitors are low.

In this kind of system, weak, insecure local managers can become dependent on headquarters for operational assistance. They'll want headquarters to assume the financial risks for new product launches and welcome the prepackaged marketing programs. If performance falls short of headquarters' expectations, the local management can always blame the failure on the quality of operational assistance or on the standard marketing program. The local manager who has clear autonomy and profit-and-loss responsibility cannot hide behind such excuses.

If headquarters or regions assume much of the strategic burden, managers in overseas subsidiaries may think only about short-term sales. This focus will diminish their ability to monitor and communicate to headquarters any changes in local competitors' strategic directions. When their responsibilities shift from strategy to execution, their ideas will become less exciting. If the field has traditionally been as important a source of new product ideas as the central R&D laboratory, the company may find itself short of the grassroots creative thinking and marketing research information that R&D needs. The fruitful dialogue that characterizes a relationship between equal partners will no longer flourish.

———— HOW TO GET THERE

When thinking about closing the gap between present and desired positions, most executives of decentralized multinationals want to accommodate their current organizational structures. They rightly view their subsidiaries and the managers who run them as important competitive strengths. They generally do not wish to transform these organizations into mere sales and distribution agencies.

How then, in moving toward global marketing, can headquarters build rather than jeopardize relationships, stimulate rather than demoralize local managers? The answer is to focus on means as much as ends, to examine the relationship between the home office and the field, and to ask what level of headquarters intervention for each business function, product, marketing mix element, and country is necessary to close the gap in each.

As *Exhibit 2* indicates, headquarters can intervene at five points, ranging from informing to directing. The five intervention levels are cumulative; for headquarters to direct, it must also inform, persuade, coordinate, and approve. *Exhibit 2* shows the approaches Atlanta and Vevey have taken. Moving from left to right on *Exhibit 2,* the reader can see that things are done increasingly by fiat rather than patient persuasion, through discipline rather than education. At the far right, local subsidiaries can't choose whether to opt in or out of a marketing program, and headquarters views its country managers as subordinates rather than customers.

When the local managers tightly control marketing efforts, multinational managers face the three critical issues listed below. In the sections that follow, we'll take a look at how decentralized multinationals are working to correct the three problems as they move along the spectrum from informing to directing.

- *Inconsistent brand identities.* If headquarters gives country managers total control of their product lines, it cannot leverage the opportunities that multinational status gives the company. The increasing degree to which consumers in one country are exposed to the company's products in another won't enhance the corporate image or brand development in the consumers' home country.
- *Limited product focus.* In the decentralized multinational, the field line manager's ambition is to become a country manager, which means acquiring multiproduct and multifunctional experience. Yet as the pace of technological innovation increases and the likelihood of global competition grows, multinationals need worldwide product specialists as well as executives willing to transfer to other countries. Nowhere is the need for headquarters guidance on innovative organizational approaches more evident than in the area of product policy.
- *Slow new product launches.* As global competition grows, so does the need for rapid worldwide rollouts of new products. The decentralized multinational that permits country managers to

EXHIBIT 2   Global Marketing Planning Matrix: How to Get There

		Informing	Persuading	Coordinating	Approving	Directing
Business functions	Research and development					
	Finance and accounting					
	Manufacturing					
	Procurement					
	Marketing					
Products	Low cultural grounding High economies or efficiencies					
	Low cultural grounding Low economies or efficiencies					
	High cultural grounding High economies or efficiencies					
	High cultural grounding Low economies or efficiencies					
Marketing mix elements	Product design					
	Brand name					
	Product positioning					
	Packaging					
	Advertising theme					
	Pricing					
	Advertising copy					
	Distribution					
	Sales promotion					
	Customer service					
Countries Region 1	Country A					
	Country B					
Region 2	Country C					
	Country D					
	Country E					

☐ Nestlé   ■ Coca-Cola

proceed at their own pace on new product introductions may be at a competitive disadvantage in this new environment.

WORD OF MOUTH

The least threatening, loosest, and therefore easiest approach to global marketing is for headquarters to encourage the transfer of information between it and its country managers. Since good ideas are often a company's scarcest resource, headquarters' efforts to encourage and reward their generation, dissemination, and application in the field will build both relationships and profits. Here are two examples:

- Nestlé publishes quarterly marketing newsletters that report recent product introductions and programming innovations. In this way, each subsidiary can learn quickly about and assess the ideas of others. (The best newsletters are written as if country organizations were talking to each other rather than as if headquarters were talking down to the field.)
- Johnson Wax holds periodic meetings of all marketing directors at corporate headquarters twice a year to build global esprit de corps and to encourage the sharing of new ideas.

By making the transfer of information easy, a multinational leverages the ideas of its staff and spreads organizational values. Headquarters has to be careful, however, that the information it's passing on is useful. It may focus on updating local managers about new products, when what they mainly want is information on the most tactical and country-specific elements of the marketing mix. For example, the concentration of the grocery trade is much higher in the United Kingdom and Canada than it is in the United States. In this case, managers in the United States can learn from British and Canadian country managers about how to deal with the pressures for extra merchandising support that result when a few powerful retailers control a large percentage of sales. Likewise, marketers in countries with restrictions on mass media advertising have developed sophisticated point-of-purchase merchandising skills that could be useful to managers in other countries.

By itself, however, information sharing is often insufficient to help local executives meet the competitive challenges of global marketing.

FRIENDLY PERSUASION

Persuasion is a first step managers can take to deal with the three problems we've outlined. Any systematic headquarters effort to influence local managers to apply standardized approaches or introduce new global products while the managers retain their decision-making authority is a persuasion approach.

Unilever and CPC International, for example, employ a world-class advertising and marketing research staff at headquarters. Not critics but coaches, these specialists review the subsidiaries' work and try to upgrade the technical skills of local marketing departments. They frequently visit the field to disseminate new concepts, frameworks, and techniques, and to respond to problems that local management raises. (It helps to build trust if headquarters can send out the same staff specialists for several years.)

Often, when the headquarters of a decentralized multinational identifies or develops a new product, it has to persuade the country manager in a so-called prime-mover market to invest in the launch. A successful launch in the prime-mover market will, in turn, persuade other country managers to introduce the product. The prime-mover market is usually selected according to criteria that include the commitment of local management, the probabilities of success, the credibility with which a success would be regarded by managers in other countries, and its perceived transferability.

Persuasion, however, has its limitations. Two problems recur with the prime-mover approach. First, by adopting a wait-and-see attitude, country managers can easily turn down requests to be prime-mover markets on the grounds of insufficient resources. Since the country managers in the prime-mover markets have to risk their resources to launch the new products, they're likely to tailor the product and marketing programs to their own markets rather than to global markets. Second, if there are more new products waiting to be launched than there are prime-mover organizations to launch them, headquarters product specialists are likely to give in to a country manager's demands for local tailoring. But because of the need for readaptation in each case, the tailoring may delay rollouts in other markets and allow competitors to preempt the product. In the end, management may sacrifice long-term worldwide profits to maximize short-term profits in a few countries.

MARKETING TO THE SAME DRUMMER

To overcome the limits of persuasion, many multinationals are coordinating their marketing programs so that headquarters has a structured role in both decision making and performance evaluation that is far more influential than person-to-person persuasion. Often using a matrix or team approach, headquarters shares with country managers the responsibility and authority for programming and personnel decisions.

Nestlé locates product directors as well as support groups at headquarters. Together they develop long-term strategies for each product category on a worldwide basis, coordinate worldwide market research, spot new product opportunities, spark the field launch of new products, advise the field on how headquarters will evaluate new product proposals, and spread the word on new products' performance so that other countries will be motivated to launch them. Even though the product directors are staff executives with no line authority, because they have all been successful line managers in the field, they have great credibility and influence.

Country managers who cooperate with a product director can quickly become heroes if they successfully implement a new idea. On the other hand, while a country manager can reject a product director's advice, headquarters will closely monitor his or her performance with an alternative program. In addition, within the product category in which they specialize, the directors have influence on line management appointments in the field. Local managers thus have to be concerned about their relationships with headquarters.

Some companies assign promising local managers to other countries and require would-be local managers to take a tour of duty at headquarters. But such personnel transfer programs may run into barriers. First, many capable local nationals may not be interested in working outside their countries of origin. Second, powerful local managers are often unwilling to give up their best people to other country assignments. Third, immigration regulations and foreign service relocation costs are burdensome. Fourth, if transferees from the field have to take a demotion to work at headquarters, the costs in ill will often exceed any gains in cross-fertilization of ideas. If management can resolve these problems, however, it will find that creating an international career path is one of the most effective ways to develop a global perspective in local managers.

To enable their regional general managers to work alongside the worldwide product directors, several companies have moved them from the field to the head office. More and more companies require regional managers to reach sales and profit targets for each product as well as for each country within their regions. In the field, regional managers often focus on representing the views of individual countries to headquarters, but at headquarters they become more concerned with ensuring that the country managers are correctly implementing corporatewide policies.

Fiat and Philips N.V., among others, consolidated their worldwide advertising into a single agency. Their objectives were to make each product's advertising more consistent around the world and to make it easier to transfer ideas and information among local agency offices, country organizations, and headquarters. Use of a single agency (especially one that bills all advertising expenditures worldwide) also symbolizes a commitment to global marketing and more centralized control. Multinationals shouldn't, however, use their agencies as Trojan horses for greater standardization. An undercover operation is likely to jeopardize agency–client relations at the country level.

While working to achieve global coordination, some companies are also trying to tighten coordination in particular regions:

- Kodak experimented by consolidating 17 worldwide product line managers at corporate headquarters. In addition, the company made marketing directors in some countries responsible for a line of business in a region as well as for sales of all Kodak products in their own countries. Despite these new appointments, country managers still retain profit-and-loss responsibility for their own markets.

Whether a matrix approach such as this broadens perspectives rather than increases tension and confusion depends heavily on the corporation's cohesiveness. Such an organizational change can clearly communicate top management's strategic direction, but headquarters needs to do a persuasive selling job to the field if it is to succeed.

- Procter & Gamble has established Euro Brand teams that analyze opportunities for greater product and marketing program standardization. Chaired by the brand manager from a "lead country," each team includes brand managers from other European subsidiaries that market the brand, managers from P&G's European technical center, and one of P&G's three European division managers, each of whom is responsible for a portfolio of brands as well as for a group of countries. Concerns that the larger subsidiaries would dominate the teams and that decision making would either be paralyzed or produce lowest-common-denominator results have proved groundless.

STAMPED AND APPROVED

By coordinating programs with the field, headquarters can balance the company's local and global perspectives. Even a decentralized multinational may decide, however, that to protect or exploit some corporate asset, the center of gravity for certain elements of the marketing program should be at headquarters. In such cases, management has two options: it can send clear directives to its local managers or permit them to develop their own programs within specified parameters and subject to headquarters approval. With a properly managed approval process, a multinational can exert effective control without unduly dampening the country manager's decision-making responsibility and creativity.

When Procter & Gamble developed a new sanitary napkin, P&G International designated certain countries in different geographic regions as test markets. The product, brand name, positioning, and package design were standardized globally. P&G International did, however, invite local managers to suggest how the global program could be improved and how the nonglobal elements of the marketing program should be adapted in their markets. It approved changes in several markets. Moreover, local managers developed valuable ideas on such programming specifics as sampling and couponing techniques that were used in all other countries, including the United States.

Nestlé views its brand names as a major corporate asset. As a result, it requires all brands sold in all countries to be registered in the home country of Switzerland. While the ostensible reason for this requirement is legal protection, the effect is that any product developed in the field has to be approved by Vevey. The head office has also developed detailed guidelines that suggest rather than mandate how brand names and logos should appear on packaging and in advertising worldwide (with exceptions subject to its approval). Thus the country manager's control over the content of advertising is not compromised, and the company achieves a reasonably consistent presentation of its names and logos worldwide.

DOING IT THE HEADQUARTERS WAY

Multinationals that direct local managers' marketing programs usually do so out of a sense of urgency. The motive may be to ensure that a new product is introduced rapidly around the world before the competition can respond or that every manager fully and faithfully exploits a valuable marketing idea. Sometimes direction is needed to prove that global marketing can work. Once management makes the point, a more participative approach is feasible.

In 1979, one of Henkel's worldwide marketing directors wanted to extend the successful Sista line of do-it-yourself sealants from Germany to other European countries where the markets were underdeveloped and disorganized, as had once been the case in Germany. A European headquarters project team visited the markets and then developed a standard marketing program. The country managers, however, objected. Since the market potential in each country was small, they said, they did not have the time or resources to launch Sista.

The project team responded by pointing out that capitalizing on potential scale economies would make its pan-European marketing and manufacturing programs superior to any programs the subsidiaries could develop by themselves. Furthermore, it maintained, the already developed pan-European program was available off the shelf. The European sales manager, who was a project team member, discovered that salespeople as well as tradespeople in the target countries were much more enthusiastic about the proposed program than the field marketing managers. So management devised a special lure for the managers. The project team offered to subsidize the first-year advertising and promotion expenditures of countries launching Sista. Six countries agreed. To ensure their commitment now that their financial risk had been reduced, the sales manager invited each accepting country manager to nominate a member to the project team to develop the final program details.

By 1982, the Sista line was sold in 52 countries using a standard marketing program. The Sista launch was especially challenging because it involved the extension of a product and program already developed for a single market. The success of the Sista launch made Henkel's field managers much more receptive to global marketing programs for subsequent new products.

————— MOTIVATING THE FIELD

Taking into account the nature of their products and markets, their organizational structures, and their cultures and traditions, multinationals have to decide which approach or combination of approaches, from informing to directing, will best answer their strategic objectives. Multinational managers must realize, however, that local managers are likely to resist any precipitate move toward increased headquarters direction. A quick shift could lower their motivation and performance.

Any erosion in marketing decision making associated with global marketing will probably be less upsetting for country managers who have not risen through the line marketing function. For example, John Deere's European headquarters has developed advertising for its European country managers for more than a decade. The country managers have not objected. Most are not marketing specialists and do not see advertising as key to the success of their operations. But for country managers who view control of marketing decision making as central to their operational success, the transition will often be harder. Headquarters needs to give the field time to adjust to the new decision-making processes that multicountry brand teams and other new organizational structures require. Yet management must recognize that even with a one- or two-year transition period, some turnover among field personnel is inevitable. As one German headquarters executive commented, "Those managers in the field who can't adapt to a more global approach will have to leave and run local breweries."

Here are five suggestions on how to motivate and retain talented country managers when making the shift to global marketing:

1. Encourage field managers to generate ideas. This is especially important when R&D efforts are centrally directed. Use the best ideas from the field in global marketing programs (and give recognition to the local managers who came up with them). Unilever's South African subsidiary developed Impulse body spray, now a global brand. R. J. Reynolds revitalized Camel as a global brand after the German subsidiary came up with a successful and transferable positioning and copy strategy.

2. Ensure that the field participates in the development of the marketing strategies and programs for global brands. A bottom-up rather than top-down approach will foster greater commitment and produce superior program execution at the country level. As we've seen, when P&G International introduced its sanitary napkin as a global brand, it permitted local managers to make some adjustments in areas that were not seen as core to the program, such as couponing and sales promotion. More important, it encouraged them to suggest changes in features of the core global program.

3. Maintain a product portfolio that includes, where scale economies permit, local as well as regional and global brands. While Philip

Morris's and Seagram's country managers and their local advertising agencies are required to implement standard programs for each company's global brands, the managers retain full responsibility for the marketing programs of their locally distributed brands. Seagram motivates its country managers to stay interested in the global brands by allocating development funds to support local marketing efforts on these brands and by circulating monthly reports that summarize market performance data by brand and country.

4. Allow country managers continued control of their marketing budgets so they can respond to local consumer needs and counter local competition. When British Airways headquarters launched its £13 million global advertising campaign, it left intact the £18 million worth of tactical advertising budgets that country managers used to promote fares, destinations, and tour packages specific to their markets. Because most of the country managers had exhausted their previous year's tactical budgets and were anxious for further advertising support, they were receptive to the global campaign even though it was centrally directed.

5. Emphasize the general management responsibilities of country managers that extend beyond the marketing function. Country managers who have risen through the line marketing function often don't spend enough time on local manufacturing operations, industrial relations, and government affairs. Global marketing programs can free them to focus on and develop their skills in these other areas.

Copyright © 1986; revised 1991.

———— DISCUSSION QUESTIONS

1. Give your views on customizing global marketing in today's global environment. What are the advantages of customization? The disadvantages?

2. Compare the advantages of customization and standardization in today's global marketing. Compare the disadvantages of both. Give an example in which the trade-offs between the two approaches would determine your marketing policy.

3. How big a role do cultural barriers play in shaping global marketing strategies? Does this vary according to industry? Give some examples.

Do You Really Have a Global Strategy?   38

GARY HAMEL AND C. K. PRAHALAD

Competition from Japan emerged in the 1970s, and in the view of the authors the U.S. response has been weak and shortsighted. Many companies, they argue, miscalculated both the timing and the workability of their opposing strategies, in part because they failed to understand what global strategy really is. The result was to fall behind and lose market share. Through a detailed analysis of the tire and television markets, the authors show that only by thinking about strategy in a more analytic light can U.S. companies overtake their competitors.

The threat of foreign competition preoccupies managers in industries from telecommunications to commercial banking and from machine tools to consumer electronics. Corporate response to the threat is often misdirected and ill timed—in part because many executives don't fully understand what global competition is.

They haven't received much help from the latest analysis of this trend. One argument simply emphasizes the scale and learning effects that transcend national boundaries and provide cost advantages to companies selling to the world market.[1] Another holds that world products offer customers the twin benefits of the low-cost and high-quality incentives for foreign customers to lay aside culture-bound product preferences.[2]

According to both of these arguments, U.S. organizations should "go global" when they can no longer get the minimum volume needed for cost efficiency at home and when international markets permit standardized marketing approaches. If, on the other hand, they can fully exploit scale benefits at home and their international export markets are dissimilar, U.S. executives can safely adopt the traditional, country-by-country, multinational approach. So while Caterpillar views its battle with Komatsu in global terms, CPC International and Unilever may safely consider their foreign operations multidomestic.

---

1. *See* Thomas Hout, Michael E. Porter, and Eileen Rudden, "How Global Companies Win Out," *Harvard Business Review* (September–October 1982).

2. *See* Theodore Levitt, "The Globalization of Markets," *Harvard Business Review* (May–June 1983).

After studying the experiences of some of the most successful global competitors, we have become convinced that the current perspective on global competition and the globalization of markets is incomplete and misleading. Analysts are long on exhortation—"go international"—but short on practical guidance. Combine these shortcomings with the prevailing notion that global success demands a national industrial policy, a docile work force, debt-heavy financing, and forbearing investors, and you can easily understand why many executives feel they are only treading water in the rising tide of global competition.

World-scale manufacturing may provide the necessary armament, and government support may be a tactical advantage, but winning the war against global competition requires a broader view of global strategy. We will present a new framework for assessing the nature of the worldwide challenge, use it to analyze one particular industry, and offer our own practical guidelines for success.

─── THRUST AND PARRY

As a starting point, let's take a look at what drives global competition. It begins with a sequence of competitive action and reaction:

- An aggressive competitor decides to use the cash flow generated in its home market to subsidize an attack on markets of domestically oriented foreign competitors.
- The defensive competitor then retaliates—not in its home market where the attack was staged—but in foreign markets where the aggressor company is most vulnerable.[3]

As an example, consider the contest between Goodyear and Michelin. By today's definitions, the tire industry is not global. Most tire companies manufacture in and distribute for the local market. Yet Michelin, Goodyear, and Firestone became locked in a fiercely competitive—and very global—battle.

In the early 1970s, Michelin used its strong European profit base to attack Goodyear's American home market. Goodyear could fight back in the United States by reducing prices, increasing advertising, or offering dealers better margins. But because Michelin would expose only a small amount of its worldwide business in the United States, it had little to lose and much to gain. Goodyear, on the other hand, would sacrifice margins in its largest market.

Goodyear ultimately struck back in Europe, throwing a wrench in Michelin's money machine. Goodyear was proposing a hostage trade. Michelin's long-term goals and resources allowed it to push ahead in the United States. But at least Goodyear slowed the pace of Michelin's attack and forced it

---

3. *See* Craig M. Watson, "Counter-Competition Abroad to Protect Home Markets," *Harvard Business Review* (January–February 1982).

to recalculate the cost of market share gains in the United States. Goodyear's strategy recognized the international scope of competition and parried Michelin's thrust.

Manufacturers have played out this pattern of cross-subsidization and international retaliation in the chemical, audio, aircraft engine, and computer industries. In each case international cash flows, rather than international product flows, scale economies, or homogeneous markets, finally determined whether competition was global or national.[4]

The Goodyear–Michelin case helps to distinguish among:

- Global competition, which occurs when companies cross-subsidize national market share battles in pursuit of global brand and distribution positions.
- Global businesses, in which the minimum volume required for cost efficiency is not available in the company's home market.
- Global companies, which have distribution systems in key foreign markets that enable cross-subsidization, international retaliation, and world-scale volume.

Making a distinction between global competition and a global business is important. In traditionally global businesses, protectionism and flexible manufacturing technologies are encouraging a shift back to local manufacturing. Yet competition remains global. Companies must distinguish between the cost effectiveness based on off-shore sourcing and world-scale plants and the competitive effectiveness based on the ability to retaliate in competitors' key markets.

——— IDENTIFYING THE TARGET

Understanding how the global game is played is only the first step in challenging the foreign competitor. While the pattern of cross-subsidization and retaliation describes the battle, world brand dominance is what the global war is all about. And the Japanese have been winning it.

---

4. When a global company uses financial resources accumulated in one part of the world to fight a competitive battle in another, it is pursuing a strategy called cross-subsidization. If a company faces a large competitor in a key foreign market, it may make sense for it to funnel global resources into the local market share battle, especially when the competitor lacks the international reach to strike back.

Money does not always move across borders, though this may happen. For a number of reasons (taxation, foreign exchange risk, regulation) the subsidiary may choose to raise funds locally. Looking to the worldwide strength of the parent, local financial institutions may be willing to provide long-term financing in amounts and at rates that would not be justified on the basis of the subsidiary's short-term prospects.

Cross-subsidization is not dumping. When a company cross-subsidizes it does not sell at less than the domestic market price. Rather than risk trade sanctions, the intelligent global company will squeeze its competitor's margins just enough to dry up its development spending and force corporate officers to reassess their commitment to the business.

It took less than 20 years for Canon, Hitachi, Seiko, and Honda to establish worldwide reputations equal to those of Ford, Kodak, and Nestlé. In consumer electronics alone, the Japanese are present in or dominate most product categories.

Like the novice duck hunter who either aims at the wrong kind of bird or shoots behind the prey, many companies have failed to develop a well-targeted response to the new global competition. Those who define international competitiveness as no more than low-cost manufacturing are aiming at the wrong target. Those who fail to identify the strategic intentions of their global competitors cannot anticipate competitive moves and often shoot behind the target.

To help managers respond more effectively to challenges by foreign companies, we have developed a framework that summarizes the various global competitive strategies (see *Exhibit*). The competitive advantages to be gained from location, worldscale volume, or global brand distribution are arrayed against the three kinds of strategic intent we have found to be the most prevalent among global competitors: (1) building a global presence, (2) defending a domestic position, and (3) overcoming national fragmentation.

Using this framework to analyze the world television industry, we find Japanese competitors building a global presence; RCA, GE, and Zenith of the United States defending domestic dominance; and Philips of the Netherlands and CSF Thomson of France overcoming national fragmentation. Each one uses a different complement of competitive weapons and pursues its own strategic objectives. As a result, each reaps a different harvest from its international activities.

LOOSE BRICKS

By the late 1960s, Japanese television manufacturers had built up a large U.S. volume base by selling private-label TV sets. They had also established brand and distribution positions in small-screen and portable televisions—a market segment ignored by U.S. producers in favor of higher-margin console sets.

In 1967, Japan became the largest producer of black-and-white TVs; by 1970, it had closed the gap in color sets. While the Japanese first used their cost advantages primarily from low labor costs, they then moved quickly to invest in new process technologies, from which came the advantages of scale and quality.

Japanese companies recognized the vulnerability of competitive positions based solely on labor and scale advantages. Labor costs change as economies develop or as exchange rates fluctuate. The world's low-cost manufacturing location is constantly shifting: from Japan to Korea, then to Singapore and Taiwan. Scale-based cost advantages are also vulnerable,

EXHIBIT
A Global Competitive Framework

	Build global presence	Defend domestic dominance	Overcome national fragmentation
1965	Access volume		
		Response lag	Response lag
1970	Redefine cost-volume relationships		
		Match costs	
1975	Cross-subsidize to win the world		Reduce costs at national subsidiary
		Amortize world-scale invest-ments	
1980	Contiguous segment expansion		Rationalize manufacturing
		Gain retaliatory capability	
1985			Shift locus of strategic responsibility
1990			

particularly to radical changes in manufacturing technology and creeping protectionism in export markets. Throughout the 1970s, Japanese TV makers invested heavily to create the strong distribution positions and brand franchises that would add another layer of competitive advantage.

Making a global distribution investment pay off demands a high level of channel utilization. Japanese companies force-fed distribution channels by rapidly accelerating product life cycles and expanding across contiguous product segments. Predictably, single-line competitors were often blindsided, and sleepy product-development departments were caught short in the face of this onslaught. Global distribution is the new barrier to entry.

By the end of the decade, the Japanese competitive advantage had evolved from low-cost sourcing to world-scale volume and worldwide brand positions across the spectrum of consumer electronic products.

RCA AT HOME

Most American television producers believed the Japanese did well in their market simply because of their low-cost, high-quality manufacturing systems. When they finally responded, U.S. companies drove down costs, began catching up on the technology front, and lobbied heavily for government protection.[5] They thought that was all they had to do.

Some could not even do that; the massive investment needed to regain cost competitiveness proved too much for them, and they left the television industry. Stronger foreign companies purchased others.

Those that remained transferred labor-intensive manufacturing offshore and rationalized manufacturing at home and abroad. Even with costs under control, these companies (RCA, GE, and Zenith) are still vulnerable because they do not understand the changing nature of Japanese competitive advantage. Even as American producers patted themselves on the back for closing the cost gap, the Japanese were cementing future profit foundations through investment in global brand positions. Having conceived of global competition on a product-by-product basis, U.S. companies could not justify a similar investment.

Having conceded non-U.S. markets, American TV manufacturers were powerless to dislodge the Japanese even from the United States.

While Zenith and RCA dominated the color TV business in the United States, neither had a strong presence elsewhere. With no choice of competitive venue, American companies had to fight every market share battle in the United States. When U.S. companies reduced prices at home, they subjected 100% of their sales volume to margin pressure. Matsushita could force this price action, but only a fraction of it would be similarly exposed.

We do not argue that American TV manufacturers will inevitably succumb to global competition. Trade policy or public opinion may limit foreign penetration. Faced with the threat of more onerous trade sanctions or charges of predatory trade tactics, global competitors may forgo a fight to the finish, especially when the business in question is mature and no longer occupies center stage in the company's product plans. Likewise, domestic manufacturers, despite dwindling margins, may support the threatened business if it has important interdependencies with other businesses (as, for example, in the case of Zenith's TV and data systems business). Or senior management may consider

---

5. *See* John J. Nevin, "Can U.S. Business Survive Our Japanese Trade Policy?" *Harvard Business Review* (September–October 1978).

the business important to the company's image (a possible motivation for GE) for continuing television production.

The hope that foreign companies may never take over the U.S. market, however, should hardly console Western companies. TVs were no more than one loose brick in the American consumer electronics market. The Japanese wanted to knock down the whole wall. For example, with margins under pressure in the TV business, no American manufacturer had the stomach to develop its own videocassette recorder. Today, VCRs are the profitability mainstay for many Japanese companies. Companies defending domestic positions are often shortsighted about the strategic intentions of their competitors. They will never understand their own vulnerability until they understand the intentions of their rivals and then reason back to potential tactics. With no appreciation of strategic intent, defensive-minded competitors are doomed to a perpetual game of catch-up.

LOOSE BRICKS IN EUROPE, TOO

Philips of the Netherlands has become well known virtually everywhere in the world. Like other long-standing MNCs, Philips has always benefited from the kind of international distribution system that U.S. companies lack. Yet our evidence suggests that this advantage alone is not enough. Philips has its own set of problems in responding to the Japanese challenge.

Japanese color TV exports to Europe didn't begin until 1970. Under the terms of their licensing arrangements with European set makers, the Japanese could export only small-screen TVs. No such size limitation existed for Japanese companies willing to manufacture in Europe, but no more than half the output could be exported to the rest of Europe. Furthermore, because laws prohibited Japanese producers from supplying finished sets for private-label sale, they supplied picture tubes. So in 1979, although Europe ran a net trade deficit of only 2 million color televisions, the deficit in color tubes was 2.7 million units. By concentrating on such volume-sensitive manufacturing, Japanese manufacturers skirted protectionist sentiment while exploiting economies of scale gained from U.S. and Japanese experience.

Yet just as they had not been content to remain private-label suppliers in the United States, Japanese companies were not content to remain component suppliers in Europe. They wanted to establish their own brand positions. Sony, Matsushita, and Mitsubishi set up local manufacturing operations in the United Kingdom. When, in response, the British began to fear a Japanese takeover of the local industry, Toshiba and Hitachi simply found U.K. partners. In moving assembly from the Far East to Europe, Japanese manufacturers incurred cost and quality penalties. Yet they regarded such penalties as an acceptable price for establishing strong European distribution and brand positions.

If we contrast Japanese entry strategies in the United States and Europe, it is clear that the tactics and timetables differed. Yet the long-term strategic intentions were the same, and the competitive advantage of Japanese producers evolved similarly in both markets. In both Europe and the United States, Japanese companies found a loose brick in the bottom half of the market structure—small-screen portables. And then two other loose bricks were found—the private-label business in the United States and picture tubes in Europe.

From these loose bricks, the Japanese built the sales volume necessary for investment in world-scale manufacturing and state-of-the-art product development; they gained access to local producers, who were an essential source of market knowledge. In Europe, as in the United States, Japanese manufacturers captured a significant share of total industry profitability with a low-risk, low-profile supplier strategy; in so doing, they established a platform from which to launch their drive to global brand dominance.

REGAINING COST COMPETITIVENESS

Philips tried to compete on cost but had more difficulties than RCA and Zenith. First, the European TV industry was more fragmented than that of the United States. When the Japanese entered Europe, twice as many European as American TV makers fought for positions in national markets that were smaller than those in the United States.

Second, European governments frustrated the attempts of companies to use offshore sources or to rationalize production through plant closings, layoffs, and capacity reassignments. European TV makers turned to political solutions to solve competitive difficulties. In theory, the resulting protectionism gave them breathing space as they sought to redress the cost imbalance with Japanese producers. Because they were still confined to marginal, plant-level improvements, however, their cost and quality gap continued to widen. Protectionism reduced the incentive to invest in cost competitiveness; at the same time, the Japanese producers were merging with Europe's smaller manufacturers.

With nearly 3 million units of total European production in 1976, Philips was the only European manufacturer whose volume could fund the automation of manufacturing and the rationalization of product lines and components. Even though its volume was sufficient, however, Philips's tube manufacturing was spread across seven European countries. So it had to demonstrate (country by country, minister by minister, union by union) that the only alternative to protectionism was to support the development of a Pan-European competitor. Philips also had to wrestle with independent subsidiaries not eager to surrender their autonomy over manufacturing, product development, and capital investment. By 1982, it was the world's largest color TV maker and had almost closed the cost gap with Japanese producers. Even so, after 10 years rationalization plans were still incomplete.

Philips remains vulnerable to global competition because of the difficulties inherent in weaving disparate national subsidiaries into a coherent global competitive team. Low-cost manufacturing and international distribution give Philips two of the critical elements needed for global competition. Still needed is the coordination of national business strategies.

Philips's country managers are jealous of their autonomy in marketing and strategy. With their horizon of competition often limited to a single market, country managers are poorly placed to assess their global vulnerability. They can neither understand nor adequately analyze the strategic intentions and market entry tactics of global competitors. Nor can they estimate the total resources available to foreign competitors for local market share battles.

Under such management pressure, companies like Philips risk responding on a local basis to global competition. The Japanese can "cherry pick" attractive national markets with little fear that their multinational rival will retaliate.

THE STRATEGIC IMPERATIVE

International companies like General Motors and Philips prospered in the fragmented and politicized European market by adopting the "local face" of a good multinational citizen. Today Philips and other MNCs need a global strategic perspective and a corresponding shift in the locus of strategic responsibility away from country organizations. That need conflicts with escalating demands by host governments for national responsiveness. The resulting organizational problems are complex.

Nevertheless, companies must move beyond simplistic organizational views that polarize alternatives between world-product divisions and country-based structures. Headquarters will have to take strategic responsibility in some decision areas; subsidiaries must dominate in others. Managers cannot resolve organizational ambiguity simply by rearranging lines and boxes on the organization chart. They must adopt fundamentally new roles.

National subsidiaries can provide headquarters with more competitive intelligence and learn about world competitors from the experiences of other subsidiaries. They must fight retaliatory battles on behalf of a larger strategy and develop information systems, decision protocols, and performance measurement systems to weave global and local perspectives into tactical decisions. Rather than surrender control over manufacturing, national subsidiaries must interact with the organization in new and complex ways.

Such a realignment of strategic responsibility takes three steps:

1. Analyze precisely the danger of national fragmentation.
2. Create systems to track global competitive developments and to support effective responses.
3. Educate national and headquarters executives in the results of analysis and chosen organization design.

This reorientation may take as long as five years. Managing it is the hardest challenge in the drive to compete successfully.

A NEW ANALYSIS

Managers must cultivate a mind-set based on concepts and tools different from those normally used to assess competitors and competitive advantage.

For example, the television industry case makes clear that the competitive advantage from global distribution is distinct from that due to lower manufacturing costs. Even when they don't have a cost advantage, competitors with a global reach may have the means and motivation for an attack on nationally focused companies. If the global competitor enjoys a high price level at home and suffers no cost disadvantage, it has the means to cross-subsidize the battle for global market share.

Price level differences can exist because of explicit or implicit collusion that limits competitive rivalry, government restrictions barring the entry of new companies to the industry, or differences in the price sensitivity of customers.

The cash flow available to a global competitor is a function of both total costs and realized prices. Cost advantages alone do not indicate whether a company can sustain a global fight. Price level differences, for example, may provide not only the means but also the motivation for cross-subsidization.

If a global competitor sees a more favorable industry growth rate in a foreign market populated by contented and lazy competitors, who are unable or unwilling to fight back, and with customers that are less price sensitive than those at home, it will target that market on its global road. Domestic competitors will be caught unaware.

The implications for these strictly domestic companies are clear. First, they must fight for access to their competitors' market. If such access is unavailable, a fundamental asymmetry results. If no one challenges a global competitor in its home market, the competitor faces a reduced level of rivalry, its profitability rises, and the day when it can attack the home markets of its rivals is hastened. That IBM shares this view is evident from its pitched battle with Fujitsu and Hitachi in Japan.

Global competitors are not battling simply for world volume but also for the cash flow to support new product development, investment in core technologies, and world distribution. Companies that nestle safely in their home beds will be at an increasing resource (if not a cost) disadvantage. They will be unable to marshal the forces required for a defense of the home market.

Not surprisingly, Japanese MNCs have invested massively in newly industrializing countries (NICs). Only there can European and American companies challenge Japanese rivals on a fairly equal footing without sacrificing domestic profitability or facing market entry restrictions. The failure of Western organizations to compete in NICs will give the Japanese another uncontested profit source, leaving U.S. and European companies more vulnerable at home.

—— NEW CONCEPTS

Usually, a company's decision whether to compete for a market depends on the potential profitability of a particular level of market share in that country. But the new global competition requires novel ways of valuing market share; for example:

- Worldwide cost competitiveness, which refers to the minimum world market share a company must capture to underwrite the appropriate manufacturing-scale and product-development effort.
- Retaliation, which refers to the minimum market share the company needs in a particular country to be able to influence the behavior of key global competitors. For example, with only a 2% or 3% share of the foreign market, a company may be too weak to influence the pricing behavior of its foreign rival.
- Home country vulnerability, which refers to the competitive risks of national market share leadership if not accompanied by international distribution. Market leadership at home can create a false sense of security. Instead of granting invincibility, high market share may have the opposite effect. To the extent that a company uses its market power to support high price levels, foreign competitors—confident that the local company has little freedom for retaliation—may be encouraged to come in under the price umbrella and compete away the organization's profitability.

CRITICAL NATIONAL MARKETS

Most MNCs look at foreign markets as strategically important only when they can yield profits in their own right. Yet different markets may offer very different competitive opportunities. As part of its global strategy, an organization must distinguish between objectives of (1) low-cost sourcing, (2) minimum scale, (3) a national profit base, (4) retaliation against a global competitor, and (5) benchmarking products and technology in a state-of-the-art market. At the same time, the company will need to vary the ways in which it measures subsidiary performance, rewards managers, and makes capital appropriations.

PRODUCT FAMILIES

Global competition requires a broader corporate concept of a product line. In redefining a relevant product family—one that is contiguous in distribution channels and shares a global brand franchise—an organization can, for example, scrutinize all products moving through distribution channels in which its products are sold.

In a corollary effort, all competitors in the channels can be mapped against their product offerings. This effort would include a calculation of the extent of a competitor's investment in the distribution channel, including investment in brand awareness, to understand its motivation to move across segments. Such an analysis would reveal the potential for segment expansion by competitors presently outside the company's strategic horizon.

SCOPE OF OPERATIONS

Where extranational-scale economies exist, the risks in establishing world-scale manufacturing will be very different for the company that sells abroad only under license or through private labels, compared with the company that controls its own worldwide distribution network. Cost advantages are less durable than brand and distribution advantages. An investment in world-scale manufacturing, when not linked to an investment in global distribution, presents untenable risks.

In turn, investments in worldwide distribution and global brand franchises are often economical only if the company has a wide range of products that can benefit from the same distribution and brand investment. Only a company that develops a continuous stream of new products can justify the distribution investment.

A company also needs a broad product portfolio to support investments in key technologies that cut across products and businesses. Competitors with global distribution coverage and wide product lines are best able to justify investments in new core technologies. Witness Honda's leadership in engine technology, a capability it exploits in automobiles, motorcycles, power tillers, snowmobiles, lawnmowers, power generators, and so forth.

Power over distribution channels may depend on a full line. In some cases, even access to a channel (other than on a private-label basis) depends on having a "complete" line of products. A full line may also allow the company to cross-subsidize products in order to displace competitors who are weak in some segments.

Investments in world-scale production and distribution, product-line width, new product development, and core technologies are interrelated. A company's ability to fully exploit an investment made in one area may require support of investments in others.

RESOURCE ALLOCATION

Perhaps the most difficult problem a company faces in global competition is how to allocate resources. Typically, large companies allocate capital to strategic business units (SBUs). In that view, an SBU is a self-contained entity encompassing product development, manufacturing, marketing, and technology. Companies as diverse as General Electric, 3M, and Hewlett-Packard embrace the concept. They point to clear channels of management accountability, visibility of business results, and innovation as the main benefits of SBU management. But an SBU does not provide an appropriate frame of reference to deal with the new competitive milieu.

In pursuing complex global strategies, a company will find different ways to evaluate the geographic scope of individual business subsystems—manufacturing, distribution, marketing, and so on. The authority for resource allocation, then, needs to reside at particular points in the organization for different subsystems, applying different criteria and time horizons to investments in those subsystems.

Global competition may threaten the integrity of the SBU organization for several reasons. A strong SBU-type organization may not facilitate investments in international distribution. To justify such investments, especially in country markets new to the company, it may have to gain the commitment of several businesses that may not share the same set of international priorities.

Even if individual SBUs have developed their own foreign distribution capability, the strategic independence of the various businesses at the country level may make it difficult to cross-subsidize business segments or undertake joint promotion. The company loses some of the benefits of a shared brand franchise.

Companies may have to separate manufacturing and marketing subsystems to rationalize manufacturing on a local-for-global or local-for-regional basis. Economic and political factors will determine which subsidiaries produce which components for the system. In such a case, a company may coordinate manufacturing globally even though marketing may still be based locally.

Companies might also separate the responsibility for global competitive strategy from that for local marketing strategy. While national organizations may be charged with developing some aspects of the marketing mix, headquarters will take the lead role in determining the strategic mission for the local operation, the timing of new product launches, the targeted level of market share, and the appropriate level of investment or expected cash flow.

GEOGRAPHY-BASED ORGANIZATIONS

For the company organized on a national subsidiary basis, there is a corollary problem. It may be difficult to gain commitment to global business initiatives when resource allocation authority lies with the local subsidiary. In this case, the company must ensure that it makes national investments in support of global competitive positions despite spending limits, strategic myopia, or the veto of individual subsidiaries.

Finally, the time limit for investments in global distribution and brand awareness may be quite different from that required for manufacturing-cost take-out investments. Distribution investments usually reflect a long-term commitment and are not susceptible to the same analysis used to justify "brick and mortar" investments.

NEW STRATEGIC THOUGHT

Global competitors must have the capacity to think and act in complex ways. In other words, they may slice the company in one way for distribution investments, in another for technology, and in still another for manufacturing. In addition, global competitors will develop varied criteria and analytical tools to justify these investments.

In our experience, few companies have distinguished between the intermediate tactics and long-run strategic intentions of global competitors. In a world of forward-thinking competitors that change the rules of the game in support of ultimate strategic goals, historical patterns of competition provide little guidance. Executives must anticipate competitive moves by starting from new strategic intentions rather than from precooked generic strategies.

It is more difficult to respond to the new global competition than we often assume. A company must be sensitive to the potential of global competitive interaction even when its manufacturing is not on a global scale. Executives need to understand the way in which competitors use cross-subsidization to undermine seemingly strong domestic market share positions. To build organizations capable of conceiving and executing complex global strategies, top managers must develop the new analytic approaches and organizational arrangements on which our competitive future rests.

DISCUSSION QUESTIONS

1. When do you think a company should "go international"? What criteria, in your view, would serve as determining factors?
2. Firms in the United States face stiff competition in their home market from foreign companies. Should their domestic marketing strategy differ from the one they use globally? Explain why or why not.
3. When American firms go up against foreign competition abroad should they use the same marketing strategy that they follow in the United States? Why or why not?

SECTION C

ETHICAL AND LEGAL ISSUES

After all is said and done,
And the market plan is run,
How profiteth the marketer,
If wrong over right has won?
– Anonymous

The most skilled marketers, employing the most effective marketing program that engenders the highest return on the investment, stand to lose it all if the temptations of the marketplace cause them to succumb to unethical or illegal practices.

Anyone with decision-making authority holds considerable power. This power carries with it the responsibility to deal fairly, equitably, and ethically with everyone—from consumers to the competition, from employees to distributors. The penalties for not doing so are high, and ignorance or conflict of interest are not exculpatory. Although management sets the tone, individuals hold the reins, and compromising ethical standards or breaking a law can result in a serious blow to the individual, the company, or both. The temptations are there—from price fixing to deceptive practices—in all areas of selling, distribution, advertising, or product policy. The readings in this section outline the legal framework and ethical dilemmas that confront marketers and their companies.

Legal Restrictions on Marketing   39
Management

PATRICK J. KAUFMANN

Marketing decisions can be greatly influenced by the state and federal laws that protect consumers, the public, and the competition. Every marketer formulating and implementing a marketing strategy needs to be aware of the existence of these constraints.

This reading summarizes the legal and regulatory dimensions of marketing in relation to the key areas of price, distribution, promotion, and product policy. It is not a complete survey of the law on the subjects covered but an introduction to the complexities of the marketing manager's legal environment.[*]

Every day marketing managers make strategy and implementation decisions that are constrained or influenced by laws and regulations designed to promote competition, protect the consumer, and enhance public welfare. Every day judges, legislators, and regulators apply, re-examine, and amend those laws and regulations in an on-going effort to create a system that serves society's interests even better. Although marketers may not always agree with the wisdom of the laws and regulations they face, it is vital for both their corporations and themselves that they become familiar with them.

One of marketing managers' most frequently voiced complaints concerns the number and breadth of the legal and regulatory restrictions that influence their strategic and implementation decisions. These restrictions range from laws that deal with collusive price stabilization to celebrity endorsements; from implied warranties to discriminatory advertising allowances, and on and on. They exist at the federal and state level, and vary by state. They are derived from statutes, judicial decisions, and the charters and rulemaking powers of many regulatory agencies and commissions. Even in the current era of deregulation and free-market economics, the body of law and regulation that affects marketers is enormous.

See also Benson P. Shapiro, "Legal and Ethical Aspects of Marketing," Harvard Business School No. 9-585-007.

This reading introduces some of the most important aspects of the marketer's legal environment. It is restricted to an examination of U.S. law but is by no means a complete treatment of it, nor even an extensive survey.[1] The focus is on general laws and regulations that affect marketers in many industries; industry-specific laws and regulations—often the most central to marketers' decisions—cannot be treated in this brief survey. It is important, however, for the marketers to become as familiar as possible with the general issues in their legal environment. They should consult internal or external legal counsel for answers to specific questions and for general guidance in the particular industry and area of responsibility.

The discussion is organized around the familiar marketing-decision variables: price, distribution, promotion, and product policy. Only legal constraints are considered; ethical issues represent an equally important but different dimension of the marketing manager's decision environment. While the law may offer rough guidance about the ethics of a particular decision or activity, mere legality cannot be equated with ethical behavior.

——— PRICE

Although most managers know that agreements between competitors to fix prices are illegal, many are unaware of how far-reaching pricing regulations are. The impact of the legal environment on pricing decisions takes two basic forms. The first are laws prohibiting certain activities that are presumed to interfere with the natural tendency of competition to push prices down toward cost plus a normal return on investment; the Sherman Act's condemnation of price fixing falls into this category. The second form are laws dealing with the behavior of specific firms—for example, decisions regarding prices charged particular customers. The Robinson-Patman Act's requirement that firms offer competing customers the same price (with certain exceptions) is in this category.

PRICE FIXING AND HORIZONTAL MARKET ALLOCATION

Questions about pricing normally fall within the purview of antitrust law. The first antitrust statute, the Sherman Act, was passed in 1890; it forbids agreements between competitors to distort the natural forces of competition. Not only agreements between competitors that fix, set, or stabilize prices, but also agreements that allocate particular markets or customers (assumed ultimately to affect prices as well) are illegal under this act. For example, competing

---

1. The applicability of U.S. antitrust law to cases involving foreign commerce is a complex question beyond the scope of this article. The general rule is that U.S. law applies when there is an impact on U.S. commerce but does not apply when that impact is a result of a foreign "act of state."

oil companies might each agree to sell their gasoline only in particular areas of the country. The obvious result of such an agreement would be to allow companies to increase prices. The argument that the purpose of such an agreement was not anticompetitive is not an acceptable defense; any agreement that fixes prices or allocates markets between competitors is illegal per se (i.e., in and of itself), and the motives of the parties are irrelevant.[2]

Furthermore, the parties need not be successful in their endeavor in order to be prosecuted; the Sherman Act also proscribes conspiracies to restrict competition. In the example above, if some of the oil companies could not be convinced to join the market-allocation scheme, they might put enough competitive pressure on local markets so that prices could not be raised. Although the scheme would fail, the conspirators could still face prosecution.

Nor is direct evidence of a formal agreement between the parties necessary. Merely sharing pricing information about specific customers, together with subsequent price stabilization, could lead a court to infer an agreement. For example, competitors who meet and agree to exchange information about customers and the prices at which they sell to them might be presumed to have done so to reduce the customers' ability to bargain among suppliers; the court could infer that the actions were designed to reduce normal price fluctuations caused by market competition.

The Sherman Act is vague and broadly interpreted. Penalties for violations can include fines of up to $1 million (per violation) for the corporation, and $100,000 fines and/or three-year prison terms for individuals. The Act covers not only agreements between competitors but also monopolization by a single firm. Monopolization occurs when a firm actively uses its dominant market power to manipulate the price of a product or otherwise restrain competition.

Another antitrust statute, the Clayton Act, allows injured parties to bring civil suits against antitrust violators and provides for successful plaintiffs to receive judgments of three times the damages proven to have been suffered due to the illicit agreements. For example, if the injured party proves that the damages suffered amounted to $1 million, $3 million is awarded. These awards are intended to punish the offender and discourage such activity, as well as to encourage private enforcement of the law. In addition to the Justice Department and injured parties, the Federal Trade Commission (FTC) can prosecute individuals and corporations for these practices. The FTC Act, making "unfair methods of competition" illegal, has been interpreted to include violations of the Sherman and Clayton acts.

---

2. All agreements between competitors (e.g., to fix prices or to allocate markets) are referred to as horizontal agreements and are per se illegal. Agreements between buyers and sellers within a channel of distribution (e.g., to set up an exclusive territory) are referred to as vertical agreements. Some are per se illegal while others are examined under a "Rule of Reason" to determine whether they are, in fact, anticompetitive.

Simply stated, therefore, marketers should avoid any discussions with competitors, especially those concerning prices, markets, and specific customers. If innocent discussions with competitors are necessary (e.g., in the creation of industry safety standards), the parties should seek legal advice to learn the best way to avoid legal misinterpretation.

RESALE-PRICE MAINTENANCE

Another form of pricing agreement prohibited under the Sherman Act, but one which does not involve competitors, is resale-price maintenance. As products reach the consumer through channels of distribution, demand for a product at any level in the channel is derived from the demand at lower levels. Assuming a two-level channel of distribution in which a manufacturer sells to retailers who sell to the consumer, demand at the manufacturer's level is derived from the demand at the retail level. The manufacturer may believe that a low retail price hurts the brand's prestige image or precludes the high levels of retail service indispensable to its marketing plan. Such service may be possible only if retail prices are high enough to provide the necessary distribution margins to pay for it. The prevailing retail price, therefore, is of great concern to the manufacturer.

In this situation the manufacturer can suggest and even advertise suggested retail prices, but may not make an agreement with the retailer about the price at which the latter sells the product. A threat to cut off the retailer's supply, together with the retailer's coerced promise to maintain the desired price, can constitute a price-maintenance agreement. Legal scholars, however, differ on whether mere compliance by the retailer in response to the manufacturer's threat (i.e., without the retailer's explicit communication of intent) constitutes an agreement.

Nonetheless, sellers are generally free to choose with whom they will do business. A manufacturer may legally choose not to sell to known price cutters, and may be able legally to stop selling to someone who has begun cutting prices. Termination of a price cutter, however, is extremely hazardous. Any attempt to use the threat of termination to curtail the price-cutting behavior, rather than merely terminating the price-cutting distributor, may be viewed as resale-price maintenance. Moreover, terminating a price-cutting distributor for unrelated reasons often results in a law suit by the angry distributor, who claims that the real reason for dismissal was refusal to maintain resale prices.

DISCRIMINATORY PRICING

Pricing-related violations of the antitrust laws can also occur without any agreement with competitors or channel members. The complex and often criticized Robinson-Patman Act (the 1936 amendment to Section 2 of the Clayton Act) precludes price discrimination (i.e., charging different customers different prices for the same product) where the effect may be to lessen competition substantially. Such an effect is assumed to exist if the customers in question are in competition. For example, if a dairy offers milk to a large chain at a lower price than to the mom and pop grocery next door, the effect is to give the chain a competitive advantage.

Discrimination between competing customers in advertising and promotion allowances is also prohibited under Robinson-Patman. For example, when a cosmetic firm offers a demonstration person to a department store, it must offer a proportionally equivalent promotion to a small competing drug store. The amount of the promotion is prorated on the basis of account size and probably would not include a demonstration person but some point-of-purchase displays or other sales aid.

There are a number of defenses to charges of price discrimination. For example, sellers can offer a discriminatory price in order to meet (not beat) a competitor's offered price to the same customer. Price differences justified by the cost efficiencies realized by selling to a particular customer are also allowed, although this exception has been notoriously hard to prove in court and usually requires detailed cost data unavailable in many companies. Volume discounts too are permitted under the statute, although they must be graduated to be functionally available to competing customers. For example, it might be difficult to justify a major price discount offered on such a large quantity that the discount is actually available only to the one customer capable of purchasing that amount.

The Robinson-Patman Act (historically called the anti-chain store act) was designed to protect small businesses from the cost advantage large chains enjoy due to tremendous buying power. Because it prevents sellers from offering discounts to certain customers, the Act can be criticized for keeping prices higher than they would otherwise be, thereby contradicting the policy expressed in the Sherman Act. In recent years neither the Justice Department nor the Federal Trade Commission has prosecuted actively under Robinson-Patman. Marketers should still beware, however, for private injured parties can bring civil actions, and treble damages are available to those who prevail.

PREDATORY PRICING

Predatory pricing is another pricing practice that may precipitate prosecution or civil litigation under the antitrust laws. Essentially, it is the attempt to enhance competitive position by driving a competitor from the market instead of improving the company's own performance. As evidence of predatory intent, courts often use patterns of pricing below variable cost. For example, if an established manufacturer with a variable cost of $5 per unit sells its product at $4 per unit in a market a competitor is trying to enter, the court may interpret the price as an intent to drive the competitor from the market. Parties engaged in predatory pricing sometimes subsidize below-cost pricing in markets where the target competition sells by using profits from less-competitive markets. (This also has been called primary-line price discrimination because the anticompetitive effect takes place on the manufacturer's, not customer's, level.) The question for the court is whether the pricing policy merely reflects fair, hard competition or is an attempt specifically to injure the competitor. Commonly heard statements by marketers about "destroying this or that competitor" make corporate attorneys cringe when coupled with significant market power and pricing behavior that is hard to justify on strictly economical grounds.

Some analysts see rules against predatory pricing, like those against price discrimination, as inconsistent with overall antitrust policy. They argue that rules against predatory pricing create an unwanted and unwarranted chilling effect on hard competition. Nevertheless, the marketer should be aware that pricing below variable cost under certain circumstances can expose the individual and firm to liability. A marketer who intends to price this way, or faces a competitor that is doing so, should consult the company's attorney.

——— DISTRIBUTION

Antitrust law also covers a number of issues involving distribution. Legal constraints on the marketer's decisions regarding the distribution system fall into three general categories: (1) product-mix requirements or restrictions, (2) territory, location, or customer restrictions, and (3) vertical pricing restrictions other than resale-price maintenance agreements.[3]

PRODUCT-MIX REQUIREMENTS AND RESTRICTIONS

Product-mix issues arise under two circumstances: (1) when a marketer refuses to sell a distributor (i.e., wholesaler, retailer, etc.) a desired product unless it also purchases another product; or (2) when a marketer tries to keep competitors' products out of the marketer's distribution outlets. The first practice is called *tying*, and the second is called *exclusive dealing*. Tying is a violation of both the Sherman Act and the Clayton Act and is per se illegal. An exclusive-dealing agreement is a violation of the Clayton Act if it may "substantially lessen competition or tend to create a monopoly."

---

3. Although it is treated differently from other types of vertical restraints, resale-price maintenance has much the same rationale behind it (i.e., to increase the amount of interbrand competition in a particular market). Consequently, many legal scholars have argued that it should be treated in the same way as territorial restrictions, instead of being per se illegal, like horizontal price fixing.

Tying is essentially an effort to use the market power of one product to help another. For tying to occur there must be two products, a requirement that they be bought together, and sufficient economic power in the tying product to restrain competition appreciably in the tied product. For example, if a maker of the dominant brand of toothbrushes enters the toothpaste business and refuses to sell toothbrushes to any distributor who does not also sell its toothpaste, the manufacturer could face prosecution. The central question would be whether the brand of toothbrushes had enough market power to allow the manufacturer to force the toothpaste on unwilling distributors.

This reasoning has been extended to include franchisor trademarks. Because the only source of the trademark is the franchisor, the trademark may have the same monopoly power as a patented product; when that power is used to require purchases of other products, prosecution for tying can result. For example, if a franchisor of an established chain of restaurants refuses to sell franchise rights to use that trademark unless the franchisee also agrees to buy napkins or paper cups (items that could easily be supplied by outside sources) from the franchisor, the franchisor could be prosecuted (or sued by franchisees) for tying. On the other hand, the franchisor may require franchisees to buy certain products, such as a special spice mixture, because to specify its contents for outside sourcing would require disclosure of trade secrets.

Exclusive dealing refers to an agreement between a manufacturer and distributor in which the distributor agrees not to carry competing brands. This agreement may be illegal if the manufacturer enforces it by refusing to sell to the distributor or refusing to grant the distributor the same price unless the latter acquiesces. The question for the court will be whether competitors have been foreclosed from a substantial line of distribution. If the amount of trade handled by the distributor or covered by the agreement is substantial—either in absolute or market-share terms—the manufacturer may be liable under the Clayton Act.

TERRITORY, LOCATION, AND CUSTOMER RESTRICTIONS

Another form of distribution restriction involves agreements about where and to whom the distributor can sell. These agreements take several forms: some specify the location from which a retailer can sell; some segment customers within an area and assign segments to specific distributors; some restrict the territories in which distributors can solicit or accept business. Generally, these types of agreements are part of a market-allocation system by which the marketer grants each distributor exclusive rights to a particular territory or customer group so that they are shielded from intrabrand competition. By doing so, the marketer hopes to provide an environment in which distributors can more effectively engage in interbrand competition. For example, a camera retailer might wish to hire expert (and expensive) retail salespeople to provide consumers with important information about the marketer's brand of camera versus other brands. The retailer may not wish to do so, however, if the benefits of providing that information are shared by other lower-cost, lower-price dealers located nearby selling the same camera. To encourage effective interbrand competition, therefore, marketers may try to limit intrabrand competition by permitting only a limited number of retailers to carry their product and limiting their ability to change location. This is sometimes referred to as selective, as opposed to intensive, distribution.

Prior to 1977, both horizontal and vertical territorial restrictions were per se illegal. In 1977 the Supreme Court, in the landmark Sylvania Case, radically changed the law concerning vertical territorial restrictions (i.e., those within the channel of distribution, not between competitors). In response to increasing competition in the television market and decreasing market share, Sylvania decided to switch to a selective distribution strategy with a limited number of distributors serving specific territories. One dealer violated the agreement by opening a new store outside its territory without Sylvania's permission. Sylvania terminated the dealer and the dealer claimed the territorial restrictions were in restraint of trade. The Court found that the test of illegality for vertical territorial restrictions was whether their negative effects on intrabrand competition outweigh their positive effects on interbrand competition. The restrictions are allowed if the net result is more overall competition in the market. This is referred to as a *Rule-of-Reason* test and is contrasted with the per se rule applicable to horizontal agreements. In Sylvania's case, the increase in dealer dedication produced by the selective distribution system had allowed Sylvania to once again become competitive with other brands; the restrictions were therefore seen to have a positive effect on interbrand competition.

—— PROMOTION

Although there are many regulations and laws dealing with specific issues of promotion and advertising, the most important statute is Section 5 of the Federal Trade Commission Act. Section 5 makes "unfair or deceptive acts or practices" illegal, while other sections of the act empower the FTC to prosecute and adjudicate such violations.

UNFAIR ACTS OR PRACTICES

The FTC's primary focus has always been on deceptive acts or practices. In the 1970s, however, a broad interpretation of the term "unfair" allowed the FTC to venture into the regulation of unscrupulous and unethical conduct. In recent years the FTC has been more restrained in its interpretation of "unfair acts or practices," confining it to instances of substantial consumer injury the consumer could not avoid by acting reasonably, and balancing the injury against any positive effects the act may have on consumers and competition.

One of the prime targets of inquiry under these criteria has been advertising for children. For example, the FTC obtained a cease-and-desist order preventing a bicycle manufacturer from running an advertisement that showed children riding their bicycles through an intersection without stopping.

DECEPTIVE ACTS OR PRACTICES

In deciding what is deceptive the FTC tries to determine whether an advertisement has the tendency or capability of deceiving even a small but significant number of credulous consumers. In doing so the commission uses both available proof and its own expertise to examine the advertisement.

It has singled out several areas for special treatment. For example, in 1980 the FTC issued a guide on the types of endorsements it considers deceptive. The guide covers both celebrity and consumer endorsements and requires, among other things, that celebrities actually use the product they endorse and that there is reason to believe they will continue to do so as long as the advertisement runs.

When an advertisement has been found to be deceptive, the FTC can issue an order requiring the company to cease running it and to alter the deceptive wording before running it again. At one time the FTC also used corrective advertising orders, compelling companies to run a specified number of additional advertisements designed to correct consumer misperceptions created by deceptive advertisements. Because FTC actions can lead to expensive legal procedures and disrupt on-going marketing programs, marketers and advertising agencies must be sensitive to the mere possibility for deception in their advertising. It is not enough that the marketer or other intelligent individuals would not be deceived; the advertisements must be considered from the perspective of the naive, credulous, or ignorant consumer.

—— PRODUCT

Four important areas of the law that impact the marketer's product policy decisions are (1) patents, trademarks, and copyrights; (2) warranties; (3) product liability; and (4) product-safety regulation. Unlike pricing and distribution issues, antitrust law does not cover these areas of the marketer's legal environment; they are, however, the subject of a broad conglomeration of statutes, federal and state regulations, and court-made law.

PATENTS, TRADEMARKS, AND COPYRIGHTS

The word *patent,* meaning open, is derived from *litterea patentes*—open letters from the king bestowing monopoly privileges for a product or manufacturing process to a favored subject. Subsequently, those rights were granted to the inventor of the product or process for a limited time only.

To be patentable under U.S. law, a product, process, or machine employed in that process must be new, nonobvious, useful, capable of doing what it claims, and adequately described in the documentation. A patent confers exclusive rights to the product, process, or machine for 17 years and cannot be renewed. The holder does not need to use a patent for it to remain intact. If another marketer intentionally or inadvertently introduces the patented product or one not clearly distinguishable from it, the patent holder can ask for an injunction and sue for damages for patent infringement. All new products, therefore, must be checked to ensure they do not infringe on existing patents.

Trademarks are similar to brands in that they embody the marketer's investment in creating a meaning or image attached to and conveyed by some mark or symbol. A trademark specifies the source of the product and provides information about the product because of its source. Trademark law, therefore, protects the consumer by ensuring that the product is made by a familiar and trusted producer. It also protects marketers by allowing them to invest in quality products and create a reputation for quality without fear of having their investments usurped.

Trademarks do not have to be registered in order to be protected from infringement. Registering a trademark, however, provides procedural protections, such as dated constructive notice to the public that such a trademark exists (i.e., the public is legally presumed to have been notified as of that date). Because trademarks may not always be registered, the marketer desiring to introduce a new mark should employ a specialist in trademark searches prior to investing in its development and then register the new trademark immediately.

If a trademark becomes a generic term, it can be lost by the company and become part of the public domain. This happened to cellophane and could happen to brands like Kleenex® or Xerox®. When the trademark stops indicating the specific manufacturer and begins to be synonymous with the product, the manufacturer's exclusive right to the trademark can be lost. The manufacturer must protect the trademark by ensuring that it is always used to refer to the source of the product and not the product itself (e.g., "Buy Kleenex® tissue").

In the same way that patents encourage invention, and trademarks encourage investment in a reputation for quality, copyright encourages the production of intellectual property. The Copyright Act of 1976 provides protection for a wide range of forms of expression, from books and music to computer programs and data bases. To be protected, any publicly distributed copies must be labeled with the symbol © (℗ for sound reproduction), the author's name, and the date first published. It is also necessary to register the work with the U.S. Copyright Office.

WARRANTIES

Warranties are based on the law of contract and covered by the Uniform Commercial Code and the Magnuson-Moss Warranty Act. A warranty is essentially a statement about a product that the buyer relies on as true. If it is not true, the seller has not sold the buyer what was promised and is in breach of contract. The buyer can then sue the seller for damages, which can include personal injury or economic damages caused by the product's failure to live up to the promised standard.

If the statement about the product is explicitly made by the seller, it is called an *express warranty*. Such a statement may take the form of a verbal or written fact, promise, description, or model. If, and only if, the buyer has relied on its truth in purchasing the product, the seller is bound by it. A product may contain no defect whatsoever and yet may not meet the standard set by the express warranty.

Other warranties are not expressly made by the seller but nonetheless become part of the bargain. If the seller is a merchant (i.e., someone in the business of selling a particular item), there is an *implied warranty* of *merchantability* for all goods sold in the course of that business. The term means that the product would pass without objection in the trade, be of fair and average quality, be of reasonably even quality and quantity across all units, be adequately packaged and labeled, and conform to affirmations on the label. Whether or not the intention is to promise these things, the marketer is deemed to have done so merely by being in business and offering the product for sale. The warranty is implied, and if the product does not meet those standards, the buyer can sue for damages.

A marketer can avoid express warranties simply by not making the statements. To avoid implied warranties a marketer must conspicuously disclaim the implied warranty of merchantability (using that term). Successfully disclaiming implied warranties in consumer sales is much more difficult than in sales to other businesses. Under the Magnuson-Moss Warranty Act, if a firm enters into a written warranty or service contract, implied warranties can be limited to the term of the written warranty but cannot be entirely disclaimed. Magnuson-Moss sets forth the specific terminology and procedures necessary to create and disclaim various warranties.

A third type of warranty ensures that the product is fit for a particular purpose. If the seller knows that the product will be used for a particular purpose (e.g., that a car will be used to pull a house trailer), and the buyer relies on the seller's knowledge of whether the product will do that job, the seller is deemed to have warranted the product fit for that purpose. As in the case of an express warranty, a product may be entirely without defect (e.g., a

four-cylinder subcompact car that performs perfectly well under normal conditions) and yet not be up to the more rigorous standard of fitness for the
purpose the buyer intends (i.e., pulling a heavy house trailer).

PRODUCT LIABILITY

While warranties are based on contract law, product liability is based
on tort law (i.e., the requirement that persons and companies exercise due care
not to injure others). Product-liability cases can be divided into two types:
product-disappointment cases and product-defect cases. Even if the product is
without defect, marketers can be held liable if they make important statements
to a buyer about the product that are untrue—and that the marketers knew or
should have known were false. This is called the *tort of misrepresentation.*

Product-defect cases arise in three ways. A manufacturer can be negligent in the way it designs, manufactures, or markets its products. Even a
product designed and manufactured with the utmost care can be made dangerous if marketed incorrectly. For example, some critics believed that one
company's policy of providing free infant formula to third-world mothers still
in the hospital produced a dangerous product. The criticism was that this
marketing strategy created dependency on a product the mother could not
afford after leaving the hospital. This caused the mothers to dilute the formula,
thereby endangering the infants' health. Negligent marketing of a product can
include failure to attach warnings or instructions necessary for safe operation,
use, or enjoyment of the product. For example, a chain saw without proper
operating instructions and warnings is a lethal product. It is, therefore, very
important for marketers to educate themselves about the dangers inherent in
each product and to make certain that full and explicit warnings and instructions accompany the product to the purchaser.

PRODUCT SAFETY REGULATION

Numerous statutes and regulations deal with specific issues of product
safety. Some states have seat-belt laws, while others outlaw the sale of
fireworks. The federal government is also involved in everything from meat
inspection to tamper-proof packaging. Marketers need to be aware of the
particular regulations pertaining to their industry.

One of the most important federal commissions, with broad jurisdiction
over many industries, is the Consumer Product Safety Commission. The CPSC
creates safety standards for individual products and bans unreasonably hazardous products. To issue a safety standard, the CPSC must find that the
standard is "reasonably necessary to eliminate or reduce an unreasonable risk
of injury associated with such product." In the case of banned products, it must
find that no feasible safety standard could be written that could adequately

protect the public from the unreasonable risk of injury. Manufacture for sale, sale, or distribution for sale of banned products or those not meeting promulgated standards is illegal. Safety standards may include requirements especially important to marketers such as those pertaining to consumer-product packaging and to the warnings and instructions that must accompany products.

The CPSC has been accused by all sides of being too aggressive or too passive; in fact, its activity generally follows the current administration's attitude toward regulation. Product-liability law and warranty law seek to redress injury once it has occurred, and they also indirectly encourage careful design, manufacture, and marketing through fear of legal liability. The CPSC, on the other hand, principally seeks to identify potential threats to consumer safety beforehand and to create rules designed to prevent injury.

——— CONCLUSION

Decisions made by marketing managers require attention to both the business and legal environment, and many issues of law and regulation have not been discussed here. Moreover, with the globalization of business, the legal environment is expanding rapidly; marketers must contend with the complexities of doing business within radically different legal systems. Although it is the ultimate responsibility of the corporate attorney to guide the marketer through the maze, a basic understanding of the legal environment will help marketers avoid wasting time and effort on marketing plans, programs, and decisions that will be vetoed by the legal department.

This discussion can do no more than familiarize the marketer in a general way with some of the more important laws and regulations relevant to marketing decisions. The books listed in Appendix A provide a more thorough survey of the law as it relates to marketing decisions. Appendix B contains excerpts from some of the most important sections of the various statutes referred to in this reading. Marketers should not, of course, use this, or any general summary, as a substitute for sound legal advice.

APPENDIX A   Bibliography on Laws Pertaining to Marketing

Blackburn, John D., Elliot I. Klayman, and Martin H. Malin. *The Legal Environment of Business.* Homewood, Ill.: Richard D. Irwin, Inc., 1982.

Howard, Marshall C. *Antitrust and Trade Regulation.* Englewood Cliffs, N.J.: Prentice-Hall, Inc., 1983.

Matto, Edward A. *A Manager's Guide to the Antitrust Laws.* New York: AMACOM, 1980.

Noel, Dix W., and Jerry L. Phillips. *Products Liability.* St. Paul, Minn.: West Publishing Co., 1980.

Stern, Louis W., and Thomas L. Eovaldi. *Legal Aspects of Marketing Strategy.* Englewood Cliffs, N.J.: Prentice-Hall, Inc., 1984.

Steuer, Richard M. *A Guide To Marketing Law.* New York: Law and Business, Inc./ Harcourt Brace Jovanovich, Inc., 1986.

Sullivan, Lawrence A. *Antitrust.* St. Paul, Minn.: West Publishing Co., 1977.

Welch, Joe L. *Marketing Law.* Tulsa, Okla.: Petroleum Publishing Co., 1980.

APPENDIX B   Excerpts from Federal Statutes Pertaining to Marketing

—— SHERMAN ACT

Section 1   Every contract, combination . . . or conspiracy, in restraint of trade . . . is hereby declared to be illegal. Every person who shall make any [such] contract, or engage in any [such] combination or conspiracy, shall be deemed guilty of a felony, and . . . shall be punished by fine not exceeding one million dollars if a corporation, or, if any other person, one hundred thousand dollars, or by imprisonment not exceeding three years, or by both.

—— CLAYTON ACT

Section 2(a)   That it shall be unlawful for any person . . . to discriminate in price between different purchasers of commodities of like grade and quality . . . where the effect of such discrimination may be substantially to lessen competition or tend to create a monopoly. . . . Provided, that nothing herein contained shall prevent differentials which make only due allowance for differences in the cost of manufacture, sale, or delivery . . . to such purchasers. [As amended by the Robinson-Patman Act of 1936]

Section 2(b)   [If a seller is found to have discriminated in his pricing, the seller can rebut the charge by] showing that his lower price ... was made in good faith to meet an equally low price of a competitor.

Section 2(d)   That it shall be unlawful for any person ... to pay or contract for ... any thing of value ... for the benefit of a customer ... unless such payment or consideration is available on proportionally equal terms to all other [competing] customers.

Section 3   That it shall be unlawful for any person ... to lease or make a sale ... or fix a price charged therefor, or discount from, or rebate upon, such price, on the condition ... that the lessee or purchaser thereof shall not use or deal in the goods ... of a competitor ... of the lessor or seller, where the effect ... may be to substantially lessen competition or tend to create a monopoly.

Section 4   That any person who shall be injured in his business or property by reason of anything forbidden in the antitrust laws [not including the FTC Act] may sue ... and shall recover threefold the damages by him sustained, and the cost of suit, including a reasonable attorney's fee.

──── FEDERAL TRADE COMMISSION ACT

Section 5(a)(1)   Unfair methods of competition ... and unfair or deceptive practices ... are hereby declared unlawful.

──── UNIFORM COMMERCIAL CODE

Section 2-313   *Express Warranties by Affirmation, Promise, Description, Sample.*
(1) Express Warranties are created as follows:
   (a) Any affirmation of fact or promise made by a seller to the buyer which relates to the goods and becomes part of the basis of the bargain creates an express warranty that the goods shall conform to the affirmation or promise ....

(2) It is not necessary to the creation of an express warranty that the seller use formal words ... , but an affirmation merely of the value of the goods or a statement purporting to be merely the seller's opinion or commendation of the goods does not create a warranty.

Section 2-314   *Implied Warranty; Usage of Trade*
(1) Unless excluded or modified, a warranty that the goods shall be merchantable is implied in a contract for their sale

if the seller is a merchant with respect to goods of that kind. . . .

(2) Goods to be merchantable must be at least such as
   (a) pass without objection in the trade . . .
   (b) . . . are of fair average quality . . .
   (c) are fit for the ordinary purpose for which such goods are used; and
   (d) [are] . . . of even kind, quality and quantity . . .
   (e) are adequately contained, packaged, and labeled . . .
   (f) conform to the promises or affirmations of fact made on the container or label if any. . . .

Section 2-315   *Implied Warranty: Fitness for Particular Purpose*
Where the seller at the time of contracting has reason to know any particular purpose for which the goods are required and that the buyer is relying on the seller's skill or judgment to select or furnish suitable goods, there is unless excluded . . . an implied warranty that the goods shall be fit for such purpose.

——— MAGNUSON-MOSS WARRANTY ACT

Section 2308   *Implied Warranties–Restrictions on Disclaimers or Modifications*
(a) No supplier may disclaim or modify (except as provided in subsection (b) of this section) any implied warranty to a consumer with respect to a consumer product if (1) such supplier makes any written warranty to the consumer with respect to the consumer product, or (2) at the time of sale, or within 90 days thereafter, such supplier enters into a service contract with the consumer which applies to such consumer product.

Limitation on Duration
(b) For purpose of this chapter [other than for "Full" warranties where implied warranties cannot be limited] implied warranties may be limited in duration to the duration of a written warranty of reasonable duration, if such limitation is conscionable and is set forth in clear and unmistakable language and prominently displayed on the face of the warranty.

━━━ CONSUMER PRODUCT SAFETY ACT

Section 2058(c) *Required Considerations and Findings*

(1) Prior to promulgating a consumer product safety rule [which creates a safety standard or bans a product], the Commission shall consider, and shall make appropriate findings for inclusion in such rule with respect to

(a) the degree and nature of the risk of injury . . .

(b) the approximate number of consumer products . . . subject to the rule;

(c) the need of the public for the consumer products subject to such rule, and the probable effect of such rule upon the utility, cost, or availability of such products to meet such need; and

(d) any means of achieving the objective of the order while minimizing adverse effects on competition or disruption or dislocation of manufacturing and other commercial practices consistent with public safety.

(2) The Commission shall not promulgate a consumer product safety rule unless it finds (and includes such finding in the rule)

(a) that the rule (including its effective date) is reasonably necessary to eliminate or reduce an unreasonable risk of injury associated with such product;

(b) that the promulgation of the rule is in the public interest; and

(c) in the case of a rule declaring the product a banned hazardous product, that no feasible consumer product safety standard . . . would adequately protect the public from the unreasonable risk of injury associated with such product.

━━━ COPYRIGHT ACT

Section 401 *Notice of Copyright*

(a) *General Requirement*: Whenever a work protected under this title is published in the United States or elsewhere by authority of the copyright owner, a notice of copyright . . . shall be placed on all publicly distributed copies . . . .

(b) *Form of Notice*: The notice appearing on the copies shall consist of the following three elements:
    (1) the symbol © ... or the word "Copyright" ...;
    (2) the year of first publication of the work ...;
    (3) the name of the owner of the copyright.

Section 408   *Copyright Registration in General*
(a) Registration Permissive: At any time during the subsistence of copyright in any published or unpublished work, the owner ... may obtain registration of the copyright claim by delivering to the Copyright Office [one copy of an unpublished work or two copies of a published work], together with the application and fee.

——— DISCUSSION QUESTIONS

1. The legal environment plays a major role in shaping marketing strategy. Price fixing, unfair acts, and deceptive practices are just a few of the restrictions that marketing managers must consider. How much influence does the manufacturer have on the retailer in these matters? How can the retailer resist unacceptable pressures and still retain an acceptable source of supply?
2. Assume a manufacturer refused to place a major product with a distributor unless the distributor also carried a lesser brand from the same manufacturer. What is this practice called and how should the distributor manage this situation?
3. As a manufacturer, assume that a retailer carrying your product attempts a bait-and-switch tactic, offering your product as a "come-on" and then persuading customers to buy a competitor's product because it nets higher retail profit. How would you contend with this situation? How important is it to not antagonize your distributors?
4. Product safety regulations play a big role in shaping manufacturing requirements, packaging, labeling, and so on. Are these regulations necessary to provide product safety to the consumer? Or can industry regulate its own practices, with customer satisfaction playing the balancing, regulatory role?

An Issue of Trust: Ethics in Marketing Management

40

MARILYN NADELHAFT

Is there a framework for evaluating marketing practices that border on, or in fact enter into, the realm of unethical behavior? Does something have to be illegal in order to be unethical? Is there a prevailing attitude of "It's done all the time" and "It's normal industry practice"? How do we resolve unethical situations without "bringing the house down on everyone" and causing innocent people to suffer? How far can a marketer carry the "buyer beware" approach? Is customer satisfaction the ultimate measurement of ethics?

In 1990 participants in an ethics workshop at the Harvard Business School focused on questions like these and on the dilemmas created for marketing managers by the seeming contradiction between ethical and economic thought. This reading provides a detailed account of the discussions that took place at the workshop.

In the long chain of events between the conceptualization of a product or service and its eventual purchase by the consumer, it is marketing, the last and most public link, that frequently attracts the closest ethical scrutiny. In the 1980s, marketing decisions—both good and bad—figured prominently in a number of highly visible incidents involving company responses to product tampering, recalls due to design flaws, and misleading or false advertising.

In the spring of 1990, case studies based on some of these controversies sparked three days of lively, thought-provoking discussion at the Harvard Business School-sponsored workshop on ethics in marketing, "The Impacts of Marketing Decision-Making." The program was organized by E. Raymond Corey, the School's Malcolm P. McNair Professor of Marketing (now emeritus), Professor John A. Quelch, and Visiting Assistant Professor N. Craig Smith. Smith noted that the focus of the workshop was to "examine major ethical issues in marketing management and identify the implications for marketing practice and public policy." The goal, he explained, "was to arrive at recommendations for improving coverage of the ethical dimensions of marketing decision making in marketing teaching and research." Forty-seven individuals attended the forum, representing a wide spectrum of colleges and universities, as well as businesses and regulatory agencies.

The conference made significant inroads toward shaping and defining a relatively new and sensitive area of study with particular ramifications for marketing managers. As Smith remarked, "Some of the most fundamental concepts in marketing management and some of the most fundamental concepts that we as marketing teachers employ and that we encourage marketing managers to employ, are really challenged when we start thinking about the underlying ethical considerations."

Amplifying that observation during his address as the seminar's keynote speaker, James E. Burke (MBA '49), chairman of the strategic planning committee of Johnson & Johnson and chairman of the Partnership for a Drug-Free America, succinctly summarized the ethical dilemma of the marketing manager: "The marketing person has to be closest to the ultimate consumer. That is what marketing is all about . . . and that means people in marketing have a particularly exquisite ethical burden."

It was, in fact, Burke's own ethical burden as CEO of Johnson & Johnson during the Tylenol crisis in 1982 that was examined during the workshop's opening session. Burke's decision to pull Tylenol from the shelves after a series of mysterious deaths in the Chicago area were traced to Tylenol capsules laced with cyanide—followed by the subsequent successful relaunch of the product—was considered by many participants to be an extraordinary business decision. Richard Tedlow, Harvard Business School professor and supervising author of the case study "James Burke: A Career in American Business," called it "one of the greatest business decisions of all time."

Ray Corey, who led the Tylenol case discussion, raised three basic issues:

- What should the CEO do, from an ethical standpoint?
- Was the decision to take Tylenol capsules off the market a good business decision?
- What factors tend to shape management decisions when the chips are down?

The group concluded that the CEO was right to pull the capsules from the shelves. Most thought it was the correct business decision, not only from a safety standpoint but also because the act of removing the capsules helped keep the public from perceiving other company products as contaminated. As Tedlow stated, Burke's decision was truly extraordinary because it "cleansed the product," providing the opportunity for a relaunch. The discussion of factors influencing Burke's action led to a consideration of corporate and personal value systems and relevant past experiences—the stories that express the corporate culture and its performance measurement and reward systems.

This examination of the actions of a highly respected manager who had "done the right thing" by integrating strong ethical values and wise business decisions set the tone for the rest of the workshop. Session after session raised intriguing and controversial ethical issues such as corporate responsibilities in the area of public health, the influence of consumers in determining a corporation's ethical standards, and ways to reconcile the persuasive intent of advertising with the overriding values of fairness and honesty. The workshop explored these issues in terms of five corporate functions: product policy, distribution, marketing communications, pricing, and the integration of marketing.

——— PRODUCT POLICY

"It is totally unethical to try to put a value on the number of lives that might be lost. If we go through a calculation where we say, 'Maybe we're going to kill ten people, and because of product liability lawsuits, we'll end up paying $100,000 a person and that's less expensive than going through a recall,' then that's an outrageous decision," said Robert Hunter, president of the National Insurance Consumer Organization, during a lively discussion of a case study on the Black & Decker Spacemaker Plus coffeemaker. Led by HBS professor Stephen A. Greyser, the case outlined a 1988 incident in which a coffeemaker caught fire, probably because the consumer did not correctly insert the water reservoir drawer. In subsequent tests, the company determined that a design flaw made the product potentially hazardous under conditions of normal use. Meanwhile, the president of Black & Decker's Household Products Group had to decide, in the middle of the holiday buying season, whether or not to recall the coffeemaker that the company's annual report had called a "major product highlight of 1988."

In speculating on what issues the group president should consider when thinking about a recall, workshop participants identified such key areas as company liability, potential danger to consumers, company image, the scope of the problem (a grave emergency or not?), and how competitors might have handled a similar situation.

Then Greyser posed an additional question. Once a company decides on a recall (which Black & Decker ultimately did), how vigorously should it be pursued? Opinions varied from recalling enough units to protect the company's position to "as thoroughly as we can." Special guests Ken Homa and Gael Simonson, the Black & Decker officials who handled the Spacemaker Plus recall, shared the specifics of their experience. Homa, vice president of Marketing and Business Planning, began by explaining that once Black & Decker found that normal use could cause the problem, the company decided to try for a 100-percent recall. "Out of inexperience in product recalls or naiveté," he explained, "we assumed that 100 percent was a reasonable goal."

This decision was made with little assistance from government agencies and in the absence of any established recall procedures—a fact that surprised Homa. "We were appalled with the response of experts who told us that even with the most aggressive action on our part, the most we could hope for was probably between 7 to 15 percent of the units would be returned," Homa said. "Given that we had established that there was a remote danger the product could lead to a fatality, that kind of response was totally unacceptable to us. We didn't know how we were going to do better, but we knew we had to try."

Gael Simonson, director of Brand Marketing and Strategy Development, then outlined the components of Black & Decker's aggressive strategy, which included draining trade channels, providing consumer incentives such as refunds and replacement coffeemakers, and implementing an unusual public relations effort utilizing press releases with such dramatic headlines as "Milwaukeans Slow to Respond to Life-Threatening Danger." But, according to Homa, the company's most significant breakthrough came when their in-house marketing department implemented a direct-marketing campaign to reach owners of the Spacemaker Plus. The combination of these factors produced a 92-percent return rate—unprecedented for a product recall.

Following the Black & Decker case, a panel consisting of Richard Tedlow, HBS assistant professor Melvyn Menezes, and Wayne State University professor Fred Morgan discussed related aspects of ethics and product policy. John Quelch served as moderator. "Product safety is defined by what each of many stakeholders—manufacturers, retailers, politicians, regulators, lawyers—says it is," Tedlow noted. "Sometimes the information never gets to the top decision makers, or gets to them long after the first instance of a problem is reported to someone lower down on the command chain." Tedlow proposed several questions for further research: How can you minimize the possibility that a product will be subject to recall? What is the best way of channeling information to appropriate decision makers? How can regulatory agencies best deploy their own limited resources, and what criteria should be applied in selecting industries for scrutiny?

Morgan discussed product safety in the context of the product-development process. He urged the incorporation of recall protocols into product planning and argued that the age of products has a bearing on safety. Finally, in addressing the border between the law and ethics, Morgan commented, "Minimal compliance with the law is an attitude that's out there. We can sit here and say that's wrong, but from a business standpoint, it's a viable position. I think there are a lot of ethical issues that don't come into play in the courtroom," he observed. "It's often just rules and regulations."

Melvyn Menezes then defined four product-policy areas with ethical dimensions: (1) design and positioning, (2) packaging and labeling, (3) recalls, and (4) the environment. With respect to design and positioning, Menezes pointed out that until very recently, people expected products to be designed safely; there was no need to include safety in the "sell." When discussing product recalls, Menezes stated that the method adopted by a corporation—and the ethical considerations involved—may vary depending on where the blame for the problem lies. If the problem leading to the recall originates outside the firm and is relatively uncontrollable (such as product tampering), the recall response will be quick and taken on ethical high ground. In contrast, a company will probably resist a recall if the problem is internal and controllable. Finally, in discussing a product's impact on the environment, Menezes made three important generalizations:

- Products should be altered to take advantage of consumers' increasing concern for the environment.
- Industry should change voluntarily to stay ahead of tightening regulations reflecting public attitudes.
- Environmental considerations are so important that they should be a part of all business decisions, even if profits suffer in the short term.

——— DISTRIBUTION

In rural Nigeria, where a recent estimate of the ratio of doctors to the rest of the population was 1 to 50,000, the treatment of malaria—the cause of 100,000 deaths a year in that country—is often through self-diagnosis and self-medication. In the early 1980s, an estimated 40 to 50 percent of malaria victims in Nigeria went untreated. Chloroquine, an extremely bitter-tasting, highly toxic drug used to treat the disease (available only by prescription in the West), is distributed through an unregulated network of Nigerian pharmacists, registered and unregistered patent medicine stores, and street vendors.

This scenario, taken from a case study on Ciba-Geigy Pharmaceuticals, provided the basis for a discussion led by Walter J. Salmon, the Stanley Roth, Sr., Professor of Retailing at HBS, on the ethical dilemmas faced in distribution, especially in the Third World. In 1983, responding to a perceived market for a better-tasting malaria treatment, Ciba-Geigy's Third World pharmaceutical company, Pharma International (PHI), was considering introducing Fevex—a tasteless, encapsulated form of chloroquine—into Nigeria. Salmon noted two ethical dilemmas highlighted by the case: What issues should PHI consider in making the new-product decision; and how should it proceed if management decides to go ahead?

Several participants talked about the ethical trade-offs involved. Although the bitter taste of chloroquine often meant that patients curtailed treatment prematurely, the introduction of a more palatable alternative might raise the risks of overdose or unintended consumption—a real danger in a country where almost half the population is under the age of fifteen.

Participants also considered other decision-making factors, including the societal benefits of introducing the drug to Nigerians, the primitive distribution channels that must be utilized, and the implications of marketing a me-too product. Many at the session felt that PHI should not channel resources toward a "new and improved" antimalarial drug, but rather toward mass education about the correct consumption of the existing drug, as well as toward improving distribution in remote areas.

HBS associate professor V. Kasturi Rangan said, "It's not a question of overdosing or underdosing. Fifty percent of Nigerians don't dose at all and that's the real issue. It also doesn't matter if it's a me-too product, because it won't be a me-too product by the time it gets to villages where the people don't even know the drug exists." Rangan also focused on the importance of analyzing the drug's societal benefits by Nigerian, not American, standards. He argued that if the main concern of the Nigerian people is to reduce fatalities, then the entire population should have access to the medication, risking some deaths from overdosing, but decreasing fatalities overall.

On the question of how PHI should proceed if they decide to introduce Fevex, most attendees agreed that an emphasis on education was important, but acknowledged the frustration inherent in trying to communicate with a largely illiterate population. With this in mind, several participants stressed the importance of making Fevex available to streethawkers, who are essential links in the Nigerian distribution chain. The drawback was that this practice might lead to such promotional gimmicks as distributing t-shirts and baseball caps bearing the Fevex logo, which might be frowned upon by the international community.

During the follow-up panel presentation, John Farley and HBS associate professor Frank Cespedes focused on the research addressing the interface of ethical issues and distribution. Farley, a professor at Columbia University's Graduate School of Business, explained the limited nature of the research base on this topic and argued that future efforts should be international in scope: "If channels of distribution occupy marginal positions in a lot of societies, then many of the things Western marketing managers will expect a channel to do, it either can't do or won't do. The notion of the friendly pharmacist helping the family, for example, is not something you can depend on to be effective in many countries." Farley proposed three areas in need of extensive research: (1) identifying a culture's basic ethical outlook on distribution channels; (2) determining what channels cost and why costs vary around the world; and (3) discovering how social issues become intertwined with distribution.

Cespedes presented a review of literature dealing with ethical and social issues in channel management. He outlined the four topics mentioned most frequently in this literature; direct marketing (including telemarketing, automated telephone sales messages, and direct response) topped the list. He characterized direct marketing as a rapidly growing field that "raises ethical issues tending to focus on privacy, confidentiality, and intrusion." The other topics he discussed were trade promotions, franchising, and what Cespedes referred to as the allied areas of gray markets (i.e., the emergence of unauthorized channels of distribution for a manufacturer's products or services), diverting (i.e., the term typically used in the consumer packaged goods industry to refer to gray markets), and parallel imports (i.e., gray markets which, due to exchange rate differences or other factors, occur internationally).

—— MARKETING COMMUNICATIONS

Protesting the phenomenal growth of state-sponsored lotteries in the United States, a July 1989 editorial in *The Economist* proclaimed, "Governments have no duty to stop people from spending their money foolishly. But they do have a duty not to encourage people to spend their money in that fashion." The quote was included in a case on the Massachusetts State Lottery that began a spirited discussion of ethics in marketing communications. Led by Robert D. Buzzell, the HBS Sebastian S. Kresge Professor of Marketing, the case touched on questions of monopoly, advertising practices, and—at the heart of the matter—the ethics of government involvement in a gambling activity.

Buzzell invited workshop participants to explore the case from a number of perspectives by assuming the roles of an investigative journalist, the state lottery's marketing director, and the governor of Massachusetts. In assessing the ethics of a state lottery, participants identified a tension between the need for additional state revenue and the implicit endorsement of gambling. Also questioned were marketing efforts targeted to the poor and uneducated—they were a kind of regressive taxation, one participant suggested. Many viewed lottery advertising as deceptive since it emphasizes the big win while barely mentioning the overwhelming odds. Others felt that most people know they have almost no chance of winning but are willing to take a chance because the potential reward is so great.

A panel introduced by HBS Lincoln Filene Professor Alvin J. Silk included professors Pat Murphy of the University of Notre Dame, Ivan Preston of the University of Wisconsin, and Rick Pollay of the University of British Columbia and expanded the analysis of ethics in marketing communications. In considering the ethical issues involved in personal selling, Murphy observed that because salespeople's salaries are often based on commissions, they may be especially susceptible to pressure to compromise their ethical beliefs. Economic pressures also have an impact on advertisers, who face ethical dilemmas in determining how persuasive their advertising should be and how responsible they are for their audience. Referring to the lottery case, Murphy suggested that the media might find it difficult to be openly critical of the lottery's advertising techniques because it is a major customer.

Examining marketing communications from a legal standpoint, Ivan Preston outlined several cases that came before the Federal Trade Commission (FTC) in the 1980s. His model of common deceptive advertising practices involved a company whose advertising conveyed the impression that its pain reliever had been proven to be "superior for headache pain." In reality, the test in question showed that the product's superiority lay in the relief of postpartum pain.

Continuing the discussion of deceptive advertising, Rick Pollay, who has served as an expert witness in trials involving the Canadian tobacco industry, shared his expertise in Canadian cigarette advertising. Pollay presented research showing that, although cigarette companies claim that their advertising is targeted toward brand "switchers," only 10 percent of smokers per year are likely to change brands. The only real growth in the cigarette market comes from new smokers, and, as a result, cigarette advertising targets young people. Pollay also noted that cigarette companies' heavy investments in advertising inhibit media reporting of the health risks of smoking.

——— PRICING

What is a "fair" price? This deceptively straightforward question was the focus of a workshop session on pricing issues. Craig Smith led a case discussion of "Amalgamated Aluminum Alloy Division," about a product manager pondering the pricing issues involved in marketing a new alloy discovered and developed by an in-house metallurgist. The new product will replace an existing company product, an alloy used primarily in aerospace and defense applications. Although its properties are not completely understood and field testing has been limited, the company believes the new alloy will cost much less to manufacture than its predecessor.

Workshop participants discussed a variety of factors that would be taken into account in deciding whether to set a new price or retain the old: the response of competitors, customers, and stockholders; the potential impact on sales volume; and reaction of the company sales force, as well as other internal repercussions. The product manager's pricing decision is further complicated by a recent companywide directive from the CEO to emphasize long-term profitability and customer relationships over short-term gain, at the same time maintaining maximum return to shareholders. At the workshop, opinion was split between advocates of a lower price, which would allow the company to share the benefits of R&D with customers while gaining an edge on its competition, and those who favored the old price so that higher profits could provide additional funds for new R&D.

Boston University's Thomas Nagle opened the subsequent panel discussion by recalling Ray Corey's observation that all of marketing—including its ethical aspects—comes to focus on the pricing decision. The product, promotion, and distribution aspects of marketing can all be justified as creating value for the consumer, Nagle observed. But pricing, he said, is the time "when you grab a chunk of that value and stick it in your pocket; that's marketing's moment of self-interest, and it can't be portrayed as service to the customer."

HBS assistant professor Gwendolyn K. Ortmeyer then presented a review of the literature on ethics and pricing. She reported two principal areas of concern: anticompetitive pricing (such as price-fixing conspiracies within industries) and consumer pricing (such as deceptive or misleading retail pricing practices). In legal terms, she explained, some practices, such as horizontal price fixing, are judged illegal per se while others are subject to the rule of reason on a case-by-case basis.

Ortmeyer also outlined major research about consumers' attitudes to pricing. How do consumers incorporate price into their decision making? How do they react to potentially misleading pricing practices? How do they decide what is a fair price?

Professor Richard H. Thaler of Cornell's Johnson School of Management then discussed consumer attitudes with a presentation entitled "What Makes a Price (Seem) Fair?" Thaler suggested that the group ask two questions: What is the fair pricing and distribution policy for a firm to adopt? and What actions will be considered fair by customers, the public, government, and other interested parties? The answers to these questions, Thaler noted, by no means coincide. "No one will accuse you of price gouging if you charge a lot for a drug that cures baldness, but they will if you charge a lot for an AIDS cure," he pointed out.

Thaler concluded by noting two major considerations for marketers. Perceptions of fairness, he said, whether or not they coincide with efficiency, constrain the actions that profit-maximizing firms can take. Secondly, in order to avoid the appearance of price gouging, firms in some cases may need to adopt innovative pricing strategies.

The conversation then turned to a hypothetical case involving the discovery of a cure for AIDS. As John Farley observed, "When you get away from wants and into the realm of needs, people's perceptions change." HBS assistant professor Patrick J. Kaufmann asked, in the case of a very expensive AIDS drug, if a firm should charge only what people could afford to pay. Richard Thaler observed that need-based pricing is rare for profit-maximizing firms and that there are obvious practical problems with such price-discrimination techniques. For one thing, he said, the drug will often be resold instead of consumed by those for whom it is intended.

W. Michael Hoffman, director of the Center for Business Ethics at Bentley College, replied: "It seems to me that, after taking into account R&D, distribution, and so forth, a fair price could be charged and justified in the case of an AIDS cure without people feeling that they're being gouged. The company might even call in others outside the company to help them establish a fair price."

HBS lecturer William McLennan agreed. "Perhaps," he said, "we aren't concentrating enough on utilizing established business principles, such as good will or a wartime kind of mobilization, in solving these problems. We need to find ways to incorporate responses that may actually help—or at least not hurt—companies in the long run, while at the same time satisfying urgent social needs."

But, Thomas Nagle responded, "That's the key point. We structure our economic system so that resources are guided by financial incentives. The imposition of ethical constraints inconsistent with those financial incentives creates a paradox: the more you apply ethical constraints to business decisions, the less efficient the system becomes in providing precisely the products deemed ethically most important. If ethical considerations are important, that's fine; but some kind of incentive must be provided to make sure they are realized."

——— INTEGRATION

A case involving an advertising agency president's attempt to woo a client with a promotional pamphlet alluding to inside information about the client's competitor provided workshop participants with an opportunity to integrate some of the concepts they had discussed earlier. The source of the inside information was two new employees of the agency who had formerly worked for the competitor. The client not only refused to hire the agency but, out of concern for its own reputation, shared the pamphlet with its competitor, which lodged a lawsuit against the agency.

Discussion leader John Quelch invited participants to address four issues:

- Was the agency's action wise or ethical?
- Was it within the boundaries of normal industry practice?
- What information should employees be allowed to bring from a previous job?
- Was the client's reaction appropriate?

The consensus was that the agency's actions were foolish and the president was "creative but untrustworthy." Some argument ensued as to whether or not his actions were egregiously unethical. Ivan Preston suggested that his error lay in the method he used to pass along the information, rather than in the nature of the message itself. "The more typical way of getting that information across," Preston noted, "would be to mention it in conversation, not to print it in a brochure." One participant countered this by asking, "Would it be more ethical for the client to have that whispered to him and then make the decision to use the agency?" Most participants felt it would not.

A few of the attendees viewed the agency's plan of attack as overzealous but not completely outside the realm of standards set within the industry. Advertising agencies "do this all the time," one participant observed. Many argued this point, asserting that the industry would not support such actions and citing specific, personal experiences with other advertising agencies.

The group acknowledged the difficulty of deciding how much information people can carry from one job to the next and still stay within the boundaries of ethical behavior. They concluded that one may bring personal experience, but not property, such as a competitor's marketing plan. Without this understanding, which many companies enforce by having employees sign written agreements, the system of fair competition would break down.

Keeping this in mind, how should the client have responded to the agency's pitch? Most participants agreed that the client should have done something and that informing the competitor and, implicitly, setting the wheels in motion for a lawsuit was a perfectly acceptable action. Michael Hoffman disagreed with the idea that a lawsuit was called for. "This was an overreaction," he said. "The more appropriate response would have been to try to find some sort of regulatory agency, if there is one, and have this handled within the industry. A lot of relatively innocent people could get hurt in this lawsuit."

The ensuing panel presentation focused first on a theoretical model designed by Texas Tech marketing professor Shelby Hunt, which provides a framework for studying why people's ethical beliefs vary. By contrasting ideas about moral obligation and the belief that individual actions are part of some preordained grand purpose/design, and considering the many other factors that influence an individual's ethical decision-making process, Hunt's model illustrates the complexity involved in making ethical judgments. For this reason, he strongly encouraged participants to focus their research on theoretical issues pertaining to ethics, rather than relying on surveys of popular opinion.

Craig Smith then presented a marketing ethics framework he has developed for evaluating marketing practices. He described its key component as a consumer-sovereignty test, which recognizes the power of the consumer in the marketplace without ignoring the power of the producer. The test examines three dimensions of consumer sovereignty: (1) the capability of the consumer [to judge the relevant information, allowing for factors of age, education, and income]; (2) the availability and quality of information; and (3) choice or the opportunity to switch products.

To illustrate the test, Smith used a case involving a developer of planned communities in Florida. The company sells the "dream" of Florida to out-of-state prospects through an elaborate direct-mail program leading to subsidized Florida site visits once a prospect has begun making payments on a piece of land. At this point, the buyer may select a model home, which the developer then builds on either the buyer's lot or another lot which the developer will trade for the buyer's lot. A number of civil lawsuits filed by homeowners alleged the company had overcharged for construction and overpriced the houses.

At issue was the fact that the company failed to tell buyers about similar houses in the community built at lower cost by local builders, and allegedly made it difficult for them to find out on their own. Yet, as Craig Smith queried, "What industry *does* require the disclosure of competitive prices?" Panel participant Steven Edwards, an attorney who was involved in the actual case, summarized its ethical bottom line with three questions:

- What should a seller do when he knows that an alternative product is "better" than his product, either in terms of quality or price?

- When does a buyer's lack of information become an ethical issue for a seller?
- Is customer satisfaction the measure of ethical values?

—— NEXT STEPS

In his closing remarks, Ray Corey outlined several recurrent workshop themes. He noted that the marketing concept itself challenges ethics, as is evident in the implicit tension between corporate and consumer responsibility and between ethical and economic thought. Also evident were the widely varying perceptions of what is ethical, and the related conclusion that a consensus on ethics is often not possible because of different priorities and interests among stakeholders.

In the long run, asked Corey, does the market usually reward ethical decision making? It did in Jim Burke's case, but Craig Smith cautioned against generalization: "Managers and students should be urged to look hard for solutions combining ethics and profits," he observed, "but such solutions cannot always be found, and hard choices need to be made with no apparent payoff in prospect."

In considering the future of teaching and research in this area, Rick Pollay remarked that it would be "helpful for both teaching and research to advance the discussion regarding the nature of our moral and ethical criteria, and the benchmarks against which we want to judge our decisions and actions." When asked if that was researchable, Pollay made reference to a list developed by the Josephson Institute for the Advancement of Ethics that identifies ten "commandments" of ethics including honesty, integrity, trustworthiness, and accountability. "Whatever the list," Pollay continued, "it is important to develop one so as not to be vague and ambiguous about what we mean when we say ethics, especially when it comes to teaching."

Drawing on his own teaching experience, Richard Tedlow posed an interesting dilemma. How does a teacher provide answers to situations where outcomes depend so heavily on individual values and modes of reasoning? In response, Shelby Hunt noted two teaching extremes to avoid. One is a preachy, holier-than-thou approach that, according to Hunt, is implied in the list generated by the Josephson Institute. The other is the hands-off approach that renders an educator "totally value-neutral." Hunt recommended that educators "attempt to get across what you feel are the mores, conventions, and ethical codes of society."

At this point one participant stressed the importance of introducing students to role models, men and women who have succeeded in balancing the demands of ethics and marketing. He explained the equal importance of reminding students that the case-study method does not provide right and wrong answers and that "ethics is reasoning and understanding—getting a grasp on issues in the hope of moving closer to right and wrong." Steven

Edwards replied, "In teaching ethics to students, I would really emphasize the process by which ethical judgments are made, rather than emphasizing answers."

Addressing directions for future research, Lynn Sharp Paine of Georgetown University reiterated the need to think more about what constitutes an ethical issue. She identified as an important research question, "What are our moral criteria?"

Participants named two other areas ripe for ethical research: the development of ethical sensitivity in a corporate setting, and the interface between ethical and regulatory issues. As Gloria Larson, deputy director of the Bureau of Consumer Protection for the FTC, explained, "Ethical decision making, or even the definition of an ethical issue, is affected by the current regulatory climate. I would argue that, in the last eight years, some of the cigarette and alcohol advertising cases—and even some of the product-recall issues—we've discussed here may not have been defined as legal violations."

In closing, Corey thanked participants and congratulated them on their dedicated effort to contribute original thought to the field: "The breadth and frankness of your discussion has given us a real thrust forward in terms of our teaching and research on ethical issues in marketing."

——— DISCUSSION QUESTIONS

1. The ultimate aim of business is profit through customer satisfaction. But in fulfilling this aim, business must look out for its own self-interests. Often the two pursuits create a dilemma that may border on unethical behavior. Why do you think this is so? How does the marketing concept contribute to the seeming contradiction between ethical and economic behavior?

2. Assume you have a unique product that customers are willing to pay a lot of money for, yet you are able to produce it for only a fraction of what you could sell it for. Do you think it is unethical to charge the highest possible price that people are willing to pay?

3. How do you view the "Everybody does it" attitude that sometimes prevails in business and other areas and results in unethical practices?

4. How much of a role do you think the government should have in regulating unfair practices in private enterprise?

5. Does something have to be illegal in order to be unethical? Give some examples.

APPENDIX

Before marketers or students can successfully analyze marketing problems, they will need to familiarize themselves with the arithmetic techniques, concepts, and terminology typically employed in marketing analysis. This appendix contains an introductory reading on quantitative methods for analyzing the economic consequences of various courses of action, in particular break-even analysis. A glossary of marketing terms and definitions is also included here.

Basic Quantitative Analysis for Marketing   41

ROBERT J. DOLAN

"Break-even analysis is a technique for assessing the risks of a proposed investment, a new product introduction, a price change, or inaction in response to competitors' moves."[1] Its main purpose is to help marketers determine the volume of sales needed for an organization to recover all related costs of producing and marketing a product. That point is reached when total revenues equal the sum of fixed and variable costs.

This reading demonstrates the advantages of quantitative analysis, explains the terminology and mechanics of calculations, and shows how break-even analysis can be used in a variety of decision-making situations.

Simple calculations often help in making quality marketing decisions. To do good "numbers work," one needs only a calculator, familiarity with a few key constructs, and some intuition about what numbers to look at. The primary purpose of this reading is the introduction of key constructs. But only repeated analyses of marketing situations and application of the concepts and techniques presented here will develop a marketer's intuition about the relevant elements of a calculation.

First we define such key constructs as variable cost, fixed cost, contribution, and margin. Next we discuss a most useful quantity: the "break-even" volume. Finally, we demonstrate how to calculate and use this quantity in making marketing decisions.

——— BASIC TERMINOLOGY

As marketers, we are usually concerned with understanding the market or demand for the product or services in question. However, if we are to assess the likely profit consequences of alternative actions, we must also understand the costs associated with doing business. For example, the manager of a firm

---

1. "Note on Break-Even Analysis in Marketing," Harvard Business School No. 9-578-072.

EXHIBIT 1
Total Cost as Function of Output

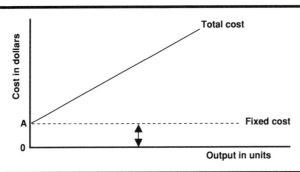

choosing a price for its new videocassette tape estimates weekly sales at different prices:

600 units	$7.50
700 units	6.00
1,000 units	5.00

Which price is best for the firm? From the data given so far, we cannot tell. We can calculate the expected revenue generated by each pricing strategy, but without cost information it is impossible to determine the best price.

We must begin, therefore, by considering key cost concepts: *variable cost, fixed cost,* and *total cost.* Second, we must combine cost information with price information to determine *unit contribution* and *total contribution. Exhibit 1* shows the relationship between a typical firm's unit output and the total cost of producing that output.

The first important feature of *Exhibit 1* is that the total cost line (the solid line) does not begin at the origin (i.e., for a zero-output level, total cost is not zero). Rather, total cost includes fixed costs (OA), represented by the length of the double-headed arrow. Fixed costs are costs that do not vary with the level of output. An example of a fixed cost is the lease cost of a plant, which is set and would be incurred even if the firm temporarily suspended production.

Although OA dollars are fixed, a second component of cost, variable cost, increases with output. As drawn in *Exhibit 1,* total costs increase in a linear fashion as output rises. In reality, it is possible for the total-cost curve to be as shown in either *Exhibit 2* or *Exhibit 3.* The former represents a situation in which each unit is cheaper to produce than the preceding one. This would occur, for example, if the firm could realize economies of scale on larger purchases of raw materials. *Exhibit 3* shows the opposite situation, in which each unit is more

EXHIBIT 2
Cost Increasing at Decreasing Rate

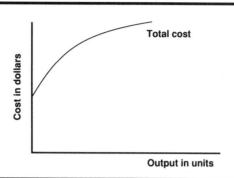

expensive to produce than the preceding one. This might occur if the firm faced a limited supply of inputs and had to pay higher unit prices as its demand increased.

While many real-world examples of *Exhibits 2* and *3* exist, we will assume that *Exhibit 1* is an adequate approximation of actual cost behavior. The total-cost line in *Exhibit 1* represents the case in which each unit costs the same. Thus, we can write

$$
\begin{array}{l}
\text{Total cost} \qquad\qquad\quad \text{Total variable} \\
\text{for output } = \text{ Fixed } + \text{ cost for output } = \text{ Fixed cost } + [k \times V] \qquad (1) \\
\text{level } V \qquad\quad \text{cost} \qquad \text{level } V \qquad\qquad (OA)
\end{array}
$$

In Equation 1, k is the cost of producing one more unit of output. It is the slope of the total-cost curve in *Exhibit 1* and does not change over the range of output shown. In summary, we first divide the firm's total cost into two parts: fixed cost and variable cost. Second, we frequently assume that the cost of producing an additional unit of output does not change, so we can write the variable cost as $k \times V$ where V is total output.

Having defined total, variable, and fixed cost, we can now introduce the concept of contribution. If k is the constant unit-variable cost and P the price received for the good or service, then

$$
\text{Unit contribution (in dollars) } = P - k \qquad\qquad (2)
$$

If V is the total number of units the firm sells, then

$$
\text{Total contribution } = (P - k)V \qquad\qquad (3)
$$

That is, total contribution equals unit contribution times unit volume sold.

If we take the V in Equation 3 inside the parentheses, we obtain

EXHIBIT 3
Cost Increasing at Increasing Rate

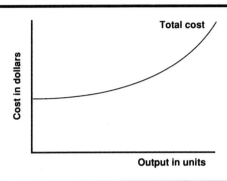

$$\text{Total contribution} = PV \text{ Total revenue } - kV \text{ Total variable cost} \qquad (4)$$

Thus total contribution is the amount available to the firm to cover (or contribute to) fixed cost and profit after the variable cost has been deducted from total revenue.

Consider these definitions in the case of the videocassette tape pricing problem. Suppose the unit-variable cost k is $4; assuming that the sales forecasts for each price level given above are correct,

At the $5 price,

$$\begin{aligned}
\text{Unit contribution} &= \$P - k = \$5 - \$4 = \$1 \\
\text{Total contribution} &= (P - k)V \\
\text{per week} &= \$1/\text{unit} \times 1{,}000 \times 1{,}000 \text{ units}/\text{week} \\
&= \$1{,}000/\text{week}
\end{aligned}$$

At the $6 price,

$$\begin{aligned}
\text{Unit contribution} &= \$6 - \$4 = \$2 \\
\text{Total contribution} &= \$2/\text{unit} \times 700 \text{ units}/\text{week} \\
\text{per week} &= \$1{,}400/\text{week}
\end{aligned}$$

At the $7.50 price,

$$\begin{aligned}
\text{Unit contribution} &= \$7.50 - \$4 = \$3.50 \\
\text{Total contribution} &= \$3.50/\text{unit} \times 600 \text{ units}/\text{week} \\
\text{per week} &= \$2{,}100/\text{week}
\end{aligned}$$

Since, by definition, the fixed cost associated with each output level is the same, the firm is best off by charging $7.50, for of the three possible prices $7.50 maximizes the total contribution. However, if the unit-variable cost were $1, the firm would be better off at the $5 price.

EXHIBIT 4
Price and Cost at Levels in the Channel of Distribution

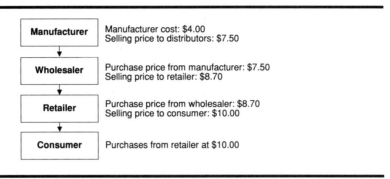

Manufacturer	Manufacturer cost: $4.00 Selling price to distributors: $7.50
Wholesaler	Purchase price from manufacturer: $7.50 Selling price to retailer: $8.70
Retailer	Purchase price from wholesaler: $8.70 Selling price to consumer: $10.00
Consumer	Purchases from retailer at $10.00

—— MARGIN CALCULATIONS

The term *margin* is sometimes used interchangeably with unit contribution. It is also used to refer to the difference between the acquisition price and selling price of a good for a member of the channels of distribution. For example, consider *Exhibit 4*, in which the videocassette tape manufacturer sells through a wholesaler, who, in turn, sells to retailers, who then sell to the public. Each of the three members of the channel of distribution (manufacturer, wholesaler, retailer) performs a function and is compensated for it by the margin it receives.

Manufacturer's margin = Manufacturer's selling price to distributors − Manufacturing cost
= $7.50 − $4.00 = $3.50

Wholesaler's margin = Wholesaler's selling price to retailers − Price paid to manufacturer
= $8.70 − $7.50 = $1.20

Retailer's margin = Retailer's selling price to consumers − Price paid to wholesaler
= $10.00 − $8.70 = $1.30

So the dollar margin is a measure of how much each organization makes per unit of goods sold.

The unit contributions and margins we have presented so far have all been in dollar terms. Sometimes it is more useful to state margins in percentage terms. Consider the retailer in *Exhibit 4*, who has a $1.30 margin for videocassette tapes. Are all items offering the retailer a $1.30 margin equally attractive? Would the retailer be interested in stocking a color television set that retails for $300 if he or she has to pay $298.70 for it? Intuitively, it seems most unlikely that the retailer would view a margin of $1.30 on a color television attractive. Thus, it may be more useful to calculate margins in percentage terms.

EXHIBIT 5
Total Cost Line with Fixed Cost = $2,000 and Unit-Variable Cost = $4

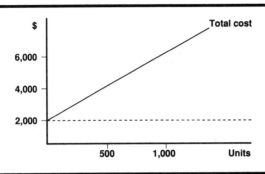

We define the retailer's percent margin as

$$\text{Retailer's percent margin} = \frac{\text{Selling price to consumers} - \text{Purchase price from wholesaler}}{\text{Selling price to consumers}}$$

$$= \frac{\text{Retailer's dollar margin}}{\text{Selling price to consumers}} \qquad (5)$$

Note that in Equation 5 the denominator is the selling price to consumers. It would have been just as logical to use purchase price from wholesaler. It is only by convention that we divide by the selling price. We always compute the percentage margin of any member of the channel by dividing its dollar margin by the price at which it sells the goods. Although this is the common definition, and we will use it throughout this discussion, it is not a universal convention.

From Equation 5 and the numbers in *Exhibit 4*, we see that

$$\text{Retailer's percent margin} = \frac{\$10.00 - \$8.70}{\$10.00} = 13\%$$

Using similar logic, the manufacturer and wholesaler percent margins in *Exhibit 4* are, respectively, 46.67% and 13.79%.

──── BREAK-EVEN VOLUME—MECHANICS

Perhaps the single most useful summary statistic one can compute from quantities defined above is the break-even volume (BEV), the volume at which the firm's total revenues equal total costs. Below BEV, the firm has a loss; above BEV, it shows a profit. *Exhibit 5* presents some hypothetical data. The BEV calculation answers questions such as "If the firm charges $7.50, how many

EXHIBIT 6
Cost, Revenue, and Break-Even Volume

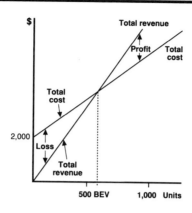

units must be sold to cover costs?" We can obtain the answer by drawing a total-revenue line, as in *Exhibit 6*. The point at which the total-revenue line crosses the total-cost line is the BEV. At volumes below BEV (to the left of BEV on *Exhibit 6*), the firm runs a loss; at volumes above (to the right), the firm shows a profit.

We can derive the BEV algebraically from the fact that at the BEV, total cost and total revenue are equal.

$$\text{Total revenue} = \text{Total cost}$$

$$\text{Price} \times \text{BEV} = \text{Fixed cost} + (k \times \text{BEV}) \tag{6}$$

Solving Equation 6 for BEV, we obtain

$$\text{BEV} = \frac{\text{Fixed cost}}{\text{Price} - k} = \frac{\text{Fixed cost}}{\text{Unit contribution}}$$

Hence, for the example shown in *Exhibit 6*,

$$\text{BEV} = \frac{\$2,000}{\$3.50/\text{unit}} = 571.43 \text{ units}$$

—— BREAK-EVEN VOLUME—APPLICATIONS

So, the BEV calculation is simple. Indeed, simplicity plus relevance are the characteristics that make BEV so frequently warranted in case analysis. It can help make decisions about unit contribution (through price or variable-cost changes) or about the appropriate level of fixed costs for a business.

EXHIBIT 7
Price and Associated Break-Even Volumes

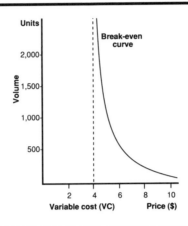

First, with respect to unit contribution, we can extend the example of the videotape manufacturer. We have shown that at a price of $7.50, the BEV is 571 units. Since

$$\text{BEV} \quad = \quad \frac{\text{Fixed cost}}{\text{Unit contribution}}$$

a price change affects the BEV. For example, at the $7 price, the BEV increases to 666.66 units. At $8, it decreases to 500 units. *Exhibit 7* shows the BEV for various price levels. From the perspective of a pricing decision, the decision maker may ask, Do I have a better chance trying to sell 2,000 units at $5 or selling 333.33 units at $10? Notice that cutting the price in half (from $10 to $5) would necessitate a sixfold increase in volume to be worthwhile. The reason for this, of course, is that this price cut would reduce the unit contribution from $6 ($10 – $4) to $1 ($5 – $4). Combined with a sense of the market size and competitors' positions, this analysis can be very useful in narrowing the feasible price range for the product.

Before considering changes in fixed costs, we should note that this type of analysis can be done for any given level of profit as well as for the break-even level. For example, if the firm's goal is to make $1,000 per time period in addition to covering its fixed costs, we can determine the volume required to achieve that goal given any particular price. At all the points on the curve in *Exhibit 7*, (Price – V.C.) x Volume = $2,000, the fixed-cost level. If the firm wants to make $1,000 per time period in addition to covering the $2,000 fixed cost, the relevant set of points becomes those satisfying (Price – V.C.) x Volume = $2,000 + $1,000 = $3,000. For any given price, the required volume is

EXHIBIT 8
Curves for Break-Even and $1,000 Profit

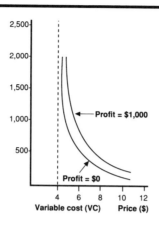

($3,000)/(Price – V.C.). *Exhibit 8* shows these points along with the break-even curve of *Exhibit 7.*

BEV is also useful in analyzing proposed changes in fixed costs. First, it can be used to aid in the decision of whether a new product should be marketed at all. For example, consider a firm estimating initial setup costs for plant and equipment and initial advertising outlays required to enter the market at $3 million. The firm also believes that unit contribution from the product will be about $1,000. Should the firm enter the market? Using BEV analysis, it is easy to see that the firm must sell 3,000 units just to cover its initial investment. Combined with some knowledge of total market size and competitive offerings, this analysis may indicate whether the $3-million investment is a good risk.

Second, BEV can help analyze the effects of proposed changes in the fixed costs of marketing an existing product. For example, the tape manufacturer is considering a $300,000 advertising campaign. Should it go ahead? Following the BEV logic and assuming a $7.50 price,

$$\frac{\text{Incremental volume required}}{\text{to justify expenditure}} = \frac{\text{Incremental expenditure}}{\text{Unit contribution}}$$

$$= \frac{\$300,000}{\$3.50/\text{unit}} = 85,714 \text{ units}$$

So for the $300,000 advertising expense to be justified, the decision maker would have to believe that the expenditure will generate incremental volume of almost 86,000 units.

—— USING THE NUMBERS

We have shown how, given certain quantities, we can calculate a quantity; that is, we can translate some facts or estimates into other facts or estimates—a process that is useful if the end result clearly suggests an action. If we put together a fixed cost of $2,000 (is this good, bad, or indifferent?) and a unit contribution of $3.50 (is this good, bad, or indifferent?) to come up with a break-even volume of 571 units (is this good, bad, or indifferent?), how do we know that the answer to the third question will not be "indifferent"?

What makes it possible to say whether 571 units is good or bad? To answer the question, we have to compare it with some other number. For example, if the total market for the product is estimated at 500 units, 571 is bad. If it's 50,000 units, 571 represents only 1.14% share, so maybe 571 is good.

The key point is this: numbers have meaning only when there is some benchmark for comparison. In marketing, such benchmarks are developed from understanding market size, growth rate, and competitive activity. The finding that BEV = 571 is, in and of itself, useless unless combined with other information in a meaningful context. The goal of quantitative analysis—making marketing policy decisions—must always be clear.

A Glossary of Marketing Terms   42

RICHARD S. TEDLOW

Many of the terms defined below have industry-specific meanings. The contextual definition of a term, of course, always takes precedence over the necessarily more general definition in this glossary.

Italics indicate cross-references; that is, terms that have their own entries in this glossary. The numbers in parentheses correspond to the sources of definitions found in the bibliographical list following the glossary. While some definitions are quoted almost directly from these sources, others are only loosely based on them.

GLOSSARY

Advertising   Any form of paid or public service presentation and promotion of ideas, goods, or services by a sponsor (8). Although word-of-mouth advertising (in which consumers tell one another about their experiences with a product or service) is a well-known phenomenon, advertising usually takes the form of mass communication. The advertiser buys space or time to send a message to a large number of unknown people with no interpersonal contact. The defining characteristic of advertising is its persuasive nature. It is not disinterested dissemination of information but is designed to convince those exposed to it of the merits of a product or service.

Advertising agency commission   The percentage of advertising costs earned by advertising agencies for their services to advertisers. Standard practice has traditionally set this commission at 15% of gross media expenditures (time, talent, facilities, space, etc.) and 17.65% of net advertising production expenses for art work, photography, typesetting, engravings, and so on (2). These standard figures are, however, often subject to negotiation.

Aftermarket   The market created by the need for new component parts for a finished product already in use. The sale of automobile tires, batteries, and air filters is an example (25).

Agent   A person or business unit that negotiates purchases or sales or both but does not take title to the goods in which it deals. Agents commonly receive remuneration in the form of a commission or fee. They do not usually represent both buyer and seller in the same transaction (8). Agents are similar to brokers, except that agents tend to have long-term relationships with their principals whereas brokers, in general, do not.

All-commodity rate   In transportation, a rate applicable regardless of the nature of the *commodities* shipped (26).

All-commodity volume (ACV)   One way in which manufacturers whose products are distributed through *supermarkets* and other food stores evaluate the effectiveness of their distribution systems. "Eighty-five percent of ACV," for example, means that a product is distributed in stores that represent 85% of the sales volume of all food-store products in an area. It does not mean that the product is carried by 85% of the stores in an area.

Arbitrage   The buying and selling of the same *commodity*, security, or foreign exchange at the same time but in two or more different markets to take advantage of differences in the prices of the item in question (26).

Auction   Offering an article to the highest of several bidders (26).

Audits   Tracking the movement of products to give manufacturers the most current sales information possible. The most important audit systems are *Nielsen* and *Information Resources, Inc.* (20).

Bait and switch   Bait advertising is "an alluring but insincere offer to sell a product or service which the advertiser in truth does not intend or want to sell." The practice of placing such advertising and attempting to switch the consumer, once in the store, to another (more profitable) product through disparagement or various other tactics is illegal (34).

Bargain basement   The lowest floor of a *department store* (often, literally the basement), which specializes in merchandise priced lower than in the store as a whole (19).

Billings   The total charges for space, time, production, and other services provided by the *advertising* agency to a client (2).

Brand   A name, term, sign, symbol, or design, or a combination of them that identifies the goods or services of a seller and differentiates them from those of competitors (8).

Break-even analysis   A technique for determining the volume of sales necessary (at various prices) for the seller to cover costs or break even between revenue and cost. Break-even analysis is used to help set prices, estimate profit or loss potential, and determine costs that will be incurred (6).

Broker   See *Agent*

Business format franchising (as distinguished from *product* or *trademark franchising*)   A type of franchise relationship in which the franchisor provides the franchisee with the total system for doing business. The franchisee receives rights to use the trademark of the franchisor and also conducts business under specific guidelines and standards covering operations, marketing, and all other aspects of the business. Some well-known examples of format franchising are fast-food restaurants, motels, and car rentals. It accounted for approximately 26% of franchise sales in 1985.

Buying allowance (Off-invoice allowance)   A *trade promotion* consisting of a short-term offer of a stated reduction in price for a certain quantity of a product purchased (29).

Buying center   The *decision-making unit* involved in a specific organizational buying decision. (See also *DMU*)

Buying group (also **buying office** or **resident buying office**)   An organization representing a group of non-competing stores formed primarily for buying merchandise. The group may be independent, store owned, or may own the stores (19).

C.B.D. Abbreviation for **cash before delivery.**   The payment of cash for a purchase before the purchase is actually delivered.

C.I.F. Abbreviation for **cost, insurance, and freight.**   These three letters signify that the items for which they stand have been included in the price quoted (26).

C.O.D. Abbreviation for **cash on delivery.**   The payment of cash for a purchase at the time of its delivery.

Cable television   A system for delivering television programming that relies upon a cable to connect the television set to a central antenna rather than upon broadcast transmission of signals directly to a residence. Because cable television does not use the air waves, it is less subject to federal regulation than the traditional transmission system, which is based on public ownership of the air waves.

Cannibalization   When a new product gains a portion of its sales at the expense of an existing product sold by the same company.

Captive distributor   A *distributor* owned by a manufacturer. The captive distributor provides a *channel of distribution* for products the parent company sells and may also carry related items made by other manufacturers.

Car card   A poster type of advertisement designed for mounting inside public-transportation vehicles, usually 11 inches high by 28 inches wide (2).

Carriage trade   The wealthy class of patrons (19).

Cash cow   One of four categories of business lines or products in a portfolio theory of *product management.* (The other three are *stars, problem children,* and *dogs.*) A cash cow is a product judged to be in the mature or decline stage of its life cycle, requiring little investment and produced at a low cost, to be "milked" for high profits in order to fund fast-growing *stars* or to invest in *stars* and more questionable *problem children* (11).

Catalog retailers   Merchants selling a variety of high-margin, branded goods, at low prices and relying on catalogs, both in their stores and mailed to customers. The customers' orders are filled from a backroom warehouse designed as a low-cost facility. Their lower prices are made possible by lower rents for out-of-the-way locations, minimal-service provision, and product offerings that are not fashion intensive.

Caveat emptor   A Latin phrase meaning "Let the buyer beware." The phrase describes a philosophy that it is and/or should be the responsibility of the purchaser to assure himself or herself of the value of a seller's wares rather than relying on the seller's word (19).

Chain discount   A series of discounts taken on a base successively decreased by preceding discounts. For example, $100 discounted by 40% plus 10% plus 2% equals $52.92, and the total amount of the discount is 47.08%: that is, $100 − 40% = $60; $60 − 10% = $54; $54 − 2% = $52.92; $100 − $52.92 = 47.08% (26).

Chain store   A group of retail stores of essentially the same type, centrally owned and with some degree of centralized control of operation (8).

Channel captain or **commander**   An organization in a *channel of distribution* that assumes leadership for firms from which it buys and/or to which it sells by absorbing risk on their behalf and generally engaging in actions designed to benefit its suppliers and customers as well as itself (14). An example of a channel commander's role would be J. C. Penney's relationship with some of its apparel suppliers. Penney's volume and importance relative to these suppliers are such that it can establish the specifications of their product, conduct inspection programs at the factory, and determine the *margin* structure.

Channel of distribution   The structure of intercompany organization units and extra-company *agents* and *dealers*, wholesale and retail, through which a product or service is marketed (8).

Circular   Printed *advertising* matter, usually from 1 to 24 pages, widely used in sales promotion (2).

Clayton Act   A federal statute passsed in 1914 that strengthened antitrust legislation by restricting such practices as price discrimination, exclusive dealing, *tying contracts*, and interlocking directorates (5).

Closed circuit   A telecast fed to receivers by cable rather than broadcast by air. Reception is controlled, limited, and not available to the public at large.

Clutter   The incidence of numerous, short commercials, particularly on television, increasing the potential level of confusion on the part of the intended recipients of *advertising* (14).

Commodity   A product category or a product that is not distinguished in the minds of potential customers from similar products produced by competitors (14).

Commodity exchange   An organization, usually owned by the member traders, that provides facilities for bringing together buyers and sellers of specified commodities, or their *agents*, to promote trades in these commodities (8).

Comparative advertising   *Advertising* that makes specific *brand* comparisons using actual product names (25).

Concentration ratio   The percentage of total output of an industry manufactured by a certain number of firms. Thus, if the four-firm concentration ratio in industry X is 40%, four firms produce 40% of the output in that industry.

Consignment sales   Sales not completed until products placed with a retailer by a supplier are sold to the consumer. Payment for goods placed on consignment is not due until such goods are resold (14).

Consumer behavior   The acts of individuals directly involved in obtaining and using economic goods and services, including the decision processes that precede and determine these acts (3).

Consumers' cooperative   A retail business owned and operated by ultimate consumers to purchase and distribute goods and services primarily to the membership (8).

Consumer credit   Funds borrowed or financial obligations incurred for periods of time—generally three years or less (6).

Consumer goods   Goods destined for use by ultimate consumers or households and in forms that can be used without commercial processing (8).

Consumer panel   See *Diary panel*

Consumer promotions   Techniques designed to attract the ultimate consumer or end user to a specific product (29).

Consumerism   A social movement seeking to increase the rights and powers of consumers and responsibilities of sellers.

Contests and sweepstakes   Two important *consumer promotion* devices. In a contest participants compete for prizes on the basis of their skill in fulfilling a certain requirement, usually analytical or creative. In sweepstakes, participants merely submit their names to have them included in a drawing of prizewinners (29).

Contracting out   The decision by a firm to have another company manufacture goods or components that it assembles and/or sells.

Contribution   The monetary (or percentage) difference between revenues realized and the variable costs incurred in the production and distribution of one or more units of a product (14).

Convenience goods   *Consumer goods* that are purchased frequently, immediately, and with a minimum of comparison. The articles are usually of small unit value and are bought in small quantities at any one time. Examples include tobacco products, chewing gum, and newspapers (8).

Convenience store   Smaller grocery stores with limited numbers of items, usually at relatively high prices, which are open long hours. These stores specialize in fill-in items such as bread, milk, and soft drinks and usually do not carry fresh meat or produce (19).

Cooperative   An establishment owned by an association of customers. In general, the distinguishing features of a cooperative are patronage dividends based on the volume of expenditures by members and a limitation of one vote per member regardless of the amount of stock owned (19).

Cooperative advertising   Local or regional *advertising*, the cost of which is shared by a national advertiser (manufacturer) and a retailer and/or wholesaler (2).

Copy   In the *advertising* world, copy usually refers to the text, written or spoken, accompanying an advertisement.

Copy testing   Preliminary trials of different copy, *advertising* appeals, or selling ideas to determine their effectiveness (2).

Cost of goods sold   The total amount of all costs related to the acquisition and preparation of goods for sale (35).

Cost per thousand (CPM)   The cost of *advertising* for each 1,000 homes reached in television or radio or for each 1,000 circulation of a publication.

Coupon   A certificate that, when presented for redemption at a retail store, entitles the bearer to a stated savings on purchase of a specific product (29).

Credit   A loan extended, often for the purpose of facilitating the acquisition of goods and services in advance of the payment.

Cumulative audience ("Cume")   The net unduplicated audience delivered by a specific program in a particular time slot over a measured period of time, usually one to four weeks (2).

DMP   Abbreviation for **decision-making process**. The process by which a *decision-making unit* (*DMU*) arrives at the decision to make a purchase.

DMU   Abbreviation for **decision-making unit**. The term can refer to a single individual but more commonly designates a group of individuals linked by a common organizational bond but separated by functional specialization, trying to reach a joint decision on a purchase. Individuals tend to take on certain roles in the buying process, such as *initiator, gatekeeper, influencer, decider, purchaser,* and *user,* descriptive of their involvement and predictive of their behavior.

Dating   The practice of giving *credit* beyond a stated period by forward dating an *invoice*. For example, a buyer technically obliged to pay for a purchase within 30 days may be given a postdated *invoice* bearing a date perhaps a month later than the actual date of purchase. In effect, the buyer now has 60 days in which to make payment. Dating is often used to encourage orders for seasonal goods well in advance of need (1).

Dealer   A firm that buys and resells merchandise at either the retail or wholesale level.

Dealer loader   A premium presented to retailers for the purchase of certain quantities of merchandise. Its purpose is to gain new distribution or to move an unusually large quantity of goods from the manufacturer to the retailer and subsequently to the consumer (29).

Deciders   Individuals who actually make the decision about a contemplated purchase (4). (See *DMU*)

Demographic segmentation   Market *segmentation* on the basis of age, sex, family size, family life cycle (e.g., young, single; young, married; young, married, youngest child under six; etc.), income, occupation, education, religion, race, nationality, and/or social class (17).

Department store   A large *retailing* business that carries a wide assortment of *shopping* and *specialty goods,* usually in the medium-to-high price range. Its products are departmentalized or segmented by categories within the store. Each department has a discrete store space allocated to it, a cash register to record sales, and salespersons to assist customers. There are two types of department stores: traditional and departmentalized specialty. The major difference is that the former carry a full line of merchandise, including consumer *durables* such as furniture and home appliances. The latter do not carry such items and focus their efforts on apparel.

Department store ownership group   An aggregation of centrally owned stores in which each store continues to be merchandised and operated primarily as an individual concern with central guidance rather than central management or direction (19).

Diary panel   A survey technique in which an individual or a family keeps a record of listening or viewing behavior or of product-purchasing activities (2).

Diffusion   The process through which a new product or service moves from its introduction to a wider acceptance in its potential market.

Direct selling   The process whereby a firm responsible for production sells to the user, ultimate consumer, or retailer without intervening middlemen (8).

Discount store   A departmentalized retail establishment utilizing many self-service techniques to sell hard goods, health and beauty aids, apparel and other soft goods, and other general merchandise. These stores operate at low margins, have a minimum annual volume of $1 million and are 10,000 square feet or over in size (12).

Discretionary income   Funds remaining after necessities are paid for out of *disposable income* (25).

Disposable income   Personal income remaining after the deduction of income taxes and compulsory payments, such as social security (8).

Distributor   A firm (or an individual) selling manufactured products either to retail outlets (*dealers*) or direct to consumers. In common parlance, distributors are often thought of as having closer and more long-term relationships with the manufacturers from which they buy than *wholesalers* do.

Dog   One of four categories of business lines or products in a portfolio theory of *product management*. (The other three are *cash cows, stars,* and *problem children.*) Dogs are low-share products in slow-growth markets. The chances of such products becoming major cash generators are not good, and they are thus often thought of as cash traps because of the investment needed to maintain their market position (11).

Drawing account   An account from which an employee is permitted to draw commissions against future sales. Deficits are accumulated and subtracted from earned commissions in later periods when there is an excess over the drawing account limit (19).

Drop shippers (or desk jobbers)   *Wholesalers* who do not handle or store the goods they sell. They take customer orders and arrange for manufacturers to ship directly to buyers. Their role is similar to that of *manufacturers'* *agents* except that they take title to the merchandise they handle and assume corresponding risks (6).

Dry goods   A broad term applied to textiles. It is generally used to include piece goods, narrow yard goods, and the textile items of women's accessories and men's furnishings (19).

Dumping   The sale of goods abroad at prices well below those charged in the country of origin. It may be done to gain the advantages of scale economies or the learning curve for the producer and/or to make it difficult if not impossible for foreign firms to compete in the market in question.

Durable goods   Goods expected to last longer than three years, such as appliances, furniture, and automobiles (1).

E.O.M., R.O.G.   Abbreviation for **end of month, receipt of goods**. This is a form of *dating* in which the net credit period begins at the end of the month and the cash discount period begins upon the purchaser's receipt of the goods (19).

80-20 rule   The common observation that 20% of products or customers often account for 80% of sales. The term is also used to express the view that 20% of the effort on a project often produces 80% of the results.

Elasticity of demand   The relative responsiveness of sales revenue to particular changes in price. When total revenue falls as prices fall or when revenue rises as prices rise, the demand for the product is said to be relatively price inelastic. When revenue rises as prices fall or when revenue falls as prices rise, demand is said to be relatively elastic (6).

Envelope (or **statement**) **stuffer**   An *advertising* leaflet, folder, or circular placed in an envelope along with its primary contents, usually an *invoice* or statement (2).

Evoked set   The range of *brands* of a product group that is seen as true alternatives by the consumer (3).

Exclusive distribution   Selling through only one *wholesaler* and/or *retailer* in a particular trading area (25).

Experiment   A scientific method of investigation used in marketing research to establish cause-and-effect relationships. Typically, an experimenter manipulates or controls one or more independent variables and observes the effect on a dependent variable. For example, a marketer might manipulate *advertising* messages (e.g., run a different messsage in equivalent markets) to determine the effects of the *advertising* messages on sales. In such an experiment, the *advertising* messages are the independent variables, and sales is the dependent variable.

F.O.B.   Abbreviation for **free-on-board**. Any agreed-upon destination to which transportation charges are paid by the vendor and at which title passes to the purchaser (19).

Factoring   The practice by which a company sells its accounts receivable at a discount to a financial institution, which then collects them.

Fair trade laws   Laws permitting *resale price maintenance*. There were at one time a number of such laws on the state level, but they were determined to be unconstitutional in 1975. *Resale price maintenance* is therefore illegal in the United States. (See *resale price maintenance*)

Family (or **umbrella**) **brand**   The use of a single *brand* name for several products (25). Kellogg, for example, uses its corporate name with all its cereals. Procter & Gamble, by contrast, does not use its corporate name to accompany its *brands;* thus Crest Toothpaste is not called Procter & Gamble Toothpaste or Procter & Gamble Crest.

Fashion   Mode of dress, etiquette, furniture, style of speech, and so on. In general, the taste of a particular segment of consumers at a particular time.

Federal Trade Commission (FTC)   Created by Congress in 1914, the FTC is an independent regulatory agency designed to police unfair competition and various corporate practices held to harm not only competitors but consumers as well. The commission's area of interest extends to *pricing* and *advertising* practices and their impact on industry concentration.

Flight   Part of an *advertising* campaign divided into segments, with lapses of time between segments (2).

Floor planning   The financing of display stocks for auto and appliance retailers by manufacturers or financial institutions (25).

Focus group   A group of 8 to 12 consumers who meet a marketer's specifications in terms of usage of or interest in a particular product category. The group is brought together with a moderator to discuss products, *promotions, advertising,* or other marketing ideas (32).

Football item   Merchandise used by *retailers* to attract customers through frequent price changes (19).

Franchising   The granting of supporting services by a supplier to a reseller in return for the sale of products or services or a specified fee. Such supporting services can include the use of a *trademark* or *brand,* merchandising assistance, advice on location, financing, and limits on the number of directly competing outlets (14).

Free-goods deal   An offer of a certain amount of a product to *wholesalers* or *retailers* at no cost but dependent on purchase of a stated amount of the same or another product (29).

Frequency   The average number of times an accumulated audience has been exposed to—or has had the opportunity for exposure to—the same *advertising* message within a measured period (26).

Full-line forcing   A type of *tying* arrangement in which the seller demands that the buyer purchase an entire line as the price of purchasing one particularly desired item in it. Full-line forcing and other *tying agreements* that do not involve *patents,* copyrights, or *franchises* are normally illegal unless the tying product is neither unique nor attractive enough to restrain competition in the tied market (34).

Functional discount   A discount from the list price to cover the middleman's *margin* (i.e., costs plus profit).

Gatekeepers   Individuals, such as purchasing agents, whose responsibility it is to be knowledgable about the range of vendor offerings useful for satisfying needs or solving problems. They largely determine which vendors get the opportunity to communicate with the decision makers making a purchase (4). (See *DMU*)

General merchandise chain   A phrase often used to describe Sears, Ward's, and Penney's—large, nationwide *chains* selling a wide variety of *consumer goods.*

Generic products   Products that have no *brand* other than the identification of their contents (25).

Geographic segmentation   *Segmentation* of a market on the basis of region, county size, city or Standard Metropolitan Statistical Area (SMSA), size, population density, and/or climate (17).

Gestalt (in *advertising*)   The phenomenon of perceiving the whole of an advertisement to have greater impact or effectiveness than the sum of its parts (2).

Gondola   A type of self-service counter with tiers of shelves back-to-back, which is free-standing between aisles of a retail store (19).

Gross margin   Sales revenue minus the *cost of goods sold.*

Gross rating points (GRPs)   The measure by which a television time buyer or advertiser evaluates its impact or clout in one or more segments of the total market. It is arrived at by multiplying reach times frequency, that is, the total number of persons exposed to an advertisement times the average number of exposures per person (2,6).

Guarantee   See *Warranty*

HBA   An abbreviation for the health-and-beauty-aid product category (19).

Hard goods   Sometimes used synonymously with *durable goods*—that is, *consumer goods* expected to last longer than three years. It may also refer specifically to consumer durables made principally from metal such as most electrical appliances, automobiles, cutlery, and tools (1).

Horizontal integration   Expansion of a company through acquisition of other companies engaged in the same stage of production of the same product. An example would be the acquisition of one retail wearing apparel *chain* by another (1).

House agency   An *advertising* agency offering full or limited service capabilities that is owned wholly or in part by an advertiser, who is typically the agency's only or most important client (2).

Implementation   Effective execution of marketing strategy at the functional (e.g., *sales force management*), programmatic (e.g., *product management*), and policy levels of the firm. Implementation involves the organization, interaction, allocation, and control necessary to carry out strategic plans efficiently and effectively.

Impulse purchase   A purchase decision made on the spur of the moment, without prior planning.

In-stock program   Maintenance by a vendor of an *inventory* of finished goods that a purchaser can buy and receive virtually immediately.

Industrial goods   Goods intended to be sold for use in producing other goods rather than to an ultimate consumer.

Industrial marketing   Marketing goods to companies (or the government or nonprofit groups) rather than to individual consumers.

Influencers   Managers with some voice in determining whether a purchase is to be made and what is to be bought (4). (See *DMU*)

Information Resources, Inc.   The market research firm that developed Behavior Scan, a service in which all stores in a market are provided with scanning equipment, and data are collected at the household level.

Initiators   Individuals who set the purchase process in motion through their recognition that a company problem can be solved or avoided through purchasing a product or service (4). (See *DMU*)

Instalment credit   Consumer credit that is repaid in periodic instalments over a period of time, with interest charged on the balance (6).

Intensive distribution   The sale of a product through a large percentage of the available *wholesale* or *retail* units in a defined market area (14).

Inventory   Unsold goods, or elements of unsold goods. Finished-goods inventory are products ready for sale, such as, for example, canned goods awaiting shipment from a factory to a *supermarket*. Work-in-process inventory are products in the process of production, such as, for example, an automobile engine prior to the final assembly of the vehicle. Raw material inventory are *commodities* still in the condition in which they were acquired from a supplier and that have not yet entered the production process. Crude oil stored at a refinery would be an example.

Invoice   A business form showing the items shipped and charges levied by the seller at the time of the shipment to the buyer (26).

Irregulars   Merchandise containing some flaw such as poor fit or poor workmanship (19).

Jobber   A term with specialized meanings in various industries but which is generally synonymous with *wholesaler* (8).

Joint venture   An arrangement in which one company shares the risks, costs, and management of a specific business project with another company (19,5). A joint venture differs from a partnership in that it is not necessarily conceived of as an on-going relationship (1).

Keystone markup   Doubling the cost to arrive at a price. Thus a men's clothing store that purchases a suit at $125 and retails it for $250 is keystoning it (19).

Knockoff   The exact or similar reproduction of another firm's merchandise (19).

Landed cost   The total cost of imported merchandise, including price paid, transportation, and crating but prior to customs duties (19).

Layaway   A method of deferred payment in which merchandise is held by the store for the customer until it is completely paid for (19).

Lease   A contract for the possession of land, buildings, machinery, *patents*, or some other item of value in return for periodic payment of a certain sum of money (26).

Letter of credit   A letter authorizing the extension of *credit* or the advance of money to the bearer, who is usually named in the letter. The *credit* or advance is charged to the person issuing the letter (26).

Licensing   The sale of the right to use some process, *trademark, patent,* or other item for a fee or royalty (25).

Line extension   A new product that is a variation on a product already offered. The new product is introduced in order to exploit the equity already built up in other product(s) in the line and/or as a competitive reaction to the strategies of other firms in a market (13).

List price   The price shown on the sales list of the seller and used as the basis from which discounts are computed for various classes of buyers (26).

Local advertising   *Advertising* appearing in one or more specific localities as distinguished from regional or national *advertising* (2).

Locker stock   The shipment by a manufacturer or *wholesaler* of extra *inventory*, which is held in a store's central warehouse unopened. As soon as the buyer removes any item held in locker stock, payment is due for the entire shipment (19).

Loss leader   Merchandise sold at a loss to attract customers (19).

Mail order chains   See *General merchandise chains*

Manifest   A shipping form used by carriers for consolidation purposes, listing all pertinent information such as consignor, consignee, commodity classification, number and weight of packages, and (sometimes) cost (19).

Manufacturers' agents or **Manufacturers' representatives**   Individuals, generally operating on an extended contractual basis, who sell, often within an exclusive territory, noncompeting but related lines of goods. They may possess limited authority with regard to prices and terms of sale. Individual agents are sometimes authorized to sell a specific portion of a manufacturer's output. The terms are generally used interchangeably (8,5).

Margin   The difference between the selling price and the acquisition cost (manufacturing cost in the case of a manufacturer and purchase cost in the case of a *wholesaler* or *retailer*) of a unit of product.

Markdown   A reduction in the established price of a product, typically in a retail outlet. The reduction percentage is determined by dividing the amount of the reduction by the original price (14).

Markdown money   Money a manufacturer pays to a *retailer* to enable the latter to put slow-selling or obsolete merchandise on sale without absorbing the loss.

Market niche   A protected segment of a market. The nature of the protection can vary. Thus a group of buyers may be particularly sensitive to price, to quality, to appeals through *advertising*, and so on. Servicing that group through the development of a special competence can enhance the competitive strength of the seller.

Market penetration   The percentage of a target market that is purchasing a company's product or service.

Market share   The ratio of a company's sales to total industry sales in a particular market. Market share can be measured in dollars or units.

Marketing   The process of planning and executing the conception, *pricing, promotion,* and *distribution* of ideas, goods, and services to create exchanges that satisfy individual and organizational objectives (24).

Marketing management   The planning, direction, and control of the entire marketing function, specifically the formulation and execution of marketing objectives, policies, programs, and strategy. Responsibilities include product development, organization and staffing to carry out plans, supervision of marketing operations, and control of marketing performance (8).

Marketing mix   Usually refers to the four pillars of marketing management: *product policy, promotion (advertising* and personal selling), *pricing,* and *channels of distribution.* For the sake of alliteration, distribution is often referred to as "place." Thus the Four *P*s.

Marketing research   A systematic investigation conducted to establish facts or to solve problems relating to the marketing of goods and services (14).

Markup   The percentage by which a seller increases the selling price of goods over the price he or she paid for them. Conventionally, markup is computed as a percentage of sales price. Thus an item a retailer purchases for $10 and sells for $15 has a 33⅓% ($5/$15) markup (1).

Mass merchandise chains   This often-used phrase has no generally agreed-upon meaning. Sometimes it is used specifically to refer to Sears, Ward's, and Penney's. At other times it is used to refer to such national or regional retail outlets as K Mart and Caldor, which are generally thought of as selling at price points below Sears, Ward's, and Penney's. Yet another use of the term includes large discount drug chains.

Matrix organization   In marketing, the assignment of responsibilities so that one group of managers (including those for sales, *advertising, marketing research,* etc.) is responsible for ensuring the contribution of specialized, differentiated, functionally oriented expertise to the marketing effort, while another (composed of product or brand managers) is responsible for integrating functional inputs to provide effective marketing programs for products, *brands,* or product lines (14).

Mean   The arithmetic average of all observations in a *sample.* It is calculated by summing the values of all observations and dividing by the number of observations (20).

Median   In statistics, the observation that is exactly in the middle of a *sample* (20). Thus, in a sample consisting of the values 1, 5, 7, 8, 9, 11, and 13, the median is 8.

Merchandise allowance   A short-term, contractual agreement through which a manufacturer compensates *wholesalers* or *retailers* for features (i.e., *advertising* or in-store displays of its products). Proof of performance, such as an *advertising* tearsheet, is generally required (29).

Merchandising   The planning and supervision involved in marketing merchandise at the places, times, and prices and in the quantities that best serve to realize the marketing objectives of the business. The term is most often heard in the retail, especially *soft goods*, trade (8).

Merchant   A business unit that buys, takes title to, and resells merchandise (8).

Mode   In statistics, the figure occurring most frequently in a *sample* (20). Thus, in a *sample* consisting of the observations 1, 1, 1, 3, 5, 7, and 9, the mode is 1.

Model   A set of inputs (often called parameters of the model), an explicit system or set of relationships for combining and manipulating those inputs, and the definition of the outputs used to summarize what happens when a specific set of values for the inputs is subjected to the relationship of the model (15).

Motivation research   A group of techniques developed by behavioral scientists, which *marketing researchers* use to study *consumer behavior*. These techniques attempt to identify the underlying purchase motives of consumers.

Multivariate analysis   A collection of procedures for analyzing the association between the values of two or more variables in a data set. For example, a researcher undertakes to interview five people in order to evaluate the effectiveness of an advertisement. He or she might ask them how often each saw the advertisement (frequency), what they remembered about it (recall), and whether they found it convincing (persuasiveness). The data set, therefore, consists of fifteen measurements: that is, five people times three variables per person. Examples of multivariate analysis include multiple regression, discriminate analysis, factor analysis, and cluster analysis.

National account   A large geographically diverse customer with high pre- and post-sales service needs.

National advertising   *Advertising* in one or more media that, individually or collectively, provides nationwide reach or exposure opportunity (2).

National brand   A manufacturer's *brand* that usually enjoys wide distribution (8).

Nielsen   The largest supplier of *marketing research*, Nielsen is best known for (a) its *retail audits*, providing information on grocery products, alcoholic beverages, toiletries, proprietary drugs, and product movement from retail stores; and (b) for its rating system of television shows. It specializes in providing services on a syndicated basis; that is, it recruits clients for a specified period of time (20). Nielsen is owned by Dun & Bradstreet.

Nondurable goods   *Consumer goods*, such as food or clothing, expected to last less than three years (1).

Non-store marketing   *Retailing* through means other than a retail store, such as catalogs, telephone orders, mail, and, more recently, cable television.

Non-tariff barriers   Restraints on international trade other than *tariffs*. Examples of such restraints are quotas, domestic government purchasing policies, and safety and technical standards (22).

Odd lot   An unbalanced assortment of styles, colors, sizes, fabrics, and quality (19).

Off-price stores   Stores that sell *brand*-name merchandise, predominantly apparel, textiles, footwear, and housewares, at well under the prices at which they are sold in *department* and *specialty stores*. Off-price stores are able to sell at lower prices because they usually offer little service and ambience is not emphasized. Often they buy manufacturer overruns or end-of-season merchandise at sharp discounts.

Oligopoly   An industry in which there are few sellers.

Open-to-buy   The amount of merchandise a buyer may order during the balance of a given period. The phrase is most common in *department store* and other *soft goods* retailing (19).

Opinion leader   A person who influences others (25).

Order-entry system   Computerized systems designed to streamline the many tasks involved in order processing: transmission of the order to the firm, *inventory* checking, customer credit checks, and preparing and shipping the product. Computerized order-entry systems are now facilitating every phase of this process (18,28).

Original equipment manufacturer (OEM)   A company that buys a product to incorporate into what it in turn makes and sells (i.e., into its own product line) (9).

Outlet store   A store specializing in job lots and clearance merchandise or owned by a manufacturer to dispose of surplus stocks (19).

Over-the-counter (OTC)   A term used to identify such proprietary drugs as cough medicine and aspirin, which can be purchased without a prescription, as opposed to "ethical" drugs, for which a doctor's prescription is needed (2).

Packer's brand   An unadvertised and unpromoted brand owned by a manufacturer, usually sold on price.

Patent   A grant of protection from would-be copiers for a definite period of time. Such a grant, made to persons who obtain certification of originality for their product or process from the Patent Office, currently extends 17 years in the United States (14).

Penetration pricing   A *pricing* strategy, based on a low price relative to actual or potential alternatives, designed to (a) stimulate purchase by several customer groups (market segments), (b) gain a large share of the market, (c) facilitate production economies, and/or (d) preempt potential competitors (14).

Personal selling   Oral sales presentations in conversations with one or more prospective purchasers.

Physical distribution   The management of the physical movement and handling of goods from the point of production to the point of consumption or use.

Planned purchase   A purchase decision made in advance of exposure to or final direct contact with a particular product (14).

Point-of-sale advertising (also **point-of-purchase, P-O-P**)   Displays of various kinds used in *retailing* at one or more in-store locations such as shelf, window, counter, wall, island, over-wire, or checkout area (2).

Positioning   The art of fitting a product to one or more segments of the broad market in such a way as to set it apart from competition and optimize opportunity for greater sales and profits (2). Positioning can exploit the tangible and/or intangible attributes of a product to influence customers' perceptions and establish a mental niche for the product. Positioning strategies can be implemented either through *advertising* and other forms of communication or through specific product attributes.

Predatory pricing   A *pricing* policy that restricts competition by driving out existing rivals or excluding potential rivals from the market (16).

Premiums   Merchandise offered free or at a low cost as a bonus to purchasers of another product (29).

Price fixing   Agreements between or among vendors to set prices, including efforts to raise, stabilize, or lower them by any one of a number of means, including splitting markets by rotating bids, maintaining uniform prices by distributing price lists to competitors, fixing certain aspects of the price mix by agreeing on markups or discounts, or various other conspiracies. All such joint efforts to "raise, depress, fix, peg, or stabilize" prices are illegal in the United States (34).

Price leader   A firm whose *pricing* policies are followed by other companies in its industry (8).

Price line   Prices set by company policy to give a range for customer choice.

Price packs   Packages that carry a stated discount.

Price point   Synonym for price. In some industries, this term is used to denote prices at which some kinds of products are traditionally sold or which are thought of as having noteworthy psychological meaning to consumers.

Pricing   The art of translating into quantitative terms (monetary units) the value of a product to a customer at a given point in time (9).

Primary demand   Demand for a product category, not just a company's own brand (25).

Prime time   The evening hours of broadcasting (from 7:30 P.M. to 11:00 P.M.), when television audience potential is greatest and rates charged advertiser are highest (2).

Private brands (or private labels)   *Brands* (or labels) owned by merchants or *agents* as distinct from those owned by manufacturers or producers (8).

Problem children   One of four categories of business lines or products in a portfolio theory of *product management*. (The others are *cash cows, stars, and dogs*.) Problem children have small relative market shares, weak cash flows, and, as a result, large needs for cash to fund fast growth (11). These products are problematic because it is particularly difficult to decide whether or not the chance for fast growth and future profits justifies the needed investment.

Product differentiation   Any difference, real or imaginary, in products, that may result in a preference for one over the other even though their prices are identical or when one is higher priced (26).

Product life cycle   The progression of a product from introduction to withdrawal. It is sometimes thought of as encompassing five stages: introduction, early growth, late growth, maturity, and decline.

Product management   The planning, direction, and control of all phases of the life cycle of products, including the creation of ideas for new products; the screening of ideas; the coordination of research for physical development of products; packaging and *branding;* introduction to the market; market development; product and marketing modification; servicing; and, eventually, deletion from the product line (8).

Product or **trademark franchising** (as distinguished from *Business format franchising*)   A type of *franchise* relationship in which the franchisor grants the franchisee the right to sell the franchisor's product and display or use the franchisor's *trademark.* Although the franchisee may receive training, *advertising,* and management assistance, the franchisee generally conducts business as an independent distributor. Common examples are automobile and gasoline dealerships. Product or trademark franchising accounted for approximately 74% of *franchise* sales in 1985.

Product policy   A product is a tangible good, service, or idea that satisfies a customer need. Product policy is the determination of the characteristics of that product. Included under product policy would be such issues as the actual features of the product, the number and variety of products to be offered and their relation to one another in the product line, services to be offered with the product, new-product introduction, elimination of mature products from the line, naming, packaging, and others (28).

Product portfolio   Products a company attempts, for strategic purposes, to manage as a group.

Product recall   The retrieval by a manufacturer of products that it has placed in the hands of *wholesalers, retailers,* or end users. Such retrieval is usually prompted by a discovery of a defect in or contamination of the product (14).

Product testing   The solicitation of reactions to products by encouraging their actual use among a sample of typical customers, if possible in a manner that allows comparison with competing products along critical dimensions (14).

Promotion   (a) The use of communication to persuade or convince potential customers. (b) All communication with the exception of *advertising* and personal selling; examples are *contests* and sales aids. (c) A short-term price cut. In certain industries the phrase "to promote a *brand"* means to cut its price (14).

Promotional item   In *retailing,* merchandise that has great price appeal to a customer because it appears to be a bargain (19).

Psychographic segmentation   The *segmentation* of a market on the basis of such aspects of the consumer as lifestyle, personality, benefits sought (i.e., convenience, prestige), user status (i.e., nonuser, user, ex-user), usage rate, loyalty status, readiness (i.e., unaware, aware, informed, interested, desirous), and/or marketing factor sensitivity (i.e., quality, price, service, *advertising*, sales promotion) (17).

Public relations   Mass communication primarily concerned with the corporation as an institution rather than as a vendor of specific items.

Publicity   Unpaid nonpersonal presentation of ideas or products (8).

Pull strategy   A marketing strategy in which the manufacturer rather than the *channel of distribution* assumes a great share of the burden for promotional efforts for simple products at low unit prices, often through the use of *advertising* directed at potential end users or buyers. Such a strategy often accompanies a fairly intensive distribution program offering low percentage *margins* to channel intermediaries (14).

Purchaser   The company employee with responsibility to obtain a product or service (4). (See *DMU*)

Push money   Payment by a manufacturer to a *wholesaler* or *retailer* in excess of the usual *margin* to provide an added incentive for sales efforts.

Push strategy   A marketing strategy in which the *channel of distribution*, rather than the manufacturer, assumes a great share of the burden for promotional effort, often through the use of personal selling. Such a strategy may accompany a selective distribution program offering high percentage *margins* to channel intermediaries and is usually directed toward the sale of relatively complex products at high per-unit prices (14).

Quantity discount   See *Volume discount*

Rack jobber (also **service merchandiser**)   A *wholesaler* who markets specialized lines of merchandise to certain types of retail stores and who merchandises, arranges, and stocks the racks on which these items are displayed. Rack jobbers are most prevalent in the grocery industry (8).

Rating   The percentage expression of the size of a television or radio program's audience. An 8 rating means that 8% of all homes with sets in the coverage area were tuned in to a particular program (2).

Recall test   A test to assess the actual communication impact of a media advertisement. Recall tests involve finding persons who are regular users of the medium in question and asking them to recall everything they can about the commercial. The administrator may or may not aid them in their recall (17).

Reciprocity   Trading sales for sales (e.g., I'll ship my steel on your railroad if you purchase steel rails from me). Such arrangements can be anti-competitive and illegal (34).

Reference group   The group to which an individual looks when forming his or her attitudes (25).

Refund   The return of part or all of payment for a product. A cash refund is just that, whereas a merchandise refund stipulates that the refund must be spent on other merchandise offered by the same seller (1).

Regression   A form of *multivariate analysis* that predicts a dependent variable as a function of one or more independent variables (20).

Relative market share   The *market share* of a product relative to the combined *market share* of the three leading competitors (11).

Reliability   A statistical term meaning repetitive consistency. A measure is said to be reliable if it consistently obtains the same result when measuring the same observation (20).

Replacement market   The market for products or components of products many of which are already in the hands of end users but which have been used up or have ceased for other reasons to operate effectively.

Resale price maintenance   The practice—legal prior to the repeal of *Fair Trade Laws* enabling legislation by Congress in 1975—of a manufacturer's requiring adherence to a prescribed price by *wholesalers* and/or *retailers* who resold its goods (14).

Reset   The periodic reorganization of shelves in a *retail* outlet. The reset process often involves intense competition for shelf space among manufacturers and their *agents*.

Retailing   Selling to the ultimate consumer (8).

Robinson-Patman Act   This legislation, passed by Congress in 1936 as an amendment to the *Clayton Antitrust Act*, made it illegal to discriminate in price between competitors purchasing *commodities* of like grade and quality where the effect of the discrimination may be to lessen competition substantially. Price differentials can be justified if it costs the seller less to transact business with a particular buyer, if the price change is based on changes in market conditions or the deterioration of merchandise, or if the seller is seeking to meet the low price of a competitor. This act is enforced by the *Federal Trade Commission* (34).

Roll out   The process by which a firm offering a product for sale in a regional market, perhaps as part of a test, extends distribution and promotion of the product to a wider geographical area (14).

Sales management (also **Sales administration** or **Sales force management**)   The planning, direction, and control of the personal selling activities of a business unit, including recruiting, selecting, training, equipping, assigning, routing, supervising, paying, and motivating a personal sales force (8).

Sample   (a) In statistics, a limited or finite number of items of data selected from a universe or population. (b) In marketing, one or more units of a product given free (or sold at a price far below market) to induce prospective buyers to try it or enable them to determine its characteristics by inspection or analysis (26).

Scanner   A device used at checkout counters of *supermarkets* and some other stores that emits a laser beam to identify automatically items marked with the *Universal Product Code* as they pass over the checkstand. Scanners speed the checkout process, reduce personnel needs, and provide valuable data on inventory movement (30).

Scrambled merchandising   The tendency of retail establishments to offer a growing number of product types, leading to increased duplication of assortments at various types of retail outlets. This has led to an increase in intertype competition, in which, for example, *supermarkets* offer drug products and discount drugstores offer food and laundry soap (14).

Segmentation   The process of identifying groups of potential customers by geographic area, common buying behavior, shared perceptions about a product or service, and/or similar use patterns of a product or service. The purpose of the process is to (a) design more efficient marketing programs to target one or more selected segments; or (b) *position* a product in relation to competition in a particular market segment (14).

Selective demand   Demand for one particular *brand* as opposed to demand for a general product category.

Selective distribution   The sale of a product or service through a carefully selected subset of all available wholesale or retail outlets in a given market area (14).

Semidurable goods   Goods expected to last between six months and three years, such as shoes (1).

Served market   The portion of the market for which a company's product is suitable and in which it is presently being targeted.

Share   For a television program, the percentage of households using television during a specific time period that is tuned to the program (23).

Sherman Antitrust Act   Passed by the U.S. Congress in 1890, this legislation prohibits (a) monopolies or attempts to monopolize; and (b) various acts, including contracts, combinations, or conspiracies, intended to restrain trade. The Sherman Act was aimed primarily at firms operating at one particular level in a *channel of distribution*, particularly manufacturers (14).

Shopping goods   Goods whose purchase entails risk perceived as sufficient to warrant a search to compare price, quality, style, and so on among a number of competing products.

Shrinkage   In *retailing*, the value of book inventory in excess of actual physical inventory. The difference represents losses from shoplifting, employee theft, breakage, and so on (19).

Skimming strategy   A *pricing* strategy to earn the highest possible per-unit profits. It is based on high initial price and successively lower prices designed to appeal in sequence to market segments placing successively greater emphasis on price (14).

Soft goods   (sometimes used as a synonym for *nondurable goods*) *Consumer goods* expected to last less than three years, such as food or clothing. It may also refer to goods that are literally soft to the touch, such as textiles (1).

Source effect   The extent to which a source influences the credibility of a message. Most citizens of the United States, for example, would be far more likely to believe a news story they read in the *New York Times* than to believe the same story appearing in *Pravda* (21).

Sourcing system   The complex of outside suppliers and internal manufacturing sources an organization requires for materials, component parts, supplies, machinery and equipment, facilities, and services (10).

Specialty goods   Goods for which a consumer is willing to expend the effort required to purchase a preferred item rather than buying a potentially acceptable substitute (14).

Specialty store   A retail store that makes its appeal on the basis of a restricted class of *shopping goods*. By its selection of these goods, it aims to differentiate itself from *department store* competition (8).

Spiff   Direct payment to a wholesale or retail salesperson as an incentive to sell a manufacturer's product.

Split run   Running different advertisements in alternating copies of the same issues of a publication to test the effectiveness of copy.

Spot advertising   Purchasing television or radio time on a station-by-station or market-by-market basis rather than across a network (23).

Star   One of four categories of business lines or products in a portfolio theory of *product management*. (The other three are *cash cows, dogs,* and *problem children.*) Stars are share leaders in growing markets, which may need cash to sustain their strong position (11).

Starch   A commercial research firm, best known for its Starch Message Report, which attempts to measure the impact of advertisements in magazines and newspapers (20).

Stockkeeping unit (SKU)   The lowest level of disaggregation at which a product can be ordered. Thus a shirt stockkeeping unit would be a particular size (collar and sleeve length) of a particular style of a particular color.

Strategic alliance   A business relationship more intimate and permanent than that of preferred vendor and major customer but short of actual merger. Firms may enter into a strategic alliance in order to develop some new, shared technology or because the size of a contemplated transaction is extraordinarily large, the sale particularly complex, the need for on-going technological backup pressing, and/or the opportunity for mutual learning great. An example is the relationship between Fujitsu Fanuc, a Japanese robot vendor, and General Motors. Their *joint venture* provided an opportunity for Fanuc to learn more about robot applications in a factory than it could as a typical vendor and gave General Motors the chance to understand robotics and to capitalize on its knowledge by selling factory robot technology to other companies.

Strategy   The pattern of objectives, purposes, or goals and major policies for achieving these goals, stated in such a way as to define what business the company is in or is to be in and the kind of company it is or is to be (6).

Super store   A store similar in general layout to a *supermarket* but much larger, averaging around 30,000 square feet compared to 18,000 square feet for the average *supermarket*. Super stores sell not only groceries but a large variety of convenience items (such as garden supplies) and even some big-ticket durables like television sets. Some super stores even offer such services as laundry and dry cleaning (28,18).

Supermarket   A large, low-price, low-margin, high-volume, self-service retail store selling food and a limited range of household products. The supermarket has annual sales of at least $2 million and is less than 30,000 square feet in size.

Survey   The organized solicitation of information or opinions from a *sample* or population of respondents for the purpose of drawing conclusions about the population (14).

Targeted gross rating points   *Gross rating points* with the base defined as a specific target group. For example, if the target market is men, ages 18–34, 100 gross rating points would mean that all the individuals in that group had been reached once, or half of them twice, or a third of them three times, and so on.

Tariff   (a) A customs duty or tax laid on goods as they enter or exit a country. These duties are either specific (i.e., according to the number or bulk of the items) or *ad valorem* (i.e., according to the value of the items). (b) A schedule of regulated rates and rules affecting the application of rates for specific products (26).

Tearsheet   An entire actual page containing an advertisement, illustration, or article clipped from a publication. Manufacturers who have *cooperative advertising* or *merchandise-allowance* programs with retailers often demand that retailers submit tearsheets as proof of performance (2).

Telemarketing   The use of telephone sales as part of a systematic plan to reduce expenditures for personal sales calls.

Test marketing   An attempt to evaluate the nature and degree of customer acceptance of a product by putting it on the market in selected areas. It may use a full-scale marketing program in those areas or try different combinations of such marketing tools as promotional appeals and special prices, varying the types or intensity of distribution to determine the most effective marketing strategy (6).

Trade association   An association of manufacturers or *dealers* engaged in a particular trade for the interchange of information, establishment of standards, and other activities of common interest to the members (26).

Trade promotion   Special short-term merchandising and/or sales support from *distributors* used to induce retailers to promote a product through *advertising* and display, or to stimulate retailers and their sales clerks to push a certain manufacturer's product rather than a competitor's product (29).

Trade show   A gathering of sellers and buyers for the purpose of displaying and surveying new products, processes, or services (14).

Trademark   A *brand* that has been given legal protection (5).

Trading area   A district within whose boundaries it is economical, in terms of volume and cost, for a marketing unit to sell a product (8).

Trading company   There are two types. The specialized trading company (*senmonshosha* in Japanese), exists all over the world and specializes by product, function, and region. Thus a firm importing footwear to the United States from Italy is a specialized trading company. The general trading company (*sogoshosha*) is diversified in terms of product, function, and region. The largest Japanese companies, such as Mitsui, Mitsubishi, and Sumitomo, trade all over the world and facilitate all aspects of transactions—including, for example, *physical distribution* and insurance. Their transactions are not limited to the family of firms of which they are a part; they move a great variety of products in and out of many countries.

Trading up   An attempt to induce a current or prospective owner of a product to purchase a more expensive model or version of the same product (14).

Transfer price   The price charged by one unit of a corporation when it supplies a product or service to another unit of the same corporation (26).

Turnover or **turns**   The total number of times during the course of a year that the average *inventory* is sold (25).

Tying contract   An arrangement in which the seller agrees to sell one product (the tying product) only if the buyer agrees to buy another product or products (the tied products). Such arrangements are subject to prosecution if they substantially reduce competition for the tied product (34).

Universal product code (UPC)   A numerical, bar-coded item-identification number that can be read by a *scanner* at the checkout counter of a store. These codes make it possible to track the store's *inventory* more efficiently (30).

Validity   The degree to which a measure is an accurate representation of the object or concept it is intended to measure.

Value added   The extent to which an organization enhances the price customers are willing to pay for its goods or services through the creation of form, place, time, or ownership utilities. Value added is determined by subtracting the cost of materials, supplies, fuel, and contract work from the value of the shipments (7).

Value pricing   *Pricing* on the basis of the buyer's perception of the value of the product rather than on the basis of sellers' costs (17).

Variety store   A retail establishment offering many kinds of merchandise at low prices with few attendant services. Woolworth's is a good example (14).

Vertical integration   The acquisition of firms or the development of divisions that carry out all stages of the production and sales processes. For example, an apparel manufacturer that purchases retail stores or establishes its own division to build and operate such stores is vertically integrating. In this case, the integration is forward, toward the consumer. If the apparel manufacturer purchases a textile company or establishes one, it is backward integrating—that is, away from the consumer.

Volume discount   An amount deducted in advance from payment due, as a reward for buying in quantity (1). There are a wide variety of such discounts. Discounts can be given on all units above a base; or they can be established stepwise, with, for example, a 5% discount on units 11 through 20, a 6% discount on units 21 through 30, and so on. Other variants include the volume rebate (a year-end refund according to the volume purchased during the year) and the growth-volume rebate (given on the difference between purchases from one year to the next).

Voluntary chain   A group of retailers, each of whom owns and operates its own store and is associated with a wholesale organization (19).

Warehouse outlet   A large retail facility located in a warehouse-type building, or with an adjoining warehouse, that competes on the basis of low prices made possible by a no-frills approach. It is located in a low-rent area, offers few if any services, and makes maximum use of vertical space in the storage of large inventories.

Warranty   An undertaking of responsibility by the seller of a good or service for the quality or suitability of the product. An express warranty (which can be written or verbal) is one based on express statements voluntarily made by the seller. One example of an express warranty is an automobile manufacturer's warranty that its vehicle will perform as promised for seven years or 70,000 miles, whichever comes first. Warranties can also be implied. An implied warranty is not made directly by the seller but is implied by law—for example, that a product sold as food is fit for human consumption.

Wholesaler   A business unit that buys and resells merchandise to retailers and other merchants, and/or to industrial, institutional, and commercial users, but does not sell to ultimate consumers.

——— SOURCES

1. Ammer, Christine, and Dean S. Ammer. *Dictionary of Business and Economics*. New York: Free Press, 1984.
2. *Ayer Glossary of Advertising and Related Terms*. Philadelphia: Ayer Press, 1972.
3. Block, Carl E., and Kenneth J. Roering. *Essentials of Consumer Behavior*. Hinsdale, Ill.: Dryden, 1979.
4. Bonoma, Thomas V., and Benson P. Shapiro. *Segmenting the Industrial Market*. Lexington, Mass.: D. C. Heath, 1983.
5. Boone, Louis E., and David L. Kurtz. *Contemporary Marketing*. Hinsdale, Ill.: Dryden, 1980.
6. Buzzell, Robert D., Robert E. M. Nourse, John B. Matthews, Jr., and Theodore Levitt. *Marketing: A Contemporary Analysis*. New York: McGraw-Hill, 1972.
7. *Census of Manufactures*, 1982.
8. Committee on Definitions of the American Marketing Association. *Marketing Definitions*. Chicago: American Marketing Association, 1963.
9. Corey, E. Raymond. *Industrial Marketing: Cases and Concepts*. Englewood Cliffs, N.J.: Prentice-Hall, 1976.
10. Corey, E. Raymond. *Procurement Management: Strategy, Organization, and Decision-Making*. Boston: CBI Publishing, 1978.
11. Day, George S. *Analysis for Strategic Market Decisions*. St. Paul, Minn.: West, 1986.
12. *The Discount Merchandiser*, June 1987.
13. Hayden, Catherine L. *The Handbook of Strategic Expertise*. New York: Free Press, 1986.
14. Heskett, James L. *Marketing*. New York: Macmillan, 1976.

15. Jackson, Barbara Bund. *Computer Models in Management*. Homewood, Ill.: Richard D. Irwin, 1979.
16. Joskow, Paul L., and Alvin K. Klevorick. "A Framework for Analyzing Predatory Pricing Policy." *Yale Law Journal* 89, No. 2 (1979).
17. Kotler, Philip. *Marketing Management*. Englewood Cliffs, N.J.: Prentice-Hall, 1980.
18. Kotler, Philip. *Principles of Marketing*. Englewood Cliffs, N.J.: Prentice-Hall, 1986.
19. Krieger, Murray. *The Complete Dictionary of Buying and Merchandising*. New York: National Retail Merchants Association, 1980.
20. Lehmann, Donald R. *Market Research and Analysis*. Homewood, Ill.: Richard D. Irwin, 1979.
21. Levitt, Theodore. *Industrial Purchasing Behavior: A Study of Communications Effects*. Boston: Division of Research, Harvard University Graduate School of Business Administration, 1965.
22. *Macmillan Dictionary of Modern Economics*. New York: Macmillan, 1986.
23. Mandell, Maurice I. *Advertising*. Englewood Cliffs, N.J.: Prentice-Hall, 1974.
24. *Marketing News*. March 1985.
25. McCarthy, E. Jerome, and William D. Perreault, Jr. *Basic Marketing*. Homewood, Ill.: Richard D. Irwin, 1981.
26. Nemmers, Erwin Esser. *Dictionary of Economics and Business*. Totowa, N.J.: Littlefield, Adams, 1976.
27. Packard, Sidney A., Arthur A. Winters, and Nathan Axelrod. *Fashion Buying and Merchandising*. New York: Fairchild, 1980.
28. Reibstein, David J. *Marketing: Concepts, Strategies, and Decisions*. Englewood Cliffs, N.J.: Prentice-Hall, 1985.
29. Shapiro, Benson P. "Improve Distribution with Your Promotional Mix." *Harvard Business Review* 55, No. 2 (1977).
30. Stern, Louis W., and Adel I. El-Ansary. *Marketing Channels*. Englewood Cliffs, N.J.: Prentice-Hall, 1982.
31. Takeuchi, Hirotaka. "A Note on Retailing Institutions." Boston: Harvard Business School Case No. 9-580-042.
32. "Test Marketing Sharpens the Focus." *Sales and Marketing Management*, March 16, 1981.
33. *The Food Marketing Industry Speaks*, 1986.
34. Welch, Joe L. *Marketing Law*. Tulsa, Okla.: Petroleum Publishing, 1980.
35. Wilcox, Kirkland A., and Joseph G. San Miguel. *Introduction to Financial Accounting*. New York: Harper & Row, 1980.

INDEX